CLOTHING THE CLERGY

CLOTHING THE CLERGY

Virtue and Power in Medieval Europe, c. 800–1200

MAUREEN C. MILLER

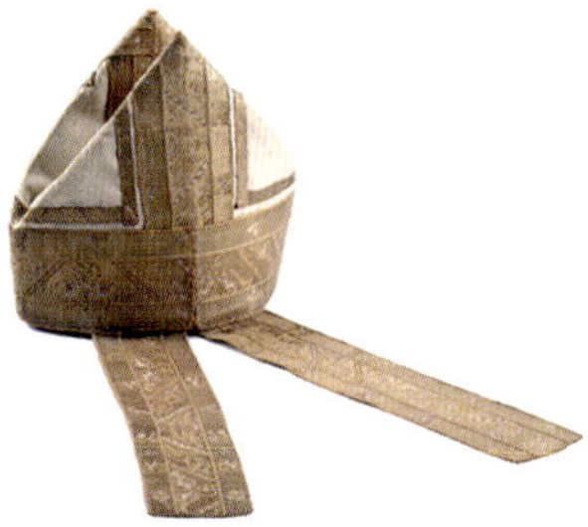

Cornell University Press · *Ithaca and London*

First published 2014 by Cornell University Press
First printing, Cornell Paperbacks, 2014

Printed in China

Library of Congress Cataloging-in-Publication Data

Miller, Maureen C. (Maureen Catherine), 1959– author.
Clothing the clergy : virtue and power in medieval Europe, c. 800–1200 / Maureen C. Miller.
pages cm
Includes bibliographical references and index.
ISBN 978-0-8014-4982-6 (cloth : alk. paper)
ISBN 978-0-8014-7943-4 (pbk. : alk. paper)
1. Church vestments—Europe—History—To 1500. 2. Clergy—Clothing—Europe—History—To 1500. 3. Clothing and dress—Social aspects—Europe—History—To 1500. 4. Power (Social sciences)—Europe—History—To 1500. 5. Authority—Religious aspects—Catholic Church—History. I. Title.
NK4850.M55 2014
247—dc23 2013036051

Cornell University Press strives to use environmentally responsible suppliers and materials to the fullest extent possible in the publishing of its books. Such materials include vegetable-based, low-VOC inks and acid-free papers that are recycled, totally chlorine-free, or partly composed of nonwood fibers. For further information, visit our website at www.cornellpress.cornell.edu.

Cloth printing 10 9 8 7 6 5 4 3 2 1
Paperback printing 10 9 8 7 6 5 4 3 2 1

For Catherine L. Miller,
who would have had a lot to say on this subject,
and for Cornelia Junfu Shonkwiler,
my sewing teacher.

CONTENTS

ILLUSTRATIONS

ACKNOWLEDGMENTS

Many institutions and individuals have made this book possible. Fellowships from the American Council of Learned Societies, the University of California President's Office, and the National Endowment for the Humanities allowed me two wonderfully intense periods of writing, while grants from the Pasold Research Fund, the Committee on Research of the University of California at Berkeley, and its Department of History made the research possible. I am grateful to the librarians of Berkeley, particularly those of its interlibrary loan unit; to the librarians and scholars of the Index of Christian Art in Princeton and of the Getty Research Institute in Los Angeles; to the textile specialists of the Abegg-Stiftung in Riggisberg, particularly Evelin Wetter and Michael Peter, and of the Istituto Superiore per la Conservazione ed il Restauro in Rome, especially Marica Mercalli and Silvia Checchi; and to the staffs of the Antonio Ratti Textile Center and Reference Library of the Metropolitan Museum of Art in New York and of the Joan Diehl McCauley Textile Study Center of the de Young Museum in San Francisco.

Seeing the liturgical vestments that survive from the Middle Ages profoundly shaped my understanding of clerical clothing: I owe a huge debt to the museum staffs that facilitated access to collections and provided the photographic materials and permissions necessary to provide readers some glimpses of the ornate style of clerical clothing explored in these pages. I thank especially Catherine Depierraz of the Abegg-Stiftung, Birgit Kandora of the Diözesanmuseum in Bamberg, and Marion Aichner of the Diözesanmuseum Hofburg in Brixen. The illustration program could not have been achieved without the support of the Abigail Reynolds Hodgen Publication Fund, Carla Hesse, the dean of social sciences, and Ethan Shagan, chair of the department of history of the University of California, Berkeley, as well as Cornell University Press. I am also grateful to Liz Kurtulik at Art Resource in New York, who patiently responded to so many requests; to Ann Higgins, who created the line drawings; to Riccardo Cristiani, who compiled the indexes; and to John G. Ackerman, director of Cornell University Press, who nurtured this project from the very beginning and brought it to fruition.

This book has been supported and shaped in special ways by the extraordinary community of scholars that is the University of California at Berkeley. I thank David Hollinger and Mary Elizabeth Berry, who as chairs of the Department of History were supportive in myriad ways, but especially in allowing me two leave years to write. My colleagues in the department and in the Program in Medieval Studies read chapters, and a particularly valiant subset offered incisive commentary on a complete draft. I thank especially Geoffrey Koziol, Susanna Elm, Maria Mavroudi, Katherine O'Brien O'Keeffe, Frank Bezner, Christopher Ocker, Diliana Angelova, John Connelly, and Victoria Frede. The Institute for International Studies at Berkeley generously made a day of discussion and critique possible through its Manuscript Mini-Conference Grant. I'm especially grateful to Kathryn L. Jasper for handling all the logistics of that day, for drawing up the bibliography, and for assistance and inspiration across many years. Other graduate students also offered valuable commentary, most notably Daniel Melleno, Giovanna Palombo, Jesse Torgerson, Joshua O'Brien, and Norman Underwood. The university has suffered dire cuts during the life of this project, yet its members' daily dedication to scholarship continues to make an extraordinary quality of intellectual life possible.

Beyond Berkeley I am most indebted to Barbara H. Rosenwein, whose detailed comments on the entire manuscript were invaluable; to R.I. Moore, whose suggestions regarding clothing and dissent helped deepen several chapters; and to Bruce L. Venarde, whose close readings and insights on gender particularly improved chapters 4 through 6. Other colleagues and communities generously commented on individual chapters: I thank Anders Winroth, Roger Reynolds, Dorothy Glass, Carol Lansing, Ron Witt, the University of California Medieval History Seminar, the Medieval Studies Colloquium at Berkeley, the Medieval and Early Modern Studies Workshop at Stanford University, the Medieval and Early Modern History Seminar at Brown University, and the Issues in Medieval Liturgy group convened by Susan Boynton at the North American Academy of Liturgy meetings. I know that I have only imperfectly assimilated the wealth of suggestions offered and that any remaining errors are mine alone.

The greatest gift of the scholarly life is the wide network of friends who share wisdom and companionship in ways great and small. They are too numerous to name, but I thank them all.

ABBREVIATIONS

THE DOUAY-RHEIMS TRANSLATION has been used for all passages of scripture since it is closest to the language of the Vulgate Latin translation most widely known in medieval Europe. Wherever possible, I have cited English translations in addition to critical editions of the sources in order to encourage students to pursue issues raised in this book. The following abbreviations facilitate reference to frequently cited works.

AASS
Jean Bolland et al., eds. *Acta Sanctorum Quotquot Toto Orbe Coluntur.* Editio nova. Paris, 1863–.

Amiet, *AS*
Robert Amiet, ed. "Une 'Admonitio Synodalis' de l'époque carolingienne: Étude critique et Édition." *Medieaeval Studies* 26 (1964): 12–82.

Andrieu, *Ordines*
Michel Andrieu, ed. *Les Ordines Romani du haut moyen age.* 5 vols. Spicilegium sacrum Lovaniense, Études et documents, fasc. 11, 23–24, 28–29. Louvain, 1931–1956; repr. 1960–1965.

BAV
Biblioteca Apostolica Vaticana, Vatican City

BMT
Bibliothèque Municipale de Tours

BnF
Bibliothèque nationale de France, Paris

BV
Biblioteca Vallicelliana, Rome

Braun, *DLG*
Joseph Braun. *Die liturgische Gewandung im Occident und Orient nach Ursprung und Entwiklung, Verwendung und Symbolik.* Frieburg im Breisgau, 1907.

CC
Corpus Christianorum, Series Latina

CCCM
Corpus Christianorum, Continuatio Mediaevalis

CHWT
David Jenkins, ed. *The Cambridge History of Western Textiles.* 2 vols. Cambridge, 2003.

CIETA
Centre International d'Étude des Textiles Anciens

CESG
Codices Electronici Sangallenses (e-codices St. Gallen, Stifsbibliothek): http://www.e-codices.unifr.ch/en

CSEL
Corpus Scriptorum Ecclesiasticorum Latinorum

DACL
Fernand Cabrol and Henri Leclercq, eds. *Dictionnaire d'archéologie chrétienne et de liturgie.* Paris, 1907–1953.

DDC
Dictionnaire de droit canonique. 7 vols. Paris, 1935–1965.

Decrees
Norman P. Tanner, ed. *Decrees of the Ecumenical Councils.* 2 vols. London, 1990.

De institutione
Hrabanus Maurus. *De institutione clericorum libri tres.* Edited by Detlev Zimpel. Freiburger Beiträge zur mittelalterlichen Geschichte. Studien und Texte 7. Frankfurt, 1996.

DMA
Joseph R. Strayer, ed. *Dictionary of the Middle Ages.* 13 vols. New York, 1982–1989.

Du Cange
Charles du Fresne sieur du Cange. *Glossarium Mediae et Infimae Latinitatis.* 7 vols. Paris, 1840–1850.

EH
Marjorie Chibnall, ed. and trans. *The Ecclesiastical History of Orderic Vitalis.* 6 vols. Oxford, 1973.

Gregory, *Letters*
The Letters of Gregory the Great. Translated by John R.C. Martyn. 3 vols. Toronto, 2004.

Haddan & Stubbs
Arthur West Haddan and William Stubbs, eds. *Councils and Ecclesiastical Documents Relating to Great Britain and Ireland.* 3 vols. Oxford, 1869–1878.

Jaffé
Philipp Jaffé, Wilhelm Wattenbach, S. Loewenfeld, F. Kaltenbrummer, and Paul Ewald, eds. *Regesta Pontificum Romanorum: Ab Condita Ecclesia ad Annum Post Christum Natum MCXCVIII.* 2 vols. Leipzig: Veit, 1885–1888.

Ladner, *Papstbildnisse*
Gerhart B. Ladner, *Die Papstbildnisse des Altertums und des Mittelalters.* 3 vols. Monumenti di Antichità Cristiana pubblicati dal Pontificio istituto di archeologia Cristiana. Vatican City, 1941–1984. Vol. 1, from late antiquity through the investiture conflict, was published in Italian with the title I *Ritratti dei Papi nell'Antichità e nel Medioevo;* vol. 2, from Innocent II to Benedict XI, was published in German, as was vol. 3, which publishes additions, corrections, and several important *Exkurse* on specific issues, including papal attire.

Liber officialis
Amalarius of Metz. *Amalarii episcopi opera liturgica omnia.* Edited by John Michael Hanssens. 3 vols. Studi e Testi 138–40. Vatican City, 1948–1950, vol. 2.

Liber pontificalis
Louis Duchesne, ed. *Le liber pontificalis.* 2nd ed. in 3 vols. with additions and corrections by Cyrille Vogel. Paris, 1955–1957.

Mansi
J. D. Mansi, ed. *Sacrorum Conciliorum Noua et Amplissima Collectio.* 53 vols. Florence, 1759–1798; repr. Graz, 1960.

Materials
James Craigie Robertson, ed. *Materials for the History of Thomas Becket, Archbishop of Canterbury*, 7 vols. Rolls Series 67 London 1875–1885.

MGH
Monumenta Germaniae Historica, with subseries:
Briefe Kaiserzeit *Briefe der deutschen Kaiserzeit. Munich*, 1949–.
Cap. *Legum sectio II Capitularia regum Francorum.* Hannover, 1881.
Cap. episc. *Capitula episcoporum.* Edited by Peter Brommer, Rudolf Pokorny, and Martina Stratmann. 4 vols. Hannover, 1984–1995.
Concilia *Legum sectio III Concilia.* Hannover, 1893–.
Const. *Legum IV Constitutiones et acta publica imperatorem et regum.* Hannover, 1893–.
Epp. *Epistolae.* Berlin, 1887–.
Epp. Sel. *Epistolae Selectae.* Berlin, 1916–.
Lib. de lite *Libelli de lite imperatorum et pontificum saeculis XI. et XII. conscripti.* Edited by Ernst Dümmler. 3 vols. Hannover, 1891–1897.
SSRM *Scriptores rerum Merouingicarum.* Edited by Bruno Krusch and William Levison. 7 vols. Hannover, 1885–1919.
SS *Scriptores* in folio. 32 vols. Hannover, 1826–1934.
SSRG *Scriptores Rerum Germanicarum in Usum Scholarum Separatim Ediit.* Hannover, 1871–.

Muthesius, *Byzantine Silk*
Anna Muthesius. *Byzantine Silk Weaving AD 400 to AD 1200.* Vienna, 1997.

Peter Damian, *Die Briefe*
Peter Damian. *Die Briefe des Petrus Damiani.* Edited by Kurt Reindel, 4 vols. MGH Briefe Kaiserzeit 4. Munich, 1983–1993.

Peter Damian, *Letters*
Peter Damian. *The Letters of Peter Damian.* Edited and translated by Owen J. Blum, 7 vols. Washington, D.C., 1989–1995.

PL
J. P. Migne, ed. *Patrologiae Cursus Completus.* Ser. Lat. 221 vols. Paris, 1844–1864.

Schatzverzeichnisse
Bernhard Bischoff, ed. *Mittelalterliche Schatzverzeichnisse.* Vol. 1, *Von der Zeit Karls des Großen bis zur Mitte des 13. Jahrhunderts.* Veröffentilichungen des Zentralinstituts für Kunstgeschichte in München, 4. Munich, 1967.

Textile Conservation
Mechthild Flury-Lemberg. *Textile Conservation and Research: A Documentation of the Textile Department on the Occasion of the Twentieth Anniversary of the Abegg Foundation.* Bern, 1988.

INTRODUCTION

We have an eager and curious observer of the clergy in Eadmer, monk of Christ Church Canterbury, friend and disciple of Saint Anselm. In 1098 he had accompanied Anselm to the southern Italian port of Bari for a papal council. "Since it was my habit from childhood," he earnestly wrote, "to consider with careful attention and commit to memory new things, especially those occurring in ecclesiastical affairs, I discreetly observed the conduct of the council, the seating arrangements, the procedures and ways of weighing issues, perhaps on my part with a more curious than perceptive mind and eye, since I had never seen such things before." And what did Eadmer notice that was worth recording? Most of his account of the council dwells on a garment "ornamented all over with gold thread": a cope, a sort of liturgical cape, worn by the archbishop of Benevento.[1] He observed that it stood out in the gathering, its costly and splendid ornamentation surpassing the garb of all the others assembled there—including the pope!

Eadmer was fascinated enough by this cope that he made inquiries about it, especially since he had as a youth heard stories from the older monks in his community about a garment given in return for a precious relic. Could this be that garment? Indeed, Eadmer discovered that it was. The cope was a gift of Æthelnoth, the archbishop of Canterbury (1020–1038), to an earlier archbishop of Benevento who had traveled to England bearing the arm of Saint Bartholomew, seeking alms to succor his famine-devastated flock. Queen Emma's generous gift to feed the starving Beneventans moved their archbishop to leave the relic in England, while the cope was an additional gift from the archbishop of Canterbury to his beleaguered wandering colleague. Certainly Eadmer's recording of the story cast his native Canterbury and the island's monarchy in a highly positive light, providing reason enough for the telling. But more striking is the fact that among all the things that a religious observer might experience and notice at a council, he was most interested in a richly ornamented ecclesiastical garment.

1. See the glossary for more information on and images of individual articles of attire.

Eadmer's digression on the archbishop of Benevento's cope offers us entrée into the meanings medieval people attributed to ecclesiastical garments. The cope adorned both churches, Benevento and Canterbury, the monk wrote, making manifest the events uniting the sees as "witness and proof" to future generations. The events uniting the sees were a bishop's heroic care for his flock, a queen's piety and generosity, and an archbishop's fraternal affection for another cleric. An association is also made between the object left by that earlier archbishop of Benevento—a precious relic of the apostle Bartholomew—and the cope. Since Bartholomew was believed to have evangelized India, the relic associated England with the frontiers of Christianity while the cope celebrated both the unity of Western Christendom as well as a special relationship between the ancient centers of the faith and its more recent converts. The great sanctity of the relic is also linked to a beautiful liturgical vestment.[2] Instead of criticizing the archbishop for ostentation—an equally plausible monastic response—Eadmer located the cope in the context of relationships of holiness, virtue, and status forged through objects. These meanings and connections are the subject of this book: clerical clothing reveals ideas about holiness and virtuous pastoral care, the influence of the frontiers of medieval Christianity on Rome, and relationships among clerics as well as between them and women.

The meanings medieval people attributed to garments, of course, are not wholly different from our own. We too receive articles of clothing from friends and family that then remind us of our relationships with them and the circumstances of the gift. But within a shared semantic range, there are important differences. Eadmer's reaction to the gold-encrusted cope would certainly not have been my own initial response, given our culture's preoccupation with clothing as an expression of individual self-fashioning and consumer spending power. After his initial notice of the cope I would have expected a story about the hubris of the Beneventan archbishop or some sort of rivalry between his see and Rome. If not for Eadmer's history of the garment, I might also have read its precious splendor as a sign of southern Italy's precocious trading connections with the Byzantine and Islamic worlds. I would not have guessed that it came from Anglo-Saxon England. Eadmer's ability to upset my expectations, in fact, opened a whole new vista into momentous changes in Western Christianity and the exercise of power in European societies.

What follows is the story of a crucial shift in Christian ideas about the appearance of its ministers, from heeding the exhortation of Jesus not to worry about clothes and the example of John the Baptist's ascetic garb to embracing the gold-embellished finery of the Old Testament priesthood. This change, evident in the ninth century, was not uncontested. It was both debated and limited, particularly in the twelfth century. Indeed, resistance to clerical finery shaped a contrast—between gold and silk vestments within

2. Eadmer, *Historia novorum in Anglia*, ed. Martin Rule, Rerum britannicarum medii aevi scriptores 81 (London, 1884), 107–10; on this council, see also Georg Gresser, ed., *Die Synoden und Konzilien in der Zeit des Reformpapsttums in Deutschland und Italien von Leo IX. bis. Calixt II 1049–1123* (Paderborn, 2006), 321–27; and R. W. Southern, *Saint Anselm: Portrait in a Landscape* (Cambridge, 1990), 279–80, 409–10.

church and dark, modest attire outside the sanctuary—that influenced the expressive uses of clothing down to the present. What the medieval clergy developed was a language of clothing claiming holiness and power. Its origins are complex, but driving forces were a desire to make the clergy virtuous in order to channel God's grace to his people, the involvement of bishops in royal governance as an aspect of their pastoral care, and the association of elite status and political authority with precious attire. These forces came together in the Carolingian era to produce what I call here the ornate style of clerical clothing, and what follows is its biography. It is recounted analytically rather than strictly chronologically. In chapter 1 I sketch its prehistory—giving a brief overview of clerical clothing in early Christianity and early medieval Europe—and identify through ecclesiastical legislation a radical change in concerns in the twelfth century. After centuries of worrying about poverty and the lack of appropriate liturgical attire in churches, ecclesiastical leaders were suddenly legislating against "superfluities." Why this change? Canon law provides some preliminary answers, but chapter 2 turns to liturgical sources to locate the origins of ornate vestments in a clerical spirituality linking what they wore to virtues they were to cultivate. Carolingian efforts at reforming the clergy fostered and diffused these ideas and practices. The visual evidence for the emergence of the ornate style is presented in chapter 3, bringing into view the social and political forces that made it acceptable to depict clerics in silks and gold. In chapter 4 I reveal the creators of the ornate style—women—and use surviving textiles to explore their relationships with clerics and the spirituality that both deepened and imperiled those relationships. The development of the ornate style during the reform efforts of the eleventh and twelfth centuries is taken up in chapter 5, which shows that despite anxieties about the relationships with women that produced them, gold and silk vestments were used to articulate ecclesiastical hierarchies and claim status for the entire clerical order. In the final chapter I return to the concerns about "superfluities" that emerged in chapter 1 and use the meanings excavated throughout the book to reveal an important debate in twelfth-century Europe about good and bad lordship that was conducted at least partially through critiques of the ornate style of clerical clothing. Although ecclesiastical claims to exercise public authority were ultimately rejected in the European tradition, clerical ideas about the virtuous power their clothing represented influenced the character of secular governance in Western societies. The afterlife of the stark and meaningful contrast between the ornate style and its sober twin, the medieval precursor of the soutane, or cassock, is traced in the conclusion.

Objects are the focus of this story: how medieval people made them, used them, understood and imagined them. Clerical clothes—actual medieval garments—survive today in sacristies, tombs, reliquaries, and museums. One aim of this book is to demonstrate the extraordinary significance of this fragile heritage in the hope of fostering the preservation and study of all medieval textiles.[3] The illustrations included here will give

3. A significant body of recent work by art historians and curators argues for the significance of these garments in the history of art. A good point of entry to this scholarship is Pauline Johnstone, *High*

a glimpse of their beauty, so we can enter into Eadmer's fascination and understand how compelling these vestments were to clerics as well as to laypeople. These surviving garments, moreover, reveal ideas and practices not recorded in written sources. They are remarkable historic artifacts with many more stories to tell. Scholars writing about medieval clothing routinely ignore these most primary of sources for their topic. I understand why. The garments are scattered all over Europe, and photographs and descriptions of them are few, often inadequate, and published in relatively rare catalogs, books, and journals. The conservation and study of historic textiles, moreover, is a rapidly evolving and highly technical discipline. I have relied on the expertise and generosity of textile specialists, and hope that any errors I have made will appear small in comparison to the interest provoked. Students and young scholars should note that I have explored only a small portion of this rich trove. There is so much more to be learned from these material sources.

Anyone writing about clerical clothing walks in the footsteps of a scholarly giant. Joseph Braun (1857–1947) was an immensely learned Jesuit with a keen interest in the material artifacts of Christian liturgy. His encyclopedic study of liturgical vestments, *Die liturgische Gewandung im Occident und Orient*, was published in Freiburg in 1907.[4] A careful historian and philologist, Braun traced the origins and development of each piece of liturgical apparel in unrivaled detail, drawing on a vast array of published and unpublished sources. Even more impressive, Braun scoured European churches and museums for surviving garments. He carefully weighed their evidence and published photographs of hundreds of vestments, some now the only surviving images of artifacts destroyed in the twentieth century's two world wars.[5] The dates of some of the garments he studied have been revised by textile specialists through more systematic technical comparisons and the use of new scientific tools such as radiocarbon analysis. But the

Fashion in the Church: The Place of Church Vestments in the History of Art from the Ninth to the Nineteenth Century (Leeds, 2002), 27–59 (on the Middle Ages). For an overview of "artifact-based," compared to other, approaches to the history of dress, see Lou Taylor, *The Study of Dress History* (Manchester, 2002), especially 3–63.

4. See the list of abbreviations for full citation. Braun also published a shorter work focusing on Western liturgical attire—*Die liturgischen Paramente in Gegenwart und Vergangenheit: Ein Handbuch der Paramentik* (Freiburg im Breisgau, 1924)—and a history of the altar: *Der christliche Altar in seiner geschichtlichen Entwicklung* (Munich, 1924).

5. Braun built on the pioneering work of Franz Johann Joseph Bock (1823–1899), who organized the first major exhibit of medieval liturgical vestments and was one of the founders of the diocesan museum of Cologne. While Bock's work clearly fostered the scientific study of medieval textiles, his practice of cutting up precious silks (e.g., the eleventh-century cloth of Saint Gereon) in order to sell pieces to other museums cast a pall over his reputation among modern scholars. His major study, *Geschichte der liturgischen Gewänder des Mittelalters*, 3 vols. (Bonn, 1856–1871), enumerates all the articles of liturgical dress and raises key issues, such as the economic and artistic importance of their material construction and their origins in Roman civil attire. But its historical perspective was not sufficiently grounded in patristic and medieval sources, and its annotation does not provide adequate references to sources or studies. On Bock and his work, see Birgitt Borkopp-Restle, *Der Aachener Kanonikus Franz Bock und seine Textilsammlungen: Ein Beitrag zur Geschichte der Kunstgewebe im 19 Jahrhundert* (Riggisberg, 2008).

erudition of this extraordinary scholar is unsurpassed. What I have written here would be impossible without it, and anyone writing about ecclesiastical attire ignores it at his or her peril.

While clearly interested in the origins of contemporary usages, Braun was much more sensitive to changes over time in liturgical apparel than many more recent authors.[6] He was most focused on changes in the forms of vestments—for example, the narrowing of the chasuble over the late Middle Ages—and readers sharing this interest should refer to his work. My focus is on a more general and significant change in the appearance of liturgical vestments that is quite evident in visual sources from the mid-ninth century. The ornate style of vestments used colorful silks and elaborate embroidered or woven decoration, often in silver or gold—the type of garment that captured Eadmer's attention. The fact that it is still with us today, and has profoundly shaped the preservation of vestments, has led to the mistaken view that Western liturgical garb has always been made of precious materials and been highly ornamented. In fact, the early church was deeply ambivalent about special liturgical attire, and even after its acceptance in the late fourth century ecclesiastical leaders repeatedly banned the use of expensive materials. The emergence of ornate vestments was not a natural development. Its origins were in specific historical circumstances and its acceptance and proliferation depended on political and religious ideas as well as social and economic structures.

My approach, in sum, is resolutely historical even though I have drawn on sources that are usually the purview of other disciplines.[7] In defining the scope of this study, I do aim to address several characteristics of work on medieval clothing over the last three decades. First is its focus on secular attire and a tendency to assume clerical clothing either was simply influenced by lay practices or was a simpler subcategory of them.[8] While members of the clergy may have shared many ideas and practices with laymen, their beliefs, education, and activities produced a distinctively ecclesiastical culture of

6. Teleology and emphasis on continuity most mark the Anglophone works on which many contemporary scholars tend to rely: Cyril E. Pocknee, *Liturgical Vesture: Its Origins and Development* (London, 1960); Janet Mayo, *A History of Ecclesiastical Dress* (New York, 1984). The Oxford Movement informed the sense of tradition in both. The best brief overview of vestments in English is Roger E. Reynolds, "Vestments, liturgical," *DMA*, s.v. More recent Catholic scholarship stresses greater variance over time, in part to make its peace with the changes wrought by the Second Vatican Council: Louis Trichet, *Le costume du clergé: Ses origines et son évolution en France d'après les règlements de l'église* (Paris, 1986).

7. Eric Palazzo, "Art and Liturgy in the Middle Ages: Survey of Research (1980–2003) and Some Reflections on Method," *Journal of English and Germanic Philology* 105 (2006): 170–84 advocates the close reading of artistic and textual evidence together, which I simply take somewhat further by considering textiles and an even wider range of texts.

8. Françoise Piponnier and Perrine Mane, *Dress in the Middle Ages*, trans. Caroline Beamish (New Haven, 1997), 114–20 treats ecclesiastical attire as a subcategory of clothing functioning as "identification markers." Similar approaches with even sharper focus on lay attire are Anne H. van Buren, *Illuminating Fashion: Dress in the Art of Medieval France and the Netherlands, 1325–1515*, with Roger S. Wieck (New York, 2011), 1–37; Stella Mary Newton, *Fashion in the Age of the Black Prince: A Study of the Years 1340–1365* (Woodbridge, 1980), 86. Sources for the study of secular dress are best treated in Mireille Madou, *Le costume civil*, Typologie des sources du moyen âge 47 (Turnhout, 1986).

clothing. My focus here will be on the secular clergy: that is, those ordained to minor or major orders and those consecrated as bishops.[9] Clerics were called "secular" because they lived in, and ministered to those in, the world (*saeculum*), as opposed to monks, who withdrew from the world to pray. Over the Middle Ages, monks increasingly took orders and some even became bishops, so there was overlap between these two groups.[10] Monasticism, as the ideal form of Christian life, also exerted a powerful influence on the clergy, but as a distinct *ordo*, or way of life, it had its own clothing practices.[11]

A second characteristic has been a concentration on cultural representations of clothing. This has produced much valuable work that I draw on throughout this book. Specialists in literature have called attention to the uses, appearances, and meanings of clothing in the medieval "imaginary."[12] Art historians have also offered valuable cultural readings of the representation of clothing in painting, sculpture, and manuscript illumination.[13] While representations are extremely important, I am also interested in what medieval people may have actually done. It's true that our sources only imperfectly capture this, but I have culled evidence from an array of historical sources—legislation, liturgical texts, charters, inventories, chronicles, and letters—to assess clothing practices.

9. The minor orders were doorkeeper, lector, exorcist, and acolyte, while the major orders were subdeacon, deacon, and priest. In the early Middle Ages, lists of the minor orders sometimes included the cantor, or *psalmista*. On their developments, see below, 34, 67.

10. By the twelfth century, roughly 65–75% of the monks in independent Benedictine houses were ordained, and the proportion in the newer reformed orders (Cluniacs, Cistercians, Carthusians) was even higher. Eadmer, our observer of the council of Bari, was certainly ordained before he was elected bishop of Saint Andrews in 1120. Giles Constable, *The Reformation of the Twelfth Century* (Cambridge, 1996), 227–31; R.W. Southern, *Saint Anselm and His Biographer: A Study of Monastic Life and Thoughts 1059–c. 1130* (Cambridge, 1966), 236.

11. On the monastic habit, see Giles Constable, "The Ceremonies and Symbolism of Entering Religious Life and Taking the Monastic Habit, from the Fourth to the Twelfth Century," in *Segni e riti nella Chiesa altomedievale occidentale, 11–17 aprile 1985*, Settimane di studio del Centro italiano di studi sull'alto medioevo, 33 (Spoleto, 1987), 771–834; on the meanings of *ordo*, see his "Orders of Society," in *Three Studies in Medieval Religious and Social Thought* (Cambridge, 1995), 251–341. The monastic profession, or *ordo*, was defined by vows to live a certain kind of religious life under a rule (*regula*), and so ecclesiastical historians usually call monks either "regulars" or "religious." Beginning in the twelfth century and accelerating in the thirteenth, new religious orders—that is, new forms of Christian communal life under rules—emerged. Their clothing practices usually sought to distinguish them from Benedictine monks and were influenced by both monastic and clerical ideas about dress.

12. Prominent examples include Susan Crane, *The Performance of Self: Ritual, Clothing, and Identity during the Hundred Years War* (Philadelphia, 2002); E. Jane Burns, *Courtly Love Undressed: Reading through Clothes in Medieval French Culture* (Philadelphia, 2002); most of the essays in *Medieval Fabrications: Dress, Textiles, Cloth Work, and Other Cultural Imaginings*, ed. E. Jane Burns (New York, 2004); and E. Jane Burns, *Sea of Silk: A Textile Geography of Women's Work in Medieval French Literature* (Philadelphia, 2009). See also Taylor, *Study of Dress History*, 90–114.

13. Cordelia Warr, *Dressing for Heaven: Religious Clothing in Italy, 1215–1545* (Manchester, 2010); Margaret McEnchroe Williams, "Dressing the Part: Depictions of Noble Costume in Irish High Crosses," and Susan L'Engle, "Addressing the Law: Costume as Signifier in Medieval Legal Miniatures," both in *Encountering Medieval Textiles and Dress*, ed. Désirée G. Koslin and Janet E. Snyder (New York, 2002), 45–63, 137–53; Eric Palazzo, *L'évêque et son image: L'illustration du pontifical au moyen âge* (Turnhout, 1999); Taylor, *Study of Dress History*, 115–49.

Combined with surviving textiles and garments, this evidence of human actions can profitably be compared with how clothing was represented. In some cases, representations accord with the physical and textual evidence, and in others they do not. Chapter 3 explores a particularly interesting chronological disjunction between when the ornate style of vestment begins to be produced and when it begins to be represented in manuscript illuminations and frescoes.

The explicit chronology of this book, c. 800–1200, is derived from the ornate style: the earliest evidence of its existence comes from the late eighth and early ninth centuries, and by the early thirteenth it is ubiquitous. I have overstepped these bounds in order to trace the earliest origins of distinctive clerical garb in Western Christianity, to chart the development of clerical attire outside the sanctuary, to elucidate ecclesiastical efforts to influence lay ideas and practices of lordship, and to sketch the historical significance of clerical clothing. The *longue durée* is still an immensely valuable perspective on historical change. An expansive geographical terrain was also necessary to tell this story. When I first began research on clerical attire, I did not intend to leave Italy, but sources and clues lured me over the Alps. "Europe" in this book comprises the Italian peninsula, England, and all the lands conquered by the Carolingians. Like Charlemagne, however, I had to retreat from the Iberian Peninsula, and so for my purposes here it is not included in "Europe." There is ample and extremely interesting ecclesiastical legislation concerning clerical clothing from Iberia, but pictorial representations of ecclesiastical garb—chiefly in manuscript illuminations, such as the "Codex Aemilianus"—proved so different from the more naturalistic depictions in other European manuscripts that they were incomparable.[14] This material merits its own study, and I sincerely hope an Iberianist will take up the challenge, especially since significant textile evidence is being recovered, conserved, and studied.[15]

Economic and material conditions also influenced my terminal date. The making of textiles in Western Europe was transformed over the twelfth and thirteenth centuries. The introduction of the horizontal loom combined with rapid urbanization and the expansion of trade created complex manufacturing industries and a sophisticated commercial market in textiles. Europeans increasingly bought cloth, rather than making it at home. Also, many aspects of clothing production that had been dominated by women since antiquity came to be practiced by men. This significantly changed the way that clerics got clothing. Before clothing production was commercialized, they were

14. John Williams, *Early Spanish Manuscript Illumination* (New York, 1977), 8–9, 59–61, 100–101; Codex Aemilianensis (976–992), Abbey of San Millán de la Cogolla, El Escorial, Real Biblioteca de San Lorenzo de El Escorial, Ref. d.I.1, 31v, Mark Lansburgh Collection in the Photo Study Collection of the Getty Research Institute. For the conciliar materials, see José Vives, ed., *Concilios Visigóticos e hispano-romanos*, España Cristiana, textos 1 (Barcelona, 1963), 73, 102, 146, 206, 374–75.

15. Metropolitan Museum of Art, *The Art of Medieval Spain AD 500–1200* (New York, 1993), 107 (no. 57); Rosa Martin I Ros, "Les vêtements liturgiques de Saint-Valère: Étude historique," *Bulletin du CIETA* 73 (1995–1996): 63–78; Mechthild Flury-Lemberg and Gisela Illek, *Spuren kostbarer Gewebe*, Riggisberger Berichte 3 (Riggisberg, 1995), 56–161.

dependent on women for their attire and for the linens necessary for the liturgy. Although women continued to make vestments, over the thirteenth century men became increasingly involved in supplying ecclesiastical needs.[16] The manufacture of silk, a key element in the ornate style, also determined the terminal date of c. 1200. Before the late twelfth century, Europeans could get silk (thread and cloth) only from centers of production in Byzantium, the Islamic world, or further east. Silk production was established in Sicily during its era of Muslim domination (c. 827–1072). Once the Normans conquered the island at the end of the eleventh century, the techniques began to diffuse in the Latin West with industries developing in northern Italian towns in the second half of the twelfth century.[17] Before c. 1200, however, silks were rare commodities, acquired at great cost and usually through elite connections. Production centers within Europe led to greater social diffusion and wider availability. In sum, before 1200 relationships were crucial to the acquisition of both mundane and precious textiles, while markets more powerfully influenced access from the thirteenth century on.

As the book's title indicates, this is a study of clerical clothing. I have preferred the term "clothing"—and synonyms with equal breadth of meaning such as dress, apparel, attire, or garments—to "costume" or "fashion." Late nineteenth- and early twentieth-century histories of dress favored "costume," partly because many authors and members of their audience were associated with the theater. These early histories tended toward taxonomy, and "costume" was used to designate a type of dress characteristic of a country, period, class, or calling.[18] Although clerical clothing in the Middle Ages did function as a means of visually distinguishing clerics, and thus articulating their calling and membership in a social group, the term's connotations of artificiality in current parlance make it unsuitable.

"Fashion" is even less appropriate. Many of those writing about the history of "fashion" never define what they mean by it, but some elements of a definition have emerged

16. John H. Munro, "Medieval Woollens: Textiles, Technology and Organization," in *CHWT*, 1:181–324, but especially 194–97; David Herlihy, *Opera Muliebra: Women and Work in Medieval Europe* (New York, 1990), 75–102.

17. David Jacoby, "Silk Economics and Cross-Cultural Artistic Interaction: Byzantium, the Muslim World, and the Christian West," *Dumbarton Oaks Papers* 58 (2004): 197–240, but especially 201–40; Anna Muthesius, "Silk in the Medieval World," in *CHWT*, 1:325–54; André Guillou, "La soie sicilienne au Xe–XIe s.," in *Bizantino-Sicula II: Miscellanea di scritti in memoria di Giuseppe Rossi Taibbi*, Istituto siciliano di studi bizantini e neoellenici, Quaderni 8 (Palermo, 1975), 285–88. For the process of silk production, see Muthesius, *Byzantine Silk*, 5–18.

18. Auguste Racinet's encyclopedic *Le costume historique*, originally published in 1888, has been translated into several languages and an English edition reprinted as recently as 2003: *The Complete Costume History: From Ancient Times to the 19th Century* (Cologne, 2003). More influential for contemporary studies were James Laver's *Taste and Fashion, from the French Revolution until Today* (New York, 1938) and *A Concise History of Costume* (London, 1969). Laver (1899–1975) was curator of the Victoria and Albert Museum's theater collection. He was interested in works of art as sources for historic dress, but used the work of social theorists such as Thorstein Veblen to bring much greater sophistication to costume history.

in more reflective scholarship.[19] Since Thorstein Veblen's *Theory of the Leisure Class* (1899), fashion has been associated with mercantile and industrial capitalism: the economic goal of profit favored rapidly changing styles in clothing to fuel consumer demand. While some historians locate the birth of fashion in the early modern period or the late Middle Ages and associate it with the dawn of modernity, medievalists see its roots in the eleventh and twelfth centuries.[20] To a certain degree, these claims for an earlier origin are related to recognition of increasing trade after the millennium. But they more directly respond to descriptions of new types of clothing among courtiers as novelties adopted for the sake of novelty and to characterizations of them as scandalous.[21] I have used the term "fashion" in discussing these elite lay uses of clothing in medieval courts because evidence suggests not only rapid change and novelty but also concerns for social distinction and favor in a competitive environment, and these characteristics are among those included in recent definitions proffered by historians and theoreticians of fashion.

Clerical clothing changed, but not rapidly and not for the sake of novelty. The change that is my primary focus here was enduring: the ornate style of liturgical attire is still with us today. Although there is some overlap in meaning between "fashion" and "style"—in the sense of visible characteristics or features, a particular make, shape, or pattern—I have used the latter because it has the connotations neither of rapid change nor of consumer choice that "fashion" has. Beyond indicating a particular manner of dress, style sometimes has the meaning of a socially or culturally approved way of dressing, and this sense is highly appropriate to my subject since attitudes toward ecclesiastical dress are at the heart of this story.[22] Style's association with writing and language also motivates my usage. The theoretical approaches that I have found most useful in understanding clerical attire are those—drawing on linguistics, communications theory, and anthropology—that explore clothing as an expressive language.[23] While more a set of

19. Ingrid Brenninkmeyer, *The Sociology of Fashion* (Paris, 1963), 4–6; Jennifer Craik, *The Face of Fashion: Cultural Studies in Fashion* (London, 1994), x–xi; Lara Svendsen, *Fashion: A Philosophy*, trans. John Irons (London, 2006), especially 12–20; Sarah Grace Heller, *Fashion in Medieval France* (Woodbridge, 2007), 16–45 offers an elaborate ten-point definition of a fashion "system."

20. Sociologists see its origins in the earliest primitive societies: Brenninkmeyer, *Sociology of Fashion*, 17–47. Heller, *Fashion in Medieval France*, 46–60 surveys many of the economic theories. See also Susan Mosher Stuard, *Gilding the Market: Luxury and Fashion in Fourteenth-Century Italy* (Philadelphia, 2006); Ulinka Rublack, *Dressing Up: Cultural Identity in Renaissance Europe* (Oxford, 2010), 7–8, 16–18.

21. See chapter 6 for a discussion of these reactions. Medieval sources use the Latin word *mos*, which has a similar range of meanings (manner, way, usage, practice) as our "fashion," a term most directly derived from Middle English, Old French, and Provençal, but also from the Latin *factio* (a making, doing; conduct) or *facere* (to make, to do).

22. On the uses of these terms, see Malcolm Barnard's introduction to his edited volume, *Fashion Theory: A Reader* (London, 2007), 3. This is the most useful of the recently published guides to the subject.

23. My evidence does not support theorizing ecclesiastical dress as a "system" or a language with a defined grammar and syntax. But Roland Barthes's theory of "connotation" as a set of associations that are the product of an individual's cultural location well describes medieval representations of and responses to dress. Umberto Eco's use of the term "code" in relation to clothing—in the loose sense of the

possibilities than invariant rules, the language of clerical clothing—the ideas and practices that developed around both liturgical attire and clerical garb outside the sanctuary—had important historical effects. I agree strongly with Peter Stallybrass and Ann Rosalind Jones that clothing—in the Middle Ages as well as in their period of the Renaissance—had an "animating and constitutive power." A person in these societies was constituted as a monarch, a priest, or a servant by being invested with garments. The widespread use of clothing for this purpose pivoted on an ancient belief in some relationship between the exterior appearance of individuals and their interior states. Although rife with tensions and unresolved contradictions, this belief meant that clothing could be "deeply put on," that it could have some inner effect and produce powerful "material memories."[24] Eadmer would certainly have agreed. What follows is some attempt to understand how and why so much was invested in clerical clothing in medieval Europe and what the effects of this economic, ideological, and emotional investment were.

meanings and ideological connotations produced—is also warranted. Roland Barthes, "Rhetoric and the Image," in *Image, Music, Text*, ed. and trans. Stephen Heath (New York, 1977), 32–51; Umberto Eco, "Social Life as a Sign System," in *Structuralism, an Introduction*, ed. David Robey (Oxford, 1973), 57–72.

24. Ann Rosalind Jones and Peter Stallybrass, *Renaissance Clothing and the Materials of Memory* (Cambridge, 2000), 1–14.

1

LET THEM EXHIBIT HOLINESS

Let no one sing [Mass] without amice, alb, stole, fanon, and chasuble. These vestments should be clean and used for no other purpose.
—*Admonitio synodalis* (early ninth century), Amiet, *AS*, 44, 77

We also enjoin that bishops as well as clergy take pains to be pleasing to God and to humans in both their interior and exterior comportment. Let them give no offence in the sight of those for whom they ought to be a model and example, by the excess, cut or colour of their clothes, nor with regard to the tonsure, but rather, as is fitting for them, let them exhibit holiness. If after a warning from the bishops they are unwilling to change their ways, let them be deprived of their ecclesiastical benefices.
—Second Lateran Council, canon 4 (1139), *Decrees* 1:197

Both these pieces of ecclesiastical legislation address what the clergy wore, but with radically different concerns. The first, most likely the product of a regional or provincial council held in Lotharingia or the southern Rhineland, strove to define minimum standards in clear and simple sentences. Concerns about seemliness and cleanliness pervade this pastoral "admonition." The fathers gathered in Rome three centuries later advocated something more complex: the cultivation of inner purity made outwardly manifest through dignified appearance and comportment with the aim of instructing others by example. What they legislated against were excesses in the style and color of clerical attire. Moreover, the Lateran canon spells out penalties and indicates who has the responsibility for correcting such abuses. While the Carolingian legislation aimed at achieving the basic necessities to sustain Christian liturgy, the twelfth-century canon sought to constrain inventive superfluity in clerical clothing.

This change in legislative aims needs to be understood in a much broader context of Christian thought about the appearance of clerics. Should they look different from laymen? If so, how? A consensus had developed by the sixth century that special attire should be worn for the celebration of Christian rites, and some unity in the appearance of early liturgical garb gradually emerged from a common late Roman heritage of garments and communication among clerics. This still left plenty of room for local traditions, which were constantly developing in dialogue with centers of power. The desire to differentiate clerics also grew over the early Middle Ages to include calls for distinctive attire outside of church and stronger visual contrasts among the various ranks of clergy serving at the altar. Carolingian monarchs and bishops intensified these processes in the ninth century by self-consciously working to "correct" ecclesiastical customs. Their seriousness about creating a Christian society focused attention on the most basic aspects of pastoral care and gave rise to more concerted efforts to produce better purveyors of it. These goals motivated subsequent generations of reformers. Those in the eleventh century concentrated on how clerics acquired their positions and on their living conditions, provoking violent conflicts over simony, lay investiture, and clerical celibacy. They did not articulate much interest in clerical clothing until the early twelfth century, when a new set of preoccupations emerged. Their concerns were to advance a public place for the clerical order acceptable to lay powers, to define the clergy as models of Christian comportment, and to assert the holiness of the entire clerical order. This latter developed out of a more intense conflation of purity with holiness and a struggle to codify its outward manifestations. Clothing was only one means to these ends, but it was one prominent in the legislation of the Western church.

After tracing the earliest development of distinctive clerical attire in Western Christianity, in this chapter I will describe the concerns about clothing articulated by ecclesiastical leaders in conciliar legislation and how they changed across the early and central Middle Ages. I locate a major change in the eleventh and twelfth centuries with at least three important aspects. First, whereas the legislation of the early Middle Ages was equally concerned with what clerics wore in church and what they wore outside of it, the decrees of the central Middle Ages focused overwhelmingly on clerical attire outside the sanctuary. To a certain degree this was because the rules and acceptable customs for liturgical vesture had been agreed on. But to a much larger degree it was due to new questions animating Western society about relations between ecclesiastical and temporal powers. Second, whereas early medieval legislation demanded the expression of respect and veneration for the holiness of the Mass though proper and seemly attire, conciliar decrees of the central Middle Ages assumed a more intimate relation between the person of the cleric and his clothing and associated both with holiness. A subtle but critical expansion of the sacred had solidified, at least ideologically. Some clerical servants of the altar in early medieval Europe were believed to have achieved holiness, but all of these servants by the twelfth century were supposed to "exhibit holiness." Third, clerical exhibition of holiness had become dichotomous by the twelfth century. Although early medieval legislation sometimes demanded that clerical vestments used within church not be worn outside of it, the legislation of the central Middle Ages much more emphatically prescribed not only that different garments be worn in these different spaces but also that these two kinds of clothing be sharply visually distinct. The liturgical expression in silk and gold vestments makes few appearances in ecclesiastical law but is obvious in the visual sources that will be the focus of chapter 3. The legal sources that are the focus of this chapter reveal the sharply contrasting plain and modest attire that was codified as the appropriate and acceptable public exhibition of clerical holiness. This contrast between a highly ornate style for one set of functions and a plain or "low" style for others became a significant contribution of clerical culture to Western uses of clothing.

The Origins of Distinctive Clerical Attire in the Christian Tradition

There are two types of distinctive clerical garb in Western Christianity. The first is liturgical vestments, which are the special garments worn when performing sacred functions. The second is what we might call clerical "street-wear," which is particular clothing worn outside of church in order to indicate clerical status. Our evidence for the former is fuller and earlier than that for the latter. But the origins of both are in the making of early Christianity, a complex process of innovation and amalgamation shaped most strongly by Roman culture. In developing liturgical attire, as in other areas of ecclesiastical material culture, early Christians chose to adapt and sacralize Roman civil traditions rather than modifying contemporary religious practices. One might regard this as natural in light of Christian hostility toward paganism and the vexed nature of Christianity's relationship with Judaism, but whole centuries of possible experimentation are simply lost to us. The sources begin to give us some sense of Christian priestly attire only in the fourth century.

The Christian priesthood itself was a creation of these obscure centuries. Although Judaism before the Roman destruction of the Temple in 70 CE had elaborately garbed priests and high priests,[1] the New Testament applied the terms "priest" (*hiereus*) and "high priest" (*archiereus*) only to Jesus. Altogether different terms are used for the leadership positions that appear in Paul's letters to early Christian communities: apostles, prophets, teachers, overseers (*episkopoi*), elders (*presbyteroi*), and servants (*diakonoi*).[2] The latter three, however, were clearly forming an official hierarchy by the early second century, and Ignatius of Antioch (c. 35–c. 107) referred to bishops as both priests and high priests as does the *Traditio apostolica*, once attributed to Hippolytus of Rome (c. 170–c. 236). This text gives ordination rites for bishops and priests that emphasize the laying

1. Exod. 28; Emil Schürer, *The History of the Jewish People in the Age of Jesus Christ (175 B.C.–A.D. 135)*, rev. English ed., 3 vols., ed. Geza Vermes, Fergus Millar, and Matthew Black (Edinburgh, 1973), 2:244; R.J. Zwi Werblowsky and Geoffrey Wigoder, eds. *The Oxford Dictionary of the Jewish Religion* (Oxford, 1997), s.v. "priestly vestments."

2. Ralph P. Martin and Peter H. Davids, eds., *Dictionary of the Later New Testament and Its Developments* (Downers Grove, Ill., 1997), s.v. "Priest, high priest"; Frank C. Senn, *Christian Liturgy: Catholic and Evangelical* (Minneapolis, 1997), 102.

on of hands (I.2, I.7), a tradition that appears in the New Testament.[3] However, none of the defining Levitical acts for the making of priests—anointing the head with holy oil, consecrating the hands, and being vested with holy vestments (Lev. 21:10)—are included.

By the late fourth century, however, the Christian hierarchy had expanded, and the clergy had definitely developed vestments for the liturgy. A clear piece of evidence is that the various clerical orders began disputing over who could wear what: canon 22 of the late fourth-century Council of Laodicea in Asia Minor prohibited subdeacons from wearing the *orarium*, or stole, a sort of liturgical scarf that developed either from the Roman *sudarium* (handkerchief, neck-cloth) or from late Roman consular insignia.[4] It is worth noting here that late antique Christians did embrace functional specializations among the clergy (doorkeeper, exorcist, lector, acolyte, deacon), a prominent feature of the Roman priesthoods.[5] And like the ritual specialists of Roman "paganism," the different orders of the Christian clergy came to have distinctive garb.

Rhetoric about Christian attire, however, emphasized difference. The fathers of the church fulminated generally against luxury and vainglory, and particularly condemned the wearing of silk, purple, and gold by Christians.[6] The Council of Narbonne in 589 specifically banned clerical wearing of purple, an expensive color associated with the emperors, but also in the late empire associated with soldiers, imperial functionaries, and provincial Roman priesthoods.[7] As late as 743 too the Roman church seemed

3. The *Traditio apostolica* is now viewed as a composite document preserving materials from perhaps as early as the mid-second century to the mid-fourth. See Maxwell E. Johnson, "The Apostolic Tradition," in *The Oxford History of Christian Worship*, ed. Geoffrey Wainwright and Karen B. Westerfield Tucker (Oxford, 2006), 32–35; Bernard Botte ed., *La Tradition Apostolique d'après les anciennes versions*, 2nd ed., Sources Chrétiennes 11bis (Paris, 1968), 40, 56; Hippolytus of Rome, *The Treatise on the Apostolic Tradition of St Hippolytus of Rome*, ed. Gregory Dix, rev. ed. Henry Chadwick (London, 1992), 3, 13. On the institutional development of the early church: Wayne A. Meeks, "Social and Ecclesial Life of the Earliest Christians," and Stuart George Hall, "Institutions in the Pre-Constantinian *Ecclesia*," both in *The Cambridge History of Christianity*, vol. 1, *Origins to Constantine*, ed. Margaret M. Mitchell and Frances M. Young (Cambridge, 2006), 153–56, 416–21; Vittorino Grossi and Angelo Di Berardino, *La chiesa antica: Ecclesiologia e istituzioni* (Rome, 1984), 79–111.

4. Mansi, 2:579; Braun, *DLG*, 608–20; Louis Duchesne, *Christian Worship: Its Origin and Evolution*, trans. M. L. McClure, 5th ed. (London, 1956), 390–94; *DACL*, s.v. "étole."

5. Not only did Roman religion have functional specializations—such as the *haruspices* who read the entrails of sacrificial animals and the *pontifices* who set the calendar and determined religious law—but each had its distinctive attire. The purple-edged toga (*toga praetexta*) was worn by magistrates as well as by several types of priests (e.g., the *pontifices*, the *arvales*), but some had more distinctive garments, such as the purple- and scarlet-striped mantle (*trabea*) of the augurs. There were also special garments for particular functions, such as the fringed tunic worn by the *quindecimviri* during the immolation of sacrificial animals. *Thesaurus cultus et rituum antiquorum*, 5 vols. (Los Angeles, 2004–2006), 5:71–72, 79, 81, 92 (Rome); 120, 124, 128–29 (provinces).

6. Roland Delmaire, "Le vêtement, symbole de richesse et de pouvoir, d'après les textes patristiques et hagiographiques due Bas-Empire," in *Costume et société dans l'Antiquité et le haut Moyen Age*, ed. François Chausson and Hervé Inglebert (Paris, 2003), 85–98.

7. Ibid., 92; Charles de Clercq ed., *Concilia Galliae A. 511–A. 695*, CC 148A (Turnhout, 1963), 254; Mansi, 9:1015.

concerned to expunge any visual references with pagan associations, prohibiting any bishop, priest, or deacon from celebrating the solemnities of the Mass "entering with a staff [*baculo*] or assisting at the altar of God with veiled head [*velato capite*]." This latter gesture, the veiling of the head to offer sacrifice, was the most common Roman religious use of clothing and it was not restricted to the priesthood: it was customary for men to pull a fold of their toga up over their heads and for women to do the same with their mantles.[8] Canon 9 of the same council banned celebrations of the Kalends of January and the winter solstice with pagan rites (*ritu paganorum*).

What did these early liturgical garments look like? Answering this question is fraught with epistemological and source problems, some of which will be confronted in chapter 3 and in the glossary provided. For the moment, however, a few orienting remarks and examples will have to suffice. As has often been noted by historians of costume, the Christian clergy adopted and adapted common articles of Roman civil attire as their new sacred clothing. The priestly chasuble (*planeta*, *casula*, *amphibalus*), for example, seems to have been a variant of the *paenula*, a simple poncho-like Roman cape widely worn as an outer garment over a tunic.[9] This tunic, the basic male garment throughout the empire, was often made of white linen and became the most basic liturgical robe, the alb.[10] The dalmatic, which became the characteristic attire of deacons, was a type of tunic—originally from Dalmatia, as the name suggests—that became widely popular throughout the empire from the late second or early third century. Narrow purple or red stripes (*clavi*) running from the shoulders to the hem usually distinguish the dalmatic from other styles of tunic, although more elaborate decorative patterns were employed.[11] In several ways, the choice of such common and widely available articles of clothing does seem perfectly natural. Before the era of legal toleration inaugurated by Constantine in 313, discretion certainly fostered the survival of Christian communities and militated against the development of highly distinctive clerical garb. With the advent of toleration, one can readily imagine a period of experimentation with what was at hand. Common garments also had the advantage of not being already freighted with religious meanings, although they certainly conveyed social and cultural statements that are very difficult to reconstruct today.

8. Toga-draped ("togate") representations of emperors in the first and second centuries often included this veiling of the head as a sign of piety. Alexandra T. Croom, *Roman Clothing and Fashion* (Stroud, 2000), 47; Richard Gordon, "The Veil of Power: Emperors, Sacrificers and Benefactors," in *Pagan Priests: Religion and Power in the Ancient World*, ed. Mary Beard and John North (London, 1990), 201–31.

9. Braun, *DLG*, 239–47; Duchesne, *Christian Worship*, 379–81; *DACL*, s.v. "chasuble."

10. The early fifth-century Council of Carthage required deacons to wear the alb during readings and when oblations were made: Mansi, 3:954 (can. 41). See generally Braun, *DLG*, 57–61; *DACL*, s.v. "aube." For archaeological evidence on tunic types in the Roman world: Alexandra Lorquin, "Le costume dans l'antiquité tardive d'après les vestiges textiles coptes," in Chausson and Inglebert, *Costume et société dans l'Antiquité*, 121–28.

11. Braun, *DLG*, 299–302; *DACL*, s.v. "dalmatique."

The ambivalence evident in early Christian texts about the emergence of liturgical vestments, however, suggests that the process was not perceived by everyone as either natural or welcome. In his *Dialogue against the Pelagians* (I.30), for example, Jerome (c. 340–420) has his heretic assert that "the glory of dress and ornament is repugnant to God." The response of the orthodox interlocutor reveals the target of Pelagian criticism: "How is it repugnant to God, I ask, if I wear a cleaner tunic or if the bishop, priest, deacon, and the rest of the ecclesiastical orders go forth to administer sacrifices dressed in shining white? Clerics and monks, beware! Widows and virgins, you are in danger, unless the crowd sees you squalid and ragged."[12] Roughly contemporary with Jerome's sarcastic defense of special liturgical attire are Sulpicius Severus's hagiographic works on Martin of Tours. As this saint was famous for having given half his cloak to a freezing beggar outside the gate of Amiens, it should not surprise us that clothing constitutes an important image in Severus's vita and dialogue on Martin's virtues. When the monk Martin is chosen bishop of Tours by popular acclaim, some people, "among these some of the bishops, who had been summoned to appoint a chief priest, were impiously offering resistance." Their objections? He was unworthy of the episcopate in their view, Severus recounts, because "he was a man despicable in countenance, his clothing was mean, and his hair disgusting." This episcopal critique of Martin's appearance is not only labeled "impious" and "madness," but Severus goes further in censuring such attitudes by having divine intervention support the virtuous Martin. In an implied critique of the usual behavior and dress of bishops, the author also praises Martin's cultivation of "the same humility in his heart, and the same homeliness in his garments" after being raised to the see. Indeed, a vignette from the *Dialogi* (2.1) in which Martin gives his own clothing to a poor man depicts the saint's usual attire for the liturgy as a tunic and a coarse chasuble (*amphibalus*).[13]

Unease about special liturgical attire afflicted even the papacy. Responding to concerns of the bishops of Narbonne and Vienne, Pope Celestine I wrote in 428 that priests and clerics should not officiate at church services "wrapped in a pallium and with limbs girded." Although some historians of dress have interpreted this letter simply as opposition to special vestments, it is better understood as evidence of two more important developments. First, Celestine is certainly echoing in a pastoral voice the concerns about vacuous pomp evident in both the Pelagian critique answered by Jerome and in Sulpicius Severus's depiction of the episcopate in Gaul. Celestine objected not so much to the

12. Jerome, *Dialogus adversus Pelagianos*, ed. Claudio Moreschini, CC 80 (Turnhout, 1990), 38. The adoption of "shining white" garments is likely responding to Mark's description of Jesus' transfiguration when "his garments became shining and exceeding white as snow" (9:2).

13. Sulpicius Severus, *Vita di Martino*, ed. Fabio Ruggiero, Biblioteca Patristica 40 (Bologna, 2003), 98–102 (9.3, 10.2); Sulpicius Severus, *Gallus: Dialogues sur les "vertus" de Saint Martin*, ed. Jacques Fontaine, Souces Chrétiennes 510 (Paris, 2006), 216–18. On Severus's attitudes generally toward the clergy, see Clare Stancliffe, *St. Martin and His Hagiographer: History and Miracle in Sulpicius Severus* (Oxford, 1982), 265–72; and on clothing imagery, Sylvie Labarre, "Le vêtement dans la *Vie de Saint Martin* (IVe s.): Signe social et valeur symbolique," in Chausson and Inglebert, *Costume et société dans l'Antiquité*, 129–41.

particular costumes that the bishops complained of, but of these priests', and their bishops', focus on exterior rather than interior states. The pope characterizes the priests as serving "more in superstitious reverence than in purity of mind," but he chides their bishops for overreacting and for missing an opportunity to teach true priestly virtues. At the very origins of Christian liturgical dress there were within the church those who embraced majesty and solemnity in the name of honoring God and those who found ornament offensive as a betrayal of Jesus' message. This division and tension remained constant in Western Christianity, flaring up repeatedly into rancorous theological and institutional clashes.

The second development evident in the letter is diversity and experimentation in creating Christian customs. From some of the pope's queries, it seems that these bishops had left the safety of their cathedral cities to visit some of their subject churches only to be shocked and appalled at what they found. "Perhaps they have this observance," suggests Celestine of the offending priests, "since they live in remote places, far from others [i.e., other clerics]." This, too, would be a frequently enacted scenario in medieval Christianity: bishops hardly ever liked what they found out in the farther reaches of their dioceses. But another papal observation suggests an interesting syncretism provoking this particular outburst of episcopal despair. "It's not surprising," Celestine wrote, "that these go against ecclesiastical custom, wrapped in the pallium and limbs girded, believing themselves to be fulfilling the faith of scripture not through the spirit but through the letter, for they did not grow up in the church, but coming from another observance brought with them that which they had in another usage."[14]

Where did these priests come from? From which "other observance" (*alia ritu*), from which "other usage" (*alia conversatione*) were they bringing these outfits? There are at least two possibilities. The "other usage" could be monastic life, and historians of early Christianity have preferred this interpretation without proffering convincing evidence to support it.[15] Did monks in early fifth-century Gaul wear belted pallia? Jerome's Latin translation of the Rule of Pachomius specifically bans the wearing of pallia. John Cassian's *Institutes*, written between 420 and 429 in southern Gaul, do emphasize that monks should gird themselves with a belt and mention that Egyptian ascetics carried staffs, *bacula*, another accessory mentioned in Celestine's letter. But Cassian refrains from recommending a particular monastic robe, instead praising the cowls (*cucullae*) and tunics (*colobia*) of Egyptian monks.[16]

14. "Sed non mirum, si contra ecclesiasticum morem faciunt, qui in ecclesia non creverunt, sed alio venientes è ritu, secum haec in ecclesiam, quae in alia conversatione habuerant, intulerunt; amicti pallio, & lumbos praecincti, credentes se Scripturae fidem, non per spiritum, sed per litteram completuros." Pierre Coustant, ed., *Epistolae Romanorum Pontificum* (Paris, 1721), 1:1066–67.

15. Léon Cristiani, "Essai sur les origines du costume ecclésiastique," *Orientalia Christiana periodica* 13 (1947): 69–79; Louis Trichet, *La tonsure* (Paris, 1990), 29–30; Robert Godding, *Prêtres en Gaule mérovingienne* (Brussels, 2001), 28.

16. Amand Boon, ed., *Pachomiana Latina*, Bibliothèque de la Revue d'histoire ecclésiastique 7 (Louvain, 1932), 37 or *PL*, 23:74; John Cassian, *De institutis coenobiorum e de octo principalium vitiorum remediis*

Another, in my view more likely, possibility is that the "other usage" is philosophy: the pallium was the gown of the philosopher. Christianity at first embraced this attire. The second-century Christian apologist Justin Martyr taught in Rome wearing the pallium, and Tertullian (c. 160–c. 225) gave up the toga for the pallium. The fact that he wrote a speech, *De pallio*, defending his change of attire demonstrates how contested this symbol of ancient learning and spiritual guidance was. Tertullian overtly claims the philosopher's mantle as Christian garb: "Be glad and rejoice, o you pallium, now that you serve a better philosophy, since you clothe the Christian."[17] Jesus himself and his apostles were depicted in this garb from the fourth century on, and perhaps this understanding of Christ as the "teacher of true philosophy" fostered the development of different apparel for the human leaders of Christian congregations. Augustine, who came to the faith via philosophical studies, referred disparagingly to philosophers in his *City of God* (13.16) as *palliati.* It seems entirely plausible that some local Christian leaders in early fifth-century Gaul came into the church from similar backgrounds, still wearing their pallia. This reading makes more sense of Celestine's identification of the pallium-wearers as "those who did not grow up in the church" (or "those who were not born in the church": *qui in ecclesia non creverunt*) and also accords with his reference to these priests carrying bacula.[18] Celestine's letter captures a moment in the emergence of liturgical vestments when the church's custom was not yet fixed or clear, and diverse notions of appropriate attire existed.

libri xii, ed. Michael Petschenig, rev. ed., CSEL 17 (Vienna, 2004), 7–16 (Lib. I); in English, *The Institutes*, trans. Boniface Ramsey, Ancient Christian Writers 58 (New York, 2000), 19–27. The Rule of Saint Augustine gives no specific provisions regarding clothes, except that they be kept together and distributed according to need and season. Of the rules postdating the letter, the evidence is mixed. Caesarius of Arles's brief rule for monks (535–542) doesn't specify the form of "religious" clothes to be worn, only that the abbot distributes them: *Sancti Caesarii Arelatensis Opera Omnia*, ed. Germanus Morin, 2 vols. (Maretioli, 1937–1942), 2:149–55. Nor are garments prescribed in the late sixth-century Rule of Columbanus, which was widely diffused in Gaul, even replacing Caesarius's rule in the monastery of Lérins: *Sancti Columbani Opera*, ed. G.S.M. Walker, Scriptores Latini Hiberniae 2 (Dublin, 1957), xxxiii, 122–69. The Rule of the Master (500–530) does use the word *pallia* to describe the monk's outer cloak (chap. 81), but chapter 55 of Saint Benedict's Rule (c. 540) prescribes the cowl (*cuculla*) and tunic (*tunica*): Adalbert de Vogüé, ed., *La Règle du Maître*, 3 vols., Sources chrétiennes 105–7 (Paris, 1964–1965), 2:330–32; Rudolph Hanslik, ed., *Benedicti Regula*, CSEL 75 (Vienna, 1960), 127–30, or Bruce L. Venarde, ed. and trans., *The Rule of Saint Benedict*, Dumbarton Oaks Medieval Library 6 (Cambridge, 2011), 178–79. Isidore of Seville (560–636) uses the term *pallium* to describe monastic garb: *Reglas monásticas de la España visigoda: Los tres libros de las "Sentencias,"* ed. and trans. Julio Campos Ruiz and Ismael Roca Melia, Biblioteca de Autores Cristianos, Santos Padres Españoles 2 (Madrid, 1971), 109–10 (chap. 12).

17. Paul Zanker, *The Mask of Socrates: The Image of the Intellectual in Antiquity*, trans. Alan Shapiro (Berkeley: University of California Press, 1995), 267–331, quote on 267; Stefan Heid, "The Romanness of Roman Christianity," in A *Companion to Roman Religion*, ed. Jörg Rüpke (Malden, Mass., 2007), 408; Delmaire, "Le vêtement," 87; T. Corey Brennan, "Tertullian's *De pallio* and Roman Dress in North Africa," in *Roman Dress and the Fabrics of Roman Culture*, ed. Jonathan Edmondson and Alison Keith (Toronto, 2008), 257–70.

18. "Nam si ad hoc ista praecepta sunt, ut taliter servarentur: cur non fiunt pariter quae sequuntur, ut lucernae ardentes in manibus unà cum baculo teneantur?" *Epistolae Romanorum Pontificum*, 1:1067.

A century later in Rome, however, there seems to be an effort, at least on the part of the author of the first redaction of the *Liber pontificalis*, to depict the use of special liturgical vestments as an ancient, papally sanctioned custom. Working probably in the 530s, the compiler attributes to Pope Stephen I (254–257) the decree that "*sacerdotes* and deacons should not use the consecrated vestments for everyday purposes but only in church." He praises Pope Sylvester (314–335) for establishing "that the deacons should wear dalmatics, and that their left arms should be covered with pallia, half wool, half linen." In what seems a concession to criticism, he further attributes to this pope the decree "that the sacrifice of the altar should not be celebrated in silk or in dyed cloth, but only in naturally produced linen, just as the body of our Lord Jesus Christ was buried in a fine linen shroud."[19]

If the emergence of liturgical vesture was contested and varied, it seems well established in the Western church in the sixth century.[20] The emergence of clerical street-wear—that is, special garb to denote clerical status outside of church—begins in the sixth century, reversing an earlier preference for indistinction. Saint Jerome (c. 345–420), in his letter to Nepotian on clerical duties, concerning lectors and acolytes urged "let their character, not their dress, be their adornment." Similarly, canon 26 of the *Statuta ecclesiae antiqua* (Gaul, c. 475) enjoined, "Let the cleric show his calling in his manner and bearing, and therefore let him not seek ornament in either clothes or shoes."[21] The Council of Agde (or Agatha, in Languedoc) in 506, however, limited the clergy to wearing clothing "which is proper to religion," and the Council of Mâcon in 583 repeated this injunction, specifying that "no cleric presume to wear a military cloak or secular clothing or shoes [*sagum aut vestimenta vel calciamenta saecularia*]." The canon goes on to prescribe thirty days' incarceration on only bread and water for any cleric

19. *Liber pontificalis*, 1:154, 171; English translation: Raymond Davis, ed. and trans., *The Book of Pontiffs* (Liverpool, 1989), 10, 15. For other evidence of distinguishing between liturgical and nonliturgical garb, see Odette Pontal, "Recherches sur le costume des clercs des origines au XIVe siècle d'après les décrets ces conciles et des synodes," *L'année canonique* 17 (1973): 773. This serial collection of papal biographies was compiled by several authors at intervals from the early sixth century into the later Middle Ages. Although it contains some apocryphal materials, its authors also recorded events of which they had first-hand experience and copied information from sources now lost. See the discussion in the introduction of Davis's translation and the authoritative annotation of Duchesne's edition.

20. In addition to the evidence already discussed, the Iberian Council of Braga in 561–563 gave specific provisions for how deacons should wear their stoles and prohibited lectors from chanting in church "in secular attire": José Vives, ed., *Concilios Visigóticos e hispano-romanos*, España cristiana, textos I (Madrid, 1963), 73; Mansi, 9:778. On the sixth century as an important period of transformation, Pontal, "Recherches," 773–78.

21. *Select Letters of St. Jerome*, trans. F.A. Wright (Cambridge, Mass., 1963), 202–3; "Clericus professionem suam etiam habitu et incessu probet et ideo nec vestibus nec calceamentis decorem quaerat." Charles Munier, ed., *Concilia Galliae A. 314–A. 506*, CC 148 (Turnhout, 1963), 171. Ambrose (d. 397) in his *De officiis* (I.83) counseled modesty, which is "promoted not by the wearing of expensive or brightly coloured garb but by plain, ordinary clothes. This way, there is no neglect of what is honourable or necessary, but equally there is no pretension towards display." Ambrose, *De officiis*, ed. and trans. Ivor J. Davidson, 2 vols., Oxford Early Christian Studies (Oxford, 2001), 167.

found "with indecent clothing or arms."[22] A similar association of secularity with weapons is clear in the first canon of the Council of Bordeaux in the mid-seventh century: "Clerics ought to wear religiously the dress conceded to them, and they should not bear or have lances, other arms, or any secular attire."[23]

The militarization of Western societies appears to be the crucial change driving the desire to visualize clerical status beyond the confines of the sanctuary. The prohibition on clerics carrying weapons was repeated in council after council over the early Middle Ages, and Carolingian royal capitularies were equally emphatic.[24] As the research of Friedrich Prinz has amply demonstrated, however, this ban was never applied to the higher clergy, who were expected to raise and lead armies in the service of the king. As Prinz noted, the *Admonitio generalis* of 789 specified that deacons and priests "should not carry weapons, but entrust themselves more to the protection of God than arms," but said nothing about bishops and abbots. Since contemporary legislation against clerics hunting explicitly named bishops and abbots, it would seem that the military obligations of the higher clergy came to constitute a special exception to the more general ban on violence and bloodshed.[25]

Although ecclesiastical legislation from the sixth century is fairly clear about what the clergy should not wear, it is ambiguous about what they should. Evidence from the eighth century suggests the concept of a particular clerical outfit. The Council of Rome in 743 enjoined the wearing of the "priestly tunic" (*tunica sacerdotale*), while a Bavarian council in 798 stated simply that "those who minister at the altar of the Lord should be different from the rest of the people." Commanding that "they should wear clerical clothes [*clericali vestitu vestiantur*]," the canon explains that "just as they ought to be different in manners [*moribus*] from secular people, so too in their clothing."[26] But what were these "clerical clothes"? The evidence suggests various interpretations of what constituted clerical garb. In his *Etymologies* (19.23), Isidore of Seville (c. 560–636) equates the *tunica sacerdotalis* with the dalmatic, but there is little evidence that this classically Roman vestment was yet widely used beyond the Alps.[27] The story of Alban's martyrdom in the *Historia ecclesiastica* suggests that English custom may have been for

22. *Concilia Galliae A. 511–A. 695*, 224; Mansi, 9:933; see also canon 6 of the Council of Metz, in 888, Mansi, 18:79.

23. *MGH Concilia* 1:156–57, 215.

24. In addition to the councils already cited, add those of Saint Jean de Losne in 673–675, Austrasia in 742, Reisbach in 798 and 800, Meaux in 845, Tours 858, Senlis in the ninth century, Freising in the mid-ninth, Reims 1049, Narbonne 1054, Rome 1059, Gerona 1068 and 1078, Poitiers 1078, Clermont 1095, and London 1138 and 1175: *MGH Concilia* 2:3, 197, 213; 3:85; *MGH Cap. episc.* 2:151, 3:86, 227; Mansi, 19:742, 830, 915, 1071; 20:495–502, 518–19, 817; 21:513; 22:150. Capitularies from 742, 758–768, 769, 789 (Admonitio generalis), 802, and the ninth-century collection of Ansegis also prohibit clerics from bearing arms: *MGH Cap.* 1:25, 41, 44, 59, 103; *MGH Cap. Nova Series* I: 466.

25. Friedrich Prinz, *Klerus und Krieg im früheren Mittelalter: Untersuchungen z. Rolle d. Kirche beim Aufbau d. Konigsherrschaft* (Stuttgart, 1971), 1–35, 81–83.

26. *MGH Concilia* 2:10 (Rome, canon 13), 199 (Reisbach, canon 7).

27. Mayo, *Ecclesiastical Dress*, 16; Braun, *DLG*, 252–58.

clerics to wear a *paenula*-like garment called the *caracalla*. In Bede's recounting of the tale, the future saint hides a fugitive priest in his home and is slowly converted to Christianity by him. When soldiers come to seize the priest, Alban puts on his cloak (*ipsius habitu, id est caracalla qua uestiebatur*), and the soldiers, thinking him the fugitive cleric, seize Alban.[28] The *Admonitio synodalis*, on the other hand, gives the impression that a priest's garb outside of church was simply a different alb than he used at Mass: "Let no one presume to sing Mass in an alb that he uses in his own employ [*qua in suos usus utitur*]."[29] Given the varied evidence of what was recognized as clerical attire, it is perhaps unsurprising that in the ninth century people still had trouble identifying priests beyond the confines of their churches. A canon of the Council of Trebra in Thuringia (895) that was incorporated into later manuscript copies of the *Admonitio synodalis* admonished, "Let priests not go about without wearing a stole or *orarium*. And if priests when traveling without a stole are robbed, wounded, or killed, let simple compensation be paid; if with a stole, triple."[30] This directly contradicts, of course, other canons restricting the stole to liturgical use, but it does suggest that reasonable doubt arose in legal cases about whether a criminal knew the ecclesiastical status of his victim.

A major impediment to establishing uniform clerical street-wear was surely the cost of clothing. Only the very wealthy were buried clothed; for the mass of the population in early medieval Europe, garments were too valuable to be thrown away.[31] They were passed down, patched, and reused. Where did the clergy get clothes? In religious communities, clothing was supposed to be provided from the revenues yielded by the lands donated to the house. The mid-eighth-century rule for cathedral clergy by Chrodegang of Metz, for example, set out precise clothing rations: priests and deacons received two tunics and two shirts each year, while minor clerics received one of each. Everyone received one pair of leather boots and four pairs of sandals, the costs of which the bishop helped subsidize through the "shoe money" (*calciaticum*) that he donated every year. Even in a community with endowed revenues, however, clothing was recycled. The senior half of the clergy received a new cloak (*cappa*) every year and passed down their old

28. Bede's account implies that the soldiers knew what a priest looked like from his clothing, but the magistrate who condemns Alban seems to have recognized him regardless of his borrowed attire. *Bede's Ecclesiastical History of the English People*, ed. and trans. Bertram Colgrave and R.A.B. Mynors (Oxford, 1969), 28–31.

29. Amiet, *AS*, 45. Somewhat clearer is the language of Bishop Riculf of Soissons in his 889 constitutions: "omnimodis prohibemus ut nemo illa alba utatur in sacris mysteriis qua in quotidiano vel exteriori usu induitur"; *MGH Cap. episc.* 2:104; Mansi, 18:81.

30. *MGH Cap.* 2:248; Amiet, *AS*, 60; *MGH Cap. episc.* 3:228.

31. Only 2–3% of excavated burials yield evidence of the corpse having been clothed. Roberta Gilchrist and Barney Sloane, *Requiem: The Medieval Monastic Cemetery in Britain* (London, 2003), 80; Gabrielle Démians d'Archimbaud, "Archéologie et vêtement médiéval: Apports et limites des recherches récentes en France méditerranéenne," in *Vêtement et sociétés 2: Actes du colloque national C.N.R.S. "Vers un anthropologie du vêtement," Musée de l'Homme (9–11 mars 1983)*, ed. Yves Delaport, special issue of *L'Ethnographie* 80 (1984): 317–18.

cloaks to the other half.[32] The situation of the average parish priest was more precarious. Rural clergy depended for their livelihoods on the tithes their parishioners were supposed to pay and on the revenues yielded by whatever lands might be attached to the church. These lands, their revenues, and even tithes, however, were quite frequently held and administered by local lords, who theoretically were supposed to provide for the support of the clergy. But how little might trickle down is evident when we get parish inventories and, in the later Middle Ages, visitation records.[33] Involuntary poverty likely afflicted some portion of the clergy in the earlier period if even in a more economically sophisticated era priests could be pitifully poor. Indeed, the *Liber pontificalis* praised the mid-eighth-century pope Stephen II for paying off the debts of the Roman clergy and providing them tunics and chasubles "so that they might all be found well-attired in God's church."[34]

What a well-to-do priest might own in the way of clothing is revealed in a ninth-century petition to the bishop of Tongres. An Irish or Scottish priest returning from Rome complained of being robbed by his traveling companions of "an alb with a stole and two corporals, one good black cloak worth three *uncie*, a tunic with two ties worth two *solidi*, a shirt worth two *solidi*, a tunic [*rocum*] worth one *uncia*, four pair of Scottish hose, one fur, and other little things that, nevertheless, I needed." He begged alms of the bishop: "Let your piety overcome the impiety of the thieves!"[35] The value of clothing is also evident in the custom of making bequests of garments. When he died in 542, Bishop Caesarius of Arles left to whoever succeeded him in the see "all the paschal vestments that were given to me . . . together with the better quality shaggy cloak, the better quality tunic, and the thick cloak, which I have left behind." The rest of his clothes, with the exception of his hooded cloak, were to be divided among his clerical and lay servants.[36] The wills of less well-to-do priests also reveal the pious practice of leaving

32. Jerome Bertram, *The Chrodegang Rules: The Rules for the Common Life of the Secular Clergy from the Eighth and Ninth Centuries, Critical Texts with Translations and Commentary* (Aldershot, 2005), 45, 74–75.

33. Carl I. Hammer, Jr., "Country Churches, Clerical Inventories and the Carolingian Renaissance in Bavaria," *Church History* 49 (1980): 5–16 reveals great variation in the material possessions of parishes; more bleak pictures are given by Charles M. de la Roncière, "Condizioni economiche del clero parrocchiale, rurale e urbano, nell'Europa meridionale, XII–XV secoli (osservazioni da lavori recenti)," in *Gli spazi economici della Chiesa nell'Occidente mediterraneo (secoli XII–metà XIV)* (Pistoia, 1999), 329–61, especially 341–42, 354–57; and Daniel Bornstein, "Spiritual Culture, Material Culture: Church Inventories in Fifteenth-Century Cortona," *Medievalia et Humanistica*, n.s. 28 (2001): 101–15.

34. *Liber pontificalis*, 1:443; English translation in *The Lives of the Eighth-Century Popes*, trans. Raymond Davis (Liverpool, 1992), 57.

35. " Homines, qui mecum erant in eadem navi, spolia mea rapuerunt, hoc est unam albam cum stola et corporalibus duobus et unam bonam nigram capam III uncias valentem, et tonicam cum fasciolis valentem II solidos, et unam camisiam II solidos valentem, et unum rocum valentem unciam, et IIII osas Scotticae vestis, et unam pelliciam et reliquas minutas causas, sed mihi necessarias." *MGH Epp.* 6:196–97.

36. "Sancto et domino meo pontifici, qui mihi indigno digne successerit, licet omnia in sua potestate sint, tamen si iubet et dignum ducit, vestimenta paschalia, quae mihi data sunt, omnia illi serviant, simul cum casula villosa meliore et tunica vel guanape quod melius dimisero. Reliqua vero vestimenta mea excepto birro auricularii mei tam clerici quam laici cum gratia et ordinatione domini episcopi sibi ipso

clothes to other clerics: the priest Martin in 1159 left to another priest, named Blancus, "one *guarnellus* [a thick cotton tunic], my leather garment, a shirt, and a pair of pants."[37]

Under such varied conditions of clerical life and livelihood, bishops probably realized that requiring their clergy to have and wear a particular outfit would pose a hardship. This is perhaps why Carolingian and later legislation instead emphasized the tonsure as the visual marker of clerical status. As Louis Trichet's careful study makes clear, the term *tonsura* meant simply to cut the hair short and, following a Pauline admonition (1 Cor. 11:14–15), this became widely associated in the West by the fifth century with entry into clerical status. The practice of shaving the top of the head, leaving a circle of hair below, emerged slightly later, in sixth-century Gaul. In early medieval sources this is called the "crown" (*corona*). The custom spread to the Iberian Peninsula and to Italy in the seventh century and is well attested throughout northern Europe in the eighth century.[38] The first canon of the Council of Aachen in 816 set out the requirement for clerical tonsure using the words of Isidore of Seville: "Indeed, I esteem the sheared head above and the circular crown left below to represent in these [receiving it] the clerical dignity and the authority of the church." This famous reforming council urged canons to cultivate moderation in attire, but did not prescribe specific garb.[39]

The desire to distinguish the clergy visually remained constant across the rest of the Middle Ages. Although there had been some ambivalence in early Christianity over adopting distinctive garb, from the sixth century concerns shifted to regulating usages in liturgical vesture and defining what was appropriate clerical attire. Conciliar legislation allows us to trace these concerns not only across the medieval centuries but also across the many Christian communities of western Europe.

Rome and Beyond: Diversity and Unity in Early Medieval Liturgical Vestments

From early in the history of Christianity, bishops gathered together to discuss and resolve problems confronting their communities, disputes of various kinds, and questions

iubente immo donante dividant." *Sancti Caesarii Arelatensis Opera Omnia* 2:284–85; *PL*, 67:1140A; English translation available in *Caesarius of Arles: Life, Testament, Letters*, trans. William E. Klingshirn, Translated Texts for Historians 19 (Liverpool, 1994), 72. Theodred Bishop of London in the late tenth century left a chasuble "and all that belongs to it" (a matching stole and maniple?) to each of four individuals, specifying the colors (one white, one red, and two yellow, one ornamented and one not) and that he had bought two of them at Pavia. In the same period Bishop Alfwold of Crediton left his cope "to Edwin the mass-priest" and a set of Mass vestments to his see. D. Whitelock, M. Brett, and C. N. L. Brooke, eds., *Councils and Synods with Other Documents Relating to the English Church, I A.D. 871–1204* (Oxford, 1981), part 1 (871–1066), 81, 385–86.

37. "[R]elinquo presbitero Blanco unum guarnellum et pellem meam et camiseam et sarabolam"; *Archivio di Stato, Bologna*, Santo Stefano busta 11, perg. 19.

38. Trichet, *La tonsure*, 33, 41–85.

39. *MGH Concilia* 2:318 (chap. 1), 404–5 (chap. 124).

about belief, practice, and discipline. Called variously either synods or councils, provincial gatherings are documented from the early third century and larger "ecumenical" meetings from Nicaea in 325. For the sake of clarity, I will use "council" here to mean a gathering of bishops and reserve "synod" for a bishop's convocation of the priests of his diocese to discuss matters of pastoral care, but the reader should note that medieval authors were not similarly consistent in the use of these descriptive terms.[40] The decisions of councils, the "canons" or rules agreed on, came to constitute a body of ecclesiastical law that in the central Middle Ages was systematized and taught, ultimately becoming the basis of a complex judicial system. Early conciliar documentation, however, is anything but systematic.[41] Often our knowledge of a council comes from a passing mention in a chronicle or letter: "We indicate, therefore," wrote Gregory the Great in September of 595, "that the priest John, who bears this letter, has been acquitted of the accusations against him. We held a council and investigated his faith, as he asked, with a very careful examination, and we did not find any sign of a false confession in him."[42] The more direct documentation produced by councils—*acta*, narrative descriptions of what took place at a gathering, often closing with a list of all the bishops who took part, and of the *canones*, or the specific regulations passed—also gives a vivid sense of the varied things councils did. Highly individual concerns, such as the accusations against John or a property dispute between two religious communities, were addressed as well as quite abstract theological issues. I underscore the multipurpose character of ecclesiastical councils at the outset of this analysis of decrees on clerical clothing to make the reader aware that we are not in the early Middle Ages dealing with a parliamentary body the primary

40. This is the modern meaning in canon law of "synod": *DDC*, s.v. "concile" and "synode."

41. Since my interest is in all medieval ideas and practices concerning clerical clothing rather than in the emergence of a code of canon law, I have relied on the evidence of modern scholarly collections attempting to recover all canons rather than on the evidence of the medieval collections compiled for specific purposes. For the early Middle Ages, I have searched *MGH Cap.* I (507–827) and II (828–927); *MGH Cap. Nova Series* I; *MGH Concilia* I (511–695), II (742–842), III (843–859), IV (860–874), and VI (916–1001); *MGH Const.* I (911–1197); *MGH Cap. episc.* I–IV; Haddan & Stubbs. These were supplemented with more recent editions: Charles Munier and Charles de Clercq, eds., *Concilia Galliae, 314–695*, 2 vols., CC 148–148A; Vives, *Concilios Visigóticos e hispano-romanos*. For the eleventh and twelfth centuries, a systematic search of Mansi was checked against and supplemented with Heinz Wolter, *Die Synoden im Reichsgebiet und in Reichsitalien von 916 bis 1056* (Paderborn, 1988); Georg Gresser, *Die Synoden und Konzilien in der Zeit des Reformpapsttums in Deutschland und Italien von Leo IX. bis. Calixt II 1049–1123* (Paderborn, 2006); Uta-Renate Blumenthal, *The Early Councils of Pope Paschal II* (Toronto, 1978); Robert Somerville, *The Councils of Urban II*, vol. 1, *Decreta Claromontensia*, Annuarium Historiae Conciliorum, supplementum I (Amsterdam, 1972); idem, *Pope Urban II's Council of Piacenza March 1–7, 1095* (Oxford, 2011); idem and Stephan Kuttner, *Pope Urban II, the Collectio Britannica, and the Council of Melfi (1089)* (Oxford, 1996); and Somerville's many useful articles on individual councils collected in *Papacy, Councils and Canon Law in the 11th–12th Centuries* (Aldershot, 1990); Odette Pontal, *Les Conciles de la France capétienne jusqu'en 1215* (Paris, 1995); and *Councils and Synods*. On the deficiencies of Mansi, see Richard Kay, "Mansi and Rouen: A Critique of the Conciliar Collections," in *Councils and Clerical Culture in the Medieval West* (Aldershot, 1997), 4:155–68.

42. 6.17: CC 140:387; Gregory, *Letters*, 2:415.

purpose of which was to legislate.[43] Even when councils did agree on canons, the subjects treated were often quite different from modern notions of legislative matter: it does seem a bit odd, as one scholar has recently reminded us, to decide the nature of the divine by a vote.[44] Participants conceived of councils, moreover, as liturgies: they were "celebrated" and ordines were drawn up to guide their enactment just as for the Mass or baptism. And just as liturgies were performances of sacred power, so too were councils. This aspect of their unique character seems particularly prominent in the early Middle Ages when one sees less evidence of attempts to make the rules agreed on usable. Canons were collected and some efforts at systematization were apparent as early as the seventh century. We also have evidence of bishops consulting collections as well as making inquiries with other prelates about specific decrees. But it was not generally until the eleventh and twelfth centuries that canons were grouped by topic and principles for resolving conflicting authoritative claims were articulated. Indeed, the repetition of canons suggests a didactic purpose of these gatherings as well as ritualized performance of episcopal power.[45] Participating in a council, one senses, was on-the-job training in how to be a bishop, much as attending faculty meetings is an education in what comes with the title of "professor." Councils, however, called down the Holy Spirit to inform their actions and words. What this meant and how it shaped what went on in councils and the documentation left by them is hard for the historian to fathom.

Although the development of conciliar legislation into a system of law was a gradual process, canons from both the early and central Middle Ages do represent at least some bishops' concerns about ecclesiastical practices at a given historical moment.[46] Gatherings of bishops may have exaggerated the extent or severity of the problems addressed, but I think we can take their descriptions of clothing as reflecting the usages of some clerics in their dioceses. The historical record of medieval conciliar decrees is certainly imperfect: many more subjects were likely discussed and statutes enacted than we know

43. A good introduction to the character and sources of early medieval councils is Gregory I. Halfond, *Archaeology of Frankish Church Councils, AD 511–768* (Leiden, 2010), 8–26.

44. Ramsay MacMullen, *Voting about God in Early Church Councils* (New Haven, 2006).

45. I thank Anders Winroth for his observations on early efforts at systematization and readers should see his *Making of Gratian's Decretum* (Cambridge, 2000) on the twelfth-century organization of ecclesiastical law. On early medieval manuscript evidence for episcopal use of canonical collections, see Rosamond McKitterick, *The Frankish Church and the Carolingian Reforms, 789–895* (London, 1977), 18–44. Boniface's 747 letter to Archbishop Cuthbert of Canterbury reveals episcopal sharing of decrees, *Die Briefe des heiligen Bonifatius und Lullus*, ed. Michael Tangl (Berlin, 1955); *MGH Epp. Sel.* 1:161–70 (letter 78); and *The Letters of Saint Boniface*, trans. Ephraim Emerton (New York, 1940; repr. 2000), 114–19; see also Halfond, *Archaeology*, 159–79. Helpful in thinking about law in premodern societies is Patrick Wormald's *Legal Culture in the Early Medieval West: Law as Text, Image and Experience* (Hambledon, 1999), especially 1–43, and on the performative aspects of conciliar gatherings, Kay, "Mansi and Rouen," 167; Johannes Laudage, "Rituel und Recht aut päpstlichen Reformkonzilien (1049–1123)," *Annuarium historiae conciliorum* 29 (1997): 287–334. Conciliar *ordines* may be found in Herbert Schneider ed., *Ordines de celebrando concilio: Di Konzilordines des Früh- und Hochmittelalters* (Hannover, 1996).

46. As Halfond nicely puts it, the decrees of councils "are less reflections of reality than reactions to it." Halfond, *Archaeology*, 218 (quote), 99–130.

of today, and any statistical analysis would be ludicrous.[47] My intent here is to draw on the evidence of conciliar legislation only to interrogate patterns of diversity and unity in the usage of clerical clothing before the millennium. Was Europe a constellation of "micro-Christianities" with strongly regional clerical cultures? In particular, to what extent did Roman customs differ from those of churches beyond the Alps?

The brief answer is that they were quite a bit different before the expansion of Carolingian power in the mid-eighth century. Whereas councils north of the Alps voiced many concerns about clerical clothing practices, Roman councils articulated none. Papal correspondence reveals a strong awareness of the distinctiveness of Roman liturgical garb and a concern to control its use. But sharing in the vestimentary splendor of the Holy See was considered a privilege only popes could grant, not a requirement of all Western churches. Indeed, the letters of Gregory the Great reveal a notion of the "custom of the universal Church" that accommodated a great deal of liturgical diversity.

Before the Carolingian era, Roman conciliar documentation shows utterly no interest in clerical attire. Over fifty councils are documented between the fourth and early eighth centuries, but they are nearly entirely dedicated to doctrinal issues. In sum, the concerns of the Roman see were much broader—really, of an entirely different order—than those of provincial councils in Francia. All of the great doctrinal controversies and "heresies"—Arianism, Donatism, Monophysitism, Monothelitism—were addressed, and much of our knowledge of Roman councils comes from papal correspondence with emperors and bishops in the eastern Mediterranean.

Other papal letters, however, do reveal concern over controlling the use of particular attire that communicated special status, most notably a white woolen scarf called the pallium.[48] This ecclesiastical garment, firmly attested from the sixth century, was granted by popes to some bishops as a sign of particular favor and special authority. In 513, for example, Pope Symmachus conferred on Bishop Caesarius of Arles "alone the right to use the pallium throughout the whole of Gaul."[49] Eventually the pallium became associated with metropolitan status,[50] and already in the sixth century some sees were

47. Robert Somerville's observations on the transmission of conciliar records in the eleventh century, as well as the manuscript evidence he has compiled on the decrees of Clermont, well summarize the limitations of our sources: Somerville, *Councils of Urban II*, esp. 20–41.

48. The reader will have noticed that this word can denote several things. Most basically, a pallium is a piece of cloth, and the *Liber pontificalis* uses it repeatedly in this sense to itemize gifts of brocades, silks, and other precious fabrics. A piece of cloth draped, toga-like, over the body as a garment was also called a pallium (as in the discussion above of Celestine I's letter of 428), as were smaller drapings of cloth, such as the papally bestowed pallium. On the latter, see Braun, *DLG*, 620–64; *DACL*, s.v. "pallium."

49. *Sancti Caesarii Arelatensis opera* 2:11 (letter 7); trans. Klingshirn, *Caesarius of Arles*, 93. The *Liber pontificalis*, redacted no later than the 530s, depicts Pope Mark (336) granting the pallium to the Bishop of Ostia and establishing that this prelate consecrates the newly elected pope, and Duchesne argues that its origins were in the fourth century: *Liber pontificalis*, 1:202; Duchesne, *Christian Worship*, 384–89.

50. That is, with archiepiscopal status: Julius von Pflugk-Harttung, ed., *Acta Pontificum Romanorum Inedita*, 3 vols. (Tübingen, 1880–1886; repr., Graz, 1958), 2:21–22, 61–63, 82–84, 97–98, 142–43, 180–81, 202–3, 228–29, 242, 257–58, 273–74, 294–95, 352–53, 359, 382–83.

accustomed to receive it as a matter of course, but in the early Middle Ages its bestowal could recognize individual merits, as in the case of Syagrius of Autun. Gregory the Great's letter concerning this case reveals that imperial consent was necessary for the granting of the pallium as well as a request from the recipient bishop.[51] Early visual evidence, such as the sixth-century San Vitale mosaic of Archbishop Maximian of Ravenna (see figure 12) and the seventh-century apse mosaic of two popes in the basilica of Sant'Agnese (see figure 13) in Rome, depict the pallium draped loosely across the back and chest, crossing on the left shoulder, with the ends hanging down on the left side. The white wool band was decorated with a black cross on either end.[52] Gregory the Great penned several strongly worded letters to Bishop John of Ravenna regarding his wearing of the pallium not just during Mass—which Gregory characterized as "the custom of the universal church"—but also in the *secretarium*, a room adjacent to the basilica where the bishop received laypeople and resolved disputes, and in processions for litanies. John stridently defended these usages as the ancient traditions of his see, and Gregory partially relented.[53] The importance of the pallium as a symbol of authority is evident in descriptions of papal depositions in the *Liber pontificalis:* the narratives of Silverius's removal from office in 537 and Constantinus's in 768 mention first the pontiff being stripped of his *pallium.*[54]

The term *pallium* is also used in the *Liber pontificalis* to denote a diaconal vestment worn over the left arm. Pope Sylvester, it recounts, "decreed that deacons should wear dalmatics in church, and that their left arms should be covered with pallia half wool, half linen."[55] It must be noted that deacons were extremely powerful figures in the Roman church. From at least the third century the city was divided into seven administrative regions with a deacon in charge of each. These regional deacons, called cardinal deacons by the eighth century, managed the patrimony and poor-relief operations of the Roman church. Many early medieval popes were elected from their ranks. Additionally, there were liturgical deacons who read the Gospel during the Mass and performed other important ceremonial roles.[56] This elevated status was thus early on denoted through

51. Concerning bestowal: 5.58, 6.18, 9.21, 9.229, 9.234, 11.39: CC 140:354–55, 388; 140A: 793, 810, 816–17, 935; Gregory, *Letters*, 392, 416, 690, 703, 707, 786. On Syagrius, 8.4, 9.214, 9.220, 9.223: CC 140A:519–20, 774, 792, 795–96; Gregory, *Letters*, 502, 678, 690, 691–92.

52. The form changed in the ninth century to the Y-shaped style dominant throughout the central Middle Ages: see Braun, *DLG*, 642–51.

53. 3.54, 5.11, 5.15, 9.168 app. 6: CC 140:200–203, 277, 280–81; 140A:726–27, 1097–99; Gregory, *Letters*, 272–77, 330, 332–33, 649.

54. *Liber pontificalis*, 1:293; the earliest papal consecration rite simply describes the Bishop of Ostia putting the pallium on the new pontiff: Andrieu, *Ordines*, 4:293, 297. On clerical degradation rituals generally, see Dyan Elliott, "Dressing and Undressing the Clergy: Rites of Ordination and Degradation," in *Medieval Fabrications: Dress, Textiles, Clothwork, and Other Cultural Imaginings*, ed. E. Jane Burns (New York, 2004), 55–69.

55. *Liber pontificalis*, 1:171, 225; see also *DACL*, s.v. "manipule."

56. Roger E. Reynolds, "Clerics in the Early Middle Ages: Hierarchies and Functions," in idem, *Clerics in the Early Middle Ages: Hierarchy and Image* (Aldershot, 1999), 1:5; Tommaso di Carpegna Falconieri,

special garb. The *pallea linostima* mentioned in the *Liber pontificalis* were most likely maniples (*mappulae*), special cloths worn over the left arm that eventually came to be used by all the major orders (subdeacons, deacons, priests, and bishops).[57] In the same exchange with John of Ravenna mentioned earlier, Gregory the Great also decried the wearing of maniples by the clergy of Ravenna, asserting that these were the sole prerogative of the Roman clergy.[58]

The Roman deacon's characteristic tunic, the dalmatic, also developed into a prestige garment. The life of Caesarius of Arles (1.42) asserts that Pope Symmachus, in addition to granting the pallium to the bishop, "also distinguished Caesarius's deacons by allowing them to wear dalmatics in the fashion of Roman deacons."[59] Gregory the Great, in a letter of 599 to Aregius, a bishop from Gaul, referred to a request the bishop made during a recent visit to Rome: "you asked that we should give permission for you and your archdeacon to use dalmatics." Explaining why he did not act immediately on the request, Gregory continued,

> But we were fully involved, and a consideration of Church custom would not let us make this new grant without consideration and suddenly. For that reason, the outcome of your request has been delayed. But as we now remember the goodness of your Beloved, we grant what you seek by the tradition of this authority of ours, and we have allowed you and your archdeacon to be decorated by the use of dalmatics, and have sent over those dalmatics, carried by our most beloved son and abbot, Cyriacus.

Gregory follows this grant with a request that Bishop Aregius take part in an upcoming council in Gaul against simony.[60] The bestowal of permission to wear special Roman liturgical garments and the provision of those garments appears to be a way the pope created closer ties with distant sees and cultivated collaborators in ecclesiastical efforts. Although visual evidence suggests that its use had become more general throughout western Europe in the ninth century, Pope Benedict VII (974–983) confirmed the privilege of the abbots of the imperial monastery of Corvey to wear the "pontificalia" of the dalmatic and *sandalia* on certain feast days.[61] Generally garments appear to have been

Il clero di Roma nel medioevo: Istituzioni e politica cittadina (secoli VIII–XIII) (Rome, 2002), 128–29; Michel Andrieu, "La carrière ecclésiastique des papes et les documents liturgiques du moyen âge," *Revue des sciences religieuses* 21 (1947): 91–95.

57. Braun, *DLG*, 515–61.

58. 3.54, app. 6: CC 140:203; 140A:1099; Gregory, *Letters*, 274–76; Martyn mistakes the *mappula* (maniple) for *mappulus* (saddlecloth).

59. "Diaconos ipsius ad Romanae instar ecclesiae dalmaticarum fecit habitu praeminere." *Sancti Caesarii episcopi Arelatensis opera* 2:313; trans. Klingshirn, *Caesarius of Arles*, 31.

60. 9.220: CC 140:792; Gregory, *Letters*, 689–90.

61. Braun, *DLG*, 251–57; Mansi, 19:55–56. In 752 Pope Stephen II granted Fulrad, abbot of Saint-Denis, the right to have six deacons in his abbey wear the dalmatic: Jaffé, 2332; *PL*, 89:1018. Such grants to abbots continued across the eleventh and twelfth centuries: Pflugk-Harttung, *Acta Pontificum*, 2:73–74, 111–12, 207, 219–20, 302–3. The "sandals" were really more like ornamental overshoes with cutouts revealing the slippers and hose beneath: see Braun, *DLG*, 159–63.

exchanged regularly among ecclesiastics as gifts. In 600 Gregory the Great sent fifteen cloaks (*lenae*) and bedding to the abbot of Mount Sinai for use in the *hierochomium*, a place for taking care of infirm holy people. He rejected a gift of vestments embroidered with palm fronds (*palmatianae*) from the bishop of Messina that he deemed too extravagant.[62] Saint Boniface received *vestimenta* from Abbess Eadburga, thanking her in a letter of 735, and Alcuin similarly thanked this "sister in Christ" Gisla for a cloak (*cappa*) she had sent him.[63] Such exchanges were certainly a way that ideas about proper vesture were shared and probably a force producing greater uniformity over time.

Other markers of status that the bishops of Rome seemed keen to control were the *campagi*, black leather slippers barely covering the heel and toe, secured with a band running from the instep over the top of the foot. Gregory the Great expressed outrage to the bishop of Syracuse in 598 about the deacons of Catania wearing these special shoes, revealing that in Sicily only the deacons of Messina had been granted this privilege long ago. They appear as episcopal attire in the earliest Roman ordines.[64]

Although at this point in our discussion it might appear that the Roman church had quite precise clerical dress regulations, in fact only the diaconate and the episcopate seem to have developed especially distinctive liturgical costumes by this time. The Roman ordination rites before their adaptation by Frankish clerics in the Carolingian era direct the bishop-elect to be dressed in dalmatic, chasuble, and *campagi*, and the candidate for the diaconate to put on the dalmatic just after he is consecrated and kissed by the ordaining bishop. Later ordination rites will associate the chasuble and stole with the priesthood, but not yet here: while the deacon being ordained a priest does exchange his dalmatic for a chasuble, this garment is also worn by the acolyte and subdeacon in this early ordo. Both of these clerical ranks are also depicted with the *orarium*, or stole. Indeed, alb, chasuble, and stole appear in this early text to be standard clerical attire for the liturgy, with the dalmatic marking off the status of the deacon and bishop, and special shoes (the *campagi*) further distinguishing the bishop.[65] One might wonder at the lack of attention given to the priesthood in early medieval Roman ordination rites, especially in light of the eleventh-century reform's exaltation of sacerdotal status. But in this period it was the city's bishop who was its chief priest: on all the major feasts of the Christian year and at the stational masses at the city's ancient basilicas, the pope consecrated the Eucharist and then it was distributed to the neighborhood churches. In the early fourth century Pope Innocent I described this custom of distributing the consecrated bread, called the *fermentum*, throughout the city that emphasized the unity of the Christian community under their bishop. While there were masses in the city's

62. 11.2 and 1.64: CC 140A:860; 140:74; Gregory, *Letters*, 737, 181. On the *palmatianae*, see Du Cange, s.v.

63. *MGH Epp. Sel.* 1:60 (no. 35); *MGH Epp.* 4:127 (no. 84).

64. 8.27: CC 140A:548; Gregory, *Letters*, 522; see also, Braun, *DLG*, 385–89.

65. Ordo 34, chap. 750: Andrieu, *Ordines*, 3:612, 605–6, 603–4; see also Cyrille Vogel, *Introduction aux sources de l'histoire du culte chrétien au moyen âge* (Spoleto, 1973), 151–54; English ed., *Medieval Liturgy: An Introduction to the Sources*, trans. William G. Storey and Niels Krogh Rasmussen (Washington, D.C., 1986), 174–76; Aimé-Georges Martimort, *Les "ordines," les ordinaires et les cérémoniaux* (Turnhout, 1991), 30.

neighborhood churches, the believer would be more likely to associate priests with penance and last rites than with the central sacrifice of the mass.[66] The pope was the central figure in the city's liturgical life.

Lest one too quickly attribute this imprecision to the partial or defective nature of our sources, it is worthwhile considering Gregory the Great's letter of October 598 to the bishop of Syracuse. Gregory has heard that some in Sicily were complaining that he was slavishly following the customs of the church of Constantinople. "When I asked him," Gregory continued, "'Which of its customs do we follow?' he replied: 'Because you have had "alleluia" said at Mass, outside the season of Pentecost, and you have decided that subdeacons should approach the altar disrobed, and that "Kyrie eleison" should be said, and the Lord's Prayer be said directly after the canon.'" Gregory denied this charge and asserted that the Roman church had "followed no other church in any of these matters." With regard to the disrobed subdeacons, the pope replied:

> That was an ancient custom of the Church. In fact I do not know why a certain pontiff of ours decided to order them to approach wearing vestments. For did your churches receive the tradition from the Greeks? From where then do they have the present custom that subdeacons should approach wearing vestments, unless it is because they learnt this from their mother church in Rome?

On the other counts, Gregory carefully pointed out how Roman usages differ from those in the Greek rite and then concluded: "We have either renewed our ancient customs or have established new and useful ones, in which we are still not shown to be imitating others."[67] Gregory, clearly, was no slave to "custom." Even when previous popes have ordered one thing—like subdeacons wearing vestments—Gregory felt free to return to a more ancient tradition or devise a new one. He also seems quite comfortable with some differences in liturgical customs: he does not criticize Greek practice, nor the fact that the Sicilian church is apparently following some customs once cultivated in Rome but now abandoned. Gregory did, in the case of Ravennate use of the pallium, defend what he saw as the prerogatives of the Roman church to concede and determine the use of this badge of honor. But proof of such a concession need not be a written privilege (although Gregory clearly would have preferred this!): the pope made inquiries and sought witnesses who could testify to the practices of the church of Ravenna and those of other churches in the East. It appears that this research bore fruit: when Bishop John was succeeded by Marinianus, Gregory conceded the pallium, specifically granting permission to wear it outside of Mass for four litanies.[68]

66. Robert Cabié, *La lettre du Pape Innocent Ier a Décentius de Gubbio (19 mars 416): Texte critique, traduction et commentaire* (Louvain, 1973), 26–28, 50–53; Sible de Blaauw, *Cultus et Decor: Liturgia e architettura nella Roma tardoantica e medievale*, 2 vols. (Vatican City, 1994), 1:30.

67. 9.26: CC 140A:586–87; Gregory, *Letters*, 561–62.

68. See n. 53 above.

In contrast to the Roman conciliar evidence, bishops beyond the Alps expressed many concerns about attire in conciliar decrees. Generally, Anglo-Saxon councils worried more about monks wearing inappropriate clothing than clerics, but the council of 786 in Mercia led by the papal legate Gregory of Ostia did admonish both canons and monks to cultivate discretion in food and clothing, and specifically prohibited canons from wearing anything "precious or dyed with Indian colors." The earlier Council of Clofesho in 747 cautioned religious leaders not to allow their communities to grow to numbers beyond those they could feed and clothe "according to the condition of their profession." It linked insufficient means to provide *vestes consuetae* to clerics and monks wearing inappropriate worldly garb, such as leg bands and shaggy Irish cloaks.[69]

Two concerns were most prominent in Francia. The first was clerics bearing arms. This issue emerged in conciliar legislation in late sixth-century Gaul and was constantly repeated through the rest of the Middle Ages. As Charlemagne's *Admonitio generalis* of 789 explained, priests and deacons "should trust more in God's defense than in weapons." The late seventh-century Council of Bordeaux invoked Psalms 43:4 to voice its objection: "For they did not get possession of the land through their own sword, nor did their own arm save them, but Your right hand and arm, and the light of Your countenance."[70] The clergy, especially those who handled the sacred elements at the altar, should be men of peace; they should not appear to threaten violence. The second issue prominent in Carolingian ecclesiastical legislation was the problem of clergy not having or using appropriate and clean liturgical garb to celebrate the Mass. A canon issued by Bishop Riculf of Soissons in 889 well summarizes these concerns: "Strive to have your ecclesiastical vestments worthily and properly prepared, namely: one or two clean albs for the divine mysteries with stoles—that is, two clean stoles—and two clean amices, and two cinctures, and just as many clean maniples, and clean altar cloths, and a silk chasuble in which to celebrate Mass."[71] That the bishop repeats "clean" (*nitidus*) six times

69. Haddan & Stubbs, 3:374, 450; *MGH Epp.* 4:22; Catherine Cubitt, *Anglo-Saxon Church Councils c. 650–c. 850* (London, 1995).

70. See above, nn. 24 and 25, on the frequency of prohibitions on bearing arms in the early Middle Ages and exceptions to the rule. In addition, the following councils in the eleventh and twelfth centuries repeated the ban: Mansi, 19:742 (Reims 1049 canon 6), 830 (Narbonne 1054 canon 15), 915 (Rome 1059 canon 10), 1071 (Gerona 1068 canon 5); Mansi, 20:460 (Winton 1076, confirming canon 12 of the Council of Winchester), 499 (Poitiers 1078 canon 10), 518–19 (Gerona 1078 canon 6), 817 (Clermont 1095 canon 4); Mansi, 21:513 (London 1138 canon 13); Mansi, 22:150 (London 1175 canon 11). For the two rationales quoted, *MGH Cap.* 1:59; *Concilia Galliae A. 511–A. 695*, 312; similar language: *MGH Concilia* 2:213; *MGH Cap. episc.* 1:187.

71. Mansi, 18:81. The following canons require proper vesture: Mansi, 3:954 (Carthage 436 canon 4); *Concilios Visigóticos*, 73 (Braga 561 canons 9, 11); *Concilia Galliae A. 511–A. 695*, 224 (Mâcon 583 canon 6), 267 (Auxerre c. 573–603 canon 13); *Concilios Visigóticos*, 206 (Toledo 633 canon 40), 374–75 (Braga 675 canon 3); Mansi, 11:156–57 (Braga late seventh century, canon 4); *MGH Cap. episc.* 3:60 (Neustria <829 chap. 2), 87–88 (Senlis ninth century chap. 8); Amiet, *AS*, 44–45 (early ninth century chap. 16, 18); *MGH Cap. episc.* 2:135 (Herard of Tours 858 chap. 34), 104 (Riculf of Soissons 889 chap. 7—also Mansi, 18:81); 2:270 (Atto of Vercelli tenth century chap. 14); Mansi, 19:374 (Stephen of Hungary 1016 canon 13), 787 (Coyaco 1050 canon 3); 20:36 (Rouen 1072 canon 5), 1123 (Poitiers 1100 canon 5–6). The following

suggests some repugnance at the filthy condition of some garb worn at altars in his diocese. Indeed, episcopal capitularies from the ninth century often required parish priests to bring their vestments with them to synod so that they could be inspected.[72] The requirement suggests that the definition of "clean" had been found to be highly variable between rural parishes and the cathedral seat. These concerns about cleanliness and propriety extended beyond vestments to include sacramental vessels, altar linens, the area around the altar, and the entire church. The chalice and paten were to be made from a "pure material" and used for no other purpose than the divine mysteries. Women were not to come near the altar or touch the sacred vessels. Mass should be said only in a consecrated church, and only holy things should be kept in the church: no harvested crops, no straw, and no animals.[73]

Some of these Frankish concerns and others are evident in the canons of the Roman council held in 826 by Pope Eugene II, but it is mainly in liturgical sources that Carolingian influence on the use of vestments is clear.[74] Michel Andrieu's work on the early Roman ordines (books of sacraments or rites) and that of Cyrille Vogel, Reinhard Elze, Niels Rasmussen, and others on the earliest episcopal books, or pontificals, have amply demonstrated the intense interest of Frankish liturgists in adapting the customs of the Roman see to their churches and their influence on the liturgy of Rome itself by the tenth century. Pepin the Short and Charlemagne actively sought "authentic" Roman liturgical and canonical texts for use in correcting practices within their vast realm. Rome's bishops were willing partners in sharing the "apostolic tradition" of Saint Peter's see as models, but they recognized that the different circumstances of other churches required modifications.[75] Carolingian ecclesiastics tailored Roman customs to the

canons additionally emphasize cleanliness: Amiet, *AS*, 44 (early ninth century chap. 17); *MGH Cap. episc.* 2:146 (Herard of Tours 858 chap. 86); Mansi, 18:81 (Soissons 889 canon 7); 3:124 (Ottobeuern late ninth-early tenth century canon 6); 1:63 (Trier 915–31 canon 5); *Councils and Synods*, part 1 (871–1066), 292–93 (Aelfric's first Old English letter to Wulfstan c. 1006), 325, 328–29 (so-called Canons of Edgar).

72. *MGH Cap. episc.* 1:106, and 3:117 (Saint Gall late ninth–early tenth century canon 7); *MGH Concilia* 6:79 (Trier 927); Mansi, 18:79 (Metz 888 canon 6). Another strategy, employed by Hincmar of Reims, was to send inspectors with the specific charge to discover, among other things, whether altar cloths and vestments "sint nitida aut in nitido loco collocentur": *MGH Cap. episc.* 2:46–47.

73. On vessels and linens: Mansi, 19:700. A late ninth-century episcopal capitulary from Munich (repeated at Troyes) required that no one other than a deacon or subdeacon should wash the altar linens, particularly not a woman, "quod maxime horret": *MGH Cap. episc.* 3:163, 170. Prohibitions against women being near the altar or sacred vessels: *MGH Concilia* 2:367, 639; *MGH Cap.* 2:52; *MGH Cap. episc.* 3:55; 2:133; 3:269 (or Mansi, 19:247); 1:64–65, 107. On churches: Mansi, 19:182; *MGH Cap. episc.* 1:62–63, 108, 110.

74. Canon 33 broadened the prohibition on women approaching the altar to exclude all laypeople from the altar enclosure (*presbyterium*) during Mass. The canons of this council show much greater interest in the state of the priesthood than appears in earlier Roman documentation, and some of the reforms promulgated at Aachen in 816—such as clerics living in a cloister attached to their church—are taken up. *MGH Concilia* 2:568–75, 581. On Frankish influence during this brief pontificate (824–827), see Jean-Marie Sansterre, "Eugenio II," *Enciclopedia dei papi*, 3 vols. (Rome, 2000–2006), 1:710–12.

75. On Carolingian interest in the Roman liturgy, see Cyrille Vogel, "Les échanges liturgiques entre Rome et les pays francs jusqu'à l'époque de Charlemagne," in *Le chiese nei regni dell'Europa occidentale e i*

liturgical needs of their churches, and some of their innovations proved enduringly popular. Several aspects of the use of liturgical garments that appear in these Carolingian adaptations of Roman rites were incorporated into a new type of liturgical book—the "pontifical," or bishop's book—that reached a mature and highly influential form at Mainz between 950 and 962. This product of the Ottonian renaissance responded to the practical needs of bishops to have in one volume the ritual directions and formulas essential to the performance of their office. This extremely useful compendium—dubbed the Romano-German Pontifical (hereafter RGP), because it combined Roman rites with Frankish usages—was immediately popular, and when introduced to Italy through the frequent visits of the Ottonian court in the second half of the tenth century, it was readily embraced in Rome. It would be further adapted in Rome in subsequent centuries, but for now let it suffice to say that an ongoing process of cultural exchange across the Alps yielded by the late tenth century a set of practices regarding liturgical attire that was an amalgam of Roman and Frankish garments, terms, and ideas.

The Frankish contribution was significant. The *Admonitio synodalis*, that ninth-century Frankish episcopal admonition to priests quoted at the beginning of this chapter, was incorporated into the RGP's instructions for holding a provincial council: the admonition, with its directives about wearing clean liturgical garments for Mass, was to be read to the assembly on the fourth day.[76] Attention to proper vesture is noticeable throughout the Frankish revisions to the Roman ordines and in the RGP. Whereas, for example, the earliest Roman ordines for a papal Mass give specific directives only for the pontiff's garb, the Frankish revision opens with instructions for what the deacons and subdeacons are to put on when the pope dons his dalmatic (albs of linen or silk over the amice), and what they are to wear if the pope does not wear a dalmatic (albs and chasubles, no amice).[77] The ordination rites allow the broadest comparison: having discussed above these directives on vestments in the earliest Roman ordines, let us consider the evidence on the uses of garments in the Frankish additions, and the RGP.

Ordo 35 (Frankish, before 925), like the earliest Roman ordination rite, ordo 34, depicts acolytes, subdeacons, and deacons wearing chasubles (*planetae*); the deacon here

loro rapporti con Roma sino all'800, Settimane di studio del Centro italiano di studi sull'alto medioevo 7, 2 vols. (Spoleto, 1960), 1:185–295, and Mayke de Jong, "Charlemagne's Church," in *Charlemagne: Empire and Society*, ed. Joanna Story (Manchester, 2005), 117–19. The extent of liturgical diversity and the loose notion of what Carolingian reformers considered "Roman" are evident in Susan A. Keefe, *Water and the Word: Baptism and the Education of the Clergy in the Carolingian Empire*, 2 vols. (Notre Dame, 2002), 1:52–69, 150–55. Both insistence on Roman apostolic tradition as a universal norm, as articulated in Innocent I's letter to Decentius of Gubbio in 416 ("Si instituta ecclesiastica"), and the position more tolerant of diversity found in Gregory the Great's writings, particularly his letter of 591 to Leander of Seville ("Respondere epistolis vestris"), remained within the Western ecclesiastical tradition and law, both being cited throughout the Middle Ages and into the modern era: see Herbert Schneider, "Rom und die liturgische Vielfalt," in *Roma fra oriente e occidente*, Settimane di studio del Centro italiano di studi sull'alto medioevo 49 (Spoleto, 2002), 1101–40.

76. Cyrille Vogel and Reinhard Elze, eds., *Le Pontifical romano-germanique du dixième siècle*, 2 vols. (Vatican City, 1963), 1:286–89 (80.51).

77. Andrieu, *Ordines*, 2:157 (4.2).

too exchanges his chasuble for the dalmatic. The most noticeable change in this Frankish adaptation is in the attention given to priestly ordination: the ordinand sheds his diaconal dalmatic, receives the chasuble from the archdeacon, and then approaches the bishop, who says the consecratory prayer over him, and then places the *orarium* around his neck and anoints his hands with chrism. In the episcopal rite, the prescribed garments of the bishop-elect remain the same (dalmatic, chasuble, and *campagi*).[78]

The changes in the RGP are more extensive. It is a much fuller text, including ordination rites for many more minor orders (*psalmista*, or cantor; doorkeeper; and exorcist; in addition to lector and acolyte) and it distinguishes not only between the minor and major orders but also between those receiving the imposition of hands (deacons, priests, bishops) and the lesser orders that did not. The subdeacon is a liminal figure here: he is grouped with the clearly major orders of deacon and priest but does not receive the imposition of hands, and his ordination rite resembles those of the minor orders in which objects symbolizing the duties of the office are bestowed. The cantor receives the antiphonary, the doorkeeper the keys to the church, the lector the book of readings, the exorcist the text of the exorcism rite, the acolyte the candlestick and candle as well as an empty pitcher, and the subdeacon an empty chalice and paten, and the pitcher, water basin, and towel used in the washing of the priest's hands.[79] Note that none of these receive vestments; indeed, the attire to be worn by any of these orders is never mentioned in the RGP. The bestowal of vestments, however, becomes a key ritual act in the ordination of deacons, priests, and bishops: deacons receive stoles, priests receive both stoles and chasubles, and bishops receive the *campagi*, sandals, the dalmatic, chasuble, and gloves.[80] Moreover, the rites include prayers said as the garments are bestowed that relate the vestment to the powers and virtues of the office. As the stole is placed on the deacon, for example, the bishop says, "Accept your stole, fulfill your ministry, for God who is powerful shall strengthen you with his grace," or "Accept the power of reading the Gospel in God's church, for both the living and the dead, in the name of the Lord."[81] As priests receive the stole, the bishop prays, "Accept the yoke of the Lord, for his yoke is sweet and his burden light [Matt. 11:30]," and as the chasuble is put on, "Accept the priestly robe through which charity is learned."[82]

Both the Carolingian dissemination of Roman texts and the popularity of practical compendiums like the RGP fostered increasing unity in the use and ideology of sacred

78. Andrieu, *Ordines*, 4:34–35, 37–40, 43. On this ordo, see Vogel, *Introduction*, 154.

79. Vogel and Elze, *Pontifical romano-germanique*, 1:15–18 (15.8–9, 14, 17, 20), 22 (16.5).

80. Ibid., 1:27, 34, 213 (16.15, 17, 30–31; 63.23).

81. Ibid., 1:27 (16.16–17): "Accipe stolam tuam, imple ministerium tuum, potens est enim Deus ut augeat tibi gratiam suam"; another variant in most manuscripts is "Accipite potestatem legendi euangelium in ecclesia dei tam pro uiuis quam pro defunctis in nomine domine." For the blessings of the stoles and chasubles, 1:24, 26–27 (16.11, 14a).

82. Ibid. 1:34 (16.30–31): "Hic reflectat orarium super humerum eorum dextrum, dicens ad eos per singulos: Accipe iugum domini, iugum enim eius suave est et onus eius leve. Hic vestiat eos casula, dicens ad unumquemque: Stola innocentiae induat te dominus. Accipe vestem sacerdotalem per quam caritas intelligitur."

vestments. Surely individual churches continued to adapt these practices to their own needs. Liturgy is an expressive language used every day by the clergy: new usages are to be expected. The important point here is that the greater interest in the proper use of vestments evident in conciliar legislation beyond the Alps was grafted onto Roman traditions in the Carolingian era and then, through continuing exchange of liturgical books and ideas, defined as "Roman." In the tenth century there was still great liturgical diversity in western Europe: the Ambrosian rites of the Milanese church and the Mozarabic traditions of Iberia are but the best-known and best-documented examples of local liturgical cultures that had developed independently over centuries. Such variability could be characterized as evidence of "micro-Christianities," but more striking to me are the myriad exchanges among clerics across significant distances that created a certain unity, a "universal" church. It was certainly more tenuous, to be sure, than the truly pan-European ecclesiastical culture that emerged in the central Middle Ages, just as the scholarly community of medievalists before the age of budget airlines and the Internet was a much smaller and more elite, slow-moving culture. But to understand the enthusiasm that reform efforts and new papal leadership aroused in the eleventh century, we should imagine the exhilarating sense of a larger world that a cleric in the entourage of his bishop might have experienced visiting a see like Mainz or Rome in the early Middle Ages.

Change in the Twelfth Century: A Contrast Defined

The reform movements of the eleventh century brought about changes in nearly every aspect of ecclesiastical life; one of the most important was a new type of council. The Roman councils of the early Middle Ages were attended by the suburbicarian bishops from the region around the city and often by other prelates from central and southern Italy. To say that they were just "provincial councils" is not entirely accurate, given that the wide connections of the Roman see brought issues to these gatherings that affected the entire church. But attendance was largely regional despite the broader and more sophisticated agendas pursued. Change began after the millennium. Popes had jointly presided with emperors over larger councils in the first half of the eleventh century, but these gatherings were called and orchestrated by imperial authority. A more significant innovation during the pontificate of Leo IX (1049–1054) was the calling of papal councils, assemblies "attended by bishops from outside the Roman ecclesiastical province and from outside the imperial territories, an assembly under the sole presidency of the pope, the decrees of which were regarded as binding on the whole of Latin Christendom."[83] These larger gatherings under papal leadership became a highly significant tool of reform and in the process forged a new understanding of the "universal

83. I.S. Robinson, *The Papacy 1073–1198: Continuity and Innovation* (Cambridge, 1990), 122, and for the emergence of papal councils and their development in the reform era, 121–45.

church." While Gregory VII's councils were attended mainly by those with matters to be decided by the assembly, Urban II's attracted so many participants that sessions had to be held outdoors. These developed into the great ecumenical councils held at the Lateran in 1123, 1139, 1179, and, most famously, 1215.[84]

Over the second half of the eleventh century and the opening decades of the twelfth, the papal reform councils were dominated by judicial cases ("punishing evildoers") and the issues of simony, clerical celibacy, and lay investiture. Several papal councils and provincial councils presided over by papal legates repeated the usual prohibitions on clerics bearing arms or relaxing their tonsures, and even the late Carolingian requirement that priests bring their vestments to be inspected. But clerical clothing was not a prominent concern.[85]

Early indicators of a new agenda begin to appear under Urban II. The council he held in Melfi (Apulia) in 1089 raised several new concerns about the clergy, and decreed: "And so that all causes of offence, all suspicions be removed from the laity, we prohibit clerics henceforth to wear cut clothing [*scissis vestibus*], and we admonish that they should not dress in ornate garments [*pomposis exuviis*]."[86] A council held in Westminster in 1102 prescribed that clerical garments should be one color and footwear well ordered (*calceamenta ordinata*).[87] Canon 8 of Pascal II's Council at Troyes in 1107 more fully foreshadows the type of legislation that becomes frequent from the 1130s, specifically prohibiting clerics to wear pointed shoes and tight garments, or to have lace on jackets or shirts.[88] The Council of Clermont in 1130 ordered "that bishops as well as clerics strive to be pleasing to God and men in their mental attitude and their bodily appearance; let them not offend the sight in the superfluity, cut, or color of their clothes—the appearance of which ought to be an example—but [wear only] what is proper to their sacredness." The councils of Reims in 1131 and of Pisa in 1135 passed nearly identical canons, and then in 1139 the Second Lateran made the decree quoted at the outset of this chapter. This canon was widely diffused because it was incorporated into Gratian's *Decretum*, an innovative compilation of canons that was used to teach ecclesiastical law in the emerging universities.[89] As I. S. Robinson has noted, such canons were part of a new program of legislation introduced by Innocent II that endured through the twelfth century. Its chief emphases were

84. Ibid., 122–25, 131.

85. Mansi, 19:742, 830, 915, 1071; 20:460, 499, 518–19, 561, 817. The Council of Compostella in 1056 reminded bishops that their vestments should reach to their heels, and one in Rouen in 1072 decreed that priests should wear both alb and stole when performing baptisms: ibid., 19:855; 20:36.

86. *Scissis vestibus* could simply mean "cut" as in tailored, but it could also mean slit or "dagged," meaning patterning through serration or creating openings to reveal another material underneath. The decrees of this council had "a not insubstantial and perhaps even a surprising diffusion": Somerville and Kuttner, *Pope Urban II*, 210–14, 256–57, 262.

87. *Councils and Synods* 1:672; also Mansi, 20:1151.

88. "Presbiteris et diaconibus longos capillos, rostratos sotulares, fixas uestes, laqueos in blialdis uel camisiis habere uel aleis seruire prohibemus." Blumenthal, *Early Councils*, 94.

89. In abbreviated form and attributed to Innocent II: Emil Friedberg and Aemilius Ludwig Richter, eds., *Corpus Iuris Canonici*, 2 vols. (Leipzig, 1879; repr., Graz, 1959), 1:860.

ecclesiastical discipline and the "dignity of the clerical estate."[90] Concern about excesses in clerical attire continued into the early thirteenth century, receiving its fullest articulation in the Fourth Lateran Council's canon 16, "On the Dress of Clerics":

> Clerics should not practice callings or business of a secular nature, especially those that are dishonourable. They should not watch mimes, entertainers and actors. Let them avoid taverns altogether, unless by chance they are obliged by necessity on a journey. They should not play at games of chance or of dice, nor be present at such games. They should have a suitable crown and tonsure, and let them diligently apply themselves to the divine services and other good pursuits. Their outer garments should be closed and neither too short nor too long. Let them not indulge in red or green cloths, long sleeves or shoes with embroidery or pointed toes, or in bridles, saddles, breast-plates and spurs that are gilded or have other superfluous ornamentation. Let them not wear cloaks with sleeves [*cappas manicatas*] at divine services in a church, nor even elsewhere, if they are priests or parsons, unless a justifiable fear requires a change of dress. They are not to wear buckles or belts ornamented with gold or silver, or even rings except for those whose dignity it befits to have them. All bishops should wear outer garments of linen in public and in churches, unless they have been monks, in which case they should wear the monastic habit; and let them not wear their cloaks loose in public but rather fastened together behind the neck or across the chest.[91]

Obviously dress here is placed in a larger context of appearances unsuitable to the dignity of the clerical estate. None of the opening admonitions, however, were new: individual canons against dishonorable work and pastimes, especially against being in taverns and gaming, were ancient and repeated frequently.[92] The requirement of tonsure and *corona* was also venerable. What is new is the attempt to inventory in such detail what kinds of clothing and accessories were considered objectionable. Most broadly, the new legislation completely redefined the "problem" of clerical clothing. Early medieval legislation addressed want and disrepair, exhorting clerics to acquire and maintain proper and clean garments for the conduct of their duties. The unseemliness this legislation combated was an appearance of impoverishment or squalor that dishonored the sacred. The Fourth Lateran canon addressed not need or want, but overabundance, "superfluity." Some of the specific items banned point to a new ecclesiastical affluence, and particular ways of visualizing that wealth, that offended the faithful. The perceived need

90. Robinson, *Papacy*, 135–36; on possible relations between the canons attributed to Reims and Pisa to those of Lateran II, see Robert Somerville, "The Canons of Reims (1131)," *Bulletin of Medieval Canon Law*, n.s. 5 (1975): 122–30 and "The Council of Pisa, 1135," *Speculum* 45 (1970): 98–114 (text of the canon on 106), both repr. in Somerville, *Papacy, Councils and Canon*, 15, 16. The Pisan canon on clothing, discovered by Somerville in Bayerische Staatsbibliothek MS Clm 11316 in Munich, was not published in Mansi.

91. *Decrees*, 1:243.

92. *MGH Concilia* 2:268, 364, 369, 572.

to ban the wearing of rings, and gold and silver buckles, confirms what many other sources tell us: the church and its clergy shared fully in the new affluence produced by the "take off" of the European economy in the central Middle Ages. But the specificity of the canons still suggests that something more than general affluence was perceived as problematic. What lay behind these detailed provisions?

Chiefly, what lay behind them was a lively and important discussion among Western Christians about clerical status, the powers claimed for it by reformers, and its visual expression in society. Chapters 5 and 6 of this book will draw the reader deeply into this conversation and consider the many voices contributing to it. But as a first step toward understanding the changes that had prompted it, we need here to consider closely the characteristics of this new legislation. Keeping in mind that conciliar decrees expressed the concerns of the very highest strata of the Western clergy—bishops and, in the Roman reform councils, the pope—this legislation reveals significant lay criticism of clerical clothing.

Several canons, indeed, overtly mention lay critique as a motivating factor behind the legislation. The Council of Melfi in 1089 explicitly stated that its prohibition of "cut" and pompous clerical clothing was enacted "so that all causes of offence (*scandala*), all suspicions be removed from the laity." The formulations of Clermont, Reims, and the Second Lateran allude to such criticism ("let them give no offence in the sight of those for whom they ought to be a model and example"). A council held at Montpellier on the eve of the Fourth Lateran, presided over by the papal legate Peter of Benevento, articulated the motivations for its decree on episcopal garb very clearly:

> Since laypeople, whose complaints have frequently been laid before us, are scandalized at the disordered appearance of certain religious persons and secular clerics, [these laypeople] not only disdain to hold ecclesiastical men in reverence, but even attack and molest them and their churches repeatedly, not believing these clerics ought to be distinguished from laypeople since they not only differ not at all from laypeople in appearance and other manners, but indeed in this and other things show themselves to be more dissolute, we decree in this synod . . .

The canon goes on to require bishops to wear long robes and linen shirts over other garments when outside and when holding court within their palaces in the presence of "outsiders."[93] Laypeople were accusing the clergy of dressing like laypeople and using this as an excuse to mistreat them and their churches (surely meaning the church's property).

In none of these canons, however, do the clergy admit the charge.[94] Even as they legislate changes to stem criticism, they do not characterize the offensive attire as

93. Mansi, 22:940.

94. The only characterization of the banned clothing as secular occurs in the chronicle of Montecassino, in which a monk conveying the results of the Council of Benevento in 1108 reported "vestimenta vero saeculari et pretiosa clericis reprehendit, et talibus uti interdixit." Blumenthal, *Early Councils*, 103.

secular: none of the proscribed garments or accessories is called "lay" or "worldly." Earlier ecclesiastical legislation, however, had used such language. Decrees from the eighth, ninth, and tenth centuries forbid the clergy to wear lay clothing (*secularia indumenta, vestimenta laicalia*). The Council of Tribur in 895 used exactly the sort of language one might expect in the twelfth century: "Clerics should not wear lay garments, that is: mantles or capes without hoods, or costly and unsuitable shoes and other vane novelties [*aliis vanitatum novitatibus*]."[95] Obviously, earlier ecclesiastical leaders had conceived of the problem in these terms. So why does the new legislation of the twelfth century articulate the lay interpretation but then subtly contest its terms? Was this just defensive legalism?

Perhaps it was. Some of the characteristics of the clothing banned do suggest lay, and more particularly, courtly influence. Indeed, as Joachim Bumke and others have richly documented, there had been a revolution in lay attire in the eleventh and twelfth centuries. Reports of new and objectionable court fashions are particularly numerous in the early twelfth century, contemporaneous with the new ecclesiastical legislation on clerical clothing. Orderic Vitalis, for example, remarked on the new trends in his *Historia ecclesiastica*. He attributed to Fulk le Rechin (d. 1109) the fashion of "shoes like scorpions' tails" and launched into a diatribe against the "new fads" of his day, wherein wanton youth "sweep the dusty ground with the unnecessary trains of their robes and mantles; their long, wide sleeves cover their hands whatever they do."[96] Similar items appear in Lateran Four's canon 16: "long sleeves or shoes with embroidery or pointed toes" (*manicis aut sotularibus consuticiis seu rostratis*). Generally Orderic and other critics complained of the contrast central to the new fashion: tightly fitted elements, revealing bodily form, paired with luxuriant amounts of fabric. In women's wear this meant a tightly fitted bodice and then a long, pleated and draping skirt; in men's, a mantle fitted on top but full and long below, and often slit open to reveal the legs. When our canons complain of "superfluity" and "cut," therefore, they may well be objecting to excessive length or use of cloth in clerical attire and more form-fitting or slit garments.[97] A decree from Innocent II's council of 1131 required clerics to wear "round," probably in the sense of full, garments (*vestes rotundae*), meaning the baggy tunics everyone wore before the new courtly fashions. The directive in the Lateran IV decree not to use red or green fabric may also be aimed at dissuading clerics from adopting the bright palette typical of courtly attire.

This prohibition is our surest indicator, moreover, that this new legislation regulated clerical street-wear, not liturgical apparel. A full two decades before the Fourth Lateran decree Lothar of Segni, before he became pope as Innocent III, had defined red and

95. *MGH Concilia* 2:12–13, 199; Mansi, 18:79; *MGH Cap.* 2:248; *MGH Cap. episc.* 3:270.

96. *EH*, 4:186–89; Joachim Bumke, *Courtly Culture: Literature and Society in the High Middle Ages*, trans. Thomas Dunlap (Berkeley, 2000),138–49; Françoise Piponnier and Perrine Mane, *Dress in the Middle Ages*, trans. Caroline Beamish (New Haven, 1997), 56–76.

97. See Somerville's commentary, Somerville and Kuttner, *Pope Urban II*, 289–92.

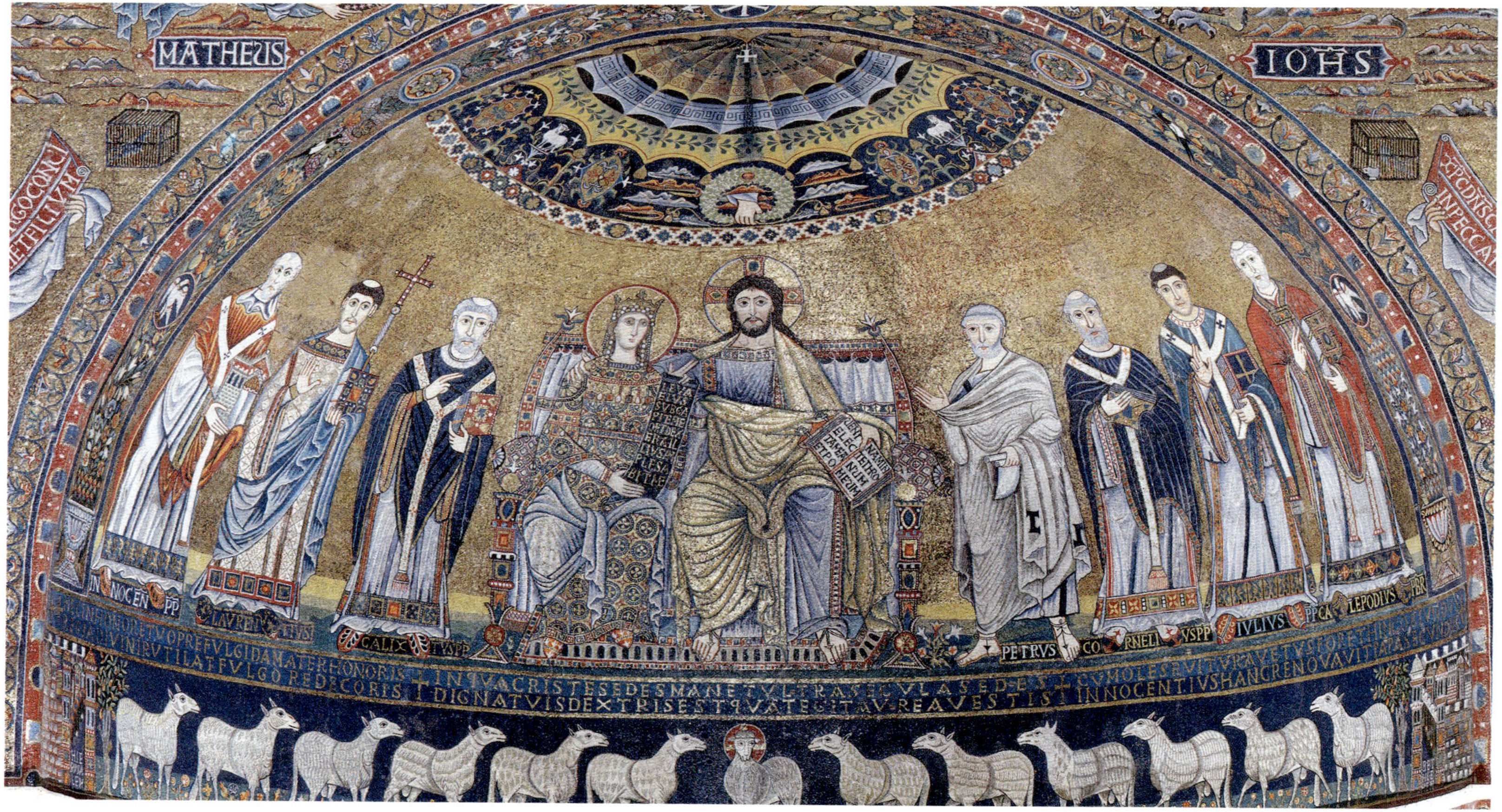

Figure 1. Apse mosaic showing the patron Pope Innocent II (far left), c. 1140–1143, Santa Maria in Trastevere, Rome. Scala / Art Resource.

green as liturgical colors (red appropriate for vestments worn on the feasts of apostles and martyrs, as well as Pentecost and the Holy Cross; green for "ordinary time").[98] The pope most associated with this new legislation on the dignity of the clerical estate, Innocent II (1130–1143), actually had himself depicted in the apse mosaic of the Roman basilica of Santa Maria in Trastevere (figure 1) dressed in a red chasuble, and two of the other ecclesiastical figures in the apse—Pope Julius I (337–352) and Saint Calepodius (d. 232)—wear green and red vestments. Indeed, all the shoes worn by the ecclesiastical figures in this mosaic are highly decorated, depicting either embroidery—explicitly banned in Lateran IV's canon 16—or appliqué work. The specification of gilded bridles, saddles, breastplates, and spurs also indicates that the legislation targeted not liturgical attire but the appearance of the clergy outside of church.

The ban on gilded saddlery and on "wearing buckles or belts ornamented with gold or silver" calls our attention to an emerging desire for contrast. The twelfth-century apse mosaic of Santa Maria in Trastevere depicts clerics not only in brightly colored and highly ornamented liturgical vestments, but also in vestments decorated with gold. The cuff of Innocent II's alb, the edging of the sleeve of his dalmatic and elements of its decorated hem are all gold, as are details of the vestments of the five other clerical figures in liturgical attire. The story of the emergence of this gold-bedecked style of liturgical attire will be told in chapter 3, but here note that this is not the rich garb targeted by twelfth- and thirteenth-century ecclesiastical legislation. The affluence of the church displayed liturgically was not censured. What was appropriate at the altar, however, seems to have been troubling outside of church.

This returns us to a question raised earlier: What, then, was appropriate clerical street-wear? Like the early medieval decrees already surveyed, this new legislation still states more clearly what clerics should not wear than what they should. The Council of Westminster in 1102 did state positively that clerical garments should be one color, and Montpellier specified long robes and linen overgarments. The Fourth Lateran, too, stipulated that bishops wear linen and twice underscored that outergarments or cloaks should be worn closed. These details are at least slightly more informative than early medieval admonitions to wear a *tunica sacerdotalis*. Materials seem to be an issue: the requirement of linen implicitly bans silk. The demand that garb be long and closed suggests that the body—and any other clothing worn beneath—should be covered.

Fortunately for us, the bishops who attended the Fourth Lateran Council were required to implement its canons, including 16, "On the Dress of Clerics." The records of thirteenth-century synods reveal them dutifully attempting to do so all over western Europe. For our purposes, what is interesting about these local synodal decrees is that

98. Michel Pastoureau, *Bleu: Histoire d'une couleur*, 2nd ed. (Paris, 2006), 35–37. The chapter on liturgical colors in Lothar of Segni's tract, "De sacro altaris mysterio," is *PL*, 217:799–802. Thomas M. Izbicki considered precisely this prohibition of red and green from Lateran IV to the fifteenth century and proffered no explanation for why these colors in particular were banned: "Forbidden Colors in the Regulation of Clerical Dress from the Fourth Lateran Council (1215) to the Time of Nicholas of Cusa (d. 1464)," *Medieval Clothing and Textiles* 1 (2005): 105–14.

they don't just repeat canon 16: they explain and interpret it in the vocabulary, lexical and sartorial, of the clergy in their local churches. Some intersperse phrases from canon 16 with more detailed requirements. Bishop Bonfilius of Siena opened his constitutions of 1232 with a chapter requiring all clerics, from "prelates and officials" to those serving in urban and rural churches or chapels throughout the diocese, to wear closed overgarments (*superna indumenta clausa, vestimenta superna clausa*). These phrases were repeated for each category of cleric serving the Sienese church. The language about basic clerical garments is more varied in other dioceses. The Synod of Trier in 1227 prescribed "properly long garments" (*vestes decenter longae*) or full cloaks (*capae rotundae*). In 1235 the bishop of Rouen decreed the use of "closed overtunics without undue pomp," specifying that they be neither too long nor too short, or the "closed cloak" (*cappa clausa*), while the bishop of London in 1237 required "properly well-proportioned garments" and *cappae clausae*.[99] The 1306 constitutions of the clergy of Fiesole suggest that the somewhat vague language in these canons about suitably long and closed garments may have been accommodating the lesser means of many clerics. This synodal legislation distinguished between the *prelati dyocesis*, required to wear the closed cloak, or *cappa clausa*, and *inferiori clerici* required simply to wear "seemly garments closed in front" (*honesta et clausa desuper . . . indumenta*).[100]

In their local reiterations of Lateran IV's clothing requirements, bishops banned some garments and styles not mentioned at the ecumenical council. Unseemly clerical attire seems to have varied regionally across Europe. The archbishop of Trier, for example, specified that clerical "long garments" or "full cloaks" be without anything unnecessary, "especially gold or silver buttons" (*superfluis maxime nodis aureis vel argenteis . . . non utantur*). At Rouen the bishop forbade his clergy to have a hood of a different fabric on their closed cloaks, while at Worcester Bishop Walter de Cantilupe in 1240 banned the wearing of the *herigaldus*, whatever that was.[101] Undoubtedly, until bishops could actually afford to provide a standard appropriate garment, clerics and their superiors sometimes disagreed over whether their garb was sufficiently closed or properly proportioned. A clearly exasperated provost and archdeacon in early fifteenth-century Salzburg spelled out in a special addendum to his bishop's synodal decrees exactly what a proper clerical garment was. It was not tight across the shoulders and chest, "as is common among laypeople." It had decent sleeves, extending only to the knuckles and no wider than a hand's width. It was not to have any side slits, and in back any opening for ease in walking should be no larger than a hand's width and a half. Abuses, he continued, such

99. Mansi, 23:32, 243, 378, 414 (*supertunicalia clausa, nec indebito apparatu utantur*), 454 (*in mensura decenti vestes*).

100. Richard C. Trexler, *Synodal Law in Florence and Fiesole, 1306–1518*, Studi e Testi 268 (Vatican City, 1971), 188, 244.

101. Mansi, 23:32, 378 (*nec deferent capucia alterius panni*), 533 (*non amplius utantur herigaldis*). According to Du Cange, the usage of *herigaldus* was unique to this council, although he suggests it was perhaps related to *herga*, a garment soldiers wore.

as short bodices, tight sleeves, multiple folds or pleats, or "sleeves" that expose the arms, would not be tolerated.[102] Thirteenth-century episcopal visitation records reveal only very partial compliance with the new standards for clerical street-wear. In the register of Eudes Rigaud, archbishop of Rouen from 1248 to 1275, clerics are constantly cited for not having a *cappa clausa* and going about unsuitably attired.[103]

Punishments varied. Rouen's archbishop stipulated that priests discovered wearing the military tunic known as the tabard or the sleeveless and slitted garment called the *garnachia*, without a *cappa clausa* over them, would be required to hand over the offensive garments so that they could be given "to lepers or other poor persons." Other bishops levied fines: five *solidi* in Tours, one-tenth of the guilty party's benefice income in Worcester (those without benefices would be blocked from being admitted to one). In the diocese of Trier, improperly attired clerics would be warned three times, and then if still recalcitrant either put in prison or, if brought into a lay court, not defended as clerics.[104] This latter penalty refers to the clerical right to be judged in an ecclesiastical court under canon law, rather than by the local lord or count. And since judicial processes generated revenue, this provision gave an incentive to any serving a local lord to police clerical garb.

And what color were these long, closed clerical cloaks? Lateran IV had not defined a normative color; canon 16 prohibited only red and green. Most of the local synodal promulgations are also silent on color, emphasizing instead length and closure. But a few, however, begin to define norms on this issue. Book 2, chapter 1 of the *Mitrale* of Sicard of Cremona, "On the Manner of Life and Dress of Ecclesiastics," specified that clerics should wear the *cappa clausa* and that it should be *nigra*, an adjective also used in the 1227 canons of Trier.[105] The Latin *niger* can mean "black," but may also mean simply "dark." There are several reasons to read it in the latter sense here. First, recent art historical studies have called attention to how the description and perception of color may be culturally conditioned, and in particular they posit a medieval conception of color recognizing degrees on a scale of brightness, between dark and light, more than of hue. This makes some sense of the ways medieval texts use the same word, such as *persus*, to describe hues from blue-black to red.[106] A discussion of licit shoes from the canons of Rouen in 1235, moreover, suggests that various dark colors were acceptable. The Rouen canon banned leather shoes unless they—presumably the upper parts—were made of "serge, or black serge [*de saja vel de sargia nigra*], or *persico*, or *bruneta nigra*."[107] The author's sequential use of two different words for serge perhaps meant that both the

102. Mansi, 28:1010.

103. Susan M. Carroll-Clark, "Bad Habits: Clothing and Textile References in the Register of Eudes Rigaud, Archbishop of Rouen," *Medieval Clothing and Textiles* 1 (2005): 81–114.

104. Mansi, 23:414, 497, 533; 24:245.

105. *PL*, 213:59–60.

106. John Gage, *Color and Meaning: Art, Science, and Symbolism* (Berkeley, 1999), 68–76.

107. Mansi, 23:371.

common variety of this durable twill fabric and the dark or black version were acceptable. We know this fabric in cotton as denim, a shortening of "serge de Nimes," so it is possible that common serge was usually woad-dyed blue.[108] *Persicus* or *persus* could mean blue, blue-black, or dark green, and *bruneta* meant dyed dark, usually brown, so *bruneta nigra* could be dark brown, brown-black, or black. What we think of as black was also not easy to produce or maintain. Even naturally black sheep's wool is not particularly resistant to light and turns a golden brown over time. Readily available gallotannins—such as oak galls, also used for ink—could be used with an iron mordant to create black, but the iron tended to weaken fibers and oak galls were expensive in the quantities needed for dyeing fabric.[109] Coarse, undyed woolen cloth can be a dark gray when various colors of natural wool are spun together: the cowl of Saint Francis preserved at Assisi was made of such undyed humble cloth.[110] Pragmatically, requiring clerics to wear dark, rather than specifically black, outerwear was probably a bishop's only hope of moderate success.

The documentary evidence, in sum, suggests the diffusion and gradual enforcement of new standards for clerical street-wear. Both the ecumenical legislation and the local attempts to convey it across the thirteenth century indicate an emerging consensus about the characteristics of appropriate clerical attire outside the sanctuary. It should be modestly long and closed so that limbs are not exposed. In sharp contrast with liturgical garb, it should neither be ornamented nor made of luxurious fabrics. Further, unlike liturgical garb, it should be darkly, not brightly, colored. What seems to have been sought is a stark visual contrast: dark, plain, and humble outside of the sanctuary, but bright, glistening, and ornamented within church. This contrast became a key element in clerical usages of clothing.

Visual sources confirm the emerging consensus articulated in conciliar decrees. The best trove of visual evidence on clerical street-wear is found in illuminated canon-law manuscripts. Since Gratian's famous twelfth-century compilation, the *Decretum*, was used as a textbook in the early law faculties, it included cases that raised and clarified key issues. These are the most consistently illustrated in luxury editions. In cases where different clerical ranks interacted or in those involving the liturgy or the sacraments, artists depicted the clergy in liturgical garb. Several cases, however, invited the representation of clerics out and about in society. Case XV, involving a homicidal priest, provided a wonderful opportunity for artists to represent how a bad cleric looked: chiefly, he showed a lot of leg! Late twelfth- and thirteenth-century manuscripts from Italy and northern France depict the murderer in a short belted tunic, sometimes with a cape that is short

108. John H. Munro, "Medieval Woolens: Textiles, Textile Technology and Industrial Organisation, c. 800–1500," in *CHWT*, 1:211.

109. Michel Pastoureau, *Jésus chez le teinturier: Couleurs et teintures dans l'Occident medieval* (Paris, 1997), 123–26; Michel Pastoureau, *Black: The History of a Color*, trans. Jody Gladding (Princeton, 2009), 90–92.

110. *Textile Conservation*, 314.

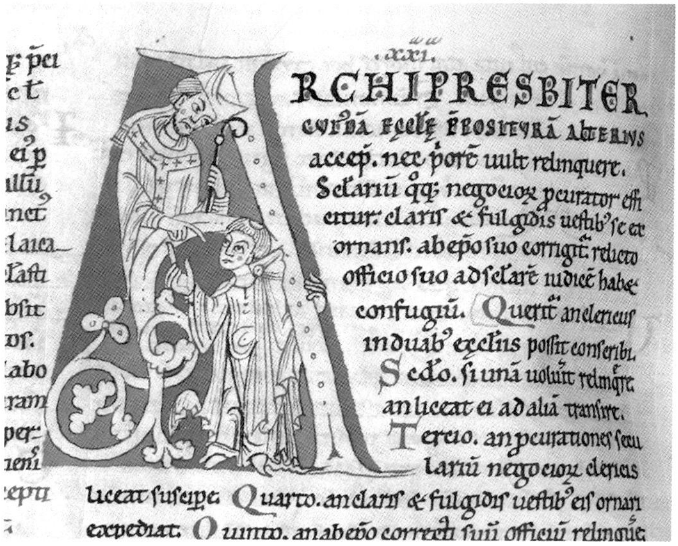

FIGURE 2. Gratian's *Decretum*, Causa XXI, MS Clm. 17161, 106v, c. 1165–1170, Bayerische Staatsbibliothek, Munich. Photo courtesy of Bayerische Staatsbibliothek Munich.

and wide open as well.[111] Case XXI focused on another kind of problematic cleric: one who accepted multiple benefices, engaged in "secular business," and was corrected by his bishop for wearing "bright and glittering clothes" *(claris et fulgidis vestibus se exornans).* A late twelfth-century south German artist ornamented the opening "A" of the passage with a severe-looking bishop pointing at a tonsured figure in a clingy, form-fitting tunic with wide decorated sleeves, pointy shoes, and an open mantle with its cascading volume of fabric dragging behind him (figure 2). Another sports a tunic with wide decorative bands pulled back to reveal an undertunic with a patterned inset and decorative hem. Several are depicted in jaunty hats, which of course cover their tonsures, and flowing tunics with lapels or gowns that are short or bright red.[112] These artistic renderings echo Lateran IV's canon 16 prohibition of "open" outer garments, those either too short or too long, made of red or green cloth, or with long sleeves, and shoes with pointed toes.

A case (XI) of civil litigation between two clerics, one about clerics drawing up wills (XII), and another (XVI) in which secular clerics challenge monastic possession of a parish church likely provide better indications of appropriate attire. Late twelfth-century and some thirteenth-century illuminations tend to depict the clerics in a simple, alb-like tunic with fitted sleeves and a cloak closed at the neck or clasped at the shoulder and draping most of the body.[113] In late thirteenth- and early fourteenth-century

111. Anthony Melnikas, *The Corpus of the Miniatures in the Manuscripts of "Decretum Gratiani,"* 3 vols., Studia Gratiana 16–18 (Rome, 1975), 2:495 (figs. 12–13), 496 (figs. 14–16); Susan L'Engle and Robert Gibbs, eds., *Illuminating the Law: Legal Manuscripts in Cambridge Collections* (London, 2001), 118 (pl. 3f).

112. Melnikas, *Corpus*, 2:655, 663 (fig. 13), 661 (fig. 8), 665 (fig. 17), 667 (fig. 21), 668 (fig. 22), pl. II.

113. Ibid., 2:387 (fig. 3), 390 (fig. 9), 391 (fig. 10), 392 (figs. 11–12), 411 (figs. 1–2), 412 (fig. 4), pl. II Causa XI, 413 (fig. 5), 523 (Figs. 10–11), and 525 (fig. 15).

manuscripts, however, a slightly different garb predominates. Clerics are depicted in long, dark, hooded gowns.[114] There are variations in how the arms are accommodated. Some have simple slits in the garment through which the arms may be extended.[115] Others have sleeves, either loose or more tightly fitted.[116] Still others have a slit opening but also a long piece of fabric, a sort of ornamental sleeve, cascading from the shoulder to the knees or lower.[117] While both of these latter variations could be considered a "sleeved cloak," I think the last is probably the *cappa manicata* condemned in Lateran IV's canon 16 and in other twelfth- and thirteenth-century canons. Two illustrations of case XI suggest this. Of the two clerics described in the case, one insists correctly on having the matter decided before an ecclesiastical judge, while the other went before a civil magistrate. The latter ends up censured by the bishop. The illustration in an early fourteenth-century northern French manuscript depicts two clerics sitting opposite one another, gesturing in argument (figure 3). The one on the left wears the truly sleeved gown while the other the likely *cappa manicata* with its flowing sleeve appendages. This cleric has five pearl buttons on the fitted sleeves of an undertunic on his extended arms. An Italian manuscript c. 1300 has an even more emphatic interpretation: the cleric wearing the draping faux-sleeved tunic pleads his case to the civil magistrate, while the cleric on the other side, in a gown with real sleeves, demurs.[118]

The issue of this *cappa manicata* returns us to the language of the ecclesiastical legislation and the lay critique that the clergy were wearing lay attire or, in the words of the Montpellier decree, differing "not at all from laypeople in appearance." Might the twelfth-century legislation have refrained from characterizing the offensive garments as lay because they believed them to be clerical? A critical term is *cappa*, or cloak. As we have seen, the dark closed cloak, or *cappa clausa*—the medieval precursor to the soutane, or cassock—emerged as the most often specified standard appropriate as clerical streetwear. The word *cappa* has a range of meanings: it can denote a cap, a hood, a hooded cloak, a cloak, or the cape-like vestment called the cope or pluvial. In the latter sense, it appears frequently in liturgical *ordines*, inventories of ecclesiastical treasuries, and lists of

114. Melnikas provides only some color illustrations, and in those plates depiction varies. Some manuscripts deploy somber shades for clerical garb, and others have quite outlandish, if beautiful, choices seemingly driven by a palette used throughout the work. One Parisian manuscript c. 1300, for example, represents a clerical *cappa manicata* in brownish-gray, while a Bolognese *Decretum* c. 1320 dresses all the figures, clerical and lay, in green, pink, purple, blue, or red. Melnikas, *Corpus*, pl. II causa X; L'Engle and Gibbs, *Illuminating the Law*, 126–32.

115. Melnikas, *Corpus*, 2:394 (fig. 16), 397 (fig. 22, second figure from left), 399 (fig. 25), 530 (figure closest to the bishop).

116. Ibid., 2:396 (fig. 19, left cleric), 398 (fig. 23, figure facing bishop), 399 (fig. 25, far left), 401 (fig. 28, right), 406 (fig. 35), 528 (fig. 20, left), 529 (fig. 22), 533 (fig. 30, left).

117. Ibid., 2:393 (fig. 13), 395 (fig. 18), 396 (fig. 19, right), 397 (fig. 21), 401 (fig. 28, on left), 527 (fig. 18), 531 (fig. 25), 532 (fig. 27).

118. Ibid., 396 (fig. 19, Paris BN Ms. Lat. 3893 f. 176v), 401 (fig. 28, Berlin, Staatsbibliothek Preussischer Kulturbesitz Ms. Lat. Fol. 6, f. 131).

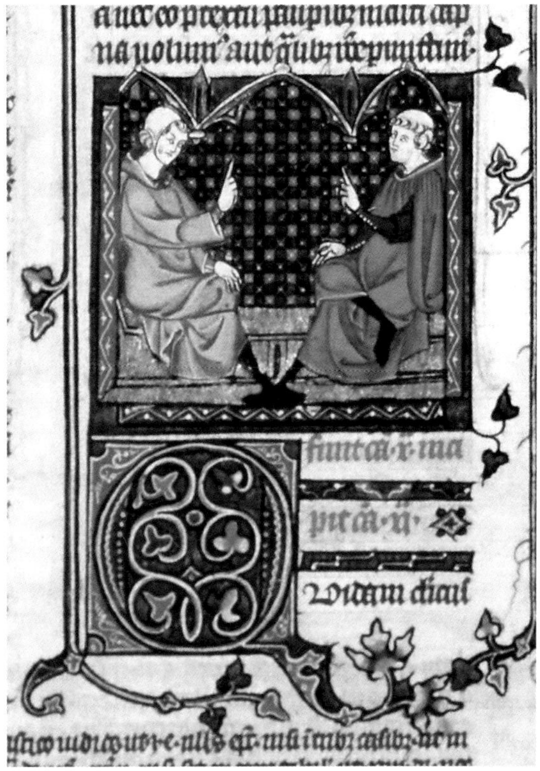

FIGURE 3. Gratian's *Decretum*, Causa XI, MS Lat. 3893, 176v, fourteenth century, Bibliothèque nationale de France, Paris. Photo by permission of Bibliothèque nationale de France.

gifts given by prelates, such as when Conrad Bishop of Hildesheim (1194–1198) donated to his church "six *cappae*, three of red velvet and three of white."[119] Even when the setting or context is not liturgical, however, the *cappa* is an ecclesiastical cloak; it is worn by monks and secular clerics. William, the reforming abbot of Hirsau, prescribed the wearing of the *cappa* at several points in his monastic constitutions from 1091, and the monks who received the Duke of Aquitaine after the election of Jordan as bishop of Limoges, according to Ademar of Chabannes, wore "silk copes" (*cappis olosericis*).[120] Orderic Vitalis, who had a lot to say about contemporary fashion, used *cappa* solely to denote ecclesiastical garb.[121] Galbert of Bruges remarked that the provost's chamberlain wore a *cappa* "following the custom of clerics" (*iuxta morem clerici*).[122] The ecclesiastical associations of this garment were so pronounced that the author of the life of Bishop Meinwerk of Paderborn, when he wanted to indicate that the bishop had disguised himself in order to

119. *Chronicon Hildesheimense*, *MGH SS* 7:858: "sex cappas, tres de examito rubeo, tres de albo." These garments are mentioned throughout *MGH Ordines de celebrando concilio*, 430, 448, 460, 487, 570, 576, 582; and *Schatzverzeichnisse*, 14–19, 21–22, 25, 27, 31, etc.

120. *PL*, 150:971, 1057, 1061; Ademar of Chabannes, *Chronicon*, lib. 3, chap. 57, CCCM 129:178.

121. *EH*, 2:64, 128, 148; 3:162, 230, 240, 242; 4:240, 312; 6:184.

122. Galbert of Bruges, chap. 35, CCCM 131:81; in the same chapter (p. 79), Galbert lists *cappas palliatas et sericas* among the items in the treasury of the canons of Saint Donatus.

observe the true behavior of the monks, used the phrase "*cappa laicalis.*"[123] In fact, a lay cloak was called a *mantellus*, a *sagum*, a *pellicium*, or *crusina.*[124] Of sixty-five occurrences of the various forms of *cappa/capa* in the MGH Scriptores, a series containing many chronicles filled with lay activities, there is only one in which a layperson wears a *cappa.* In a story in the chronicle of Burchard of Ursberg of how Otto IV held court in 1209 to investigate wrongdoing and impose justice, "many knights," reports Burchard, "fled in the night." The count of Grafenbach, however, was violently brought before the emperor and "the *cappa* that he had put on was shamefully torn to pieces, causing fear of the ruler to fall upon the barons and knights." Here it seems the count had been trying to disguise himself to escape royal justice. Was the tearing of the *cappa* done "shamefully" (*turpiter*) because of the garment's ecclesiastical associations?[125] Usage of the word *cappa/capa* in twelfth- and early thirteenth-century texts overwhelmingly characterizes the garment as ecclesiastical attire.

References to the condemned sleeved cloak, the *cappa manicata*, beyond those in the ecclesiastical legislation under discussion, are quite rare. They suggest, however, divergent clerical opinions about this garment. William Fitzstephen, in his life of Thomas Becket, seems defensive about the chancellor's wearing of it. He described the prior of Leicester reproving Thomas, saying, "What is this *capa manicata* you wear? This garment is more for those who carry falcons. You are an ecclesiastic, with not one but many dignities: archdeacon of Canterbury, dean of Hastings, provost of Beverley, canon here and there, also archiepiscopal procurator, and, as is frequently heard at court, you will be archbishop." Fitzstephen emphasizes Thomas's humble response to the rumors of his imminent preferment and carefully describes the setting of the prior's comment. He points out that the chancellor had been ill, and that when he was finally on the mend, but still convalescing, he sat down to a game of chess, "having put

123. *Vita Meinwerci episcopi Patherbrvnnensis* chap. 152, *MGH SSRG* 59:81.

124. Charlemagne wore a *sagum*, and Einhard explains that the *clamys* the emperor donned in Rome was a mantle: "id est manto vel mantello." Einhard, *Vita Karoli Magni* chap. 23, *MGH SSRG* 25:28. Monarchs after the investiture controversy challenged their sacred status are sometimes depicted as wearing a *cappa*, as in Roger of Hovedon's reference to Richard I: *Chronica magistri Rogeri de Houedene*, ed. William Stubbs, 4 vols. (London, 1868–1871), 3:93. In the twelfth-century Latin romance, the *Ruodlieb*, cloaks are *pellicia* or *crusine/chrusenne; cappa* is used to denote a hood: C.W. Grocock ed. and trans., *The Ruodlieb* (Warminster, 1985), 48–49, 56, 60–61, 100–101, 120–21, 142–43, 158–59, 166–67, 215. Gerhoh of Reichersberg, in his letter to Innocent II (1130–1143) on how secular clerics differ from regulars, reminded his readers that "the sacred canons instruct all clerics not to wear lay clothing, that is, a mantle or other garb without a *cappa*" (cum omnibus clericis sacri canones precipiant, ut non laicalibus vestibus utantur, id est, mantello sive aliis sine cappa), *MGH Lib. de lite* 3:232.

125. *Die Chronik des Propstes Burchard von Ursberg*, ed. Oswald Holder-Egger and Bernhard von Simson (Hannover, 1916), *MGH SSRG* 16:97. Donning the *cappa* as strategic disguise is attested elsewhere: Orderic Vitalis reported that King Louis had his knights disguise themselves "nigris capis amicti" in order to take the ford of Nicaise. There are a handful of undeniably lay usages. In Gislebert of Mons's *Chronicon Hanoniense*, *cappae* are received as payment for feudal dues: *MGH SSRG* 29:297. Goffredo Malaterra and Roger of Hovedon each use *cappa* twice when describing laypeople: see Du Cange, s.v. "capa."

on a *capa manicata*." The chancellor was not, therefore, wearing the garment in a public or official setting.[126] William Durand (1230–1296) in his *Rationale*, a liturgical commentary he wrote while bishop of Mende in order to better train the priests of his diocese, referred to the garment when trying to explain the double meaning of the white tunic worn for baptism: "Hence, this garment is double, like a *capa manicata*, because of its double holiness, namely the blessedness and glory possessed." The reference is somewhat obscure—does Durand mean that the *capa manicata* has double sleeves, the actual arm covering and the ornamental tail?—but note that nearly a century after the prohibition of Lateran IV this bishop thought that his priests would know what this garment was and that reference to it would help them understand the meaning of baptism.[127] That it was still much worn by clerics is also suggested by late medieval condemnations of it.[128]

John of Salisbury's *Historia pontificalis* also reveals disagreement among clerics about what was appropriate attire and, specifically, about this twelfth-century legislation against particular garments. In his opening description of the Council of Reims in 1148, John notes that all the decrees to be promulgated were approved "by general consent, with one exception": a canon banning the clergy's use "of various furs" (*variarum pellium*) was opposed by Reynold of Hildesheim and other German bishops. Indeed, the text of the canon that has come down to us does not mention furs, condemning instead "*inhonesta varietate colorum*."[129] The German bishops' objections could, reasonably, have been based on differing circumstances, the harsher climate of northern Europe requiring the use of furs for warmth. It seems harder to imagine, however, a similar defense of the sleeved cloak, which is perhaps why it was specifically banned.

The crucial point here is that it was condemned as an excessive and inappropriate *clerical* garment and not as a piece of lay attire worn by clerics. The clergy were creating and wearing new kinds of garments, such as the *cappa manicata*, and modifying others through the use of new colors, fabrics, and types of ornamentation. Clerical

126. The description further suggests that Thomas had changed outfits in order to play the game, but it is unclear whether the author is implying that the change occurred because he had just arisen from his sickbed or withdrawn from a more public setting. William Fitzstephen, *Vita S. Thomae* in *Materials*, 3:25–26.

127. "Vnde uestis ipsa duplex est, quasi in modum cape manicate, quia sancti duplica, scilicet beatudinem et gloriam, possidebunt" (lib. 6, cap. 83, pars 16). *Guillelmi Duranti Rationale divinorum officiorum*, ed. A. Davril and T.M. Thibodeau, 3 vols. (Turnhout, 1995), CCCM 140A:420.

128. Thomas of Cobham's condemnation in his early fourteenth-century *Summa de arte praedicandi* of those who "preach in lay clothes, as in the *cappa manicata* or in other odious garb," is one example: "si predicet in habitu laicali, ut in cappa manicata uel in alia ueste deformi": Thomas of Cobham, *Summa de arte praedicandi*, ed. Franco Morenzoni (Turnhout, 1988), CCCM 82:69 (III.458).

129. Chibnall, apparently unable to imagine that John's rendition could diverge from the promulgated canon, translated "*variarum pellium*" as "multi-colored cloaks." The Latin reads: "Nam cum usus uariarum pellium clericis interdiceretur, et plurimi interrogati sibi complacere responderent, Raginaldus de Heldenesham et alii Teutones reclamauerunt decretum hoc nec placere presentibus nec posteris placiturum." John of Salisbury, *Memoirs of the Papal Court*, ed. and trans. Marjorie Chibnall (London, 1956; repr. 1962), 8; Mansi, 21:714.

culture was definitely evolving in dialogue with the laypeople clerics served in their churches, and clearly innovations in clerical attire had provoked lay criticism. The new kind of conciliar legislation of the twelfth and early thirteenth centuries was responding to this. To a certain degree, however, this careful legal language may suggest a more intractable problem than mere lay influence: the superfluity and excess condemned were clerical creations, not simply incautious borrowing from lay attire. What fostered this particular form of clerical creativity? Why were clerics inventing new types of garb? A key clue lies in the demand articulated in the Second Lateran Council's decree: the clergy were to "exhibit holiness" and wear "only what is proper to their sacredness." But what looked holy? And how were these outer signs related to interior spiritual states?

2

A CLERICAL SPIRITUALITY

In modern kidnap dramas, the victim's struggle when initially seized often leaves some trace that later becomes a significant clue in leading to his or her liberation. A witness notices some detail, the victim drops something, or the violence of the struggle creates key forensic evidence: we know as viewers and readers to pay close attention to the clues embedded in this scene. Paul of Bernreid's account of the kidnapping of Pope Gregory VII during the Christmas Eve service of 1075 provides us the abundance of details we expect as modern consumers of action-packed thrillers, and some that seem likely to become highly significant. Gregory is saying Mass in the Basilica of Santa Maria Maggiore where a Nativity scene has been constructed near the main altar so that all may contemplate the event in salvation history being commemorated. The armed men make their move at a moment when there is plenty of movement in the church to mask their approach: Communion is being distributed. A great shout goes up when the intruders are detected, but their immediate threatening violence cows and confuses the people: "ranging through the church with drawn swords, striking at those whom they could reach, they converged on the site of the crib, where the excellent pope was seated." Entering the sanctuary by force, "breaking down those little doors with their cruel hands," one of the malefactors strikes the pope, wounding him on the forehead. They start dragging him from the church, "stripping him of his pallium and chasuble, of his dalmatic and tunicle"; "clad only in his alb[, his amice,] and his stole," they throw him on a horse and make their getaway.[1]

1. I. S. Robinson, ed. and trans., *The Papal Reform of the Eleventh Century: Lives of Pope Leo IX and Pope Gregory VII* (Manchester, 2004), 296–97; Johann Matthias Watterich, ed., *Pontificum Romanorum Vitae*, 2 vols. (Leipzig, 1862; repr. 1966), 1:501: "Tandem exutum pallio et casula, seu dalmatica et tunica, eum camisia tantum amictum et stola, ut furem tractum post dorsum cuiusdam sacrilegi posuerunt." I give a modified version of Robinson's translation of the passage here. He leaves out the amice, perhaps finding the length of this list of vestments a bit much.

Since there are no crime scene investigators in the eleventh century, the broken sanctuary doors are not likely to lead to Pope Gregory's rescue. The forehead wound may be significant, but it could also just explain to us why the pope was not able to resist his abductors. Paul's enumeration of each of the vestments stripped off the pontiff, and his equally precise description of those he was still wearing as he was dragged out of the church, seem more likely clues. Why does the reader need to have each of the vestments named? Why did the kidnappers strip Gregory only of his outer vestments, leaving him in alb, amice, and stole? The stole, in particular, would have been easily removed if they had already managed to wrangle him out of a chasuble, dalmatic, and tunicle. As modern readers, you know you are now going to have to be patient until the significance of these details becomes clear at the end of this chapter. In the meantime, we have to try to enter the mental world of Paul's medieval readers.

This life of Pope Gregory was written more than four decades after the pontiff's death by a priest who had been active in reforming circles in early twelfth-century Germany.[2] The language of composition, Latin, and the polemical tone of the work suggest that Paul's primary audience was other ecclesiastics active in the ongoing struggle for reform. What meanings might such readers attach to each of the vestments Paul mentions, and to their violent removal in a sacred space? It is significant that these are liturgical objects and that the action takes place in liturgical space, even during a liturgy, because what we know of the education of clerics in this era suggests that it was heavily liturgical. By the end of the twelfth century, the young men who would become clerics might go off to study in cities like Bologna and Paris, where lively confluences of masters and students were congealing into universities. But before such opportunities for study emerged, and even after for the less affluent, training to become a priest was a matter of apprenticing yourself to experienced clerics under the watchful discipline of a bishop. It was a long liturgical internship. Whether mastering scripture or the skills necessary to serve and govern the church, participatory learning was the norm.[3] Saint Ubaldus of Gubbio, for example, was given over as a child to the cathedral church where his paternal uncle was a canon. He studied *divinae litterae* and was "brought up under

2. The vita was most likely completed in 1128 in Regensburg. See Robinson's careful reconstruction of Paul's career and the circumstances surrounding the writing of the life: Robinson, *Papal Reform*, 64–82.

3. Pierre Riché, *Education and Culture in the Barbarian West from the Sixth through the Eighth Century*, trans. John J. Contreni (Columbia, S.C., 1976), 122–29, 279–90, 404–21, 458–77; Keefe, *Water and the Word*, 1:31–38; Christopher M. Bellitto, "Revisiting Ancient Practices: Priestly Training before Trent," in *Medieval Education*, ed. Ronald B. Begley and Joseph W. Koterski (New York, 2005), 35–49. C. Stephen Jaeger's excellent work on changing educational ideals over this period focuses on the most elite strata of clerical learning. But even at this level, where pastoral care was not always the primary goal, personal ("charismatic," as he puts it) presence and practical experience dominated pedagogy before the rise of the universities. See *The Envy of Angels: Cathedral Schools and Social Ideals in Medieval Europe, 950–1200* (Philadelphia, 1994), 21–27, 36–64, 76–87, 180–95. Better on the average experience of parochial clergy, and the limited role of book-learning in their apprenticeship, is Joseph Goering, *William de Montibus (c. 1140–1213): The Schools and the Literature of Pastoral Care*, Pontifical Institute of Mediaeval Studies, Studies and Texts 108 (Toronto, 1992), 60–62.

ecclesiastical discipline." Unhappy with the laxity of religious life at the cathedral, as an adolescent he sought greater rigor at another local church, one that later became a regular canonry. Bishop John was so impressed with Ubaldus's religiosity, however, that he recalled him to the cathedral and made him prior, a position that gave him charge of the training of the clergy. Ubaldus went on to reform the chapter, and in 1129 became bishop himself.[4] Other bishops were not as fortunate as John was to have a local saint at hand to improve clerical life and training. When disappointed with the results of this informal system, some bishops wrote or commissioned works to use in the education of their clergy. These tracts took the form of commentaries on the liturgy and liturgical apparatus that were the daily focus of clerical life.

The allegorical meanings attributed to vestments in these tracts certainly shaped the response of Paul's audience to his narrative of the abduction of Gregory VII. In the first part of this chapter I will describe the emergence and development of this genre of commentaries on the meaning of clerical garments. Then we will consider the effects of these attempts at educating the clergy, tracing the articulation of an enduring set of spiritual practices relating to vestments and vesting. Two key ideas were broadly influential. The first was that vestments represented clerical virtues, and this led to the creation of rituals for vesting and prayers to be recited as these sacred garments were put on. The second influential idea was that the priesthood of the New Testament superseded that of the Old, suggesting some relationship between the garments worn by the medieval clergy and those made for Aaron and his sons. The intersection of both these ideas with customs associating certain vestments with particular functions or offices fostered more extensive use of vestments in ordination rites and the creation of new insignia. Collectively, these ideas and practices contributed to a heightened sense of the holiness of vestments. They were cultivated quite intensely by eleventh-century reformers intent on asserting the sacred status of the clergy and making clerics themselves conform to higher ideals.

Educating Clerics

One of the most enduring Christian manuals of clerical education is Gregory the Great's *Pastoral Care* (*Regula pastoralis*). Written at the end of the sixth century, this little book made a crucial association between the Old Testament account of the vestments of Aaron and the virtues to be cultivated by Christian priests. "The voice of God enjoined," wrote Gregory,

> that on the breast of Aaron the breastplate of judgment should be set, bound with fillets. The import of this was that the heart of the priest should in no way harbour dissolute thoughts, but only right reason should rule and restrain it, nor should he

4. *AASS*, 3 Mai: 630–31.

> entertain any indiscreet or unprofitable thought. One who is set up for a model to others should ever, by the strictness of his way of life, display what a wealth of reason he carries in his breast.

The description of the high priest's garb in Exodus might well attract Christian exegetes, as it is rich in colorful detail. God commanded the Israelites

> that they may make Aaron's vestments, in which he being consecrated may minister to me. And these shall be the vestments they shall make: a rationale and an ephod, a tunic and a strait linen garment, a mitre and a girdle. They shall make the holy vestments for thy brother Aaron and his sons, that they may do the office of priesthood unto me.

The ephod was to be made of "gold and violet [*hyacinthum*] and purple and scarlet twice dyed, and fine twisted linen, embroidered with diverse colors" (Exod. 28:3–5). Rightly so, commented Gregory,

> so that it may be evident with what great variety of virtues the priest should be conspicuous. Thus, in the vesture of the priest the gold is resplendent beyond all else; so should he especially shine beyond all others in the understanding of wisdom. Hyacinth is added, brilliant with the colour of the skies, that by every matter which he penetrates with his understanding, he may not stoop to the base favours of earth, but rise up to the love of heavenly things. . . . With the gold and blue of the vesture, there is also mingled purple. That is to say, the heart of the priest, while hoping for those high matters about which he preaches, should repress in itself the remotest suggestions of vice. . . . Now, to gold, blue, and purple is added twice-dyed scarlet, to signify that in the eyes of the Judge of the heart all that is good in virtues must be adorned with charity, and that everything that is resplendent in human eyes must in the sight of the Judge within be lit up with the flame of love coming from the heart. Moreover, because this charity embraces both God and neighbour, its radiance is, as it were, of a double hue. . . . But while the mind is intent on the precepts of charity, it remains, beyond doubt, that the flesh must be mortified by abstinence. Consequently, fine-twisted linen is joined with the twice-dyed scarlet. Now, fine linen comes from the earth with radiant hue. And what else is designated by linen but chastity, radiant in the comeliness of bodily cleanness?

Gregory had more, too, to say about the rationale or breastplate. The description in Exodus is exquisitely detailed: we learn its dimensions; its fastening via golden chains, hooks, rings, and purple fillets; and the names of the twelve gemstones to be affixed in rows, symbolizing the twelve tribes of Israel descended from Jacob's sons. Gregory takes the names of these patriarchs engraved on the breastplate's gems as a reminder for clerics "to meditate unceasingly on the lives of those elders. The priest then walks blamelessly, when he is ever contemplating the examples of the fathers who preceded him, when without interruption he regards the footsteps of the Saints." Another descriptive detail that attracted Gregory's and later exegetes' attention was the hemming of the high priest's tunic with bells. Exodus recounts that the tunic was a deep blue, the bottom bordered with pomegranates interspersed with little bells. Aptly also, comments Gregory, the "little bells are fixed to the vesture, that even the works of the priest should loudly proclaim his way of life in the sound of his speech."[5]

This section of Gregory's *Pastoral Care* had a powerful influence on later interpretations of vestments. It was among the excerpts from patristic sources on clerical life that were issued with the decrees of the reforming Council of Aachen in 816, and thus circulated widely in the Carolingian realm.[6] Three other early texts were also highly influential. Jerome's letter to Fabiola commenting on Aaron's vestments provided later authors a great deal of etymological and descriptive material, but it made only very general comments beyond the literal meaning of the text and did not connect the Levitical to the Christian priesthood. Isidore of Seville's *Etymologies* were used similarly.[7] Bede's *On the Tabernacle* (c. 721–725), however, drew on all of these sources and provided a much more complete exegesis of Exodus 28. He provided allegorical interpretations of many more details: the size of the rationale "indicates the indefatigable and constant effort of pious intention"; its diversity of gems "designates the manifold grace of the various virtues which should always appear in the heart of a priest, arranged in harmonious succession"; their arrangement in three rows "that we ought to hold fast to unfeigned faith in the Holy Trinity." Following Gregory's lead, the venerable Bede quite thoroughly interpreted Aaron's vestments as symbols of the virtues to be cultivated by Christian priests.[8]

Carolingian authors made significant interventions in this developing tradition. First, instead of organizing their narratives around Aaron's vestments as described in Exodus 28, they took the vestments of the Christian priesthood as their framework. This innovation was due to the strongly liturgical emphasis of the Carolingian reform. What both secular and ecclesiastical leaders wanted in the eighth and ninth centuries was for clerics "to know and understand liturgical texts and rituals, especially those of

5. Gregory the Great, *Pastoral Care*, trans. Henry Davis, Ancient Christian Writers 11 (Westminster, Md., 1950), 46–54 (2.2–4); for the critical edition, see *Règle Pastorale*, ed. Floribert Rommel, 2 vols., Sources Chrétiennes 381–82 (Paris, 1992), 1:176–78, 184–86, 190–92.

6. *MGH Concilia* 2:346–47.

7. Jerome, *Sancti Eusebii Hieronymi Epistulae*, ed. Isidore Hilberg, 3 vols., CSEL 54–56 (Vienna, 1910–1918), 1:586–615 (letter 64); Isidore of Seville, *Etimologie o origini*, ed. Angelo Velastro Canale, 2 vols. (Turin, 2004), 2:584–91 (book 19.21–22), which gives the critical edition of W.M. Lindsey and an Italian translation; in English, *The Etymologies of Isidore of Seville*, trans. Stephen A. Barney, W.J. Lewis, J.A. Beach, and Oliver Berghof (Cambridge, 2006), 383. Barton Brown's 1983 dissertation completed at New York University, "'Enigmata Figurarum': A Study of the Third Book of the 'Rationale Divinorum Officiorum' of William Durandus and Its Allegorical Treatment of the Christian Liturgical Vestments" (PhD diss., NYU, 1983) traces connections among many of these tracts, with some difficulties in translations, but his perspective is strongly teleological, considering earlier tracts as forerunners of Durand.

8. Bede, *De tabernaculo*, ed. David Hurst, CC 119A (Turnhout, 1969), 97–129; *Bede: On the Tabernacle*, trans. Arthur G. Holder (Liverpool, 1994), 111–45 (3.3–10).

the Roman rite." This provoked a veritable "flood" of liturgical treatises.[9] In taking Christian vestments as their starting point, however, Carolingian liturgists recycled and reframed earlier exegesis of Aaron's attire. The effect of this creative rearrangement of texts was to connect Christian vestments more directly not only to priestly virtues, but also to the Jewish high priest's garments.

The three most influential liturgists of the era all wrote commentaries on vestments: Hrabanus Maurus (d. 856) in his *De institutione clericorum libri tres*, Amalarius of Metz (d. c. 850) in the *Liber officialis*, and Walafrid Strabo (d. 849) in his *Libellus de exordiis et incrementis quarundam in observationibus ecclesiasticis rerum*. The latter, historical in its approach, was the briefest and least popular among contemporaries and later medieval authors and scribes. Walafrid makes a few comments on the emergence of the chasuble, dalmatic, and stole—drawing on the *Liber pontificalis*, Gregory the Great's letters, and conciliar canons—and then observes that "different people have added different things to sanctified vestments either to imitate items which priests of an earlier period used or to express an allegorical meaning; our predecessors have sufficiently elaborated the significance of each item we now use."[10] He clearly meant his teacher Hrabanus and Amalarius, both of whom provided allegorical meanings for each vestment.

Each, however, usually provided different meanings. Hrabanus, for example, equated the amice with the *ephod* and then followed Bede in making it a symbol of the purity of the priest's good works. Amalarius started from the fact that the amice was wrapped around the neck, and since the voice comes from here, the garment is a sentinel of the voice, reminding priests not to say sinful things.[11] Hrabanus posits a similar meaning for the stole, also worn around the neck, but links it to preaching since it is bestowed only on those entrusted with this office. A different route is taken by Amalarius, who emphasizes the deacon's wearing of the stole and his duty to read the Gospel. Invoking Jerome's commentary on Matthew 11:30 ("For my yoke is sweet and my burden light"), he

9. Roger E. Reynolds, "Liturgy, Treatises on" in *The Dictionary of the Middle Ages*, ed. Joseph R. Strayer, 13 vols. (New York, 1982–1989), 7:627. Liturgical commentaries were already established in the Orthodox tradition and several of these texts may have influenced the Carolingian tracts. Parts of the *Mystagogie* of Maximus the Confessor (d. 662) that were included in the influential commentary of Germanus, Patriarch of Constantinople (d. 733)—not those concerning vestments—were definitely translated into Latin by Anastasius Bibliotecarius during his sojourn in Constantinople in 869–870 and later sent to Charles the Bald. But other portions of these works may have been known earlier through florilegia. Amalarius of Metz went to Constantinople in 813 (seven years before writing his own liturgical commentary) and may then have been exposed to this Orthodox tradition. More scholarship in this area is needed. See Germanus of Constantinople, *On the Divine Liturgy*, ed. and trans. Paul Meyendorff (Crestwood, N.Y., 1984), 9–16, 64–67; René Bornert, *Les commentaires byzantins de la divine liturgie du VIIe au XVe siècle*, Archives de l'orient chrétien 9 (Paris, 1966), 29–39, 82–90, 124–50, 161–69.

10. Alice L. Harting-Correa, *Walafrid Strabo's "Libellus de exordiis et incrementis quarundam in observationibus ecclesiasticis rerum": A Translation and Liturgical Commentary*, Mittellateinische Studien und Texte 19 (Leiden, 1996), 152–53.

11. *De institutione*, 309 (1.15); *Liber officialis*, 239 (2.17).

reads the yoke as the Gospel, "which is Christ," and thus the stole as a symbol of this "light burden" to proclaim the Gospel.[12] Both agree that the alb, or *camisia*, means bodily discipline or continence, although as usual they arrive by different paths—Hrabanus via the whiteness of linen and Amalarius following Bede.[13] The chasuble produces slightly different readings. Hrabanus starts with Isidore's etymology of *casula* being a diminutive of *casa*, or house, and goes on to equate this "little house" with love: just as the chasuble covers over and protects everything under it, so love surpasses all the virtues, securing and illumining them. Amalarius notes that the chasuble was worn by all clerics, "and so it ought to signify the works that are the duty of all clerics: hunger, thirst, wakefulness, want, reading, chanting of the psalms, prayer, manual labor, teaching, silence, and the rest." Calling these collectively the "works of righteousness," he quotes Bede: "The sacred vestments of Aaron which Moses made for him are the works of righteousness and holiness."[14]

The latter gesture is typical of how Amalarius connects Christian vestments to those of the Jewish high priesthood.[15] His attempts are more persistent than Hrabanus's. At the opening of his section on vestments in the *De institutione*, Hrabanus announces that he will be comparing "the clothing of the modern priest to the ancient garb of the Old Testament."[16] But after identifying the amice as the *ephod bad* and invoking both Jerome and Bede to link the alb to the high priest's linen tunic, Hrabanus's comparison peters out. Amalarius was more consistently and creatively engaged with exegesis of Exodus 28. Like Hrabanus, he turns to the letter to Fabiola to define the linen tunic and repeats Jerome's explanation of why it was fitted and narrow. "In this regard, their vestment differs from ours," remarks Amalarius, "because that one was tight and ours is loose." As usual, however, there is a further meaning:

> For truly, these priests of the Old Testament were bound tight in the spirit of their servitude, concerning which Paul said: "For you have not received the spirit of bondage again in fear" [Rom. 8:15]. Indeed, because the Son freed us, we are free; we do not receive the spirit of servitude in fear, but the spirit of adopted sons. Therefore, theirs is narrow; ours loose, because of the freedom that Christ won for us.[17]

12. *De institutione*, 311–12 (1.19); *Liber officialis*, 242–43 (2.20).

13. Both also see the belt, or *cingulum*, as signifying continence or chastity. *De institutione*, 310–11 (1.16–17); *Liber officialis*, 239–41 (2.18), 247 (2.22).

14. *De institutione*, 313–14 (1.21); *Liber officialis*, 241–42 (2.19).

15. Brown notes this characteristic of Amalarius's commentary: "'Enigmata Figurarum,'" 140.

16. "De veste ergo sacerdotali moderno ad antiquum veteris testamenti habitum comparationem facientes, secundum maiorum sensum quid mystice significet, persequamur": *De institutione*, 309 (1.14).

17. *Liber officialis*, 240 (2.18): "In eo discrepat vestimentum istud a nostro, quod illud strictum est, nostrum vero largum. Etenim hi in veteri testamento spiritu servitutis erant astricti, de quo dicebat Paulus: *Non enim accepistis spiritum servitutis in timore*. Nos vero quia Filius liberavit, liberi sumus; non accepimus spiritum servitutis in timore, sed spiritum adoptionis filiorum, ac ideo sit illorum strictum, nostrum largum, propter liberatatem qua Christus nos liberavit."

Amalarius is not above fudging, however, when he wants correspondence. He asserts the "rule" that the pope wore two tunics in addition to the alb so that the number of his vestments adds up to eight, the same number as Aaron's.[18]

This new sort of liturgical commentary was intimately connected to Louis the Pious's support for clerical reform. Both Hrabanus and Amalarius wrote their tracts in the wake of the reform council held in Aachen in 816, the latter dedicating his *Liber officialis* to Louis. Hrabanus's *De institutione* more clearly arose out of the experience of teaching. Master of the school at the abbey of Fulda, Hrabanus recounted in the prologue that he wrote the commentary to satisfy the insistent questions of his brothers in Holy Orders. He also dedicated and sent it to Archbishop Haistulf of Mainz.[19] This collaboration between monastic scholars and bishops charged with the education and supervision of the secular clergy was typical of Carolingian reforming efforts.[20] After a lull in the composition of liturgical commentaries, the genre was strongly revived in the eleventh and twelfth centuries, and in this period bishops themselves were the primary authors. Bishop Bruno of Segni, for example, wrote his *De sacramentis* for Walter of Maguelonne. The two met just after Walter had been elected bishop in 1104 or 1105. A stimulating conversation on the book of Exodus, in particular the relationship of the Old Testament priesthood to the order in their own day, led Bruno to promise Walter a written commentary. The *Tractatus de sacramentis, mysteriis et ritibus ecclesiae* was the result; it treated the rites for consecrating churches, baptism, confirmation, and episcopal consecration.[21] John of Ivry wrote his *De officiis ecclesiasticis* while bishop of Avranches (1060–1067), announcing in its prologue his hope that it would contribute to the reform of his diocese.[22] At the end of the twelfth century, Bishop Sicard of Cremona (1185–1215) wrote his

18. Although the opening of Exodus 28 lists only six vestments, Christian exegetes counted eight by including the linen underbreeches (Exod. 28:42) and the gold plate inscribed and affixed to the miter (Exod. 28:36–37). Isidore of Seville's section on priestly vestments in the *Etymologies* (19.21) began "Octo sunt in lege genera sacerdotalium vestimentorum" and the Romano-Germanic Pontifical (81) later included an "Expositio octo vestium Aaron primi pontificis": Isidore, *Etimologie*, 2:584; Vogel and Elze, *Pontifical romano-germanique*, 1:292–300. Amalarius's application of this to papal attire is in his *Liber officialis*, 247 (2.22).

19. Amalarius probably composed the first version of his *Liber officialis* c. 820–822; he sent it to Louis the Pious sometime after April 5, 823: Allen Cabaniss, *Amalarius of Metz* (Amsterdam, 1954), 52. Hrabanus sent his tract to Archbishop Haistulf in 819: see Zimpel's introduction to his edition and the prologue itself: *De institutione*, 7–8, 11–33, 281; for further bibliography, see Helmut Spelsberg, *Hrabanus Maurus: Bibliographie* (Fulda, 1983).

20. Monasticism from its earliest texts imbued the habit and its parts with symbolic meanings, but this tradition remained quite rudimentary in comparison to the florid development of clerical allegorization of vestments traced here. Partly this was because the monastic habit was simple, while liturgical garments were numerous. Another obvious accelerant in the clerical tradition was this exegetical interest in Exodus 28. On monastic garb, see Constable, "Ceremonies and Symbolism," 771–834, but especially 808–33.

21. William L. North, "In the Shadows of Reform: Exegesis and the Formation of a Clerical Elite in the Works of Bruno, Bishop of Segni (1078/9–1123)" (Ph.D. diss., University of California, Berkeley, 1998), 324–30.

22. Richard Allen, "'A Proud and Headstrong Man'. John of Ivry, Bishop of Avranches and Archbishop of Rouen, 1060–79," *Historical Research* 83, no. 220 (2010): 201–2.

Mitrale for the education of his clergy, and this tradition reached its apogee in William Durand's *Rationale*, written for the clergy of Mende when he was their bishop. Surviving in two recensions, the first c. 1285 when Durand was promoted to the see and the second, more widely diffused edition in 1291 when he actually came to Mende, the *Rationale* was used as a standard textbook for the rest of the Middle Ages.[23]

And this is just a sample. Allegorical commentaries on vestments were included in the sermons of Ivo Bishop of Chartres, the theological works of Hugh of St. Victor, and Peter Comestor's *Historia scholastica*.[24] Short versions also circulated with anonymous expositions of the Mass, such as the eighth-century one once attributed to Germanus of Paris.[25] Many exemplars are entirely derivative, either regurgitations of Amalarius or pastiches that intermingle bits of the *Liber officialis* with some of Hrabanus's *De institutione*.[26] But there were some more creative interpretations within this genre across the twelfth century, namely Honorius Augustodunensis's *Gemma animae* (c. 1097–1110), Bruno of Segni's *Tractatus de sacramentis* (c. 1105), Rupert of Deutz's *Liber de divinis officiis* (c. 1109–1112), and Pope Innocent III's *De sacro altaris mysterio* (1195–1197). These four provided most of the material for the thirteenth-century compilations, notably Durand's *Rationale*.[27] The innovations of this reform era take two general forms.

First, multiple allegorical meanings were posited using the physical characteristics of the vestment as keys to understanding its significance. Akin to the *distinctiones* being made in the exposition of legal texts and sacred scripture, twelfth-century liturgical commentators presented various meanings of vestments organized around their parts and qualities.[28] Honorius, for example, tells us that the humeral or amice stands for hope of heaven but goes on to specify that

23. *Guillelmi Duranti Rationale Divinorum Officiorum*, ed. A. Davril and T.M. Thibodeau, 3 vols. CCCM 140A (Turnhout, 1995), vii–x. On Sicard, Maureen C. Miller, *The Bishop's Palace: Architecture and Authority in Medieval Italy* (Ithaca, N.Y., 2000), 243, with bibliography.

24. On these, see Brown, "'Enigmata Figurarum,'" 156–60, 176–78; he also discusses commentaries by John of Avranches (152–53) and Hildebert of Lavardin (154–56).

25. Josef Andreas Jungmann, *Missarum Sollemnia: Eine genetische Erklärung der römischen Messe*, 5th ed., 2 vols. (Vienna, 1962), 1:59; an English translation of the second edition is available: *The Mass of the Roman Rite: Its Origins and Development (Missarum Sollemnia)*, trans. Francis A. Brunner, 2 vols. (New York, 1951–1955), 46; Pseudo-Germanus, *Expositio antiquae liturgiae gallicana*, ed. E.A. Ratcliff, Henry Bradshaw Society Publication 98 (London, 1971), 23–25; Yitzhak Hen, *The Royal Patronage of the Liturgy in Frankish Gaul to the Death of Charles the Bald (877)* (Woodbridge, 2001), 5–7.

26. A good example is the much-copied *Liber quare*; its *quaestiones* (242–53) on sacred vestments repeat, in condensed form, the meanings assigned by Amalarius in his *Liber officialis:* George Polycarp Götz, ed., *Liber qvare*, CCCM 60 (Turnhout, 1983), 97–104; on the popularity of the text, see Roger E. Reynolds, "Liturgical Scholarship at the Time of the Investiture Controversy: Past Research and Future Opportunities," in *Law and Liturgy in the Latin Church, 5th–12th Centuries* (Aldershot, 1994), 18:116–17.

27. V.I.J. Flint, *Honorius Augustodunensis of Regensburg*, Authors of the Middle Ages 6 (Aldershot, 1995), 106–10, 138; North, "In the Shadows of Reform," 325, 329; John H. Van Engen, *Rupert of Deutz* (Berkeley, 1983), 58–67; Brown, "'Enigmata Figurarum,'" 160–73, 183–88, 291, 302.

28. On *distinctiones* as new tools in school pedagogy but also popular literature, see Goering, *William de Montibus*, 69–71. Richard H. Rouse and Mary A. Rouse, "*Statim invenire:* Schools, Preachers, and New Attitudes toward the Page," in *Renaissance and Renewal in the Twelfth Century*, ed. Robert L. Benson and

> through the edges of the humeral we understand that faith and works are connected in two ways to hope: both cross the breast, one showing and the other hidden, because faith and works are joined in one, but faith is hidden in the heart whereas works are manifest for the instruction of those around us. For one end is concealed and the other is visible because our works shine forth for others whereas our intention before God is hidden within. The breast is girded by the humeral because it is through hope for our celestial home that perverse thoughts are restrained in the heart of the priest. The two ties that fasten the amice across the breast are fear of punishment and the desire for life, which the Holy Spirit engraves on our heart. This vestment is white because all things are brilliant in the presence of the Lord.[29]

Bruno of Segni gives a similarly detailed reading of the pallium, equating it with the breastplate or rationale described in Exodus. Symbolizing the burden of the episcopal office, it also reminded the bishop of the wisdom so essential to his job. After these general meanings, Bruno develops an elaborate string of allegories about its folds, which recall the contrast between this life and the next; its long ends, symbolizing the cares and anxieties of office; and even the three pins used to affix it to the chasuble, that are the faith, hope, and love needed to carry out his duties well.[30] Rupert of Deutz found meaning in different parts of the pontifical sandals: their straps should remind us of John the Baptist saying that he was not worthy to bow down to loose the shoes of the one to come after him, and their ties of the inestimable love by which the divine word joined itself to flesh.[31] These uses of the physical characteristics of vestments to expound their meanings constituted a powerful pedagogical tool in teaching clerical virtues and simple theological principles.

Second, Christological meanings become more and more prominent.[32] Rupert's commentary on the vestments in the *De divinis officiis* most clearly demonstrates this development. The stole represents the priest's obedient service to the Son of God, and recalls particularly how obediently Christ suffered and died. "The chasuble signifies the vestment of the great priest, our Christ, the vestment of the true Aaron, to the edge of which ran down the oil that is placed on the head [Ps. 133:2], first running down into Aaron's beard." The oil, Rupert explains,

> is the Holy Spirit, whose plenitude is in the head, namely Christ, and then flows first into the apostles as if into the beard, then into the whole church and to its least

Giles Constable (Cambridge, Mass., 1982), 201–25 place the "distinctions" in the context of emerging memory and finding aids to support pastoral work, particularly preaching.

29. Honorius Augustodunensis, *Gemma animae*, book 1, chapter 201, in *PL*, 172:604–5.

30. Bruno of Segni, *Tractatus de sacramentis ecclesiae, mysteriis atque ecclesiasticis ritibus*, in *PL*, 165:1105–7; North, "In the Shadows of Reform," 354–56, 358.

31. *Liber de divinis officiis*, ed. Hrabanus Haacke (Turnhout, 1967), 20 (1.24).

32. Braun, *DLG*, 701, 705.

> members as if to the very edge of the vestment. The chasuble, therefore, stands for the vestment of Christ, which is the church.[33]

Bruno of Segni also offers some simpler Christological meanings. The crossing of the stole over the breast should remind the priest of the crucifixion, and the ring given to a bishop is a sign that he is the vicar of Christ, who rules and guards over Christ's bride, which is the church.[34] In his *De sacro altaris mysterio*, Innocent III went through the vestments twice, first presenting the Christological significance of each (drawing heavily on Rupert), then setting out in the second list how each vestment represented the virtues the priest should cultivate.[35]

Allegorical tracts on the meaning of vestments, in sum, were closely associated with attempts to reform the clergy in both the Carolingian era and in the central Middle Ages. Their direct influence on one highly articulate priest is evident in Peter Damian's letter 28 to his teacher, the hermit Leo of Sitria. Also known as the *Liber "Dominus vobiscum,"* the letter was a response to a specific liturgical question: When a priest says Mass alone, should he use the form "the Lord be with you [plural]" (*"Dominus vobiscum"*) and should he himself utter the responses usually said by the people? Damian describes the origins of the question in the practice of hermits, like his teacher Leo, performing Mass in their cells. Some of these, Damian explains,

> as if arguing with themselves, reply: "Are we to ask a blessing of the stones or from the boards of the cell, or to say to them 'The Lord be with you'?" on the other hand, others fear that if in any way they should abandon the traditional ecclesiastical *ordo* they would sin for having lessened the length of divine service.

The situation Damian was addressing, however, was not only a hermit's dilemma. One of the novel results of the emphasis in the eleventh century on the status of the priesthood was the idea that the priest should recite all the parts of the Mass. Essentially, the Mass went from being necessarily a community celebration to being also a priestly devotion. Even if the deacon, subdeacon, lector, and choir were present and performing their specific roles, the priest should quietly recite their parts as well, contemplating their meaning and significance. This devotional understanding of the Mass may have had its origins in the increase in votive Masses—that is, a Mass said for a special purpose, such as the benefit of a deceased loved one's soul, or the healing of a sick friend, or the end of

33. *Liber de divinis officiis*, 18–19 (1.22): "Casula magni sacerdotis nostri Christi uestimentum significat, illud uestimentum ueri Aaron, cuius *in oram descendit unguentum, quod est in capite*, primum descendens *in barbam ipsius Aaron*. Quod est illud uestimentum? Sancta ecclesia catholica. . . . Vnguentum autem regale et sacerdotale Spiritus sanctus est, cuius tota plenitudo est in capite scilicet Christo, atque inde primum in apostolos quasi in barbam, deinde in totam ecclesiam et usque in extrema membra ecclesiae quasi in oram uestimenti descendit. Casula ergo uestimentum Christi, quod est ecclesia, significat."

34. *Tractatus de sacramentis*, in *PL*, 165:1104, 1108.

35. *PL*, 217:787–96; Brown, "'Enigmata Figurarum,'" 184–86.

a drought. Another factor may have been the increased tendency for monks—like the hermits Damian was addressing directly—to take Holy Orders.[36] Whatever its precise origins, the practice is reflected in the emergence of a new liturgical book: the plenary missal. In the early Middle Ages, many books were necessary to perform the Mass. The sacramentary was the celebrant's book, giving the prayers the priest spoke, particularly the canon or Eucharistic prayer. The readings proclaimed by the deacon (the Gospel) and subdeacon or lector (the epistle, and in non-Roman rites also an Old Testament reading) were each gathered into one or more volumes called evangeliaries, lectionaries, or epistolaries. The cantors and the *scola cantorum* also had their own books. The gradual or Mass antiphonal had the "proper" chants, those that varied according to the feast day (such as the introit, offertory, and Communion antiphons), to which were often added the "ordinary" or unchanging chants sung at every Mass (such as the Kyrie Eleison, the Sanctus, the Agnus Dei). The *cantatorium* was a book with the soloist's parts, chiefly the responsories sung between the reading of the epistle and Gospel. A book gathering all these parts together, the plenary missal, emerged from the eleventh century, facilitating the priestly devotion of reciting all these parts.[37]

This devotion may be one reason Damian's letter had a wide circulation in the Middle Ages and was printed very early.[38] For our purposes, Damian's response is interesting because in the course of answering the specific liturgical question about "Dominus vobiscum," he brings up the allegorical meanings of vestments and shows how they were related, in a clerical mind-set, to far weightier issues. To recite the words of the liturgy, for Damian, is to participate in the mystical unity of the church: "If they are one who believe in Christ, then wherever an individual member is physically present, there too the whole body is present by reason of the sacramental mystery."[39] After giving several other examples of how the language of the liturgy reminds participants of the unity and power of the church, he equates "spiritual insight" with understanding the symbolism behind things "that on the surface seem frivolous and trivial." Damian asks, "When one

36. Jungmann, *Missarum Sollemnia*, 1:137–41, 273–306; *Mass*, 1:103–7, 207–33; Cyrille Vogel, *Introduction aux sources de l'histoire du culte chrétien au moyen âge* (Spoleto, 1973), 87–89; English ed., *Medieval Liturgy: An Introduction to the Sources*, trans. William G. Storey and Niels Krogh Rasmussen (Washington, D.C., 1986), 105–6, 134. Arguments were included in Mass commentaries, however, defending the custom of having at least a priest, deacon, and subdeacon to perform the liturgy; see Roger E. Reynolds, "A South Italian Liturgico-Canonical Mass Commentary," *Mediaeval Studies* 50 (1988): 626–70 and in *Law and Liturgy in the Latin Church, 5th–12th Centuries* (Aldershot, 1994), 12:636–37.

37. The most concise description of these books and their development is now Eric Palazzo, *A History of Liturgical Books from the Beginning to the Thirteenth Century*, trans. Madeleine Beaumont (Collegeville, Minn., 1998); for the books discussed here see 21–27, 63–75, 83–101, 107–10. An excellent brief overview of the transformation of liturgical books generally in this era is Niels Krogh Rasmussen, "Célébration épiscopale et célébration presbytérale: Un essai de typologie," in *Segni e riti nella chiesa altomedievale occidentale: 11–17 aprile 1985*, Settimane di studio del Centro italiano di studi sull'alto medioevo, 33 (Spoleto, 1987), 581–607.

38. Another reason would be the panegyric to the eremitical life that closes the tract: see Blum's note in Peter Damian, *Letters*, 1:255.

39. Ibid., 263; Peter Damian, *Die Briefe*, 1:256–57.

looks at the priestly vestments, is he likely to find in them anything to admire if he fails to understand the symbolism there contained?" He then rattles off a whole list of such symbolic meanings of vestments: someone with spiritual insight

> will reflect on the reason why the alb reaches to the heels and why the amice should always be made of linen; he will consider the meaning of the cincture and of the stole; at the same time he will examine why it is that the dalmatic is shaped in the form of a cross, why the chasuble is put on over all the other vestments, and why the maniple, which is used to clean away the spiritual rather than the physical discharge from eyes or nose, is worn on the left arm.

This series of allusions closely follows the order and substance of a widely copied late ninth-century *expositio missae* by Remigius of Auxerre that was included as book 40 in the Pseudo-Alcuin's liturgical commentary, the *Liber de divinis officiis*.[40] "The profound meaning of allegorical contemplation," concludes Damian, "is contained in the functions of public worship." These functions, moreover, are authoritative. Early in the tract he asserts that the words of the liturgy like "Dominus vobiscum" may not be omitted "just as nothing may be subtracted or added to the authority of divine Scripture."[41] Damian connects this belief in the authoritative character of ecclesiastical traditions by introducing an example from canon law. If the custom of the church appears illogical according to human reason—such as the ban on twice-married men from becoming priests even while a priest who has committed fornication may come to function as a priest again—then its deeper "mystery of interior grace" must be sought. This admonition to seek the allegorical, symbolic meaning behind the church's customs is not just about ecclesiastical discipline for Damian; it is about preserving the "mystical unity" of the church.

The allegorical interpretations of vestments included in liturgical commentaries influenced clerical culture, contributing to the development of a spirituality centered on these material objects. Not only did this eleventh-century priest know one version of these commentaries on vestments well enough to incorporate them into a letter, but he

40. Peter Damian, *Die Briefe*, 1:269–70; he also shows familiarity with Amalarius's discussion of the maniple in the *Liber officialis* by including the phrase "oculorum vel narium pituita," a detail not in the Pseudo-Alcuin. On Damian's use of the *De divinis officiis*, see John J. Ryan, "Pseudo-Alcuin's *Liber de divinis officiis* and the *Liber 'Dominus vobiscum'* of St. Peter Damiani," *Mediaeval Studies* 14 (1952): 159–63. The alb reaches to the heels because good works are carried through to perfection and one who perseveres will be saved. The amice is made of linen as a reminder that just as much work is necessary to make linen white, much effort is necessary to cleanse the body of sin and make it pure. The cincture means discretion; the stole reminds preachers that they bear the yoke of Christ. The cross shape of the dalmatic recalls to the wearer that the world is his crucifixion. The chasuble is put on over all the other vestments because it stands for love (*charitas*), which exceeds all other virtues. The maniple is used to clean away "humors" because it represents the present life, full of desires that should be cleansed. For another example of an educated cleric's engagement with this tradition, see *The Letters and Poems of Fulbert of Chartres*, ed. and trans. Frederick Behrends (Oxford, 1976), 159 (letter 88).

41. Peter Damian, *Letters, 1–30*, 261; Peter Damian, *Die Briefe*, 1:255.

understood them as exemplifying the spiritual quest incumbent upon clerics to seek the mystical unity of the church in their understanding of and deference to ecclesiastical tradition. Other prelates probably found Damian's deft use of mystical meanings to buttress ecclesiastical authority quite appealing, but they also took more tangible lessons from allegorical interpretations of vestments.

Creating New Apparel: The Rationale

One of the most elaborately described articles of the high priest's attire in Exodus 28 is the breastplate, or "rationale of judgment." It was to be embroidered in various colors and have mounted on it four rows of gemstones, set in gold, and engraved with the names of the children of Israel.[42] Two gold chains, four gold rings, and purple fillets secured it to the ephod. This important ornament of the Jewish high priest posed a particular challenge for liturgical commentators; it was not easily correlated with a Christian vestment. The Pseudo-Germanus and Bruno of Segni both equated it with the pallium,[43] but this seems to have been deemed insufficient. The lack of an equivalent to the high priest's rationale led to the creation of a new piece of episcopal ornament called the rationale.[44]

This ingenious addition to the standard garments of ecclesiastical vestiture is well known to those who have studied vestments. Joseph Braun provided an overview of its use and forms, while more recently Klemens Honselmann assembled significant documentary and visual evidence.[45] Their findings merit discussion here because the creation of the rationale is such an exquisite example of ideas giving birth to apparel. Most of the standard liturgical vestments had their origins in everyday Roman garments that

42. The first row was to have a sard (a red stone), topaz, and emerald; the second, a carbuncle (another deep-red stone), a sapphire, and a jasper; the third, a ligurius, agate, and amethyst; and in the fourth row, a chrysolite, onyx, and beryl. See Exod. 28:17–23.

43. Pseudo-Germanus, *Expositio*, 23; Bruno of Segni, *Tractatus de sacramentis* in *PL*, 165:1105–6. There are some similarities to the pallium in how the rationale was used by the papacy, and the privilege of wearing it was sometimes granted along with the pallium: Helmut Beumann, "Das Rationale der Bischöfe von Halberstadt und seine Folgen," in *Kirche und Reich: Beiträge zur früh- und hochmittelalterlichen Kloster-, Bistums- und Missionsgeschichte*, ed. Irmgard Fees, Bibliotheca eruditorum: Internationale Bibliothek der Wissenschaften 33, ed. Domenico Maffei, Horst Fuhrmann (Goldbach, 2004), 43–59.

44. The name "rationale" comes from the Vulgate: Jerome translated the high priest's breastplate, or *logion*, as *rationale*.

45. Braun, *DLG*, 676–700; Klemens Honselmann, *Das Rationale der Bischöfe* (Paderborn, 1975). Honselmann gathers together sources making any possible allusion to the rationale; I have been more selective in using his evidence, distinguishing between references to the high priest's attire and sources (such as inventories, images) more clearly refering to an actual ornament worn by medieval bishops. Honselmann's work has led to further research on its origins: Klaus Gamber, "Das Superhumerale der Regensburger Bischöfe in seiner liturgiegeschichtlichen Entwicklung," in *Ecclesia reginensis: Studien zur Geschichte und Liturgie der Regensburger Kirche im Mittelalter*, Studia patristica et liturgica quae edidit Institutum Liturgicum Ratisbonense 8 (Regensburg, 1979), 184–98, arguing that it was a development of a "Gallican pallium."

were then modified for ecclesiastical use. Early medieval clerics took what was at hand and, as we have seen, they generated an enormous range of spiritual meanings for the garments they used. In the case of the rationale, spiritual meanings came first: exegesis of Exodus 28, particularly attempts to allegorically correlate the vestments of the Jewish high priesthood with those of the Christian clergy, gave rise to a new episcopal ornament. Walafrid Strabo alluded to such a creative process in the mid-ninth century: "different people have added different things to sanctified vestments," he wrote, "to imitate items which priests of an earlier period used."[46] Would that we had all these experiments!

The earliest references to the rationale as something worn by Christian bishops come from the second half of the tenth century. Sometime after 984, Bishop Hildeward of Halberstadt wrote to Bishop Adalbero II of Metz in response to an inquiry the latter had made via a mutual acquaintance. Apparently, Adalbero was interested in "that special gift of the divine altar . . . called, namely, the rationale of learning and truth." Hildeward goes on to reveal that this "special gift" had been granted to his see by Pope Agapetus (II, 946–955). Since, of course, it could not be divided, Hildeward wrote that he had arranged for an "exemplar" to be sent to Adalbero.[47] Although this word could indicate a pattern or image, surely Hildeward meant a copy or reproduction, for he goes on in the letter to ask Adalbero to send his church an ampulla of the blood of Saint Stephen, the patron saint of both Metz and Halberstadt, and a "modest part" of the relics of Saint Glossinde. Lest we think Hildeward too forward, the bishop does explain the reason for this pious request. Recalling that Metz had been preserved from the ravages of the Huns long ago by divine protection, Hildeward pleads for a share in the relics because his see is pressed in upon from all sides by Slav invasions. Might Pope Agapetus have been moved to send this rationale and the special privilege of wearing it to a previous bishop of Halberstadt because of the violent attacks his see was facing?

More likely it was offered to mollify the see during Otto I's attempts to have ecclesiastical organization overhauled to consolidate his eastern conquests. The king's initial plan was to have Magdeburg raised to an archbishopric, effectively demoting Halberstadt, once the premier see in the region, and subtracting it from the archdiocese of its traditional metropolitan, Mainz. The opposition of Archbishop Wilhelm of Mainz, acridly articulated in a letter to Pope Agapetus II in 955, seems to have led to reconsideration of this plan. Otto was successful in having Pope John XII elevate Magdeburg in

46. Harting-Correa, *Walafrid Strabo's "Libellus de exordiis,"* 152–53. While the form of the rationale may have developed from a "Gallican pallium," the use of the term *rationale* to denote a special episcopal ornament was clearly influenced by the liturgical commentary tradition.

47. "Proinde ad declarandum in vos nostre dilectionis igniculum, divini, cui indigni deservimus, altaris speciale donum, doctrine videlicet et veritatis rationale vocatum, venerabilis pape Agapeti decreto sibi collatum, prout nobis vestra claritas per fratrem communiter nostrum Meinzonem iniunxit, quia unum dividere non potuimus, exemplar illius, vobis devotissime direximus, id ipsum aut illius simile, si iusseritis, quantocius missuri"; Honselmann, *Das Rationale*, 106–7.

967 to an archbishopric, but Halberstadt remained under Mainz.[48] As we see both from Adalbero of Metz's inquiries about the rationale and from Hildeward's intention to send him a copy, neither prelate seemed to have felt that papal permission was necessary to wear this new ornament. A few sees—Aquileia in 1027, Naumberg in 1119, Paderborn in 1133, Liège in 1135, and Monreale in Sicily in 1182—did receive papal privileges, but the evidence for bishops having a rationale or having themselves depicted in it is more extensive.[49] Indeed, the varied regional forms the rationale took suggest that its use spread through contact with neighboring prelates rather than with Rome. In the eleventh and twelfth centuries it seems largely a German fashion, but in the thirteenth century bishops are depicted wearing it in France and England.[50] With the exceptions of Aquileia and Monreale, Italian bishops seem to have had less interest in the rationale.

Although some metropolitans added the rationale to their pontifical garb, Braun argued that the new ornament mainly functioned as an episcopal counterpart to the archiepiscopal pallium.[51] But why might bishops be so intent on further distinguishing themselves, particularly by constructing themselves as high priests after the pattern of Exodus? The Old Testament distinguished between ordinary priests, who wore four white linen garments, and the high priest, who donned an additional four richly ornamented items: the blue tunic hemmed with pomegranates and bells, the ephod, the breastplate (rationale), and a golden inscribed diadem set into his headdress. When liturgical commentators started seeking parallels between Christian vestments and the garments described in Exodus, the Levitical distinction between priests and high priests was lost. The amice, for example, which priests wore, was equated with the ephod.

This equation of the Jewish high priest with the ordinary Christian priest in the liturgical commentaries reflected an increasing emphasis within Western Christianity on the special powers of the priesthood. Mainly fueled by a greater mystical sense of the Eucharist coming out of theological reflection and debate during the ninth and the eleventh centuries,[52] the special status being accorded the priesthood led to a narrower understanding of orders. Whereas *ordo* was used in the early Middle Ages to denote an

48. Ibid., 26–27, 105–6; Beumann, "Das Rationale," 240–43; Timothy Reuter, *Germany in the Early Middle Ages, c. 800–1056* (London, 1991), 163–64.

49. Honselmann, *Das Rationale*, 28, 107, 117–21. Auxerre, Bamberg, Speyer, Limoges, Augsburg, Salzburg, Regensburg, Trier, Magdeburg, Würzburg, Münster, Hildesheim, Strasburg, Zweifalten, Prague, Cologne, Mainz, Meissen, Bremen, Constance, and Osnabruck used it with no known papal privilege: 89–90, 108, 110–11, 122; plates 1–2, 32–35. Minden claimed in the thirteenth century to have received the rational from Pope Leo III and Eichstatt in the fourteenth from Saint Boniface: 28, 141, 131–32. See also Beumann, "Das Rationale," 250–70.

50. Honselmann, *Das Rationale*, plates 44 (Paris), 45–46 (Chartres), 53 (Worcester), 55 (Ely). One of the earliest pieces of liturgical evidence for the rationale now appears to come from a tenth-century Canterbury pontifical: Nicholas Orchard ed., *The Sacramentary of Ratoldus (Paris, Bibliotèque nationale de France, lat. 12052)*, Henry Bradshaw Society 116 (London, 2005), clxx, 238 (1084).

51. Braun, *DLG*, 694–97.

52. Jaroslav Pelikan, *The Christian Tradition: A History of the Development of Doctrine*, vol. 3, *The Growth of Medieval Theology (600–1300)* (Chicago, 1978), 184–204; Charles M. Radding and Francis Newton, *Theology, Rhetoric, and Politics in the Eucharistic Controversy, 1078–1079: Alberic of Monte Cassino against*

office or ministry—and thus was used to describe a wide range of functions, such as lectors, exorcists, abbesses, bishops, and monarchs—from the late eleventh century, some reform councils insisted that only the diaconate and the priesthood were sacred orders sanctioned by Christ.[53] Out of these reform debates came a definition of the "minor" (doorkeeper, lector, exorcist, acolyte) and "major" (subdeacon, deacon, priest) orders conceived as stepping-stones to the power to confect the Eucharist. The priesthood became the defining *ordo:* "that sacrament which is the most excellent of them all," Berno of Reichenau (d. 1048) observed, "namely the body and blood of Christ, is consecrated daily by priests as well as by bishops, and it is no holier when done by the latter than when done by the former."[54] Early medieval lists of the orders had included bishops at the pinnacle, but the theologians and canonists of the eleventh and twelfth centuries removed them, redefining the episcopate as an office to which one was consecrated, not ordained.[55] While not exactly a demotion, given the significant sacramental and other powers attached to the office, these changes in the conception of episcopal status seem likely to have nurtured desires to heighten visually the distinction between ordinary priests and priests serving as bishops.

But what did this new distinguishing ornament look like? Since no one in western Europe had seen a Jewish high priest's "breastplate of judgment," medieval clerics had only the Latin translation of Exodus and their imaginations to use in designing the rationale. The only extant example from our period, a rationale from the mid-eleventh century in the Bamberg cathedral treasury, did take from the description in Exodus the idea that it should be embroidered. What survives today is sewn onto a sixteenth-century chasuble, but originally the purple-blue silk backing with gold embroidery was, like later extant versions, a sort of short scapular put on over the head (figures 4 and 5).[56] Front and back panels are joined by circular pieces that rest on the shoulders. The shoulder roundels contain the only other reference to Exodus 28. Between the inner circle and the outer are half-figure bust portraits of the twelve sons of Israel who are represented, in the Exodus description, by the twelve gems. Although not named in Exodus, the artist of

Berengar of Tours (New York, 2003), 3–20; Gary Macy, *The Theologies of the Eucharist in the Early Scholastic Period* (Oxford, 1984), 18–43.

53. E.g., Benevento, 1091. On the narrowing definition of "orders," see Gary Macy, *The Hidden History of Women's Ordination: Female Clergy in the Medieval West* (Oxford, 2008), 89–110.

54. In his *Libellus de quibusdam rebus ad missae officium*, chapter 2 (*PL*, 142:1061), as cited in Pelikan, *Growth of Medieval Theology*, 185.

55. Roger E. Reynolds, "Clerics in the Early Middle Ages: Hierarchies and Functions," and "'At Sixes and Sevens'—and Eights and Nines: The Sacred Mathematics of Sacred Orders in the Early Middle Ages," both in *Clerics in the Early Middle Ages: Hierarchy and Image* (Aldershot, 1999), 1:1–31; 3:669–84; and idem, *The Ordinals of Christ from Their Origins to the Twelfth Century*, Beiträge zur Geschichte und Quellenkunde des Mittelalters 7 (Berlin, 1978) 100–112, 134–51, 162–63.

56. A mid-fourteenth-century rationale from Regensburg has a similar form and imagery. The only other medieval exemplar, from late fourteenth-century Cracow, takes a very different form and was beaded: Honselmann, *Das Rationale*, plates 4–6.

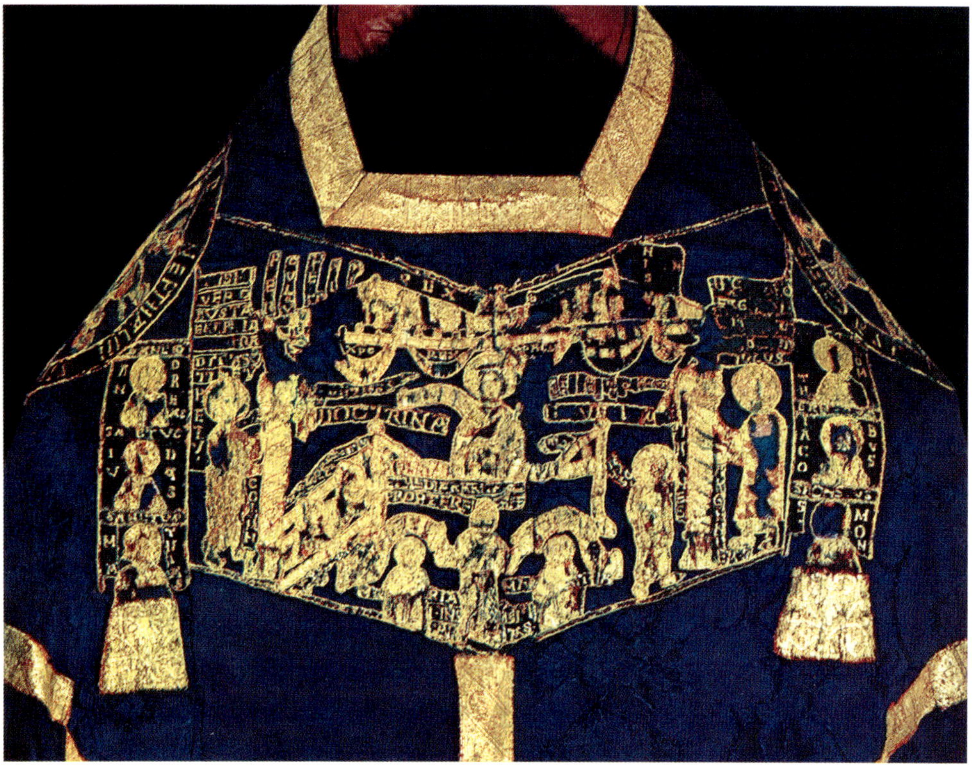

FIGURE 4. Rationale (front), c. 1050, cathedral treasury, Bamberg. Diözesanmuseum Bamberg / Verein für Geschichte und Altertumskunde Westfalens, Abteilung Paderborn.

the rationale has embroidered, in capital letters, the names of each of the sons of Israel under their images along the outer edge of the roundel: RUBEN, ASER, MANASES, LEVI, ISACHAR, and IOSEPH around left shoulder, and IUDAS, GAD, NEPHTALIM, SIMEON, ZABULON, and BENIAMIN around the right. Within the inner circle are pairs of figures referencing Psalm 85:11: "Mercy and truth have met each other; justice and peace have kissed."[57]

Although incorporating few details from the description in Exodus 28, the design was itself an exercise in exegesis. The images both front and back allude to passages in the Song of Songs (3:9–11) and Revelation (5:6 and 19:11), and most of the numerous inscriptions are also scriptural. The visual complexity of the design and the amount of text incorporated suggest that it was created for a sophisticated clerical audience. The choice of the Song of Songs as the key motif on the front of the rationale suggests further that this audience was mature: Saint Jerome, Isidore of Seville, Hrabanus

57. See Wilhelm Messerer, *Der Bamberger Domschatz in seinem Bestande bis zum Ende der Hohenstaufen-Zeit* (Munich, 1952), 69; see 67–70 in this work for the full description and transcription of the inscriptions, along with plates 72 and 73; the latter plate includes the shoulder roundels, which Honselmann does not. For color images, see Honselmann, *Das Rationale*, plates 1–2.

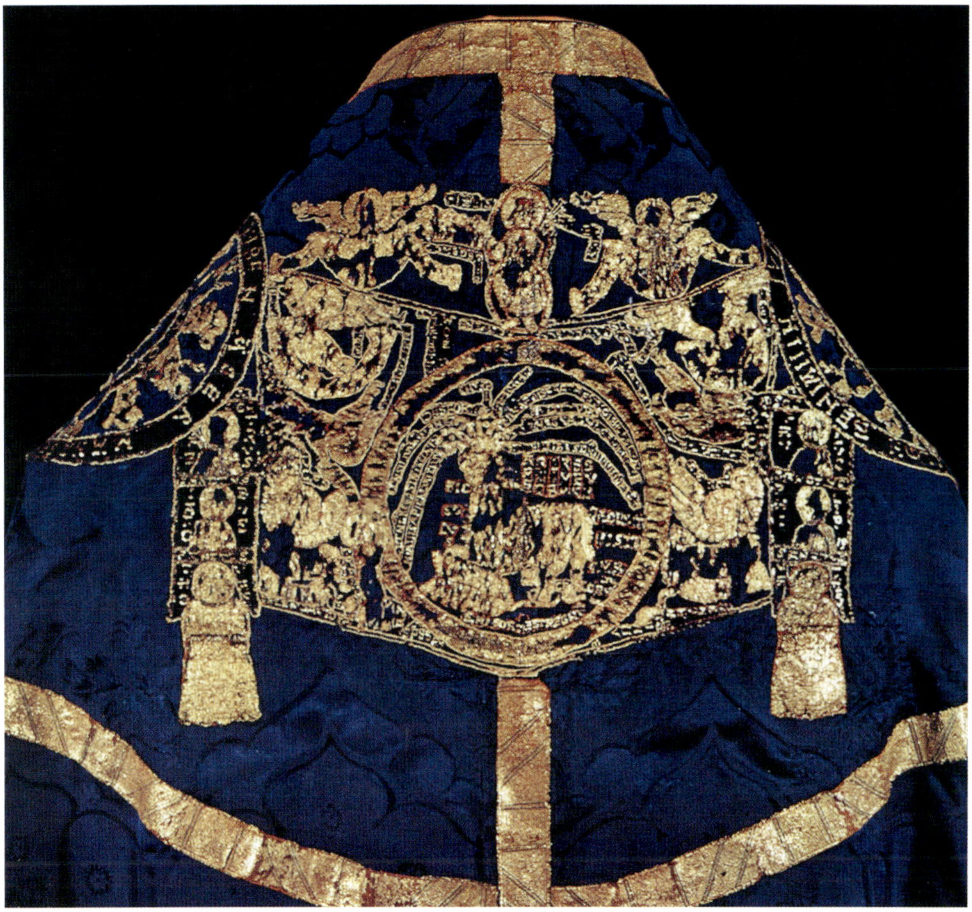

FIGURE 5. Rationale (back), c. 1050, cathedral treasury, Bamberg. Diözesanmuseum Bamberg.

Maurus, and other exegetes continued a Jewish tradition of restricting study of this amorous text to those over thirty who had already studied all the other books of the biblical canon.[58]

At the center of the front panel is an image of Jesus holding a scroll and scepter, an inscription above his head proclaiming that he is "Christ the Peaceful King." Flanking him are the words "DOCTRINA E(T) VERI(T)AS," exactly those used to identify the "rationale of learning and truth" in Hildeward's letter to Adalbero. The half-bust of the savior sits on the litter (*ferculum*) or palanquin of Solomon, an identification made certain by the inscription that begins vertically at top left, "FERCULU(M) FECIT SIBI REX SAL(OMON D)E L(IG)NIS (L)IB(A)N(I)" (King Solomon has made him a litter of the wood of Libanus; Song of Sol. 3:9). Its silver columns and purple steps are also depicted and labeled. Just beyond the columns at the edge of the scene are Saints Peter (left) and Paul (right), surrounded by inscriptions, not all of them still legible. On the banners extending toward Christ,

58. Ann W. Astell, *The Song of Songs in the Middle Ages* (Ithaca, N.Y.), 27.

however, each apostle speaks in his own words: Peter, as quoted in Matthew (16:16), says "You are Christ, the Son of the living God," while Paul, from his letter to the Galatians (6:14), cries out, "[But God forbid that I should] glory save in the cross of our Lord Jesus Christ." Beyond these apostles are side panels with more: the apostles Andrew, Jude, and Matthias on the left, and Bartholomew, James, and Simon on the right. Directly below the figure of Christ, the passage from the Song of Songs continues, "the midst he covered with charity for the daughters of Jerusalem" (Song of Sol. 3:10), and a figure labeled "FINIS P(RAE)CEPTI KARITAS" (The end of the commandment is charity; 1 Tim. 1:5). The figures of Martha and Mary flank KARITAS.

Christian exegetes, ever since Origin's massive third-century commentary, allegorized the bride of the Song of Songs as *ecclesia*, the church, joined in mystical union with Christ.[59] In the passage used on the rationale, the litter of Solomon was also understood as a metaphor for the church, and Christ here appears as the new Solomon, whose wisdom exceeds that of the Old Testament king. Through his church the savior "himself may be carried throughout the world." By labeling Christ the "peaceful king," the creator of this rationale showed acquaintance with an interpretation that was incorporated into the gloss of Anselm of Laon (c. 1050–1117), later known as the *Glossa ordinaria:* "the peaceful one [Christ] towards whose bed I hasten has strengthened me in this way, and has done this by means of a litter, that is, by means of the apostles whom he sent for our salvation and by whom he is carried as if on a throne."[60] Thus, Christ is flanked by Peter and Paul, while bands framing the panels of the rationale contain images of the rest of the apostles, all attendant on the litter bearing Christ. As an episcopal ornament, the words and images on the rationale identify the bishop as an apostle, one who brings Christ's salvation to the people, but it also identifies him with Christ. During his ritual of consecration the bishop received a ring that symbolized his union with his church, so he is also the *sponsus*, the bridegroom, who in the Song of Songs is Christ.[61]

Not only do the words and images on the rationale present allegorical or "mystical" interpretations just like those woven for sacred vestments, but the inclusion of the figure "Karitas" also directly intersects with those meanings. The word is in the passage from the Song of Songs, but it was also the meaning of the chasuble to which the rationale was

59. Ibid., 1–41; E. Ann Matter, *The Voice of My Beloved: The Song of Songs in Western Medieval Christianity* (Philadelphia, 1990), 86–111, especially 106–9 on exegesis during the eleventh-century reform era.

60. The columns were also understood as leaders of the church, silver because they are "learned in the clarity of the divine word"; the steps of the litter were allegorized as "those people by means of whom a person is able to climb first to the virtues and afterward to the holy of holies": *The "Glossa Ordinaria" on the Song of Songs*, ed. and trans. Mary Dove (Kalamazoo, Mich., 2004), 73–75 and ix–xiii on the compilation of the gloss.

61. On the development of this idea in this period: Megan McLaughlin, "The Bishop as Bridegroom: Marital Imagery and Clerical Celibacy in the Eleventh and Early Twelfth Centuries," in *Medieval Purity and Piety: Essays on Medieval Clerical Celibacy and Religious Reform*, ed. Michael Frassetto (New York, 1998), 209–237. The gloss's interpretation of the Song of Songs as sanctioning and promoting the active ministry of clerics has been underscored by Suzanne LaVere, "From Contemplation to Action: The Role of the Active Life in the *Glossa Ordinaria* on the Song of Songs," *Speculum* 82 (2007): 54–69.

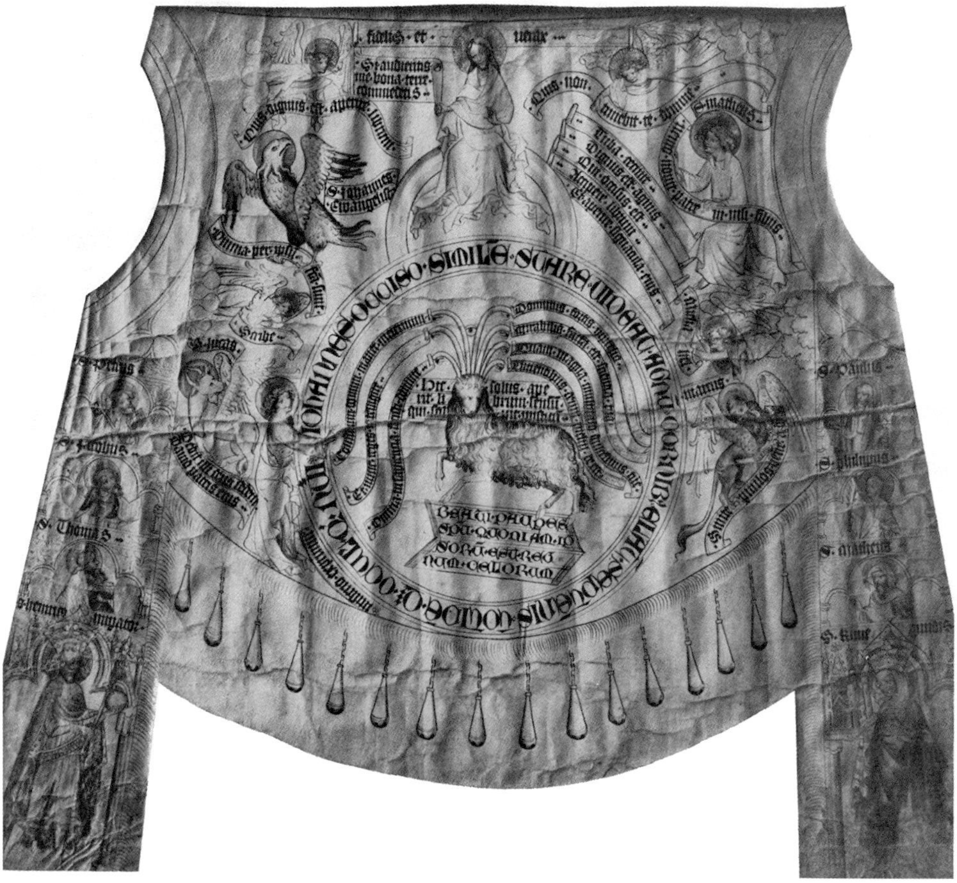

FIGURE 6. Drawing of the Bamberg rationale (back), fifteenth century. Bibliothek Stroß Pommersfelden, Kunstsammlungen Graf von Schönborn / Vereins für Geschichte und Altertumskunde Westfalens Abteilung Paderborn.

attached: "we understand this garment," wrote Hrabanus Maurus, "to be love [*charitatem*], which surpasses all the virtues."[62] The figures of Martha and Mary flanking KARITAS represented the two sides of the episcopal office, the active and contemplative lives: love, or charity, brings them together for *karitas*, another inscription reminds the prelate, "is the end of the commandment."

The words and images on the back of the Bamberg rationale have suffered more from the ravages of time, but a drawing made in the fifteenth century helps in deciphering them (figure 6). Some themes and images carry over from the front: the framing outer bands with apostles continue with Peter, James, and Thomas along the left, and Paul, Philip, and Matthew on the right. The figures and inscriptions at the very top pick up the theme of *ecclesia*. Around a double mandorla with God in majesty is the

62. *De institutione*, 313 (1.21).

inscription: FIDELIS ET (V)ERAX, referencing Revelation 19:11: "And I saw heaven opened: and behold a white horse. And he that sat upon him was called faithful and true; and with justice does he judge and fight." Although the horse is not represented here, it was commonly understood as the church, its rider being Christ.[63] Again, the bishop as ruler of a church acts as Christ; "faithful and true," he judges and does battle. Two angels hover on either side, speaking their lines from the Apocalypse: "Who shall not fear you, O Lord?" (Rev. 15:4), says one, addressing the righteous warrior Lord, while the other asks, "Who is worthy to open the book?" (Rev. 5:2). Just below, at the center of the panel, is the lamb (Christ) opening the book. This is the lamb of Revelation 5:6: "And behold in the midst of the throne and of the four living creatures and in the midst of the ancients, a lamb standing, as it were slain, having seven horns and seven eyes: which are the seven Spirits of God, sent forth into all the earth." The structure of the rationale seems to refer to the opening phrase, with Christ enthroned on the litter on its front, with the outer bands of apostles or "ancients" framing the front and back panels, and with the four symbols of the evangelists—the "living creatures" of Mathew's angel, Mark's lion, Luke's ox, and John's eagle—positioned around the circle of the lamb.[64] An inscription around the lamb's head tells us that "this one alone opens the book that freed the mystical meaning," while the open book below proclaims, "Blessed are the poor in spirit for theirs is the kingdom of heaven." Sprouting from the lamb's head are the seven horns and seven eyes "which are the seven Spirits of God sent forth into all the earth." Here they send out scrolls inscribed with passages from the psalms.[65]

If the front of the rationale associated the bishop with the apostles who spread Christ's word and with Christ himself as the bridegroom of the church, this side of the rationale identifies the bishop with the apocalyptic Christ who battles those arrayed with the Antichrist. According to the *Glossa ordinaria*, his armaments are learning and example, values at the heart of the ethos of the cathedral schools of the eleventh century—and Bamberg was seat of one of the foremost. So this Christ is also the slain lamb, the one worthy to open the book, to make manifest the mysteries of God's word. Glosses on this "book" identify its exterior as the Old Testament, where God's truth was set out in simple, less perfect words, whereas the interior of the book, its more secret but more perfect meaning, is the New Testament. The book embroidered here is opened by the slain lamb to Matthew 5:3, the Sermon on the Mount, in which Christ declared the kingdom of heaven

63. Bede, *De tabernaculo*, 15; Bede, *On the Tabernacle*, 14 (1.4); *Biblia latina cum glossa ordinaria: Facsimile Reprint of the Editio Princeps (Adolph Rusch of Strassburg 1480/81)*, 4 vols. (Turnhout, 1992), 4: Apoc. 5, 1, "Septem."

64. Messerer, *Der Bamberger Domschatz*, 69; Honselmann, *Das Rationale*, plate 28.

65. (DOMINE) OMNIA IN SAPIENCIA FECIS(TI) ([O Lord,] you have made all things in wisdom; Ps. 104:24); ET N(UN)C REGES INTELLIGTIE (= intelligite) (And now, O you kings, understand; Ps. 2:10); CONSILIU(M) D(OMI)NI MANET (IN ETERNUM) (The counsel of the Lord stands [forever]; Ps. 33:11); D(OMI)N(U)S FORTIS ET POTENS IN PRELIO (The Lord who is strong and mighty in battle; Ps. 24:8); (MIRABI)LIS FACTA EST SCIENCIA TUA (Your knowledge has become wonderful to me; Ps. 139:6); Q(UAM) MAGNA MULTITUDO DULCEDINIS TUE (How great is the multitude of your sweetness; Ps. 31:20); T(IM)ENTIBUS D(OMI)N(U)M NIHIL DEEST (To those fearing God, nothing is wanting; Messerer, *Der Bamberger Domschatz*, 69).

to belong to the humble, those "poor in spirit." The symbols of the evangelists that surround the image of the lamb on the rationale underscore the priority of the New Testament over the Old, just as the Christian priesthood of the one wearing the rationale superceded the high priesthood of Exodus and the breastplate described there.

The emphasis on the book and the evangelists on the back of the Bamberg rationale surely also refered to the ritual for consecrating a bishop. From the early tenth century, the Frankish rite usually included the direction that after his presentation to the people and their acclamation of assent to his election, the bishop-elect bowed forward. The archdeacon then "placed the [codex] of the four Gospels over his neck and between his shoulder blades." In this position, the consecrator, usually the metropolitan, and at least three other bishops placed their hands on his head and the consecration prayer was proclaimed. This long prayer addresses God, recalling how he had instructed Moses about the priestly garb and

> ordered Aaron, the elect, to be dressed in a mystical amice amidst the sacred rites, in order that generations to come might understand the discernment of judgment from the example of the ancients and the erudition of your teaching might not be lacking to any age, since among the ancients, the appearance itself of the signs received reverence, while in our day the experience of things is more certain than the enigmas of signs. Indeed, the dress of that earlier priesthood is the adornment of our mind, and it is no longer the dignity of dress that commends the episcopal glory to us, but rather the splendor of souls. For at that time they sought things that were pleasing to the carnal gaze rather than the things which should be understood within them. And therefore we ask, O Lord, that you grant this grace to this, your servant, so that whatever those veils signified in the glitter of their gold, in the brilliance of their gems, and in the variety of their manifold workmanship, this may shine forth in his behavior and actions.[66]

By placing the symbols of the evangelists on the back of the rationale, precisely where the Gospel book would have been placed during the bishop's consecration, the designers

66. "Deus qui, Moysen famulum tuum secreti familiaris affatu, inter cetera caelestis documenta culture de habitu quoque indumenti sacerdotalis instruens, electum Aaron mystico amictu vestiri inter sacra iussisti, ut intellegentiae sensum de ex[em]plis priorum caperet secutura posteritas, ne eruditio doctrinae tuae ulli deeset aetati, cum et apud veteres reverentiam ipsa significationum species obtineret et apud nos certiora essent experimenta rerum quam enigmata figurarum; illius namque sacerdotii anterioris habitus nostrae mentis ornatus est et pontificalem gloriam non iam nobis honor commendat vestium sed splendor animorum, quia et illa, quae tunc carnalibus blandiebantur obtutibus, ea potius quae in ipsis erant intellegenda poscebant. Et idcirco huic famulo tuo, quem ad summi sacerdotii ministerium elegisti, hanc, quesumus, domine, gratiam largiaris, ut, quicquid illa velamina in fulgore auri, in nitore gemmarum, in multimoda operis varietate signabant, hoc in eius moribus actibusque clarescat." Andrieu, *Ordines*, 4:44–45 (35.68). This consecration prayer, and the instruction to place the Gospel book on the elect's back, were incorporated into the Romano-Germanic Pontifical, Vogel and Elze, *Pontifical romano-germanique*, 1:216–8 (63.31–35), and then into the Roman pontifical of the twelfth century: Michel Andrieu, ed., *Le Pontifical romain au moyen âge*, 4 vols., Studi e testi 86–88, 99 (Vatican City, 1938–1941), 1:147 (10.21–23). I've used here the translation of this prayer done by North, "In the Shadows of Reform," 327–28, with some additions and modifications.

linked this novel episcopal ornament with the ritual actions that established his new status.

The consecratory prayer itself offers a guide to reading the rationale: it exhorts the bishop to set his sights beyond the earthly beauty of his vestments to the adornments of the mind, the "splendor of souls," that should "shine forth in his behavior and actions." Indeed, one of the most striking things about the Bamberg rationale is how it is designed to provoke the generation of spiritual meanings. Whereas liturgical commentators had to start with the names and material characteristics of traditional vestments in order to develop allegories about priestly virtues, the makers of the Bamberg rationale crafted into its physical substance and appearance a complex array of invitations to allegorization. The prompts were numerous and sewn right into the object. Perhaps because the name of the ornament would immediately make the link to the high priest's vestment, the Bamberg artists felt free to embed a more complex layer of physical characteristics as stimuli for contemplation. How would all these complex signs have been read? Although the fabric is crowded with texts, none are complete: they serve as prompts, relying on the clerical reader to know the rest of the passage. This was also how liturgical books cued the prayers and psalms that every cleric was assumed to know. Some of the images on the rationale—like the lamb with its seven horns and eyes—would have functioned similarly: the viewer would move from image directly to known texts. Other images work in conjunction with inscriptions that identify them and prompt the scriptural allusion. From the juxtaposed references to biblical texts, the learned clerical viewer could then take the next step, which was to discern the mystical sense by assembling the multiple symbolic meanings into some new whole.

Although the bishop surely knew the meanings embroidered on this ornament that he wore, the construction of the piece addressed others: one could not read the inscriptions or view the imagery when wearing it. All these inscriptions and imagery, therefore, were addressed primarily to those standing in close proximity to the prelate during Mass. That is, the rationale was meant to be read by the clergy attending the bishop, reminding them of his special status as a high priest among priests, and his special responsibility to bring the Gospel to his *ecclesia*. It is worth underscoring at this point that the educational efforts we have been considering constructed a culture peculiar to the clergy. While some of these ideas certainly filtered through to the laity, a cleric even in only minor orders had developed knowledge and expertise that profoundly altered his frames of reference and mode of understanding the world. For the acolyte standing beside him holding a candle, the bishop's rationale was surely an engaging puzzle. But it could be, and I think it was designed to be, much more: an aid to spiritual contemplation.

As such an aid, the Bamberg rationale is a particularly complex example. Two other versions using the same imagery from the Song of Songs and Revelation survive from fourteenth-century Regensburg and seventeenth-century Munich, both probably reworkings of earlier rationales closer to the Bamberg design. But the varied forms the rationale took in medieval Europe reveal the diversity and dynamic character of the clerical spirituality linked to vestments. Two early eleventh-century images of the bishop of

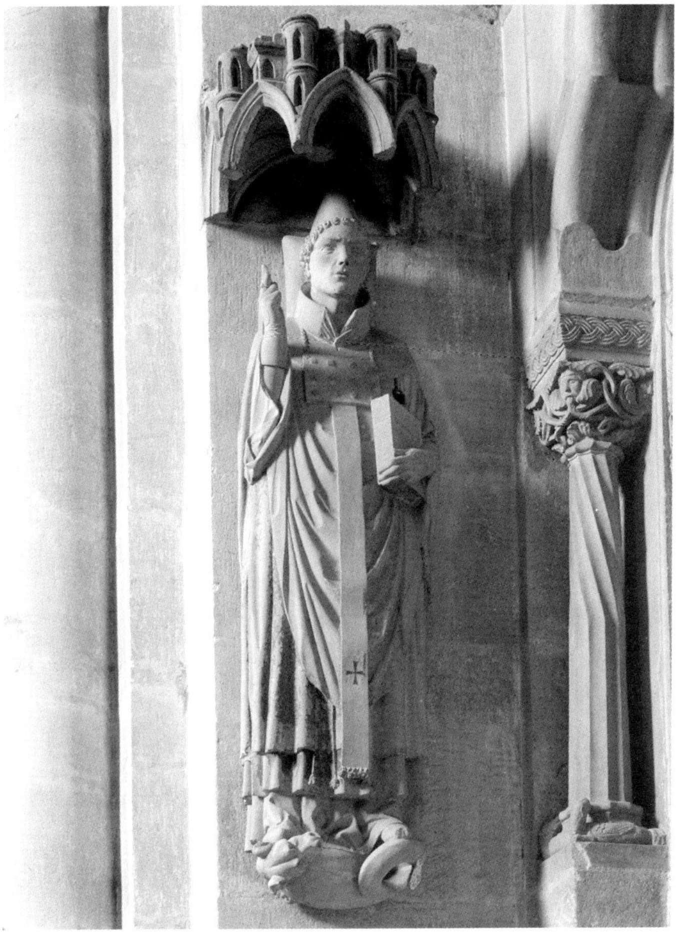

FIGURE 7. Funerary statue of Pope Clement II, thirteenth century, cathedral, Bamberg. Diözesanmuseum Bamberg.

Minden depict a decorated band around the shoulders, while in Bamberg itself we see an altogether different design of the rationale on the funerary statue of Pope Clement II in the cathedral (figure 7). This thirteenth-century interpretation more literally follows the description in Exodus 28. The rationale is a rectangular breastplate hanging on a chain around the pontiff's neck, with twelve gems or stones arranged in three rows. Other thirteenth-century sculptural programs at Chartres, Reims, and Worcester preserve similar depictions of the rationale.[67] It seems more this form that, in turn, entered the liturgical commentary tradition. Once the rationale was an element of episcopal vestiture, liturgical commentators began to include it in the lists of vestments for which they offered "mystical" meanings. Honorius Augustodunensis's *Gemma animae*, written in the

67. On the Minden rationale, see chapter 3, 123–24; Sigrid Müller-Christensen, *Das Grab des Papstes Clemens II. im Dom zu Bamberg* (Munich, 1960), 25, 31, and plates 1–2; Honselmann, *Das Rationale*, plate 43 (Bamberg), 45 (Chartres), 47–52 (Reims), 53 (Worcester).

early twelfth century, was the first liturgical commentary to include the rationale. After giving a condensation of the description from Exodus, Honorius informs his readers that the rationale "is worn on our vestments as an ornament, which with gold and gems is affixed to chasubles over the breast." "It reminds the prelate," Honorius continues,

> that he ought to cultivate honor in judgment, to carry out his duties with the gold of wisdom, the hyacinth of spiritual insight, the purple of endurance in Christ (who measures heaven by the span); [he ought] to radiate learning and truth; to shine with the gems of virtue; to imitate the twelve apostles in holiness; and remember the whole people in sacrifice.[68]

While the bishop may well have reflected on all these things as he wore his golden ornament studded with gems, a layperson not immersed in this clerical culture of allegorization might reasonably understand the rationale as a superfluous flaunting of ecclesiastical wealth. The lay critiques of clerical clothing mentioned by the legislation considered in chapter 1, as we have seen, focused on clerical attire worn outside of church. But the extravagances in clerical street-wear they censured may have developed from the same mentalities and cultural practices that created innovations like the rationale. From a clerical perspective, adding things to vestments "to imitate items which priests of an earlier period used," as Walafrid Strabo put it, was engaging in a spirituality of allegorical meaning that used material objects to cultivate and, in Peter Damian's terms, participate in the mystical unity of the church. They had been taught from a tender age to do this; such practices were at the heart of the educational project that formed them.

Liturgical commentaries on vestments were clearly favored by ecclesiastical reformers as a means of educating the clergy. From what we have seen thus far, it is clear that they definitely influenced clerical culture on the elite level. A highly educated cardinal like Peter Damian incorporated them into his theological arguments, and someone, perhaps close to the papal court, was inspired by them to create a new episcopal ornament similar to the high priest's breastplate. Pope Agapetus II, it appears, found this new creation a useful diplomatic tool, as did later pontiffs who issued privileges to wear it. Bishops, moreover, embraced the rationale, and at least one, Sicard of Cremona, commented on its meanings in the tract he wrote for the education of his clergy. The great number of liturgical commentaries written over the Middle Ages suggests that this genre was favored by those in charge of educating clerics. But did the average cleric take any of it to heart?

68. "Hoc in nostris vestibus praefert per ornatum, qui auro et gemmis summis casulis in pectore affigitur. Monet autem pontificum ratione vigere, auro sapientiae, hyacintho spiritualis intelligentiae, purpura patientiae in Christum (qui coelum palmo mensurat) tendere debere, doctrina et veritate radiare, gemmis virtutum coruscare, duodecim apostolos sanctitate imitari, totius populi in sacrificio recordari." Honorius Augustodunensis, *Gemma animae* 1.213 in *PL*, 172:608. Sicard of Cremona also included the rationale in his allegorization of vestments, drawing heavily on Honorius: *Mitrale* 2.5 in *PL*, 213:77–78. Honselmann's evidence for the diffusion of the rationale disproves Brown's contention that it was a mark of imperial allegiance rejected by papal supporters: "'Enigmata Figurarum,'" 266.

Priest Books and Vesting Prayers

The books used by priests suggest that allegorical thinking about vestments had a significant impact on clerical culture well below the elite level. They usually include not the didactic explications of vestments composed for their edification, but a more active appropriation of the concepts imparted: simple prayers to be said when putting on vestments.[69] These vesting prayers are usually attached to the opening of the *ordo missae*, a text giving condensed instructions for the saying of daily Mass. The earliest extant set of prayers is from the late ninth century, but it is during the eleventh century that examples become common and widely diffused.[70] They seem, therefore, to emerge out of the Carolingian interest in teaching clerics the meaning of liturgical words, objects, and actions, but their diffusion and establishment as a common practice was accomplished during the eleventh century. Like many of the changes linked to the eleventh-century reform movements, these prayers took root in clerical practice and flourished. The recitation of vesting prayers was a devotion enjoined upon priests that endured until the Second Vatican Council made it optional in 1965.

A small manuscript in the Vatican Library's collection provides a good introduction to the priest-book genre. Pierre Salmon, in his catalog of the library's liturgical manuscripts, rightly labeled Vatican codex Ottoboniensis Latinus 6 an "*enchiridion sacerdotale*," a priest's manual.[71] The volume fits comfortably in your hands, its seventy-five folios roughly eight inches by five and a half, the size of many paperback editions today. It's not

69. An introduction to these using one particularly developed example is Joanne M. Pierce, "Early Medieval Vesting Prayers in the *Ordo Missae* of Sigebert of Minden (1022–1036)," in *Rule of Prayer, Rule of Faith: Essays in Honor of Aidan Kavanagh, O.S.B.* (Collegeville, Minn., 1996), 80–105: see also the author's "Sacerdotal Spirituality at Mass: Text and Study of the Prayerbook of Sigebert of Minden (1022–1036)" (Ph.D. diss., University of Notre Dame, 1988).

70. Vesting prayers are also attested in the Orthodox tradition, but later (thirteenth century on): Warren T. Woodfin, *The Embodied Icon: Liturgical Vestments and Sacramental Power in Byzantium* (Oxford, 2012), xxxi, 104, 287–89 (a set of vesting prayers as published in the sixteenth-century *textus receptus* of the Orthodox rite).

71. Pierre Salmon, *Les manuscrits liturgiques latins de la Bibliothèque Vaticane*, 5 vols., Studi e testi 251, 253, 260, 267, 270 (Vatican City, 1968–1972), 2:122 (no. 292). Salmon gives a partial transcription in "L'*Ordo missae* dans dix manuscrits du Xe au XVe S," in *Analecta liturgica: Extraits des manuscrits liturgiques de la Bibliothèque Vaticane; Contribution à l'histoire de la prière chrétienne*, Studi e testi 273 (Vatican City, 1974), 198–200. This genre has received little scholarly attention, but see Frederick S. Paxton, "*Bonus Liber*: A Late Carolingian Clerical Manual from Lorsch (Bibliotheca Vaticana MS Pal. Lat. 485)," in *The Two Laws: Studies in Medieval Legal History Dedicated to Stephan Kuttner*, ed. Laurent Mayali and Stephanie A.J. Tibbetts, Studies in Medieval and Early Modern Canon Law 1 (Washington, D.C., 1990), 8–9; Keefe, *Water and the Word*, 1:23–31; Sarah Hamilton, "The *Rituale*: The Evolution of a New Liturgical Book," in *Studies in Church History* 38 (2004): 75–86; Yitzhak Hen, "Knowledge of Canon Law among Rural Priests: The Evidence of Two Carolingian Manuscripts from around 800," *Journal of Theological Studies* 50 (1999): 117–34; Yitzhak Hen, "A Liturgical Handbook for the Use of a Rural Priest (Brussels BR 10127–10144)," in *Organizing the Written Word: Scripts, Manuscripts and Texts: Proceedings of the First Utrecht Symposium on Medieval Literacy, Utrecht, 5–7 June 1997*, ed. Marco Mostert (Turnhout, forthcoming)—I thank the author for sending me a copy of this article.

pretty. The parchment is of low quality: edges uneven, holes on some pages, with rough ruling prickings along the edges. At least two hands, neither particularly fine, copied the collection of texts in the late tenth or early eleventh centuries, perhaps in or near the abbey of Nonantola.[72] The largest piece in the manuscript (31r–68v) is a section of a seventh-century mosaic of biblical and patristic texts, Defensor of Ligugé's *Liber scintillarum.* Organized by topic—"on penitence," "on humility," "on abstinence," and so forth—the work's brief quotations from scripture and the fathers were handy fodder for preachers.[73] The smaller excerpts also reveal the interests and needs of priests: the Venerable Bede's computistical tract (how to calculate the dates of Easter and other moveable feasts), Isidore of Seville on penitence and the origin of clerical offices, and excerpts relating to the clergy from a collection of canons.[74] The liturgical texts all focus on the Mass. After an *ordo missae* (9v–11r) there is an abbreviated version of the Mass commentary (*expositio missae*) of Remigius of Auxerre included as book 40 in the Pseudo-Alcuin's liturgical commentary, the *Liber de divinis officiis* (11v–14v).[75]

The vesting prayers are embedded in an opening ritual of preparation for Mass. This preparatory rite opens with the chanting of several psalms, beginning with "Quam dilecta" (Ps. 84), "How lovely are your tabernacles, O Lord of Hosts! . . . Blessed are they that dwell in your house." Then the rite continues with psalms asking God's forgiveness and help: "Benedixisti" (Ps. 85), "Convert us, O God our Savior: and turn off your anger from us"; and "Inclina" (Ps. 86), "Incline your ear, O Lord, and hear me." The final psalm in the sequence, "Credidi" (Ps. 116), asks the priest to remember what he is about to do: "I will take the chalice of salvation . . . I will sacrifice to you the sacrifice of praise." After reciting the "Kyrie Eleison" and the Lord's Prayer, this section concludes with five versicles, also drawn from the book of Psalms:

> Let your mercy, O God, be upon us. (Ps. 33:22)
> You will turn, O God, and bring us to life. (Ps. 85:7)

72. BAV Ottobon. Lat. 6 measures 206 mm x 140 mm; Salmon dated it to the tenth century, Reynolds to "X/XI": Roger E. Reynolds, "Excerpta from the Collectio Hibernensis in Three Vatican Manuscripts," *Bulletin of Medieval Canon Law* n.s. 5 (1975): 2. For the qualities of the parchment, see folios 6, 11, 14, 58. On 28v there is a list of the abbots of Nonantola.

73. BAV Ottobon. Lat. 6, 31r–68v. The manuscript text begins several lines into chapter 3, and includes all of chapters 4–10, 12–17, 27–28, 33–34, 44–45, 49–55, 68–71; see *Defensoris Locogiancensis Monachi "Liber scintillarum,"* ed. Henricus M. Rochais, CC 117 (Turnhout, 1957), 13–54, 60–80, 111–16, 134–37, 157–62, 165–80, 222–34.

74. Fols. 1r–9r give excerpts from the *Collectio canonum Hibernensis.* See Reynolds, "Excerpta," 3, n. 14 for a complete list of the chapters included, and the edition by Herrmann Wasserschleben, *Die irische Kanonensammlung* (Leipzig, 1885). The excerpts on 11r–v and 29r–30v, also identified by Reynolds, are from Isidore of Seville's *De ecclesiasticis officiis* 1.15.1–3, 1.18. Fols. 15r–22v have Bede's *De natura rerum* (chapters 21–51) and all of his *De temporibus;* 23r–26r have another computistical tract. Fols. 68v–75v contain several brief excerpts on penance: a sermon attributed to Augustine (no. 393, *PL*, 39:1713–44, "De poenitentibus") and several chapters on sin and repentance from Isidore of Seville's *Sententiarum libri tres,* book 2, chapters 3, 12–14, 16–17, and 22; *PL*, 83:602–3, 613–20, 624–25.

75. *PL*, 101:1246–71.

Show us, O Lord, your mercy. (Ps. 85:8)
And enter not into judgment with your servant. (Ps. 143:2)
Hear, O Lord, my prayer. (Pss. 102:2, 143:1)

The composition of this preparatory rite varied. Some manuscripts reveal a ritual less involved than the prescriptions in Ottoboniensis Latinus 6. An early eleventh-century ordo from Saint Martin of Tours and one from Figeac (or Moissac), for example, simply give a prayer for the priest to say as he washes his hands and then the vesting prayers.[76] Others were significantly more complex. An eleventh-century version from Hamburg preserved in Vallicelliana B 141 and studied by Niels Rasmussen includes a long (seventy-one-line) litany that begins with an alphabet of virtues ("Archangelorum eternitas; Bonitas patriarcharum; Caritas sacerdotum . . ."), then invokes patriarchs, prophets, and apostles before moving onto the acts of the Savior. One from Reichenau dating to the eleventh century includes an even longer litany, invoking more than two hundred named saints, after the vesting sequence.[77] The inclusion of litanies reveals the assumed collective character of this preparatory rite: the priest intoned the petition and the other clerics gathered with him in the sacristy responded, "Pray for us" or "Have mercy on us."[78] Some manuscripts also include rubricized directions that the versicles be chanted antiphonally,[79] and William Durand's thirteenth-century pontifical specifies

76. Edmund Martène, *De Antiquis Ecclesiae Ritibus Libri Tres*, 4 vols. (Antwerp, 1763–1764), 1:192 (ordo 7), 193 (ordo 8); Aimé-Georges Martimort, *La documentation liturgique de Dom Edmond Martène: Étude codicologique*, Studi e testi 279 (Vatican City, 1978), 151, 218, 312 (nos. 191, 323, 551, 552); Aimé-Georges Martimort, "Additions et corrections à *La documentation liturgique de Dom Edmond Martène*," *Ecclesia orans* 3 (1986): 88; BMT Diocèse 1, fol. 7v is Martène's ordo 7 and BnF MS lat. 2293, fol. 12v is ordo 8. The prayers are the same: "Lavabo inter innocentes manus meas et circumdabo altare tuum, Domine. Asperges me Domine hysopo et mundabor; lavabis me et super nivem dealbabor" (Ps. 26:6, 51:9) (I will wash my hands among the innocent and I will compass your altar, O Lord. Sprinkle me with hyssop, O Lord, and I shall be cleansed, wash me and I shall be made whiter than snow.) This prayer also appears in the earliest version of vesting prayers in a ninth-century sacramentary from Amiens (BnF MS lat. 9432), although this rite contains many more psalms than these later French examples: Victor Leroquais, "L'Ordo Missae du sacramentaire d'Amiens," *Ephemerides Liturgicae* 41 (1927): 439.

77. Niels Krogh Rasmussen, "An Early 'Ordo Missae' with a 'Litania Abecedaria' Addressed to Christ (Rome, Bibl. Vallicelliana, Cod. B. 141, XI. Cent.)," *Ephemerides Liturgicae* 98 (1984): 198–211; Joaquim O. Bragança, "O 'Ordo Missae' de Reichenau," *Didaskalia: Revista da faculdade de teologia de Lisboa* 1 (1971): 137–61.

78. A rite in a tenth-century manuscript from Corbie specifies that the bishop "ingredietur quoddam oratorium," where the first opening prayer is said, and then a second "dum introeierit secretarium," where he vests. Later versions locate the entire rite in the sacristy. The Corbie rite also specifies in the rubrics that "quidem minister" recites the versicles and the bishop responds. Martène, *De Antiquis Ecclesiae Ritibus*, 1:202 (ordo 11), 171 (ordo 2), 221 (ordo 23); Martimort, *La documentation*, 97, 313 (nos. 106, 555), 310 (no. 544), 148–49, 317 (nos. 187, 567); Orchard, *Sacramentary of Ratoldus*, 189 (836, 837), 236 (1070). A very different tradition developed in the Orthodox rite with vesting occurring at the altar: Woodfin, *Embodied Icon*, 8–9, 13, 19.

79. BAV Archivio S. Pietro F 11, fol. 91v; BV cod. F 4, fol. 2v; also the Minden ordo: Pierce, *Sacerdotal Spirituality*, 150–53. BAV Chigi D V 77, fol. 70v instructs that psalms be sung "cum circumastantibus clericis," as do the pontifical given by Humbert bishop of Paris to Halinard abbot of Sainte-Benigne in

that a deacon and subdeacon assist the bishop in putting on his vestments.[80] A priest by himself could certainly do the simpler versions of these preparatory rites, but the manuscript evidence suggests that they were quite often performed with other clerics.

Historians of the liturgy have rightly emphasized the penitential and purificatory aspects of these rituals of preparation for the Mass. Commenting on the prayer "Largire sensibus nostris," often included with "Lavabo inter innocentes" at the washing of hands, Joanne Pierce pointed out the explicit connection made "between exterior washing of the body (hands) and both interior purification of the mind as well as growth in holiness" that "sets the tone for the rest of the vesting actions and prayers to follow."[81] The concern with cleansing the celebrant of sin is evident in the psalm "Benedixisti," but even more so in the prayers included in a complex version such as the ordo of Minden: most were drawn from penitential rites.[82] The vesting prayers continue purificatory themes but also construct the virtuous celebrant.

This is well illustrated in the prayers for putting on the amice (*amictus*, *ephod*, *superhumerale* or *humerale*), a linen rectangle with slender ties attached to either end (at the top). It was wrapped around the neck and shoulders, the ends crossing over the chest, and then affixed by passing the ties around the back and securing them in front. The more easily washable amice protected the rest of the vestments from direct contact with the skin.[83] In Ottoboniensis Latinus 6, as in many other versions, more than one prayer is given, presumably to give the priest options in performing the rite. Two are given here. The first, shorter version implores, "Rend, O Lord, my garment and wrap me in joy," while the longer asks, "Protect my shoulders, O Lord, with the grace of the Holy

1036, the Minden ordo, and the ordo of Bishop Warmond of Ivrea. Mariano Dell'Omo, "*Litaniae sanctorum, Libellus precum, Ordo Missae* di S. Vincenzo al Volturno (Biblioteca Apostolica Vaticana Chig. D V 77," *Mediaeval Studies* 70 (2008): 248; Martène, *De Antiquis Ecclesiae Ritibus*, 1:204 (ordo 12), 209 (ordo 14); Martimort, *La documentation* 313 (no. 556) and 138–39, 314 (nos. 170, 558); Pierce, "Sacerdotal Spirituality," 157; Bonifacio Baroffio and Ferdinando Dell'Oro, "L''Ordo Missae' del vescovo Warmondo d'Ivrea," *Studi Medievali*, ser. 3, 16 (1975): 809.

80. Andrieu, *Le Pontifical romain*, 3:633–34.

81. Pierce, "Early Medieval Vesting Prayers," 85–86. The prayer in full is "Largire sensibus nostris omnipotens Deus, ut sicut hic exterius abluuntur inquinamenta manuum, sic a te mundentur interius pollutiones mentium et crescat in nobis augmentum sanctarum virtutum." See also Jungmann, *Missarum Sollemnia* 1:354–59; *Mass*, 1:271–76.

82. Pierce sets this out particularly well in her commentary on the Minden ordo: see "Sacerdotal Spirituality," 284–89. "Apologiae," prayers expressing a sense of unworthiness and sometimes including an actual confession of sins, have figured prominently in the reigning hypothesis on the evolution of the *ordo missae*. The key work is Boniface Luykx, *De oorsprong van het gewone der Mis* (Utrecht, 1954), translated into German by Johannes Madey and published as "Der Ursprung der gleichbleibenden Teile der heiligen Mess (*Ordinarium Missae*)," in *Priestertum und Mönchtum*, ed. Theodor Bogler (Maria Laach, 1961), a special issue of *Liturgie und Mönchtum* 29 (1961): 72–119. His work and its influence are ably summarized by Pierce in her article "The Evolution of the *Ordo Missae* in the Early Middle Ages," in *Medieval Liturgy: A Book of Essays*, ed. Lizette Larson-Miller (New York, 1997), 10–13. Orthodox vesting prayers, in contrast, consist in scriptural quotations: Woodfin, *Embodied Icon*, 287–89.

83. Braun, *DLG*, 21–52; Roger E. Reynolds, "Clerical Liturgical Vestments and Liturgical Colors in the Middle Ages," in *Clerics in the Early Middle Ages*, 6:1–2.

Spirit and gird my spirit, all sins having been removed, [so that I might] sacrifice to you, God, [who] lives and reigns forever."[84] Another prayer that appears in several eleventh-century manuscripts reveals a new mode of donning the amice: "Place upon my head, O Lord, the helmet of salvation to conquer and overcome diabolical errors and the fury of my persecuting enemies."[85] The amice in this fashion is first draped over the head, secured, and then pushed back off the head to create a collar visible above the other vestments. A version found in manuscripts from the Basilica of Santa Maria in Trastevere in Rome and from the monasteries of Montecassino and San Vincenzo a Volturno also alludes to this way of wearing the amice: "Cover my head, O Lord, with the shade of holy faith and drive away from me the clouds of ignorance."[86] As in this version found around Rome, most of these prayers pair positive conditions the priest summons (holy faith, salvation, grace, joy) with negative attributes he seeks to expiate (ignorance, sin, error). The prayers also relate closely to ritual acts: they name the parts of the body touched by the vestment (shoulders, head) and use verbs evoking the actions of donning the garment (*circumdare*, *praecingere*, *obumbrare*).

For the next vestment to be put on, the long white linen tunic known as the alb (*alba*, *camisia*, *camisus*),[87] Ottoboniensis Latinus 6 gives the most commonly found vesting prayer: "Clothe me, O Lord, in the vestment of salvation and gird me with the breastplate

84. "Ad humerale oratio / Conscinde domine saccum meum et circumdame laeititia. Item. Humeros meos / sci spiritus gratia protege domine renesque meos uitiis omnibus expulsis precinge tibi ad sa/crificandum deo iuuenti et regnanti in secula seculorum." BAV Ottobon. Lat. 6, 9v. These prayers are also found in the Reichenau, Minden, and Stavelot ordines: Bragança, "O 'Ordo Missae' de Reichenau," 139; Pierce, "Sacerdotal Spirituality," 157; Martène, *De Antiquis Ecclesiae Ritibus*, 1:210 (ordo 15); Martimort, *La documentation*, 303, 314–15 (nos. 207, 559) and "Additions," 88.

85. "Oratio ad amictum / Pone domine galeam salutis in capite meo . ad ex/pugnandas et superandas cunc/tas diabolicas fraudes . omnium/que inimicorum meorum seuitiam su/perandas. Amen." BAV Arch. S. Pietro F 11 A, 93v; Salmon, *Les manuscrits*, 2:4 (no. 3); Armando Petrucci, "Censimento dei codici dei secoli X–XII," *Studi Medievali*, ser. 3, 11 (1970): 1125. Also with slight variations in another sacramentary from Saint Peter's, and in the Besançon, Troyes, Tours, Figeac-Moissac, Hamburg, and Modena ordines: BAV Arch. S. Pietro F 15, 103r; J. Lemarié, "Le Pontifical d'Hugues de Salines, son 'Ordo Missae' et son 'Libellus precum,'" *Studi Medievali* ser. 3, 19 (1978): 374; Martène, *De Antiquis Ecclesiae Ritibus*, 1:190 (ordo 6), 192 (ordo 7), 193 (ordo 8); Martimort, *La documentation*, 151, 214–15, 218, 311–12 (nos. 316, 323, 549, 551); BMT Diocèse 1, 7v; BV cod. B 141, 31r–v; Rasmussen, "Early 'ordo missae,'" 202; Ludovico Muratori, *La Liturgia Romana Vetus*, 2 vols. (Venice, 1748), 1:87; BnF MS lat. 2293, 12v.

86. "Ad ammictum / Obumbra domine caput meum obumbraculo sancte fidei . et ex/pelle a me nubila ignorantie": BV cod. F 4, 2v–3r; Petrucci, "Censimento," 1067; BAV Ottobon. Lat. 576, 218r; Salmon, *Les manuscrits*, 2:126 (no. 305); BAV Chigi D V 77, 69v; Dell'Omo, "*Litaniae*," 246; Salmon, *Les manuscrits*, 1:131 (no. 261); Martène, *De Antiquis Ecclesiae Ritibus*, 1:204 (ordo 12); Montecassino, Archivio della Badia 127, p. 313. Still other versions may be found in BAV Vat. Lat. 4775, 58r–v (an eleventh-century sacramentary from Arezzo: Salmon, *Les manuscrits*, 2:28 [no. 44]); BAV Vat. Lat. 4770, 114r (an eleventh-century missal from the monastery of San Bartolomeo di Musiano in Bologna: Salmon, *Les manuscrits*, 2:156 [no. 401]); BnF MS lat 9436 (Réserve), 5r; and Martène, *De Antiquis Ecclesiae Ritibus*, 1:186 (ordo 5) (a mid-eleventh-century sacramentary from St. Denis); Martimort, *La documentation*, 99, 311 (nos. 109, 548), and "Additions," 85 and 1:203 (ordo 11) (a Corbie *sacramentary* from the second half of the tenth century, once attributed to Abbot Ratoldus, now in BnF MS lat. 12052); Martimort, *La documentation*, 97, 313 (nos. 106, 555); Orchard, *Sacramentary of Ratoldus*, 236 (1075), also published in *PL*, 78:240.

87. Braun, *DLG*, 57–92; Reynolds, "Clerical Liturgical Vestments," 2.

of fortitude." Variants substitute "the robe of justice" or "garment of joy" for the *lorica fortitudinis*.[88] Two other versions are given in Ottoboniensis Latinus 6 that also appear in the ordines of Stavelot and Minden. "Gird me, O Lord, with the armor of faith," reads one, "so that having been shielded from the arrows of iniquity, I might have the strength to preserve righteousness and justice." The other more directly associates a purified state with the alb: "Omnipresent and eternal God, I humbly beseech you in order that having cast off the deception of all evasions and put on this white garment, I might be worthy to follow you into the realm of true joy."[89] This long white tunic was secured with a sash-like belt called a cincture (*cingulum, zona, baltheus*),[90] and, not surprisingly, most of the prayers for this accessory stressed chastity: "With the cincture of faith and the virtue of chastity, O Lord, gird the loins of my heart and body, extinguishing in them, drying out, the humor of lust so that the honor of complete chastity may continually abide in them."[91] Other versions associate the cincture with justice and liken the action of securing it to arming for battle: "Fasten most powerfully upon my thigh, O Lord, your sword, so that I may be able manfully to vanquish your enemies with the steadfast hope of eternal truth."[92]

88. "Ad albam. Indueme domine / vestimento salutis et circumdame lorica fortitudinis," BAV Ottobon. Lat. 6, 9v. The same prayer is given in the ordines of Reichenau, Stavelot, Salzburg, Rome-San Pietro, San Vincenzo al Volturno, and Montecassino. Amiens, Troyes, and Figeac-Moissac substitute "indumento iusticiae"; Bologna substitutes "indumentum laetitiae," while Tours, Rome-S. Pietro, and Rome-Santa Maria in Trastevere add both "tunica justiciae" and "indumento laetitiae"; another eleventh-century Tours missal from Saint-Gatien has "vestimento justitiae et spiritali intellectu." Bragança, "O 'Ordo Missae' de Reichenau," 139; Martène, *De Antiquis Ecclesiae Ritibus* 1:210, 207, 204; BAV Arch. S. Pietro F 11 A, 93v, Arch. S. Pietro F 15, 103r; Chigi D V 77, 70r, and Ottobon. Lat. 576, 218r; Dell'Omo, "*Litaniae*," 246; Montecassino, Archivio della Badia, 127, p. 313; Leroquais, "L'Ordo Missae," 439; Martène, *De Antiquis Ecclesiae Ritibus*, 1:190, 192, 194; BAV Vat. Lat. 4770, 114r; BMT Diocèse 1, 7v; BAV Arch. S. Pietro F 15, 103r; BV cod. F 4, 3r; BnF MS lat. 9434, 18r; BnF MS lat. 2293, 12v.

89. "Circumdame domine / fidei armis ut ab iniquitatum sagittis erutus, valeam aequitatem et iustitiam custodire": BAV Ottobon. Lat. 6, 9v; Martène, *De Antiquis Ecclesiae Ritibus*, 1:210; Pierce, "Sacerdotal Spirituality," 158. Minden also includes "Omnipotens sempiterne Deus te suppliciter exoro ut fraude omnium obfusca / torum exutus alba veste indutus te sequi merear ad regna ubi vera sunt gaudia."

90. Braun, *DLG*, 101–17; Reynolds, "Clerical Liturgical Vestments," 2–3.

91. "Ad zonam. Praecinge, Domine, cingulo fidei et virtute castitatis lumbos mei cordis et corporis, et exsiccando extingue in eis humorem libidinis, ut jugiter in eis sit honor totius castitatis": Martène, *De Antiquis Ecclesiae Ritibus*, 1:190 (Troyes), 192 (Tours), 194 (Figeac-Moissac); BnF MS lat. 2293, 12v; BMT Diocèse 1, 7v; Leroquais, "L'Ordo Missae," 439; Lemarié, "Le Pontifical d'Hugues de Salines," 374; BV cod. F4, 3r (Santa Maria in Trastevere).

92. The formula "Circumcinge lumbos meos, Domine, zona iusticiae, et circumcide uitia cordis et corporis mei," is found in BAV Ottobon. Lat. 6, 9v; Bragança, "O 'Ordo Missae' de Reichenau," 184; Pierce, "Sacerdotal Spirituality," 158; Martène, *De Antiquis Ecclesiae Ritibus*, 1:210 (Stavelot). The martial version—"Accinge Domine gladium tuum super femur meum potentissime, ut viriliter posim contra inimicos duos dimicare spe firma veritatis aeterne"—is found in Ottobon. Lat. 6, 9v; BAV Vat. Lat. 4775, 58v (Arezzo); and Martène, *De Antiquis Ecclesiae Ritibus*, 1:210 (Stavelot). Mindfulness and purity are themes of another version: "Domine accinge in me custodiam mentis mee . ne ipsa mens infletur spiritu elationis" (Equip me, O Lord, with a watchfulness for my soul, lest my mind be warped by a prideful spirit): BAV Chigi D V 77, 70r; Dell'Omo, "*Litaniae*," 246; Martène, *De Antiquis Ecclesiae Ritibus*, 1:204 (San Vincenzo al Volturno), 207 (Salzburg); BnF MS Latin 820, 5v; BAV Arch. S. Pietro F 11 A, 93v, and Ottobon. Lat. 576, 218r (Montecassino).

Some collections composed for bishops insert here prayers for the tunicle and the dalmatic, vestments associated with subdeacons and deacons but also worn by prelates as a sign of their place at the summit of the orders with authority over them. Prayers used for the alb, chasuble, and even cincture in other series tend to be applied to the tunicle as well.[93] The prayers for the donning of the dalmatic are more unique. The Minden prayer book offers, "Having been clothed in this vestment, the emblematic rite of the venerable fathers, woven in the shape of the cross with purple stripes, I humbly beg that I might, through the commemoration of your passion, be made perpetually pleasing to you, Lord Jesus Christ, who lives and reigns forever."[94] The Pontifical of Hugh of Salins gives a version that makes no explicit reference to the distinctive appearance of the dalmatic, but instead invokes the words of Paul in his letter to the Ephesians (4:24): "Put on me O Lord the new man, who according to God is created in the justice and holiness of truth."[95]

Justice was the most frequently invoked virtue in prayers for donning the stole (*orarium, stola*). This long (around eight feet), thin band of linen or wool was worn by priests around the neck, with both ends falling down the front of the body and usually secured by the ties of the cincture.[96] It was associated generally with priestly status, but especially with the administration of the sacraments. "Place the stole of justice around my neck, O Lord, and purify my soul of all sinful corruption," implores the most common prayer, continuing in some versions to ask God to "break the chain of my sins, so that having taken up the yoke of your service, I might be worthy to attend you with fear and reverence."[97] Another resounds, "Restore to me, I beseech you O Lord, the stole of

93. The Minden prayer book refers to the tunicle as the *subtilis* and gives the "Indue me Domine uestimento salutis et circumda me lorica fortitudinis" prayer, as does the Besançon pontifical (adding "indumento laetitiae" too); the Troyes ordo gives the "Rogo altissime Deus" prayer more commonly used for the chasuble and the Hamburg ordo offers the "Praecinge Domine" prayer most often said for the cincture. Pierce, "Sacerdotal Spirituality," 159; Besancon: Lemarié, "Le Pontifical d'Hugues de Salines," 375; Troyes: Martène, *De Antiquis Ecclesiae Ritibus*, 1:190; BV cod. B 141, 31v; Rasmussen, "An Early 'Ordo Missae,'" 202.

94. "AD DALMATICAM. Indumento hoc typico priscorum patrum ritu in modum crucis tramitibus purpureis contexto uestitus humiliter postulo. ut ex commemoratione passionis tuae fiam tibi domine Jesu Christe iugiter gratiosus. QUI VIVIS." Pierce, "Sacerdotal Spirituality," 159.

95. "AD DALMATICAM. Indue me domine nouum hominem qui secundum deum creatus est in iustitia et sanctitate ueritatis." Besancon: Lemarié, "Le Pontifical d'Hugues de Salines," 375.

96. Braun, *DLG*, 562–620; Reynolds, "Clerical Liturgical Vestments," 6–7. Deacons wore it too, but in a different fashion: the stole rested on the left shoulder, crossing the body diagonally with the ends joined at the right hip.

97. "Ad Stolam. Stola iustitiae circumda domine ceruicem meam / et ab omni corruptione peccati purifica mentem meam et disrumpe uincula / peccatorum meorum. ut iugo tuae seruitutis innexus [sic: innixus] valeam cum timore et / reverentia tibi famulari": BAV Ottobon. Lat. 6, 9v. This formula is also found in the ordines of Reichenau, Minden, St. Denis, Tours, Salzburg, Stavelot, Arezzo, San Vincenzo al Volturno, St. Peter's Basilica in Rome, Montecassino, Santa Maria in Trastevere in Rome, Modena, and Tours-St. Gratien: Bragança, "O 'Ordo Missae' de Reichenau," 139; Pierce, "Sacerdotal Spirituality," 159; Martène, *De Antiquis Ecclesiae Ritibus*, 1:187, 192, 207, 210; BnF MS lat. 820, 5v; BnF MS lat. 9436 (Réserve), 5r; BMT Diocèse 1, 7v; BAV Vat. Lat., 4775, 58v; BAV Chigi D V 77, 70r; Dell'Omo, "*Litaniae*," 247; BAV Arch. S. Pietro F 11 A, 93v; Montecassino, Archivio della Badia, 127 p. 313; BAV Ottobon. Lat. 576, 218r; BV cod. F 4, 3r; Muratori, *La liturgia romana*, 1:87; BnF MS Latin 9434, 18r.

immortality that I lost through the transgression of the first parents, and because with this ornament I entered, however unworthy, your holy ministry, grant that with it I may deserve to rejoice forever."[98] The reference here to the laying on of the stole during the ordination rite underscores the role of this vestment in constructing and symbolizing priestly status.

The chasuble (*planeta*, *casula*) also came to be bestowed during priestly ordination, although throughout the Middle Ages it could be worn by other clerics for particular liturgies.[99] The stole, by contrast, was always a marker of priestly status and would be worn without the chasuble for administering sacraments such as baptism, penance, and last rites. Still, in another manual—Vatican manuscript Archivio San Pietro H 58—only one vesting prayer is given, on the volume's very first folio, and it is for the chasuble. A form of the prayer appears in one of the earliest, and most eccentric, versions of vesting prayers in a sacramentary copied in the second half of the tenth century at the monastery of Corbie. In this exemplar and in an eleventh-century pontifical from Besançon and a missal from Bologna, the prayer is designated for recitation when putting on the cincture.[100] In Archivio San Pietro H 58, however, the wording is slightly different and the rubric clearly indicates that the prayer is to be said "when the chasuble is put on":

> I entreat you, God most high, holy father, to grant me the tunic of chastity, gird and encircle my loins with the cincture of your love, and enflame the innermost recesses of my heart with the fire of your affection so that I may be able to intercede for my sins and merit forgiveness of sins for those of your people gathered here, and offer peaceful offerings for each. [I ask you] also gently to sustain me rashly approaching [your altar]. Through Jesus Christ our Lord your only-begotten son who lives with you.[101]

98. "Ad stolam. Redde mihi, Domine, obsecro, stolam immortalitatis quam perdidi in praevaricatione primi parentis, et quia cum hoc ornamento accessi, quamvis indignus, ad tuum sanctum ministerium, presta ut cum eo letari merear in perpetuum." This version is found in the Amiens, Besançon, Troyes, Figeac-Moissac, Rome-S. Pietro, and Hamburg ordines: Leroquais, "L'Ordo Missae," 440; Lemarié, "Le Pontifical d'Hugues de Salines," 375; Martène, *De Antiquis Ecclesiae Ritibus*, 1:190, 194; BnF MS lat. 2293, 12v; BAV Arch. S. Pietro F 15, 103v; BV cod. B 141, 31v; Rasmussen, "An Early 'Ordo Missae,'" 202. Still another version is "Stola iucunditatis circumda, Domine, cervicem meam, et ab omni corruptione cordis et corporis purifica Deus mentem meam": Leroquais, "L'Ordo Missae," 440; Martène, *De Antiquis Ecclesiae Ritibus*, 1:194 (Troyes).

99. Braun, *DLG*, 149–247; Reynolds, "Clerical Liturgical Vestments," 5.

100. Orchard, *Sacramentary of Ratoldus*, 237 (1078), also in Martène, *De Antiquis Ecclesiae Ritibus* 1:203, and in *PL*, 78:240; Lemarié, "Le Pontifical d'Hugues de Salines," 374–75; BAV Vat. Lat. 4770, 114r.

101. "Oratio quando vestitur pla/netam. Rogo te altissime deus /pater sanctae . ut me toni/cam castitatis dig/neris ac cingere . et meos lum/bos balteo tui amoris am/bire . et renes cordis mei /tue caritatis igne urere . / ut pro peccatis meis possim /intercedere . et astantis/populi peccatorum ueniam/ promereri. ac pacificas sin/gulorum hostias immola/re . me quo que audacter / acedentem . leniter susci/pere per Iesum Christum dominum nostrum /tuum unigenitum filium/qui te cum uiuit." BAV Arch. S. Pietro H 58, 1r. Neil Roy is preparing an edition and study of this interesting manuscript, and I thank him for sharing some of his observations on it. Salmon in his catalog of Vatican liturgical manuscripts—*Les manuscrits*, 3:60 (no. 149)—assigned it to "s. XI–XII," but in a subsequent study argued that it was composed in the

The prayer more commonly found entreats, "Robe me, O Lord, with the ornament of humility, love, and peace so that having been completely fortified with virtues I might be able to withstand sins and enemies of mind and body."[102]

In most sets of vesting prayers, the final vestment to be put on was the maniple (*mappula, manipulum, fano, sudarium*). Some early ordines (Amiens, Ottoboniensis Latinus 6, Bologna) lack a prayer for the maniple, and in others (Troyes, Figeac-Moissac) it comes earlier in the series, before the chasuble and just after the donning of the stole.[103] The maniple was, in form, a smaller version of the stole: it was a band of cloth about a yard long that was draped over the left arm. Into the Carolingian era it served as a functional handkerchief: Amalarius recommends it for removing eye and nose mucus as well as excess saliva.[104] But it became ornamental, and highly ornamented, from the tenth century.[105] Its original use to capture phlegm may be evoked in the most common prayer for it: "Give me, O Lord, right understanding and a pure voice so that I might be able to accomplish your praise."[106] Another suggests its use as a towel: "Give me, O Lord, virtue

first half of the eleventh century, "en 1026 ou peu après," and was used in the Basilica of the Holy Apostles in Rome: Pierre Salmon, "Un 'Libellus Officialis' du XIe siècle," *Revue Bénédictine* 87 (1977): 257–88; idem, "Un témoin de la vie chrétienne dans une église de Rome au XIe siècle: Le *Liber Officialis* de la basilique des Saints-Apôtres," *Rivista di Storia della Chiesa in Italia* 33 (1979): 65–73. Petrucci in his "Censimento," 1132–33, assigns it to the tenth century; Roy, Bernhard Bischoff, and Roger Reynolds concur: see Reynolds, "Excerpta," 4–9, and Roger E. Reynolds, "Penitentials in South and Central Italian Canon Law Manuscripts of the Tenth and Eleventh Centuries," *Early Medieval Europe* 14 (2006): 66–67. A paleographical analysis, however, dates one part of the manuscript to the late tenth or early eleventh century and the rest to the beginning of the second half of the eleventh century: Paola Supino Martini, *Roma e l'area grafica romanesca (secoli X–XII)* (Alessandria, 1987) 73–75. Several scholars have studied the penitential materials in the manuscript: Ludger Körntgen, "Ein italienisches Bußbuch und seine fränkischen Quellen: Das anonyme Paenitentiale der Handschrift Vatikan, Arch. S. Pietro H 58," in *Aus Archiven und Bibliotheken: Festschrift für Raymund Kottje zum 65. Geburtstag*, ed. Hubert Mordek (Frankfurt, 1992), 189–205; Hamilton, "*Rituale*"; and Adriaan Gaastra, "Between Liturgy and Canon Law: A Study of Books of Confession and Penance in Eleventh- and Twelfth-Century Italy," (Ph.D. diss., Utrecht University, 2007).

102. "Ad casulam. Indue me domine ornamento hu/militatis. caritatis. et pacis. ut undique munitus uirtutibus possim resistere / uitiis et hostibus mentis et corporis per te Iesu Christe": BAV Ottobon. Lat. 6, 9v. The same form appears in the ordines of Reichenau, San Vincenzo al Volturno, Salzburg, Rome-S. Pietro, Montecassino, Hamburg, and Rome-S. Maria in Trastevere: Bragança, "O 'Ordo Missae' de Reichenau," 184; BAV Chigi D V 77, 70r–v; Dell'Omo, "*Litaniae*," 248; Martène, *De Antiquis Ecclesiae Ritibus*, 1:207; Arch S Pietro F 11 A 93v–94r; Montecassino, Archivio della Badia, 127 pp. 313–14; BAV Ottobon. Lat. 576, 218r; BV cod. B 141, 31v, and also Rasmussen, "An Early 'Ordo Missae,'" 202; BV cod. F 4, 3r. Two other close variants are in the Minden and St. Denis ordines: Pierce, "Sacerdotal Spirituality," 160; BnF MS lat. 9436 (Réserve), 5r; Martène, *De Antiquis Ecclesiae Ritibus*, 1:187. A very different tradition works off Matt. 11:30: "Iugum enim tuum, Domine, suave est et bonus tuum leve; presta ut sic illud deportare valeam qualiter consequi possim tuam gratiam." Leroquais, "L'Ordo Missae," 440 (Amiens); Martène, *De Antiquis Ecclesiae Ritibus*, 1:190 (Troyes), 192 (Tours), 194 (Figeac-Moissac); BnF MS lat. 2293, 12v; BMT Diocèse 1, 7v; BAV Arch. S. Pietro F 15, 103v.

103. Martène, *De Antiquis Ecclesiae Ritibus*, 1:190, 194; BnF MS lat. 2293, 12v.

104. *Liber officialis*, 249 (2.24).

105. Braun, *DLG*, 515–61; Reynolds, "Clerical Liturgical Vestments," 6.

106. "Ad fanonem. Da mihi, Domine, sensum rectum et uocem puram, ut implere possim laudem tuam": Bragança, "O 'Ordo Missae' de Reichenau," 440; Martène, *De Antiquis Ecclesiae Ritibus*, 1:207

to wipe away all impure blemishes from my hands so that I may be worthy of serving you free of mental and bodily defilement."[107]

The constant refrain in these prayers about worthiness, freedom from sin, purity of mind and body goes to the heart of the anxieties driving the eleventh-century reform movements. The reasons for heightened concern about the worthiness of priests and the efficacy of the sacraments they offered were complex. The violence and invasions of the late ninth and tenth centuries certainly wreaked havoc on ecclesiastical institutions as well as on the population more generally, and perhaps made salvation seem a more tenuous proposition. Strong demographic expansion from the late tenth century and across the eleventh led to a rapid multiplication of churches, outpacing the capacity of bishops to train and provide adequate priests. Since they took place in the sacristy, at least not in direct view of the people, these preparatory rites for the Mass and vesting prayers would not likely have calmed lay qualms, but as a frequently repeated ritual they constantly reminded clerics of the values they were supposed to uphold. The connections made between virtues and articles of clothing, however, might as easily raise concerns as quell them. Can unchaste flesh be made chaste by donning an alb and belting it tightly? The contrast between the appearance of holiness and a cleric's local reputation might engender only greater doubt and cynicism. In the second half of the eleventh century the hierarchy adopted a theology of grace that emphasized its origin in Christ and downplayed the condition of its conduit, the priest. Still, as these prayers entreated, the hope was for greater convergence between interior states and exterior appearances.

Another theme in these vesting prayers is justice and peace. Donning a "robe of justice," a chasuble of "humility, love, and peace," or a "stole of justice," the priest asks "strength to preserve righteousness and justice." Three decades ago now, R.I. Moore called attention to the increasing importance of priests in communities as settlements multiplied and social tensions with them. The priest's role as mediator and arbitrator within his parish and on its behalf was ever more needed, and his relationships, therefore, were more carefully scrutinized. "In these conditions," Moore observed, "the priest's concubine represented something more than an affront to public decency," and his ties to local lords, financial or familial, could call into question his ability to bring true peace or anything resembling justice to his community. The role of bishops in orchestrating peace councils and their attempts to enforce a peace or truce "of God" only raised expectations that the local clergy foster these conditions too.[108] Little wonder,

(Salzburg), 210 (Stavelot); BnF MS lat. 820, 5v; BAV Chigi D V 77, 70v (San Vincenzo al Volturno); Dell'Omo, "*Litaniae*," 248; BAV Arch S Pietro F 11 A, 94r (Rome-S. Pietro); BAV Ottobon. Lat. 576, 218v (Montecassino); BV cod. F 4, 3r (Rome-S. Maria in Trastevere).

107. "Da, Domine, virtutem manibus meis ab abstergendam omnem maculam immundam, ut sine polutione mentis et corporis tibi servire valeam": Martène, *De Antiquis Ecclesiae Ritibus*, 1:210 (Stavelot); Pierce, "Sacerdotal Spirituality," 161 (Minden); and with slightly different wording, Rome, BV cod. B 141, 31v. and Rasmussen, "Early 'Ordo Missae,'" 202 (Hamburg).

108. R.I. Moore, "Family, Community and Cult on the Eve of the Gregorian Reform," *Transactions of the Royal Historical Society* 5/30 (1980): 49–69, quote on 61; on the peace movement, see his *First European Revolution, c. 970–1215* (Oxford, 2000), 58–64.

then, that priests prayed for the wisdom and strength to do justice and bring peace. The allegorical references to armaments are also significant in this respect. As conciliar legislation repeatedly insisted, clerics were not to bear arms, putting them in a vulnerable position similar to most members of the communities they served. Vestments, by making visible a priest's consecrated status, did afford him some protection, but it was not for this that he prayed when vesting. His alb and "armor of faith" was put on to "preserve righteousness and justice," while his cincture was fastened as if girding on God's "most powerful sword" so that he was able "manfully to vanquish your enemies." Was the church an independent authority that could stand up against unjust worldly rulers? Gregory VII thought so, and the allegorization of vestments as new kinds of armaments constructed the priest as a new sort of elite standing in sharp contrast to the nobility, whose violence and arbitrary exercise of power were so often lamented.

Liturgical Effects: Ordination Rites

The clerical spirituality of sacred vestments that developed out of liturgical commentaries in turn came to influence liturgical practice.[109] As elucidated in chapter 1, Frankish interest in liturgical dress yielded changes in ordination rites. Ordo 35 (Frankish, before 925) gave many more specific directions for removing and donning vestments, particularly in the rite of priestly ordination: having taken off his diaconal dalmatic, the ordinand was vested in the chasuble by the archdeacon and in the stole by the bishop. Such uses of clothing as constitutive acts in the ordination rites for the major orders continued to expand. In the Romano-Germanic Pontifical (RGP), deacons received stoles, priests received both stoles and chasubles, and bishops received the *campagi*, sandals, the dalmatic, chasuble, and gloves.[110]

The importance of these acts in the creation of sacred orders is visually evident in the late tenth-century Beneventan scroll (*rotulus*) known as the Pontifical of Landulf (Biblioteca Casanatense 724 [B I 13]).[111] Written and illustrated for Archbishop Landulf (957–984), the *rotulus* contains a dozen images of the actions accompanying the rites of ordination to the various clerical grades. Careful study of these images in relation to the text of the Beneventan scroll and other ordination texts by Myrtilla Avery, Roger

109. A connection made by Andrieu, *Ordines*, 1:476–85, and Roger E. Reynolds, "The *De Officiis VII Graduum*: Its Origins and Early Medieval Development," in *Clerical Orders in the Early Middle Ages: Duties and Ordination* (Aldershot, 1999), 2:135.

110. See above, chapter 1, 29, 32–33, and accompanying annotation. Bestowal of the habit was long part of monastic rituals of profession, but when and how it happened varied a good deal. This variation continued well after clerical usages became more consistent, although the strong constituative meaning of putting a garment on is evident earlier in monasticism. See Constable, "Ceremonies and Symbolism," 791–808.

111. On the exultet rolls generally, see Thomas Forrest Kelly, *The Exultet in Southern Italy* (New York, 1996); on the Landulf roll in particular, Guglielmo Cavallo, *Exultet: Rotoli liturgici del medioevo meridionale* (Rome, 1994), 75–84.

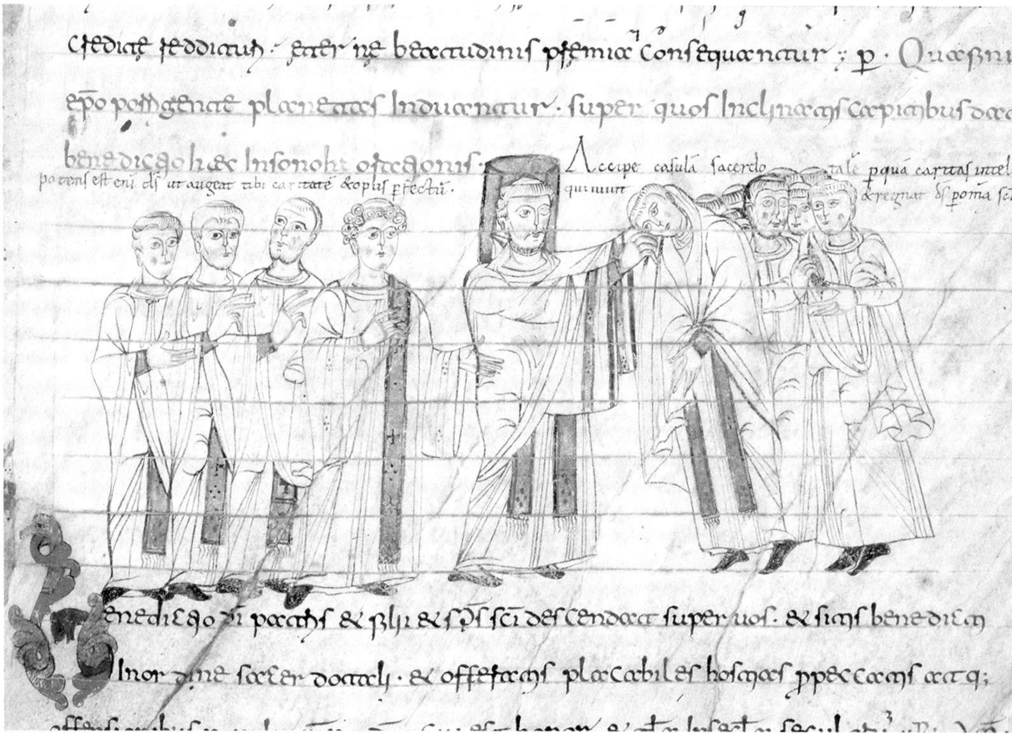

FIGURE 8. Landulf Pontifical, detail, bestowal of chasubles, Biblioteca Casanatense 724, 957–984, Rome. Biblioteca Casanatense.

Reynolds and others, has established them as a unique source for actual liturgical practice: the rubrics above each of the illustrations were not formulaic, "suggesting that they follow the ceremony actually used by Landulf."[112] Two of the four images of the ordination rite for priests depict the bestowal of vestments: after an image of the ordinands prostrating themselves as the ordination prayer is said over them, there are depictions of Landulf putting the chasuble over the head of a candidate while others line up behind him holding their chasubles (figure 8), and of the bishop placing the stole on the neck of another, again, with others in line proffering their stoles (figure 9). The final scene illustrates the anointing of the hands with holy oil. The illustration of the rite for deacons combines two scenes in one panel: the giving of the stole and the recitation of the ordination prayer.

These prayers in the Pontifical of Landulf invoke the virtues of the order conferred without explicitly linking them to the vestment bestowed.[113] The RGP, however, takes

112. Roger E. Reynolds, "Image and Text: The Liturgy of Clerical Ordination in Early Medieval Art," in *Clerics in the Early Middle Ages*, 8:34.

113. For the text of the Landulf Pontifical ordination rites, see Roger E. Reynolds, "The Ritual of Clerical Ordination of the *Sacramentarium Gelasianum Saec. VIII:* Early Evidence from Southern Italy," in *Clerical Orders in the Early Middle Ages*, 12, addenda, 19–24.

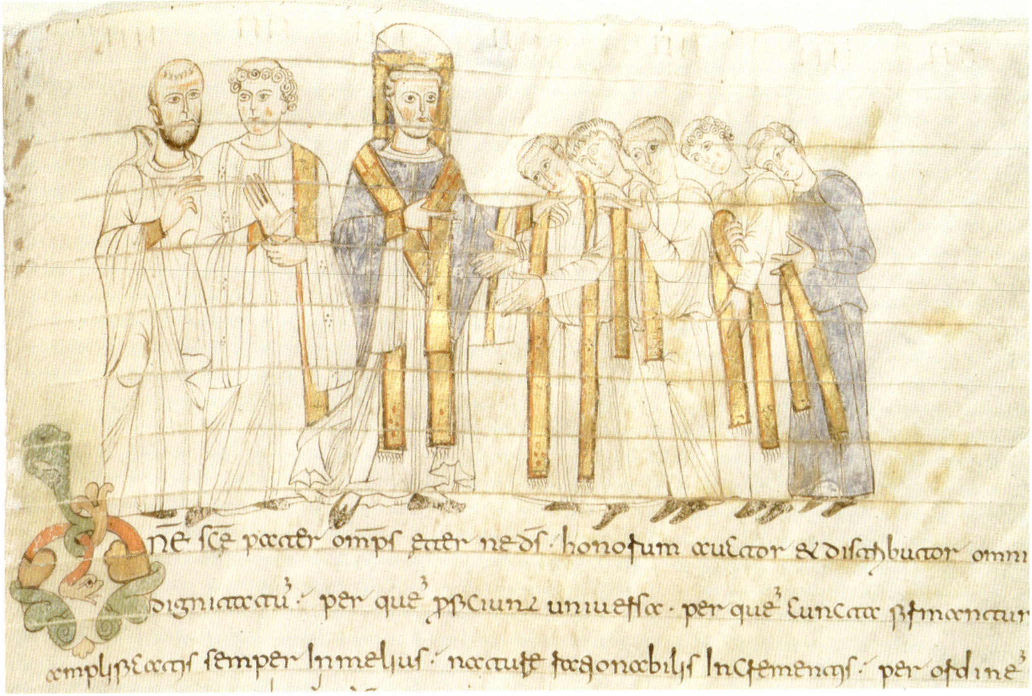

FIGURE 9. Landulf Pontifical, detail, bestowal of stoles, Biblioteca Casanatense 724, 957–984, Rome. Biblioteca Casanatense.

this further step. As priests receive the stole, for example, the bishop prays, "Accept the yoke of the Lord, for his yoke is sweet and his burden light [Matt. 11:30]," and as the chasuble is put on, "Accept the priestly robe through which charity is learned."[114] Placed in the context of the liturgical commentary tradition and its effects, these words surely seem familiar. Amalarius of Metz, in his commentary on the stole in the *Liber officialis*, invoked the same passage from Matthew and defined the stole as a symbol for the "light burden" of proclaiming the Gospel. The most common vesting prayer said as priests donned the stole referred not only to this symbolism, but to the rite of ordination: "Place the stole of justice around my neck, O Lord, and purify my soul of all sinful corruption; break the chain of my sins, so that having taken up the yoke of your service, I might be worthy to attend you with fear and reverence."[115] The association of the chasuble with *charitas* (charity or love) also came out of the commentary tradition: "we understand this garment," wrote Hrabanus Maurus, "to be love [*charitatem*], which surpasses all the virtues."[116] The vesting prayers, too, refer to this virtue.

114. Vogel and Elze, *Pontifical romano-germanique*, 1:34 (1630–31): "Hic reflectat orarium super humerum eorum dextrum, dicens ad eos per singulos: Accipe iugum domimi, iugum enim eius suave est et onus eius leve. Hic vestiat eos casula, dicens ad unumquemque: Stola innocentiae induat te dominus. Accipe vestem sacerdotalem per quam caritas intelligitur."

115. See above, 56–57, 83.

116. *De institutione*, 313 (1.21).

Later pontificals continued these customs and added to them. The evidence of the Roman pontifical of the twelfth century is particularly important. Pope Gregory VII was well aware of the impact on the Roman liturgy of the Frankish influences codified in the Romano-Germanic Pontifical. Commenting on the correct number of psalms and readings to be performed during the office, he observed that "the Romans began to do it a different way, especially from that time in which the governance of this church was given over to Germans." "We, however," Gregory continued, "investigating the Roman *ordo* and the ancient custom of our church, ordered that it [the office] be done just as we have set out above, imitating the ancient fathers."[117] Gregory's "correction" of the office was part of a broader movement for liturgical reform among his Roman supporters. Both Cardinal Deusdedit and Anselm of Lucca included much-pruned versions of the ordination rites from the RGP in their canon law collections.[118] Significantly, however, they did not remove the usages regarding vestments.

These were incorporated into the Roman pontifical of the twelfth century, and thereafter into the thirteenth-century pontifical of the papal curia and William Durand's, the latter of which became the basis for the first printed edition.[119] In the twelfth-century Roman pontifical, for example, the stole is bestowed on the new deacon with the prayer,

> Accept the shining white stole from the hand of the lord, having been purified of all the filth of sin in the sight of the divine majesty, so that the example of your manners in [this] life may be offered to all and the community dedicated in the name of Christ may, by imitating you, acquire an upright exemplar.[120]

Several manuscripts also include an interlude in which the new deacon is given and puts on the dalmatic, and this addition was carried forward in a majority of the manuscripts of the pontifical of the thirteenth-century Roman Curia and in Durand's pontifical.[121] The priestly ordination rite retains the bestowal of the stole with the prayer based on Matthew 11:30 and the vesting in chasuble with a prayer invoking the ordinand's new

117. "Romani autem diuerso modo agere ceperunt, maxime ab eo tempore, quo Teutonicis concessum est regimen huius ecclesie [uidelicet Lateranensis] statuimus fieri sicut superius prenotauimus antiquos patres imitantes." The paragraph containing this passage was copied into the mid-twelfth-century ordo of the Lateran basilica: *Bernhardi Cardinalis et Lateranensis Ecclesiae Prioris Ordo Officiorum Ecclesiae Lateranensis*, ed. Ludwig Fischer, Historische Forschungen und Quellen 2–3 (Munich, 1916), 77. It comes from the *Regula canonicorum Gregorii VII papae*, dating probably from 1074, and surviving in a manuscript (Vat. Lat. 629) copied between 1095 and 1099: Germain Morin, *Études, textes, découvertes: Contributions a la littérature et a l'histoire des douze premiers siècles* (Maredsous Abbey [Belgium], 1913), 457–65. On the Gregorian reform of the liturgy, see also Andrieu, *Ordines*, 1:519–25; Vogel, *Introduction*, 204–14 and *Medieval Liturgy*, 249–51; H.E.J. Cowdrey, *Pope Gregory VII, 1073–1085* (Oxford, 1998), 319–20.

118. Andrieu, *Ordines*, 1:519–22, 4:117–19; Victor Wolf von Glanvell, ed., *Die Kanonessammlung des Kardinals Deusdedit* (Paderborn, 1905; repr., 1967), 231–33.

119. Vogel, *Introduction*, 204–14, and *Medieval Liturgy*, 252–56.

120. "Accipe stolam candidam de manu domini, ab omnibus vitiorum sordibus purificatus in conspectu divinae maiestatis, ut omnibus vita conversationis tuae prebeatur exemplum, plebsque dicata Christi nomine possit imitando te imitationem acquirere iustam." Andrieu, *Le Pontifical romain*, 1:133 (9.13).

121. Ibid., 1:134 (916); 2:341 (10.11); 3:362 (12.13).

power of transforming bread and wine into the body and blood of Christ as well as the virtues he should exhibit in fulfilling the duties of his office. Andrieu notes that in the Roman manuscript, Vatican Ottoboniensis latinus 270, a thirteenth-century hand added yet another prayer in the margin: "Accept the priestly garment which represents the fruit of good works."[122]

Such marginal additions to manuscripts also reveal the assimilation of the rite for creating subdeacons to its status as a major order akin to the diaconate and priesthood. The reformers had insisted that subdeacons, since they assisted at the altar like deacons and priests, should cultivate celibacy. But some canonists were less convinced that the subdiaconate was a major order, and with good reason, given the conflicting canons from the patristic era. Different opinions persisted into the late twelfth century, but two decrees attributed to Pope Innocent III definitively established that the subdiaconate was a "sacred order."[123] As Roger Reynolds has demonstrated, the confusion over the status of the office was reflected in substantial variation in ordination rites. The pattern from the eleventh century, however, was to make the rite more like those for the other major orders—and this meant conferring a vestment. The so-called Egbert pontifical and the Romano-Hispanic pontifical of Vic (c. 1100) add the maniple to the list of things given to the subdeacon during his ordination, while in the twelfth century several add the tunicle.[124] This sort of evidence proliferates for the thirteenth and fourteenth centuries. To the ample list provided by Reynolds, one could add Rome, Biblioteca Casanatense 614 and British Library Cotton Tiberius C.I. The latter is a composite manuscript containing parts of a twelfth-century Roman pontifical with some prayers in Anglo-Saxon added (158v–159v, 199v–200r). After the list of the usual instruments given to the subdeacon is the marginal addition: "on giving the maniples. With the bestowal, laying on, of these maniples, O Lord, we pray that your servants [names] thus may serve in earthly conduct in such manner that following the example of the early fathers they may merit in the future to rejoice forever."[125] Casanatense 614 is a twelfth-century

122. Ibid., 1:136 (9.21–23): "Accipe vestem sacerdotalem per quam designatur fructus bonorum operum." The pontifical of the Roman Curia (13th century) gives for the chasuble either "Stola innocentie induat te dominus," or "Accipe vestem sacerdotalem, per quam caritas intelligitur. Potens est enim dominus augere tibi caritatem et opus perfectum." Durand's pontifical gives only the second: 2:346 (10.24); 3:368 (13.11).

123. Roger E. Reynolds, "The Subdiaconate as a Sacred and Superior Order," in *Clerics in the Early Middle Ages*, 4:1–39; Charles Hilkin, "Necrological Evidence of the Place and Permanence of the Subdiaconate," in *Ritual, Text and Law: Studies in Medieval Canon Law and Liturgy Presented to Roger E. Reynolds* (Aldershot, 2004), 51–66.

124. Reynolds, "Subdiaconate," 33–39, and the table following these pages. All three forms of the Pontifical of the Roman Curia in the thirteenth century include the giving of the tunicle or the tunicle and maniple, while the pontifical of William Durand prescribes bestowing the amice, the maniple, and the tunicle: Andrieu, *Le Pontifical romain* 2:335–36 (9.6–7); 3:357 (11.16–18).

125. London, British Library, Cotton Tiberius C I, 154v: "[a]d dandas mappulas. /[i]nvestione haru[m] /[m]appularu[m] subnixe /[] d[omi]ne dep[re]cam[ur] ut /[?]i famuli tui . N . sic /[ap]p[er]ent[ur] in te[m]porali /[c]onversatione. Qu[a]tin[us] /[e]xe[m]plo prio[rum] patru[m] /[in] futuro mereantur /[g]audere p[er]hennit[er]. P[er]." Wear along the edge of the page has obliterated the first letter or letters of each line.

pontifical in Beneventan script with many marginal additions in a fourteenth-century hand. On folio 90v a line leads the eye from the end of the subdiaconal consecrating prayer up to the top margin where the addition reads,

> On giving the maniple to him. Accept this maniple, fulfill your ministry; truly, may God who is powerful fill you with grace. On [giving] the alb or tunic. May the Lord clothe you in the tunic of delight, the garment of joy.[126]

The last phrase, *indumetum laetitiae*, echoes the vesting prayers for the alb.

The use of vestments as potent symbols in ordination rites and, in particular, the restriction of this use to the major or "sacred" orders of priest, deacon, and subdeacon suggest a growing sense of the sacredness of the garments themselves. In the rites for the minor orders, the constitutive act was the *traditio instrumentorum*, the giving of the symbols of office. The doorkeeper received a key, the lector a book, the exorcist a scroll, and the acolyte a candlestick, a candle, and an empty vessel. The subdeacon received an empty chalice and paten, in addition to a pitcher, basin, and sometimes a towel.[127] It is not just the number of objects given to the subdeacon that suggests his status is considerably beyond that of the acolyte. Some of his objects—namely, the chalice and paten—were quite specifically blessed. While the earliest Roman church dedication *ordo* (42, c. 700–750) "baptizes" only the altar, the Frankish version (41, c. 750–775) included a generic benediction for everything used on it.[128] Early sacramentaries also included blessings or consecrations for the altar and things used on it: the paten, chalice, and the *linteaminum*. Included in this last category were the linens that covered the altar but also "vestimenta pontificalia sacerdotibus et levitis ornamenta," meaning the vestments by which priests and deacons are distinguished, or with which they are furnished.[129] The Romano-Germanic Pontifical of the mid-tenth century went a step further and added specific blessings for vestments as a class; for albs, chasubles, stoles, and cinctures; and for stoles.[130] These blessings were retained in the Roman pontifical of the twelfth century, several manuscripts specifying that the vestments be sprinkled with holy water and

126. Rome, Biblioteca Casanatense, cod. 614, 9v: "ad dandum manipulum ei . Accipe mani/pulum imple ministerium tuum potens est / enim deus ut/ augeat t[ibi] gra[tiam]/ ad albam seu/ tunicam./ tunicam iocun/ditatis indum[en]/tum letitie in/duat te d[omi]n[u]s." On this manuscript, see Robert Amiet, "Catalogue des livres liturgiques manuscrits conservés dans les archives et les bibliothèques de la ville de Rome" *Studi Medievali*, ser. 3, 27 (1986): 980; Petrucci, "Censimento," 1127–28.

127. See Reynolds, "Subdiaconate," 33–39 on the considerable variation in the objects given.

128. Andrieu, *Ordines*, 4:397–402 (42), 339–47 (41), especially 346 for the "linteamina vel omnia ornamenta ecclesiae, seu vasa sacra quaecumque ad cultum Dei ad ecclesiam pertinere."

129. The eighth-century Gelasian sacramentaries have separate prayers for the chalice, paten, "lentiaminum" and a general benediction "ad omnia in usu basilice": Leo Cunibert Mohlberg, ed., *Liber Sacramentorum Romanae Aeclesiae Ordinis Anni Circulu (Cod. Vat. Reg. lat. 316/ Paris Bibl. Nat. 7193, 41/56) (Sacramentarium Gelasianum)*, Rerum Ecclesiasticarum Documenta, Series maior, Fontes 4 (Rome, 1968), 109–10; Patrick Saint-Roch, ed., *Liber Sacramentorvm Engolismensis: Manuscrit B.N. Lat. 816. Le Sacramentaire Gélasien d'Angoulême*, CC 159C (Turnhout, 1987), 363–65.

130. Vogel and Elze, *Pontifical romano-germanique*, 1:152–54 (40.79–81).

incensed. Twelfth- and thirteenth-century missals and pontificals include even more special variants for individual vestments.[131]

That the stole was singled out early on for special benediction should not surprise us given its association with the two orders—diaconate and priesthood—increasingly thought of as especially sacred. *Ordo* 36 (Rome, 880–900) reveals the custom of incubating the stoles to be bestowed in diaconal and priestly ordinations on the "confession" or tomb of Saint Peter. Just as the pope was placing his hands on the head of the ordinand, the archdeacon is instructed "to remove from the confession the stoles, which had been placed there the day before, and put them on them [the ordinands]."[132] The benediction for stoles common to most manuscripts of the RGP prays,

> O Lord, omnipotent God, who in the beginning created things useful and necessary to men, and who ordered your servant Moses to have linens and other ornaments made for priests and deacons serving the tabernacle of the covenant, and who filled him with the spirit of wisdom for accomplishing this, deign to sanctify, bless, and consecrate this ornament for the use of your minister. Deign also to fill the servants of your altar who wear this worthily with the sevenfold Holy Spirit, and through this blessed stole of chastity and garment of eternal joy adorn them in the fruit of good works appropriate to ministers of immortality.

This particular sacred vestment represented in a special way the distinctive sacramental role of the priesthood.

Which is why Paul of Bernreid, in recounting the kidnapping of Gregory VII, made sure his clerical audience knew that the pope still had on his stole. The outer vestments stripped off the pontiff—his pallium, chasuble, dalmatic, and tunicle—each had special meanings, but collectively would be recognized as the full vestiture of the bishop of Rome for a solemn liturgy. He wore in layers the garments of all the sacred orders: the subdeacon's tunicle, the deacon's dalmatic, the priest's chasuble, plus the pallium. The latter was, from the sixth century, a special marker of papal status that came to be bestowed on other bishops with special authority. Descriptions of papal depositions in the *Liber pontificalis* emphasize the stripping off of the pallium as a key act in unmaking the pope.[133] Paul's

131. Andrieu, *Le Pontifical romain*, 1:201 (20.1–3); 2:451–52 (23.1–2); 3:520–21 (9.1–5); BAV Vat. Lat. 7818, 176r.

132. "Accedens autem archidiaconus tollit orarios de confessione, qui de esterna die repositi sunt ibi, inponet super eos." Andrieu, *Ordines*, 4:198 (36.19). A "confessio" in Roman usage could be any niche, usually below the altar, that allowed contact with the relics or tomb venerated in the church. See Sible de Blaauw, *Cultus et decor: Liturgia e architettura nella Roma tardoantica e medievale*, 2 vols., Studi e testi 355–56 (Vatican City, 1994), 1:84. Saint Peter's, of course, came to be the most visited confessio of the city, and ordo 36 specifies (Andrieu, *Ordines*, 4:197 [36.13]) that the ordination rituals described took place "ad sanctum Petrum."

133. See above, chapter 1, 27. On rites of clerical degradation in general, see Roger E. Reynolds, "Rites of Separation and Reconciliation in the Early Middle Ages," in *Segni e riti nella chiesa altomedievale occidentale, Spoleto 11–17 aprile 1985*, Settimane di studio del Centro italiano di studi sull'alto medioevo 33 (Spoleto, 1987), 405–33, and in *Law and Liturgy* 10, especially 421–22.

readers surely understood Pope Gregory's abductors as assaulting the special status of the pontiff and attempting to depose him. The mention of each of the outer garments, however, suggests not just an assault on the pope's status, but an attempt to strip him of the virtues these vestments represented in clerical spirituality. But could they really remove his *charitas?* Or his dedication, like the "new man" of Paul's letter to the Ephesians, to the justice and holiness of truth? Or his "breastplate of fortitude"?

Paul of Bernreid's description of Pope Gregory's captivity suggests not. He endured "excessively harsh treatment," taunts and threats. Just as the "dress of that earlier priesthood" to which clerical garments were likened, was "the adornment of our mind," the virtues symbolized by Gregory's vestments were within him: they could not be removed. When a Roman crowd came to his aid, besieging the tower where the pontiff was imprisoned, his captor, the Roman noble Cencius Stephani, suddenly threw himself at Gregory's feet, begging for mercy and confessing his sin. The "most merciful pope, pious soul that he was," reminded the "traitor" of all the exhortations to repentance that he had already received and ignored: "Nevertheless, the door of life still stands open to you, if only your heart is converted." Paul's clerical audience would recognize in this admonition for conversion of heart a standard element in the rites for administering the sacrament of penance.[134] The captor Cencius "again confessed that he was guilty and wretched, promising to perform without hesitation everything that was enjoined upon him." Gregory forgave "like a father" the injuries inflicted on him, but for the expiation of the sinner's offense against God and the church he enjoined a pilgrimage to Jerusalem. Paul's audience would also have known that this sacrament was usually performed in alb and stole. Although the pope's abductors had attempted to strip the pontiff of his office and virtues by removing his outer vestments, really they readied him to minister as a pastor to his persecutors. But the conclusion of the story underscores the perfidy of this sinner: "that wicked Judas . . . failed to perform what he had promised."[135]

Paul's narrative of the kidnapping of Gregory VII is immediately followed in the vita by an account of the pontiff's "dealings with King Henry": the kidnap story foreshadows the investiture struggle. The inconstancy of the sinner-king, like that of the captor Cencius, is a key theme in Paul's rendition of the conflict. But so, too, is the attempted deposition of Pope Gregory VII fomented at the Council of Worms early in 1076. This is made, in Paul's recounting, the opening of the struggle. The pope's pastoral efforts to guide the young king like a father are "rewarded" with an unprovoked assault on the pontiff's status. By foreshadowing this attempted deposition by Henry IV with the violent abduction and defrocking of the pope at Christmas Eve Mass in 1075, Paul used the imagery of sacred vestments to make both into (unsuccessful) assaults on the pontiff's

134. The actions narrated in the vita do not precisely and completely follow any of the various rites of penance practiced in this period. But some of the elements represented—the physical prostration and tears of the sinner, the admonition to "convert the heart"—do occur commonly in many of them: Sarah Hamilton, *The Practice of Penance, 900–1050* (Woodbridge, 2001), 104–72, but especially 112–14.

135. Robinson, *Papal Reform*, 298–301; Watterich, *Pontificum Romanorum Vitae*, 1:502–5.

priesthood and priestly virtues. In the context of the clerical spirituality that had developed around vestments, Paul's imagery seems a masterful way of fostering identification with the papacy and mobilizing support for the reform agenda. The pontiff's garments are those familiar to all clerics; their meanings and associations are invoked in the drama of the saint-pope's travail.

Paul of Bernreid's deployment of vestment imagery in his rendition of Pope Gregory VII's life is an apt metaphor for the broader reform movements' relationship with the clerical spirituality of liturgical dress. The origins of this spirituality may be traced all the way back to the patristic era, to Jerome's exegesis of Exodus 28 and to Gregory the Great's association of Aaron's vestments with the virtues and powers of the Christian priesthood. But these ideas were creatively reconfigured and widely diffused through the liturgical commentaries of the Carolingian era. These liturgical tracts may not have had the immediate effect their authors and patrons had hoped for, but they proved to be fertile material for another generation of reformers. Two innovations in the spirituality they fostered were particularly significant. First, while continuing to generate complex, theologically sophisticated interpretations and devotions, eleventh-century reformers also embraced and fostered simpler practices. Vesting prayers and rituals of vesting could be understood and practiced by the common clergy. As a tool of clerical reform, they had a transformative potential far beyond that of the liturgical commentaries. Second, the increasing affluence of Western society generally, and the church particularly, after the millennium allowed ecclesiastics in the eleventh century to develop a rich material culture that enhanced and deepened the clerical spirituality of vestments. Gregory the Great's comment on Exodus 28 that "in the vesture of the priest, the gold is resplendent beyond all else" became a material reality in the Christian vestments of the central Middle Ages. It is to the surviving garments and depictions of vestments in the era of reform that we must now turn.

3

RESPLENDENT IN GOLD

Among the earliest surviving liturgical vestments in medieval Europe are a stole and maniple found in 1827 in the tomb of Saint Cuthbert in Durham, England (figure 10). They are made of gold and silk. Full-length figures of prophets and saints, identified through inscriptions, are embroidered with silk thread dyed in shades of blue, red, green, and brown. These saintly figures appear to float on a sea of gold. Finely hammered strips of nearly pure gold were wrapped around red silk fibers to create each gold thread. These individual threads were then laid side by side—as many as 128 per inch—and attached with tiny couching stitches in red silk to form undulating expanses of shimmering gold. Inscriptions on the reverse ends of these golden vestments reveal, however, that they were not originally created for the saint. Queen Ælfflaed (c. 900–c. 918) had them made for Frithestan, bishop of Winchester (909–931). So these were conceived and executed as vestments for a living bishop.

We don't know whether Frithestan ever received them, but in 934 King Æthelstan presented them to Saint Cuthbert at a recognition of his relics.[1] During the same visit the king gave the saint's community a manuscript of the *Lives of Saint Cuthbert* written by the Venerable Bede (Cambridge, Corpus Christi College MS 183). A full-page dedication on folio 1v shows Æthelstan presenting the book to Saint Cuthbert (figure 11).[2] Although the king brought ornate golden vestments to Cuthbert's tomb, the saint is depicted in the manuscript very plainly attired in an alb and reddish-purple chasuble. Why was clerical attire *depicted* more simply than what the physical evidence demonstrates some clerics were wearing by the early tenth century?

1. Maureen C. Miller, "The Significance of Saint Cuthbert's Vestments," *Studies in Church History* 47 (2011): 90–102.

2. Mildred Budny, *Insular, Anglo-Saxon and Early Anglo-Norman Manuscript Art at Corpus Christi College, Cambridge: An Illustrated Catalogue*, 2 vols. (Kalamazoo, Mich., 1997), 1:177; Margaret Rickert, *Painting in Britain: The Middle Ages* (Baltimore, 1954), 36.

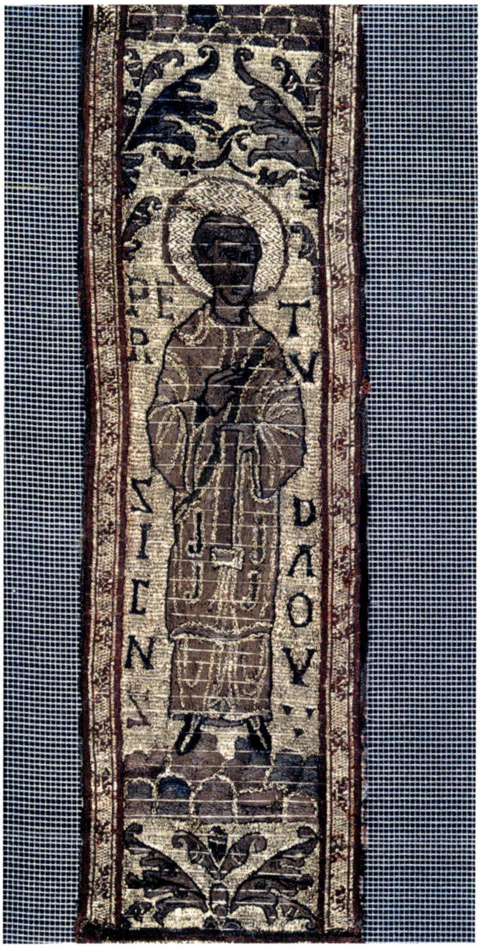

FIGURE 10. Maniple of Saint Cuthbert, detail of Peter the Deacon, c. 909–918, cathedral, Durham. Photo by permission of Durham Cathedral.

The relationship between rulers and bishops is at the heart of this disparity. Depictions of clerical attire in frescoes, mosaics, and manuscripts tend to communicate ideals more consistently than realities, and status hierarchies strongly influence representation. Still, a highly significant change in ideals can be traced across our period. In late antiquity and into the early Middle Ages, clerical attire was portrayed as made of ample fabric, some of it dyed, but it was not depicted as ornamented or made of precious materials. From the mid-ninth century this began to change, and by the late eleventh century highly ornate vestments adorned with gold were depicted throughout western Europe as appropriate clerical attire. The involvement of bishops as partners with kings in the governance of Christian society seems to correlate with changes in how ecclesiastical attire was represented in Western art, but the theology and spirituality of sacred vestments discussed in chapter 2 also contributed to the change.

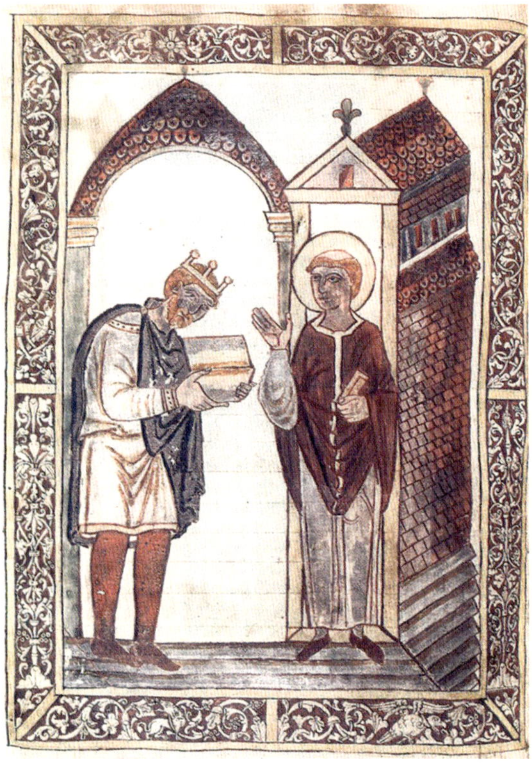

Figure 11. King Æthelstan presenting the volume of Bede's *Lives of Saint Cuthbert* to Saint Cuthbert, Winchester, c. 934, Corpus Christi College MS 183, 1v, Cambridge. Photo by permission of Corpus Christi College.

Rules and Conventions in Depicting Clerical Attire: c. 500–850

Two pieces of early ecclesiastical legislation suggest that some clerics did wear liturgical vestments made of expensive materials, but that the practice met with disapproval. The first redaction of the *Liber pontificalis* (c. 530s) attributed to Pope Sylvester (314–335) a decree banning the use of silk or dyed cloth in liturgical garb, and a 786 Anglo-Saxon council prohibited clerics from wearing clothing that was "precious or dyed with Indian colors."[3] Were these strictures heeded? The survival of liturgical garments from before the tenth century is extremely rare, but images of clerical clothing can at least illumine conventions of representation, what it was socially and culturally acceptable to depict. Even in this category, evidence is limited.[4] Full-length images of clerics that reveal their clothing in any detail are few before the millennium: most figural art depicted biblical figures and stories. From the eighth century, northern Europe provides manuscript illuminations of clerics, but in late antiquity our sources are Italian, and overwhelmingly

3. See above, chapter 1, 31.

4. I have used the Index of Christian Art in gathering and assessing the evidence for the depiction of clerical clothing, focusing on wall paintings, mosaics, and manuscripts because images in other media (ivories, glass, sculpture) tend not to offer sufficiently detailed renderings. Works in which the clerical garb is largely the reconstruction of later restorations have also been eliminated from consideration: notably, the depiction of Pope Felix VI (526–530) in the apse mosaic at the Basilica of Ss. Cosma e Damiano,

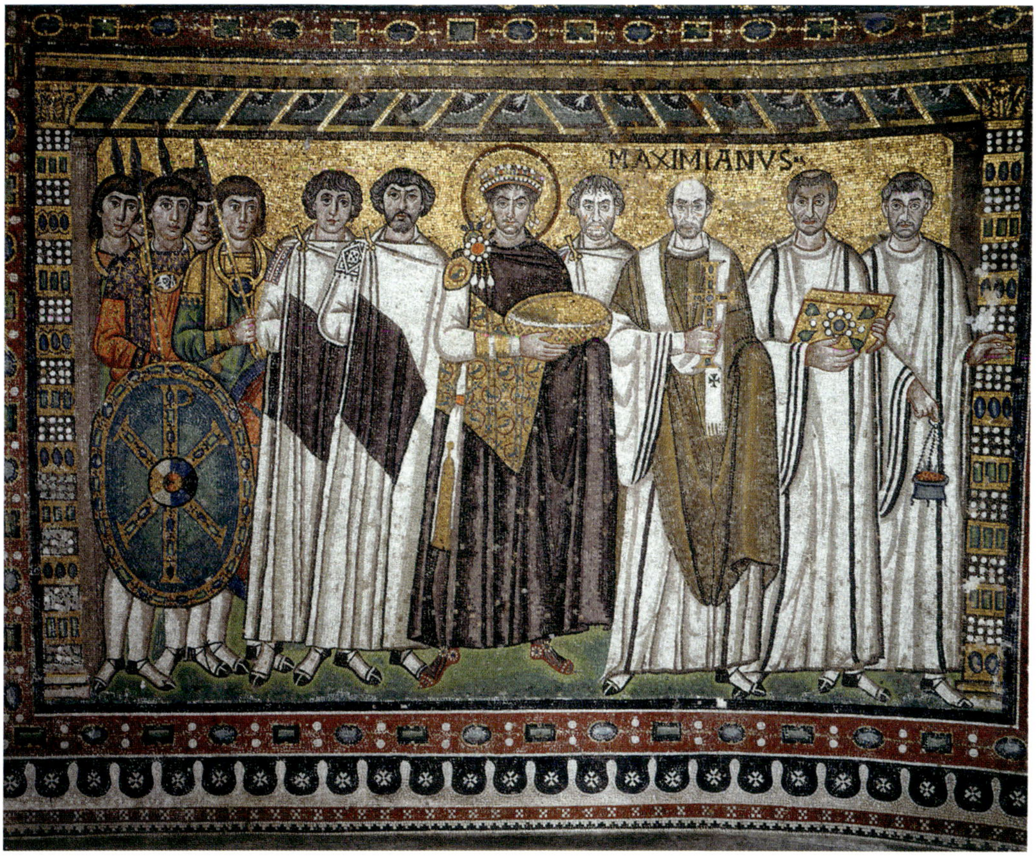

FIGURE 12. Justinian, Maximian, and deacons, mid-sixth century, San Vitale, Ravenna. Alfredo Dagli Orti / The Art Archive at Art Resource, NY.

Roman. This limited visual evidence falls somewhere in between the practices that provoked the legislation above and the ideal that it defined. It represents clerics wearing dyed fabrics, but without the kind of ornament lavished on the attire of sacred personages and lay elites.

Let's start by considering a familiar face (figure 12). One of the most well-known works of late antique art, the mosaic of the emperor Justinian and his court in the Church of San Vitale in Ravenna, prominently features a portrait of Archbishop Maximian (546–557) accompanied by two deacons.[5] All three ecclesiastics wear slender black *campagi* on their feet

Rome; the mosaics on the outer arch of San Lorenzo fuori le Mura, Rome; and the apse depiction of Saint Apollinaris at Sant'Apollinare in Classe, Ravenna. See Guglielmo Matthiae, *Mosaici medioevali delle chiese di Roma*, 2 vols. (Rome, 1967), 1:152; Walter Oakeshott, *The Mosaics of Rome from the Third to the Fourteenth Centuries* (Greenwich, Conn., 1967), 145; Friedrich Wilhelm Deichmann, *Ravenna: Hauptstadt des spätantiken Abendlandes* 3 vols. (Wiesbaden, 1958–89), 1:340, plate 289.

5. Deborah Mauskopf Deliyannis, *Ravenna in Late Antiquity* (Cambridge, 2010), 223–50; Patrizia Angiolini Martinelli ed., *La Basilica di San Vitale a Ravenna: Atlante* (Modena, 1997), 226; Irina Andreescu-Treadgold and Warren Treadgold, "Procopius and the Imperial Panels of S. Vitale," *Art Bulletin* 79 (1997): 708–23.

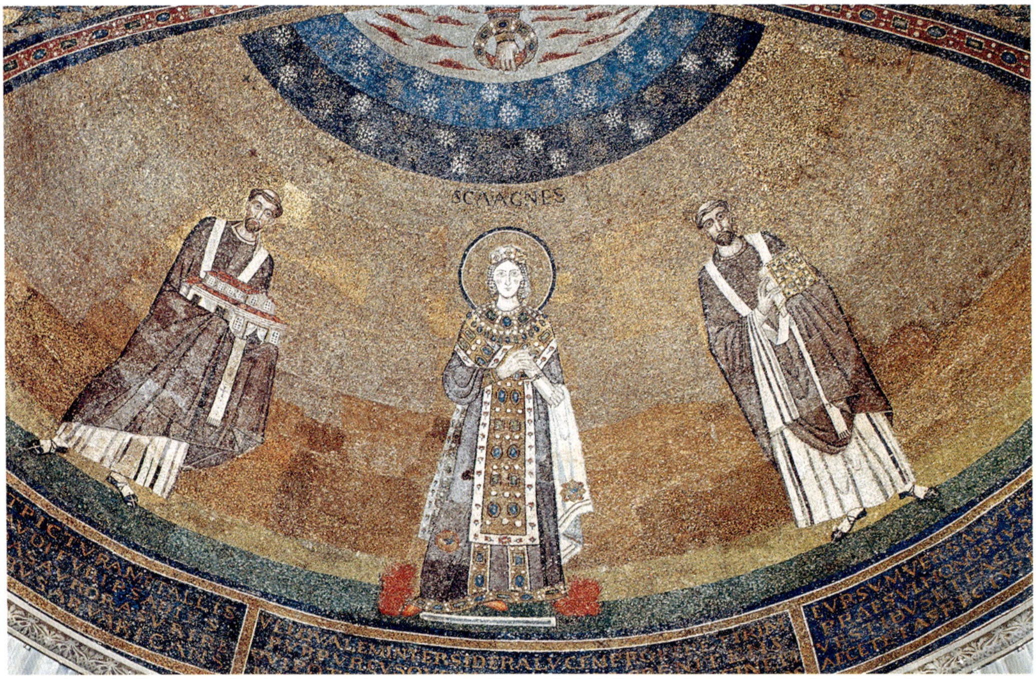

FIGURE 13. Apse mosaic, c. 625–638, Sant'Agnese, Rome. Scala / Art Resource, NY.

and white dalmatics with black *clavi* down the front and three black stripes emphasizing the elongation of their sleeves. Maximian's chasuble is olive green, with folds in its fabric indicated on the mosaic in tan and black tesserae. Only a small black cross and a fringed end decorate the white pallium, symbol of his archiepiscopal authority. Ornament is lavished not on the clergy's clothes, but on sacred objects: the gold- and gem-studded cross in Maximian's hand and the golden bejeweled book cradled by the deacon next to him.

Simplicity also characterizes ecclesiastical vesture in Roman mosaics. The earliest images of clerics are at Pope Honorius I's (625–638) church of Sant'Agnese fuori le Mura and at the chapel of San Venanzio at the Lateran built by Pope John IV (640–642) (figures 13 and 14). This native of Dalmatia secured the relics of several saints from his homeland and built San Venanzio off the Constantinian baptistery to house them. The honored saints, their patron Pope John, and his successor, Pope Theodore I (642–649), who completed work on the chapel, are all represented in the mosaic apse and arch. At Sant'Agnese, Honorius and another pope (most commonly identified as Symmachus) flank the virgin martyr in the glittering apse (figure 13).[6] Both wear full chasubles in a deep purple over dalmatics, slender black *campagi* on their feet, and white pallia with fringed ends and small red crosses. From the viewer's distant perspective on the floor

6. Richard Krautheimer, *Rome, Profile of a City, 312–1308*, 2nd ed. (Princeton, 1983), 89–98; Matthiae, *Mosaici*, 1:169–79, 191–94; Oakeshott, *Mosaics*, 148, 150–52. The heads of both popes in the Sant'Agnese mosaic are the work of restorers, but the garments are original: Gabriella Delfini Filippi, "Per la storia del restauro musivo nel secolo XIX: L'esempio di Sant'Agnese," *Storia dell'arte* 65 (1989): 87–94.

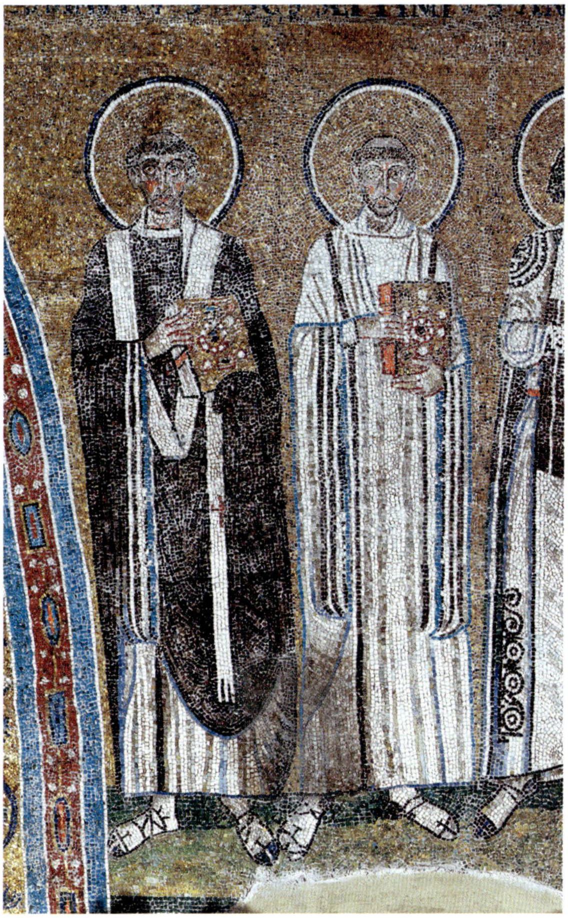

FIGURE 14. Saints Maurus and Settimius, arch mosaic, c. 640–649, Chapel of San Venanzio, Constantinian baptistery at the Lateran, Rome. Photo by Andrea Jemolo.

below, the gentle curve of the apse seems to intensify the elongation of these standing figures and the long, straight folds of their vestments. The deacon Saint Settimius portrayed on the arch at San Venanzio appears as a mass of vertical lines: the purple *clavi* of his dalmatic race down to the hem, the stripes on his sleeves emphasize their length, light blue and beige lines suggest ample but preternaturally orderly folds of fabric. Bishop Maurus beside him has a similarly lined dalmatic under his deep purple chasuble, the tesserae of which run mostly in long vertical rows. The deep loop of his white pallium and its long hanging end contribute to the saintly bishop's appearance of placid height.

Some of the ecclesiastics mentioned above—Maximian at Ravenna and Honorius I at Rome—were alive when the images were created and were patrons of these artistic projects. But clerics venerated as saints—Maurus and Settimius at San Venanzio, both haloed—were not attired in richer or more ornate vestments. Ornament is reserved in these mosaic programs for other sacred personages and lay elites. Saint Agnes is radiant between the two simply attired popes flanking her in the apse. She wears not only a jewel-encrusted *loros* and headdress, but also a robe decorated with a golden roundel with a bird within it and an ornamented hem. The white mantle draped over her left arm also has embroidered designs along the edge. Unsurprisingly, in the San Vitale mosaic, the emperor Justinian's attire is richly ornamented. A gold *tablion* (either embroidered or of gold fabric with a woven pattern) decorates his purple chlamys, which is clasped on his right shoulder with a gold brooch featuring a large red stone surrounded by pearls. Maximian's chasuble seems a dull brown in comparison to the shimmering attire of his ruler. But even less exalted lay figures than the emperor—whose head is haloed at San Vitale—are depicted with precious ornament. Frescoes from a mid-eighth-century chapel in Santa Maria Antiqua in Rome reveal the donor, Theodotus, in an unadorned chasuble but his family members wearing patterns that resemble those woven into precious silks: roundels with flowers ornament the mantle of the small female figure, while the man to her left has a red robe with medallions (figure 15).[7]

It's worth pausing for a moment to consider patterns in surviving silks and artistic renderings of them. The depictions of the clothing of Theodotus's relatives represent typical features of eighth- and ninth-century Byzantine silk production: rows of large, nearly contiguous medallions with figures within them. Medallions ringed with white dots faithfully portray a Sasanian motif, the "pearl roundel." These large-scale designs were technically complex, requiring weavers' assistants and looms with a variety of devices that lift warp threads at planned intervals to produce patterns. Artistic renderings, indeed, are much simpler than the designs in surviving fragments that feature animal and human figures (figure 16). But when an artist represented a fabric covered with roundels, he was communicating that the individual was clothed in the most expensive silk. Characteristic of the next tier down in silk production were overall patterns with small motifs, sometimes also called small-scale repeat patterns. Typical schemes have rows of hearts, crosses, or flowers, sometimes set in lattice divisions to amplify the diapering effect of the repeat pattern (figure 17). Artists used cross-hatching to represent these diaper patterns and little clusters of dots to let the viewer recognize a fabric with an overall repeat motif.[8]

7. Guglielmo Matthiae, *Pittura romana del medioevo*, 2 vols., new ed. with *Aggiornamento scientifico e bibliografia* by Francesco Gandolfo (Rome, 1988), 1:138–47; Pietro Romanelli and Per Jonas Nordhagen, *Santa Maria Antiqua* (Rome, 1999), tav. 32; Josef Wilpert, *Die römschen Mosaiken und Malereien der kirchlichen Bauten vom IV.–XIII. Jahrhundert*, 4 vols. (Freiburg, 1916–1917), 4:183. I present here Wilpert's plate of this much deteriorated fresco because it more clearly shows the clothing. Wilpert used photographic enlargements made from negatives shot shortly after the frescoes were excavated and then had an artist, Carlo Tabanelli, apply gouache colors or gold and silver tints in front of the originals. In the late 1970s, Per Jonas Nordhagen conducted a minute comparison of several of Wilpert's plates with originals recently restored or newly accessible, concluding that the plates are "highly accurate and convey a truer picture of the refinements of the original than any black and white photography." Nordhagen also gave Wilpert's plates "high marks . . . for their precision both in the delineating of the subject matter and in the rendering of colours." Given the deterioration of many of these works of art since their excavation and Wilpert's attention to evidence of restorations and alterations, the plates in his *Die römischen Mosaiken und Malereien* provide important documentation. Per Jonas Nordhagen, "Working with Wilpert: The Illustrations in *Die römischen Mosaiken und Malereien* and Their Source Value," *Acta ad Archaeologiam et Artivm Historiam Pertinentia*, Series Altera in 80 5 (1985): 247–57.

8. John Peter Wild, "The Later Roman and Early Byzantine East, AD 300–1000," in *CHWT*, 1:148–51. The plates in Anna Muthesius's *Byzantine Silk* offer the best visual introduction to the patterned silks avidly sought by western Europeans.

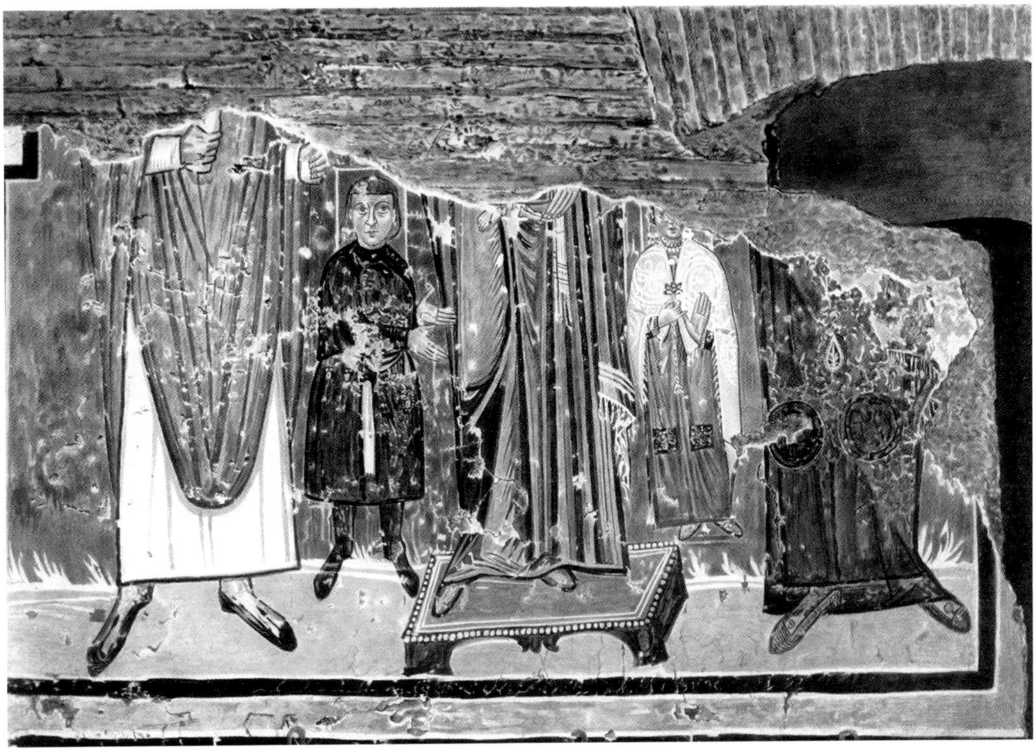

FIGURE 15. Donor portrait, c. 741–752, Theodotus Chapel, Santa Maria Antiqua, Rome. From Josef Wilpert, *Die römschen Mosaiken und Malereien der kirchlichen Bauten vom IV.–XIII. Jahrhundert*, 4 vols. (Freiburg, 1916–1917), 4:161–62. By permission of Doe Library, University of California, Berkeley.

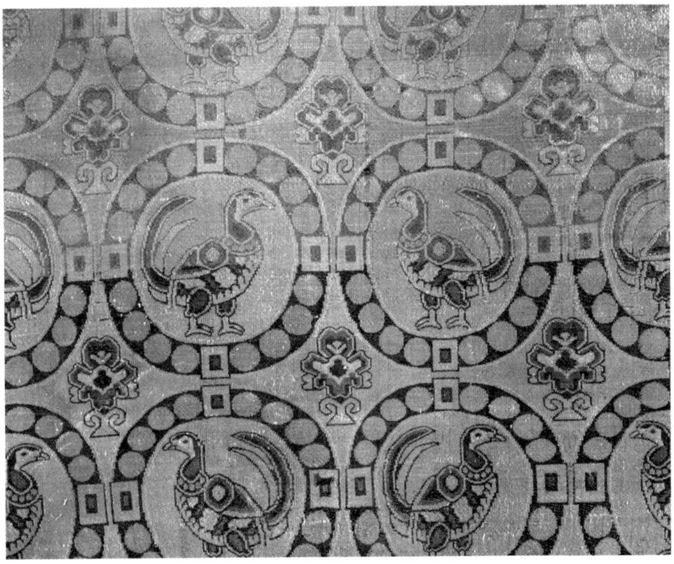

FIGURE 16. Textile fragment with large-scale medallion pattern (pheasant in pearl roundels), 680–900. Digital image © 2012 Museum Associates / LACMA. Licensed by Art Resource, NY.

All silks, but particularly these patterned silks, were prestige luxury objects in western Europe.

Such valuable fabrics were donated to numerous Roman churches by pontiffs across the early Middle Ages, so it is not the case that ecclesiastics did not have access to luxury textiles. What the evidence of the *Liber pontificalis* indicates, however, is that such fabrics were used to adorn altars and churches, not clerical bodies. They are most frequently mentioned being used as *vela*, "veils" hung from architraves and between columns to create spatial divisions within churches, and as altar coverings.[9] No examples of these papal gifts to Roman churches have survived, but one given by Bishop Anno of Verona (750–780) to the church of SS. Fermo e Rustico in his city has. The Velo di Classe (so-called because it was conserved in a monastery in Classe) now consists in three bands embroidered with roundel portrait busts of local saints and of early Veronese bishops. One band has the figures arrayed horizontally and would have hung along the top front of the altar, whereas the other two have the figures cascading vertically to be draped down the sides. The figures are embroidered in silk with inscriptions identifying them in gold thread.[10]

Although clerical attire in these earliest images is depicted as relatively unadorned, it certainly was represented as more colorful than the "shining white" garments for the celebration of the Mass that were defended by Jerome in the early fifth century. Indeed, the visual evidence suggests that the ban on using dyed cloth for liturgical vestments attributed to Pope Sylvester (314–335) in the *Liber pontificalis* was entirely disregarded for chasubles. While a theory of liturgical colors—that is, colors considered appropriate for the saint's day or feast (e.g., red for martyrs)—did not emerge until the late twelfth century, some spiritual associations may certainly have promoted colored garb earlier.[11] Whether these earliest-depicted late-antique liturgical garments, white or colored, were made of plain silk cannot, of course, be discerned in these works of art.[12] But they were

9. The *vestes* listed in the *Liber* are *vestes altaris: Liber pontificalis*, 1:418–19, 421, 432, 435, 500; 2:2–3, 8–11; John Osborne, "Textiles and Their Painted Imitations in Early Medieval Rome," *Papers of the British School at Rome* 60 (1992): 312–21. The lists in the *Liber pontificalis* are so lengthy and detailed that Paolo Delogu did an economic study of them: "L'importazione di tessuti preziosi e il sistema economico romano nel IX secolo," *Roma medievale—aggiornamenti*, ed. Paolo Delogu (Florence, 1998), 123–41. Only in the twelfth century are vestments found among the gifts made by popes to Roman churches: the *Descriptio lateranensis ecclesiae* recorded that Pope Innocent II (1130–1143) gave a fine cloth woven of gold to the basilica, from which altar cloths and a chasuble were made, while Anastasius IV (1153–1154) donated a white chasuble hemmed all around with a precious gold embroidery: Roberto Valentini and Giuseppe Zucchetti, eds., *Codice topografico della città di Roma*, 4 vols., Fonti per la storia d'Italia 81, 88, 90, 91 (Rome, 1940–1953), 3:349, 352.

10. Carlo Cipolla, "Il Velo di Classe," *Le gallerie nazionali italiane* 3 (1897): 194–249; for color photos, Francesco Butturini, *La pittura frescale dell'anno mille nella diocesi di Verona* (Verona, 1987), figs. 18–21. On the transfer of this tradition to northern Europe and its continuation, see C. R. Dodwell, *Anglo-Saxon Art: A New Perspective* (Ithaca, N.Y., 1982), 129–69.

11. Roger E. Reynolds, "Clerical Liturgical Vestments and Liturgical Colors," in *Clerics in the Early Middle Ages: Hierarchy and Image* (Aldershot, 1999), 6:10–15.

12. Of the very few ecclesiastical tunics preserved as relics of late antique saints, half are linen and half are silk: Braun, *DLG*, 260–61; Ernst Wackenroder, ed., *Die Kunstdenkmäler des Kreises Saarburg im auftrage des Provinzialverbandes der Rheinprovinz* (Düsseldorf, 1939), 242–44 [on the Taben dalmatic];

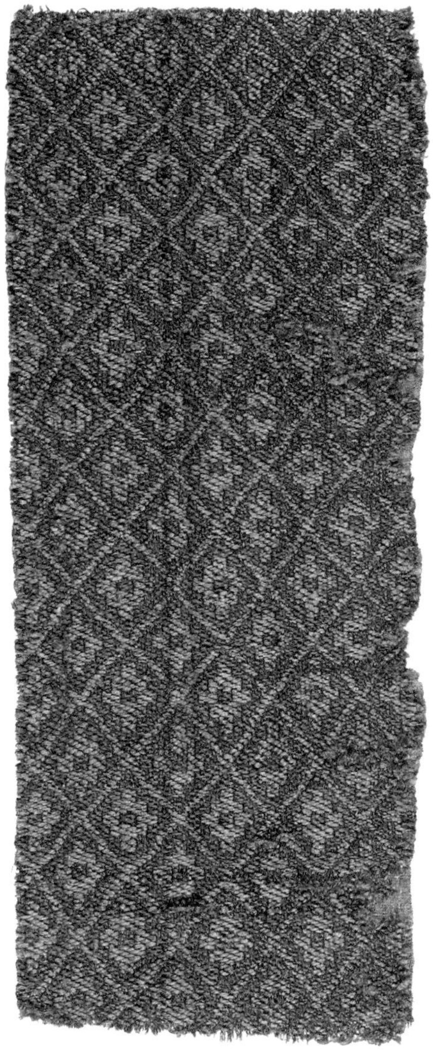

FIGURE 17. Textile fragment with small-scale repeat pattern, twelfth–thirteenth centuries. Bayerisches Nationalmuseum 55/219, Munich.

not depicted as having been made of the most coveted and prestigious silks woven with patterns, whereas lay attire was. Perhaps the lack of ornamentation was some concession to those ambivalent about special liturgical garb and opposed to ostentation. At the least, these early Christian representations suggest that the clergy were expected to be visually distinct from the laity, distinguished not only by certain types of clothing (chasubles, dalmatics) but also by its lack of ornament. The images that survive suggest the cultivation of a solemn and stately appearance, but without rich adornment.

Mechthild Flury-Lemberg, "Le vêtement funéraire de saint Servais de Maastricht," *Bulletin du CIETA* 70 (1992): 37–44 [linen tunic]; Hero Granger-Taylor, "The Two Dalmatics of Saint Ambrose," *Bulletin du CIETA* 57–58 (1983): 127–73; Alberto de Capitani d'Arzago, *Antichi tessuti della basilica ambrosiana*, Biblioteca de "l'Arte," n.s. 1 (Milan, 1941). Both of the Ambrosian dalmatics are silk; for the linen-wool tunic of Saint Caesarius, see next note.

Figure 18. Tunic of Saint Caesarius of Arles, sixth century, Arles. Photo courtesy of Anastasia Ozoline.

The relics of one late antique bishop provide some confirmation of these attitudes. Caesarius of Arles entered monastic life at Lérins as a youth and was consecrated bishop of Arles in 502 or 503. He was active regionally in councils and received the pallium from Pope Symmachus in 514. He was venerated as a saint soon after his death in 542. First buried in the Basilica of Sainte-Marie outside the city walls, his remains were disturbed and recovered at least twice: once when the city was sacked in the ninth century (by Vikings and/or Muslims, as tradition has it) and again during the French Revolution. Both times, body parts and the clothing in which he was buried were recovered and repackaged, so to speak, for veneration. The wooden box in which the saint's clothing was preserved was opened in a recognition of the relics on September 11, 1997, and for the first time in centuries the contents were studied, restored, and conserved. Discovered inside were the fragmentary remains of a plain brown tunic made of a wool and linen blend (figure 18), and two pallia wrapped in silk. One of the pallia was of wool with a light red cross embroidered in silk thread on both sides of one end (figure 19), the other of a wool-linen blend (figure 20). Radiocarbon testing confirmed that these textiles date to the sixth century, while the silks in which they were wrapped, several red silk crosses, and a piece of tapestry weaving sewn onto the pallia were from the thirteenth century.[13]

These results prompt several observations. First, Caesarius appears to have been buried in a plain brown tunic with two pallia: one entirely plain, the other with small red crosses on one end. The latter corresponds to the pallium as represented in the mosaics considered here. The tunic is considerably more humble in form and appearance, however, than the garb depicted. We know from Caesarius's will that he had other clothing. He left to his successor in his see "all the paschal vestments that were given to

13. Anastasia Ozoline, *Trésors de la Gaule chrétienne: histoire et restauration des reliques textiles de saint Césaire d'Arles (470–542)* (Arles, 2008), 17, 37, 46, 60, 87, 105.

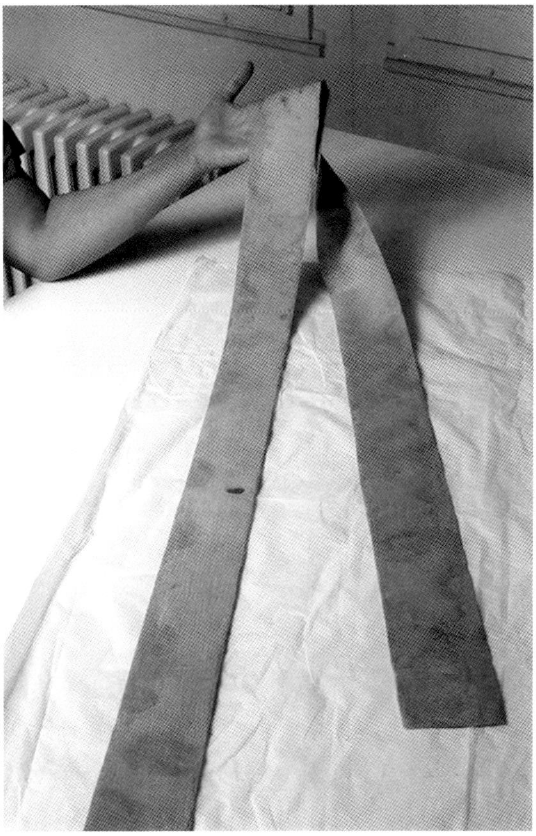

FIGURE 19. Pallium "chrismé" of Saint Caesarius of Arles, sixth century, Arles. Photo courtesy of Anastasia Ozoline.

me . . . together with the better quality shaggy cloak, the better quality tunic, and the thick cloak, which I have left behind." The rest of his clothes, with the exception of his hooded cloak, were to be divided among his clerical and lay servants.[14] The value of clothing surely factored into Caesarius's decisions in this document and likely into those of his followers who prepared his body for burial. But attitudes and sensibilities probably did too: even a high-ranking cleric could fittingly enter eternity in a plain brown tunic. The inclusion of the pallia were his markers of status—his connection to Rome, papal recognition of his ministry, and his local authority—and they are modest in appearance.

The thirteenth-century additions indicate a significant change in sensibilities. Most relics came to be wrapped in silks, so the discovery of later silks enveloping the pallia is not surprising. More significant is that those who handled the relics in the thirteenth or fourteenth centuries thought it was appropriate to sew ornaments onto them. One red silk cross was added to the wool pallium with the embroidered cross. Three red silk crosses were sewn onto the plain wool and linen pallium in addition to two pieces of tapestry work in gold and silk thread. The addition of these ornaments suggests that to

14. See chapter 1 above, 22–23.

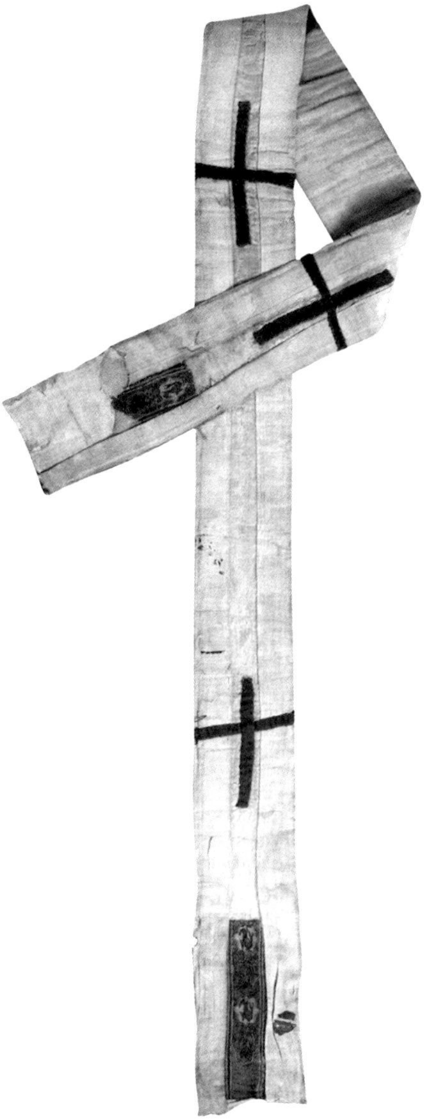

FIGURE 20. Pallium "aux Lièvres" of Saint Caesarius of Arles, sixth century with later additions, Arles. Photo courtesy of Anastasia Ozoline.

thirteenth- or fourteenth-century clerics, Caesarius's pallia were too plain. They needed golden embroidery and silk to be appropriate to a holy bishop.

In artistic depictions of clerics, evidence of these changing sensibilities begins with the Carolingians. It is slender over the first half of the ninth century, and abundant from the second half of the ninth century on. In the tenth century Anglo-Saxon examples become numerous, while in the eleventh century Rome embraced the change. From the twelfth century, ecclesiastical garb is depicted throughout Europe as made of precious silks and adorned with woven gold bands and colorful embroidery. While it was the excesses of Baroque clerical vesture that Fellini so brilliantly satirized in *Roma*'s ecclesiastical fashion show, cultural acceptance of ornate liturgical garb was established much earlier, from the ninth to the eleventh centuries.

After Caesarius, we have little information for northern Europe until the Carolingians. Figural art was extremely rare among the Merovingians: the one surviving depiction of bishops on an ivory plaque has only half-figures that don't reveal their attire. Insular art, too, preferred interlace designs and animal figures to naturalistic renderings of human forms. But from the reign of Charlemagne both wall paintings and manuscript illuminations provide images of clerical garb. The little church of Saint Benedikt in Mals, built c. 816 in the Vinschgau Valley in the Tyrol, for example, features early ninth-century wall paintings of Saint Gregory the Great and Saint Stephen dressed in ecclesiastical vestments. The latter, as is customary, is attired as a deacon in a dalmatic with double-line red *clavi* and sleeves, while Gregory wears a similar dalmatic with a red chasuble and white pallium over it.[15] Ecclesiastical vesture here appears comparable to contemporary images in Rome where red chasubles are common in early ninth-century mosaics and the pallium is affixed in a Y form.[16] Two bishops in the crypt of the abbey church of Saint-Germain at Auxerre (841–859) are similarly depicted.[17] Some manuscript paintings also depict ecclesiastical garb without ornament. Two manuscripts of Hrabanus Maurus's *De laudibus sanctae crucis* from the Fulda scriptorium, both dating to the second quarter of the ninth century (Amiens, Bibliothèque de la Ville, 223, 2v and BAV Reg. Lat. 124, 2v), depict the author, dressed as a monk, accompanied by Alcuin in a dalmatic, presenting his work to an enthroned bishop, variously identified. The pallium is strangely knotted in each to achieve the Y form, but the prelate's alb, dalmatic, and chasuble are plain.[18]

Two earlier Carolingian manuscripts, however, show the beginnings of change. Both were created in Italy in the late eighth century. A collection of homilies commissioned by Bishop Egino of Verona between 796 and 799 (Berlin, Staatsbibliothek, Phill. 1676), and presented by him to the city's cathedral, contains full-page portrait paintings of

15. Butturini, *La pittura*, 89–90 (presented as *comparanda*).

16. The range of chasuble colors depicted in eighth- and ninth-century Rome expands, with red and yellow being most common: Wilpert, *Die römischen Mosaiken und Malereien*, 4:154, 192–93. The pallium came to be fastened to the chasuble with three pins, one at each shoulder and in front at the intersection of the Y: Braun, *DLG*, 644–47.

17. Christian Sapin, ed., *Peindre à Auxerre au Moyen Âge IXe–XIVe siècle. 10 ans de recherché à l'abbaye Saint-Germain d'Auxerre et à la cathédrale Saint-Étienne d'Auxerre* (Auxerre, 1999), 123–25.

18. A slightly later manuscript (Vienna, Österreichische Nationalsbibliothek, Cod. 652, 1v) of the same text depicts multiple crosses and other patterned ornament on the pallium of the episcopal figure, labeled in a later hand "Otgerius episcopus Maguntinus." For this image and one of BAV Reg. Lat. 124, 2v, see Julius von Schlosser, *Eine Fulder Miniaturhandschrift der K. K. Hofbibliothek* (Vienna, 1892): 32–34, 52–53; for a color image of Amiens, Bibliothèque de la Ville, 223, 2v, see Hrabanus Maurus, *Louanges de la Sainte Croix*, ed. Michel Perrin (Paris, 1988), 38. An early ninth-century manuscript produced in Rome, the Codex Juvenianus (Rome, Biblioteca Vallicelliana, B.25/2, 2r), also contains a presentation miniature: the scribe and artist, the subdeacon Juvenianus, dressed in a plain white alb, offers his volume to Saint Lawrence: Alberto Zonghetti, "Il codice di Gioveniano," *Arte medievale* n.s. 4 (2005): 21, 26–28 (image of 2v on 26).

Augustine of Hippo (figure 21), Leo the Great, Gregory the Great, and Ambrose of Milan, all in episcopal garb and attended by clerics. Leo's, Gregory's, and Ambrose's chasubles (ochre, red, and green) are consonant with the wider array of colors used in Rome at this time, but like contemporary Roman attire they are unadorned. Augustine's, however, is amazingly rich and marks a significant departure: the saint's dalmatic is a deep purple with gold *clavi*, while the red fabric of his chasuble is covered with tiny golden crosses.[19] All four fathers of the church depicted in the Egino Codex were venerated as saints, so why is Augustine the only one represented as clothed in precious silk?

His representation is distinctive in other ways. Gregory and Ambrose are shown seated, poised to write in codices open before them. Leo sits enthroned holding an open book and flanked by two clerics. Augustine, however, has an audience. He sits enthroned, but turning to his left, inclining his head, gesturing with his right hand and holding an open book with his left. On that book, we the viewers can read "In principio erat verbum," "In the beginning was the word," the opening of the Gospel of Saint John. Seated before Augustine is a scribe, and we can read on his open book, "Audistis fr(atre)s k(arissi)mi," "You have heard, dearest brothers," which are the opening words of the first homily in the manuscript, a fragment of Augustine's sermon against the Pelagians. The scribe, however, isn't writing. He holds an inkwell in his left hand and a *calamus* in his right, but he has lifted his right hand to his chin in a pensive gesture. He gazes up at Augustine, as do the two clerics standing behind him. A deacon on the saint's right also gazes at him intently and beckons the viewer into the scene with his right hand. As Michael Camille pointed out in his insightful interpretation of this image, Augustine's communicative gesture and the rapt attention of those around him emphasize the importance of hearing the spoken word. But I would go further and suggest that this painting depicts Augustine as a teacher, particularly a teacher of clerics—and the clerics are all depicted here as young men. Augustine was considered a model bishop because his clergy lived a communal life with him. Possidius, in his life of the saint, depicts the clergy gathered around him to hear his teaching.[20] It was precisely this model that was being promulgated anew when Bishop Egino commissioned this manuscript. Charlemagne's *Admonitio generalis* in 789 required bishops to establish schools, and although there is evidence of a school at the Veronese cathedral as early as the sixth century, Egino was surely working to improve it. The texts of the manuscript itself, homilies of the fathers, were well suited to the education of the clergy,

19. Joachim Kirchner, *Beschreibende Verzeichnisse der Miniaturen-Handschriften der preussischen Staatsbibliothek zu Berlin. Erster Band, Die Phillipps-Handschriften* (Leipzig, 1926), 6–9; Michael Camille, "Word, Text, Image in the Early Church Fathers in the Egino Codex," in *Testo e imagine nell'alto medioevo*, Settimane di studio del Centro italiano di studi sull'alto medioevo 41, 2 vols. (Spoleto, 1994) 1:65–92 with plates following (by far the best published images of these illuminations). The author-portraits of Augustine and Leo once faced each other, and both have gold on their vestments. The portraits of Gregory and Ambrose also faced one another but are less ornamented. I thank Drs. Eef Overgaauw and Kurt Heydeck of the Handschriftenabteilung of the Staatsbibliothek in Berlin for a fuller description of the gold illumination on this folio, and Dr. Lawrence Nees for his extremely helpful observations on this manuscript.

20. Possidius, *Vita Augustini*, 25.1, 22.6, 15.1, in A. A. R. Bastiaensen, *Vita di Cipriano, Vita di Ambrogio, Vita di Agostino*, 2nd ed. (Milan, 1981), 194, 186–88, 166.

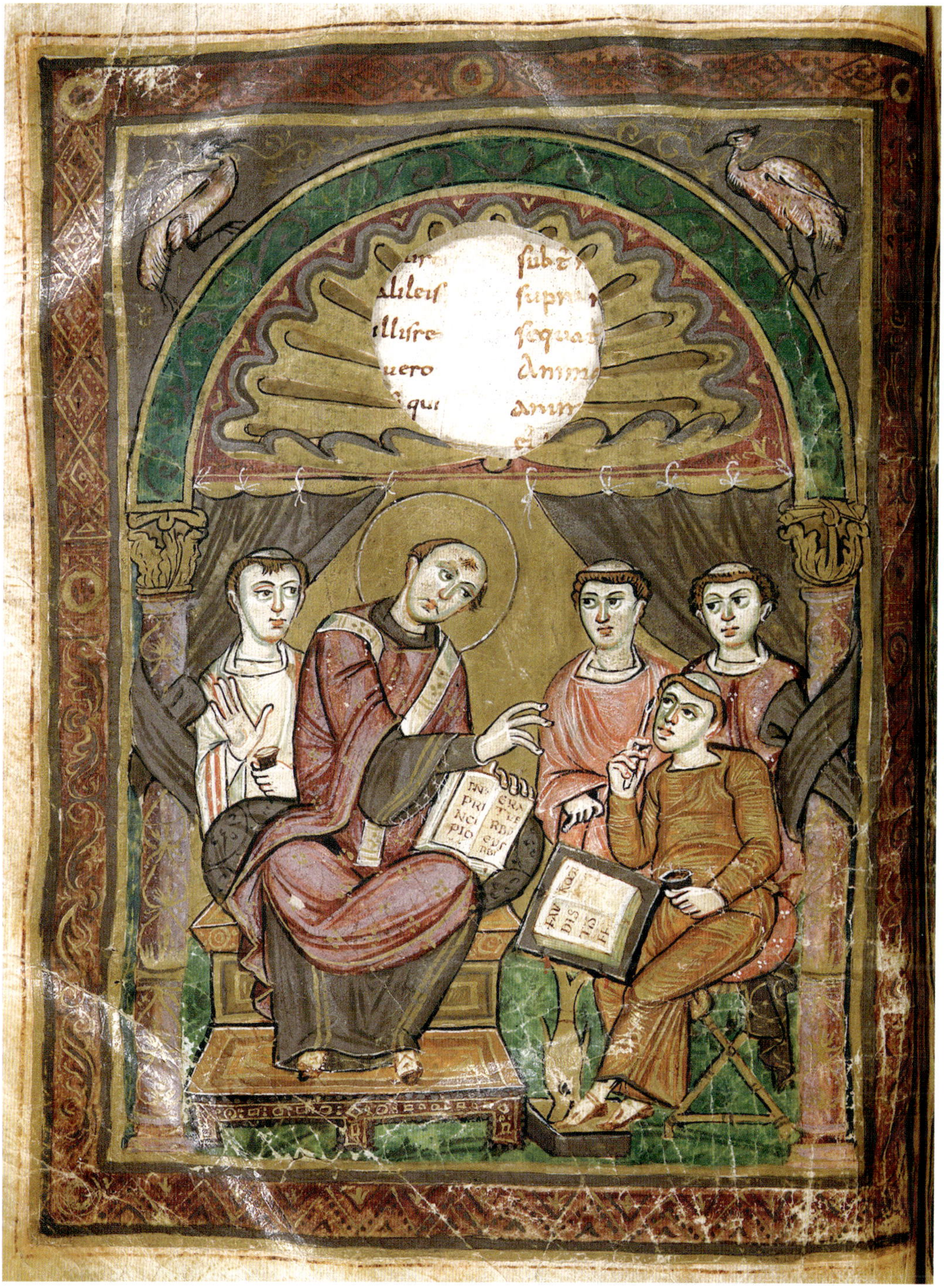

Figure 21. Saint Augustine of Hippo, Egino Codex, c. 796–799, Deutsche Staatsbibliothek MS Phill. 1676, 18v, Berlin. bpk Berlin / Handschriftenabteilung, Staatliche Museen / Art Resource, NY.

and in fact Egino says in his prologue—just preceding this image of Augustine—that he drew it up for those needing to learn (*hoc opusculum indoctis adsumpsi*).[21] Bishop Egino instructs the Veronese clergy, through his teaching and with this book, just as Saint Augustine instructs the clergy pictured here with his teaching and with the book he dictates. Perhaps the richness of Augustine's vestments simply calls attention to the value of sacred teaching. But could it also valorize Egino's act of patronage?

Another collection of homilies from Vercelli (Biblioteca Capitolare, CXLVIII/8) raises that question, for the more richly adorned vestments depicted in this manuscript are the donor's. The volume contains the homilies of Gregory the Great, and the saint is shown on folio 9v with a purple chasuble and white pallium and dalmatic. Multiple crosses ornament the pallium and dalmatic, and they are silver, as are the drapery lines. The patron who commissioned the manuscript is depicted similarly, but with even more costly ornament. Folio 7v shows the deacon Davidpertus escorted by Saint Peter to present the book to Christ. His dalmatic has crosses similar to those on Gregory's vestments, but Davidpertus's are of gold and silver, with the drapery folds in silver too.[22] It seems quite striking, even presumptuous, that his vestments are more ornate than those of a venerated father of the church.

A scene that also may imply patronage provides the earliest example of luxurious clerical clothing in Carolingian wall painting. The abbey church of St. Johann in Müstair, today in the Swiss canton of Graubünden, was built in the last quarter of the eighth century and decorated in the first half of the ninth century with the most extensive cycle of wall paintings to survive from the Carolingian era. Most of the scenes are drawn from the Old Testament or the ministry of Jesus, but there are two scenes that depict clerical clothing. These scenes are identified by some art historians as depicting the ordination and "liturgical meal" of Saint Stephen and by others as episodes in the life of Saint Vigilius, a fourth-century bishop and martyr. The first scene (figure 22), all agree, is of an ordination rite. The artist has chosen to dress the central grouping at the altar not in classical attire, as biblical characters usually are, but in liturgical vestments. One haloed figure, bending toward the altar as hands are laid on him, is dressed in a white dalmatic with red double-lined *clavi* and a bright red chasuble, with two bands of white over his shoulders and chest that should be a stole. Another haloed figure stands just behind, his right hand stretched out in blessing toward the ordinand's head and an open book in his left: he wears a white dalmatic and a bluish-gray chasuble with one white band of what presumably is a stole over his right shoulder. A deacon in a yellowish-tan dalmatic

21. Walter Berschin and Alfons Zettler, *Egino von Verona* (Stuttgart, 1995), 1–38; Ronald G. Witt, *The Two Latin Cultures and the Foundation of Renaissance Humanism in Medieval Italy* (Cambridge, 2012), 41–44; for Egino's prologue, Réginald Grégoire, *Homéliaires liturgiques médiévaux: Analyse de manuscrits* (Spoleto, 1980), 191–92.

22. Noemi Gabrielli, "Le miniature delle omelie di San Gregorio," in *Arte del primo millennio: Atti del II convegno per lo studio dell'arte dell'alto medio evo tenuto presso l'Università di Pavia nel settembre 1950*, ed. Edoardo Arslan (Turin, 1951), 301–2; Fabrizio Crivello, *Le 'Omelie sui Vangeli' di Gregorio Magno a Vercelli: Le miniature del ms. CXLVIII/8 della Biblioteca Capitolare* (Florence, 2005), 63–68, plates I–III.

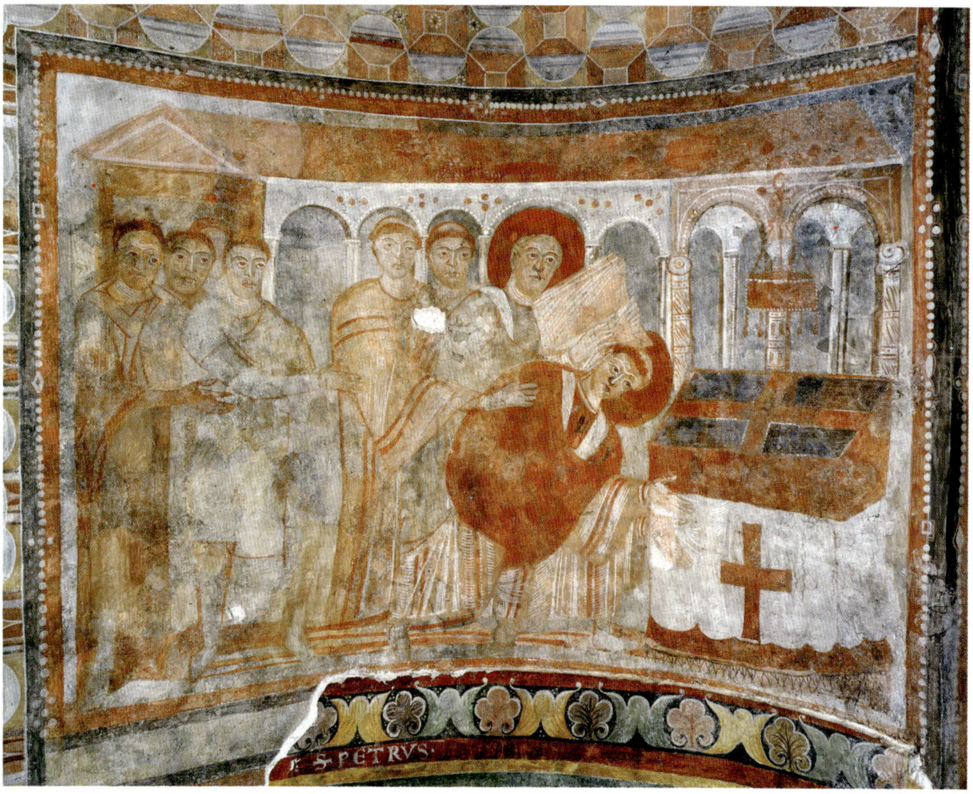

FIGURE 22. The ordination of Saint Stephen or Saint Vigilius, east wall, south apse, c. 800–825, St. Johann, Müstair. © Stiftung Pro Kloster St. Johann in Müstair & © Michael Wolf, Leipzig.

with red double-lined *clavi* also extends his right hand, while another tonsured figure, whose body is not represented, looks on. The attire of both saints is unornamented, but the colored dalmatic in this scene is a harbinger of changes to come.[23]

The next scene (figure 23), however, shows a haloed figure in very different attire: a bright-red tunic covered with the medallions used to represent the most precious woven silks. Half the scene is missing, but what remains depicts the saint enthroned,

23. Jürg Goll, Matthias Exner, and Susanne Hirsch, *Müstair: Die mittelalterlichen Wandbilder in der Klosterkirche* (Munich, 2007), 103–5, 208. These art historians maintain a long-standing identification of the subject as Saint Stephen. Others, including Marèse Sennhauser-Girard and Kirsten Ataoguz, argue more persuasively for the locally venerated martyr-bishop Vigilius. Both sides have used the liturgical attire as evidence, but I do not think it can be decided on this basis. While it is true that Stephen is usually depicted in the diaconal dalmatic, Matthias Exner has rightly pointed out that some early medieval ordination rites have the deacon at his ordination garbed in chasuble and dalmatic. A fragmentary inscription with the words *sanctus* and *episcopus* seems to me more probative, as well as the fact that neither scene has any precedent in the iconography of Stephen. I thank Kirsten Ataoguz for sharing her thoughts on the issue, and her dissertation, with me: Jenny Kirsten Ataoguz, "The Apostolic Commissioning of the Monks of Saint John in Müstair, Switzerland: Painting and Preaching in a Churraetian Monastery" (Ph.D. diss., Harvard University, 2007), 108–15.

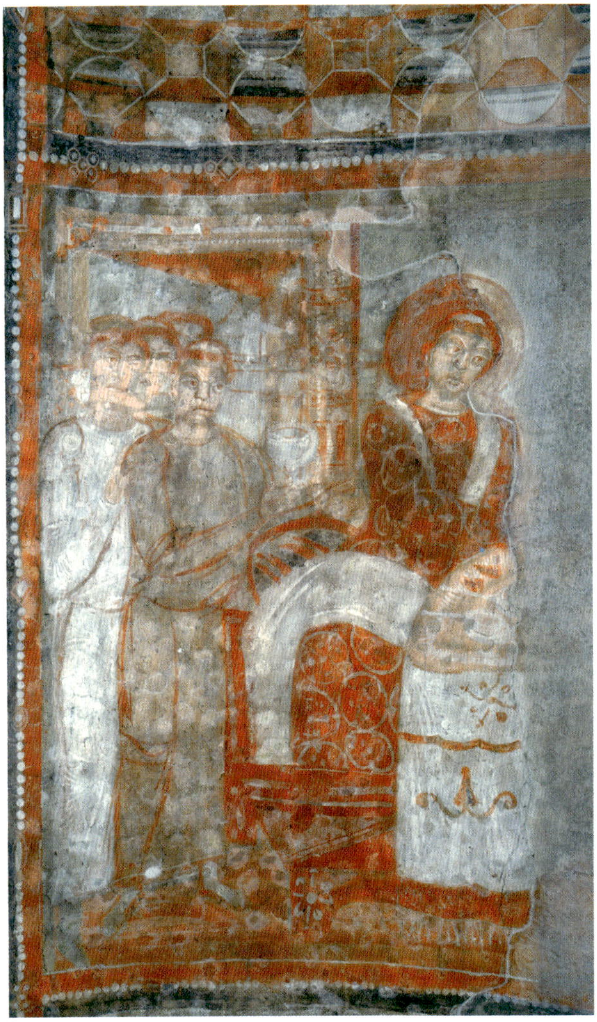

Figure 23. "Liturgical meal," east wall, south apse, c. 800–825, St. Johann, Müstair. © Stiftung Pro Kloster St. Johann in Müstair & © Michael Wolf, Leipzig.

leaning toward a table to his left. A white cloth lies over his lap, while a tonsured figure on the saint's right hands him a cup. Other figures enter through an open door. Those identifying this as a scene in the life of Saint Stephen label it a "liturgical meal": Might it be a widow's banquet? Acts 6:1–6 states that Stephen and six others were ordained in order to relieve the apostles of the responsibility of distributing food, and it was the feeding of widows that had raised the issue.[24] If the figure is Stephen, perhaps he is depicted in rich garb to portray him as a bounteous provider for poor widows? Citing a passage in one version of the life of Saint Vigilius that describes him founding a

24. Goll, Exner, and Hirsch, *Müstair*, 104, 209. We know from Gregory of Tours (*Historiae* 2:17) that an earlier cycle on Stephen's life decorated the church built at Clermont-Ferrand in the fifth century by the widow of Bishop Namatius, so it seems reasonable that the feeding of widows would be among the saint's virtues represented: Gregory of Tours, *Histoire des Francs livres I–VI*, ed. Henri Ormont (Paris, 1886), 51.

sanctuary for the poor and infirm next to his church, Kirsten Ataoguz has suggested that this scene may instead depict the holy bishop's ministry there. Perhaps his episcopal charity is represented as following Christ's injunction in Luke 14:15 to invite the poor, the maimed, the lame, and the blind when a feast is made. The depiction of the saint as patron, the maker of the feast, may explain his silk attire.

These three earliest examples of ornate clerical attire—Augustine in the Egino Codex, the donor portrait in the Vercelli homilies, and the ambiguous Müstair fragment—may use the depiction of precious materials to connote patronage. I have devoted some time to them here because these unrepresentative depictions contain vital clues to a massive change to come. We'll return to them. But the key point is that they constitute a minority in what survives: the norm evident in the limited evidence before the mid-ninth century is for clerics to be depicted clothed as plainly as their late antique forebearers. A letter of Alcuin to Æthelhard, archbishop of Canterbury, in 801 illumines these representational norms. The archbishop appears to have been planning a visit to Charlemagne's court. "If you come to my lord king," wrote Alcuin, "warn your companions, especially the clerics, to respectfully attend to every aspect of religious observance in clothing and in ecclesiastical discipline so that wherever you go you set a good example. Do not let them wear gold or silk clothing in the king's presence; let them go forth in humble attire following the custom of servants of God." Alcuin, originally from York, indicates here that Anglo-Saxon clerics were already accustomed to wearing gold and silk—a precious cultural observation to which we will return below. But for now note that Charlemagne did not tolerate such clerical attire at his court. Similar attitudes are attributed to his son and successor, Louis the Pious, by the anonymous biographer usually called the Astronomer. After praising Louis's efforts to ensure that the "state might shine forth more brilliantly in holy teaching and practice," the Astronomer reports that bishops and clerics abandoned "belts outfitted with golden bindings and jeweled daggers, refined clothing, and ankles decked out with spurs" because the emperor "considered it to be quite monstrous if someone deputed to the ecclesiastical troop [*familia*] should aspire to the ornaments of worldly glory."[25]

New Attitudes, c. 850–1050

The unadorned ecclesiastical attire demanded by Charlemagne and Louis the Pious, and the iconoclastic leanings of the Carolingian court, probably account for the few visual depictions of such garb before the mid-ninth century. Their successors seem not to have fostered similar restraint. Highly ornamented ecclesiastical apparel figures prominently in late Carolingian miniatures.

25. I thank Mayke de Jong for both these citations: *MGH Epp.* 2:375 (letter 230); *MGH SSRG* 64:378 (chap. 27), and Thomas F.X. Noble, *Charlemagne and Louis the Pious* (University Park, Penn., 2009), 255–56. *Familia* can also mean household, here surely the clergy serving the court.

The most spectacular of these is the presentation miniature in the Vivian Bible (BnF MS Lat. 1, fol. 423) (figure 24). The manuscript was created at Saint Martin of Tours and presented by the monks and their lay abbot Vivian to Charles the Bald in 845 when the king visited to confirm the monastery's privileges. Seventeen figures are depicted; none is haloed. The king's throne does float on a bank of clouds that also supports four royal attendants. Eleven tonsured figures, all in liturgical attire, stand on the ground below in a semicircle: three of these on the left proffer the Bible while the others look on and gesture. All the full-length figures wear bluish albs and white dalmatics with fringed red *clavi* and, on the seven frontally depicted ecclesiastics, the ends of gold stoles with red fringe extend below their dalmatics. Six hold maniples, some purple and others white and gold. The chasubles present a riot of colors: pink, shades of lavender, warm ocher, bright red, and a deeper garnet. Five are flecked with designs to indicate that they are made of patterned silks, and several have gold or silver bands trimming their hems, necklines, and front.[26]

In exactly the same period, this same scriptorium produced the earliest depiction of the clerical orders (figure 25). The full-page painting opens the manuscript (Autun, Bibliothèque municipale MS Lat. 19bis, 1v) and prefaces the text of the ordination rites in this sacramentary dedicated to Raganaldus, abbot of Marmoutier in 845. The artist divided the page, depicting a bishop, priest, and deacon as the "major orders" in the upper register and a doorkeeper, lector, subdeacon, exorcist, and acolyte (each holding a symbol of their office) as the "minor orders" in the lower register.[27] Each of the figures representing the minor orders is labeled, while an inscription in golden capitals across the top of the upper register proclaims that "it is the bishop's privilege to confer the ecclesiastical *honores per ordinem*, and that those who receive them must serve virtuously."[28] Although the figures are clearly representative types rather than individuals, they are all haloed—a strong visual assertion of a sacred status imparted in ordination—and each grouping is hierarchically arranged. Four of the figures wear vestments entirely of gold:

26. Marie-Pierre Laffitte and Charlotte Denoël, eds., *Trèsors carolingiens: Livres manuscrits de Charlemagne à Charles le Chauve* (Paris, 2007), 84, 103–5; Wilhelm Köhler, *Die karolingischen Miniaturen: Im Auftrage des Deutschen Vereins für Kunstwissenschaft*, 7 vols. (Berlin, 1930–1960), 1:396–401; Herbert L. Kessler, "A Lay Abbot as Patron: Count Vivian and the First Bible of Charles the Bald," in *Committenti e produzione artistico-letteraria nell'alto medioevo occidentale*, Settimane di studio del Centro italiano di studi sull'alto medioevo 39 (Spoleto, 1992), 647–75; Paul Edward Dutton and Herbert L. Kessler, *The Poetry and Paintings of the First Bible of Charles the Bald* (Ann Arbor, 1997), 71–87. Kessler shows how ecclesiastical resistance to the appointment of lay abbots is manifest in the muted depiction of Vivian (the lay figure on the right) in contrast to the four figures just below him, praised in the poem as the virtuous "leaders" (identified as Tesmundus, Sigwald, Aregarius, and the poet).

27. The doorkeeper holds keys, the acolyte a candlestick, the lector and the exorcist books, and the subdeacon a chalice and a pitcher.

28. Roger E. Reynolds, "The Portrait of the Ecclesiastical Officers in the *Raganaldus Sacramentary* and Its Liturgico-Canonical Significance," *Speculum* 46 (1971): 434. Reynolds provides the most detailed description of the image. The text of this important sacramentary has been published both in CC (159B), Odilo Heiming, ed., *Liber sacramentorum augustodunensis* (Turnhout, 1984) and by Joseph Décéaux, *Le sacramentaire de Marmoutier (Autun 19 bis) dans l'histoire des sacramentaires carolingiens du IXe siècle* (Vatican City, 1985).

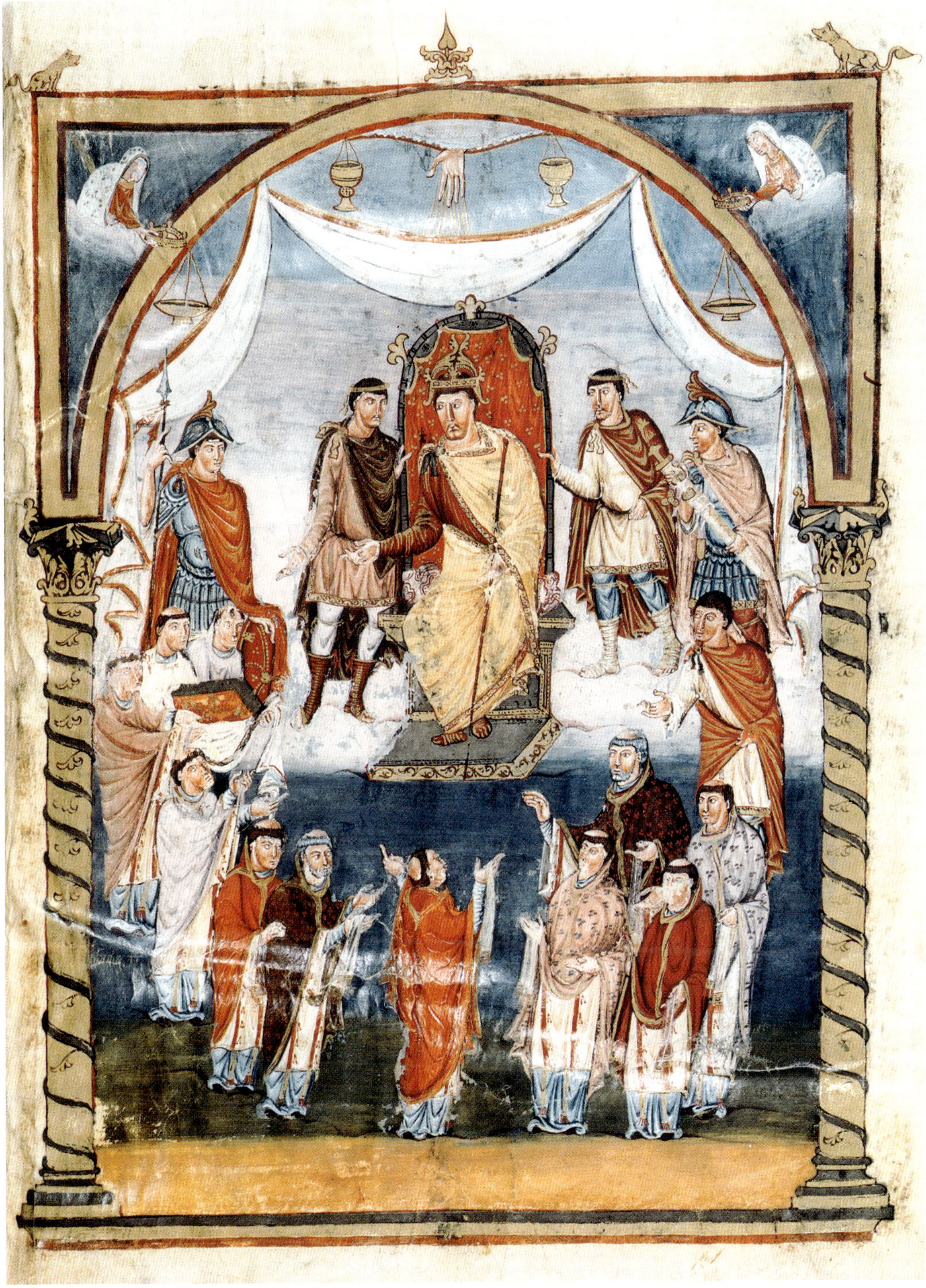

Figure 24. Dedication page, Vivian Bible, c. 845, Bibliothèque nationale de France MS Lat. 1, 423, Paris. © DeA Picture Library / Art Resource, NY.

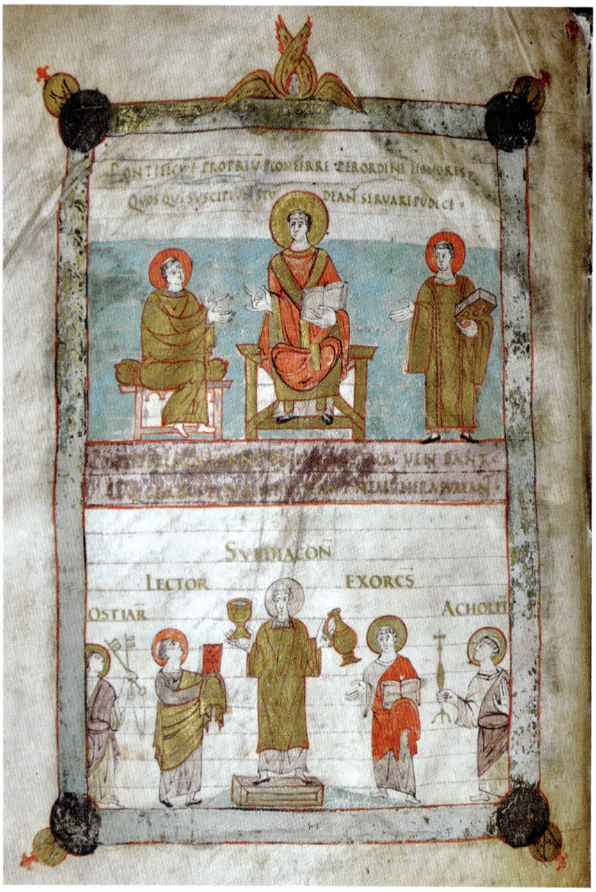

FIGURE 25. Raganaldus Sacramentary, c.845, Bibliothèque Municipale MS 19bis, 1v, Autun. Photo courtesy of the Bibliothèque d'Autun.

the priest, deacon, subdeacon, and lector. The bishop wears a vermillion chasuble at the apex of the image, balanced in the array below by red and pink vestments.[29]

Tours was not the only scriptorium depicting clerics in luxurious vestments: examples survive from the "court school" of Charles the Bald and from Saint Gall. Folio 2v of the Metz Sacramentary (Paris, BnF Lat. 1141), for example, presents three standing figures, all nimbed, with the hand of God descending from the clouds to crown the central figure. Dressed in purple boots, crimson stockings, a short patterned silk tunic, and a red and gold mantle, this figure is recognized as Charles the Bald being crowned king of Lotharingia in 869. The two bishops flanking him wear light-blue albs and white dalmatics with fringed red *clavi*. The ends of their golden stoles peak out from below the dalmatics and one is further ornamented with white, pearl-like dots. Both hold maniples ornamented

29. The garment worn over the albs of the doorkeeper, lector, exorcist, and acolyte has perplexed historians of liturgical attire. It could be a depiction of the "*planeta plicata*," a mode of wearing the chasuble in which it is folded and draped over the left shoulder during certain liturgical acts, or a "sindon" attested once as something in which acolytes were wrapped (*involuti*) as they carried liturgical vessels: Braun, *DLG*, 167–68.

with gold, and visible just below them are the gold-decorated ends of cinctures. Their chasubles—one lavender, the other purple—have golden hems and drapery lines, while golden bands (or golden pallia) decorate the front.[30] The Psalter of Charles the Bald (Paris, BnF Lat. 1152, 4r) depicts Saint Jerome clothed in a dark-purple chasuble with drapery lines of gold, an alb with a gold-ornamented hem, and a reddish-purple patterned silk dalmatic with gold stripes and golden rosettes.[31] Another miniature of Jerome from the second half of the ninth century—this one in the Golden Psalter of Saint Gall (St. Gall, Stiftsbibliothek, Cod. Sang. 22, p. 14)—presents the saint in white and gold vestments: the alb has gold ornamented cuffs, and the maniple, stole, and shoes are purple and gold.[32]

The very few fragments of wall painting that survive from this era do not contain any images of clerics, but other evidence supports dating the origins of a new acceptance of ornate liturgical attire in the second half of the ninth century. Inventories of church treasuries reveal a number of interesting patterns. First, precious vestments appear earliest at the great abbeys. Charlemagne's friend Angilbert, abbot of Saint-Riquier, endowed this monastery with gold-ornamented albs and stoles, and silk dalmatics and chasubles as early as 790.[33] Silk and gold vestments also turn up around 800 at the monastery of Saint Bavo in Ghent and in 811 at Staffelsee Abbey in Bavaria. Considered in light of Alcuin's warning to Æthelhard and the Astronomer's comments on Louis the Pious, this evidence suggests that it was the wearing of ornate attire in the emperor's presence, at court, that was objectionable. Wearing it within a monastery to beseech God on behalf of king and kingdom appears to have been more palatable, at least to lay elites. During the reign of Charles the Bald, silk vestments begin appearing in the inventories of cathedrals, chapels, and parishes. Circa 830–840, half of the chasubles belonging to the Cathedral of Würzburg were made of silk as well as twelve maniples. A chapel near Bonn had a green silk chasuble in 886, and in 899 the parish church in Mauern near Freising inventoried three chasubles: one of linen, one of wool, and one of silk.[34] A canon issued by Bishop Riculf of Soissons at a diocesan synod he held in 889 demonstrates more than mere toleration: it actually enjoined his clergy to wear silk. "Strive to have your ecclesiastical

30. *Sakramentar von Metz. Fragment. Ms. Lat. 1141, Bibliothèque nationale, Paris. Vollst. Faks.-Ausg.* (Graz, 1972), 2v; also Laffitte and Denoël, *Trèsors carolingiens*, 26 (color photo); Köhler, *Die Karolingischen Miniaturen*, 5 (ed. Florentine Mütherich), 9–10, 168. The manuscripts attributed to the "court school" were actually created in different centers due to the peripatetic nature of Charles's court: Rosamond McKitterick, "The Palace School of Charles the Bald," in *Charles the Bald. Court and Kingdom*, ed. Margaret T. Gibson and Janet L. Nelson (Oxford, 1981; repr., Adershot, 1990), 326–38. Corbie and Saint Denis have been suggested as the scriptoria responsible for this unfinished sacramentary, which was preserved in the cathedral treasury of Metz until the seventeenth century.

31. Amédée Boinet, *La miniature carolingienne, ses origins, son développement: Planches* (Paris, 1918), pl. 94b; Laffitte and Denoël, *Trèsors carolingiens*, 108–12; Köhler, *Die Karolingischen Miniaturen*, 5 (ed. Florentine Mütherich), 9–10, 138.

32. CESG, St. Gallen, Stiftsbibliothek, Cod. Sang. 22, 14.

33. *MGH SS* 15.1:177.

34. *Schatzverzeichnisse*, 36–38, 90–91, 109, 38–39, 58–59. Inventories survive from parishes from the late eighth century, so the appearance of ornate vestments at cathedrals and parishes is not an artifact of the mere diffusion of the practice of compiling inventories.

vestments worthily and properly prepared," the bishop commanded, specifying that each church have "a silk chasuble in which to celebrate Mass."[35] Across the tenth century, the number of ornate vestments multiplies and the language of description intensifies. In 903 the bishop of Passau acquired "a purple cope decorated with gold, a purple chasuble made of costly silk, two stoles with a maniple ornamented with gold and gems."[36]

Increasing trade in the Carolingian world may have made silk more available,[37] but what made it acceptable for the clergy to wear such luxurious garb? Two developments explain these changing attitudes and the patterns in the visual evidence. First, as described in chapter 2, Carolingian liturgists from the 820s directly related contemporary clerical vestments to those of Aaron and his sons described in Exodus 28, which were made of "gold and violet and purple and scarlet twice dyed, and fine twisted linen, embroidered with diverse colors." Essentially, they provided a powerful intellectual and spiritual rationale for their own vestments to be equally ornate: they were the priesthood of the new covenant superseding that of the old. As the liturgical commentaries written by Amalarius of Metz and Hrabanus Maurus circulated and were deployed by reformers to educate the clergy, the idea spread that the virtue of Christian clerics was put on and displayed through colorful vestments ornamented in gold.[38]

Parallel to this development was another that reinforced and extended it. As Steffen Patzold has compellingly argued, a new and much more powerful model of the episcopal office emerged in the reform councils of the 820s culminating in the Synod of Paris in 829. No longer just royal servants, bishops came to be defined as the king's collaborators in exercising *ministerium*, care of the salvation of the people committed to them. All sorts of texts increasingly speak of episcopal *auctoritas* across the ninth century. If bishops were not just servants and emissaries to carry out the king's will but collaborators in his governance of the empire, shouldn't they share in sartorial splendor? As the empire fractured and royal power weakened, moreover, bishops even more assertively exercised and formulated their authority. Hincmar archbishop of Reims in 881 went so far as to abandon the sense of complementary royal and episcopal roles in exercising *ministerium:* he argued for the superiority of bishops.[39]

Both these developments yielded new attitudes toward ornate vestments. Concerns about maintaining status hierarchies are still evident. Even when the clergy surrounding Charles the Bald are dressed in gold and silks, the king's superior secular and sacred

35. See chapter 1, above.

36. "Totum apparatum suum, id est sicut ipse paratus ad missam solitus fuerat stare, pluviale purpureum auro paratum, casulam purpuream siricam de sirico precioso, stolas II cum anfanone auro et gemmis paratum": *Schatzverzeichnisse*, 120.

37. E. Sabbe, "L'importation des tissus orientaux en Europe occidentale au haut moyen age (IXe et Xe siècles)," *Revue belge de philologie et d'histoire* 14 (1935): 811–48.

38. On the diffusion of copies of Hrabanus Maurus's *De institutione* to sees all over the empire, see Zimpel's introduction: *De institutione*, 95–112, 120–23, 160–230. The sections on clerical attire were particularly excerpted.

39. Steffen Patzold, *Episcopus: Wissen über Bischöfe im Frankenreich des späten 8. bis frühen 10. Jahrhunderts* (Ostfildern, 2008), 46–184, 509–44.

status is visually pronounced: dressed in imperial regalia, he is haloed, crowned by the hand of God, and enthroned among the clouds. The new assimilation of clerics to the sons of Aaron surely did not erase all anxiety about them assuming finery originally thought proper only for elites. The diverse social origins of clerics were an issue, and this is evident in chapter 28 of the Astronomer's life of Louis the Pious. Just before the section lauding Louis for insisting that clerics not wear "the ornaments of worldly glory," another reveals that the king also thought that they should not be of servile status. If it happened that "any of servile status should, on account of knowledge and probity, be elevated to the ministry of the altar, they should first be manumitted by their own masters."[40] The Astronomer may here be responding to another biographer of Louis, Thegan, who contended that Bishop Ebbo of Reims "had descended from generations of slaves" and lamented "the awful custom of making the highest bishops out of the lowest servants."[41] But clothing was very much linked to status, and references to clerical backgrounds emerge in other Carolingian texts.[42] The tension between modest social origins and rich attire may be one reason the earliest depictions of ornate vestments underscore acts of patronage since such roles—commissioning manuscripts, presiding over feasts—presumed the wealth of elites. Indeed, one suspects that clerics from elite families, especially those for whom the choice of an ecclesiastical career was not entirely their own, were among the most interested in more ornate garb.

The greater acceptance of ornate liturgical attire that emerged in the late Carolingian Empire passed directly to the Ottonians, who brought it to new heights. They also developed more methodically the ideas about the episcopal role in governance that Patzold underscored.[43] Although the artist of the Gero Codex (Darmstadt, Universitäts- und Landesbibliothek, Hs. 1948), working at Reichenau before 969, was clearly drawing on models from Charlemagne's court school preserved at nearby Lorsch, he still depicted the priest commissioning the manuscript in rich vestments (fol. 6v). Gero appears offering the codex to Saint Peter wearing a gold-embellished chasuble, with a matching golden stole and a highly ornamented gold maniple. Even the end of his cincture, often not depicted at all, stands out in red and gold.[44] The most

40. See note 25 above.

41. *MGH SSRG* 64:204, 232 (chap. 20, 44); Noble, *Charlemagne and Louis*, 204, 211.

42. While Notker wrote approvingly of Charlemagne promising studious boys "of the middling and lower sort" bishoprics, he censured impudent bishops who wore precious silks. *MGH SSRG* n.s. 12:4, 22 (1.3, 20); Noble, *Charlemagne and Louis*, 61, 74.

43. Timothy Reuter offered important nuance to the idea of the *Reichskirche* as a "system," but extensive involvement of the episcopate in Ottonian rule is undeniable. Timothy Reuter, "The 'Imperial Church System' of the Ottonian and Salian Rulers: A Reconsideration," *Journal of Ecclesiastical History* 33 (1982): 347–74; Gerd Althoff, *Otto III*, trans. Phyllis G. Jestice (University Park, Penn., 2003), 20–22.

44. Matthias Puhle, ed., *Otto der Grosse: Magdeburg und Europa* (Mainz, 2001), 232–37 (color photo, 234); Henry Mayr-Harting, *Ottonian Book Illumination: An Historical Study* (London, 1991), 25–26. The Cologne school also supplies numerous examples: Peter Bloch and Hermann Schnitzler, *Die ottonische Kölner Malerschule*, 2 vols. (Düsseldorf, 1967–1970), 1:13, pl. 2 (Evergerus Lectionary); 32, pl. V (Ambrosiana C.53 sup); 39, pl. 97 (St. Gereon Sacramentary), 46–47, pl. 119 (Hitda Codex); 54, pl. XI (Giessen Universitätsbibliothek 660); 61, pl. 219 (Gundold Gospel Book).

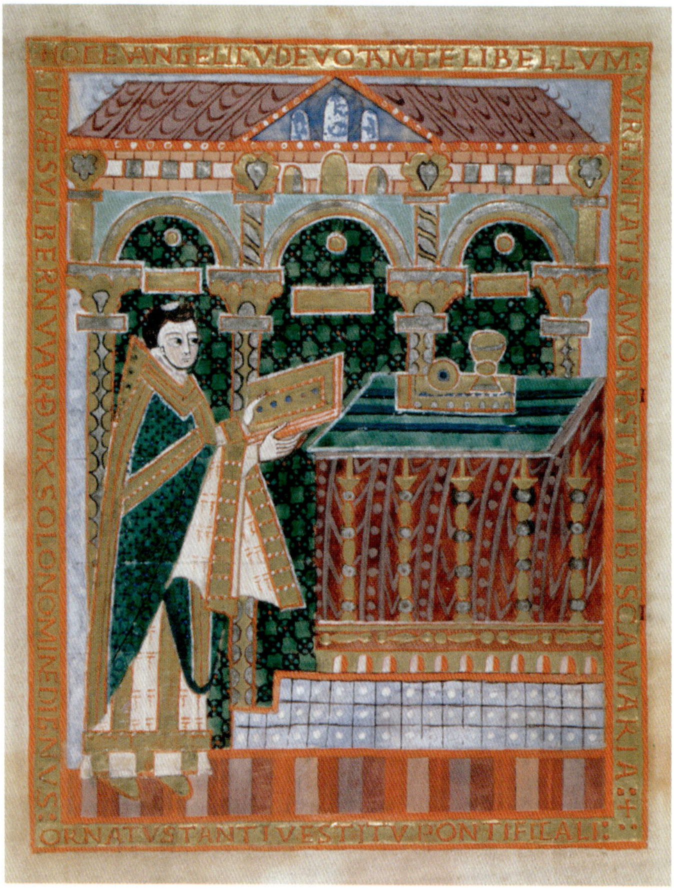

Figure 26. Dedication page, Gospel Book of Bishop Berward of Hildesheim, c. 1015, Domschatz DS 18, 16v, Hildesheim. © Bildarchiv Foto Marburg / Dom-Museum Hildesheim / Art Resource, NY.

extreme example of the rich style, however, is the donor portrait of Bernward bishop of Hildesheim in the Gospel book he commissioned for his see c. 1015 (Hildesheim, Domschatz 18, 16v) (figure 26). Depicted offering his book at an altar against an architectural backdrop, the bishop's youthful wide-eyed face seems dwarfed by the heft of his garments. Only his alb is without ornament. His shoes are entirely of gold, and the ends of his stole are solid gold finished with red fringe. A broad band of gold hems his dalmatic, two equally wide *clavi* in gold race down its front, and its long sleeves are also edged with bands of gold decorated with pearl-like dots. Similar gold bands ornament the back, front, and neckline of his chasuble, with silver disks at the back neckline similar to those adorning the binding of the book he proffers. The artist has meticulously painted repeat patterns on the fabrics to indicate woven silks: the green chasuble has tiny blue crosses on the body and blue rosettes on the outer edge, while the white dalmatic is flecked with red lines.[45]

45. Ulrich Knapp, *Buch und Bild im Mittelalter* (Hildesheim, 1999), 6; Michael Brandt, *Das kostbare Evangeliar des heiligen Bernward* (Munich, 1993), 27–30, pl. 5. Other sumptuous examples: the Egbert Psalter, especially fol. 17r, and also the Egbert Codex, 2r (both in Franz J. Ronig, ed., *Egbert Erzbischof von*

One might discount this opulent appearance as simply a by-product of exuberant illumination, but even in manuscript paintings not adorned with gold or silver leaf, artists took care to depict ornament on ecclesiastical vestments. Lines with circles between them or lines of dots suggest woven bands on hems, while clusters of white dots or cross-hatching mimic patterned fabrics.[46] This visual shorthand for woven and embroidered ornament was even deployed on more resistant surfaces. An ivory plaque (figure 27) of Bishop Sigebert of Minden (1022–1036) depicts a decorative hem band on his dalmatic, ornament on his shoes, various patterns on his maniple, and the intricate form of his rationale. Even the two crouching clerics at his feet have ornamental bands carved at the neck, sleeves, and hem of their tunics.[47]

This ivory carving of Bishop Sigebert and another painted version reflect the connection between ornate ecclesiastical garb and the liturgical commentary tradition discussed in chapter 2. Both this ivory plaque and a dedication portrait once graced the prayer book (*Liber precum*) that Sigebert compiled for himself. They depict the bishop wearing a rationale. This version of the high priest's "breastplate of judgment" appears to have little in common with the description in Exodus 28, although it was probably embroidered. The vesting prayers contained in this manuscript are the first set to incorporate this new episcopal ornament. "Give me your truth, oh Lord," he was to pray while donning it, "to maintain it steadfastly and worthily open the doctrine of truth to your people."[48] A further visual development of this connection may be found in the Uta Codex (Munich, Bayerische Staatsbibliothek, Clm. 13601), a Gospel lectionary produced around 1025 in Regensburg. Folio 4r (figure 28) depicts Saint Erhard celebrating Mass amid a set of complex subscenes and inscriptions. In addition to gold-embellished vestments, Erhard wears an immense gold rationale. As Adam S. Cohen has pointed out, its two semicircles labeled *veritas* and *doctrina* follow the instruction in

Trier 977–993: Gedenkschrift der Diözese Trier zum 1000. Todestag, 2 vols. [Trier, 1993], 1:20, 23–24, 59, 84); the Gospel Book of Otto III, 24r and the Sacramentary of Henry II, 11r (in Michael Brandt and Anne Eggebrecht, *Bernward von Hildesheim und das Zeitalter der Ottonen: Katalog der Ausstellung Hildesheim 1993*, 2 vols. [Hildesheim, 1993], 1:55, 59); and Munich, Clm. 14272, 1r (Adam S. Cohen, *The Uta Codex: Art, Philosophy, and Reform in Eleventh-Century Germany* [University Park, Penn., 2000], 42–43 and pl. 16).

46. Two Milanese Psalters provide an excellent example of how an artist copying an image that used gold to indicate rich ornament substituted patterns and colors when precious metals were not available: Angelo Paredi, "Nota storica sui Salteri milanesi del IX secolo," in *Miniature altomedievali lombarde* (Milan, 1978), plates 3 and 29. Good tenth-century examples are the frontispiece miniature in Saint Gall, Stiftsbibliothek 86 (p. 6), the portrait of Bishop Braulio of Saragossa and Saint Gregory the Great in Einsiedeln, Stiftsbibliothek, 167 (p. 1) and 156 (1v): CESG; Puhle, *Otto der Grosse*, 265–70. A pen-and-ink drawing of Pope Sylvester celebrating Mass in the mid-eleventh-century Prüm Pericope (Manchester, John Rylands University Library, Lat. 7, 130r/135r) covers the pontiff's chasuble and the clothes of his clerics in comma-like smudges: Montague Rhodes James, A *Descriptive Catalogue of the Manuscripts in the John Rylands Library at Manchester* (Manchester, 1921), pl. 13.

47. *Rhein und Maas: Kunst und Kultur, 800–1400*, 2 vols. (Cologne, 1972–1973) 1:183.

48. The dedication portrait is Berlin, Staatsbibliothek Preussischer Kultur-besitz, theol. lat.qu.3 frag. See Pierce, "Sacerdotal Spirituality," 17–34, 42–45, 112, 161; a color photo of the dedication painting may be found in Brandt and Eggebrecht, *Bernward von Hildesheim*, 99.

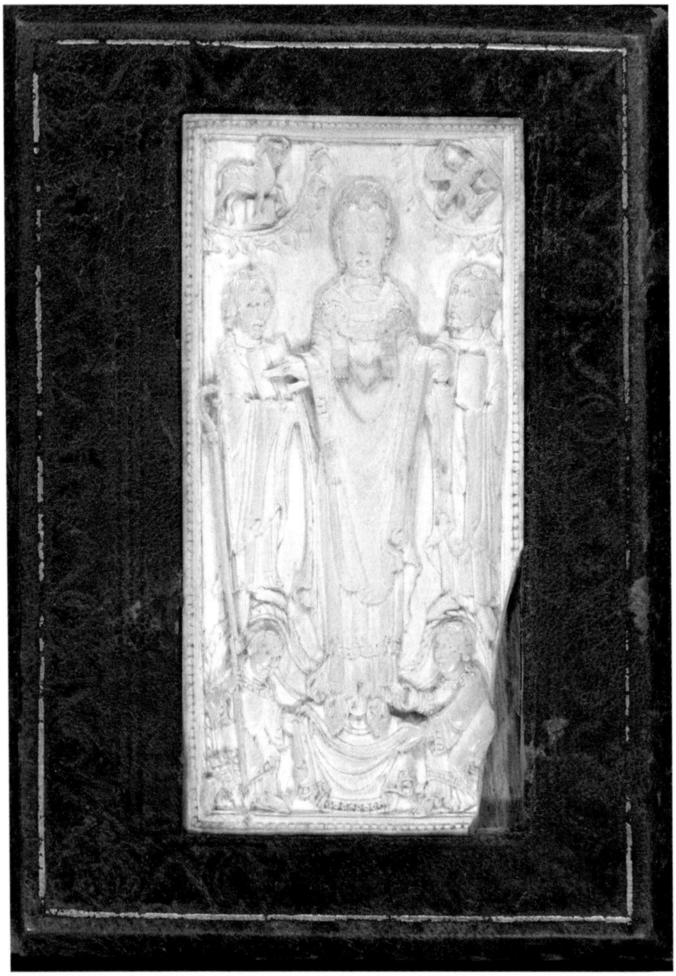

FIGURE 27. Ivory relief from the prayer book of Sigebert of Minden, 1022–1036, Inv. Ms.germ.qu 42, Staatsbibliothek, Berlin. bpk Berlin / Staatsbibliothek zu Berlin, Stiftung Preussischer Kulturbesitz / Ruth Schacht, Manuscript Division / Art Resource, NY.

Exodus 28:30, "You shall put on the rationale of judgment doctrine and truth." The bands proclaim the bishop's status (ΙΗΡΑΡΧΗΙΑ / "hierarchy" and *sacer principatus* / "holy supremacy") and posit his sacramental powers as a bridge from the old Mosaic law to the future of eternal life. Following the Exodus description more literally, the image crowns Erhard with a turban embellished with a gold triangle, the *lamina aurea* (Exod. 28:36–38).[49]

The Ottonians' relations with the Byzantine court, particularly through the marriage of princess Theophano to Otto II, may have furthered the development of this ornate liturgical attire. The gift exchanges leading up to the union and Theophano's dowry certainly brought more prestige silks into the western empire. The extraordinary purple eagle-silk chasuble believed to have belonged to Bishop Albuin of Brixen

49. Cohen, *Uta Codex*, 81–87 and color plate 5.

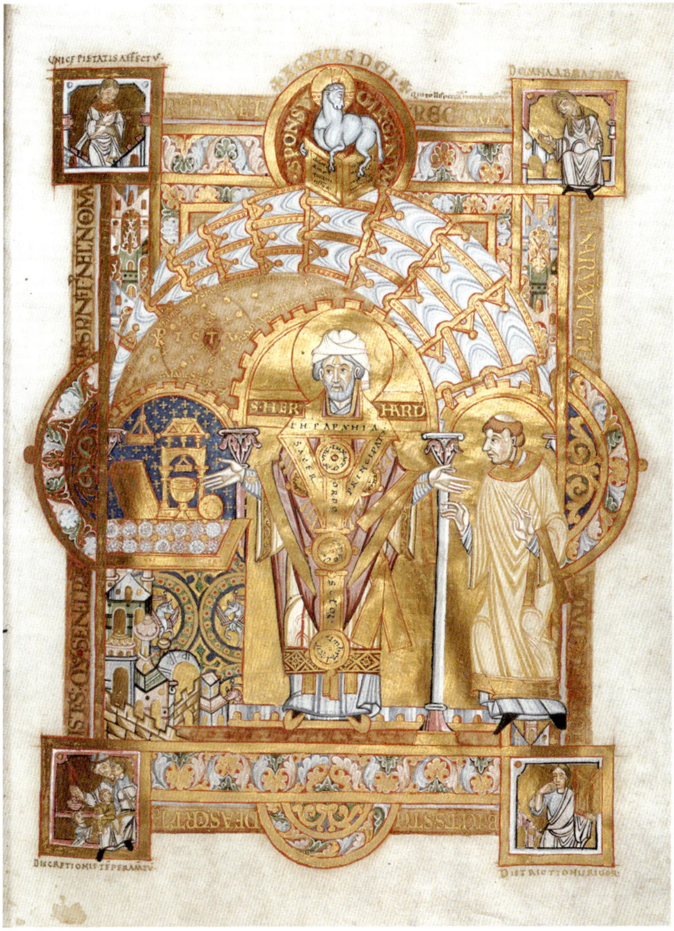

FIGURE 28. Saint Erhard celebrating Mass, Uta Codex, Regensburg, c. 1025, Bayerische Staatsbibliothek Clm 13601, 4r, Munich. Photo courtesy of Bayerische Staatsbibliothek Munich.

(975–1006), for example, was made from a Byzantine fabric that could only have come from an imperial workshop in Constantinople (figure 29). Its complex large-scale woven design of imperial eagles, the high quality of workmanship, and the use of the costliest murex dye to create the purple silk thread class it among the tightly controlled silks reserved for the court and often distributed as diplomatic gifts.[50] It seems reasonable to ask at this point whether more than just materials came from the East: Were Western clerics copying an ornate style of liturgical garb from Byzantium? The Carolingians, after all, also had contact with Constantinople.

50. Mechthild Flury-Lemberg, "Die Adlerkasel in Brixen, ein bedeutendes Zeugnis frühchristlicher Paramentik," in *Am Anfang war das Auge: Kunsthistorische Tagung anläßlich des 100 jährigen Bestehens des Diözesanmuseums Hofburg Brixen*, ed. Leo Andergassen, Veröffentlichungen der Hofburg Brixen 2 (Brixen, 2004), 298–309; Mechthild Flury-Lemberg and Gabriel Vial, "La chasuble aux aigles de Bressanone, un témoignage important de paramentique du christianism des premiers siècles," *Bulletin du CIETA* 82 (2005): 30–50.

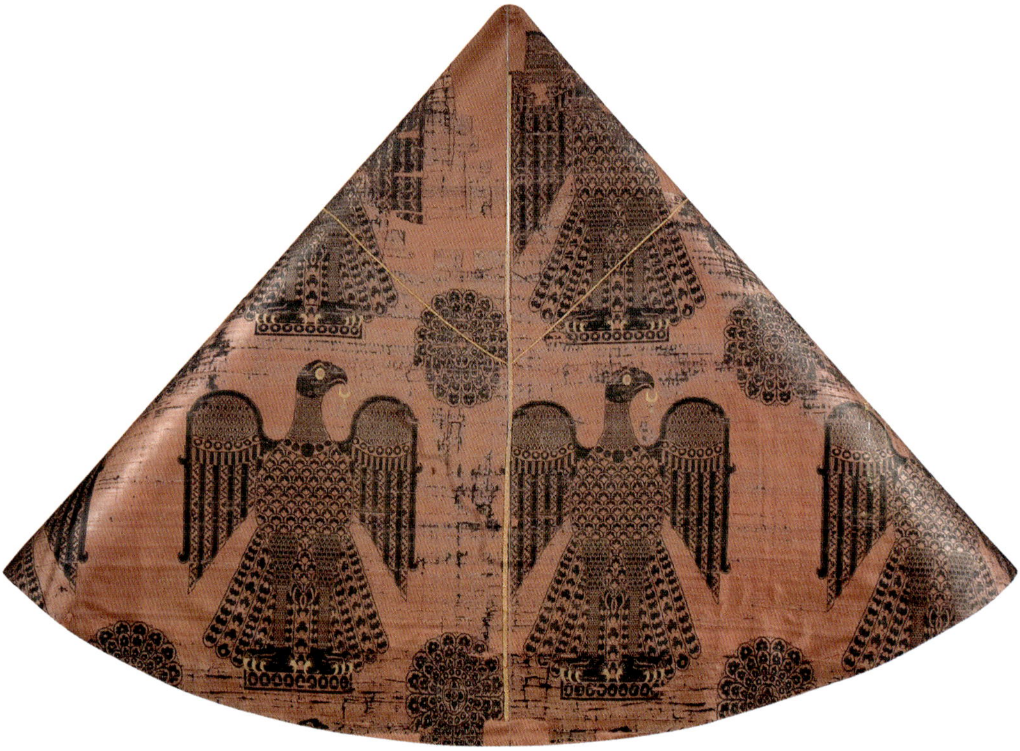

FIGURE 29. Eagle chasuble, c. 975–1006, Diözesanmuseum Hofburg, Brixen. Photo courtesy of Diocesan Museum Hofburg, Bressanone (Brixen), Italy.

The Sources of the New Style

Although the evidence is mixed and on many points too vexed to offer a definitive conclusion, I do not think Western clerics were copying Byzantine vestments. They admired, and went to lengths to obtain, Byzantine materials—chiefly high-quality silks, particularly those with complex woven designs. But it seems more likely that the ornate style of liturgical garb, with its extensive use of embroidery and woven ornamental bands, came from Anglo-Saxon sources and that its "barbarian" origins are one reason it appears in Italy only very late. Indeed, if Greek models were primary influences, one would expect to see the style first in Italy: there was a significant Greek colony in Rome, and Greek-rite monasteries were numerous and among the most richly endowed in the city. Although their numbers declined in Rome after the Carolingian conquest, in the early eleventh century Sant'Anastasio was still an entirely Greek-speaking community and Greek-rite churches remained numerous in southern Italy.[51]

The chief problem in assessing Byzantine influence is the difficulty in knowing what the Orthodox clergy were actually wearing between the late eighth century and the end of

51. Giulia Barone, "Chierici, monaci e frati," in *Roma medievale*, ed. André Vauchez (Rome, 2001), 191–92.

the twelfth. Whereas Western liturgical garments survive in ever-increasing numbers from the early tenth century—largely because of the Western cult of relics—no Byzantine vestments from before the late twelfth century have been preserved.[52] There are textile fragments that survive in Egypt—sometimes called Coptic, but more accurately late antique and early Islamic—but their partial nature and controversial dating offer no secure evidence. Most of the fragments are woven decorative bands or roundels, which may have been used on ecclesiastical garments but could just as plausibly have adorned secular attire. Even the fragments depicting biblical scenes cannot be assumed to have been fashioned for ecclesiastical garments.[53] The late fourth-century bishop Asterios of Amasia in Asia Minor famously complained of rich men and women wearing clothes decorated with Gospel stories, and the empress Theodora in the San Vitale mosaics is represented wearing a mantle hemmed with images of the magi.[54] Even fragments agreed to be remains of liturgical vestments are problematic. Five pieces of a linen band decorated with scenes from the life of Jesus unearthed at Achmim (Panopolis) in Upper Egypt at the end of the nineteenth century have been identified by several scholars as parts of an episcopal *omophorion* (equivalent to the Western pallium). The archaeologist who discovered it assigned a sixth-century date; comparable designs from a fragment in London suggest a date anywhere from the fifth to the eighth centuries; and most recently a date in the eleventh or twelfth century has been advanced on the basis of the intermingling of striped fabric and images.[55] It could, on the one hand, be an example of pre-iconoclastic liturgical attire or, on the other hand, one representing Egyptian Christian practice under Islamic rule four centuries after the empire lost this region. If the latter, is it representative of what Byzantine clerics wore?

If we take the earlier dating for this omophorion, it suggests that some bishops did wear ornamented vestments before the seventh-century and iconoclastic crises. The question then is whether they did after iconoclasm. The Second Council of Nicaea in 787, which restored the veneration of icons, specifically sanctioned "revered and holy images"—meaning those of Jesus, Mary, angels, and holy men—"in the holy churches of God, on sacred instruments and vestments, on walls and panels, in houses and by public

52. Warren T. Woodfin, "Liturgical Textiles," in *Byzantium: Faith and Power (1261–1557)*, ed. Helen C. Evans (New York, 2004), 297–303. Byzantine inventories are also late (1200–): Woodfin, *Embodied Icon*, 279–86.

53. Kurt Weitzmann, ed., *Age of Spirituality: Late Antique and Early Christian Art, Third to Seventh Century* (New York, 1979), 460–63, cat. 412–13, roundels with Joseph stories; *Byzantium: An Oecumenical Empire* (Athens, 2002), 284, cat. 149, St. Mark roundel, and 286–87, cat. 152, a tunic fragment with haloed figure; Massimo Capuani, *Christian Egypt: Coptic Art and Monuments through Two Millennia* (Collegeville, Minn., 2002), fig. 6 [unnumbered page], Jonah. There are several late antique-early Islamic tunics that survive from Egypt that could be dalmatics, but could just as easily be secular garb: Sabine Schrenk, *Textilien des Mittelmeerraumes aus spätantiker bis frühislamischer Zeit* (Riggisburg, 2004), 148–58.

54. Pauline Johnstone, *The Byzantine Tradition in Church Embroidery* (London, 1967), 8; Warren Woodfin, "Late Byzantine Liturgical Vestments and the Iconography of Sacerdotal Power" (Ph.D. diss., University of Illinois at Champagne-Urbana, 2002), 47–48.

55. Ludwig Wamser, ed., *Die Welt von Byzanz: Europas östliches Erbe; Glanz, Krisen und Fortleben einer tausendjahrigen Kultur* (Stuttgart, 2004), 134–35. I thank Lawrence Nees for calling this example to my attention.

ways."[56] Was figural ornament revived on liturgical vestments in response to this decree? Warren T. Woodfin directly confronted this question—analyzing all the extant textual, visual, and physical evidence—and concluded that "there was no such revival."[57] There seems to be, therefore, no proximate Byzantine precedent for the early tenth-century stole and maniple of Saint Cuthbert that opened this chapter.

Woodfin, however, concentrated specifically on figural embroidered ornament, and the Western style of ornate liturgical garb included other elements. When, for example, do depictions of Byzantine liturgical attire include gold ornament and patterns representing high-end silks and woven or embroidered adornments? Very few images, of course, survived the iconoclastic period (726–843), but those that do reveal the same representation of ecclesiastical attire as at Ravenna and Rome.[58] The depictions of vestments produced just after the restoration of images continue to represent them without ornament. Most significant is the evidence of the *Sacra parallela* (Paris, BnF MS Gr. 923), an early ninth-century florilegium: its derivative miniatures, based on earlier archetypes, constitute "epitomes of vast lost miniature cycles" from the iconoclastic and pre-iconoclastic periods. As it was created in the late classical style of manuscript illumination that used gold for all clothes as well as other features, the *Sacra parallela* cannot help date the use of gold to distinguish clerical garb, but its visual vocabulary for ornament (dots, gemlike geometrical shapes) is deployed only on images of kings and of liturgical objects (books) and structures (churches). The *omophoria* have only small crosses on them.[59]

At the end of the tenth century and in the eleventh, in mural paintings, mosaics, and manuscript illuminations, patterned decoration begins to appear on the ends of the *epitrachelion* (stole), on the cuffs of the *sticharion*, and on a cloth hung over the cincture called an *encheirion*. The early eleventh-century mosaics at the church of Hosios Lucas (Greece), both mosaics and paintings at Hagia Sophia in Kiev, and paintings at the Panagia ton Chalkeon in Thessaloniki and the church of the monastery of Eski Gümüs in Cappadocia all contain images of holy bishops with vestments adorned in this fashion.[60]

56. *Decrees*, 1:135–36; Woodfin, "Late Byzantine Liturgical Vestments," 55–56.

57. Woodfin, *Embodied Icon*, 35.

58. Christopher Walter, *Art and Ritual of the Byzantine Church* (London, 1982), 9–10; Wolfgang Fritz Volbach and Max Hirmer, *Early Christian Art* (New York, 1962), pls. 124–25, 127, 217.

59. Kurt Weitzmann, *The Miniatures of the Sacra Parallela Prisinus Graecus 923*, Studies in Manuscript Illumination 8 (Princeton, 1979), vii, 10, 14–15, 23–25, plates 125–37, 142–43, 151. A ninth-century manuscript of the homilies of Gregory of Nazianzus (Paris, BnF MS Gr. 510) that was illustrated between 880 and 883, for example, contains several images of priests in *sticharion* (a white undertunic equivalent to the alb), *phelonion* (chasuble), and *omophorion* (pallium): the only adornment is one or more crosses on the latter: Sirapie Der Nersessian, "The Illustrations of the Homilies of Gregory of Nazianzus Paris Gr. 510: A Study of the Connections between Text and Image," *Dumbarton Oaks Papers* 16 (1962): 196, [unpaginated] pls. 1, 3, 10, 16.

60. Ernst Diez and Otto Demus, *Byzantine Mosaics in Greece: Hosios Lucas and Daphni* (Cambridge, Mass., 1931), figs. 26–31; Hrihoriy Logvin, *Kiev's Hagia Sophia* (Kiev, 1971), pls. 69, 128, 144, 175, 187, 190, 203–4, 208, 211–13; Karoline Papadopoulos, *Die Wandmalereien des XI. Jahrhunderts in der Kirche Panagea ton Chalkeon in Thessaloniki* (Graz, 1966), figs. 6–7; Catherine Jolivet-Lévy, *Les églises byzantines de Cappadoce: Le programme iconographique de l'abside et de ses abords* (Paris, 1991), 278–81, plates 152–53.

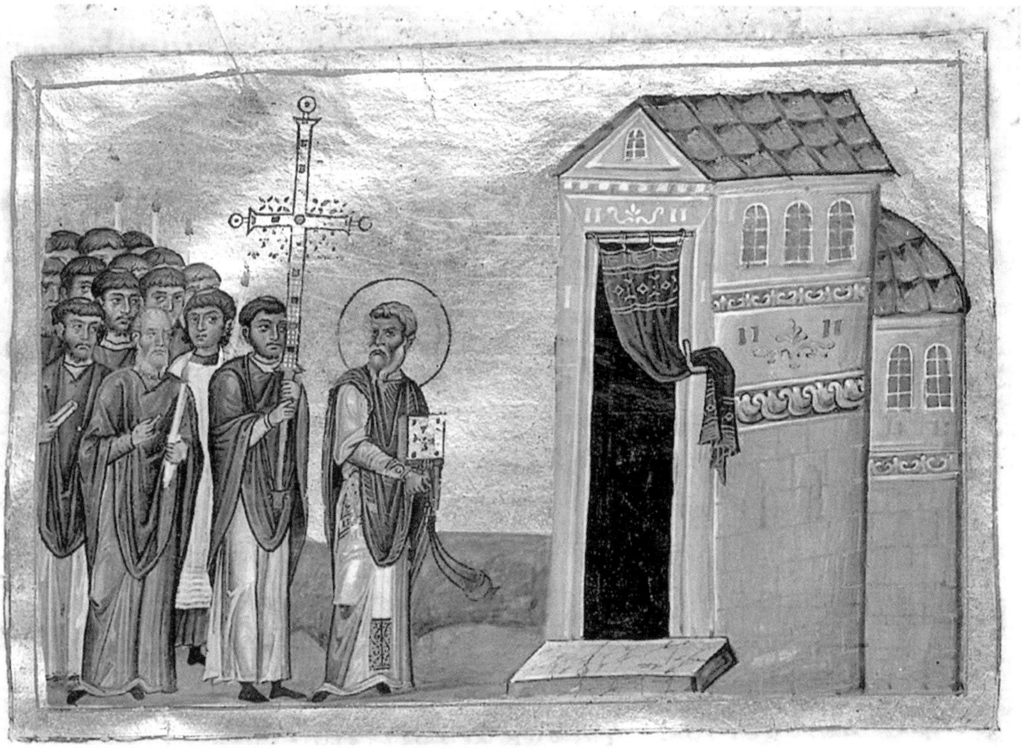

FIGURE 30. Menalogion of Basil II, c. 986, Vat. gr. 1613, p. 142, Biblioteca Apostolica Vaticana, Vatican City. Patterned decoration appears only on two items of the haloed figure's vestments: the end of the *epitrachelion* and the *encheirion* hanging from his cincture just below his right elbow. © 2012 by permission of the Biblioteca Apostolica Vaticana, with all rights reserved.

The most important manuscript evidence is the *Menologion* of Basil II (BAV Vat. gr. 1613), a collection of lives of the saints illustrated c. 986. The same types of ornamentation are abundantly attested in it (figure 30). Although only one of the seventy bishops depicted has any gold on his vestments (the crosses on the omophorion of Bishop Aristion of Alexandria, page 9)—despite the lavish use of gold throughout the manuscript—a depiction of Saint John Chrysostom in a Sinai manuscript of his homilies (Monastery of Hagia Ai Katerine, Cod. 364) dated 1042–1050 ornaments his cuffs, epitrachelion, and encheirion with gold leaf.[61] It is not until the late twelfth century, however, that Orthodox vestments are depicted as made of patterned silks.[62] In sum, whereas visual evidence for such ornament begins in the ninth century in the West, comparable visual evidence from the Byzantine Empire begins only in the late tenth century and does not really reach Carolingian

61. *El "Menalogio" de Basilio II Emperador de Bizancio (Vat. gr. 1613)* (Madrid, 2005), good examples of decorated sticharion cuffs, 46, 160, 246; ornamentation of the epitrachelion, 47, 142, 152, 177, 409; decorated encheirion, 44, 74, 142. For the Sinai manuscript, *Byzantium: An Oecumenical Empire*, 86–87.

62. Erica Cruikshank Dodd, *The Frescoes of Mar Musa al-Habashi: A Study of Medieval Painting in Syria*, Studies and Texts 139 (Toronto, 2001), 17, plates VIII, XVIII, 17, 19b, 23b; Helen C. Evans, *Byzantium: Faith and Power (1261–1557)* (New York, 2004), 54, 60, 146, 194, 226.

levels until the late twelfth. Although visual depiction lags somewhat behind the physical and documentary evidence of ornate liturgical garb in the West, the Byzantine visual evidence seems too late to posit the empire as a likely source of the new Western style.[63]

Western travelers to the East also record no observations on the attire of Greek clerics. This is less surprising in works by pilgrims who focused on the sacred sites they visited than in those of ecclesiastical diplomats. Charlemagne, for example, sent Amalarius of Metz on a legation to Constantinople in 813. The *Versus marini*, or "Sea Poem," he wrote about the trip dwelled on the rigors of travel, but comments sprinkled throughout his other works indicate, unsurprisingly, that this Carolingian liturgist noted particular usages of the Byzantine rite. In his *Liber de ordine antiphonarii*, for example, he mentions having attended services on the Epiphany in Hagia Sophia and heard the psalm "Hodie si vocem eius audieritis" sung at the beginning of the Mass.[64] Interestingly, Amalarius related in a letter to Abbot Hilduin of St. Denis that he and his traveling companion on the legation—Peter, the abbot of Nonantola—discussed differences in liturgical practice during their voyage. But the differences they debated were those *within* western Europe (as to when ordinations were performed) not between the Western and Byzantine rites.[65] A century and a half later, Bishop Liutprand of Cremona's famous account of his legation to Constantinople in 968 is only slightly more revealing. He lamented that imperial officials seized from him five very valuable pieces of purple silk that he had bought for ecclesiastical use. His anecdote illustrates merely that there was a market in fine silk in the capital that was not entirely controlled by the palace, as well as that this Lombard bishop was keen to acquire precious silks.[66]

Most of the evidence we have for the emergence of this ornate style, in fact, comes not from the East but from the far West of Europe. Beyond the decree attributed to Pope Sylvester in the *Liber pontificalis*, the only early medieval ecclesiastical legislation against

63. This same evidence led Warren Woodfin in his dissertation to suggest that the influence of Western models of ecclesiastical attire likely led to the development of figural decoration on Byzantine vestments. Woodfin, "Late Byzantine Liturgical Vestments," 64 (1191–1192 embroidered vestment), 137–43 (Western influence). In his book, however, he attributes changes in vesture to broader intellectual and cultural developments within the empire and to the influence of the imperial court. He places the beginnings of change even later than I do, concluding that the "system of clerical vesture as it emerged from the period of iconoclasm remained virtually unchanged for well over two centuries." Woodfin, *Embodied Icon*, 4 (quote), 208–13.

64. He mentions the annual veneration of the cross in Constantinople in his tract on the Mass. *Amalarii Episcopi Opera Liturgica Omnia*, ed. John Michael Hanssens, 3 vols., Studi e Testi 138–140 (Vatican City, 1948–1950), 1:280; 3:57.

65. Ibid., 1:342.

66. *Relatio de legatione Constantinopolitana* chaps. 54–55, *MGH SSRG* 41:204–6; on the nature of imperial control, see David Jacoby, "Silk in Western Byzantium before the Fourth Crusade," *Byzantinische Zeitschrift* 84/85 (1991–1992): 452–500; Angeliki E. Laiou, "Exchange and Trade, Seventh–Twelfth Centuries," in *The Economic History of Byzantium*, 3 vols. (Washington, D.C., 2001), 2:718–19. In chapter 9 of the *Relatio* Liutprand mocks a procession to Hagia Sophia, recording that the nobles were "dressed in tunics that were too large for them and were also because of their extreme age full of holes," and that "no one except [the emperor] Nicephorus wore any jewels or golden ornaments." But the author's anti-Byzantine perspective and failure to distinguish lay and clerical attire render the observation useless for liturgical garb.

ornamented vestments comes from Iberia and Anglo-Saxon England. The earliest documentary and textile evidence of gold-decorated vestments is found in Anglo-Saxon England and in the northwesternmost parts of Francia (today's Normandy and Belgium) just across the channel and the North Sea. In addition to the 851 reference to gold-ornamented stoles and maniples at St. Bavo's in Ghent, work carried out in the late twentieth century on some of the silk and decorative braid fragments from Cuthbert's tomb suggest they were part of an early ninth-century dalmatic.[67] The earliest surviving example of gold embroidery in western Europe is preserved at the church of St. Catherine in Maaseik (in what is today Belgium) as a relic associated with two Merovingian sisters, Harlindis and Relindis, who supposedly were consecrated abbesses of a convent they founded by the Anglo-Saxon missionaries Saints Boniface and Willbrord. The so-called chasuble *(casula)* of Harlindis and Relindis is a rectangular patchwork of woven and embroidered pieces, the most stunning of which use gold and silk thread to decorate a series of arcades with interlace, floral, and animal motifs and affix tiny pearls. The late ninth-century *Vita sanctarum Harlindis et Relindis* relates that the sisters were trained at a convent in Valencina (probably Valenciennes on the Scheldt) in "work which is accustomed to be done by female hands in various ways and varied adornment, namely sewing and weaving, designing and working, and arranging gold and pearls on silk." The style and patterns of the embroidered decoration, however, suggest that they were made in southern England in the late eighth or the early ninth century.[68] This early evidence, moreover, stands at the beginning of a long tradition: throughout the Middle Ages, England was known for fine needlework. *Opus anglicanum*, or "English work," meant exquisite embroidery, and ecclesiastical vestments decorated with it were sought after and highly prized. The cope that so transfixed Eadmer at Bari was ornamented by English embroiderers.

Alcuin's words of warning to Archbishop Æthelhard in 801 confirm not only that such gold and silk embroideries were being produced in southern England at that time, but also that it was culturally acceptable for clerics to wear them. His admonition to the archbishop not to allow his clerics to "wear gold or silk clothing" in Charlemagne's presence presumes either that the Canterbury clergy were known for their finery or that any Anglo-Saxon prelate, wanting to make a good impression, would normally wear "gold or silk clothing." In these customs, ecclesiastics were partaking of a broader Anglo-Saxon culture of display. The treasures of Sutton Hoo and the more recently discovered Staffordshire hoard illustrate the taste for gold and silver adornment among Anglo-Saxon elites: precious metals decorated weaponry, rings, pins, brooches, and bands. Although there were plenty of clerical critiques of this taste, from Aldhelm to Alcuin, there is nothing in Anglo-Saxon sources comparable to the Frankish praise in Einhard's famous

67. Hero Granger-Taylor, "The Weft-Patterned Silks and Their Braid: The Remains of an Anglo-Saxon Dalmatic of c. 800?" in *St. Cuthbert, His Cult and His Community to AD 1200*, ed. Gerald Bonner, David Rollason, and Clare Stancliffe (Woodbridge, 1989), 303–27.

68. Mildred Budny and Dominic Tweddle, "The Early Medieval Textiles at Maaseik, Belgium," *Antiquaries Journal* 65 (1985): 353–89, especially 354–55, 364. A color photo of the embroidery is widely available in Lawrence Nees, *Early Medieval Art* (Oxford, 2002), 127.

life of Charlemagne for the rustic simplicity of their national dress.[69] The Anglo-Saxon taste for ornament—particularly multicolored decorative bands—was noted by Paul the Deacon in his history of the Lombards and has been amply confirmed by textual, visual, and archaeological sources.[70] The Maaseik *casula* also offers fascinating evidence of the early demand for silk in the Anglo-Saxon world. One of the pieces in the patchwork relic is a red and green silk twill with figures of King David enthroned within roundels and identified with the inscription DAV/ID. The Latin inscription, in capitals comparable to late eighth- and early ninth-century Anglo-Saxon display scripts, and a number of other early fragments of patterned weaving, indicate that highly skilled silk weaving was likely being practiced in the West at this very early date using imported silk thread.[71]

As on the Continent, however, the depiction of clerics in golden vestments lags behind the documentary and physical evidence for its use. Generally, naturalistic renderings of the human figure enter insular and Anglo-Saxon illumination late, but the contrast between the gold-embroidered vestments King Æthelstan offered to Saint Cuthbert in 934 and the depiction of the saint in the manuscript the same king commissioned is still significant. Although the Alcuin letter and other evidence above indicate that Anglo-Saxon clerics were wearing ornate vestments, the norms of depiction in England do not change until the benedictional of Æthelwold (963–984) (London, British Library, Additional MS 49598) (figure 31). This luxury manuscript was distinctive in many ways, but its depiction of priests in gold-ornamented vestments will by now seem familiar to the reader. The bishop blessing his congregation on folio 118v wears gold shoes, a gold stole and maniple, and an alb and chasuble decorated with golden bands.[72] Subsequent depictions of clerics in manuscripts and in wall paintings regularly include ornament.[73] The Æthelwold benedictional is one of a number of deluxe liturgical books that came out of royal support for reform in the mid-tenth century. After the devastation of particularly sustained Viking incursions in England from the 860s, the support of King Eadger (959–975) for the initiatives of Archbishop Dunstan of Canterbury, Bishop Æthelwold of Winchester, and Oswald bishop of Worcester and then archbishop of York brought renewal to the English church. Their reforms did favor monastic institutions, but renewed influence from the Continent also

69. Textile evidence from inhumation burials from the fifth to the seventh centuries "clearly indicates that the clothing of the various tribes differed," particularly in weave patterns: Lise Bender Jørgensen, "Textile Industries of the Early Medieval World to AD 1000: The Continental Germans," *CHWT*, 1:118–20 (quote on 118).

70. Gale R. Owen-Crocker, *Dress in Anglo-Saxon England*, rev. ed. (Woodbridge, 2004), especially 237, 246–51, 283–86; Dodwell, *Anglo-Saxon Art*, 24–43, 170–87.

71. Budny and Tweddle, "Early Medieval Textiles at Maaseik," 367–70; Robin Fleming, "Acquiring, Flaunting and Destroying Silk in Late Anglo-Saxon England," *Early Medieval Europe* 15 (2007): 127–53.

72. Saint Swithin is also depicted, on folio 97v, in golden vestments, as are saints Gregory, Benedict, and Cuthbert on 1r: Robert Deshman, *The Benedictional of Æthelwold* (Princeton, 1995), 138–43, plates 1, 32, 35.

73. J.J.G. Alexander, A *Survey of Manuscripts Illuminated in the British Isles*, 6 vols. (London, 1975–1996), vol. 2, Elzbieta Temple, *Anglo-Saxon Manuscripts 900–1066* (London, 1976), 63, fig. 180 (Lambeth Palace 200); 96, fig. 247 (BL Stowe 944); Roger Rosewell, *Medieval Wall Paintings in English and Welsh Churches* (Woodbridge, 2008), 13–14, 69, 115, 170, 202.

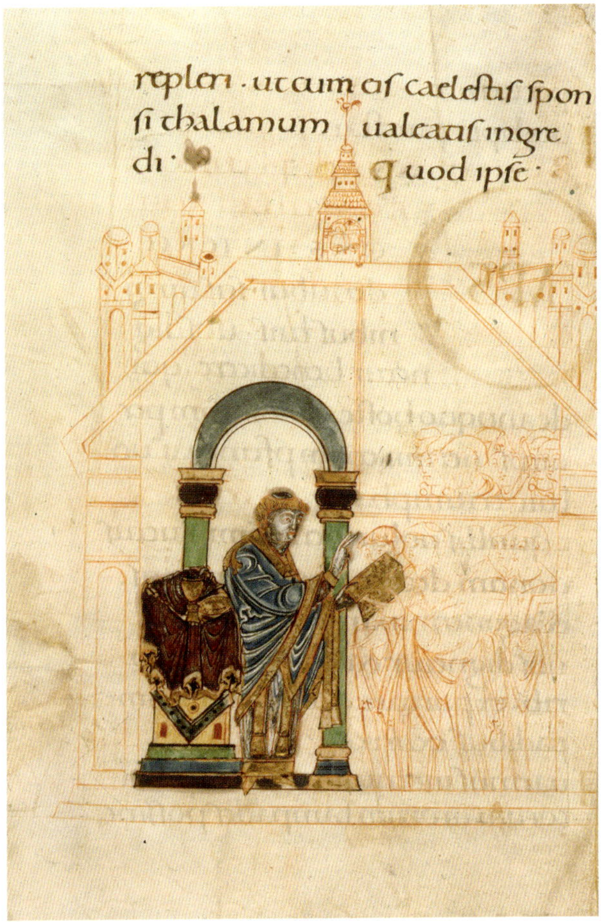

FIGURE 31. Benedictional of Æthelwold, 963–984, Add. MS 49598, 118v, British Library, London. HIP / Art Resource, NY.

yielded greater episcopal power. As Mary Frances Giandrea has pointed out, several sources from this mid-tenth-century movement "envisioned earthly rulership as a joint exercise between consecrated kings and bishops."[74] In sum, when the ninth-century Carolingian ideas about bishops as collaborators with temporal rulers in governance arrived in England through continental reform contacts, the clergy began to be depicted in golden vestments.

Affirmation, Contrast, and Holiness

Depictions of the new ornate style of liturgical vesture start cropping up in Italy from the late tenth century. The earliest suggests Ottonian influence. Sometime between 969 and 970, Archbishop Landulf I of Benevento commissioned the scroll of

74. Mary Frances Giandrea, *Episcopal Culture in Late Anglo-Saxon England* (Woodbridge, 2007), 52; John Blair, *The Church in Anglo-Saxon Society* (Oxford, 2005), 292–95, 341–54; and Catherine Cubitt, "The Tenth-Century Benedictine Reform in England," *Early Medieval Europe* 6 (1997): 77–94.

ordination rites discussed in chapter 2 (see figures 8 and 9). Not only does this unique roll illustrate the bestowal of vestments in priestly and diaconal ordinations, it used gold leaf to decorate them. Landulf's archiepiscopal pallium is golden, as are all the stoles, and some ornamental bands on dalmatics and albs. The capitals declaring the scroll to have been made by Landulf are also in gold. Scholars who have studied the roll link the commissioning of this opulent and innovative text to Landulf's promotion to metropolitan status.[75] But it also coincides with his rule of both the Principality of Benevento and Capua and the Duchy of Spoleto and Camerino under Ottonian suzerainty. When the reigning prince and duke, Pandulf Ironhead, was captured by Byzantine forces at the Battle of Bovino in 969—part of a series of campaigns undertaken with Otto I—Archbishop Landulf administered the principality and duchy on behalf of Pandulf's wife and young son. The prince was ultimately released as part of the negotiations that gained the Byzantine princess Theophano for Otto II.[76] Another early portrayal of ornamented vestments in Italy is also directly associated with imperial rule. The apse frescoes in the Basilica of Aquileia include not only the image of its imperially appointed patriarch Poppo (1019–1045) but also depictions of the emperors Conrad I, Conrad II, his son Henry (the future Henry III), and Empress Gisela. Poppo's pallium, like those of Saints Hermagoras and Hilarius, is richly decorated with roundels and pearl-like dots.[77]

Similar ornament is depicted in Rome from the mid-eleventh century. Most notable are the frescoes in the lower church of San Clemente. The subdeacons attending Saint Clement at his Mass (figure 32) have golden bands and roundels on their tunicles, and the dalmatic and chasuble of the saint himself are in patterned silks with decorative hem-bands. The papal vestments depicted in the panel devoted to the legend of Saint Alexius (figure 33) are equally ornate with roundels indicating an elaborately patterned silk for his chasuble. The mosaics in the early twelfth-century upper basilica of San Clemente depict Saint Lawrence in a dazzling dalmatic of diapered silk with golden bands, flecked with gemlike colored squares, along the hem, sleeves, and neckline. The apse mosaics from the 1140s in Santa Maria in Trastevere (figure 1) offer a similar depiction of Lawrence's dalmatic, plus five other ecclesiastics in elaborately ornamented vestments.[78] More than simply Roman artistic conservatism, of course, explains this chronology: the reformers dominating the city in this period were noted for their exalted interpretations of ecclesiastical authority. How a style artistically associated with notions of episcopal collaboration with imperial rule was reinterpreted and deployed by reformers for their own purposes

75. Guglielmo Cavallo, *Exultet: Rotoli liturgici del medioevo meridionale* (Rome, 1994), 75–85.

76. Chris Wickham, *Early Medieval Italy: Central Power and Local Society 400–1000* (London, 1981), 155–56; Barbara M. Kreutz, *Before the Normans: Southern Italy in the Ninth and Tenth Centuries* (Philadelphia, 1991), 102–6.

77. The basilica was rebuilt by Poppo, an inscription dating its completion to 1031. A restoration in 2006–2007 removed over-painting done in previous interventions allowing secure assessment of the character of the original early eleventh-century frescoes: Sergio Tavano, ed., *La Basilica di Aquileia: Gli affreschi dell'abside maggiore* (Udine, 2008), 113–17, 121–24, plates 2, 5–8, 27.

78. Serena Romano, *La pittura medievale a Roma, Corpus*, vol. 4, *Riforma e tradizione 1050–1198* (Milan, 2006), 139, 146, 213, 308–9.

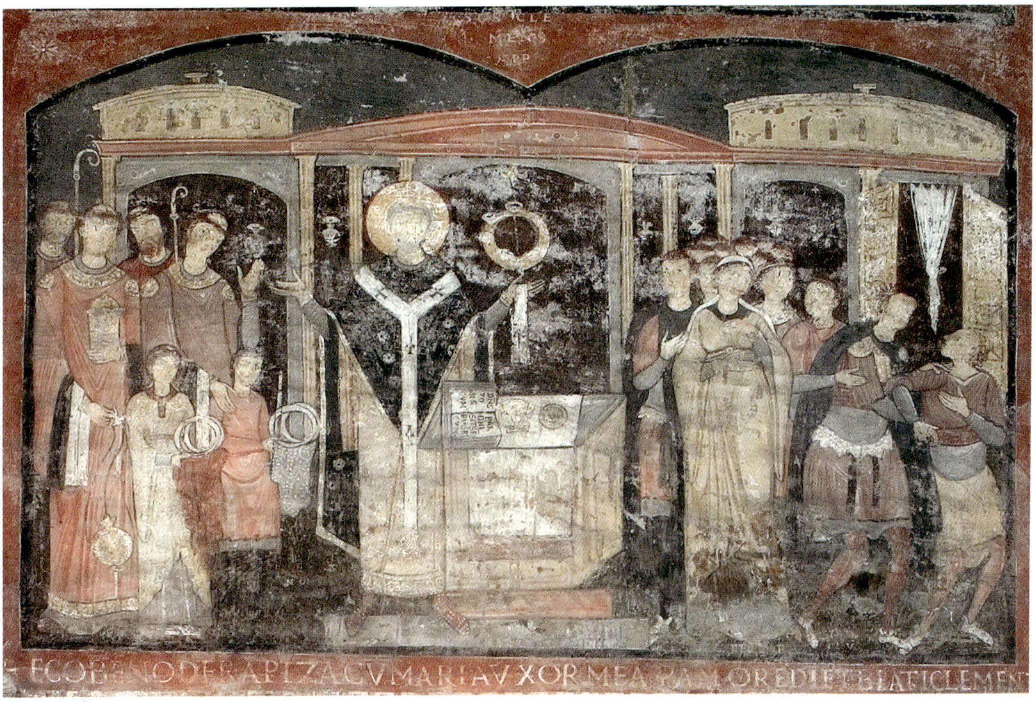

Figure 32. Saint Clement's Mass, c. 1090–1100, lower basilica of San Clemente, Rome. Photo courtesy of the Istituto Superiore per la Conservazione ed il Restauro, Archivio Fotografico Documentazione Restauri, Rome.

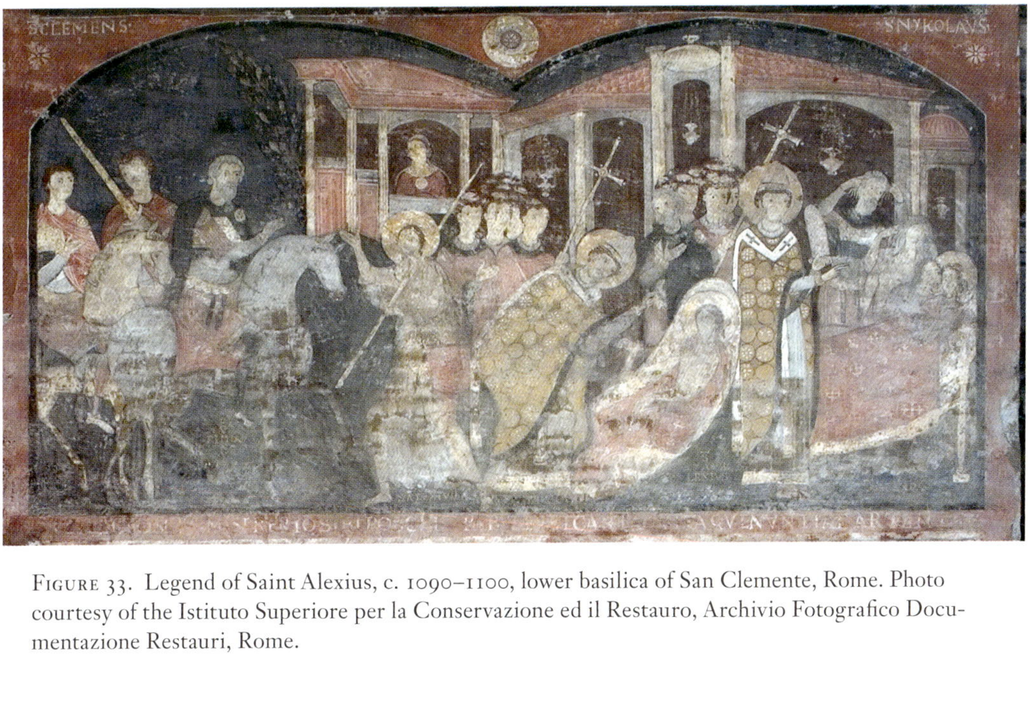

Figure 33. Legend of Saint Alexius, c. 1090–1100, lower basilica of San Clemente, Rome. Photo courtesy of the Istituto Superiore per la Conservazione ed il Restauro, Archivio Fotografico Documentazione Restauri, Rome.

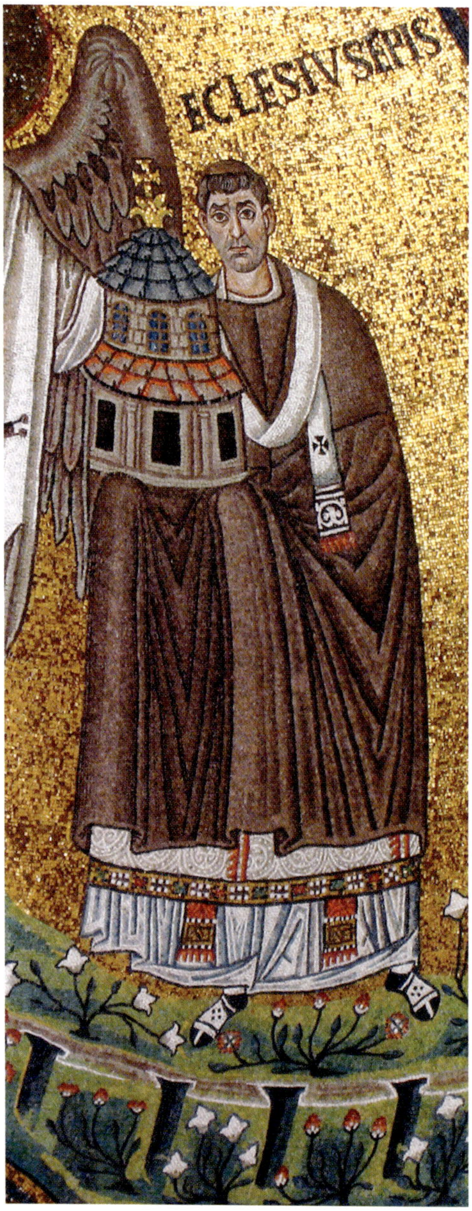

FIGURE 34. Bishop Ecclesius offering his church to the Virgin, mid-sixth century with twelfth-century restorations, San Vitale, Ravenna. Photo courtesy of Scott McDonough.

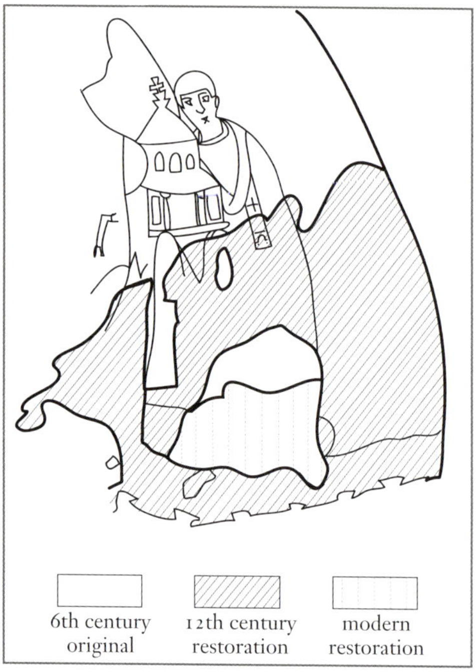

FIGURE 35. Restorations to the figure of Bishop Ecclesius offering his church to the Virgin, San Vitale, Ravenna. Drawing by Ann Higgins based on Andreescu-Treadgold, "The Emperor's New Crown and St. Vitalis' New Clothes," 153, fig. 3.

I will leave to chapter 5. For now, it is enough to note that the change in artistic depictions of sacred vestments in Italy conforms to the pattern already traced in northern Europe. Only when bishops were acknowledged as rulers, whether in collaboration with emperors or in competition with them, was it acceptable to depict them in gold and precious silks.

Indeed, by the twelfth century clerical vestments throughout Europe were represented as made of precious silks and ornamented with golden and embroidered bands. An apt example of the change in sensibilities is provided by the late antique mosaics at San Vitale in Ravenna, our starting point in this long story of the depiction of vestments.

After six centuries, quite a few tesserae had fallen out, particularly from the mosaics on the curved apse. This prompted a series of repairs in the twelfth century, discernible through the different size and type of tesserae used. The image in San Vitale's apse of Bishop Ecclesius offering the church to Christ was heavily "restored," the entire lower portion of his body (from the model church down) completely redressed (figures 34 and 35). An ornamented end was added to his late antique pallium, and the bishop was provided a sumptuous dalmatic and a decorated hem in keeping with current styles.[79]

The depiction of ornate vestments throughout Europe by the twelfth century represents a normalization of the ornate style of liturgical garb. The process we have been tracing in the visual record resonates in inventories: many churches had such attire. References to gold-embellished and silk vestments increase markedly in the second half of the tenth century, reach their peak between 1000 and 1150, then drop off somewhat.[80] The decline may indicate only that a certain saturation point had been reached: a church could only use and store so many vestments. Clerics continued to be depicted in ornate vestments over the rest of the medieval period and into the modern era, and extremely costly and beautiful garb continued to be commissioned and donated.

But it is worth considering whether the slight decline in the number of ornate liturgical vestments cataloged in surviving ecclesiastical inventories after the mid-twelfth century might indicate a certain ebbing of enthusiasm for the ornate style or a new ambivalence about it. Although the ecclesiastical legislation reining in "superfluity" (discussed in chapter 1) focused on clerical street-wear, increased lay criticism of excess in all clerical clothing may have prompted the conciliar discussions that resulted in the canons we have. What clerics wore outside the sanctuary, after all, was not essential to the spirituality of sacred vestments that had formed generations of ecclesiastics by the twelfth century. The gold-ornamented silk liturgical garments, however, were at the very heart of clerical spirituality and priestly self-image. The canny legislator in me can imagine the twelfth-century bishops gathered in councils opting to clamp down on excesses in clerical street-wear in order to protect their use of the ornate vestments that were so infused with spiritual meanings. A range of sources we'll look at in chapter 6, moreover, indicates that criticism of "superfluity" in clerical attire was coming not just from some laypeople: monastic and clerical tracts across the twelfth century questioned the wealth being poured into ecclesiastical garments and the pompous vanity such attire fostered. While the ornate style appears in our visual sources to have triumphed all over Europe by the twelfth century, textual sources register new opposition and ambivalence.

It seems fitting, moreover, that ambivalence or divided opinion about ornate clerical garb expressed itself in the marked contrast in culturally accepted styles of clerical

79. The differences in style and tesserae are discernible in the excellent photographs now available in *La Basilica di San Vitale*, 253; for an analysis of these medieval repairs in the apse, see Irina Andreescu-Treadgold, "The Emperor's New Crown and St. Vitalis' New Clothes," *Corso di cultura sull'arte ravennate e bizantina* 41 (1995): 151–53, 177–78.

80. This analysis is based on the inventories published in *Schatzverzeichnisse*.

clothing: gold and brightly colored silk vestments within church on the one hand, and simple, darkly colored "closed cloaks" outside the sanctuary on the other. The licit topography of these two contrasting styles of clerical garb is even more important when considered in its ideological and political landscapes. As I have argued in this chapter, the visual record of how clerics were represented suggests that the ornate style became accepted only with the diffusion of the idea that clerics were partners with kings and princes in the governance of God's people. When clerics became collaborators with kings in the exercise of rulership, their wearing of gold and silk was deemed appropriate. Ideas governed representation. Yet the twelfth-century legislation against superfluity, which mandated drab and dark attire when clerics were outside of church, meant that they could not wear their gold and silk finery in precisely the places they most directly exercised governing roles. When at the royal court or even when presiding at their own courts in the presence of laypeople—"in public" (*in publico*) as canon 16 of the Fourth Lateran Council repeated twice—ecclesiastic collaborators in royal governance were not to display the expensive semiotic indicators of their status and power.

There are two important aspects to this delimitation. First, it insisted visually that ecclesiastical status and power was spiritual: the expensive visual indicators of silk and gold were restricted to the altar, to liturgical space and actions. The situational limit that the twelfth- and early thirteenth-century ecclesiastical legislation placed on ornate clerical garb made rich and ornamented clothing acceptable for the Mass and liturgical processions, but not permissible for day-to-day, nonliturgical functions. This circumscribed the general idea fostering greater acceptance of clerical finery: the notion that the clergy participated in the governance of society. They may through their prayers and sacramental role administer God's grace, and through penance discipline and govern their flock. In this sphere they could wear vestments resplendent in gold. But in nonliturgical settings they were to appear modest and humble. In a certain sense, the plain style of clerical street-wear sartorially returned the clergy to servant status when exercising temporal powers delegated by kings and princes.

Second, the delimitation occurred when clerical claims to status and power were becoming more fully realized. When the representation of clerics in ornate vestments became acceptable in the mid-ninth century, ecclesiastical power was still highly dependent on temporal rulers. Late Carolingian and Ottonian bishops were powerful because of the lands and jurisdictions delegated to their sees by monarchs—who also appointed them and removed them at will. In this political world, the idea of ecclesiastics as collaborators in governance meriting the golden finery of magnates posed little threat. But Europe after the investiture contest was a very different political world. Popes in the twelfth century were actual, not just theoretical, monarchs in their own right, who claimed—and at times managed to assert—their superiority over temporal rulers. Bishops were not as pliable to the royal will either. And as the twelfth-century advanced, the ecclesiastical presence at court increased as emergent royal bureaucracies came to depend on educated clerics to implement the king's decrees. In this political world, Europeans might well have had second thoughts about clerics looking like rulers. So spatially delimiting their wearing of ornate garb visually undermined the more real power they were increasingly exercising.

The development of the two contrasting styles of clerical clothing not only participated in medieval debates about power but also in shifting emphases within Christian ideas about the appearance of holiness. The rise and diffusion of the ornate style of liturgical attire from the ninth to the twelfth centuries associated holiness with beautiful and precious materials. Ascetic movements within Christianity, however, had long associated holiness with rough simplicity in attire, and monastic reform movements periodically reaffirmed this view. The twelfth-century lay critique of "superfluity" in clerical clothing was certainly influenced by this perspective and achieved at least more clearly defined standards in ecclesiastical legislation for simple and modest clerical street-wear. The more concerted post-Lateran IV campaign across the thirteenth century to disseminate and enforce these norms for clerical attire outside the sanctuary occurred in dialogue with the rise of the mendicants. Holy men and women renouncing wealth and dedicating themselves to the care of the poor and sick appear in the twelfth century, but the orders founded by Francis of Assisi and Dominic of Guzmán in the early thirteenth century gave this critique of a more affluent society new force and prominence. Implicitly or explicitly, the friars' way of life was also a critique of the secular clergy. Clothing figured prominently in this critique. Thomas of Celano's first life of Francis (book 1, chapter 39) directly linked holiness to the friars' appearance.

> Followers of most holy poverty, because they had nothing, loved nothing, they feared in no way to lose anything. They were content with one tunic, patched at times within and without; in it was seen no refinement, but rather abjectness and cheapness, so that they might seem to be completely crucified to the world. Girt with a cord, they wore poor trousers, and they had the pious intention of remaining like this, and they wished to have nothing more.[81]

Saint Francis himself, in his very first rule for the order in 1221, stipulated that anyone entering their company sell all they owned and give the proceeds to the poor. Then he would receive "two tunics without a hood, a cord and trousers."[82]

To the dismay of many of Francis's earliest followers, even the Franciscans became more like other religious orders over the late thirteenth and fourteenth centuries. Still, they retained a reputation for a more austere way of life than their peers in the secular clergy, and were preferred by popes as well as the lowliest Christians for some pastoral roles. It might be surprising, then, to peek inside the sacristy of the church of San Francesco at Pisa in the mid-fourteenth century. An inventory allows us to do so. The chasubles alone number eighty-five, some decorated with "dragons and griffins of gold," others

81. St. Francis of Assisi, *Writings and Early Biographies*, ed. Marion A. Habig, 4th rev. ed. (Quincy, Ill., 1991), 261.

82. Ibid., 32. Novices also wore a "caperon," a kind of overgarment extending down to the cord; fully professed friars could have one tunic with a hood.

with "green parrots," and still others with "leopards of gold." The friars also had "a solemn cope of white silk embroidered with fine gold."[83] Some might characterize these ornate vestments as a sign of mendicant decline, of how quickly the generations of Franciscans after Francis abandoned his ideals. But one might also understand it as simply abiding by the accepted contrast of ornate liturgical attire in church and humble attire—in this case extremely humble—outside the church "in public." But if Francis's rule required the friars to give up all they owned and receive only two tunics, a cord, and trousers, where did the Pisan vestments come from? Who made these ornate liturgical garments? It's time to look more closely at the garments themselves.

83. Chiara Balbarini, "Gli arredi della sacrestia di San Francesco attraverso gli inventari trecenteschi," in *Il Francescanesimo a Pisa (secc. 13–14) e la missione del Beato Agnello in Inghilterra a Canterbury e Cambridge (1224–1226): Atti del Convegno di studi, Pisa, Chiesa di San Francesco, 10–11 marzo 2001* (Ospedaletto [Pisa], 2003), 124–26.

4

WOMEN AND MEN

IT IS A TRIBUTE to the pioneering work in textile conservation of the Abegg-Stiftung that its chief conservator, Mechthild Flury-Lemberg, was called to Assisi in 1980 to clean the cowl of Saint Francis.[1] The tattered garment had been exposed for veneration without dust protection for some time and was very dirty. "The appearance of this garment with its thirty-one large and small patches left a deep, lasting impression on me," she wrote: "it is certainly one of the shabbiest I have ever seen." The many patches piqued her interest. Some were sewn on "carelessly in different ways using simple whip stitch."[2] Several fabrics had been used, seemingly following the brothers' tradition of using pieces of old garments to repair their cowls. Nineteen of the patches on Francis's tunic, however, were of the same rough, brownish cloth and they had been sewn on by the same, more expert hand. This mystery mender revealed herself when the conservator visited the convent of Santa Chiara across town. Among other relics of Saint Clare, the convent preserves her cape: it is made from the same rough, brownish cloth used to patch Francis's tunic. The pieces had been taken from the lower edge of the back. Did Clare repair Francis's cowl during his lifetime or "beautify" the pitiful garment after his death? Noting the undamaged state of the seams on Clare's repairs, Flury-Lemburg inclined toward the latter.

The question focuses us on the intimate aspects of clothing. Garments touch the body. They absorb its fluids, wear and tear with its movements. Our modern consumer culture has nearly extinguished the arts of making and mending. We buy and we discard

1. As she notes, since the saint often was moved to give away his own garments to the poor, there are several of his cowls conserved as relics. The one under discussion has been in Assisi since at least 1350 and displayed for some time now in the lower church of San Francesco, near the saint's tomb. The Abegg-Stiftung, founded by collector Werner Abegg in 1961, has been at the forefront of textile conservation methods, the study of historic textiles, and training of specialists in this rapidly developing field. *Textile Conservation*, 314–17.

2. Ibid., 314.

in impersonal exchanges. That culture was beginning to emerge in the later Middle Ages with the development of complex textile industries; vibrant local, regional, and international markets; and used clothing vendors. But for the period under consideration, most clothing was made at home. From spinning to weaving, sewing to mending, textiles and garments were the products of women's work. This basic fact must inform our understanding of clerical clothing.

Opera Muliebra: The Creators of Liturgical Garb

In a now-classic monograph, David Herlihy showed how the making of cloth and clothes, from antiquity into the central Middle Ages, was "women's work" (*opera muliebra*). For free men, such tasks as spinning and weaving were considered demeaning and were thus inflicted as a humiliating punishment on convicts or war captives. Women produced textiles at home or, on large estates and in elite households, in workshops called *gynaeceum* in classical Latin (from the Greek *gynaikeion*, or women's quarters) and *genecium* or *genitium* in medieval documents. These workshops were largely staffed with female slaves, *ancillae*, and they endured through the central Middle Ages.[3] The church fully participated in these economic conventions.

Dioceses and monasteries usually held estates with workshops that could produce cloth and garments. We get a glimpse of these valuable assets in a gift to the cathedral clergy of Verona: in 813 Bishop Ratoldus gave them revenues from a long list of estates, among them garments that come from the *ginitio*.[4] Female slaves toiling on estates owned by dioceses and monasteries likely provided the cloth that covered altars and the bodies of clergy and religious. Women's monasteries seem also to have provided for some monks' needs. The life of Saint Lobin, a sixth-century monk who later became bishop of Chartres, relates that a girl in a female monastery mended the holy man's tunic. In the early twelfth century, Abelard's rule for Heloise's convent of the Paraclete dictated that the women's house should be under the supervision of the "brothers" in a male monastery and that the nuns should "confine themselves to what can suitably be done indoors by women, such as making clothes for themselves and the brothers."[5] More problematic were the cloth and garment needs of local churches. Those in urban centers

3. David Herlihy, *Opera Muliebra: Women and Work in Medieval Europe* (New York, 1990), 1–12, 18–21, 34–39, 75–91; Susan Mosher Stuard, "Ancillary Evidence for the Decline of Medieval Slavery," *Past & Present* 149 (1995): 3–28. The use of unfree female labor in textile production even enters imaginative literature: E. Jane Burns, *Sea of Silk: A Textile Geography of Women's Work in Medieval French Literature* (Philadelphia, 2009), 23–25, 30–31.

4. Vittorio Fainelli, ed., *Codice Diplomatico Veronese*, 2 vols. (Venice, 1940–1963), 1:131 (doc. 102): "De vestimentis quae de pisile, vel ginitio veniunt, decimam parte." The donation expresses particular solicitude for the sustenance of the clergy.

5. Herlihy, *Opera Muliebra*, 38; Terence P. McLaughlin, "Abelard's Rule for Religious Women," *Mediaeval Studies* 18 (1956): 259–60; Betty Radice trans., rev. M. T. Clanchy, *Letters of Abelard and Heloise* (London, 2003), 156–57.

may have been able to buy or barter to fulfill their needs, but churches in rural communities had fewer options. A canon in the collection of Ansegis (827) instructed priests to exhort the women of their parishes to make linens for the altar.[6] Donations were an important source for vestments and altar linens, but other legislation suggests they were not always sufficient. A basic problem was that the household structures that kept laymen fed and clothed were considered inappropriate to the clergy: they threatened the cultic purity increasingly at the heart of the priestly office. The major orders of the clergy were supposed to be chaste and therefore not live with women. How did the church respond to this problem?

Over the early Middle Ages, it did so by admonition and usually by not enforcing its own prohibitions against clerical marriage and concubinage. Examples of married priests, and even bishops, abound in early medieval documentation, as do mentions of women cohabitating with clerics.[7] Although ecclesiastical historians have tended to focus on the threat these women and their children posed to church property and resources, their labor surely contributed to a priest's ability to serve his church. Some ecclesiastical legislation tacitly acknowledged the need for the household services provided by women while insisting that clerics live separated from them. The only exceptions for coresidence were in the case of "a mother, or a sister, or an aunt, or other persons above suspicion." Several decrees of a council at Tours in 567 make clear that clerics needed women's textile work. "Let no cleric presume to have an unrelated woman [*extraneam mulierem*] in his house on the pretext of the need for making clothing or for the purpose of keeping house," canon 10 stated flatly.[8] The next canon, while affirming the exemption for female kin ("mother or sister or daughter"), prohibited clerics from having in their homes "for the purpose of taking care of things" their own slave girl (*ancillam propriam*), a widow, or a woman living like a nun (*quasi sanctimonialem*). Yet another canon decreed that the bishop should be surrounded by clerics in his residence and that his wife (*coniugem* in canon 13, *episcopiam* in canon 14) and her maidservants should have a separate abode. A similar rule was laid down for priests, deacons, and subdeacons: all should dwell and pray alone in their cells. Their wives and female slaves should live elsewhere.[9] Physical separation is demanded, but the wives and slaves are not relinquished: the women are still "theirs." A canon noted by Herlihy and included in Regino of Prüm's early tenth-century collection of ecclesiastical law opens by prohibiting priests from

6. *MGH Cap. Nova Series* 1:511: "CXLVI De linteis altaribus praeparandis. Ut presbiteri per parrochias suas feminis praedicent, ut linteamina altaribus praeparent."

7. Gabriella Rossetti, "Il matrimonio del clero nella società altomedievale," in *Il matrimonio nella società altomedievale: 22–28 aprile 1976*, Settimane di studio del Centro italiano di studi sull'alto Medioevo, 24 (Spoleto, 1977), 533–37; the canonical legislation is well surveyed in John E. Lynch, "Marriage and Celibacy of the Clergy: The Discipline of the Western Church; An Historico-Canonical Synopsis," *Jurist* 32 (1972) 14–38, 189–212.

8. *Concilia Galliae A. 511–A. 695*, 179: "Nullus deinceps clericorum pro occasione necessitatis faciende vestes aut causa ordinandae domus extraneam mulierem in domum suam habere praesumat."

9. Ibid., 179–84. Canon 20 uses the terms *presbiteria*, *diaconissa*, and *subdiaconissa* to identify the wives (*uxores*) of clerics.

having women in their houses, giving the usual exception for a mother, aunt, or sister. It then continues, "But if concerning these [women] he has a permissible need related to the necessary support of the priest, he may have a house in the village or estate, distant from places the priest frequents, and there let him supply them those things that are needed."[10] The last phrase led Herlihy to suggest that the priest's house of women was a workshop for producing textiles.

When our sources do identify the makers of liturgical vestments, they are women. Eustadiola of Bourges, a wealthy seventh-century widow and saintly abbess, was praised by the author of her vita for her generosity, including the "holy vestments and precious altar cloths" that she made "with her own hands with her girls [*puellis*]."[11] The ninth-century bishop Prudentius of Troyes extolled the contributions of his "best helper" (*optimam adjutricem*) and "collaborator" (*collaboratricem*), the unmarried woman Maura. "Who gave the altar cloths?" he asked,

> Maura! Who used her own wealth to buy the priestly garments? Maura! I hold more precious than gold or topaz the linen garment she made for me with her own hands. She spun, fashioned, whitened it, and asked humbly that it be worn for the sacred solemnity of the Mass.[12]

As Fiona Griffiths has pointed out and this quotation underscores, liturgical textiles were a way for women to be present at the altar. The pious women named and praised for their handiwork were all elites. But the "girls" who worked with Saint Eustadiola and the unnamed weavers of the linen Maura fashioned (*deposuit*) into a garment for Prudentius were likely slaves.

10. Herlihy, *Opera Muliebra*, 38; Regino of Prüm, *Libri duo de synodalibus causis et de ecclesiasticis disciplinis*, ed. F. G. A. Wasserschleben and Wilifried Hartmann (Darmstadt, 2004), 82 (liber 1, chap. 105); also in *PL*, 131:211–12: "Inhibendum et modis omnibus interminandum est ut nullus sacerdos eas personas feminarum, sicut et in canone insertum continetur, de quibus suspicio esse potest, in domo sua habeat: sed neque illas quas canones concedunt (quia instigante diabolo etiam in illis scelus frequenter perpetratum reperitur, aut etiam in pedissequis illarum), scilicet matrem, amitam, sororem. Sed, si quis de his habuerit talem necessitatem patientem, cui sit necessitas sustentatio presbyteri, habeat in vico aut in villa domum longe a presbyteri conversatione et ibi eis subministret, quae necessaria sunt." On Regino, see *History and Politics in Late Carolingian and Ottonian Europe: The Chronicle of Regino of Prüm and Adalbert of Magdeburg*, trans. Simon MacLean (Manchester, 2009), 6–7.

11. Fiona Griffiths, "'Like the Sister of Aaron': Medieval Religious Women and Liturgical Textiles," in *Female Vita Religiosa between Late Antiquity and High Middle Ages: Structures, Norms and Developments*, ed. Gert Melville and Anne Müller, Vita regularis: Ordnungen und Deutungen religiosen Lebens im Mittelalter, 47 (Zurich, 2011), 353. I thank the author for sharing her research with me before its publication. Where I have translated more of the source or provided slightly different translations than Griffiths, I give the source citation: *Vita Eustadiolae* in *AASS*, Jun. II (June 8), 133, chap. 3. Lois L. Huneycutt also noted women's gifts of vestments and underscored how their liturgical gifts allowed women to be present at the altar: "'Proclaiming Her Dignity Abroad': The Literary and Artistic Network of Matilda of Scotland, Queen of England 1100–1118," in *The Cultural Patronage of Medieval Women*, ed. June Hall McCash (Athens, 1996), 155–74, especially 159–61.

12. Griffiths, "'Like the Sister of Aaron,'" 351; Prudentius of Troyes, *Vita S. Maurae* in *AASS*, Sep. VI (Sept. 21), 275–76, chaps. 3, 5.

From the ninth century, ecclesiastical legislation prohibited women from physically entering the church sanctuary and approaching the altar, even to gather its linens for washing. Indeed one canon decreed that a church's deacons and subdeacons should launder sacred cloths.[13] Women continued, however, to make and donate liturgical textiles. Hedwig (d. 994), widow of Duke Burchard II of Swabia, made a cope, a stole, and an alb ("decorated with scenes from the marriage of Mercury to Philology"!) for the monastery of St. Gall, while Queen Margaret of Scotland (d. 1093) made "copes for singers, chasubles, stoles, altar cloths, and other sacred vestments."[14] Several references make clear that it was the fine embroidery and weaving with gold thread that were particularly valued in women's making of vestments. The wealthy Thuringian widow Paulina (d. 1107) had scarcely any equal "in the making of gold borders and stoles."[15]

All this evidence indicates that women, particularly pious elite women, were the creators of the new ornate style of liturgical attire that comes into view in the mid-ninth century and is ubiquitous throughout Europe by the late eleventh. Although imported silks were often used, two prominent elements of the style were particularly associated with women's textile skills in northwestern Europe: embroidery and woven bands. The most prized used precious materials: silk and gold thread, pearls and gems. But these decorative techniques could also be executed in lesser fibers. Ornamental braids, bands, and belts were made by an ingenious and highly portable method called "tablet weaving" that used a set of four-holed wooden or bone tablets to work weft thread (figures 36–39). The apparatus could be carried on a woman's belt and, whenever she had time, secured to any convenient fixed point (a post, a tree) to allow her to weave. The association of such work with virtue—eschewing idleness, industriously providing—permeates medieval sources.[16] In these texts, women's virtue and skill created the beautiful ornate vestments that represented clerical virtue.

These women artists probably designed and executed many vestments, particularly more common ones, on their own. But several pieces of evidence indicate that women collaborated with clerics in producing liturgical attire. A passage in Eadmer of Canterbury's life of Saint Dunstan posits male religious as designers of sacred vestments. At the

13. *MGH Cap. episc.* 1:65, 107, 215, 240; 3:163.

14. Griffiths, "'Like the Sister of Aaron,'" 353, 351; *Vita Margaritae* in *AASS*, Jun. II (June 10), 320, chap. 7: "cappae cantorum, casulae, stolae, altaris pallia, alia quoque vestimenta sacerdotalia"; Ingebord of Denmark, queen of France, sent a chasuble to the dean of Amiens in the early thirteenth century asking that solemn masses be said in it on the feast of the Virgin: Joan Ferrante, ed. and trans., *Epistolae: Medieval Women's Latin Letters*, http://epistolae.ccnmtl.columbia.edu/letter/434.html.

15. Griffiths, "'Like the Sister of Aaron,'" 353; Jane Tibbetts Schulenburg, "Holy Women and the Needle Arts: Piety, Devotion, and Stitching the Sacred, ca. 500–1150," in *Negotiating Community and Difference in Medieval Europe: Gender, Power, Patronage and the Authority of Religion in Latin Christendom*, ed. Katherine Allen Smith and Scott Wells (Leiden, 2009), 83–110. In Chrétien de Troye's *Erec et Enide*, the heroine is depicted presenting to the church "an impressive chasuble completely embroidered in fine gold thread" (*Et une grant chasuble ovree; / Tote a fin or estoit brosdee*): Burns, *Sea of Silk*, 34.

16. Owen-Crocker, *Dress in Anglo-Saxon England*, 283–86; *CHWT*, 1:19, 128–29, 134; Valerie L. Garver, *Women and Aristocratic Culture in the Carolingian World* (Ithaca, N.Y., 2009), 224–68; Herlihy, *Opera Muliebra*, 6, 56–59, 76.

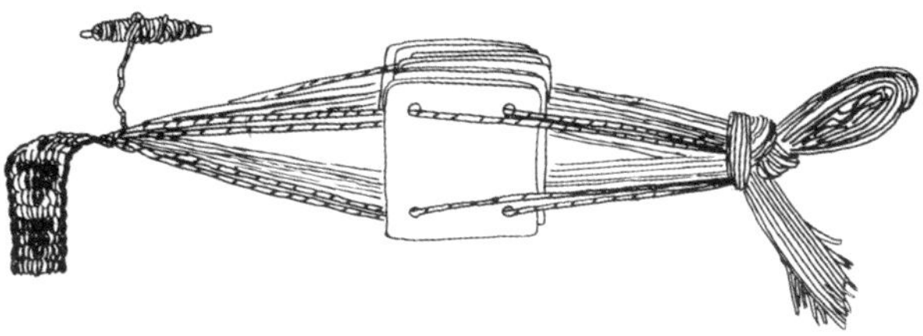

Figure 36. Tablet weaving. Drawing by Gale Owen-Crocker from *Dress in Anglo-Saxon England*, 283, fig. 228, reproduced here with her permission.

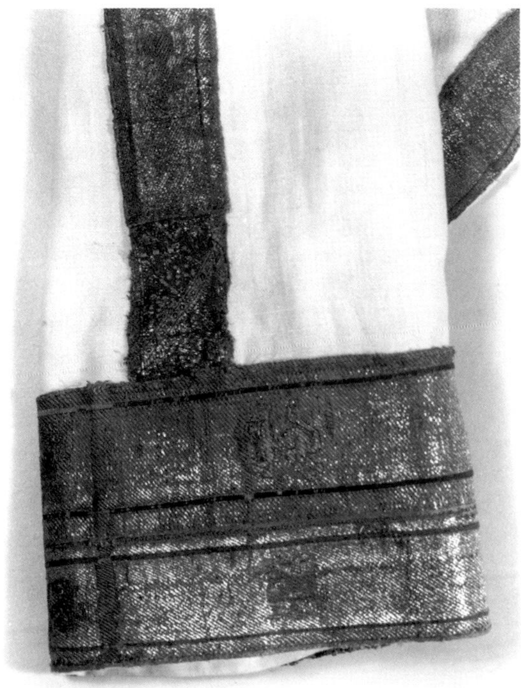

Figure 37. Alb of Saint Bernulf of Utrecht, eleventh century with later additions, Museum Catharijneconvent, Utrecht. Detail of tablet-woven bands used to patch wear on right sleeve from the documentation of its conservation at the Abegg-Stiftung, Riggisberg, Switzerland. © Abegg-Stiftung, CH-3132 Riggisberg / photo: Anne Javor.

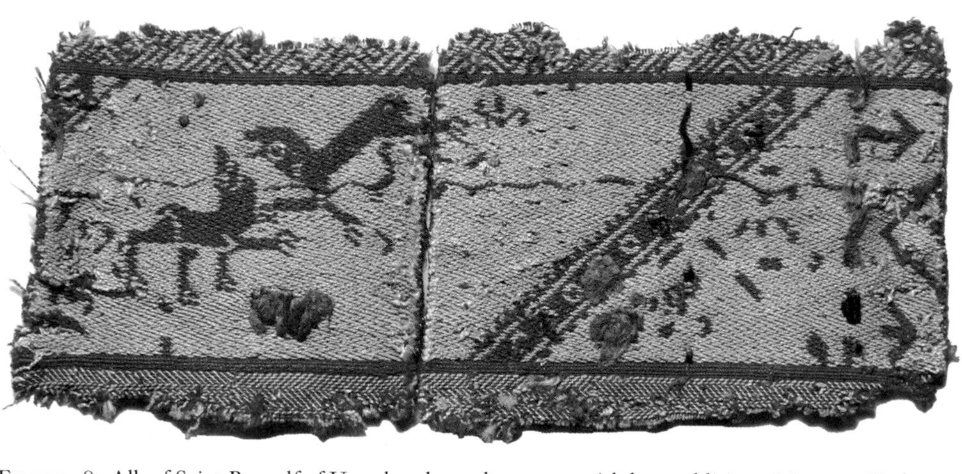

Figure 38. Alb of Saint Bernulf of Utrecht, eleventh century with later additions, Museum Catharijneconvent, Utrecht. Detail of upper tablet-woven band used to patch wear on right sleeve (right side) from the documentation of its conservation at the Abegg-Stiftung, Riggisberg, Switzerland. © Abegg-Stiftung, CH-3132 Riggisberg / photo: Anne Javor.

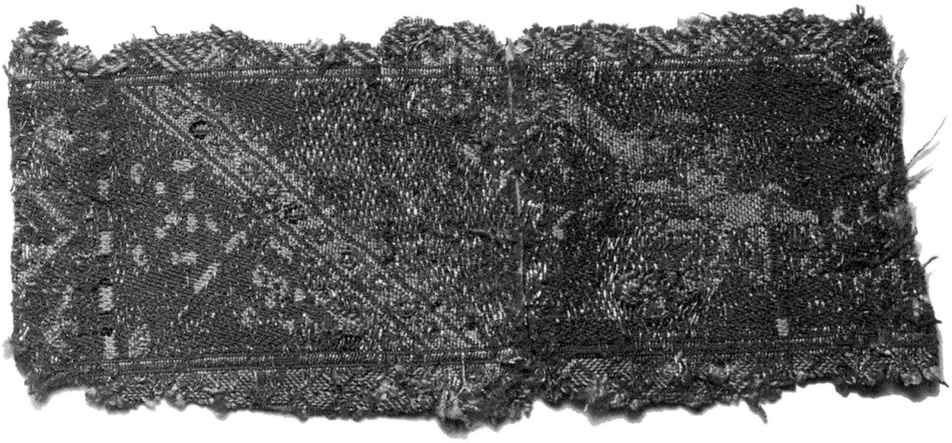

FIGURE 39. Alb of Saint Bernulf of Utrecht, eleventh century with later additions, Museum Catharijneconvent, Utrecht. Detail of upper tablet-woven band used to patch wear on right sleeve (reverse side) from the documentation of its conservation in at the Abegg-Stiftung, Riggisberg, Switzerland. © Abegg-Stiftung, CH-3132 Riggisberg / photo: Anne Javor.

end of a section praising Dunstan for having avoided idleness by excelling in the arts (painting, sculpting, casting), Eadmer relates that the saint drew up a design for a stole "with his craftsman's skill" so that "a certain matron," Æthelwynn, then "could copy it in golden thread."[17] While the design and sewing stages of such ventures could be completed at a distance, Eadmer tells this story about Dunstan's time at court, suggesting that clerics attached to a court collaborated with its elite women on ecclesiastical textile projects. One can easily imagine this kind of collaboration in the production of the Bamberg rationale or of Saint Cuthbert's stole and maniple.

A different sort of collaboration is revealed in clerical correspondence. In a letter to Countess Adela of Blois, Baudri abbot of Bourgueil asked her to make him a "cope which shining Phrygian gold surrounds, the cope which honors the breadth of the chest with gems." After both flattering her and exhorting her to "adorn ministers and enrich the treasuries of the church," he closes with "make sure the cope is not missing its fringe."[18]

17. Eadmer of Canterbury, *Lives and Miracles of Saints Oda, Dunstan, and Oswald*, ed. and trans. Andrew J. Turner and Bernard J. Muir (Oxford, 2006), 60–61.

18. Clerical requests begin much earlier. A letter of Ermentrud of Orleans in 847 reveals that Pardulo, bishop of Laon, had requested a stole from her: Ferrante, *Epistolae: Medieval Women's Latin Letters*, http://epistolae.ccnmtl.columbia.edu/letter/1002.html; Baudri's letter is http://epistolae.ccnmtl.columbia.edu/letter/95.html. In 1107 Baudri sent his more famous letter to the countess describing her chamber, and in this letter too he asks her to send him "a cope and, if it pleases you, a tunic": ibid., http://epistolae.ccnmtl.columbia.edu/letter/94.html. Griffiths discusses other letters requesting vestments in her "'Like the Sister of Aaron,'" 348, as does Jeffrey F. Hamburger, *Nuns as Artists: The Visual Culture of a Medieval Convent* (Berkeley, 1997), 204–6. The *Gesta Treverorum* records Bishop Poppo of Trier (1016–1047) sending fabric to a canoness commissioning her to make pontifical stockings (caligae) for use in solemn liturgies: *MGH SS* 8:175. Although Therese Latzke argued in 1970 that such requests were literary tropes,

One could not really call Baudri the designer of this cope, if it was ever produced. But we get a glimpse here of how ecclesiastical leaders cultivated relations with elite women in order to procure rich and impressive vestments for themselves and their churches. Significant amounts of wealth clearly flowed to churches through such relationships: when Archbishop Christian of Mainz (1249–1251) inventoried his cathedral's treasure, he valued one of the silk copes embroidered with gold and gems at sixty marks and related that an old, worn cope yielded three and a half marks of gold when melted down. Bishops undertook such inventories precisely because the garments could provide needed funds, either in this direct fashion or through using them as collateral for loans.[19] Note also that ecclesiastical leaders were the supplicants in such relationships and women were the patrons who decided which prelates and churches to favor with the fruits of their textile workshops.

The character of these collaborative relationships between the women makers of vestments and the male clerics who wore them is worth interrogating. If the wearing of vestments was central to a clerical spirituality about the cultivation of virtue, how did collaboration with women to produce these garments figure in this spirituality? A first clue is offered by Goscelin of Saint-Bertin's praise of Saint Edith (d. 984) in the life he wrote c. 1080:

> Indeed, like the sister of Aaron [Ex. 15:20] and the sister of the priests of God, she embroidered with flowers the pontifical vestments of Christ with all her skill and capacity to make splendid. Here purple, dyed with Punic red, with murex and Sidonian shellfish, and twice-dipped scarlet [Ex. 25:4, 26:1, etc.] were interwoven with gold; chrysolite, topaz, onyx and beryl and precious stones were intertwined with gold; union pearls, the shells' treasure, which only India produced in the east, and Britain, the land of the English, in the west, were set like stars in gold; the golden insignia of the cross, the golden images of the saints were outlined with a surround of pearls. Her whole thought was Christ and the worship of Christ.[20]

subsequent research on material culture and on letters of thanks have documented women's gifts. Therese Latzke, "Der Topos Mantelgedicht," *Mittellateinisches Jahrbuch* 6 (1970): 109–31.

19. Two embroidered altar frontals were valued at 100 and 60 marks, and Christian interjects after the valuation of the cope at 60 marks, "And so for this it will be able to be pledged" (*sic enim et obligari poterat*): *Schatzverzeichnisse*, 52. The economic value of vestments is clear in Paul of Bernreid's story of the simoniac bishop of Bamberg gathering together "a considerable sum of money and a store of precious metal and vestments" in order to try to bribe the pope. Paul of Bernreid, *Life of Pope Gregory VII* in Robinson, ed., *Papal Reform*, 291; Watterich, ed., *Pontificum Romanorum Vitae*, 1:496.

20. "Pontificalia nempe Christi indumenta, ut soror Aaron et sacrorum Dei germana, tota arte deflorabat et honorificentia. Hic purpura, punico, murice et Sidoniis conchiliis imbuta, coccusque bis tinctus auro intexitur; crisolitus, topazius, onix et berillus lapidumque genera preciosa auro innectuntur; concharum preci‹osar›um uniones, quos sola India ab ortu solis et sola Anglorum Britannia ab occasu producit, auro instellantur; aurea crucis insignia, aurea sanctorum ambientibus margaritis informantur simulacra. Tota intentio sua Christus, et Christi cultus." André Wilmart, "La légende de Ste Édith en prose et vers par le moine Goscelin," *Analecta Bollandiana* 56 (1938): 69; translation by Michael Wright in Goscelin of Saint-Bertin, *Praise of Saint Edith* in *Writing the Wilton Women: Goscelin's Legend of Edith and the "Liber Confortatorius,"* ed. Stephanie Hollis (Turnhout, 2004), 38.

Several important things are worth noting. First, Goscelin uses the language and imagery of Exodus, so central to the priestly spirituality of sacred vestments, not only to describe the saintly woman's work but also to make Edith herself "like a sister of Aaron." He incorporates the female makers of liturgical attire into the clergy's Old Testament warrant for the ornate attire they wore. Second, the final sentence—"Her whole thought was Christ and the worship of Christ"—suggests that the making of sacred vestments was itself a form of spirituality, a meditation on Christ and praise of him.[21]

Other lives of holy women also make this connection. The earliest vita of Matilda, wife of Henry, king of East Francia (918–936), emphasized this royal saint's constant good works. On feast days she read, and "on weekdays, when work is permitted, she engaged in prayer or the singing of psalms that she always did while pressing on with her handiwork."[22] Less privileged women, such as the thirteenth-century beguine Marie d'Oignies, were also depicted praying as they sewed. "While she worked with her hands or spun," Jacques de Vitry observed, "she had a Psalter set before her and sweetly said Psalms to Our Lord."[23] This learned cleric, later bishop of Acre, worked to gain ecclesiastical sanction for communities of pious laywomen like Marie who lived in private homes and supported themselves mainly through cloth making. Saint Godelieve, for example, according to her male biographer, was persecuted by her husband (who eventually had her murdered), and "consoled the grief in her soul with distaff, spindle and loom."[24]

The cult of the Virgin Mary elaborated more complex models of a female spirituality of textile work. Stories about the weaving and spinning of the Blessed Virgin that circulated in western Europe originated in an eighth-century apocryphal Latin text, the Gospel of Pseudo-Matthew. Full of all sorts of details about the holy family and the infancy of Christ, Pseudo-Matthew related that Mary spent her youth living a secluded and holy life as one of the virgins of the temple of Jerusalem. She spent her days praying and weaving. When she was betrothed to Joseph, she and six other maidens were commissioned to spin the wool for the veil of the temple. Foretelling the royal ancestry of her son and the blood of his passion, Mary spins the purple wool. As Gail McMurray Gibson has pointed out, these stories were extremely important in the representation of the Virgin and the Annunciation: she is frequently depicted spinning the purple wool at the moment the

21. Ibid., 11, 66. Interestingly, this sentence appears in the version of the text created for the nuns at Edith's abbey of Wilton, while it was excised in the version Goscelin presented to Archbishop Lanfranc of Canterbury.

22. "Cotidianis vero diebus, quibus operari licet, orationi aut psalmodie incumbens, ut semper solebat, manuum tamen instabat operibus." Bernd Schütte, ed., *Die Lebensbeschreibungen der Königin Mathilde* (Hannover, 1994), 130.

23. "The Middle-English Version of Jacques de Vitry's *Life of St. Marie d'Oignies*," trans. Sarah McNamer in Thomas Head, ed., *Medieval Hagiography: An Anthology* (New York, 2001), 719. The Latin is "quod etiam dum operaretur manibus, dum manum suam mitteret ad fortia, & digiti ejus apprehenderent fusum, psalterium ante se positum habebat, ex quo Psalmos Domino suaviter eructabat." *AASS*, Iun. IV, 643 (June 23).

24. "Nunc colo et fusis, nunc tela maerorem sui animi solatur." Drogo van Sint-Winoksbergen, *Vita Godeliph*, ed. Nikolaas-Norbert Huyghebaert (Tielt, 1982), 44; trans. Bruce L. Venarde in Head, *Medieval Hagiography*, 365.

angel Gabriel appears. The motif attracted not only artists but also clerical authors. Since the veil of the temple was torn in two (Luke 23:45) at the moment of Jesus' death, the Virgin's spinning at the Annunciation linked her textile work to the mystery of Christ's incarnation and bloody sacrifice. Another tradition from Pseudo-Matthew that was developed both iconographically and theologically was that Mary knitted a seamless tunic for the baby Jesus that magically grew along with his body to adulthood. This seamless tunic, of course, is the one mentioned in the Gospel of John (19:23) for which the soldiers at the Crucifixion drew lots. The idea of the Virgin spinning and weaving to clothe the Messiah was naturally combined with her role in the incarnation and God's salvific plan for mankind: "The young Christ is given the seamless tunic, the garment of his passion, by the mother who also gave him the garment of his human form."[25] As Gibson also noted, this led William Durand in the *Rationale*, the liturgical commentary written for the instruction of his diocesan clergy, to compare Mary's womb to the sacristy: "The priest proceeds from this place [*sacrarium*], where he puts on his vestments, out into public because Christ, proceeding from the Virgin's womb, came into the world."[26]

Miracle stories also link the textile-working fame of the Virgin to the clerical spirituality of sacred vestments. The Dominican friar Thomas of Cantimpré's mid-thirteenth-century exempla collection, the *Bonum universale de apibus*, includes a story about Thomas Becket (d. 1170). When the saintly archbishop of Canterbury was in exile at Pontigny, the story goes, the hair shirt and breeches he wore secretly under his clothing needed repair. Thomas did not want anyone in his household to know his secret. "He was wanting," the account continued, "none other than a certain most holy woman recluse [*reclusam sanctissimam*] in Canterbury who on a certain day abided outside the end of the church choir as if for the sole purpose of repairing his breeches." He was anxiously despairing of a solution when suddenly the Blessed Virgin appeared. She greeted him and comforted him. Then "she sat down next to him, received the breeches from his hands, and most fittingly repaired the tear."[27] Several aspects of the story merit emphasis. First, only very holy women could repair these very intimate elements of clerical attire: when Thomas's regular *reclusa sanctissima* is unavailable, none other than the Blessed Virgin herself fills in. Second, the implications for the repair or making of regular

25. Gail McMurray Gibson, "The Thread of Life in the Hand of the Virgin," in *Equally in God's Image: Women in the Middle Ages*, ed. Julia Bolton Holloway, Constance S. Wright, and Joan Bechtold (New York, 1990), 46–54, quote 50; Elizabeth Coatsworth, "Cloth-Making and the Virgin Mary in Anglo-Saxon Literature and Art," in *Medieval Art: Recent Perspectives; A Memorial Tribute to C. R. Dodwell*, ed. Gale R. Owen-Crocker and Timothy Graham (Manchester, 1998), 8–25. For more examples from the later Middle Ages, see Hamburger, *Nuns as Artists*, 186–87.

26. CCCM 140:23 (Lib. 1, cap. 1, par. 38): "Sacerdos a loco in quo vestes induit ad publicum procedit quia Christus, ex utero Virginis procedens, in munum venit."

27. *Materials*, 2:293. The *Cantigas de Santa María* contain a story about Saint Ildefonsus receiving an alb from the Blessed Virgin, who instructs him to wear it on her feast days. This scene was depicted on a cope orphrey: Evelin Wetter, "Defining a Model of Worship: An Embroidered Orphrey with Depictions Based on the *Cantigas de Santa María*," in *Iconography of Liturgical Textiles in the Middle Ages*, ed. Evelin Wetter, Riggisberger Berichte 18 (Riggisberg, 2010), 89–99, but especially 92.

vestments are not spelled out, but the general point seems to be that female holiness is a requirement for handling the special garments of holy men. Most intriguingly, the archbishop has a relationship with a holy woman built around his secret wearing of ascetic garb, an aspect of this tale to which we will return.

For now, note that Thomas of Cantimpré, Durand, and Goscelin of Saint-Bertin link the clerical spirituality of vestments to stories of pious and holy women's textile work. The Blessed Virgin and other women saints manifest their purity and piety by spinning and weaving. Their textile work is either associated with prayer or characterized as a prayerful activity. It is significant that these ideas appear in hagiographic and devotional texts written by clerics. They posit a pious and prayerful origin for the sacred vestments that constructed clerical virtue.

But did women consider their own textile work a form of prayer or a spiritual practice? Several scholars have noticed important differences in emphases between male clerical descriptions of female spirituality and the women's own presentation of their religious experiences.[28] So we should not take clerical assertions of women's prayerful handiwork as adequate proof of a women's spirituality of sacred vestments. But some evidence from women's writings does support a connection between textiles and spiritual life. Agnes of Harcourt, for example, in her life of Isabelle of France (written 1280–1285) recorded that

> this blessed and excellent lady in her childhood very willingly stayed in her chamber and learned to understand divine Scripture and did not want to go to the entertainments where the wives of her brothers and the other ladies went, and when she was instructed sufficiently in her letters, she would study to learn how to work with silk and would make stoles and other apparel for the holy church.[29]

This female author writing about the early signs of holiness in another elite woman portrays textile work as a path of preparation parallel or related to scriptural study, but definitely secondary to direct understanding of God's word. When describing Isabelle's adult life of prayer and charitable actions, however, Agnes does not mention her sewing. Women authors sometimes used textile metaphors to describe their literary and intellectual efforts, as when Hrosvit, a tenth-century canoness at Gandersheim, wrote in defense of her poems on the lives of the saints: "When I began to weave the threads, I did not know that there were doubts about the material I intended to work with."[30] Several female mystics—Hildegard of Bingen, Mechthild of Magdeburg, and Julian of Norwich—describe and allegorize clothing in their visions. But only Julian uses imagery

28. Catherine M. Moody, ed., *Gendered Voices: Medieval Saints and Their Interpreters* (Philadelphia, 1999); John Coakley, *Women, Men, and Spiritual Power: Female Saints and Their Male Collaborators* (New York, 2006), especially 220–24.

29. *The Writings of Agnes of Harcourt: The Life of Isabelle of France and the Letter on Louis IX and Longchamp*, ed. and trans. Sean L. Field (Notre Dame, Ind., 2003), 54–55. An inventory of the abbey of Longchamp's goods reveals several vestments sewn by Isabelle: Sean L. Field, *Isabelle of France: Capetian Sanctity and Franciscan Identity in the Thirteenth Century* (Notre Dame, Ind., 2006), 128.

30. Ferrante, *Epistolae*, http://epistolae.ccnmtl.columbia.edu/letter/20.html.

from making clothing or textiles (souls are "knit" to Christ), and she never allegorizes her own needlework.[31] The general tropes, moreover, are not prominent in any way parallel or equal to the use of food imagery analyzed by Caroline Walker Bynum in *Holy Feast, Holy Fast.*[32] Some women, in sum, may have viewed their textile work, particularly the making of ecclesiastical vestments, as a pious devotion. To the extent that they did, what I have been calling a clerical spirituality could be considered a shared set of spiritual practices cultivated by both the women makers of the garments and the clergy. But the scarcity in women's own writings of textile imagery imbued with spiritual significance or depictions of women praying as they sewed leads me to conclude that the portrayals of women virtuously and prayerfully making vestments derive more from clerical needs than from women's ideals or practices.

Courtly narratives give another perspective and possible explanation. They reveal that while some women may have sung psalms as they sewed, others sang "weaving songs" (*chansons de toile*). These survive as lyric poems in Old French, most incorporated into romances. Both the narratives in which they are embedded and the lyrics depict women singing them as they bend over their needlework, and usually younger women learning from their elders. Sewing is not the only subject: yearning for love is too. Jean Renart's early thirteenth-century romance *Guillaume de Dole*, for example, introduces the tale's heroine, Liënor, doing needlework with her mother. They are making vestments for poor churches. The song they sing portrays another mother and daughter at such work: "with golden thread they make golden crosses." The mother, who knows of her daughter's love of a certain young man, sings to her,

> Learn, daughter, to sew and to weave,
> and to raise gold crosses in the orphrey.
> You'd best forget about the love of Doon.[33]

These more worldly texts certainly suggest that many women talked and sang of their lives and love while they did spinning, weaving, sewing, and embroidery. But they also

31. Hildegard of Bingen, *Scivias* 3.6, 3.8, and *Liber divinorum operum simplicis hominis* 1.4.72, *PL*, 197:628B, 653A, 856A; Mechthild of Magdeburg, *Das fließende Licht der Gottheit*, 1.2, 1.44, 1.46, 2.4, 3.1, 4.12, 4.22, 4.27, 5.23, 6.1, 7.27, 7.64–65, ed. Gisela Vollmann-Profe, Bibliothek des Mittelalters 19 (Frankfurt am Main, 2003), 22, 58, 66–70, 84–86, 152, 264, 290, 300, 370–72, 426, 582, 662–64; Julian of Norwich, A *Revelation of Love*, 5.3, 6.35–37, 17.19–21, 51.80–264, 53.18–53, 58.11–12, 65.7–8, 68.6–7, ed. Nicholas Watson and Jacqueline Jenkins (University Park, Penn., 2006), 139, 145, 181, 277–87, 294–95, 307, 327, 335. I thank Barbara Newman for her insights and suggestions on this issue. Michael Bangert, "The Metaphor of the Vestment in the Writings of Gertrud of Helfta (1256–1302)," in *Iconography of Liturgical Textiles*, 129–39, discusses many types of clothing, but mostly monastic garb, using the term "vestment," and in none of his examples is Gertrud interpreting her *own* textile work.

32. Bynum presents abundant evidence from the writings of Hadewijch, Beatrice of Nazareth, Catherine of Siena, and Catherine of Genoa: Caroline Walker Bynum, *Holy Feast and Holy Fast: The Religious Significance of Food to Medieval Women* (Berkeley, 1987), 150–86.

33. Herlihy, *Opera Muliebra*, 58–59; Nancy A. Jones, "The Uses of Embroidery in the Romances of Jean Renart: Gender, History, Textuality," in *Jean Renart and the Art of Romance: Essays on Guillaume de Dole*, ed. Nancy Vine Durling (Gainesville, Fla., 1997), 24; E. Jane Burns, *Courtly Love Undressed: Reading through Clothes in Medieval French Culture* (Philadelphia, 2002), 88–118.

reveal that parts of the clerical ideal were well established in lay culture. The *chanson* they sing is actually entitled "A Girl and Her Mother Sit Making an Orphrey," and it is premised on the theme of the mother instructing her daughter in virtue as she teaches her embroidery. But these narratives also introduce tensions in the clerical ideal: women's work making vestments may be virtuous, and perceived as a way of teaching virtuous conduct, but not every woman sewing may have been thinking virtuous thoughts!

Surviving Vestments

The new style of opulent vestment that women created in collaboration with clerics was remarkably successful and enduring. The previous chapter showed that depictions of clerics in vestments made of precious silks and ornamented with gold emerged first in the Carolingian Empire in the mid-ninth century and then spread throughout Europe by the late eleventh. Depiction, however, lagged behind the actual existence of ornate vestments: they are documented in Carolingian inventories about a half a century before they are pictured in manuscript illuminations, and in Anglo-Saxon sources about a century and a half before they are represented. The evidence of surviving vestments confirms this rough chronology of the emergence of the new style in the late eighth and early ninth centuries, but the evidence is not plentiful. Indeed, the very success of the new ornate style of liturgical garb and the clerical spirituality associated with it profoundly shaped the corpus of vestments that has survived today.

Not surprisingly, most of what we know about is in museums. General art museums, usually for a textile or fashion collection, acquire vestments primarily with an eye to the beauty or rarity of their materials and workmanship. So those made of technically complex patterned silks or decorated with very fine embroidery tend to be conserved and displayed. The medieval and Renaissance galleries of the Victorian and Albert Museum in London, for example, feature several chasubles made of silk velvet and the spectacular Syon cope with its elaborately embroidered scenes from the lives of Christ and the Blessed Virgin. Diocesan museums collect chiefly on geographical and historical grounds: art and artifacts from the ecclesiastical territory of the diocese or historically associated with the see. The cathedral treasury usually forms the core of the collection along with the contents of the bishop's palace and works that once graced churches throughout the diocese. The vestments in these collections were conserved either because they were the finest apparel the cathedral (or subsidiary church) had or because they were associated with a prominent figure in the history of the see. So the diocesan museum in Bamberg devotes an entire room to the burial garments of Bishop Suidger (1040–1047), who became Pope Clement II in 1046, while the diocesan museum of Brixen features the silk vestments of the cathedral, the most spectacular being the "eagle silk" chasuble of Bishop Albuin.

Often these two motives for conservation are entwined. A good example is the stunningly beautiful "Saint Vitalis" chasuble conserved today at the Abegg-Stiftung museum (figure 40). Before its acquisition by textile collector Werner Abegg, it was conserved for

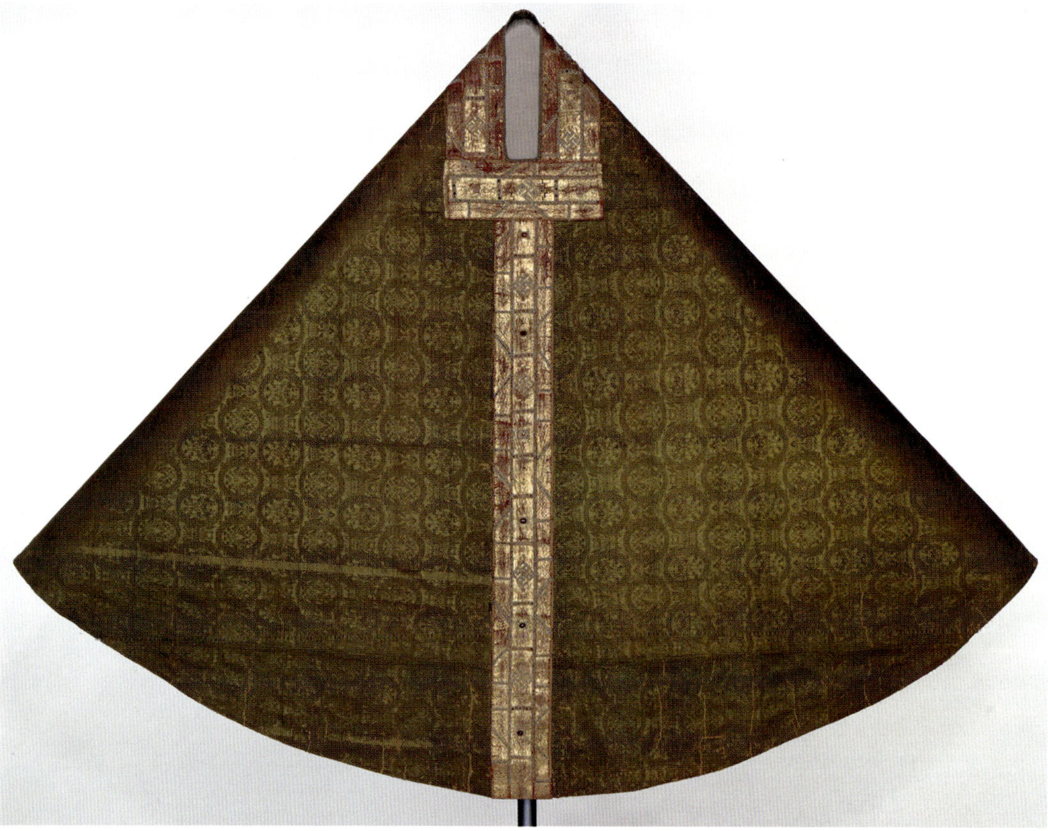

FIGURE 40. Vitalis chasuble (front view), eleventh century, inv. no. 232, Abegg-Stiftung, CH-3132 Riggisberg. © Abegg-Stiftung, CH-3132 Riggisberg, 2000 / photo: Christoph von Viràg.

centuries by the archiepiscopal abbey of St. Peter, Salzburg. The shimmering green fabric is an incised silk samite with a pattern of oval medallions enclosing griffins with eagles' beaks and lions' feet (figure 41). Golden tablet-woven bands, connected with bands of pearl decoration, border the neckline and run down the front. These were further embellished with gold embroidery incorporating pearls and tiny precious stones (figures 42 and 43). The artistry displayed by the women who made this chasuble and the costly materials employed easily explain its conservation. Its traditional association with Saint Vitalis provides other reasons. Vitalis was the second bishop of Salzburg and the abbot of St. Peter's abbey; he died sometime before 730. The materials of the garment make it impossible, however, for Vitalis to have worn it. The fabric is comparable to silks datable to the eleventh or twelfth centuries and the pearl embroidery technique is typical of early eleventh-century German works. Its measurements, the width of the fabric used, and the way in which it was tailored are compatible with a date in the eleventh century. So why was it called the chasuble of Saint Vitalis? Perhaps because it was worn to celebrate his feast day or because at some point in the modern era it looked "medieval" enough for someone to think it was Vitalis's.

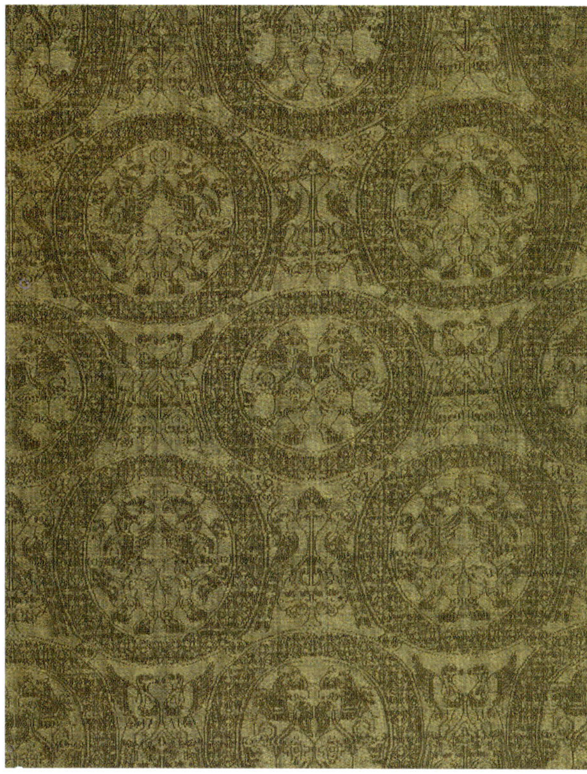

FIGURE 41. Vitalis chasuble, detail of silk pattern, eleventh century, inv. no. 232, Abegg-Stiftung, CH-3132 Riggisberg. © Abegg-Stiftung, CH-3132 Riggisberg, 2000 / photo: Christoph von Viràg.

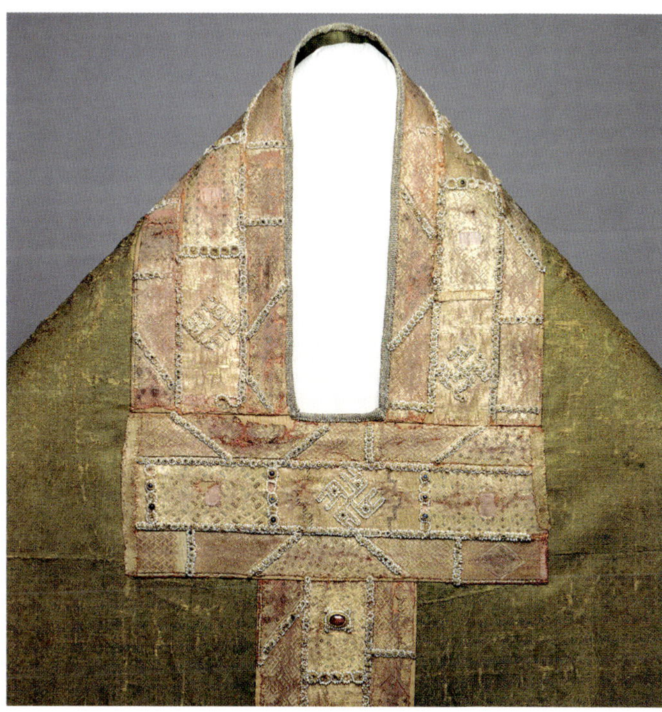

FIGURE 42. Detail of neckline with tablet-woven strips and pearl embroidery, eleventh century, inv. no. 232, Abegg-Stiftung, CH-3132 Riggisberg. © Abegg-Stiftung, CH-3132 Riggisberg, 1986 / photo: Hans Kobi.

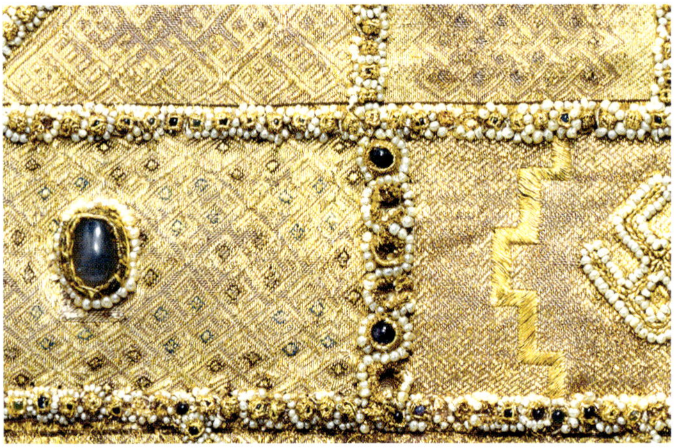

FIGURE 43. Detail of pearl- and precious-gem-embroidered ornament, eleventh century, inv. no. 232, Abegg-Stiftung, CH-3132 Riggisberg. © Abegg-Stiftung, CH-3132 Riggisberg, 2000 / photo: Christoph von Viràg.

The frequent association of medieval vestments with medieval saints in many cases helped preserve them, especially if they were not as beautiful as the Vitalis chasuble.[34]

In other cases, such as that of the linen alb of Saint Bernulf, the bishop of Utrecht (1028–1056), in the Utrecht Catharijneconvent museum (figure 44), study of the garment's style yields "no evidence to contradict its having been created in the mid-eleventh century, as is traditionally believed."[35] Details of its construction, however, suggest a more complex story. The sleeve insets, the side gores, and the general cut of the alb make an early eleventh-century date possible, so the plain, base garment could plausibly have been worn by the saint. What is striking about the alb, however, is its decoration. Seven different widths of golden tablet-woven bands ornament the neckline, cuffs, shoulder and sleeve seams, and hem—and these date, at the earliest, from the late twelfth century. The saint's cherished garment could have been "updated" for continued ceremonial use. We've already

34. *Textile Conservation*, 158–75; Karel Otavsky and Anne E. Wardwell, *Die Textilsammlung der Abegg-Stiftung, Band 5: Mittelalterliche Textilien II: Zwischen Europa und China* (Riggisberg, 2011), 142–48. Other examples where technical analysis of the materials dates the vestment to a period long after the life of the saint with whom it is associated are the *casula* (really a cope) of Saint John Angeloptes (d. 439) in the museum of the Cathedral of Ravenna (silk, at the very earliest tenth century); the chasuble of Saint Wolfgang (d. 994) (silk, eleventh century); the Saint Ebbo (d. 750) chasuble at Sens (tenth-century Byzantine silk); a cope, two dalmatics, and a chasuble of Saint Valerius of Saragossa (d. 315) (materials thirteenth-century and later); and a cope of Saint Moderanno, bishop of Rennes (d. 730–750?) (materials late tenth or early eleventh century). Adolfo Venturi, "Museo del duomo di Ravenna: La 'casula' di Giovanni Angeloptes," in *Le Gallerie Nazionali Italiane: Notizie e documenti* 3 (1897): 258–60; *Sakrale Gewänder des Mittelalters: Ausstellung im Bayerischen Nationalmuseum München 8. Juli bis 25. September 1955* (Munich, 1955), 16–17 (cat. no. 16), plate 9; Muthesius, *Byzantine Silk*, 189 (cat. M78), plates 44A, 92B–95B; Karel Otavsky and Muhammad A'bbas Muhammad Salim, *Mittelalterliche Textilien I: Ägypten Persen und Mesopotamien Spanien und Nordafrika* (Riggisberg, 1995), 190–93; Rosa Martin I Ros, "Les vêtements liturgiques de Saint-Valère: Étude historique," *Bulletin du CIETA* 73 (1995–1996): 63–78; Donata Devoti and Giulia Meucci, "Il piviale di San Moderanno," in *Il filo della storia: Tessuti antichi in Emilia-Romana*, ed. Marta Cuoghi Costantini and Iolanda Silvestri (Bologna, 2005), 67–71.

35. *Textile Conservation*, 190–93. The style and embroidery technique of the chasuble of Bishop Bernhard of Hildesheim (d. 1153) also lend "credence to the traditional assumption that the chasuble was made in the first half of the twelfth century." Ibid., 197.

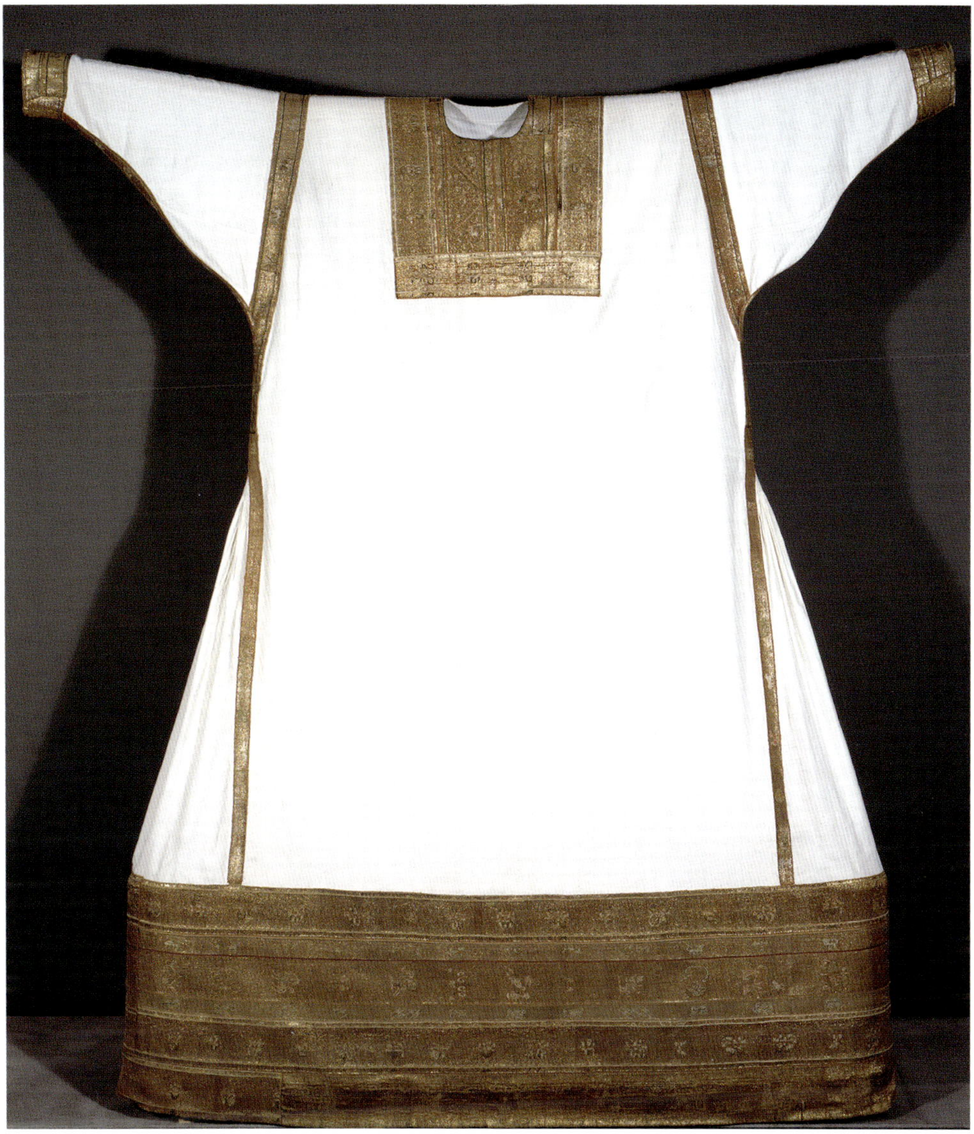

FIGURE 44. Alb of Saint Bernulf of Utrecht, eleventh century with later additions, Museum Catharijneconvent, Utrecht. Photo courtesy of Museum Catharijneconvent, Utrecht.

seen in the last chapter how ornaments were sewn onto the sixth-century vestments of Saint Caesarius of Arles by those who venerated his remains in the thirteenth century. At some point, it seems likely that the alb of Saint Bernulf was conserved in Utrecht because of its heavy golden embellishments as much as its associations with a local holy man.

Note that both of these motives for conservation—beautiful ornamentation and ideas linking holiness with vestments—were central features of the new ornate liturgical garb and the spirituality underwriting it. This is one reason the evidence for the plain style that preceded it in late antiquity comes largely from written sources and from mosaics, frescoes, and manuscript illuminations: only a handful of ecclesiastical garments survive from before the tenth century.[36] The body of textile evidence for medieval ecclesiastical vesture illuminates, basically, the central and later Middle Ages. Like most of the rest of our sources too, it has an elite bias: the vestments of leading prelates whose tombs have been excavated are more numerous than garments of ordinary priests. Indeed, vestments conserved in museums give an exaggerated impression of the success and opulence of the ornate style of liturgical garb.

Some leaven is offered by the collection of vestments surviving from the church of Castel Sant'Elia in northern Lazio. The relative modern obscurity of the tiny town of Castel Sant'Elia and the humble character of most of its vestments helped preserve them as a group. Indeed, collections of more ornate and valuable vestments were often sundered in the modern era as ecclesiastical institutions fell on hard times and sold them off piecemeal.[37] But ideas about the holy also helped keep the Castel Sant'Elia collection intact. The vestments originally belonged to the Benedictine monastery of Sant'Elia, led in the sixth century by the saints Anastasius and Nonnosus. Although none of the garments in the collection date to the era of these venerated abbots, by the early modern period the entire trove of twenty-six vestments was associated with these two saints and conserved as relics. Most of the garments date to the twelfth and early thirteenth centuries—probably from the renovation of the church under Abbot Bovo c. 1126 to the suppression of the monastery in 1258—although several were evidently altered in the later Middle Ages or in the early modern era.[38] The twelfth-century renovations of the church reveal considerable wealth and connections to a papal or curial milieu, and several pieces within the collection of liturgical vestments also suggest a prosperous monastery. An abbatial miter embroidered with silk and gilt-silver thread and two pairs of elaborately decorated leather liturgical sandals—all dating from the early thirteenth century—are the most precious pieces.[39] So the Castel Sant'Elia collection reveals what kind of vestments a prosperous Benedictine abbey had in the twelfth and thirteenth centuries and not what an "average" or even poor church might have owned. Still, few of the Castel Sant'Elia vestments could be characterized as ornate.

36. See chapter 3, 104n12, 106–7.

37. The textile treasures of the ancient Benedictine monastery of Saint Peter in Salzburg were sold off in the 1930s, some through the dealer Adolph Loewi and others through private collectors: the Vitalis chasuble was purchased by Werner Abegg; a beautiful thirteenth-century miter by the Metropolitan Museum in New York; and a silk chasuble with an inscription recording its donor, Emperor Henry II (r. 1014–1024), by the Museum of Fine Arts in Boston. Sandra L. Rosenbaum, "The Role of a Dealer in the Development of Collections: Loewi-Robertson, Inc., A Case Study," *Bulletin du CIETA* 67 (1989): 89–101; Karin von Lerber, "A Medieval Bell-Shaped Chasuble from St. Peter in Salzburg," *Journal of the Museum of Fine Arts, Boston* 4 (1992): 27–51.

38. Several of the large bell-shaped chasubles were cut down to the narrower shape popular in the later Middle Ages, and obviously fourteenth- and fifteenth-century brocaded orphreys were added to two of the albs. Maureen C. Miller, "The Liturgical Vestments of Castel Sant'Elia: Their Historical Significance and Current Condition," *Medieval Clothing and Textiles* (forthcoming). See also Joseph Braun, "Der Paramentenschatz zu Castel S. Elia," *Zeitschrift für christliche Kunst* 12 (1899): 291–302, 343–56; Luisa Mortari, "Il Museo di Arredi Sacri a Castel S. Elia," *Bollettino d'arte* 41 (1956): 275–77; Marica Mercalli and Silvia Checchi, eds., I *paramenti liturgici di Castel Sant'Elia: La loro storia e la cronaca del restauro* (Rome, 2012).

39. Mercalli and Checchi, *I paramenti liturgici*, 67–72, 88–99, 130–33.

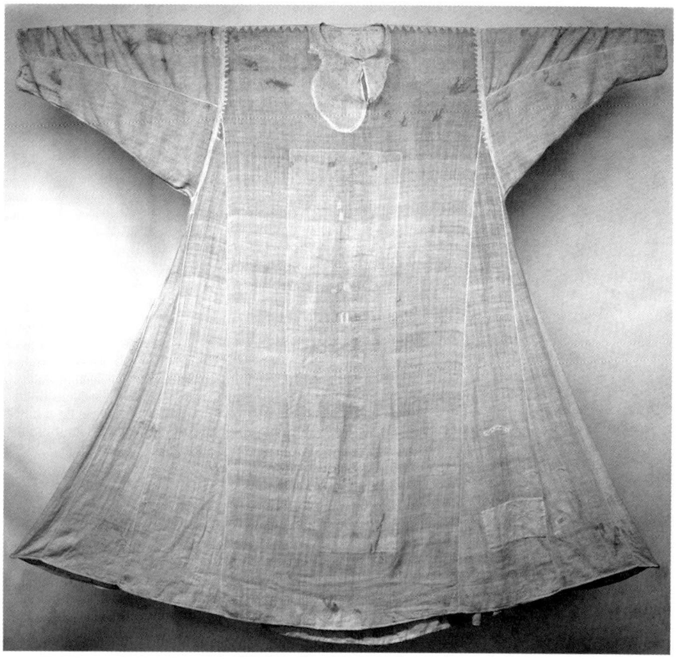

FIGURE 45. Alb, twelfth–thirteenth centuries, Museo della Spiritualità "Abate Giovanni Rosavini," Castel Sant'Elia. Photo courtesy of the Istituto Superiore per la Conservazione ed il Restauro, Laboratorio Restauro e Conservazione Manufatti Tessili, Rome.

All five of the albs were entirely plain in the central Middle Ages with orphreys having been added at the bottom front to two of them only in the fourteenth and fifteenth centuries (figure 45).[40] Of the eleven medieval chasubles, the base fabric of more than half (63 percent) is plain, and rather coarse, linen or cotton. One is entirely plain with no surviving ornamentation. The others have "runners" (*stoloni*) on front, back, or both, and some of these are of colored silk. But they could also be dyed strips of the same base material, as in the case of number 00174793, a cotton bell chasuble with a blue cotton runner down the back (figure 46). It is impossible to determine, of course, when even these simple bands were added,[41] so one has to entertain the possibility that even in a well-to-do Benedictine community such as Castel Sant'Elia the priest's chasuble might be plain, undyed linen or cotton.

Some inventories of church treasuries from the twelfth and thirteenth centuries reveal a similar mix of ornate and plain liturgical garb. The Cathedral of Bamberg in the second quarter of the twelfth century, for example, had many more chasubles than did Sant'Elia—forty as compared to eleven—but the same percentage were unornamented.[42] The proportions vary in this very small sample from a low of 21 percent ornate chasubles at the

40. Braun judged both decorative panels to be late medieval, describing one as a blue and white brocatelle of the fourteenth or fifteenth centuries ("ein weissblauer Brokatell dürfte allerdings erst dem XIV. oder gar XV. Jahrh. angehört haben"). Braun, "Der Paramentenschatz," 355.

41. Given the lack of uniformity or even symmetry in the presence of these "runners" (some only on one side, some with a lateral crosspiece, but some without), one hypothesis the restorers suggest is that these bands—especially those of silk—were added to stabilize the fabric more than to decorate the garment. The weight of the fabric worn or hung leads to distension, a phenomenon influencing the decision to create storage for most of the vestments so that they can lie flat. Mercalli and Checchi, *I paramenti liturgici*, 148.

42. The inventory of 1127 lists "casule XL ex hiis XV auro ornate" (63% plain, 37% ornamented with gold), while one dated roughly to the second quarter of the twelfth century catalogs "Casule albe II, una

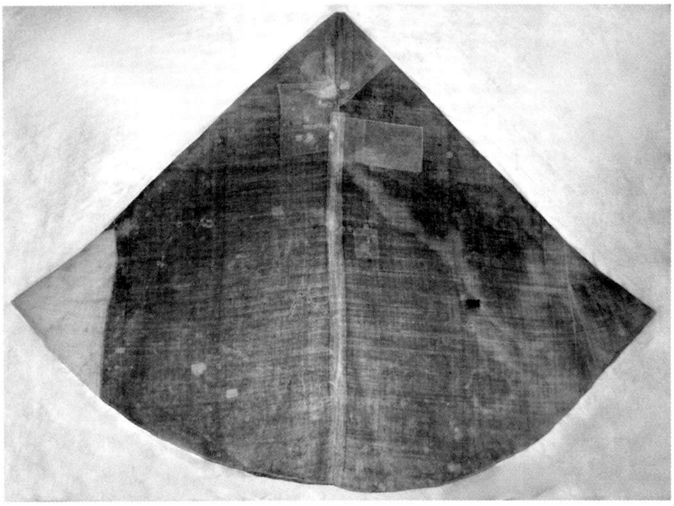

FIGURE 46. Cotton chasuble, twelfth–thirteenth centuries, Museo della Spiritualità "Abate Giovanni Rosavini," Castel Sant'Elia. Photo courtesy of the Istituto Superiore per la Conservazione ed il Restauro, Laboratorio Restauro e Conservazione Manufatti Tessili, Rome.

collegiate church of Enger in the first half of the twelfth century to a dazzling 67 percent at the imperial monastery of Prüfening in 1165, but most common was a mix of roughly one-third ornamented to two-thirds plain. What was considered distinctively ornate, however, also varied. The Cathedral of Bamberg, like most of the institutions with surviving inventories, divided garments into those decorated with gold ("*auro ornato*" or "*aurifrigiato*") and those not. Using this criterion, rather than the proportion of silk to linen or cotton, only one of Sant'Elia's eleven chasubles would have been considered ornate.[43] The early twelfth-century inventory of the imperial canonry of Gandersheim is nearly unique in giving a detailed gradation: its chasubles "entirely woven of gold" (three) were distinguished from those "decorated with gold but not all over" (nine), from those of silk without any gold (thirteen), and finally from those made only of wool (six).[44] The language of distinction within medieval inventories generally suggests that most churches had everyday (*cottidianus, usualis, communis*) liturgical garb and then a smaller percentage of more precious festal (*festivus, principalis, preciosus*) attire, although a few more bluntly distinguished simply between good and bad (*casule bone et male*) or better (*meliores*) and meaner (*viliores*) vestments.[45] This evidence from inventories and from the surviving vestments of Castel Sant'Elia needs to be balanced against the artistic representations of liturgical garb discussed in chapter 3 and the vast majority of vestments preserved in museum collections. The ornate style we have been chronicling was an extremely important development in the history of clerical clothing and it spread throughout Europe by the late eleventh century. But for even relatively prosperous churches such as Sant'Elia,

cum aurifrigio, altera sine. Virides II, I cum aurifrigio, altera sine, purperee II cum aurifrigio, vetuste VI" (67% plain, 33% ornamented with gold): *Schatzverzeichnisse*, 18–19.

43. At least one church, that of Saint Sebastian in Magdeburg, did distinguish liturgical garments made of wool and linen from those made *de pallio* (of silk): ibid., 51. For the one Castel Sant'Elia chasuble with some metallic (gilt silver) decoration, see Mercalli and Checchi, *I paramenti liturgici*, 64–67, 124–28.

44. *Schatzverzeichnisse*, 35: "III Casule per totum auro intexte, VIIII alie auro ornate, sed non per totum, sine auro serice XIII, sex lanee."

45. Ibid., 27, 61, 79, 92, 97, 101, 106.

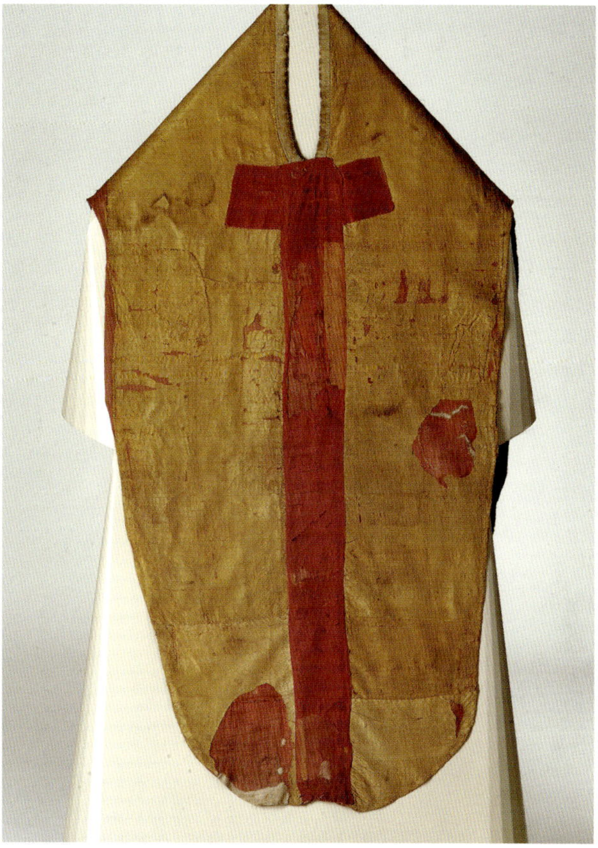

FIGURE 47. Silk chasuble (twelfth century?) altered in the fourteenth–fifteenth centuries, Museo della Spiritualità "Abate Giovanni Rosavini," Castel Sant'Elia. Photo courtesy of the Istituto Superiore per la Conservazione ed il Restauro, Laboratorio Restauro e Conservazione Manufatti Tessili, Rome.

silk- and gold-embroidered vestments were likely reserved for solemn feast days, while daily Mass was said in unornamented linen or cotton albs and chasubles.

Further, while museums showcase the most beautiful surviving exemplars of the new style, the Castel Sant'Elia collection shows us a lower end of ornate and the afterlife of a church's finest attire. The chasuble cataloged as number 00174801 clearly began its life as the sort of bell-shaped chasuble typical of the eleventh and twelfth centuries: the sharp slope of its shoulders and the slit form of its neck opening are comparable to other exemplars from this era (figure 47). The base fabric is a fine gold-colored samite silk, lined with red linen, and ornamented with a runner of red silk down the back and a runner in the same material down the front with a horizontal piece just under the neck opening.[46] This chasuble was cut down at some point in the later Middle Ages when a narrower form, leaving the arms more free than the full bell-shape, came into style. The original gold silk bell chasuble also may have been worn out or damaged because the fabric in the surviving vestment is pieced. Such recycling of older garments was surely common in ecclesiastical institutions. The scribe inventorying the Bamberg Cathedral treasury in 1127 gives a rare description of such a process when trying to explain the number of copes. He recorded eighty-four but added, "There were eighty-nine, but of these

46. *I paramenti liturgici*, 110–12.

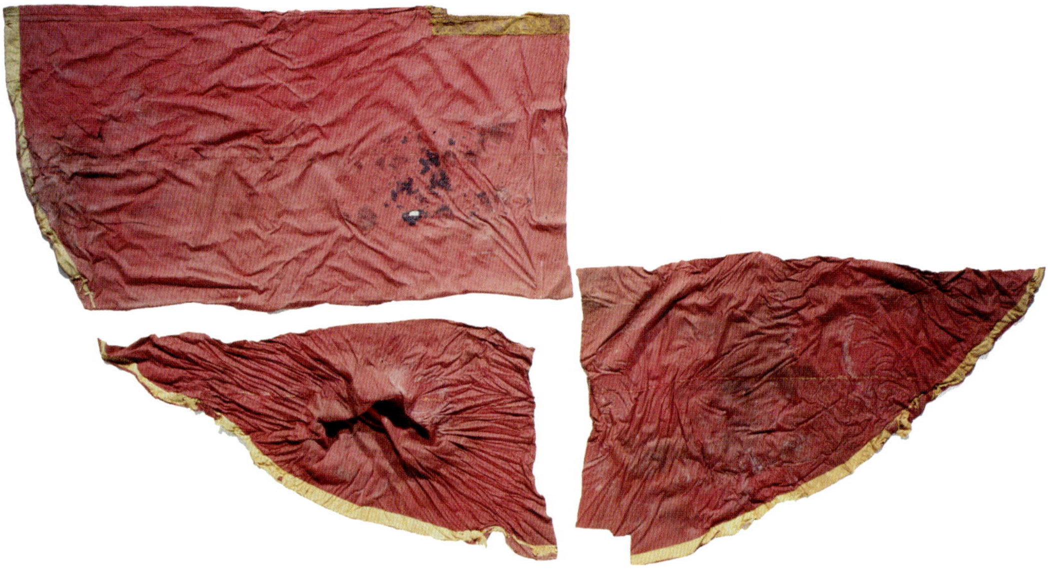

FIGURE 48. Pieces of red silk used to wrap the relics of Saint Anthony of Padua, c. 1200–1250, Basilica di Sant'Antonio, Padua, under conservation at the Abegg-Stiftung. © Abegg-Stiftung, CH-3132 Riggisberg / photo: Hans Kobi.

twenty-three were destroyed, from the pieces of which joined together we made those whole copes that we added to the rest."[47] The results of such repiecing in this Castel Sant'Elia chasuble are not so aesthetically pleasing, although the original vestment was also clearly not of the quality of the Saint Vitalis chasuble. So not all ornate vestments should be imagined as on par with the spectacular workmanship of museum pieces. But the historical value of surviving textiles goes far beyond the empirical check they provide to the images of medieval life gleaned from artistic and textual representations. Surviving garments, even less beautiful ones—like this Castel Sant'Elia chasuble or Saint Francis's tunic—are historically significant for the stories they have to tell.

Shared Knowledge and Concealed Relationships

One such story is about the spirituality of sacred vestments and how women participated in it. While most of the evidence presented in chapter 2 was from written sources, surviving textiles reveal several clerical practices that are not captured in texts. Reliquary vestments are a case in point. Texts show us that ideas linking vestments and clerical virtues developed into spiritual practices, such as vesting prayers, the bestowal of garments in ordination rites, and the blessing of vestments. Once all vestments were

47. *Schatzverzeichnisse*, 18: "Cappe LXXXIIII, quarum XXVI aurifrigio sunt composite. LXXXIX quidem fuerunt, sed ex hiis XXIII annichilate fuerunt, ex quibus frustra colligentes, quasdam integras cappas fecimus et quibusdam cappis reliqua induximus."

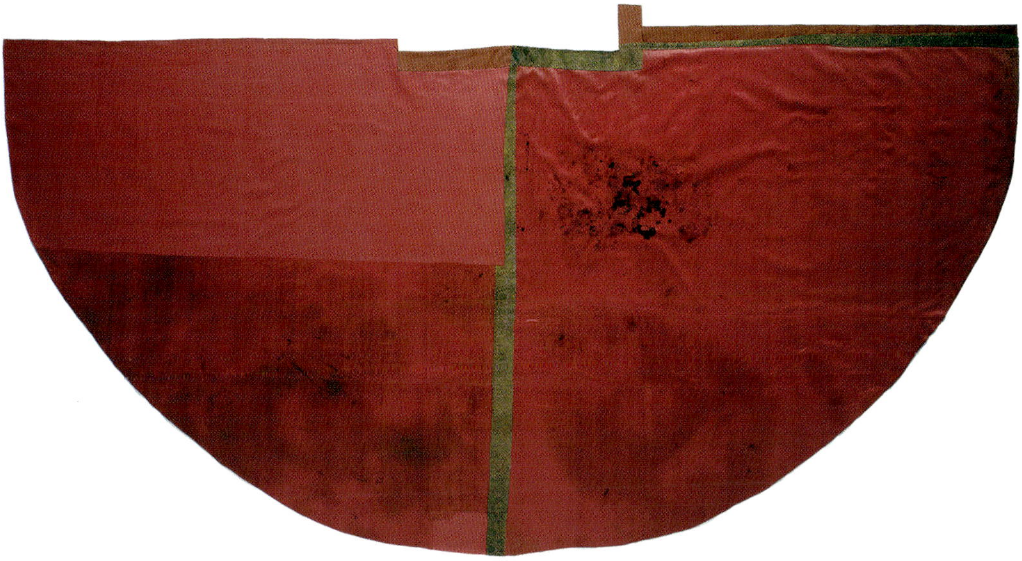

FIGURE 49. Bell-shaped chasuble reconstructed at the Abegg-Stiftung from the three pieces of red silk used to wrap the relics of Saint Anthony of Padua, c. 1200–1250, Basilica di Sant'Antonio, Padua. © Abegg-Stiftung, CH-3132 Riggisberg / photo: Hans Kobi.

blessed, however, the desire for holiness in clerical attire generated other practices and expressions. Textiles show us the development of a class of especially sacred vestments.[48]

Ecclesiastical institutions that just happened to have a vestment associated with a patron saint tended to develop that resource. So the cathedral clergy of Utrecht, believing they had the alb of their holy eleventh-century bishop Bernulf, not only used it for special feasts, but added ornament to it. That one vestment was clearly regarded as more especially sacred than other sacred vestments, and its appearance was upgraded to articulate its status. Note that this was not their only option. In late antiquity and the early Middle Ages, clothes associated with holy men—like the tunic and pallia of Saint Caesarius of Arles, or the dalmatics of Saint Ambrose of Milan—were buried with them or carefully placed in a container and venerated at an altar. Even after the emergence of the clerical spirituality of sacred vestments and the ornate style of liturgical attire, garments were buried with clerics believed to be holy. When Anthony of Padua's relics were opened in 1981, in preparation for the 750th anniversary of the saint's death, for example, his physical remains were discovered to have been divided into three parcels, each wrapped in a piece of red silk. Those pieces of silk, in the skilled hands of the conservators, were revealed to have been cut from his chasuble (figures 48 and 49).[49] But instead of burying

48. There is New Testament warrant, of course, for the holiness of Jesus working through his clothing when in Mark 5:28–34 a woman afflicted with bleeding touched his cloak and was healed. Although he tells the woman her faith has healed her, the text says that when she touched his garment Jesus "realized that power had gone out from him." In Acts 19:11–12, similar powers are attributed to Paul: "even handkerchiefs and aprons that had touched him were taken to the sick, and their illnesses were cured and the evil spirits left them."

49. *Textile Conservation*, 296–310. Buried after his death in 1231 in the church of Santa Maria Mater Domini in Padua, Anthony's remains were transferred 32 years later to the new basilica built in his honor.

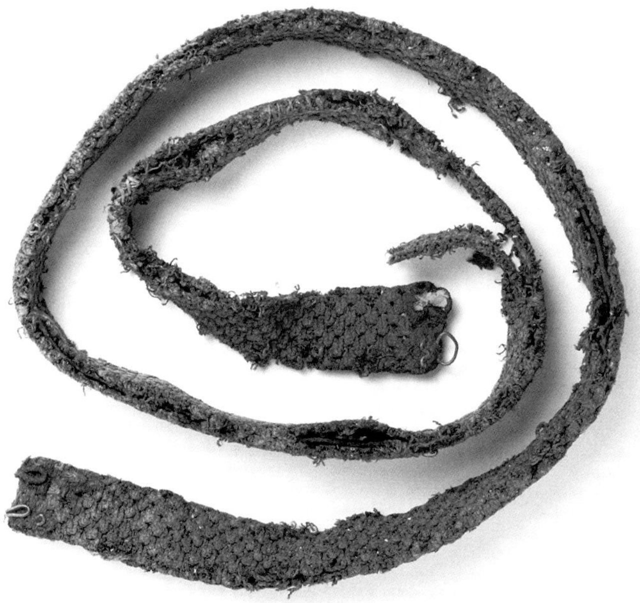

FIGURE 50. Cincture relic, eleventh–sixteenth centuries, Archiepiscopal Abbey of Saint Peter, Salzburg, before conservation at the Abegg-Stiftung. © Kunstsammlungen der Erzabtei St. Peter / © Abegg-Stiftung, CH-3132 Riggisberg / photo: Hans Kobi.

vestments associated with revered clerics, some clerical communities preserved the memory of deceased brothers by continuing to wear their liturgical garb. These were the supersacred vestments among the sacred vestments in the sacristy.

When they wore out, new vestments were made to hold the venerated pieces. These new vestments were, in effect, both liturgical garments and reliquaries. A cincture from the Abbey of St. Peter at Salzburg, associated variously with Saint Vitalis or Saint Rupert, provides a first example (figures 50–52). It was reset twice. The innermost original relic was a medieval tablet-woven band of dark blue silk. Sometime between the eleventh and thirteenth centuries, its fragments were enclosed in a silk filet net—clearly allowing some visible contact with the relic, but also making it possible to wear it. Again in the sixteenth century a silk macramé tube was created to enclose the relic and its now venerable first resetting. It could still be used as a cincture into the twentieth century.

A baroque chasuble, belonging to the Cistercian monastery of St. Urban in the canton of Lucerne and called the chasuble of Saint Ulrich (bishop of Augsburg, 923–973), provides another example of this process (figures 53–56). Under the eighteenth-century silk of the chasuble, conservators discovered many fragments of various fabrics stitched onto a kapok and linen base. Most of the fragments were of a purple, tenth- or eleventh-century, Islamic silk, some with pieces of a golden tapestry-woven border. Like so many puzzle pieces, the fragments could be reconstructed to form the type of

The three bundles of his remains were created at that time and placed in a wooden chest within the altar where he is venerated. The chasuble—of early thirteenth-century Sicilian silk with gold orphreys—showed signs of wear: it was probably one the saint wore in life and that clothed him in his initial burial.

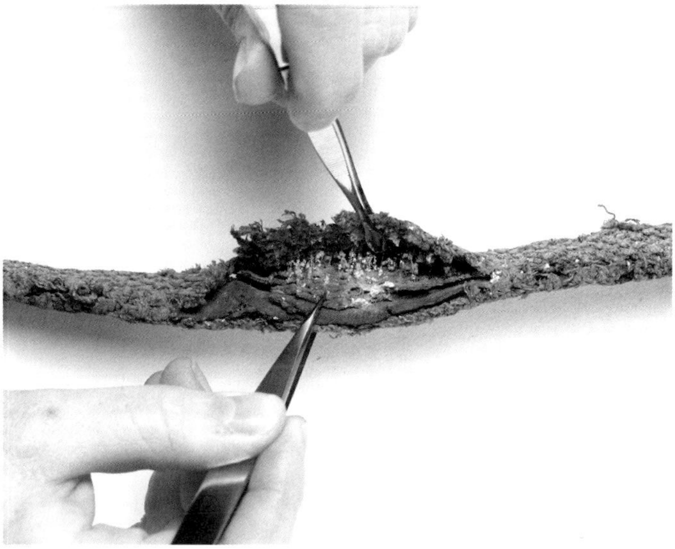

FIGURE 51. Damaged area of outer sixteenth-century covering through which the inner contents of the cincture relic were visible, Archiepiscopal Abbey of Saint Peter, Salzburg. © Kunstsammlungen der Erzabtei St. Peter / © Abegg-Stiftung, CH-3132 Riggisberg / photo: Hans Kobi.

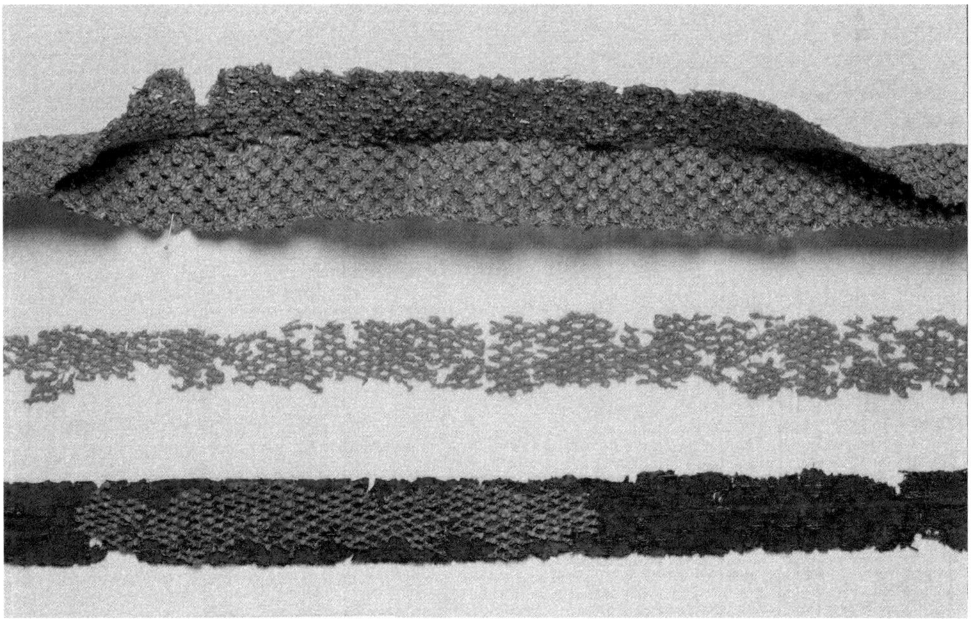

FIGURE 52. Cincture relic, Archiepiscopal Abbey of Saint Peter, Salzburg: from bottom, the tablet-woven relic with silk net covering adhering to portions; the silk filet cover, eleventh–thirteenth centuries; second macramé covering, sixteenth century. © Kunstsammlungen der Erzabtei St. Peter / © Abegg-Stiftung, CH-3132 Riggisberg / photo: Hans Kobi.

bell-shaped chasuble typical of Saint Ulrich's time. Apparently, when the saint's chasuble began to disintegrate, its pieces were gathered together and enclosed within a new vestment so that Ulrich's chasuble could still be worn.[50]

50. Ibid., 282–84, 448–53. Additionally, a chasuble, dalmatic, stole, and maniple buried with Saint Ulrich are preserved in Augsburg, and two other chasubles—one silk, the other linen with silk

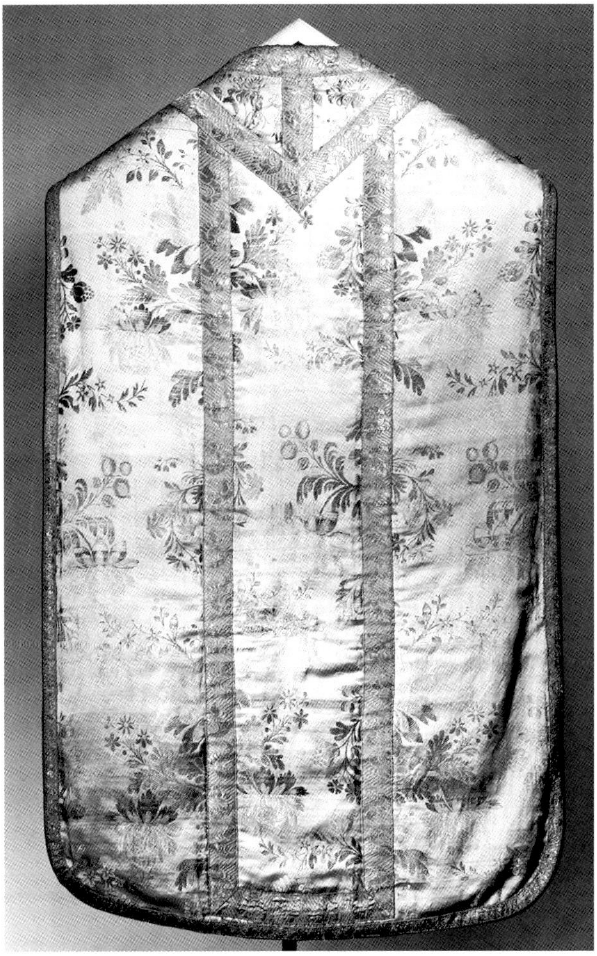

FIGURE 53. Back of the eighteenth-century Saint Ulrich chasuble before conservation, Monastery of Saint Urban, Saint Urban. By permission of the monastery of Saint Urban / © Abegg-Stiftung, CH-3132 Riggisberg / photo: Anne Javor.

Both these examples raise interesting questions about visibility, knowledge, and gender relations. By the eighteenth-century resetting of the fragments of Saint Ulrich's chasuble, a man could have helped the clergy of St. Urban's fashion the reliquary vestment. From the late Middle Ages, men came to dominate the more prestigious functions in textile production, like weaving, and from the late thirteenth century male tailors were fashioning some liturgical garments.[51] But in the early and central Middle Ages, women would have been collaborating with clerics to keep their especially sacred vestments wearable. Such projects would have provided very rare moments of direct access to relics

decoration—associated with the saint survive: Sigrid Müller-Christensen, "Liturgische Gewänder mit dem Namen des heiligen Ulrich," in *Augusta 955–1955: Forschungen und Studien zur Kultur- und Wirtschaftsgeschichte Augsburgs* (Munich, 1955), 53–60.

51. Herlihy associated male involvement in textile work with the revival of towns and dated the beginning of their takeover of the higher skilled tasks from the late twelfth century, but it is in the thirteenth and fourteenth centuries—in guild records and account books—that evidence of increasing male

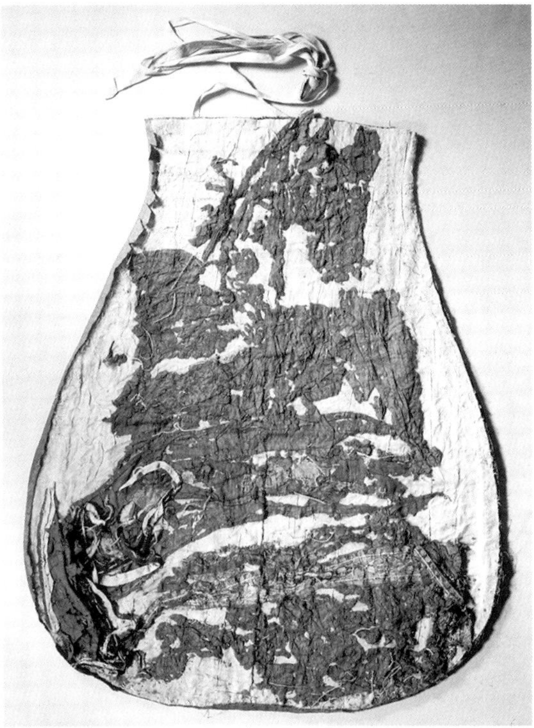

FIGURE 54. Lining of the front of the Saint Ulrich chasuble with remnants of early medieval silk discovered during conservation, Monastery of Saint Urban, Saint Urban. By permission of the monastery of Saint Urban / © Abegg-Stiftung, CH-3132 Riggisberg / photo: Anne Javor.

for women who were not even allowed to enter the sanctuary or approach the altar. Not just any woman, as the Becket miracle suggests, would be called in for such a task. What sort of spiritual experience was it for her? Surely to be asked would itself be a meaningful affirmation of virtue and skill; perhaps it came as the fruit of a long spiritual friendship with a cleric. Once women's labors had retrofitted the relic, so to speak, they had a particular knowledge of it: they knew of the sacred fragments of silk lying invisibly below the surface of a beautiful chasuble or at the inner core of a much-reworked cincture. They knew, and the clerics who wore them knew. This was a very special form of shared knowledge. Our sources give us no glimpses into what this meant to either side of the partnership, or how that shared knowledge conditioned other interactions, or how either women or clerics used this knowledge. But its existence is undeniably announced by the physical evidence.

infiltration of textile work mounts: *Opera Muliebra*, 92–97, 147–48, 161–62, 185–91; Kay Staniland, *Embroiderers* (Toronto, 1991), 7–14; Sylvia Hogarth, "Ecclesiastical Vestments and Vestmentmakers in York, 1300–1600," *York Historian* 7 (1986): 2–11. Unlike other kinds of women's work increasingly performed by men in the later Middle Ages, textile work remained a mark of feminine virtue: Ruth Mazo Karras, "'This Skill in a Woman Is by No Means to Be Despised': Weaving and the Gender Division of Labor in the Middle Ages," in *Medieval Fabrications: Dress, Textiles, Clothwork, and Other Cultural Imaginings*, ed. E. Jane Burns (New York, 2004), 89–104.

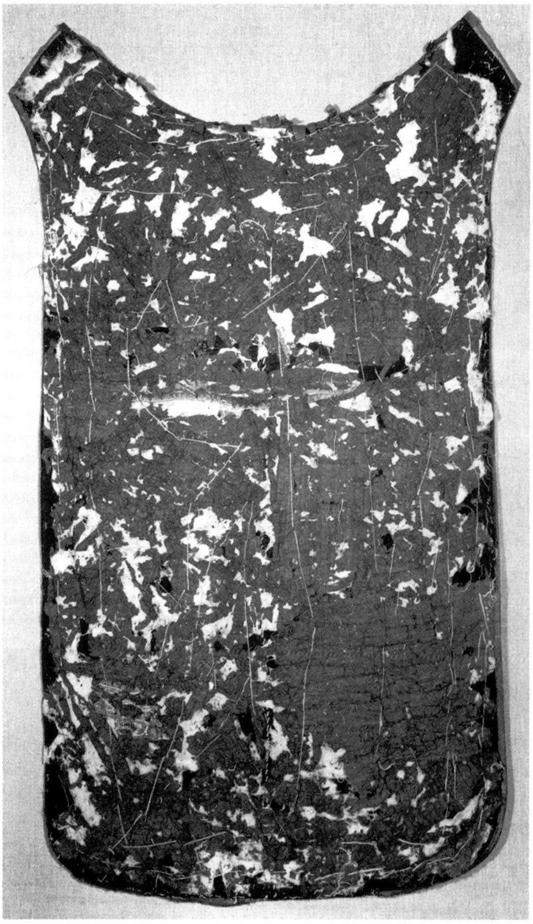

Figure 55. Lining of the back of the Saint Ulrich chasuble with remnants of early medieval silk discovered during conservation, Monastery of Saint Urban, Saint Urban. By permission of the monastery of Saint Urban / © Abegg-Stiftung, CH-3132 Riggisberg / photo: Anne Javor.

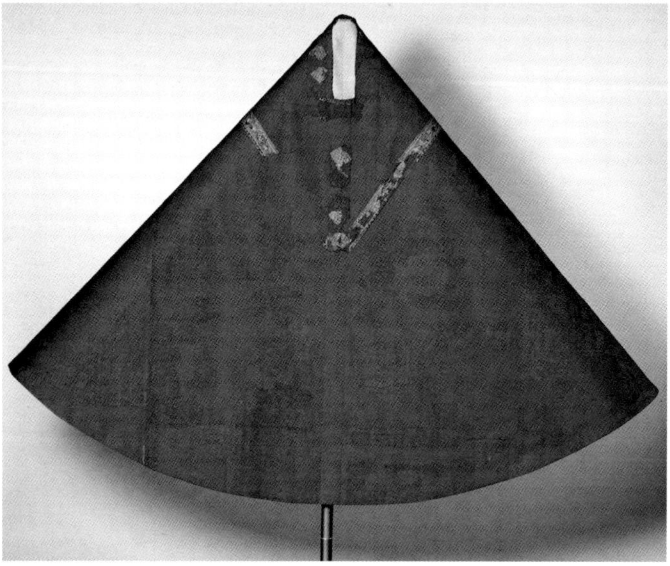

Figure 56. Early medieval silk fragments found within the Saint Ulrich chasuble, reconstructed on a backing of cotton fabric by conservators at the Abegg-Stiftung, revealing the front of the bell chasuble. Monastery of Saint Urban, Saint Urban. By permission of the monastery of Saint Urban / © Abegg-Stiftung, CH-3132 Riggisberg / photo: Hans Kobi.

Woven and embroidered inscriptions on vestments tell a similar story. On the back of both ends of the golden stole and maniple recovered from Saint Cuthbert's tomb are inscriptions telling us "Ælfflaed had this made / for the pious bishop Frithestan." Queen Ælfflaed was wife of the West-Saxon king Edward the Elder from roughly 900 until he put her aside in either 917 or 918 to marry Eadgifu.[52] Created a few decades earlier for the bishop of Augsburg was a golden cincture proclaiming in red silk capitals, "The most holy resplendent Queen Emma bestowed this cincture on Witgarius full of holy inspiration" (figure 57).[53] Some inscriptions were less personalized. A tenth-century stole from Trier with paired half-figures of apostles asked simply, "Pious pastor, holy bishop, remember me."[54] But many bore women's names. The most elaborate is a late medieval cincture from the St. Marien church in the Baltic city of Gdańsk. Worked in gold and silk thread on a linen ground is a long inscription, each of its thirty-eight words separated from the next by a cross. It begins quoting Jesus in Luke 14:16–17, "A certain man made a great supper and invited many. And he sent his servant at the hour of supper to say to them that they were invited, that they should come: for now all things are ready." It continues with the words of Proverbs 9:5, "Come, eat my bread and drink the wine which I have mingled for you." Finally, the maker addresses the reader directly: "Pray for me, Katharina of Ummen."[55] The woman's voice addressing the cleric wearing

52. ÆLFFLAED FIERI PRECEPIT / PIO EPISCOPO FRIDESTANO. Frithestan was bishop of Winchester from 909 to 931, dating the stole to the period 909–918: see Maureen C. Miller, "The Significance of Saint Cuthbert's Vestments," *Studies in Church History* 47 (2011): 92. For a general consideration of inscriptions in textiles, see Elizabeth Coatsworth, "Text and Textile," in *Text, Image, Interpretation: Studies in Anglo-Saxon Literature and Its Insular Context in Honour of Éamonn Ó Carragáin*, ed. Alastair Minnis and Jane Roberts (Turnhout, 2007), 187–207.

53. Emma of Bavaria was married to the late Carolingian king Louis the German (d. 876), and Witgarius was bishop of Augsburg from 858–887: *Sakrale Gewänder*, 14 (cat. 4) and plate 1; Braun, *DLG*, 110; Valerie L. Garver, "Weaving Words in Silk: Women and Inscribed Bands in the Carolingian World," *Medieval Clothing and Textiles* 6 (2010): 34–40, presenting not only the Witgarius *cingulum* but also a band with the name of a female donor, Ailbecunda, and three invocations of the name of the Lord; Eric J. Goldberg, "*Regina nitens sanctissima Hemma:* Queen Emma (827–876), Bishop Witgar of Augsburg, and the Witgar Belt," in *Representations of Power in Medieval Germany, 800–1500*, ed. Björn Weiler and Simon MacLean, International Medieval Research 16 (Turnhout, 2006), 57–95. Goldberg's assertion that the belt once contained a relic of the Blessed Virgin has since been disproved through the research of Renate Mäder, which shows how the Witgarius belt and both fragments of the Ailbecunde belt came to be stored together and considered relics of the Blessed Virgin in the modern era: Melanie Thierbach ed., *Der Augsburger Dom in der Barockzeit: Katalog zur Sonderausstellung im Diözesanmuseum St. Afra 29. April–26. Juli 2009* (Augsburg, 2009), 200–201. I thank Valerie Garver for sharing her research on this issue with me.

54. PIVS PASTOR S(anctus) EP(iscopus) / MEMENTO MEI: Michael Brandt and Anne Eggebrecht, *Bernward von Hildesheim und das Zeitalter der Ottonen: Katalog der Ausstellung Hildesheim 1993*, 2 vols. (Hildesheim, 1993), 2:187–88 (cat. IV-32); other examples are an eleventh- or twelfth-century stole from Andechs with the inscription "IN NOMINE DN ORA PRO ME": *Sakrale Gewänder*, 26 (cat. 38) and plate 50; and a fragment of a thirteenth-century stole with the inscription (P)URIFICA MENTES BONE PRESUL PRESBITERI AUMENTI: Gerhard Römer, *Die mittelalterlichen Paramente im Kloster St. Marienberg in Helmstedt* (Helmstedt, 1982), 10–11.

55. Homo + quidam + fecit + cenam + magnam + vocavit + multos + et + misit + servum + suu(m) + h(ora) + cene + dicere + invitatis + ut + venirent + quia + iam + parata + sunt + omnia + venite + comedite + panem + meum + et + bibite + vinum + quod + miscui + vobis + orate + pro + me + Katharina + de + ummen. Braun, *DLG*, 108–9 (photo 108, fig. 47); Walter Mannowsky, *Der Danziger Paramentenschatz: Kirchliche*

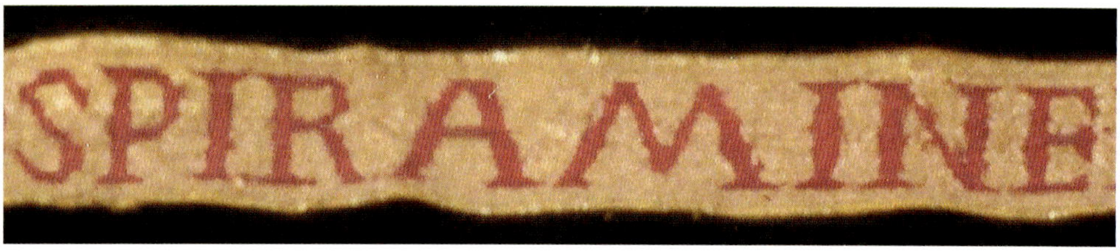

FIGURE 57. Detail of Witgarius cincture, c. 858–876, Diözesanmuseum St. Afra, Augsburg. Photo courtesy of the Diözesanmuseum St. Afra and the journal *Medieval Clothing and Textiles.*

her handwork is most clear in an inscription woven into an eleventh- or twelfth-century cincture preserved at Andechs in Bavaria. The inscribed exhortation mimics—and evidently shows knowledge of—the form of vesting prayers, but addresses the cleric rather than God: "As you gird yourself with the belt of justice, good father, so may you worthily bless the mystical bread."[56]

The readers could only be clerics. These inscriptions on vestments incorporating women's names and words would have been concealed. All of these inscriptions are found on cinctures or stoles. Queen Ælfflaed's words are on the stole ends, but on the backs: they would have been facing the cleric's shins. Unless worn with only an alb, even the large capitals of Queen Emma's inscription would have been entirely covered by the chasuble any priest would have worn at Mass. On a bishop like Witgarius, they would have been covered by still another dalmatic layer.[57] Katharina's inscribed cincture would address the cleric belting it on in the sacristy. When he stood at the altar or processed among the people, it would have been entirely concealed by the tunicle, dalmatic, and/or chasuble worn over it.

An entirely different mode of address is evident in one set of Mass vestments commissioned for the women's Benedictine monastery of Göß by the abbess Chunegunde II in the mid-thirteenth century. Inscriptions emblazon each piece and several would have been highly visible. One encircling an image of the Blessed Virgin on the back of the

Gewänder und Stickereien aus der Marienkirche (Berlin, 1983), 15. Garver presents a ninth- or tenth-century example from Speyer alluding less directly to scripture: [BENEDIC]TIONEM SICVT ISAC BENEDIXIT JACOB MANV [SUA] or "Blessing just as Isaac blessed Jacob [with his own] hand": "Weaving Words," 41.

56. ZONA IVSTICIE SIC TE . PATER OPTIME . CINGE [blank space] VT DIGNE PANEM BENEDICAS MYSTERIALEM: *Sakrale Gewänder*, 24–25 (Cat. 31). The vesting prayer version is "Circumcinge lumbos meos, Domine, zona iusticiae, et circumcide uitia cordis et corporis mei" (see above, chapter 2).

57. Valerie Garver asserts ("Weaving Words," 36) that "Witgar's belt is rare evidence for the names of donor and owner being visible on an ecclesiastical vestment, for when this belt was worn, its two names would have appeared at the bottom of either side of its hanging ends." She hypothesizes a middle section inserted between the two surviving pieces now sewn together 34). Several kinds of evidence, in my view, make her reconstruction implausible. First, no representation of a cleric from the Carolingian era shows the ends of a cincture extending out from under the dalmatic or chasuble (only the ends of the stole). In the Ottonian era, only the Erhard Mass image in the Uta Codex shows four ends extending below the dalmatic, but the image is too unrealistic in so many other features to be taken as reflective of normative practice. The physical evidence of surviving cinctures also does not support Garver's reconstruction. Two intact thirteenth-century cinctures measure 68.5 inches and 72 inches, neither long enough to

cope announces Chunegunde as the donor of both the cope and the chasuble under it. The dalmatic, too, "was made by Abbess Chunegunde," and in addition to this Latin inscription it bore one in German asserting that "the heavenly queen and her child shall help the one who has adorned her with a cloth of silk, her and her companions."[58] Although likely only used on the memorial day of the convent's founder, Adela, these inscriptions ensured that those attending the Mass—and not just the clergy wearing the vestments—remembered the abbess's gifts. Altar frontals, many of which also record the names of female artists and donors, similarly kept women visually present in the sanctuary. These overt embroidered attributions follow the broader conventions of patronage and, significantly, show women in their textiles making the same forthright declarations and invocations as male donors in other media. As Fiona Griffiths has very rightly underscored, these women also "asserted their claim to the altar," and by including images of themselves achieved a kind of sacramental participation.

This participation was accomplished more broadly by virtue of the fact that all the vestments worn at the altar were the carefully wrought creations of women's skill and devotion. I remain, however, more intrigued by the less visible inscriptions.[59] Katharina, in her embroidered cincture, quotes scripture to the priest girding himself for Mass, and the verses she presents complement those of the prefatory psalms in the vesting rite that remind the celebrant of the sacrifice he is about to offer. Through these embroidered words she seems to participate in the more intimate preparation of the celebrant. Then, hidden under other vestments, her name and prayer are present at the altar. The inscriptions of Ælfflaed and Emma announce their relationships with specific, named prelates: Frithestan and Witgarius. And, interestingly, the women in their voices declare the prelates worthy: Ælfflaed singles out Frithestan as "pious," and Emma asserts that Witgarius was "full of holy inspiration." Elite women in these instances were acting as arbiters of clerical virtue, singling out the ecclesiastical males that rose to *their* standards of piety and inspiration. This suggests an important role for women, particularly women of means, in fostering reform. They were not only present at the altar: through their gifts, of textiles and other resources, women could decide what kinds of clerical piety and inspiration should be furthered. The secret assistance of the holy recluse and the Blessed Virgin in Becket's quest for virtue is of a slightly different sort. Saint Thomas's ascetic practices, his personal project to tame his body and desires, required female assistance. The construction of the story—which all pivots around his household not

encircle the waist and reach a man's shins. In the fifteenth century, they nearly double in length; then one might plausibly argue for visibility. See Braun, *DLG*, 106–10.

58. For all these, see Griffiths, "'Like the Sister of Aaron,'" 359–60, 370–71. Pictures of the chasuble (plate 113), dalmatic (plates 117–18), and cope (fig. 119) are published in Marie Schuette and Sigrid Müller-Christensen, *The Art of Embroidery* (London, 1963), 72–75. There is also a stole in the Catharijneconvent museum in Utrecht, made in Germany before 1200, that has an inscription identifying its maker: ODILIA ME FECIT. *Ornamenta ecclesiae: Kunst und Künstler der Romanik; Katalog zur Ausstellung des Schnütgen-Museums in der Josef-Haubrich-Kunsthalle, Köln, 1985*, ed. Anton Legner, 3 vols. (Cologne, 1985), 2:441.

59. Owen-Crocker has also noted the tendency for women's inscriptions in Anglo-Saxon artifacts to be hidden: "Anglo-Saxon Women: The Art of Concealment," *Leeds Studies in English* 33 (2002): 31–51.

knowing—suggests that the laxer standards of the secular clergy surrounding the archbishop might impede his personal quest for greater virtue. Whereas the secrecy of Ælfflaed's and Emma's judgments about clerics masks their roles in encouraging and rewarding virtuous priests, the secrecy in the Becket tale seems about women providing the infrastructure through which holy men achieve sanctity. Both relationships posit women, through their collaborations with virtuous clerics, as arbiters and supporters of high standards. If secrecy, as Karma Lochrie defined it, is "intentional concealment that structures social and power relationships," then the social and political ramifications of women's relationships with clerics through textiles are more important than the mere fact of concealing their material expressions.[60] Indeed, the concealment of these relationships reveals the awareness of opposition to them.

We know that close spiritual relationships between clerics and elite women generated politically motivated "rumors" of impropriety. Lampert of Hersfeld reported that Matilda of Canossa's frequent contact with Pope Gregory VII after separating from her husband, Duke Goffredo of Lotharingia, provoked gossip and "suspicion of an unholy love." "The talk," Lampert reported, "had the pope night and day shamelessly rolling about in Matilda's arms and speculated that preoccupation with these furtive papal trysts kept her from contracting another marriage after the death of her spouse."[61] Lampert discounts the allegations, clearly showing that the political uses of fears of impropriety were as real as the actual possibility for "unholy love." But anxieties about these relationships generated not just gossip, but laws. Dyan Elliott has pointed out that fears of pollution of sacred spaces by sacrilegious sexual acts within them become prominent only in the eleventh century and initially were envisioned as clerical offenses.[62] Early canons punishing clerics for sexual acts "within the walls of the church" labeled their partners *scorta*—harlots or whores—but we should recognize this as a discursive strategy and not an accurate sociological observation: by definition, any woman who would shamefully tempt a cleric to sin in this manner was a "whore." For both the laywomen making vestments and the clergy wearing them, concealing inscriptions advertising their ties was probably prudent.

The courtly romances, moreover, suggest some other meanings associated with women's embroideries that may be at work. Embroidery is generally used in such tales, as when Jean Renart introduces Liënor in *Guillaume de Dole*, to signal aristocratic femininity and virtuous upbringing. In several, however, an "embroidery subplot" provides female characters escape, even if temporary, from male authority: when a heroine is expelled from her household or abandoned in the forest by a father or husband, she is able to provide for herself by practicing embroidery, usually with other women (a sort of *gynaeceum* in the forest). The heroines "are described as naturally gifted embroideresses,

60. Karma Lochrie, *Covert Operations: The Medieval Uses of Secrecy* (Philadelphia, 1999), 6.
61. *MGH SSRG* 38:283–84.
62. Dyan Elliott, "Sex in Holy Places: An Exploration of a Medieval Anxiety," *Journal of Women's History* 6/3 (Fall 1994): 9–11.

and they quickly achieve economic success."[63] A similar trope also appears in Jacques de Vitry's life of the beguine, Marie d'Oignies: "Our Lord had given her such abundant grace and skill in working that she far surpassed her companions, so much so that she was able to make a living both for herself and for one companion through her diligence."[64] In the courtly romance, however, needlework is not just a means for women to support themselves: it can be used to achieve other ends. In *Guillaume de Dole*, Liënor learns that the evil seneschal, who has impugned her virtue to the emperor, is in love with the chatelaine of Dijon, a lady who had hitherto repulsed his advances. Through a valet, Liënor sends the seneschal an embroidered belt, representing it as having been sent by the chatelaine, who regrets having ignored his entreaties and begs him to wear it under his clothing. He puts it on and goes to court. There the wronged heroine Liënor accuses the seneschal before the emperor of having raped her and taken her belt as a trophy. The embroidered belt, which the seneschal took for a secret love token, is revealed on his person and taken by the court as proof of his base crime.[65] Note that here too female agency is working toward good, but by exposing and censuring male immorality rather than simply rewarding virtue. In ecclesiastical struggles for reform, such power would be a frightening prospect for some.[66]

The secular courtly association of women's embroidery with both female power and secret love tokens is a frame, therefore, that must be considered in understanding the concealed aspects of women's relationships with clerics regarding sacred vestments. On the one hand, the use of embroidered objects as love tokens in romance would constitute another motive for the women's inscribed vestments to be concealed. On the other hand, were they given to clerics meant as tokens of affection? Linked to financial support, such affection and esteem for clerical virtue could be a powerful force for influencing individuals and institutions within the church. Resistance to this power led eventually to a rupture in the collaborative spiritual and material relationships between clerics and women around clothing. Notions of virtue were crucial.

As we saw in early medieval legislative attempts to require clerical continence and yet still meet the needs of churches for textiles, spatial separation of clerics from the women who wove and sewed their garments was the only imagined solution. Distance was to ensure virtue. The spirituality of sacred vestments that developed from the ninth century, however, complicated what before may have been viewed as a more straightforward, practical socioeconomic challenge of acquiring liturgical textiles. As vestments came to symbolize clerical virtue, they gradually became more costly and complex to create. Their role in constructing clerical virtue also demanded female virtue, and this fostered collaborative spiritual relationships between clerics and women for the purpose

63. Jones, "Uses of Embroidery," 17.

64. Head, *Medieval Hagiography*, 725.

65. Jones, "Uses of Embroidery," 25–27.

66. Interestingly, when women begin recording their own visions in the twelfth century, clerical sins are among the things revealed to them: Elizabeth of Schönau, *Liber visionum* 2.25–26, in *Die Visionen der Hl. Elisabeth und die Schriften der Abte Ekbert und Emecho von Schönau*, ed. F. W. E. Roth (Brün, 1884), 51–52.

of procuring liturgical textiles. There were, however, inherent tensions in this model. It could breach separation and generate suspicion of "unholy love." The only solution imagined, by either men or women it seems, was concealment. This covering up of relationships of friendship, prayer, and patronage between women and clerics contributed to the impression that churches and their magnificent liturgies were entirely clerical creations. Distance and discretion, moreover, could not reliably control the new complexities of these relationships.

Consider a story about Archbishop Poppo of Trier (1016–1047) in a continuation of this see's episcopal *Gesta* or "deeds" written in the early twelfth century. Megan McLaughlin has discussed this source with great insight in a broader consideration of episcopal sexuality, but the role of textiles in the narrative will be my focus.[67] There was, just outside Trier, a congregation of canonesses established by King Dagobert for one of his daughters. Archbishop Poppo sent a piece of fabric to one of the canonesses to make a pair of pontifical stockings (caligae) for him to wear when celebrating solemn feast days. The canoness, according to the clerical author of the *Gesta*, "desiring to have them partake of her lewdness, poisoned them with what kind of magic art I do not know," and sent them back all sewn up. As soon as he put them on, Poppo was overcome with lust for the woman. He pushed the disturbing and unexpected thoughts from his mind and quickly took off the stockings. Not saying anything, he called over one of his priests and gave him the caligae to put on. The priest put them on, and then immediately stripped them off, exchanging a look with his archbishop, but saying nothing. One by one the other clerics present tried them on, "suffered similar things," but were too embarrassed to say anything. One has to wonder here why every cleric in the sacristy had to try them on, but finally a "prefect of the city" appeared and the bishop ordered him to don them. This fellow bellowed with incredible rage, declared that he had been bewitched, and demanded an explanation. Poppo revealed who was the cause of this evil. The clergy were outraged at this attack on their church. The canoness was thrown out of her community, the archbishop imposed a harsh penitential regimen on her remaining sisters, and they one by one abandoned the house. As McLaughlin notes, the narrator presents the story as linked to a penitential pilgrimage to Jerusalem that the archbishop undertook, the "sin" prompting the journey being the collapse of the women's community under his care. Nothing is said in the *Gesta* about what happened to the community's property, which must have been substantial given that it was a royal foundation, but male ecclesiastics (*clerici religiosi*) replaced the women who had been driven or pressured out. Bewitched stockings seem a created pretext for a hostile takeover or repurposing of a well-endowed women's religious house.

This tale reveals the dangers for women and the tensions within the spirituality of sacred vestments. Setting aside the obvious clerical projections of guilt at sexual urges

67. Megan McLaughlin, "The Bishop in the Bedroom: Witnessing Episcopal Sexuality in an Age of Reform," *Journal of the History of Sexuality* 19 (2010): 17–34, especially 28–29.

onto an innocent woman, note that the canoness was hardly in a position to refuse the archbishop's request that she sew his stockings. He had the power to destroy her and her community. This raises the issue of how freely given, in fact, were many of the vestments "donated" by lay or religious women. Did bishops regularly demand liturgical textiles from the women of their dioceses? The story obviously shows the dark side of linking female virtue to clerical virtue through sacred garments by asserting that clerical failings must be due to women's sinfulness. And in a strange way it affirms the troubling intimacy of clothing noted at the start of this chapter: in the clerical imagination, a garment made by female hands could soak up its maker's "lewdness" (*inpudicitia*) and communicate it to otherwise virtuous clerics. Was this because, in this case, Poppo put on the stockings immediately (*mox*) on receiving them rather than blessing them first? Or is a more powerful, blessing-resistant female pollution being posited? Even if we regard the story as simply a fanciful ex-post-facto rationalization—the *Gesta* having been compiled in the early twelfth century—of the see's attack on a women's religious community, the imagined vector of liturgical garb and the power attributed to both the maker and the object are striking. Clothing can have strong effects on the wearer and consequences for the maker.

Women created the ornate style of liturgical garments that became the focus of clerical spirituality. While textual sources reveal the relationships clerics had with women in order to procure garments, surviving textile evidence reveals other aspects of these relationships that appear in no textual source. Through the creation of reliquary vestments and through inscriptions sewn into the more hidden pieces of liturgical garb, some women participated in the clerical spirituality of sacred vestments. The power this gave them, however, proved deeply unsettling.

Ultimately, the commercialization of textile production allowed the clergy to acquire liturgical garments without depending on relationships with women. The introduction of the horizontal loom to western Europe in the late eleventh century and rapid urbanization led to the emergence of complex textile industries from the twelfth century on that produced for both domestic and export markets.[68] Men increasingly gained control of the most lucrative sectors, although women in large numbers still worked within these industries and women retained dominance in silk manufacture. Domestic production continued, but the radical increase in urban industrial output commercialized the textile sector: cloth could be bought and garments purchased or commissioned. Although churches continue to this day to receive gifts of liturgical textiles from women, and women were definitely commissioned to make vestments across the later Middle Ages,

68. The earliest evidence of the horizontal loom in Europe comes in the Talmudic commentary of Rashi of Troyes (c. 1040–1105); this new loom produced better-quality, more densely woven cloths of far longer lengths, and its mechanization of the manipulation of the warp threads through foot peddles and heddle-harnesses led to a rapid increase in productivity. See John H. Munro, "Medieval Woollens: Textiles, Technology and Industrial Organization," in *CHWT*, 1:194–97.

clerics did not have to rely on women for the garments they wore. Pope Urban IV (1261–1264) had his own gold embroiderer at the curia, a man called Gregory of London.[69] While the commercialization of textile and clothing manufacturing increasingly allowed many clerics to acquire clothing without entering into close relationships with women, movements for ecclesiastical reform impelled the clergy to dispense with women who threatened their claims to virtue. Surviving textiles, moreover, offer a new perspective on these efforts at reform, and it is to them we need now to turn.

69. Staniland, *Embroiderers*, 12.

5

REFORM

WOMEN HAVE BEEN at the heart of debates about the reform movements of the eleventh century, usually called "Gregorian" after Pope Gregory VII (1073–1085). Their relationships with clerics were at issue in demands for clerical celibacy, a central and deeply felt reform principle for many laypeople, religious, and clerics. The effects of these reform movements, in both the short and the long term, have been viewed as a disaster for European women. For the wives and partners of those in major orders—priests, deacons, subdeacons—the immediate results were often destitution or enslavement. The reforming pope, Leo IX (1049–1054), according to Peter Damian, decreed that the "damnable women" living with priests in Rome be made slaves of the Lateran (papal) palace.[1] The long-term results of reform were also grave. The valorization of extreme rhetorics of purity and pollution normalized a misogyny that eroded women's access to property, dignity, and even religious life.[2]

A key difficulty in understanding reform, however, has been the easy resort to simplistic dichotomies. We like a good story of clashing principles, of good versus evil, of

1. "In plenaria plane synodo sanctae memoriae Leo papa constituit, ut quaecunque damnabiles feminae infra Romana moenia reperirentur presbyteris prostitutae, ex tunc et deinceps Lateranensi palatio adiudicarentur ancillae." Peter Damian, *Die Briefe*, 3:280; Peter Damian, *Letters*, 5:278. Most of these women probably fled the city, but if the wives or concubines of priests were enslaved by the papal household, it seems likely that among their chores would be the production of cloth and clothing.

2. Anne Llewellyn Barstow, *Married Priests and the Reforming Papacy: The Eleventh-Century Debates* (New York, 1982), 178–80; Paul Beaudette, "'In the World but Not of It': Clerical Celibacy as a Symbol of the Medieval Church," and Michael Frassetto, "Heresy, Celibacy, and Reform in the Sermons of Ademar of Chabannes," in *Medieval Purity and Piety: Essays on Medieval Clerical Celibacy and Religious Reform* (New York, 1998), 23–46, 131–48; Jo Ann McNamara, "The Herrenfrage: The Restructuring of the Gender System, 1050–1150," in *Medieval Masculinities: Regarding Men in the Middle Ages*, ed. Clare A. Lees (Minneapolis, 1994), 3–29; Dyan Elliott, "The Priest's Wife: Female Erasure and the Gregorian Reform," in *Fallen Bodies: Pollution, Sexuality, and Demonology in the Middle Ages* (Philadelphia, 1999), 81–106; Maureen C. Miller, "Masculinity, Reform, and Clerical Culture: Narratives of Episcopal Holiness in the Gregorian Era," *Church History* 72 (2003): 25–52.

epic conflict leading to a new world order. The Gregorian reform and investiture conflict have very easily been plotted in these satisfying tropes. A major reason is that the violent political conflict between the empire and papacy generated Europe's first propaganda war, producing a body of texts that have long captivated historians and established a basic framework for understanding events. As research has moved beyond the sharply polarized views of the literate propagandists, numerous problems with the general narrative have accrued, particularly concerning reform.[3] They can't be resolved here, but the nontextual evidence of textiles offers valuable new avenues toward understanding reform and, in particular, its gendered aspects. Reformers used the ornate style to further several ends: the maintenance of patronage, the improvement of the clergy, the visual articulation of hierarchies, and the advancement of clerical claims to status. Ornate attire was a shared language of power understood by clerics as well as laypeople. Among clerics, in particular, ornate liturgical vestments and the spiritual practices associated with them were aspects of an ecclesiastical culture shared across the many divides created by intense debates over reform, including those of the investiture conflict.

A Shared Language of Power

We need to begin with an obvious question. Why did the ornate new style of liturgical garb survive reform? It had been enthusiastically embraced and developed to new luxuriance by the imperial church. Surviving textiles underscore this connection. The Saint Vitalis chasuble, discussed above, would have been worn by the archbishop of Salzburg, who was also abbot of Saint Peter's and a leading imperial vassal.[4] The bishops of Brixen, a suffragan diocese of Salzburg, were renowned for the gorgeous purple eagle-silk chasuble (chapter 3) believed to have belonged to the holy bishop Albuin (975–1006). This bishop was a member of the Aribonen, a leading Bavarian kindred, and was close to Emperor Henry II, who likely bestowed on him the beautiful Byzantine silk vestment with its immense imperial eagles and gold trim. The same emperor appointed another Aribonen, Aribo, archbishop of Mainz in 1021 where he surely wore the gold Byzantine silk chasuble bearing the name of his predecessor, Archbishop Willigis (975–1011).[5] By the mid-eleventh century, the ornate style was also an imperial style.

The most complete surviving set of vestments to give us a sense of the style of the imperial church on the eve of the investiture contest comes from a tomb in the

3. Maureen C. Miller, "The Crisis in the Investiture Crisis Narrative," *History Compass* 7 (November 2009): 1570–80; Maureen C. Miller, "Reform and New Religious Movements," in *A Companion to the Medieval World*, ed. Carol Lansing and Edward English (Oxford, 2009), 211–30.

4. It was the preeminent see in Bavaria from the late eighth century and held extensive lands and comital authority in the eleventh century: Warren Brown, *Unjust Seizure: Conflict, Interest, and Authority in an Early Medieval Society* (Ithaca, N.Y., 2001), 14, 83–84; John B. Freed, *Noble Bondsmen: Ministerial Marriages in the Archdiocese of Salzburg, 1100–1343* (Ithaca, N.Y., 1995), 5–17.

5. Ute Bednarz, *Kostbarkeiten aus dem Domschatz zu Halberstadt* (Halle an der Saal, 2001), 32–33 (inv. 218).

Bamburg Cathedral. Here was buried Suidger, a member of Henry III's chapel from 1035 and bishop of Bamberg from 1040 to 1047. Fatefully, he accompanied his monarch to Italy in 1046, and, after a messy schism involving three papal claimants was resolved at Sutri, Suidger ended up being raised to the see of Saint Peter in a gathering dominated by the king. Taking the name Clement II, one of his first acts as pope was to crown his patron emperor. After a papacy of only a little over nine months, he died at Pesaro on October 9, 1047, but was interred at his beloved see of Bamberg. His tomb was opened in 1942.

Three pieces of the prelate's burial garments were associated with the papal office and will be discussed below. The rest are entirely consonant with other surviving eleventh-century vestments and contemporary depictions of imperial bishops. It is the state of their conservation and completeness as a set that are remarkable. The fabric of the alb, being closest to Suidger's corpse, entirely disintegrated, leaving only a few fragments of silk bands that decorated the sleeves. But Clement's cincture, stole, dalmatic, chasuble, and pontifical stockings (caligae) endure relatively intact. All were made of high-quality silks with large, complex, woven patterns: addorsed panthers and griffins grace golden-yellow boot-like stockings (figure 58). The chasuble and dalmatic are also made of yellow-gold silks (figures 59 and 60). Ovals enclosing floriate designs were woven into the fabric of the chasuble (figure 61); the pattern is very similar to that in the golden silk used to make the Archbishop Willigis chasuble. The dalmatic is made of an unpatterned, light-yellow silk with high sheen. The

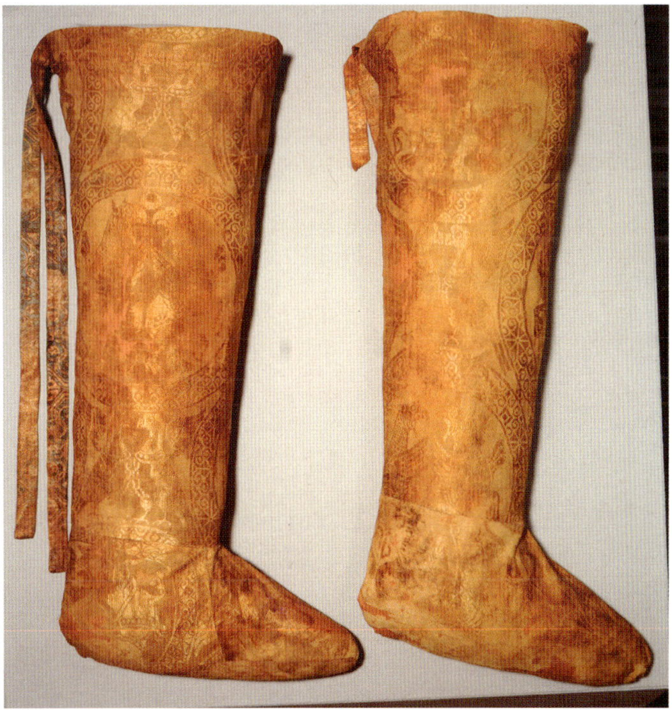

FIGURE 58. Pontifical stockings of Pope Clement II, eleventh century, Diözesanmuseum, Bamberg. By permission of the Diözesanmuseum Bamberg.

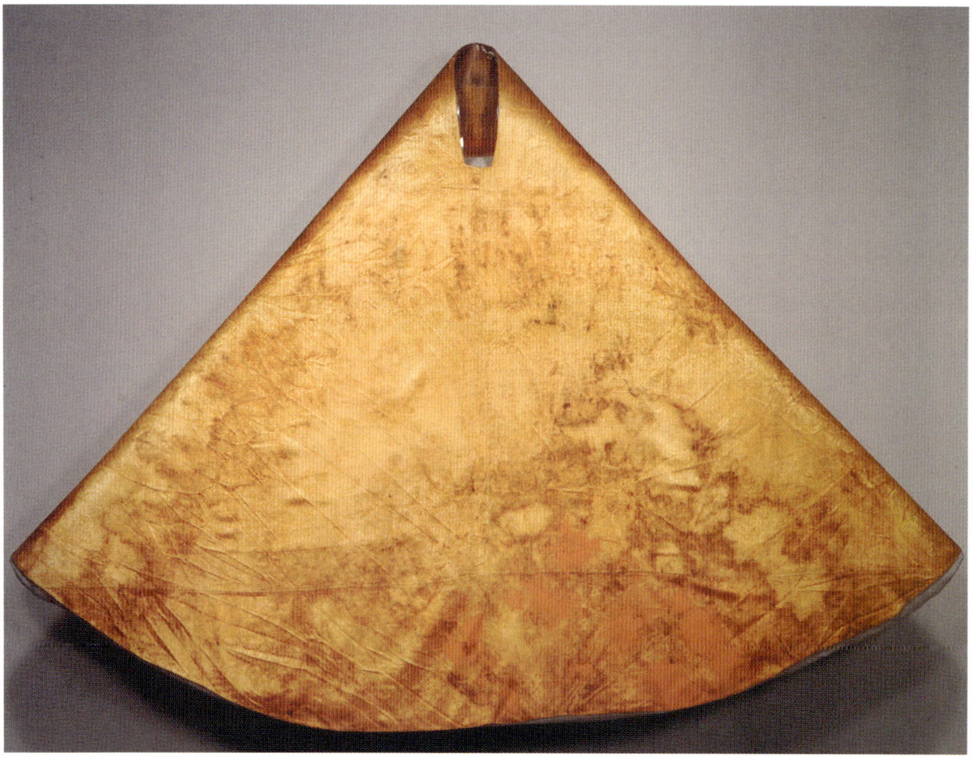

FIGURE 59. Chasuble of Pope Clement II, eleventh century, Diözesanmuseum, Bamberg. By permission of the Diözesanmuseum Bamberg.

stole and cincture are decorated with geometric and animal figures embroidered in gold thread.[6]

Like other imperial bishops, Suidger supported reform, and as Pope Clement II he convened a Roman synod in 1047 that renewed prohibitions of simony.[7] His patron, Emperor Henry III, also raised Bruno of Toul to the Holy See as Leo IX (1049–1054). His longer pontificate is usually considered the critical turning point that placed the papacy and Rome at the forefront of European-wide reforming initiatives. Although many writing about reform distinguish papal and imperial parties, this shorthand derived from the heated invective of the later investiture contest cannot be read back over the entire eleventh century, and even during Henry IV's war with Pope Gregory VII such categories obscure many important shared perspectives. As Ian Robinson has reminded us, even those who raised their voices and pens in protest against Gregory VII—figures such as Sigebert of Gembloux, Wido of Ferrara, Benzo of Alba, and Wibert of Ravenna—strongly supported and worked for reform goals such as the

6. Sigrid Müller-Christensen, *Das Grab des Papstes Clemens II. im Dom zu Bamberg* (Munich, 1960), 37–39, 41–49, 52, 57.

7. Mansi, 19:627–28; Peter Damian, *Die Briefe*, 1:498 (letter no. 40).

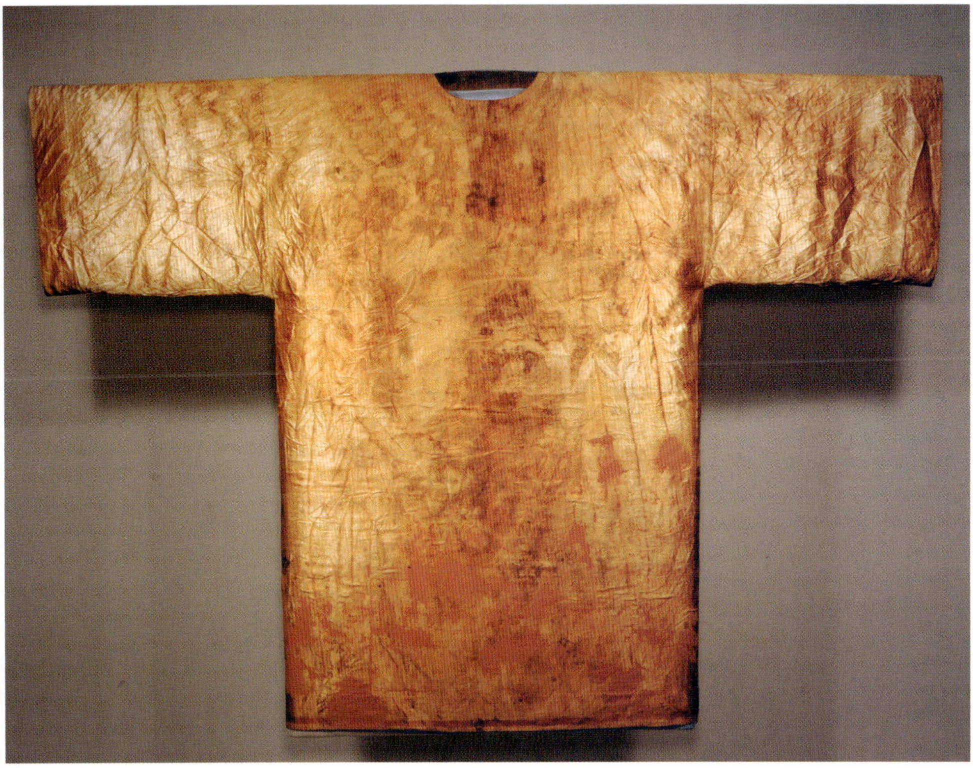

FIGURE 60. Dalmatic of Pope Clement II, eleventh century, Diözesanmuseum, Bamberg. By permission of the Diözesanmuseum Bamberg.

FIGURE 61. Detail of silk pattern in the chasuble of Pope Clement II, eleventh century, Diözesanmuseum, Bamberg. By permission of the Diözesanmuseum Bamberg.

eradication of simony and clerical marriage. They condemned Gregory's violent and coercive methods as well as his slanderous disregard for the royal office, but they, too, supported reform.[8] Indeed, just as today it would be rare to find someone against tax reform or educational reform, in the eleventh and twelfth centuries it would be difficult to find someone against ecclesiastical reform. The question was what kind of reform and how it was to be achieved. Even in the midst of acrid debate and violent confrontations, there were many shared traditions, beliefs, and customs that united ecclesiastics. One might more profitably view the late eleventh- and early twelfth-centuries as a struggle to find common ground within the church among the many views of reform aired and debated, rather than as a battle between two camps, either papal and imperial or "reformed" and "unreformed." Indeed, the fact that the church manifestly did emerge more powerful from the conflict—despite having had to compromise on high-profile issues, most notably lay investiture—should make us curious about the forces that kept ecclesiastics united. A deeply held faith undoubtedly explains the cohesion of the most committed, but a shared clerical culture was a critically important force uniting the rank and file.

The ornate style of liturgical vestments was an element in that shared clerical culture. Indeed, it was a shared language of holiness and power. As such, it is an excellent example of the common ground found during the struggles over reform and investiture. But the ornate style did not merely survive: it was also more intensely developed by advocates of reform. I noted in chapter 3 that the style entered artistic representations latest in Italy, the earliest evidence linked to assertions of Ottonian imperial power in the peninsula during the late tenth century, but the strongest to Rome in the late eleventh and early twelfth centuries. This pattern in the visual evidence is meaningful. The ornate style may have come to Italy with the imperial entourage, but it was most cultivated in Rome during precisely the period of the most intense conflicts over reform. Why was this so? The wearing of golden vestments by leading clerics allied with imperial power visually articulated their collaboration in the governance of society and their status. The mimetic character of lordly authority made shared sartorial splendor part of the lingua franca of power, and this was surely an important reason it was embraced and further developed by reformers.

In the eleventh century, most ecclesiastics recognized that no version of reform would be accomplished by renouncing status and power. Indeed, the exalted and special status of the clergy was a theme the more extreme "Gregorians" shared with Henry IV's adherents. Gregory VII famously asserted not only that there is "nothing in this world more pre-eminent than priests" but also that "a greater power is granted to an exorcist when he is constituted a spiritual emperor to drive out demons, than may be bestowed upon anyone of the laity on account of secular domination."[9] The bishops who

8. I.S. Robinson, "Reform and the Church, 1073–1122," in *The New Cambridge Medieval History IV c. 1024–c.1198*, part 1, ed. David Luscombe and Jonathan Riley-Smith (Cambridge, 2004), 276–81.

9. *Epp. sel.* 2.2:555; *The Register of Pope Gregory VII 1073–1085*, trans. H.E.J. Cowdrey (Oxford, 2002), 391 (8.21).

denounced Gregory VII at Worms in 1076 also did so on the grounds of their own status and that of all the clergy. They said to Gregory, "You have taken from the bishops, as far as you could, all that power which is known to have been divinely conferred upon them through the grace of the Holy Spirit, which works mightily in ordinations." They argued, further, that his "arrogant usurpation of new power . . . may destroy the rights due the whole brotherhood."[10] Interestingly, they go on in this letter to criticize Gregory for filling "the entire Church, as it were, with the stench of the gravest of scandals, rising from your intimacy and cohabitation with another's wife," alluding to his relationship with Matilda of Canossa, and they signaled their fear of female power and influence in papal reform circles: "the general complaint is sounded everywhere that all judgments and all decrees are enacted by women in the Apostolic See, and ultimately that the whole orb of the Church is administered by a new senate of women."[11] The words of these imperial bishops gathered at Worms offer important evidence of the shared concerns that united ecclesiastics and the antipathies that fueled conflict. Incendiary words, however, have dominated narratives of reform. Let us consider how the material and visual language of clothing was deployed in these debates.

The Ornate Style as an Instrument of Reform

It was not priests' concubines that worried the bishops at Worms but elite women like Matilda funneling resources to versions of reform they supported. The role of women's patronage in the success of reform institutions has not been systematically studied, mainly because the topic is vast but also perhaps because it may seem perverse to call attention to their efforts supporting movements that had such deleterious effects for women. But how could women of the eleventh century have foreseen reform's long-term ramifications? Liturgical garments figured in the spiritual relationships between clerics and women that we considered in the last chapter. One root of those relationships was every church's need of vestments, but textiles were assuredly only part of what women provided. To begin this consideration of how ornate vestments were used by reformers, I would like to explore some evidence that supports the perception voiced by the imperial bishops at Worms. Churchmen always needed to cultivate elites, and they often focused their attention on women as a means of influencing their husbands and sons. Although both sides in the disputes of the investiture contest were surely working their networks of alliances, the fathers at Worms may be offering us a clue that the more radical reformers in Rome were more effectively recruiting elite women—and the resources

10. Theodor E. Mommsen and Karl F. Morrison, trans., *Imperial Lives and Letters of the Eleventh Century* (New York, 2000), 148.

11. Ibid., 149: "In qua re verecundia nostra magis quam causa laborat, quamvis haec generalis querela ubique personuerit: omnia iudicia, omnia decreta per feminas in apostolica sede actitari, denique per hunc feminarum novum senatum totum orbem ecclesiae administrari." Henry IV, *Die Briefe Heinrichs* IV, ed. Carl Erdmann (Leipzig, 1937), *MGH Deutsches Mittelalter* 1:68.

they could wield—to their cause. What follows is, admittedly, speculative, but the evidence suggests to me that women liked giving ornate vestments—both out of pride in their handiwork and from a desire to be present at the altar through their gifts—and that prelates requested them as a way of initiating or deepening a relationship with a patron. Requesting vestments seems a medieval form of what contemporary professional fund-raisers call "the ask," or an initial invitation to give that one hopes will lead to bigger things.

Why might women have been reasonable targets for reformers seeking support for their projects? A first reason is that women traditionally preserved the memory of family members through the commemoration of the deceased, and so they were particularly concerned that the liturgies performed on behalf of their kin were efficacious.[12] Although they were never the dominant sources of income, women were keen to support institutions cultivating a particularly praiseworthy Christian life. This made women strong supporters of reformed monasticism. Agnes of Burgundy, for example, made several gifts to the reform monastery of Cluny in her own name but also influenced her husband, William V, Duke of Aquitaine, to make donations to the abbey. In 1062 she and her daughter successfully petitioned Pope Alexander II to extend apostolic protection to a Cluniac dependency in Poitou. Constance, daughter of Duke Robert I of Burgundy, played an even more important role, not only through direct gifts to Cluniac monasteries but also by interesting her husband, Alfonso VI of Castile, in establishing dependencies of the reform congregation in Spain.[13] Women were also important early supporters of the hermitage of Fonte Avellana in the Italian Apennines. A mother, Rozia, and her four sons in 1057 donated to Peter Damian, prior of Fonte Avellana, numerous lands to found the daughter house of San Bartolomeo, while on January 28, 1062, Ermengarda and her daughter Berta donated lands in Cagli to the hermits. Just after Damian's death, Beatrix and Matilda of Canossa took the entire congregation of Fonte Avellana under their protection.[14] The Cistercians, too, received many substantial donations from women.[15]

But real property was not the only thing religious communities needed, and many reformers were ambivalent about accepting it because of the responsibilities and relationships it entailed. Although charters of donation have, reasonably enough, been the

12. On the role of women in the preservation of family memory and care for deceased relatives' souls, see Valerie L. Garver, *Women and Aristocratic Culture in the Carolingian World* (Ithaca, N.Y., 2009), 68–121.

13. Constance Brittain Bouchard, *Sword, Miter, and Cloister: Nobility and the Church in Burgundy, 980–1198* (Ithaca, N.Y., 1987), 142–48.

14. Celestino Pierucci and Alberto Polverari, eds., *Le carte di Fonte Avellana*, 5 vols., Thesaurus Ecclesiarum Italiae IX.1 (Rome, 1972) 1:26–30, 39–42, 88–90 (nos. 11, 16, 34). I thank Kathryn L. Jasper for her observations on this subject.

15. Constance H. Berman, "Women as Donors and Patrons to Southern French Monasteries in the Twelfth and Thirteenth Centuries," in *The Worlds of Medieval Women: Creativity, Influence, and Imagination*, ed. Constance H. Berman, Charles W. Connell, and Judith Rice Rothschild (Morgantown, W.Va., 1985), 53–68; Erin L. Jordan, "Gender Concerns: Monks, Nuns, and Patronage of the Cistercian Order in Thirteenth-Century Flanders and Hainaut," *Speculum* 87 (2012): 62–94.

focus of historical inquiries into ecclesiastical patronage, the letters and chronicles documenting women's relations with advocates of reform reveal a range of other kinds of support. A good example is Orderic Vitalis's account of a visit to his Norman abbey of Saint-Évroul by Queen Matilda I, wife of William the Conqueror. According to Orderic, she decided to visit because she "had heard good reports of the observance of the monks." Such reports must have been borne out by Matilda's experience at the monastery because she left a mark of gold on the altar asking to be remembered in the monks' prayers. Further, she left instructions and funds to build a refectory so the monks could share their meals together. Finally, "she also gave a chasuble decorated with gold and pearls and a fine cantor's cope."[16] Note that no lands were given or charters drawn up: these gifts would be entirely lost to history if Orderic had not recorded them. The fact that Matilda left cash and vestments is also significant. These were things women could more easily alienate than land.[17]

Other means of support are also evident in the life of Countess Adela of Blois (c. 1067–1137). This daughter of William the Conqueror was actually countess of Blois, Chartres, and Meaux through her marriage into the princely Thibaudian dynasty. Her husband, Stephen-Henry, went on the First Crusade and died in 1102 at the Battle of Ramla. Adela's extended regency during his absence and her widowhood after his death afforded her a greater sphere of independent action than many women experienced. She did use that freedom to give lands and other economic resources (e.g., mills, rights to hay) to myriad ecclesiastical institutions. Many of these were specifically associated with reform, most notably the monk-hermits of Tiron, the abbey of Marmoutier and its dependencies, and the Cluniac nunnery of Marcigny.[18]

Beyond such direct alienations of property and rights, however, the countess also acted as a protector: at the request of Bishop Ivo of Chartres, she took under her protection both his newly reformed house of Augustinian canons, Saint Jean en Vallée, and a leper hospital at Grand-Beaulieu.[19] This is a form of patronage Gregory VII asked of his spiritual daughters: in 1073 he wrote to Countess Adelaide of Turin commending to her "care and defense" the monasteries of Fruttuaria and San Michele della Chiusa. "For high rank of office and fullness of power have been granted to you by the Lord," wrote Gregory, "so that they might be spent in the service of himself and of his own, and so that you, by willingly imparting your carnal things, may deserve participation in their spiritual things."[20] Gregory's language here is important: Adelaide may participate

16. *EH*, 3:240–41.

17. Another example is Queen Matilda I of England's donation of bells, and the funds to complete or restore the cathedral's roof, to the see of Chartres, revealed in Bishop Ivo's letter of thanks: Joan Ferrante, ed. and trans., *Epistolae: Medieval Women's Latin Letters* http://epistolae.ccnmtl.columbia.edu/letter/412.html. It is through another letter of thanks that we know she also sent a golden candelabra to Bishop Hildebert of LeMans: ibid., http://epistolae.ccnmtl.columbia.edu/letter/416.html.

18. Kimberly A. LoPrete, *Adela of Blois, Countess and Lord (c. 1067–1137)* (Dublin, 2007), 96, 128, 377, 408–12.

19. Ibid., 249–50, 252–53.

20. MGH *Epp. sel.* 2.1:59; *Register of Pope Gregory VII*, 42 (1.37).

(*participium merear*) in the spiritual work of the monks (*spiritualibus eorum*) by taking them under her protection.

Adela of Blois also acted as a mediator—intervening decisively to reconcile her brother, King Henry I of England, with Archbishop Anselm of Canterbury—and this is another form of support Gregory VII solicited from Empress Agnes, mother of Henry IV, and the Countesses Beatrix, Matilda, and Adelaide.[21] Indeed, relationships were critical—and here we can begin to understand how liturgical textiles figured in reform. Adela was able and willing to act as a mediator not only because she had welcomed the archbishop when disagreements with his monarch over lay investiture forced him into exile, but also because she had developed a close spiritual relationship with Anselm. Eadmer of Canterbury reported that Adela chose Anselm as "the instructor and tutor of her life." In this case, the archbishop's adversity yielded a relationship with an elite woman that aided him and his cause. While the movements of bishops and monks might allow for the initiation of relationships with elite women who would support their efforts, more often the movement of letters had to suffice. And requests for liturgical vestments were an accepted way for prelates to initiate or deepen a relationship with an aristocratic woman who was in the position to offer support. In Adela's case, it's unclear whether she ever granted Baudri of Bourgueil's request for a rich cope, but she definitely donated a chasuble to the Augustinian canons of Saint Jean des Vignes in Soissons, whom she also supported through interventions and other gifts.[22]

The accession to power of Adela's sister-in-law, Matilda of Scotland, offers an excellent example of a reformer seeking patronage. After she married Henry I in 1100 and was crowned queen, Matilda received a letter from Bishop Ivo of Chartres. The bishop's opening suggests this was his first approach to her: "Since we know from your reputation that you are one of the prudent women, though we are physically far apart, the odor of good opinion has made you present to us and excited us to loving the charity which the bridegroom of chaste minds ordained in you." He declares that he sends to "her liberality" two of his canons "who will tell you about the needs of our church and receive the favor God will inspire in your heart." He ends with a direct personal request: "I ask also that, in order to impress the memory of your excellence more sharply on my mind, you send an alb or some other priestly garment to my smallness which is fitting for a queen to give and a bishop to wear in celebration of the divine sacraments."[23] Ivo implies that he will wear what she sends and it will remind him of her. The request for a vestment seems here also an invitation to a more intimate spiritual relationship.

While some reformers dedicated to a Christlike life emphasizing austerity and simplicity eschewed ornate vestments, others did not. One reason was that affirming and developing the ornate style of vestments confirmed and deepened relations with key

21. LoPrete, *Adela*, 176; I. S. Robinson, *Henry IV of Germany, 1056–1106* (Cambridge, 1999), 108, 125–26, 132, 148–49, 154–55, 160–65.

22. LoPrete, *Adela*, 134, 199.

23. Ferrante, *Epistolae*, http://epistolae.ccnmtl.columbia.edu/letter/411.html.

supporters: the women who made them. But liturgical attire also served more direct reform goals: the improvement of the clergy. In chapter 2 I described the emergence of spiritual practices using liturgical garb, most notably vesting prayers and the bestowal of vestments in ordination rites, while in chapter 4 I discussed the wearing of reliquary vestments. This clerical spirituality of sacred vestments developed out of commentaries on the liturgy that were written for educational purposes. Their aim, originating in the reform councils of the early ninth century, was the betterment of the clergy. Both these liturgical commentaries and the spiritual practices that emerged from their use were further developed by eleventh- and twelfth-century reformers.

I emphasized in chapter 2 that after a tenth-century lull in the composition of new liturgical commentaries, reformers of the late eleventh and twelfth centuries revived the genre. These new compositions were more numerous and were more frequently written by the bishops who were responsible for oversight of the secular clergy.[24] But the earlier Carolingian commentaries continued to be copied too, indicating their continued relevance and utility. From the ninth and tenth centuries, twenty-nine copies of Hrabanus's *De institutione* and twenty-four copies of Amalarius's *Liber officialis* survive, but at least thirty-four new copies of each were also made across the eleventh and twelfth centuries.[25] One might wonder why advocates of reform in the late eleventh and twelfth centuries composed new liturgical commentaries when clearly some of their contemporaries found the older Carolingian texts still valuable. New trends in spirituality and new audiences, in fact, fueled the production of these new texts. I underscored in chapter 2 that Christological meanings were more prominent in the eleventh- and twelfth-century commentaries on liturgical vestments, and this reflects a general change in spirituality. This characteristic of the new commentaries may be considered merely an updating of the older textbooks. But the eleventh- and twelfth-century liturgical commentaries on sacred vestments were also more complex, positing multiple allegorical meanings for each garment. These multiple meanings were also specifically keyed to the material characteristics of the vestments, which suggest the influence of both the physical use of the garments in the devotion of vesting prayers and the scholastic practice of enumerating aspects in *distinctiones*.

It's worth pausing a moment to assess what this evidence tells us about the use of vestments as tools of reform. Continuities in aims and means are evident between the

24. While the Carolingian reforms inspired three major liturgical commentaries—those of Hrabanus Maurus, Amalarius of Metz, and Walafrid Stabo—the movements of the late eleventh and twelfth centuries produced at least eleven: the *Libellus de quibusdam rebus ad missae* of Berno, abbot of Reichenau (d. 1048); the *Liber de officiis ecclesiasticis* of John, bishop of Avranches (1061–1067); the *Micrologus* of the canonist Bernold of Constance (d. 1100); the late eleventh-century *Liber quare;* the *Tractatus de sacramentis*, written c. 1105 by Bruno, bishop of Segni (1079–1123); the *Gemma animae*, composed c. 1097–1110 by the theologian Honorius Augustodunensis; the *De divinis officiis*, written c. 1109–1112 by the monastic theologian Rupert of Deutz (d. 1129); the *De sacramentis*, written by the regular canon and master of the Paris school of Saint Victor, Hugh (d. 1141); the *Summa de ecclesiasticis officiis*, composed c. 1160 by the twelfth-century liturgist John Beleth; the *Tractatus de sacramentis altaris* of Stephen, bishop of Autun (1112–1136); and the *Mitrale* of Sicard, bishop of Cremona (1185–1215).

25. See *De institutione*, 160–230; *Liber officialis*, 1:28–35.

Carolingian and later "Gregorian" reforms. Both movements gave priority to improving the learning and piety of the secular clerics who delivered pastoral care to the laity, and both pursued this goal through the production of didactic tracts—on vestments and other liturgical matters—that could be used in training these clerics. The new qualities of the eleventh- and twelfth-century texts, however, suggest two important ways in which the "Gregorian" reforms differed from the earlier Carolingian efforts. First, the multiplication of allegorical meanings of vestments raised expectations for clerics intellectually and morally. They increased the number of things the priest in training needed to learn and multiplied the virtues he was supposed to cultivate. In this respect, the eleventh-century movements for reform did not just renew Carolingian efforts: they raised standards. The continued copying of the older, simpler commentaries of the Carolingian reforms indicates awareness of different levels of attainment: for some priests, knowledge of Hrabanus or Amalarius would yield at least competence. The composition of the new more complex commentaries reveals not only the existence of an audience of clerics able to meet higher standards but also the desire to encourage those with greater aptitude. Despite all the complaints about the clergy after the millennium, the tracts used to train them indicate a higher "basic" level of knowledge than that expected of their early medieval forebears.

The attention these newer commentaries gave to the material characteristics of vestments reveals a second important difference between Carolingian and "Gregorian" reform. These later reformers were more aware of the power of objects to stimulate devotion and form behaviors. The increased frequency with which vesting prayers were copied in eleventh- and twelfth-century manuscripts suggests this too. As noted in chapter 2, this clerical devotion of prayerfully summoning virtues with the donning of each liturgical garment endured into the twentieth century. This indicates at least a belief in the efficacy of these spiritual practices in forming clerical values and behaviors. They certainly did not make all clerics virtuous pastors, but their potential for influencing clerical behaviors has been bolstered by experimental cognitive science. Researchers in this field have recently coined the term "enclothed cognition" to "designate the systematic influence of clothes on the wearer's psychological processes and behavioral tendencies." In studies, it was found that wearing a type of clothing associated with certain qualities, such as a medical doctor's lab coat associated with scientific carefulness and attentiveness, actually did significantly influence the wearer's performance of tasks requiring sustained attention. These experiments reveal that physically wearing a garment with symbolic values has a much more potent effect on behavior than simply seeing or identifying with it.[26] The dissemination of the practice of vesting prayers across the eleventh and twelfth centuries and the more extensive use of vestments in ordination suggest that the reformers of this era understood that wearing garments associated with clerical virtues might help clerics exhibit those virtues in their ministry. Liturgical

26. Hajo Adam and Adam D. Galinsky, "Enclothed Cognition," *Journal of Experimental Social Psychology* 48 (2012): 918–25 (quote on 919). I thank Laura Smoller for calling this research to my attention.

vestments could, as Peter Stallybrass and Ann Rosalind Jones argue, be "deeply put on" and produce powerful "material memories."[27]

The wearing of reliquary vestments also likely functioned to influence clerical behavior. One of the *Cantigas di Santa María*, a collection of poems and tales about the Blessed Virgin composed at the court of King Alfonso X of Castile (r. 1252–1284), tells the story of Saint Ildefonso, archbishop of Toledo (657–667). Mary held this prelate especially dear because of his praise of her and his defense of the doctrine of her virgin motherhood in his sermons and other writings. As a sign of her special favor, she bestowed on Ildefonso "a vestment cut exactly to his measure which she brought from Paradise." The story identifies the vestment specifically as an alb and includes the Virgin's instruction that the archbishop should wear it to say Mass on her feast days. The Blessed Virgin also told Ildefonso as she gave him the garment that if anyone tried to take his place and put on the alb, God would take vengeance on the usurper. The story concludes that after Ildefonso "had departed from this world, the treacherous don Siagrio became archbishop. To his undoing, he dared to put on that garment and was at once killed and condemned, just as the Virgin had said."[28] While it's possible that the Virgin wanted no one but Ildefonso to wear the alb, the story seems more a cautionary tale about an unworthy prelate—the treacherous (*fallido*) don Siagrio—daring to put on the holy prelate's vestment. Interestingly, the relationship between the Virgin, Queen of Heaven, and a prelate who sings her praises and then is rewarded with a special vestment, mimics relationships between aristocratic women and prelates who send them poetry (e.g., Baudri of Bourgueil, Hildebert of Lavardin) in hopes of receiving ornate vestments. The dissemination of stories like this taught not only that holy clerics have particularly holy garments, but also that bad clerics risk divine censure if they dare put on a holy man's vestment. If one believed in the power of relics, the expectation that a reliquary vestment be worn on a particular feast might well influence a cleric's behavior.

The most prominent ways in which reformers used vestments as instruments of reform, however, were to reinforce and clarify hierarchies within the clergy and to make claims for the elevated status of the entire clerical estate. The language of clothing proved a subtle and flexible means to visualize these aspects of reform ideology.

While hierarchies generally were perceived as natural in the medieval world, reformers tended to view the articulation of hierarchical order within the clergy as essential to discipline and to the enforcement of higher standards. The issue was central to the investiture conflict: Rome wanted control over the appointment of bishops in order to make them responsive to the pope's mandates rather than to their monarch's. The same principle applied at the diocesan level. For a bishop to reform his clergy, he needed first

27. Ann Rosalind Jones and Peter Stallybrass, *Renaissance Clothing and the Materials of Memory* (Cambridge, 2000), 1–14.

28. José Filgueira Valverde, ed., *Cantigas de Santa María: Códice Rico de El Escorial Ms. escurialense T.I.1*(Madrid, 1985), 11–12; Kathleen Kulp-Hill, trans., *Songs of Holy Mary of Alfonso X, the Wise: A Translation of the Cantigas de Santa Maria* (Tempe, 2000), 4.

to have direct control over them. This meant wresting rights to appoint priests away from the lay owners of proprietary churches and from monasteries or other institutions whose properties included churches.[29] Scholars have long been aware that the number of major and minor clerical orders, the expectations of those in them (particularly the demand for celibacy of those in major orders), and the distinction between the clerical and lay orders were clarified over the eleventh and twelfth centuries.[30] The latter process is most visible in Rome where quasi-lay minor clerical orders were more numerous than the four (doorkeepers, lectors, exorcists, and acolytes) that came to be defined as canonical. They included, for example, persons called *mansionarii* and *virgarii*, whom we might call sacristans. They maintained the church building, especially lighting, guarded its treasure, rang bells, but also had liturgical roles (holding candles, sprinkling holy water, preparing chrism). According to Bonizo of Sutri, Pope Gregory VII viewed these "extra" minor orders as a "bad custom" (*pessima consuetudo*) of the Roman church and worked assiduously to extirpate them.[31]

This bottom border between those who were clerics and those who were laypeople was, of course, visually articulated by the tonsure and by the long, dark closed cloak, or *cappa clausa*. This long-sought visual distinction of the clergy from the laity through a distinctive garment worn outside of church was only very slowly achieved (see above, chapter 1). The distinction within the clergy between the major (priest, deacon, subdeacon) and minor orders was made principally by the imposition of celibacy on the major orders but also through the use of vestments in ordination rites. Priests received the stole and chasuble, deacons the dalmatic, and subdeacons the maniple and sometimes the tunicle too. Those in the minor orders received other material symbols of their duties: the doorkeeper received a key, the lector a book, the exorcist a scroll, and the acolyte a candlestick, a candle, and an empty vessel. What is important to note here is that the bestowal of liturgical vestments in ordination rites was associated with the higher status of the major orders. Remember that these vestments were blessed and that these sacred objects representing clerical virtues were, therefore, more specially associated with those who had embraced celibacy: priests, and those preparing for the priesthood through service at the altar. Liturgical textiles also emphasized the priesthood in the eleventh and twelfth centuries. The greatest creativity within the development of the ornate style was focused on distinguishing among priests: new distinctive attire emerged

29. I provide a detailed example of this process in *The Formation of a Medieval Church: Ecclesiastical Change in Verona, 950–1150* (Ithaca, N.Y., 1993), 117–41.

30. Many of Roger E. Reynold's essays have dealt with this topic, most particularly "Clerics in the Early Middle Ages: Hierarchies and Functions," and "The Portrait of the Ecclesiastical Officers in the *Raganaldus Sacramentary* and Its Liturgico-Canonical Significance," both in *Clerics in the Early Middle Ages*, 1:7–13 and 7:432–42. The results of this process of ordinal definition for women are treated by Macy, *Hidden History*, with a good summary of the broader changes on 23–35.

31. Roger E. Reynolds, "Clerics in the Early Middle Ages: Hierarchies and Functions," in *Clerics in the Early Middle Ages*, 1:7–13; Tommaso di Carpegna Falconieri, *Il clero di Roma nel medioevo: Istituzioni e politica cittadina (secoli VIII–XIII)* (Rome, 2002), 138–45.

for the highest priest—the pope—and for bishops.[32] The other notable area of development, however, affected the other end of the hierarchy.

A key reason for the development of new vestments and insignia for the top of the clerical hierarchy was the association of ornate attire with the exercise of power. Reformers built on ideas developed from the late Carolingian era about the roles of bishops in rulership and fully shared by imperial bishops in the eleventh century. Their use of vestments to enlarge upon and extend in new directions the imperial model of shared temporal and spiritual governance is most obvious in the development of the distinctive vestments of the pope. The key developments began to emerge in the ninth and tenth centuries, but became prominent only in the eleventh century. Although the late eighth-century forgery known as the Donation of Constantine (*Constitutum Constantini*) asserted that the first Christian emperor had given to Pope Sylvester I (314–335) the right to wear imperial regalia, there is only fragmentary evidence of real use of it before the eleventh century. The many depictions of popes in late antique and early medieval Roman mosaics present them in alb, dalmatic, chasuble and pallium. The latter was an important sign of papal office, but from late antiquity it had been shared with favored bishops and, especially, with archbishops, who came to see it nearly as a right of their metropolitan office. Suidger/Clement II was buried with one in Bamberg, and it should be interpreted as a symbol of his papal office. The bishops of Bamberg did not receive the pallium until Suidger's successor, Hartwig, was granted it in 1053.[33] Only fragments of the wool base of Clement II's pallium survive, attached to four blue-black silk crosses that adorned it. Of the insignia supposedly granted to the papacy in the *Constitutum Constantini*, the imperial "crown" and red mantle (*clamys purpurea*) have been considered the most important.

The amount of verbiage in the *Constitutum* concerning papal headwear may suggest that the late eighth-century forger was accommodating an established practice. Constantine supposedly decreed that Pope Sylvester and all his papal successors should use "the diadem or crown [*diademam videlicet coronam*], made from purest gold and precious gems, which we wear." When Sylvester would not allow a crown of gold to be placed over his clerical "crown"—that is, the tonsure—the emperor placed on his head "a splendid miter [*frigium*] in shining white as a symbol of the Lord's resurrection."[34] Some

32. A similar development of new vestments and insignia at the top of the ecclesiastical hierarchy occurred in the Greek East: Woodfin, *Embodied Icon*, 4, 13–32.

33. See Alexander Freiherr von Reitzenstein, "Papst Clemens II. und sein Grabmal im Bamberger Dom," in Müller-Christensen, *Das Grab des Papstes Clemens II*, 14–15.

34. "Decrevimus itaque et hoc, ut isdem venerabilis pater noster Silvester, summus pontifex, vel omnes eius successores pontifices diademam videlicet coronam, quam ex capite nostro illi concessimus, ex auro purissimo et gemmis pretiosis uti debeant et eorum capite ad laudem dei pro honore beati Petri gestare; ipse vero sanctissimus papa super coronam clericatus, quam gerit ad gloriam beati Petri, omnino ipsam ex auro non est passus uti coronam, frygium vero candido nitore splendidam resurrectionem dominicam designans eius sacratissimo vertici manibus nostris posuimus, et tenentes frenum equi ipsius pro reverentia beati Petri stratoris officium illi exhibuimus; statuentes, eundem frygium omnes eius successores pontifices singulariter uti in processionibus ad imitationem imperii nostri." Horst Fuhrmann, ed., *Das Constitutum Constantini, MGH, Fontes iuris Germanici antiqui in usum scholarum* (Hannover, 1968) 10:91.

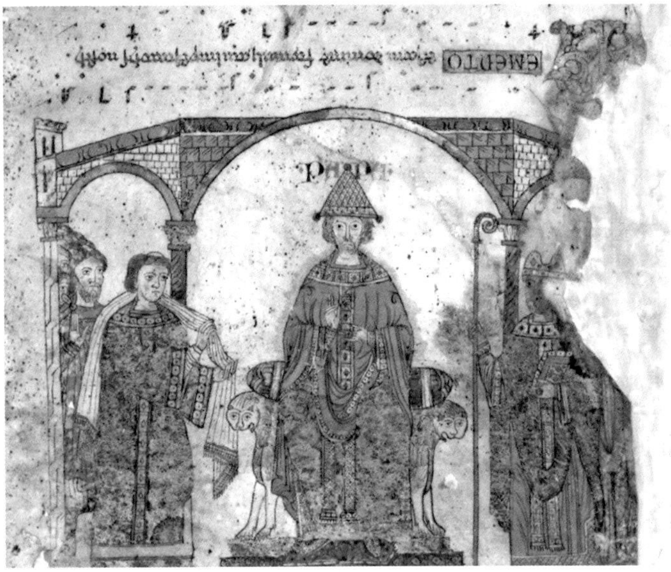

Figure 62. Image of pope enthroned with head covering (*regnum*) in the Barbarini Exultet, c. 1087, Vat. Barb. lat. 592, 5r, Biblioteca Apostolica Vaticana, Vatican City. © 2012 by permission of the Biblioteca Apostolica Vaticana, with all rights reserved.

evidence for a papal headgear may be found in the late ninth and tenth centuries. Liturgical Ordo 36 (880–900) instructs that after a new pope is enthroned and then acclaimed on the steps of Saint Peter's, a *regnum* is placed on his head. A coin of Pope Sergius III (904–911) depicts a conical hat, and a century and a half later a similar headgear appears on an image of a pope in an Exultet roll, now in the Vatican but probably produced at Montecassino (figure 62). From the mid-eleventh century the evidence, both liturgical and visual, quickens. The terms *regnum*, *frigium*, and *corona* are used into the twelfth century when the modern nomenclature, *thyara* or tiara, emerges. Depictions remain fluid until the pontificate of Boniface VIII (1294–1303), whose numerous commissioned portraits established the three-tiered "triregno" tiara as the iconic papal "crown" (figure 63).[35] Clement II's burial garb, unfortunately, offers little physical evidence to add to this picture. Whatever covered his head disintegrated leaving only fragments of a silk band attached to the remains of two fringed lappets. The fringed ends are similar to those found on eleventh- and twelfth-century episcopal miters, but the papal tiara can also be depicted with lappets.[36]

Concerning the red papal mantle, however, Clement's grave is unequivocal: the pope was buried in a bright-red silk cope with a wide green silk border (figure 64). The same large (20.5 cm) roundel pattern enclosing addorsed panthers and griffins is woven into

35. Ladner, *Papstbildnisse*, 3:270–307, but especially 275, 282–83; Agostino Paravicini Bagliani, *Le chiavi e la tiara: Immagini e simboli del papato medievale*, La corte dei papa 3 (Rome, 1998), 66–74; Lucinia Speciale, *Montecassino e la riforma Gregoriana: L'exultet Vat. Barb. lat. 592*, Studi di arte medievale 3 (Rome, 1991), 125–37.

36. Müller-Christensen, *Das Grab des Papstes Clemens II*, 53 and plates 55–56.

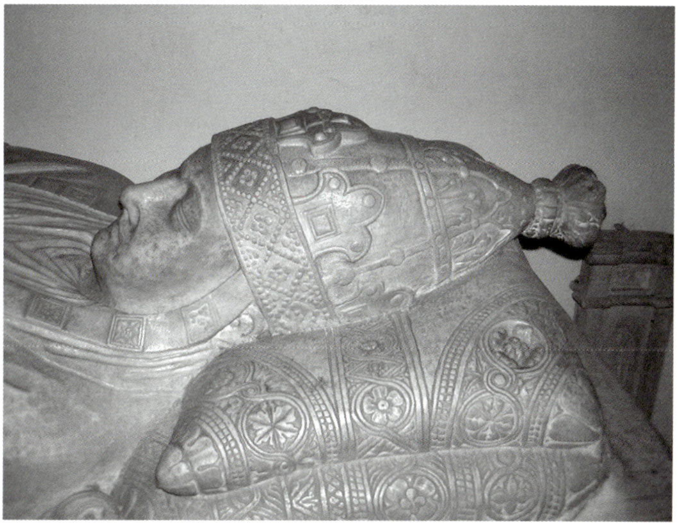

Figure 63. Tomb of Boniface VIII, 1303, Saint Peter's Basilica, Vatican City. Photo by the author.

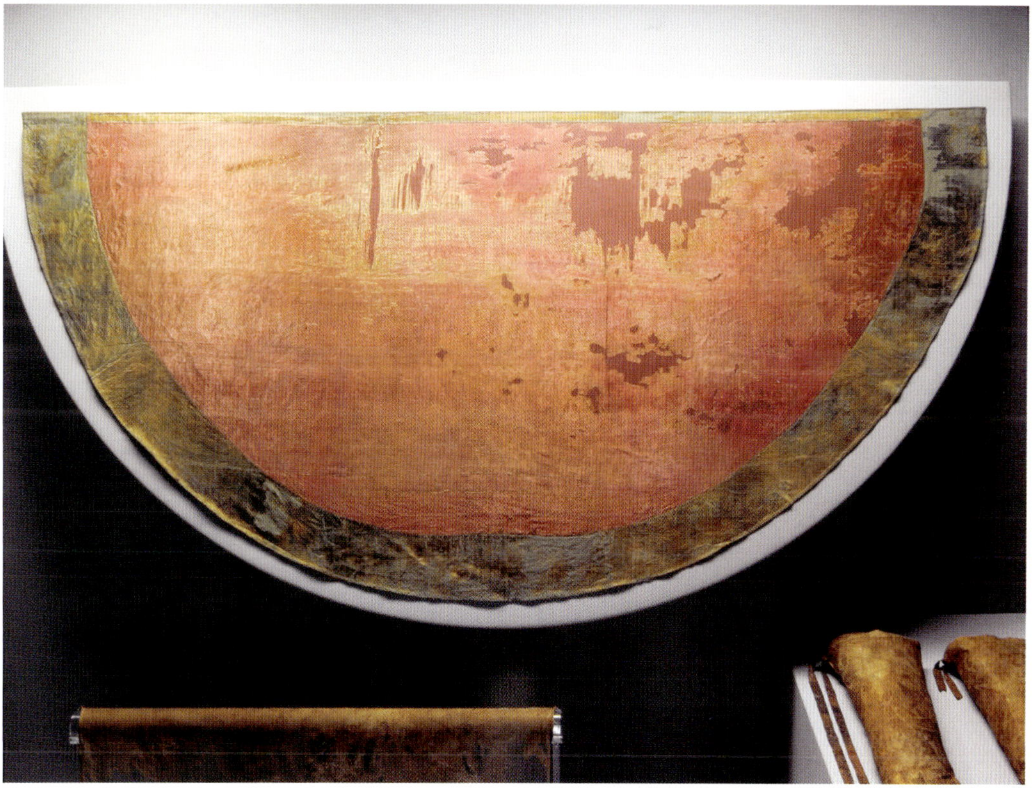

Figure 64. Cope of Pope Clement II, eleventh century, Diözesanmuseum, Bamberg. Diözesanmuseum Bamberg.

both silks, and it matches the yellow-gold silk used in the pontifical stockings. These patterns are typical of Persian silks c. 1000 and comparable to the silk used in the eleventh-century Vitalis chasuble and the Bernward (993–1022) chasuble in Hildesheim.[37] The brilliant red of Clement's mantle was definitely a mark of his papal office and a reference to the special symbols and authority believed to have been accorded it by Constantine. Some contend that Gregory VII was the first pope attested to have used the red mantle. The papal right to wear the imperial regalia was indeed reiterated in the famous *Dictatus papae* in Gregory's register, and the biography of Gregory in the *Liber censuum* did record that, after he was acclaimed pope by the Roman people, the unwilling but worthy Gregory "was enthroned in the seat of Saint Peter, having been robed in the red mantle, as is customary, and adorned with the papal miter."[38] Although this life was drawn from the *Liber ad amicum* written by Gregory's contemporary, Bonizo of Sutri, this detail was not in Bonizo's *Liber*. It was likely added by the twelfth-century redactor of this vita, Boso cardinal deacon of SS. Cosma e Damiano (d. 1178).[39] Braun also noted that in 1062 Peter Damian's letter to Cadalus of Parma, acknowledged by the imperial court as Pope Honorius II after the death of Nicholas II, chided him for having "the miter and red cope according to the custom of the Roman pontiffs."[40] So Damian clearly thought of it as papal custom before Gregory's pontificate. Then, of course, there is the textile evidence: Clement II, an unambiguously "imperial" pope, wore the red mantle.

I underscore this point because connecting the use of this potent vestimentary symbol to Gregory VII, or even to Peter Damian, places the origins of the expansive monarchical authority achieved by the papacy over the twelfth and thirteenth centuries in the more extreme reform ideology of Gregory VII and his supporters. If the use of a key symbol of papal monarchy really began with Clement II or his predecessors, a rather different genealogy must be considered. A regal papacy seems to have been what more traditional imperial reformers wanted too: another piece of common ground.

Reformers didn't only use garments to articulate a much more powerful interpretation of the papal office. They also widened the vestimentary claims for status previously focused on the major orders, particularly the priesthood, to all clerics. In medieval art, bishops are the most frequently depicted of the clerical ranks. Some deacons are portrayed, but orders lower than that—subdeacons, acolytes, or readers, for example—do not regularly appear in manuscript illuminations or wall paintings. These general conventions are what make a number of murals, painted in and around Rome in the late eleventh and twelfth centuries, particularly significant: they depict not only subdeacons and clerics in minor orders but also groups of clerics.

37. Ibid., 40–41, plates 21–24, 64–69.

38. Bagliani, *Le chiavi e la tiara*, 61–62; *Register of Pope Gregory VII*, 149 (2.55a); *Liber pontificalis*, 2:361.

39. *Liber pontificalis*, 2:361; DBI 13:270–74, s.v. Bosone. This Cardinal Boso was also papal camerarius to Pope Adrian IV (1154–1159).

40. Braun, *DLG*, 351; Peter Damian, *Die Briefe*, 2:523 (no. 88). For background on Honorius II's election, see Robinson, *Henry IV of Germany*, 40–43.

The visual shorthand for the clerical entourage is what you might call the mountain of tonsures. In the late eleventh-century panel in the lower basilica of San Clemente, which tells the story of Saint Alexius, for example, the pope and his troop of clerics are represented twice, at center and on the right (figure 33). In each grouping, the viewer can see the faces and partial bodies of three tonsured figures and then the tops of more tonsured heads receding into the distance behind them.[41] One figure in each group carries a processional cross, a role usually assigned to a lesser cleric, and their attire—tunics over albs—also suggests a crowd of clerics in lower orders. These representations emphasize the clergy as a corporate group—"the whole brotherhood," as the bishops at Worms put it—as well as their relationship with their bishop. The latter is a significant theme in several reform discourses: the bishop should live always surrounded by clerics as a guarantee of chastity and he should gather clerics around him to train and provision his diocese with priests.

The attire of these lesser clerics in these reform-era frescoes in and around Rome is colorful and ornamented. Those in the Saint Alexius panel wear reddish-pink tunics with black bands at the neckline and sleeves, while those in two other panels in the same church (depicting Saint Clement's Mass and the translation of his body) sport similarly brightly hued tunics with yellow-gold orphreys at the hem, neckline, sleeves, and shoulders (figure 32). In the late twelfth-century fresco at Anagni depicting its bishop, clergy, and people welcoming the body of Saint Magnus, the cleric holding the aspersory, a vessel filled with holy water, and the aspergillum with which to sprinkle it, is dressed in a yellow-gold silk tunic decorated with large medallions (figure 65).[42] In the late twelfth- or early thirteenth-century apse frescoes of San Silvestro in Tivoli, two clerics accompanying the saint as he subdues the dragon—both holding candles, and one also swinging a thurible—are dressed in brightly colored tunics. The thurifer wears the same pinkish-red color so evident at San Clemente, but with bright-blue bands on the sleeves of his tunic, while his companion is garbed in green.[43]

Surviving vestments and inventories indicate that the colorful silks and golden embroidery used for chasubles and dalmatics in the tenth and eleventh centuries were being deployed on tunicles and albs in the twelfth and thirteenth centuries. A Milanese inventory describing the gifts donated to its cathedral by Pope Urban III (1185–1187), a native of the city, includes a red subdiaconal tunicle, while thirteenth-century inventories from Lucca reveal *tunicelle* in purple and indigo, in red, yellow, and green samite. The cathedral in Pisa had nineteen subdiaconal tunicles in the thirteenth century, among them three red, two green, one of dark blue, and several with stripes: "one dark red with

41. The technique is also used in two scenes in the translation of Saint Magnus cycle (by the "Primo Maestro," late twelfth century) in the crypt at Anagni: Giacocchino Giammaria, ed., *Un universo di simboli: Gli affreschi della cripta nella cattedrale di Anagni* (Rome, 2001) 30, 38, plates 44, 47, 48.

42. Ibid., plate 47.

43. The dating of these frescoes is also contested; I concur with Francesco Gandolfo's verdict in the *Aggiornamento* to Matthiae, *Pittura romana*, 2:277–79. My thanks to Don Luigi Francesco Casolini, rector of the Church of San Silvestro, for access to the frescoes.

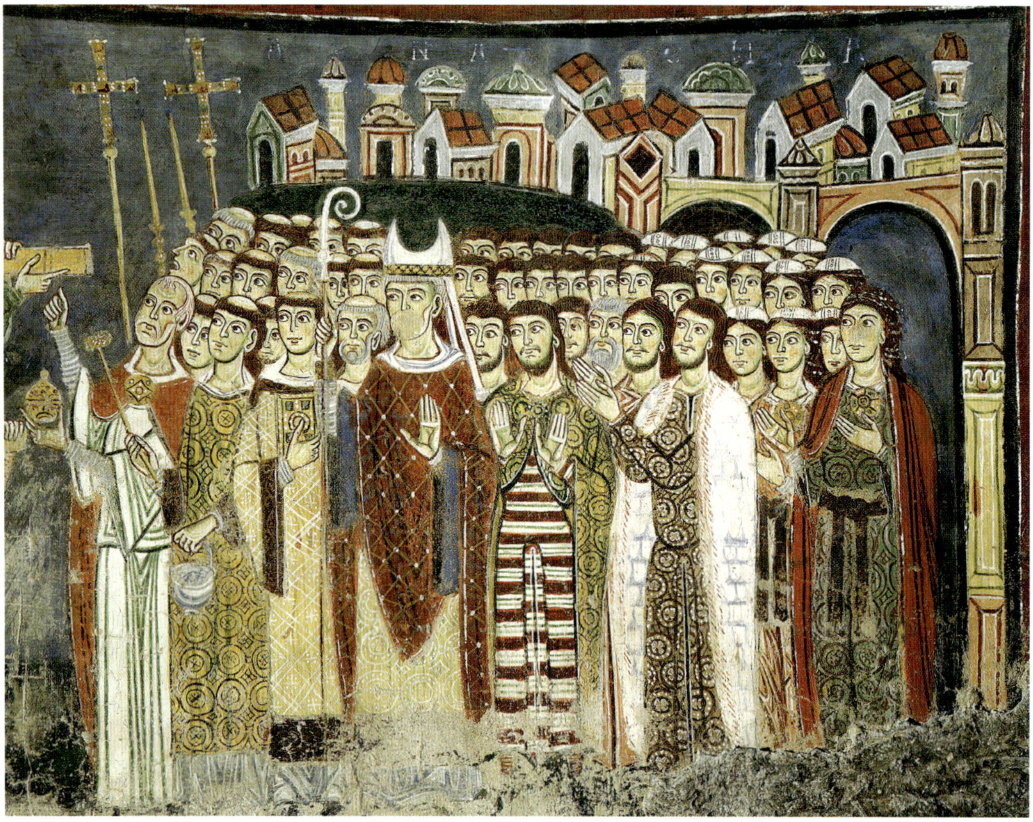

FIGURE 65. The bishop and people of Anagni greet the relics of Saint Magnus, late twelfth century, cathedral crypt, Anagni. Alfredo Dagli Orti / The Art Archive at Art Resource, NY.

stripes of gold," "one bright red with gold stripes," and "one dark blue striped with gold and various reds." German inventories reveal similar colors and still more elaborately decorated fabrics. Most evocative are the descriptions in an inventory dated 1233 from the cathedral canonry of Würzburg. Among the vestments listed are "a red alb with lions," "two old red albs with yellow birds," "a tunicle of red samite-silk with an edging-band with small lions and eagles," and another of "baldachinus [a silk tissue interwoven with gold thread] with circles in which there are snares."[44] A vestment (figure 66) dating from the second half of the twelfth century and preserved in the cathedral treasury at Halberstadt brings to life these descriptions: made of red silk samite, the tunic has golden stripes down the front and sides and gold-embroidered roundels

44. Otto Lehmann-Brockhaus, *Schriftquellen zur Kunstgeschichte des 11. und 12. Jahrhunderts für Deutschland Lothringen und Italien* (New York, 1938), 630–31, no. 2667; P. Guidi and E. Pellegrinetti, eds., *Inventari del vescovato della cattedrale e di altre chiese di Lucca*, Studi e testi 34 (Rome, 1921), 120–21, 180; Riccardo Barsotti, ed., *Gli antichi inventari della cattedrale di Pisa* (Pisa, 1959), 20. A late twelfth-century inventory from Bamberg notes a tunicle in red, one in white, and two in green; a list from early thirteenth-century Trier gives evidence of green, yellow, and red tunicles, plus one "with red and white stripes" (*subtilem virgulatam cum albo et rubeo*). *Schatzverzeichnisse*, 19, 96.

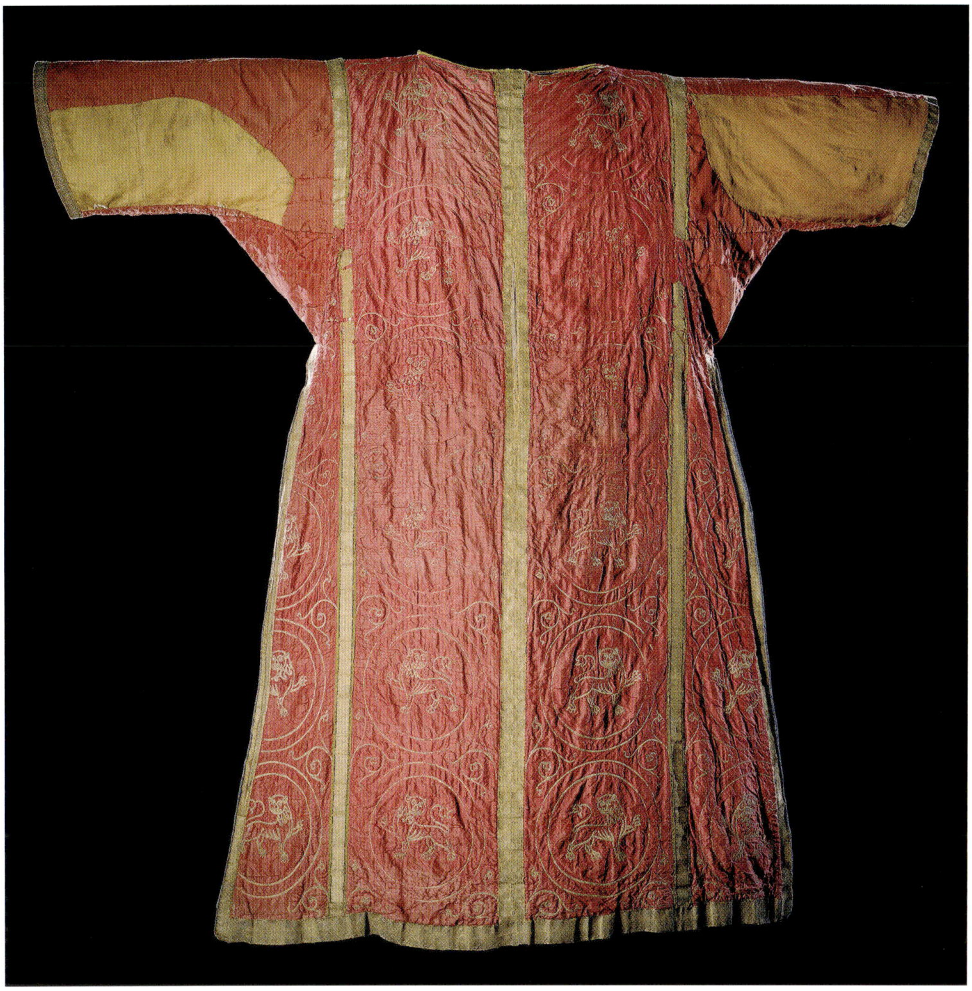

Figure 66. Red dalmatic with lions, Inv.-Nr. 117, c. 1150–1200, cathedral treasury, Halberstadt. © State Office for Heritage Management and Archaeology Saxony-Anhalt, Juraj Lipták.

enclosing lions.[45] The thirteenth-century *tunicelle* surviving at Göß, Maastricht, and Anagni were all elaborately decorated, the latter with opus anglicanum scenes from the lives of saints.[46]

The elite bias of surviving vestments makes it impossible to gauge from the textile evidence alone whether the minor clergy's vestments became more generally ornate, and

45. It has been called a dalmatic but its lack of *clavi* and form make it just as likely a tunicle—and, as Braun first noted, dalmatics and tunicles become indistinguishable in the central Middle Ages: Bednarz, *Kostbarkeiten aus dem Domschatz zu Halberstadt*, 50–51; Braun, *DLG*, 290.

46. Marie Schuette and Sigrid Müller-Christensen, *The Art of Embroidery* (London, 1963), 304; Annemarie Stauffer, *Die mittelalterlichen Textilien von St. Servatius in Maastricht*, Schriften der Abegg-Stiftung Riggisberg 8 (Riggisberg, 1991), 167–68; Luisa Mortari, *Il Tesoro della Cattedrale di Anagni* (Rome, 1963), 32–33, figs. 39–42.

it is rare to be able to discern in an inventory precisely who wore what. But the numbers of ornamented albs and tunicles recorded in cathedral inventories suggest that the lesser clergy may sometimes have appeared as richly garbed as the Roman wall murals depicted. An inventory of the Augsburg cathedral's vestments in the first half of the twelfth century records a total of thirty-two albs, "fifteen with ornament, seventeen without." Although the percentage of gold-embellished albs was lower at Würzburg (13 percent) and Bamberg (9 percent), some inventories indicate sets of ornamented albs specifically for different clerical ranks: "six ornamented albs with the best apparatus [e.g., matching cincture and amice]: two for priests, two for deacons, and two for subdeacons."[47] One Italian inventory mentions both *tunicelle* and *tonicelle subdiaconales*, raising the possibility that there were specifically subdiaconal tunicles and then tunics worn by minor clerics performing special functions (e.g., acolytes bearing candles or crosses in processions).[48]

Although the evidence is uneven, the notions lurking in it are important enough to merit consideration. In chapter 3 we saw that concerns about the diverse social origins of the clergy were associated in the Carolingian era with resistance to clerics wearing fine attire. Such concerns were still alive in the eleventh century, but growing insistence on the sacredness of orders fed claims for both clerical distinction and superiority. This was not just a clerical concern: laypeople, too, supported changes in clerical deportment—celibacy the most obvious—that distinguished those in orders from those not. Whether the distinction implied by orders yielded superior status—and if so, of what kind?—were much more vexed and divisive issues. The fresco of the clergy and people of Anagni welcoming the relics of Saint Magnus makes obvious that the minor cleric with the holy water wears silks equal to the city's nobles: the minor cleric's tunic is in a golden fabric nearly identical to that of the mantle worn by the layman right next to the bishop.[49] Were even minor orders so spiritually ennobling that a young cleric, possibly even one from a middling or peasant background, might be the equal of the town fathers? The more generalized visual assertion of status for the clergy, even the minor clergy, in the San Clemente and other late eleventh- and twelfth-century frescoes is significant in this regard. Ecclesiastical reformers, remember, were making extreme claims for the superior status of the clergy on the basis of their spiritual powers. While individual churches could decide to reserve the most ornate liturgical attire for the major orders, the desire for beauty in the liturgy may have worked slowly to accomplish visually the higher status of the clergy Gregory VII asserted. The ornate style of liturgical garb may also have contributed to the church's ability to function as a vehicle for male social mobility.

47. *Schatzverzeichnisse*, 16, 18, 111; "VI camiscii parati cum optimo apparatu, videlicet II preitili et II diaconili et II subd(iaconili)"; Guidi and Pellegrinetti, *Inventari del vescovato*, 121.

48. Guidi and Pellegrinetti, *Inventari del vescovato*, 120–21.

49. This same lay figure wears a striped knightly tunic with a slit in front and behind so that it could be worn astride a horse. The couple next to him wear tunics depicted as made of expensive red and gold patterned silks with large roundels, the male's mantle perhaps decorated with heraldic devices and trimmed with fur. Françoise Piponnier and Perrine Mane, *Dress in the Middle Ages*, trans. Caroline Beamish (New Haven, 1997), 57–61.

But what of the status of women? As the silent or silenced partners in the creation of these status-claiming garments, what could women have gained? Perhaps hope for a better life for their sons. Friendships with clerics and gifts of textiles may have smoothed the way into a clerical career for sons. Guibert of Nogent's mother worked tirelessly for her son's advancement, turning not only to lay allies but also to the clerics of her chapel.[50] Ties with the clergy could also have helped a woman's family in acquiring leases on ecclesiastical lands or contracts to provision needed goods for churches and other ecclesiastical institutions. Perhaps the prayers clerics offered or their spiritual encouragement, counsel, and friendship were enough. Robert of Arbrissel's letter to Countess Ermengarde of Brittany (1109) reveals an elite version of such support and encouragement, but the circumstances around it also point up the limitations of such relationships. Although Robert was infamous for attracting women followers and refusing to return unhappy wives to the husbands they had left, he had no sway with the ecclesiastical court that denied Ermengarde's suit for an annulment of her own marriage. He counseled her to accept and to obey.[51] Although the relationships between women and clerics that involved textiles may have had some advantages for women and their families, most of the uses and developments of the ornate style empowered clerics, and particularly those holding the highest offices.

For those at the top of the ecclesiastical hierarchy, the eleventh and twelfth centuries yielded a lot of new finery. We've already considered the example of the rationale in chapter 2, but there were other new markers of episcopal status that were more widely diffused: namely, pontifical sandals and stockings, pontifical gloves, and the miter. The slender black Roman slippers called *campagi* (chapter 1) were an early mark of episcopal distinction that became muddied as they crossed the Alps. The terminology changed to *sandalia*, and although late tenth-century popes were granting privileges to abbots to wear them, Frankish use and legislation seems not to have limited this footwear to bishops. Over the eleventh century, however, bishops slowly reasserted their prerogative to wear these special liturgical sandals and the knee-high stockings (caligae) worn with them. The forms that we know from the eleventh and twelfth centuries differ considerably from the early medieval black Roman *campagi* and the white stockings (*udones*) worn with them. The stockings (caligae) from Clement II's burial appear more like brightly colored silk boots (figure 58). The sandals of this period had cork soles covered in leather with leather uppers, usually several tongues converging on the ankle leaving cutouts through which the material of the caligae showed (figure 67). The uppers were usually embellished with embroidery.[52]

50. And to the abbot of Saint-Germer: *Monodiae* 1.4, 1.7, 1.19: Guibert de Nogent, *De vita sua*, ed. Edmond-René Labande (Paris, 1981), 26–28, 42, 166.

51. Bruce L. Venarde, ed. and trans., *Robert of Arbrissel: A Medieval Religious Life* (Washington, D.C., 2003), 68–79.

52. On liturgical footwear generally, see Braun, *DLG*, 384–424; on the lexical complexity of the term "caligae," see Simon Tugwell, "*Caligae* and Other Items of Medieval Religious Dress: A Lexical Study," *Romance Philology* 61.2 (Spring 2007): 1–23. Other surviving examples of caligae are *Vestiduras ricas: El monasterio de las Huelgas y su época 1170–1340, del 16 de marzo al 19 de junio de 2005 Palacio Real de Madrid* (Madrid, 2005), 197–98; Muthesius, *Byzantine Silk*, color plate 188A (M1105) and b/w plate 128B (M1387); Brigitta Schmedding, *Mittelalterliche Textilien in Kirchen und Klöstern der Schweiz* (Bern, 1978), 96–100.

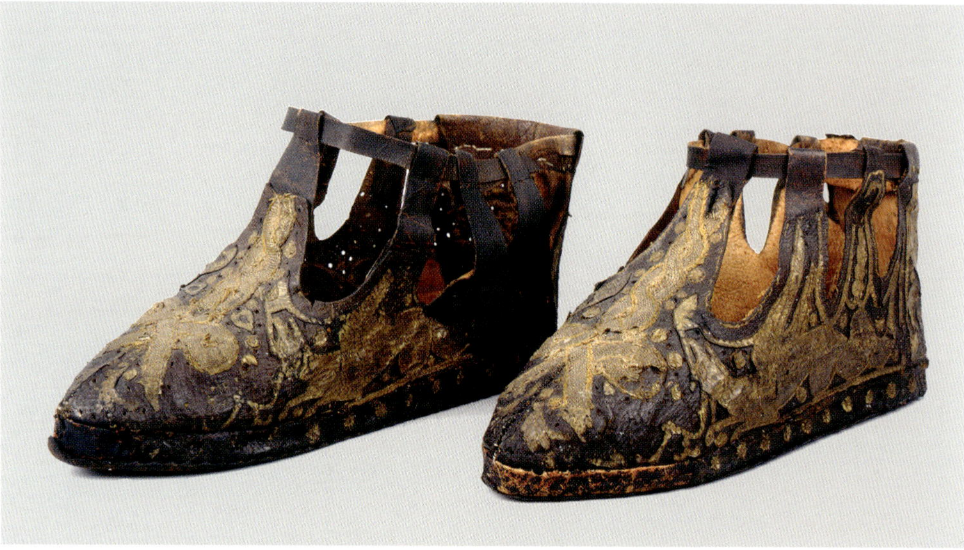

FIGURE 67. Liturgical sandals made of red leather with appliquéd gilt leather decoration, twelfth century, inv. 1825, Royal Museums of Art and History, Brussels. © RMAH.

Like sandals, pontifical gloves are mentioned more frequently over the eleventh century and by the early twelfth are established as special signs of episcopal rank. Unlike episcopal footwear, however, they do not appear to have had a late antique or early medieval Roman forebear. Called in the documents *chirothecae*, *manicae*, *inconsutiles*, or the clearly Germanic *wanti*, they are first firmly attested in a tenth-century inventory of the cathedral treasury of Monza and in the will of Riculf of Eln (d. 915). Surviving examples from the twelfth and thirteenth centuries were made of fine silk thread worked in a sort of loop technique with a needle that produced a seamless tight mesh. Usually woven or embroidered silk cuffs were added, and often a decorative medallion was affixed to the back of each hand (figure 68). One of these gold medallions, inscribed with a Lamb of God, survives from Clement II's gloves, and a pair of gloves conserved in the diocesan museum in Brixen incorporated a Byzantine enamel with the Virgin and Christ child.[53]

Examples of sandals, Schmedding, *Mittelalterliche Textilien*, 100–102; Jutta Frings and Jan Gerschow, *Krone und Schleier: Kunst aus mittelalterlichen Frauenklöstern* (Munich, 2005), 289–90; Mercalli and Checchi, I *paramenti liturgici*, 69–72, 88–99; *Sakrale Gewänder*, 16 and plate 5; Sophie Desrosiers, *Musée National du moyen âge—Thermes de Cluny, Catalogue: Soieries et autres textiles de l'antiquité au XVIe siècle* (Paris, 2004), 246–47; Maria Andaloro ed., *Nobiles officinae: Perle, filigrane e trame di seta dal Palazzo Reale di Palermo*, 2 vols. (Catania, 2006), 1:258.

53. Braun, *DLG*, 359–84; *Textile Conservation*, 244–46 (cat. 65, 18); Müller-Christensen, *Das Grab des Papstes Clemens II*, 52, plates 51–52; *Vestiduras ricas*, 193–94; *Sakrale Gewänder*, 25–26; Flury-Lemberg and Illek, *Spuren*, 146–55. Agnes Branting and Andreas Lindblom, *Medieval Embroideries and Textiles in Sweden* (Uppsala, 1932), 85–86, catalogs the burial garments of Andreas Sunesson, archbishop of Lund, who died in 1228, including gloves with circular images, one of a blessing hand inscribed P[ER] ME SACRANTVR SI QUE SACRA RITE PVTANTVR (Through me is sanctified that which is ritually considered to be holy), and the other a lamb with a star-bedecked flag inscribed PERPETVE DONO VITE BENEFACTA CORONO (I crown good deeds with the gift of eternal life).

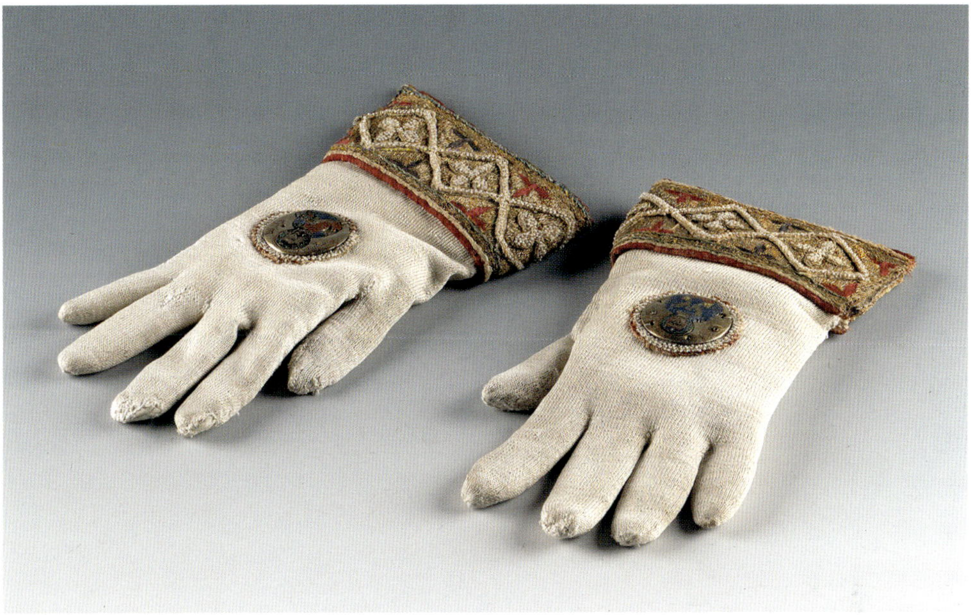

FIGURE 68. Pontifical gloves, c. 1200, Diözesanmuseum Hofburg, Brixen. Photo courtesy of Diocesan Museum Hofburg, Bressanone (Brixen), Italy.

The final and most distinctive new episcopal accoutrement was the miter. Its origins are murky and disputed. The term *mitra* in classical Latin was used to describe the turbans of various Eastern peoples. Although Jerome used *cidaris* (diadem) and *tiara* to describe the headdress of the high priest in his Vulgate translation of Exodus 28, the Old Latin (*Vetus Latina*) version also uses *mitra*.[54] In 1025, when the artist of the Uta Codex (Munich, Bayerische Staatsbibliothek, Clm. 13601) depicted Saint Erhard saying Mass in a sort of turban (see figure 28), he was linking the Western episcopate to the Old Testament high priesthood. But the form of the episcopal miter in the West appears more likely to have developed from the conical papal crown that is depicted from the mid-tenth century.[55] Over the eleventh and twelfth centuries in different parts of Europe, its form varied from a sort of trapezoidal cap, to a double-"horned" model, to the more triangular version (figure 69) that became taller over the later Middle Ages.[56] All these forms made it a distinctive and highly visible head covering, but ornamentation increased its impact. Form was achieved and maintained through an interior base of parchment that was then covered with white linen or silk. By the end of the twelfth century its characteristic embellishments were well established. A band called the *circulus*—tablet

54. *Bibliorum Sacrorum Latinae Versiones Antiquae seu Vetus Italica*, ed. Paul Sabatier, 3 vols. (Reims, 1743–1749; repr., Turnhout, 1981), 1:193. My thanks to Michael Herren for assistance on this issue.

55. Braun, *DLG*, 432–49, 495–96. Iberian roots have also been proposed: Roger E. Reynolds, "Vestments, Liturgical," in *DMA*, 12:403–4.

56. Twelfth-century miters are between 19 and 22 cm tall (7.5"–8.5"), while thirteenth-century versions measure 24 to 26 cm (9.5"–10"). Braun, *DLG*, 468.

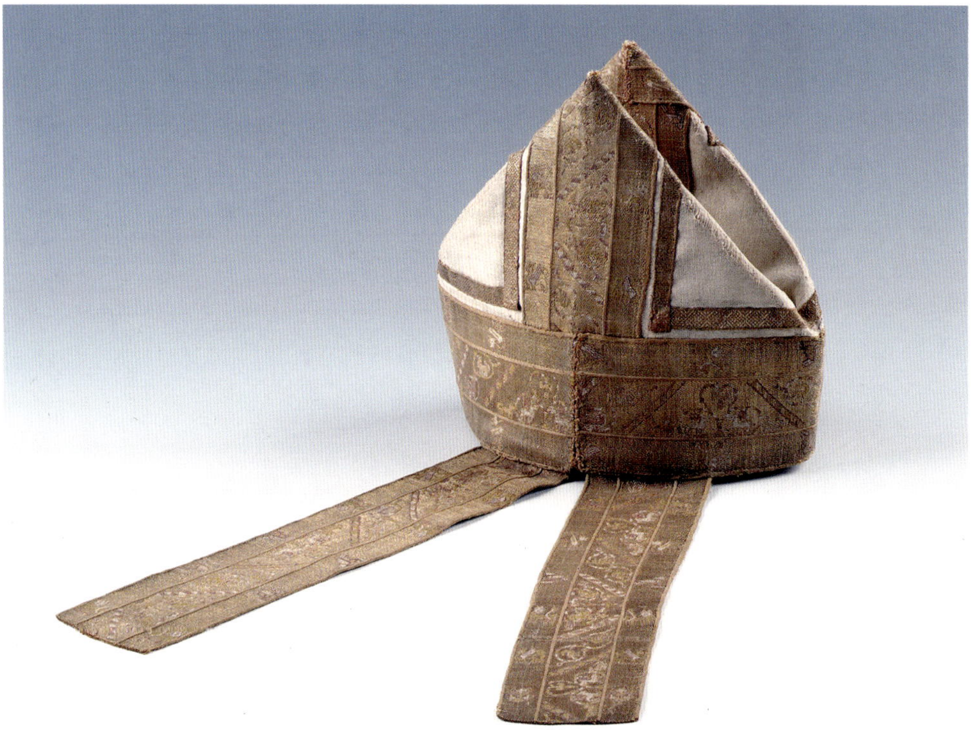

FIGURE 69. Miter of Bishop Bruno von Kirchberg, mid-thirteenth century, Diözesanmuseum Hofburg, Brixen. Photo courtesy of Diocesan Museum Hofburg, Bressanone (Brixen), Italy.

woven, often of gold—circled the base of the miter while a vertical stripe of decoration called the *titulus* emphasized the height of its peak on both front and back. Both of these could widen to the point where little linen or silk was showing. Additionally, from the back base of the *circulus* hung two tail-like bands, today called lappets but in medieval Latin described by various terms (*fasciae*, *fimbriae*, *infulae*, and many more). A foot to a foot and a half long, the lappets usually finished in fringe and provided yet more opportunity for embroidered or woven ornament.[57]

57. Early surviving examples are Karel Otavsky and Anne E. Wardwell, eds., *Die Textilsammlung der Abegg-Stiftung, Band 5: Mittelalterliche Textilien II: Zwischen Europa und China* (Riggisberg, 2011), 154–63; Muthesius, *Byzantine Silk*, color plate 63A–B (M83); *Sakrale Gewänder*, 25 with plate 53; 26, 27 with plate 58; *Textile Conservation*, 248–50; Flury-Lemberg and Illek, *Spuren*, 156–73; Mercalli and Checchi, *I paramenti liturgici*, 129–37; Mortari, *Il Tesoro*, 33–35 and plates 43–44; *Vestiduras ricas*, 188–90; Bednarz, *Kostbarkeiten aus dem Domschatz zu Halberstadt*, 72–73, 80–81; *Matilde di Canossa, il papato, l'impero: Storia, arte, cultura alle origini del romanico*, ed. Renata Salvarani and Liana Castelfranchi (Cinisello Balsamo, 2008), 377–78, 394, 395–96; Giuliana Ericani and Paola Frattaroli, eds., *Tessuti nel Veneto: Venezia e la terraferma* (Verona, 1993), 307–10; Marie Schoefer-Masson, "Etude et restauration d'une mitre du milieu du XIIe siècle dont les fanons comportent un décor en tissu dit de Palerme," in *Interdisciplinary Approach to the Study and Conservation of Medieval Textiles*, ed. Rosalia Varoli-Piazza (Rome, 1998), 30–31;

More than just status, however, could be communicated in the decoration of the miter. From the late twelfth century, figural ornament was incorporated. Most simply, a standing figure of Christ, the Virgin, or a holy bishop could be added to the *titulus*. But more elaborate schemes quickly emerged. The *circulus* might feature busts of the twelve apostles in arched segments running about the base.[58] Or the entire expanse of both front and back of the miter might be given over to a scene from the life of a saint. Most striking in this regard are a series of late twelfth- or early thirteenth-century miters featuring the murder of Thomas Becket (1118–1170). This famous archbishop of Canterbury was in the midst of a dispute with King Henry II over ecclesiastical prerogatives when four knights, inspired by their monarch's rage at the intransigent prelate, brutally killed him in his cathedral on December 29, 1170. Horror at the crime and miracles at Becket's tomb led to his canonization in 1173 and to extensive veneration throughout western Europe. At least three Becket miters survive: one originally from the Cistercian convent of Seligenthal now in the Bayerisches Nationalmuseum in Munich (figure 70), another in the treasury of the Cathedral of Sens, and still another originally in the treasury of Hugo d'Oignies at the Augustinian canonry of Saint Nicholas in Oignies and today at Namur. All three share similar compositional and technical features. Three knights are arrayed on the left, while on the right are the altar with a chalice on it and the saint's stricken body. On the Munich and Sens versions, Thomas faces his assailants; on the Namur miter, he faces the altar. A hand of God reaches toward the saint from a cloud at the miters' peak. The embroidery in silver-gilt and dark silk thread is executed on white silk twill over a layer of linen tabby using the alignment and couching techniques of opus anglicanum. These stylistic and technical similarities suggest that they were part of a series, most likely produced in England. The Munich and Sens miters have the stoning of Saint Stephen on the other side. These two are missing their lappets, so it's not clear which scene was on the front, but the Namur miter has the martyrdom of Saint Lawrence on the front and the Becket scene on the back.[59] In the medieval church, of course, this would be the side facing the congregation when the bishop faced the altar.

The choice of scenes is obviously highly significant for a head covering. A bishop, head of his church, was consecrated with the hands of other bishops placed on his head. The slicing off of the top of Becket's head—a bloody detail included in Edward Grim's eyewitness account as well as in others—not only killed the archbishop but struck down the head of the English church.[60] An attack on any of its members might be construed as

Branting and Lindblom, *Medieval Embroideries*, 86, 135 (Archbishop Sunesson's with the inscription BENEDICTIO DOMINI SUPER CAPUT. For a rare surviving miter with its leather carrying case, see Jonathan Alexander and Paul Binski, eds., *Age of Chivalry: Art in Plantagenet England 1200–1400* (London, 1987), 471.

58. Alexander and Binski, *Age of Chivalry*, 470–71.

59. Caroline Vogt, "Episcopal Self-Fashioning: The Thomas Becket Mitres," in *Iconography of Liturgical Textiles in the Middle Ages*, ed. Evelin Wetter, 117–25. (Riggisberg, 2010).

60. *Materials*, 2:437. William of Canterbury's account also makes references to the head in his rendition of Becket's exchanges with the knights: ibid., 1:133.

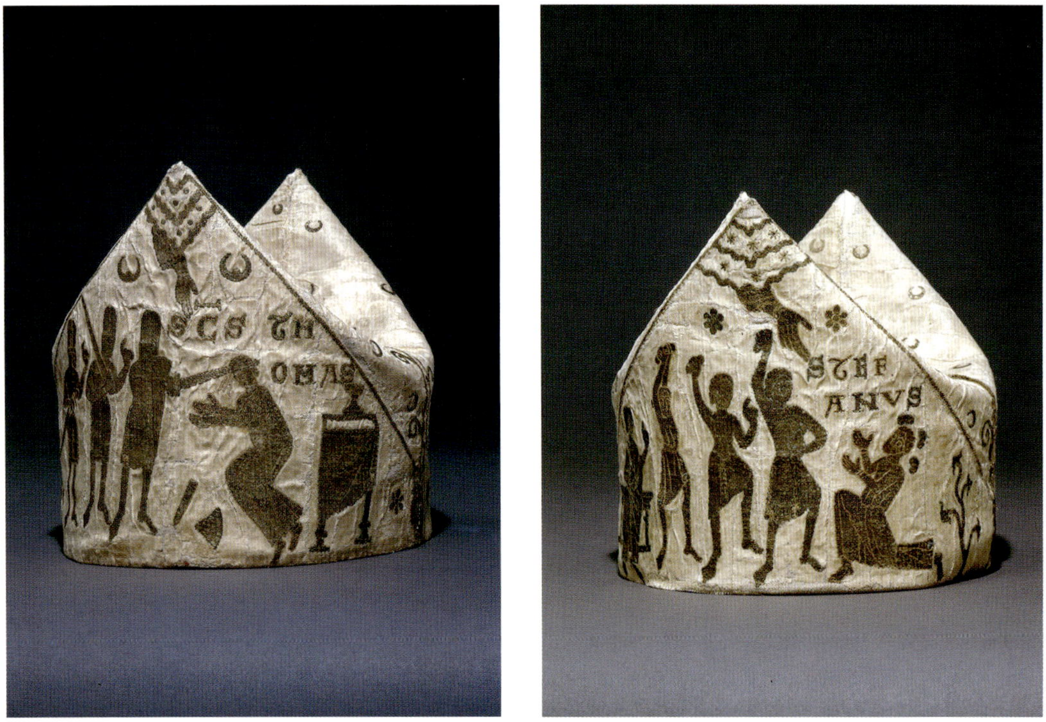

FIGURE 70. Becket miter from the Kloster Seligenthal bei Landshut, inv. no. T 17, c. 1200?, Bayerisches Nationalmuseum, Munich. Photo courtesy of the Bayerisches Nationalmuseum.

an assault on the church more generally, but an attack on its head was unmistakably so, and this particular archbishop—everyone knew—had been defending the rights and prerogatives of his church against royal aggression. The right in question—of clerics to be judged in ecclesiastical rather than lay courts—was based on the reform-era logic that ordination, even to the lowest of the minor orders, gave clerics a special sacred status and that a lower (i.e., lay) power could not judge a higher (i.e., sacred) power. The intersection of clerical with social status also figured significantly in Becket's life and death. From a wealthy merchant family, young Thomas's career was crucially advanced when he became a cleric in the household of Archbishop Theobald of Canterbury. Having ordained Thomas a deacon in 1154 and entrusted him with the office of archdeacon of Canterbury, Theobald recommended him for the position of chancellor to the realm's new king, the young Henry II. It was Henry, of course, who a decade later made Becket archbishop of Canterbury, and so their dispute was highly personal as well as political. According to Grim's account, it was Henry's lament to his courtiers that they allowed their lord "to be treated with such shameful contempt by a low-born cleric [*plebeo quodam clerico*]" that propelled Becket's assassins to Canterbury.[61] For other bishops to wear an image of Becket's martyrdom on such a prominent symbol of their episcopal

61. Ibid., 2:429.

office was an act of identification that functioned on many levels. It aligned the wearer with Becket's defense of his church unto death, with his willingness to confront temporal powers to protect sacred authority, and with his particular protection of his clergy and clerical status. One wonders whether those who had bettered their status through the church would have been particularly drawn to such an accessory. That one of these miters had been preserved in the treasury of the goldsmith Hugo d'Oignies suggests a connection to Jacques de Vitry, who donated the collection of relics that form the heart of the *trésor* and bankrolled Hugo's creation of their metalwork and enamel settings.[62] Like Thomas, Jacques seems to have come from a well-to-do but not aristocratic background and he achieved power and renown through an ecclesiastical career.[63] He entered orders and was educated at the University of Paris, became a canon regular at Saint Nicholas in Oignies, and ultimately rose to be bishop of Acre until Gregory IX in 1229 made him Cardinal Bishop of Frascati.[64] A bishop's choice to wear a Becket miter might derive from highly personal devotion to the saint or identification with perceived shared challenges in the episcopal office, but it could also be a more aggressive act in certain circumstances. Becket himself tended to show up in full pontifical regalia when summoned to court by his king. Wearing a Becket miter in the presence of temporal lords might be perceived as something more than a conversation starter.

Other miters decorated with figural scenes also emphasize martyrdom, usually pairing the stoning of Saint Stephen with Saint Lawrence's death on a grill.[65] These choices of imagery, moreover, echo themes in eleventh- and twelfth-century episcopal hagiography. Pierre Toubert first called attention to a specifically "Gregorian" model of the holy bishop in eleventh- and twelfth-century saints' lives. A key theme was the holy bishop's struggle against evil laymen, particularly those exercising temporal power. A count has his knights beat up holy Berardus, bishop of Marsi, and throw him into an empty cistern, and another evil count kidnaps the saintly Bruno, bishop of Segni, and maltreats him in a tower.[66] The theme of episcopal persecution at the hands of laymen intensifies across the twelfth century: Bishop Ubaldus of Gubbio is assaulted by workmen and attacked by his own citizens, while English bishops such as Anselm of Canterbury and Hugh of Lincoln manfully defend the properties and immunities of their churches against lay predations. Paul of Bernreid obviously deploys this trope in depicting Cencius's kidnapping of Gregory VII as the prelude to Henry IV's persecution of the saintly pope. When Christological allusions are overlaid, episcopal suffering is represented as crucifixion for the salvation of the church: after years of persecution at the hands of

62. Christiane Malaise-Heger, *Le tresor du Prieuré d'Oignies: Chefs d'oeuvre de l'orfevrerie mosane* (Liege, 1983), 2–5.

63. Philipp Funk, *Jakob von Vitry: Leben und Werke*, Beiträge zur Kulturgeschichte des Mittelalters und der Renaissance, 3 (Leipzig, 1909), 7–8.

64. Ibid., 119.

65. Vogt, "Episcopal Self-Fashioning," 119–21.

66. Pierre Toubert, *Les structures du Latium medieval: Le Latium méridional et la Sabine du IXe à la fin du XIIe siècle* (Rome, 1993), 807–29.

communal officials, Bishop Lanfranc of Pavia's demise from administrative exhaustion and illness is cast as a passion play.[67] In the context of such models of episcopal holiness, putting martyrdom scenes on miters is not surprising. The ornate style proved a supple visual language for expressing reform ideology.

During the eleventh and twelfth centuries, the ornate style of liturgical garb was used in efforts to improve clerical morality and behavior, to promote the corporate identity of the clergy, to demarcate it from the laity, and to claim superior status for all its members. It was a unifying element in a shared clerical culture that embraced a broad spectrum of reform ideologies, from those who supported gradual steps in collaboration with secular rulers to those holding more radical "Gregorian" positions demanding immediate compliance and the use of coercion to achieve it. New types of garb were developed to clarify and visualize the different orders in the clerical hierarchy. Women made all of this. In doing so they not only articulated clerical claims to status and power in a strangely ventriloquistic fashion, but they also empowered the clerical hierarchy through the wealth invested in liturgical garb and conveyed to ecclesiastic institutions. Did any of them regret the gifts given? We don't know. But the claims for clerical status made by reformers and the articulation of these claims through ornate garb did increasingly provoke opposition, and so it is to critiques of clerical clothing that we must now turn.

67. Miller, "Masculinity, Reform," 44–50; Maria Pia Alberzoni, "'Murum se pro domo Dei opposuit': Lanfranco di Pavia († 1198) tra agiografia e storia," in *Il difficile mestiere di vescovo (secoli X–XIV)*, Quaderni di Storia Religiosa (Caselle di Sommacampagna, 2000), 47–97, but especially 87–96, which narrate Lanfranco's persecution by the commune and his death, from the text of his vita preserved in Biblioteca Ambrosiana di Milano H 230, 100r–102r.

6

GOOD LORDSHIP

Witnesses to the murder of Thomas Becket recorded that his assailants left his body where it lay and then plundered the archbishop's residence. "They rooted through the chambers," William Fitzstephen wrote, "dashed writing desks and letter boxes to pieces, and carried off gold and silver vessels, money and gold, bulls of the lord pope, rings, books, and precious clothes, among these copes, tunics, and dalmatics which ought to adorn churches." They also carried off the "clothes, books, silver, and luggage" of his clerics.[1] Plunder was an ancient tradition, but what the knights did at Canterbury—murder and plunder—were also characteristic expressions of a mode of power that was dominant throughout Europe from the late ninth to the twelfth century. Lordship, domination over people, was exercised by many means, including violence. Plunder supported lordship, but was also expressive: it sent a message. In this case, as Thomas Bisson has pointed out, sacking Becket's residence was particularly meaningful. King Henry II, at whose bidding the assassins acted, or considered they acted, had recently been reminded that the spoliation of deceased prelates was a "bad custom." The destruction specifically of writing tables and letter boxes and the looting of papal bulls, books, rings, and vestments were an attack on Becket's own exercise of lordship. These were the implements and symbols of ecclesiastical power. Contemporaries recorded the plunder of his clergy because it, too, was meaningful. They were the agents of the archbishop's lordship. The conflict between Becket and his king was, indeed, a "crisis of lordship."[2]

Earlier in his important book, Bisson raises the question of whether the culture of clerical lordship was different from that of lay lordship. It's easy to cite infamous

1. *Materials* 3:144. John of Salisbury's letter 305 also includes these details: *The Letters of John of Salisbury*, ed. and trans. W.J. Millor and C.N.L. Brooke, 2 vols. (Oxford, 1979), 2:732–35.

2. Thomas N. Bisson, *The Crisis of the Twelfth Century: Power, Lordship, and the Origins of European Government* (Princeton, N.J., 2009), 485.

individual examples to suggest that it wasn't. The men who became bishops were usually from the same families that produced castellans, counts, and kings. They brought the tastes, habits, and skills of their lordly backgrounds to ecclesiastical office and many were far from saintly. But they also were schooled in the church and usually spent their young adulthood in episcopal households. Did this make a difference? More than my optimism as an educator suggests it could.

Several chapters, especially the last, have emphasized the ways in which ecclesiastical attire expressed claims to status, power, and rulership. But we need at this juncture to return to the concerns of chapter 2: the construction of clerical virtue through the spirituality of sacred vestments. Could virtue coexist with the exercise of power? This question is as meaningful today as it was in medieval Europe. Christianity had long harbored doubt that it could: the refusal to accept office was often interpreted as a sign of sanctity. Many of the twelfth-century's most eloquent religious voices argued that princely courts were not places for priests. But the crises of lordship that Bisson describes and examines begged for solutions, just as the individuals impoverished, intimidated, maimed, and killed by lords exercising their lordship cried out for mercy. Monks and monasteries often suffered the predations of lay lords, but it was the secular clergy who were constantly caught up in the crises of lordship. Both lords and their victims were part of their "flocks." What was a good shepherd to do?

The clergy's responses were often, to be sure, inadequate. But across the eleventh and twelfth centuries they tried to articulate a different kind of lordship. Clothing figured in these attempts, and the relationship between clerical clothing and lordship is most apparent in critiques of ecclesiastical garb. Such critiques reveal both the expectation that bishops should act differently as lords and the virtues that should characterize their lordship. The distinctive attire of the clergy symbolized claims both to holiness and to power. These are reasons why Becket's murderers made off with his clothes. But let us begin with a wide-angle lens: How did the appearance of lay and ecclesiastical lords differ?

The Look of Lordship

Seals are a good measure of lordly representation. "Until the ninth century," Brigitte Bedos-Rezak explains, "sealing was the exclusive prerogative of rulers (popes, emperors, and kings)." As the idea of episcopal collaboration in rule gained acceptance in the second half of the ninth century, bishops in Germany and France began to use seals. Dukes and counts began sealing in the tenth and eleventh centuries, first in Germany and then in France and England, with the practice then spreading among all those calling themselves lords (*domini*). The iconography of the seals of lay lords is remarkably consistent. The overwhelming majority (95 percent) surviving in France from 1050–1250 depicts an armed warrior on horseback. Some early exemplars represent the lord with a gonfalon or

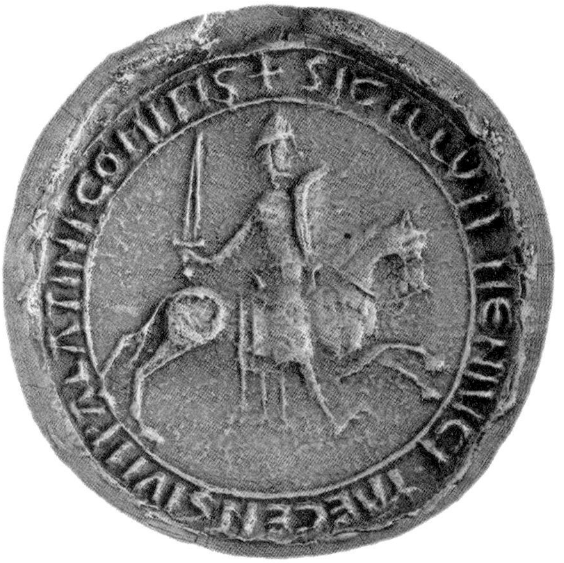

FIGURE 71. Seal of Henry the Liberal, Count of Champagne, 1168, D 566, Archives nationales, Paris. Archives Nationales France / photo by Christophe Jobard.

flag-lance to denote his leadership of the host, but sword and shield quickly became the standard symbols of lay power (figure 71).[3]

The iconography of the seals of bishops and archbishops is also consistent, but it differs radically from that of lay lords (figure 72). The prelate is either standing or seated on a throne (technically his *cattedra*, but clearly a borrowing from royal seals). He has his crosier in one hand and with the other either offers a blessing or holds a book. He is dressed for Mass, with alb, dalmatic, chasuble, stole, and maniple. By the late twelfth century, he is usually wearing a miter. The archbishop displays his pallium as well.[4]

Since the purpose of seals was "to authenticate the contents of documents and render them executive," they "had to reflect precisely the dignity of its owner who therefore chose to depict on it what was most representative of his power."[5] For lay lords, this was the capacity to do violence. On their seals they brandish weapons and wear armor. This capacity had several connotations. It could communicate a claim to exercise executive martial power and public authority. Whether such power was truly delegated from a king or simply asserted, the capacity to do violence had two further, and conflicting, connotations. The mounted warrior-lord might defend those he dominated: they looked

3. Brigitte Bedos-Rezak, "The Social Implications of the Art of Chivalry: The Sigillographic Evidence (France, 1050–1250)," in *Form and Order in Medieval France: Studies in Social and Quantitative Sigillography* (Aldershot, 1993), 6:1–2 (quote at 2). At the end of the twelfth century and across the thirteenth, sealing became a more broadly diffused practice for authentication and the expression of identity, but imagery was quite class specific.

4. Arthur Giry, *Manuel de diplomatique* (Paris, 1894), 636, 646; P.D.A. Harvey and Andrew McGuinness, A *Guide to British Medieval Seals* (Toronto, 1996), 63–69; Beatrice Marnetté-Kühn, *Mittelalterliche Siegel der Urkundenfonds Marienberg und Mariental* (Braunschweig, 2006), 72–79, 83–108.

5. Bedos-Rezak, "Social Implications," 2.

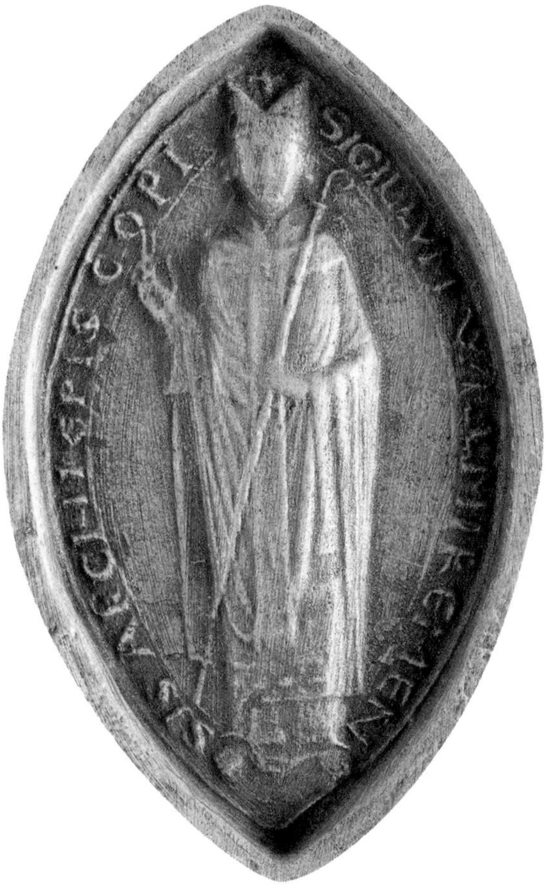

FIGURE 72. Seal of William of the White Hands, archbishop of Reims, 1183, D 6343, Archives nationales, Paris. Archives Nationales France / photo by Christophe Jobard.

to him for protection and often fled to his fortified enclosures when war or invasions threatened. But he might also use violence to subject individuals and communities to his rule and to exact or extort wealth from them to support himself and his followers.[6]

The clergy, on the other hand, were prohibited from bearing arms by ecclesiastical legislation promulgated repeatedly from the early Middle Ages. Chronicles and *chansons de geste* certainly yield examples of fighting clerics, particularly in the tenth and eleventh centuries, and even a bishop that didn't bear arms personally had men who could on his behalf. But the church at least promoted an ideal of nonviolent leadership. Prelates represented their power on their seals as pastoral and spiritual. The crosier represented the bishop's teaching authority, and it resembled a shepherd's crook to underscore his pastoral care. Either the blessing or the book communicated that his power was spiritual: he could offer God's grace and the promise of salvation revealed in scripture. Some lay

6. *Monodiae* 3.11: Guibert de Nogent, *De vita sua*, 362–63; Thomas N. Bisson, "The Feudal Revolution," *Past and Present* 142 (1994): 14–21 and his *Tormented Voices: Power, Crisis, and Humanity in Rural Catalonia, 1140–1200* (Cambridge, Mass., 1998).

viewers may have understood that the prelate's vestments represented priestly virtues since we know that bishops preached on their meanings at the ordinations of clerics and in synods.[7] They very likely at least believed them to be holy since saints' lives and preaching anecdotes (*exempla*) recount their miraculous powers. The air suspends Saint Dunstan's chasuble as he disrobes so it will not touch the ground, and bishops protect their flocks from dragons by lassoing them with their stoles.[8] Bishop Ratherius of Verona revealed this expectation in his *Praeloquia*, which he wrote while imprisoned in a tower from 934–936 by his lord, Hugh of Provence, then king of Italy. Referring to a royal token called a *wiffa* that protected the bearer from any avenging sword, Ratherius bemoaned violent assaults on bishops. "What clearer *wiffa* do you want," he exclaimed,

> than the crown [tonsure] which they wear on their heads? The stole, chasuble, cincture, stockings, and sandals—even if you could understand no other symbolic meaning in them, what do they mean if not the clearest marks of God's protection and veneration, when you see bishops wear them in distinctive fashion?[9]

Even if the finer points of meaning in seal representations were not accessible to all, the ideal representations of lay and ecclesiastical lordship were starkly different. One can be cynical about ideals, and surely there were many who did not live up to them, but both in our own society and in the past they can have power.

Medieval Christianity had a long tradition of critiquing violence and its worldly ends. But it did more than simply denounce: it created alternative institutions. Benedict of Nursia opened his rule for monastic life by addressing "whoever, renouncing his own will in order to fight for the Lord Christ, the true king, takes up the brilliant and mighty weapons of obedience." The monastery is a *schola*, an elite regiment, in which monks are waging war (*militans*) under a rule and an abbot.[10] A similar rhetoric pervades the clerical spirituality of vestments. Instead of worldly armor, the cleric puts on the *galea salutis*, the helmet of salvation, the *lorica fortitudinis*, the cuirass or breastplate of fortitude, and *fidei arma*, the shield or armor of faith.[11] When he secures his cincture over his alb the cleric

7. Ivo of Chartres, sermon 3, "De significationibus indumentorum sacerdotalium," *PL*, 162:519–27; Hildebert of Lavardin, sermon 132 (De diversis 45), "De ordinatione clericorum," *PL*, 171:926–28.

8. Eadmer of Canterbury, *Lives and Miracles of Saints Oda, Dunstan, and Oswald*, ed. and trans., Andrew J. Turner and Bernard J. Muir (Oxford, 2006), 122–23; *Vita Pavatii 6*, *AASS*, Iul. 5, 541; Samantha Kahn Herrick, *Imagining the Sacred Past: Hagiography and Power in Early Normandy* (Cambridge, Mass., 2007), 85–86.

9. Ratherius of Verona, *Praeloquia* 4.12, in *The Complete Works of Rather of Verona*, ed. and trans. Peter L.D. Reid (Binghamton, N.Y., 1991), 131, with slight modifications; CCCM 46A, 116: "Perspicaciorem quam desideras wiffam, quam eam quam capite gestant coronam? Stola uero, planeta, dalmatica, cingulum, caligae, et sandalia quid tibi, etiamsi nil intus aliud intellegere ualeres, nisi manifestissima diuinae tuitionis pariter et uenerationis, dum contra ceterorum consuetudinem eos his uti cernis, tibi produnt insignia?"

10. *The Rule of Saint Benedict*, 2–3, 8–9, 16–17 [prologue, chap. 1].

11. A *galea* is what Caesar's troops don before battle in the *Gallic Wars* (2.21), and a *lorica* is what Aeneas's warriors win and wear in the *Aeneid* (5.259, 12.276). The vesting prayer (see above, p. 81) quotes Eph. 6:17.

girds on the Lord's sword so that he might vanquish God's enemies. So when a bishop appears on his seal vested for Mass, he is armed and ready for combat, just as the lay lord on his seal is. He is representing himself as a different kind of lord.

The emphasis on justice in vesting prayers and allegorical tracts on vestments underscores the relationship between clerical clothes and lordship. The priest dons the *stola iusticie*, the stole of justice, which is also the yoke of the Lord's servitude. Kings and princes, lords, were supposed to protect and do justice, as were bishops, too, as collaborators in governance. Clerical rhetoric about vestments identified their justice with God's—since they controlled the sacraments believed to be necessary for salvation—but they also associated it with humility, love, and peace. The secular clergy not only posited a different kind of lordship, they also created mechanisms to try to empower it. Although the early church had denied the sacraments to those who ignored its sanctions, it was during the eleventh and twelfth centuries—during the "crisis of lordship"—that Christianity's coercive "spiritual weapons" were refined and much more frequently used. An interdict was a ban on the performance of essential religious services (Communion, absolution of sins, Christian burial) usually within a certain geographical area. It penalized an entire community or specific groups within it through deprivation of the sacraments, but it did not entirely cut individuals off from the church. Excommunication, a more extreme measure, was usually directed at individuals and it did place the person outside the church and its saving grace. Moreover, other Christians were prohibited from having anything to do with the excommunicate: social as well as spiritual shunning was entailed. It was only during the reform era that these two types of ecclesiastical censure were being distinguished and defined in church law. Both were characterized by the formula *anathema sit*, "let him/her be anathema," and were frequently deployed together.[12] Changes in the usage of each contributed to their definition, and it was precisely the perceived plague of bad lordship in the late tenth and early eleventh centuries that hastened this process. The peace councils of this period were mostly called by bishops with the declared aim of limiting violence. Their canons—prohibiting the invasion of property, seizure of livestock, assault of unarmed persons, and the taking of serfs as hostage to demand payment—catalog the "bad customs" of lordship. But how to enforce them? "If there shall be any," concluded the bishops gathered at Le Puy in 994, "who shall have broken this agreement and refused to abide by it, let him be excommunicated and anathematized and excluded from communion with the holy church of God until he

12. *DMA*, s.vv. "excommunication" and "interdict"; Elisabeth Vodola, "Sovereignty and Tabu: Evolution of the Sanction against Communication with Excommunicates. Part I: Gregory VII," in *The Church and Sovereignty c. 590–1918: Essays in Honor of Michael Wilks*, ed. Diana Wood (Oxford, 1991), 35–55; Elisabeth Vodola, *Excommunication in the Middle Ages* (Berkeley, 1986), 1–43; Cyrille Vogel, "Buße und Exkommunikation in der Alten Kirche und im Mittelalter: Ein historischer Überblick," *Concilium* 107 (1975): 446–52. Excellent examples of episcopal use of these "weapons" in the exercise of lordship may be found in Brian A. Pavlac, "Excommunication and Territorial Politics in High Medieval Trier," *Church History* 60 (1991): 20–36.

makes satisfaction. If he does not make satisfaction and he dies, no priest may bury him and he may not be buried within a church."[13]

Gregory VII famously used excommunication to try to coerce King Henry IV and his supporters to obey ecclesiastical decrees. Bisson quite rightly declares the investiture conflict "the first crisis of a new world in the making" and sees it as a consequence of the radical expansion and new character of lordship from the late ninth century.[14] Both sides understood the conflict to be about the exercise of power. Partisans on both sides accused their opponents of bad lordship. Henry saw his selection and investiture of bishops as a time-honored royal right, while Gregory denounced it as a bad custom clearly prohibited by ecclesiastical law. And, the pope insisted, "the Lord said, 'I am the truth and the life.' He did not say, 'I am the custom,' but 'the truth.'"[15] Indeed, by the late eleventh century the pope and others had come to view kings and princes as deriving "their origin from men ignorant of God who raised themselves above their fellows by pride, plunder, treachery, murder—in short, by every kind of crime."[16] For their part, royal supporters viewed Gregory's release of Henry's subjects from their vows of fidelity to him as an audacious example of the pope's arbitrary use of power. Sigebert of Gembloux accused the pontiff of using "tyrannical violence" in order to enforce reform.[17]

Considering Lordship and Influencing It

The reform movements and investiture conflict not only quickened the development of ecclesiastical mechanisms of coercive power, but also invigorated a conversation about good and bad lordship that had begun in the tenth century when this mode of power was becoming dominant throughout Europe.[18] The nature of that discussion is clearest among ecclesiastics who vigorously debated aspects of their own lordship but also polemically attacked their lay rivals. This was not a mere war of words: there is considerable evidence that clerics were trying to change lay ideas and practices regarding their

13. Henry Doniol, ed., *Cartulaire de Sauxillanges* (Paris, 1864), 52–54; trans. Maureen C. Miller, *Power and the Holy in the Age of the Investiture Conflict* (Boston, 2005), 37–38. Bishops were not uniformly altruistic or peaceful actors in these events. Thomas Head has called attention to a case in which a bishop used a threat of force to procure peace and another where a bishop's ambitions for his noble family clearly trumped other motives: Thomas Head, "Peace and Power in France around the Year 1000," *Essays in Medieval Studies* 23 (2006): 1–17; see also Dominique Barthélemy, "The Peace of God and Bishops at War in the Gallic Lands from the Late Tenth to the Early Twelfth Century," *Anglo-Norman Studies* 32 (2009): 1–23; Warren C. Brown, *Violence in Medieval Europe* (Harlow, 2011), 99–132.

14. Bisson, *Crisis*, 203, 205.

15. *The Epistolae Vagantes of Pope Gregory VII*, ed. and trans. H.E.J. Cowdrey (Oxford, 1972), no. 67, 151.

16. Miller, *Power and the Holy*, 108.

17. Bisson, *Crisis*, 204–7; Robinson, "Reform and the Church," 278.

18. John Van Engen, "Sacred Sanctions for Lordship," in *Cultures of Power: Lordship, Status, and Process in Twelfth-Century Europe*, ed. Thomas N. Bisson (Philadelphia, 1995), 203–30.

exercise of power. Orderic Vitalis, for example, recounted that in 1088 Odo, the bishop of Bayeaux, gave a long exhortation to Duke Robert Curthose of Normandy, to the applause of all present, urging him to "stand up for the peace of holy mother church and for the defense of the poor and helpless."[19] While the impact of this one sermon was quite limited, other indicators suggest that clerical efforts in the long run had influence. Some lay lords, too, seemed eager to engage clerics on issues when it suited their interests: Duke William V of Aquitaine, for example, wrote to Bishop Fulbert of Chartres early in 1021 about oaths of fidelity, eliciting a brief but detailed analysis of the duties of vassals.[20] The lay side of this conversation is difficult to hear since our surviving sources are overwhelmingly ecclesiastical, but vernacular poetry and imaginative literature offer some evidence. Let's begin with the ecclesiastical sources and then turn to those associated with lay culture.

Episcopal defenses of the conduct of their own lordship reveal many of the themes in this debate. As Ian Robinson has pointed out, the group of "episcopal polemics" surviving from the period of the investiture conflict is far larger than the papal and imperial tracts that tend to receive more attention. He also demonstrates that, despite their originally circumscribed local circulation, they were quite intellectually significant: they established principles essential both to papal lordship (such as the idea that bishops must be consecrated with papal authority to be legitimate) and to the resolution of the investiture conflict (namely, the "legal distinction between care of souls and custodianship of bodies").[21] They reveal several ideas about good lordship.

The most prominent theme was a perceived duty not only to safeguard but also to extend the property and rights of their sees. Whereas Gregory the Great's *Pastoral Care* had focused on how the bishop should admonish various kinds of people in different spiritual states, sources from the ninth century on emphasized the care of property as an important aspect of the prelate's care of souls. Property supported the religious life, liturgy, and ministry, particularly poor relief. Episcopal hagiography from the tenth and eleventh centuries extolled the bishop's defense of the lands and rights of his see and his improvement of the diocese's resources. Prelates were praised not only for constructing churches but also for building roads and bridges. Bishop Ermongol of Urgell (1010–1035), who perished building a bridge over the Segre River, was one of many who served their flocks by creating infrastructure "fit for posterity and on that account pleasing to God."[22] Some of the polemical tracts written by or about bishops during the investiture

19. *EH*, 4:150–55.

20. The duke was looking for ammunition in a dispute with one of his men, some details of which are revealed in a remarkable *conventum* between the two: Jane Martindale, "Conventum inter Willelmum Comitem Aquitanorum et Hugonem Chiliarchum," *English Historical Review* 84 (1969): 528–48. For Fulcher's letter, see *The Letters and Poems of Fulbert of Chartres* ed. and trans. Frederick Behrends (Oxford, 1976), 90–93 (no. 51).

21. I. S. Robinson, *Authority and Resistance in the Investiture Contest: The Polemical Literature of the Late Eleventh Century* (Manchester, 1978), 151, 168, quotation on 183.

22. Jeffrey A. Bowman, "The Bishop Builds a Bridge: Sanctity and Power in the Medieval Pyrenees," *Catholic Historical Review* 88 (2002): 1–16; on the evidence of the *gesta episcoporum*, see Michel Parisse,

conflict define good episcopal lordship in a similar fashion. Weinrich of Trier's defense of Archbishop Udo (1066–1078) praised his persistent efforts against the "robbers of the church," while Norbert's life of Bishop Benno II of Osnabrück applauded his building of firm roads through marshy regions of his diocese.[23] A tract and a letter defending Benno's various allegiances during the investiture conflict invoked the bishop's duty to protect the rights of his church.[24] Archbishop Anselm of Canterbury's anxious letter of January 1095 about his disagreements with his king reveals the same sensibility. His overriding concern, in the face of William Rufus's "arbitrary justice," was not to accede to any diminution of the lands of his church.[25]

This ideal of patrimonial stewardship, of course, was anchored in an understanding of prelacies as offices, a notion that survived in the church even as its leaders ruled by personal command as lords. The renewed emphasis on official obligations would prove significant in the long run to the reemergence of something resembling government in Europe. Within the ideal of patrimonial stewardship was also a sense of accountability: Archbishop Anselm voiced awareness that he acted "in the sight of God," to whom he must answer for any diminishment of his see. Such beliefs in divine accountability also conditioned relations with his king. When William showed his anger and made clear that Anselm "had lost his love," the archbishop replied "that I preferred him to be angry with me than God with him."[26]

German episcopal polemics promoted two other ideas. One was that lords should not treat subordinates as slaves. In 1075 Gregory VII invoked a scriptural ideal urging submission to the Roman church, "who does not hold her subjects as slaves but receives all as sons."[27] But he was accused the very next year by Henry IV of having "trodden underfoot the rulers of the holy church, the archbishops, bishops and priests, . . . like slaves ignorant of what their lord is doing."[28] The king here was referencing John 15:15, where Jesus promised to share with his followers all that he knew of his Father because they were friends, not slaves who could not understand their lord's actions. German bishops repeatedly appealed to the fraternal cooperation that should govern relations among bishops, including the bishop of Rome, and objected to Gregory's autocratic disregard of their traditional judicial prerogatives.[29] In the twelfth century, Peter the Venerable also

"Princes laïques et/ou moines, les évêques du Xe siècle," in *Il Secolo di ferro: Mito e realtà del secolo X*, Settimane di studio del Centro Italiano di studi sull'alto medioevo, 38 (Spoleto, 1991), 482–92.

23. Robinson, *Authority and Resistance*, 152–53.

24. Ibid., 156–60; also the case of Theoderic of Verdun, 153–56.

25. *The Letters of Saint Anselm of Canterbury*, ed. and trans. Walter Fröhlich, 3 vols. (Kalamazoo, Mich., 1993), 2:86–90 (no. 176).

26. Ibid., 88, 87.

27. *The Register of Pope Gregory VII 1073-1085*, trans. H. E. J. Cowdrey (Oxford, 2002), 157 (2.63); Bisson, *Crisis*, 40.

28. Carl Erdmann, ed., *Die Briefe Heinrichs* IV (Leipzig, 1937) *MGH Deutsches Mittelalter* 1:15; Theodor E. Mommsen and Karl F. Morrison, trans., *Imperial Lives and Letters of the Eleventh Century* (New York, 2000), 150 (letter 12); Robinson, *Authority and Resistance*, 169.

29. Robinson, *Authority and Resistance*, 169–72.

upheld the idea that relations between ecclesiastical lords and their subordinates should be familial rather than servile. The abbot of Cluny admitted that monks were sustained by the labor of dependent peasants, but asserted "they do not vex them with exactions or insupportable burdens, and if they see them in need they sustain them from their own goods. They consider them not as slaves and bondwomen, but as brothers and sisters."[30]

The other aspect of ecclesiastical lordship that the German episcopal polemics raised was its use of the violence of others. Sigebert of Gembloux (c. 1030–1112) supported many of the objectives of Gregory VII and his allies, but fiercely criticized the means used to achieve their ends. The pope had encouraged laypeople to shun simoniac and unchaste priests, and this led to violent physical assaults on clerics and looting of ecclesiastical property. Gregory had also encouraged the subjects of Henry IV to rise up against him. With "impious and profane" disregard for justice and order, according to Sigebert, Gregory's "tyrannical violence" in pursuit of reform yielded bitter fruit: "you see the Lord's flock miserably scattered and their shepherds inciting the wolves against them." Another ecclesiastical use of the violence of others that Sigebert critiqued would have a long and baleful history. Sending thousands of European knights to conquer the Holy Land in 1095 didn't impede the papacy from redirecting lordly violence to achieve more local ends. Count Robert of Flanders, just returned from the First Crusade in 1103, received a new remission of sins from Pope Paschal II for a campaign against "the chief of heretics," Henry IV. His devastation of the dioceses of Cambrai and Liège provoked Sigebert to upbraid the pope for his use of the "Gregorian" tactic of directing the violence of *milites beati Petri* against so-called schismatics.[31]

"Knights of Saint Peter" and crusades were part of ecclesiastical efforts to channel the violence of European lordship and redirect it to supposedly more lofty ends. These efforts included the cultural project that comes to be known as chivalry. While there were certainly secular sources for the ideals and rituals of knighthood,[32] ecclesiastical influence was powerful and it accelerated in the eleventh century. Indeed, as the work of Jean Flori has revealed, there was an episcopal *ordo* for arming knights in 1093. It included blessings of the standard (*vexillum*), the lance, the sword, and the knight himself. Then, continues the rubric,

30. "Rusticorum namque legitimis et debitis solummodo seruitiis ad uitae subsidia utuntur, nullis exactionibus uexant, nichil importabile imponunt, si eos egere uiderint, etiam de propriis sustentant. Seruos et ancillas non ut seruos et ancillas set ut fratres et sorores habent." *The Letters of Peter the Venerable*, ed. Giles Constable, 2 vols. (Cambridge, Mass., 1967), 1:87 (letter 28). Bisson presents cases where the treatment of peasants on ecclesiastical holdings, or those influenced by reformers (e.g., Matilda of Canossa), appears to have been better than in neighboring lay lordships: *Crisis*, 125, 138–39, 224, 362, 365.

31. I. S. Robinson, *Henry IV of Germany, 1056–1106* (Cambridge, 1999), 311; Robinson, *Authority and Resistance*, 175–79.

32. See Régine Le Jan, "Frankish Giving of Arms and Rituals of Power: Continuity and Change in the Carolingian Period," in *Rituals of Power from Late Antiquity to the Early Middle Ages*, ed. Frans Theuws and Janet L. Nelson (Leiden, 2000), 281–309; C. Stephen Jaeger, *The Origins of Courtliness: Civilizing Trends and the Formation of Courtly Ideals, 939–1210* (Philadelphia, 1985), 3–4, 113–14; Maurice Keen, *Chivalry* (New Haven, 1984), 66–71.

> the bishop girded him [with the sword], saying: "Accept this sword, conferred on you with the blessing of God, with which, through the virtue of the Holy Spirit, may you be worthy to oppose and vanquish all your enemies and all adversaries of the holy church of God, with the help of our Lord Jesus Christ, who is with you."

The bishop then bestowed the shield and prayed that the warrior saints Maurice, Sebastian, and George protect the knight.[33] Chronicles offer some evidence of bishops performing this ritual, although it is limited to the very highest levels of the nobility. Orderic Vitalis, for example, recorded that Archbishop Lanfranc of Canterbury presented the young King Henry I "for knighthood for the defense of the kingdom, invested him with the hauberk, placed the helmet on his head and girded him with the belt of knighthood in the name of the Lord as a king's son born in the purple."[34] Many knights—perhaps most—preferred entirely secular ceremonies. John of Marmoutier's description of the knighting of Geoffrey of Anjou in 1128 reveals some of the elements of what becomes the classic dubbing ceremony: a ritual bath, the dressing of the young man in a golden tunic and purple cloak, the bestowal of spurs, shield, and sword. It is the king, however, who oversees this ceremony, making Geoffrey a knight. No clerics participate.[35]

The influence of ecclesiastical ideas and practices accrued, however, particularly through the vernacular romances of the late twelfth and thirteenth centuries. Many of those who composed and copied these stories for courtly entertainment were clerics and, even if only in minor orders, they were obvious vectors of the religious influence so evident in these tales. In the *Prose Lancelot* or *Vulgate Cycle*, composed in c. 1215–1235, the Lady of the Lake instructs the young Lancelot in the virtues of knighthood by explaining the allegorical meanings of his arms. His shield covers the knight, as he must protect the church. His helmet shields his head, and so must the knight shield holy mother church from all who seek to harm her. The knight's sword is double-edged, signifying that he is the servant of God and of the people.[36] If this sounds familiar, one of the earliest manuals of chivalry, Ramon Llull's *Llibre de l'orde de cavalleria* (1274–1276), makes the connection to clerical vesting overt. Llull was seneschal of the future King James I of

33. "Deinde cingat eum episcopus dicendo: Accipe hunc gladium cum Dei benedictione tibi collatum, in quo per virtutem spiritus sancti resistere et eicere valeas omnes inimicos tuos et cunctos sanctae Dei ecclesiae adversarios, adiuvante domino nostro Iesu Christo, qui tecum." Jean Flori, "Chevalerie et liturgie: Remise des armes et vocabulaire 'chevaleresque' dans les sources liturgiques du IXe au XIVe siècle," *Le moyen âge: Revue d'histoire et de philologie* 84 (1978): 275–78, 437 (quote).

34. *EH*, 4:120–21; for other examples, see Joachim Bumke, *Courtly Culture: Literature and Society in the High Middle Ages*, trans. Thomas Dunlap (Berkeley, 1991), 240–41.

35. Paul Marchegay and André Salmon, eds., *Chroniques d'Anjou*, 2 vols. (Paris, 1856–1871; repr., New York, 1965), 1:234–36; Keen, *Chivalry*, 64–65; Bumke, *Courtly Culture*, 234–35.

36. H. Oskar Sommer ed., *The Vulgate Version of the Arthurian Romances*, 8 vols., Carnegie Institution of Washington Publication 74 (Washington, D.C., 1908–1916), 3:113–16; Norris J. Lacy, "The Evolution and Legacy of French Prose Romance," in *The Cambridge Companion to Medieval Romance*, ed. Roberta L. Kreuger (Cambridge, 2000), 169–73.

Majorca, a great enthusiast for tournaments, and composer of troubadour songs. A series of visions in 1263, however, led to a total conversion of life. He entered the Franciscan order, wrote numerous theological and mystical tracts, and ultimately died trying to convert Muslims. Llull knew both the knightly and ecclesiastical worlds well. He began his chapter on the knight's arms by reminding the reader that the priest prepares to say Mass by putting on the vestments symbolizing his office, and since "the office of the priesthood and of chivalry have much in common," so every piece of knightly armor has meaning. The sword has the semblance of a cross to signify Christ's sacrifice, so the knight should destroy all enemies of the cross. His helmet symbolizes the knight's dread of shame, his hauberk protection against vice and sin, his spurs swiftness and diligence, his gorget obedience, and his dagger trust in God. Allegorical meanings of twenty-one pieces of the knight's equipment are provided.[37] By the fourteenth century these same ideas appear in lay manuals of chivalry. The *Livre de chevalerie* written by Geoffroi de Charny, a Burgundian knight active in the first phase of the Hundred Years' War, also gives Christian meanings for every action in the dubbing ceremony.[38]

Several hagiographic works suggest an attempt to propagate ecclesiastical ideals of good lordship through the veneration of saintly lay lords. The life of Saint Gerald of Aurillac (d. 909) by Odo of Cluny (d. 942) is the most famous example. It depicts Gerald surrounding himself with upright laymen and clerics, hearing and investigating the pleas of the wronged, vigorously pursuing bandits and murderers, but always tempering his justice with mercy. He attempts to settle disputes through negotiation, but when that fails he tries to avoid casualties as he uses "his strength to bow the neck of the wicked." Even if his knights plundered and looted, Gerald did not. There were no frivolous entertainments or buffoonery at Gerald's table and he dressed soberly, "in the old fashion," in wools and linens. His tenants and clerics, Odo assures us, "loved him dearly as a father" and brought him little gifts of wax. The mid-eleventh-century life of Count Bouchard of Vendôme by the monk Eudes of Saint-Maur praised this lay lord as "a loyal defender of the churches, a giver of alms, a consolation to the poor, and a most pious helper of monks, clerics, widows, and virgins serving God in convents."[39]

37. Ramon Llull, *Llibre de l'orde de cavalleria*, ed. Albert Soler i Llopart (Barcelona, 1988), 9–10 (on the date of the work), 201–6. An English translation made by William Caxton from a French version of Llull's Catalan text still seems to be the basis of the modern English translations in print. The Caxton text was republished by the Early English Text Society (original series vol. 168): *The Book of the Ordre of Chivalry*, ed. Alfred T. P. Byles (London, 1926; repr., Oxford, 1971), 66–89. Another similarity with clerical vesting practices is that weapons, even outside the context of a dubbing ceremony, were blessed. From the second half of the tenth century, pontificals include blessings for arms and battle standards: Flori, "Chevalerie et liturgie," 266–74; Bumke, *Courtly Culture*, 292–93; Derek A. Rivard, *Blessing the World: Ritual and Lay Piety in Medieval Religion* (Washington, D.C., 2009), 156–57, 160–66.

38. *The Book of Chivalry of Geoffroi de Charny: Text, Context, and Translation*, ed. and trans. Richard W. Kaeuper and Elspeth Kennedy (Philadelphia, 1996), 167–71.

39. Gerard Sitwell, ed. and trans., *St. Odo of Cluny, Being the Life of St. Odo of Cluny by John of Salerno and the Life of St. Gerald of Aurillac by St. Odo* (London, 1958), 107–14, 116, 122–23, 128–29; Odo of Cluny, *Vita sancti Geraldi Auriliacensis: Édition critique, traduction française, introduction et commentaires*, ed.

The idea that lay lords should defend the church, of course, was elaborated in the late eleventh century to include holy places outside of Europe, particularly those associated with the life of Christ. The possibilities for conquest and the extension of European lordships made this version of Christian knighthood much more successful than hagiographic models of elite rule such as the *Life* of Saint Gerald. Indeed, the clearest evidence of ecclesiastical ideas about lordship having some influence on lay mentalities is the enthusiasm for crusading and the military religious orders that emerged in the twelfth century. Even if many answered the call to crusade for gain or adventure, some—most famously Raymond of Saint-Gilles, count of Toulouse—seem to have been motivated by piety and desire to fight in defense of the church and sacred places.[40] Military orders, such as the Templars, founded in c. 1120, and the knights of the Hospital of St. John (or Hospitallers) that emerged in the 1130s, generated rules that required their brethren to attend services, cultivate poverty and chastity, and serve the church.[41]

The numbers who joined the military orders were quite limited, however, and recruiting for Crusades after the first was never easy, so the attraction of laymen to ecclesiastical ideals of lordship should not be overestimated. Most of the troubadour poetry by lay lords, in fact, reveals no interest in these ideals. The sirventes of Bertran de Born, a lesser lord in the Limousin, are often critical of lords—for cowardice, lack of military skill, inconstancy, and stinginess—but celebrate warfare as a pleasurable pastime and praise killing. Indeed, those of the Catalan lord Guillem de Berguedà reveal fierce hostility toward the clergy.[42] Although this evidence is meager, that of other attempts to gauge the influence of clerical discourses on lay ideas, most notably sexuality, suggest an uneven and limited impact.[43] That the clergy were attempting to influence lay ideas and

Anne-Marie Bultot-Verleysen, Subsidia hagiographica 89 (Brussels, 2009), 156–68, 172, 180–82, 190 (chaps. 13–20, 25, 33, 40); Bumke, *Courtly Culture*, 291–92.

40. Marcus Bull, *Knightly Piety and the Lay Response to the First Crusade: The Limousin and Gascony, c. 970–c. 1130* (Oxford, 1993), and more concisely in his article "The Roots of Lay Enthusiasm for the First Crusade," *History: The Journal of the Historical Association* 78 (1993): 353–72; Giles Constable, "Medieval Charters as a Source for the History of the Crusades," in his *Crusaders and Crusading in the Twelfth Century* (Farnham, 2008), 93–116, but especially 110–15; Michael McCormick, "The Liturgy of War from Antiquity to the Crusades," in *The Sword of the Lord: Military Chaplains from the First to the Twenty-First Century*, ed. Doris L. Bergen (Notre Dame, Ind., 2004), 45–67. David Couch gives an excellent appraisal of the religiosity of William Marshal in *William Marshal: Court, Career and Chivalry in the Angevin Empire 1147–1219* (London, 1990), 185–94.

41. Alan Forey, "The Military Orders, 1120–1312," in *The Oxford Illustrated History of the Crusades*, ed. Jonathan Riley-Smith (Oxford, 1997), 184–216, esp. 208–11; Giles Constable, "The Military Orders," in *Crusaders and Crusading in the Twelfth Century* (Farnham, 2008), 165–82.

42. Catherine Léglu, "Moral and Satirical Poetry," in *The Troubadours: An Introduction*, ed. Simon Gaunt and Sarah Kay (Cambridge, 1999), 55–60; Karen Wilk Klein, *The Partisan Voice: A Study of the Political Lyric in France and Germany, 1180–1230*, Studies in General and Comparative Literature 7 (The Hague, 1971), 92–98, 169–80; *The Poems of the Troubadour Bertran de Born*, ed. and trans. William D. Paden, Jr., Tilde Sankovitch, and Patricia H. Stäblein (Berkeley, 1986), 114–18, 122–26, 186–212, 234–38, 276–80, 328–30, 338–44, 356–74, 430–32.

43. John W. Baldwin, *The Language of Sex: Five Voices from Northern France around 1200* (Chicago, 1994), 225–29.

practices of lordship, however, is unquestionable, as is the long-term significance of the successes they achieved.

Critiquing Clothing

Histories of fashion routinely discuss the critiques of lay clothing found in monastic chronicles, and sometimes even mention critiques of clerical attire. But they either miss much of their meaning by viewing them narrowly in the framework of fashion or restrict their analyses to moral and social values, emphasizing their similarities more than differences.[44] These critiques were not just about clothing. They were about the virtues requisite for good lordship. They were all based on the common belief that exterior appearance was related to interior states, and most derided clothing excesses as rooted in pride and vanity. But beyond these basic commonalities, different ideas about lords and lordship are expressed. Critiques of clothing are found in many different genres: chronicles, letters, tracts, theological works, and poetry.[45] My analysis here, however, is organized to emphasize the backgrounds of the critics and the types of clothing they criticized, moving from monastic critiques of lay, monastic, and clerical clothing to clerical critiques of their own attire.

Let's begin with the monastic chroniclers and their critiques of lay clothing. One of the earliest and most frequently cited is Rodulfus Glaber's diatribe on the "strange manners and clothes" that were brought into the kingdom of France c. 1000 through the marriage of Robert II to Constance of Arles. This noblewoman from Provence was, according to Glaber, accompanied by "a great flood of strange men . . . flippant and vain fellows." They wore "indecent hose and shoes," were beardless, and had odd haircuts. Since Glaber also critiqued their weapons and the equipment of their horses, we know they were at least knights if not noble relations of Constance and therefore lords themselves. Lest the reader think that their new fashions were simply "superstitious vanities," Glaber corrects this

44. Henri Platelle, "Le problème du scandale: Les nouvelles modes masculines aux XIe et XIIe siècles," *Revue belge de philologie et d'histoire* 53 (1975): 1071–96; Frédérique Lachaud, "Dress and Social Status in England before the Sumptuary Laws," in *Heraldry, Pageantry and Social Display in Medieval England before the Sumptuary Laws*, ed. Peter Coss and Maurice Keen (Woodbridge, 2002), 105–23; Frédérique Lachaud, "La critique du vêtement et du soin des apparences dans quelques oeuvres religieuses, morales et politiques, XIIe–XIVe siècles," in *Le corps et sa parure: The Body and Its Adornment*, Micrologus 15 (Florence, 2007), 61–85.

45. Many occur in works often classed and discussed as "court criticism," but not all critics of courtly life discussed clothing, and critiques of attire were not restricted to this important body of texts. On court criticism, see Jaeger, *Origins of Courtliness*, 176–94; Bumke, *Courtly Culture*, 415–23; Laurence Harf-Lancner, "Les malheurs des intellectuels à la cour: Les clercs curiaux d'Henri II Plantagenêt," in *Courtly Literature and Clerical Culture*, ed. Christoph Huber and Henrike Lähnemann (Tübingen, 2002), 3–18; Claus Uhlig, *Hofkritik im England des Mittelalters und der Renaissance* (Berlin, 1973), 27–136; Rolf Köhn, "'Militia Curialis': Kritik am geistlichen Hofdienst bei Peter von Blois und in der lateinischen Literatur des 9.–12. Jahrhunderts," in *Soziale Ordnungen im Selbstverständnis des Mittelalters, 1. Halbband*, Miscellanea mediaevalia 12/1 (Berlin, 1979), 227–56.

benign view: they were the "brand-marks of Satan." Their evil, moreover, was not generic; it specifically concerned lords, their men, and violence. Those cultivating the new fashions were "totally devoid of good faith and respect for agreed peace." Worse still, "their evil example was seized upon avidly by the whole people of France." Rampant bad lordship in early eleventh-century France, according to Glaber, was a plague brought into the kingdom by a foreign woman. The heroic verses Glaber composed to express his hatred of the "wicked behavior" makes its critique of lordship quite clear:

> Behold, our people now mock past generations,
> Mix pleasure and debauchery and call them manners,
> Fear not scandal and scorn serious matters,
> Spurning honour, the guide of just men.
> This life now produces tyrants [*tyrannos*] with strange bodies,
> Faithless and foolish men, with clothes too short for them.
> While the republic [*respublica*] groans under soft petticoat rule,
> Fraud, theft, and all infamy reign supreme in the world,
> Saints are not honoured nor the sacred worshipped.
> The sword, plague, and famine rage all about,
> And the impiety of men uncorrected spares no one.[46]

The blaming of Constance and her "*consilium muliebre*" for the kingdom's woes in Glaber's history becomes a more direct emasculation of fashionably dressed lords in twelfth-century critiques. Orderic Vitalis's famous rant against "frivolous" Angevin attire explained that "at that time effeminates set the fashion in many parts of the world, foul catamites, doomed to eternal fire," while William of Malmesbury, commenting on fashionable flowing locks, complained that knights were "transforming themselves to look like women."[47] This suggested, of course, that they were unfit to rule. Orderic lamented the new hairstyles too. They "grew long and luxurious locks like women," he wrote,

> and loved to deck themselves in long, over-tight shirts and tunics. . . . Our wanton youth is sunk in effeminacy, and courtiers, fawning, seek the favours of women with

46. Rodulfus Glaber, *The Five Books of the Histories and the Life of St William*, ed. and trans. John France (Oxford, 1989), 166–69 (book 3, chap. 40). See also William of Volpiano's sermon on the same theme, 290–91 in the same volume. Rodulfus wrote this part of his history c. 1036–1041 (xlv). In 1043, Abbot Siegfried of Gorze bemoaned similar fashions in a letter to Poppo, the abbot of Stavelot, about King Henry III's intention to marry Agnes of Poitou. Siegfried believed the marriage to be incestuous and wanted Poppo to admonish the king about its dangers. He concludes his argument with a lament about "the shameful custom of the vulgar French . . . in the cutting of beards, in the shortening and deforming of clothing, execrable to modest eyes, and many other novelties." Siegfried reasoned that these exterior indicators were alarming "since we see pillaging, oath-breaking, treacheries, and various kinds of deceitfulness gradually increasing, and we fear these are merely the indicators of worse evils to come." Wilhelm von Giesebrecht, *Geschichte der deutschen Kaiserzeit*, 6 vols. (Leipzig, 1877–1895), 2:718.

47. *EH*, 4:189; William of Malmesbury, *The Historia Novella*, ed. and trans. K.R. Potter (London, 1955), 6.

> every kind of lewdness. They add excrescences like serpents' tails to the tips of their toes where the body ends, and gaze with admiration on these scorpion-like shapes. They sweep the dusty ground with the unnecessary trains of their robes and mantles; their long, wide sleeves cover their hands whatever they do.

This fashion report erupts in Orderic's narration of the "uncontrolled wickedness" that reigned in Normandy under Duke Robert Curthose, who "was so idle and frivolous that he never governed justly and effectively as he ought to have done." The duke's ineffective and costly alliance with Fulk le Rechin, Count of Anjou, to subdue Maine is the specific example of bad lordship that prompts Orderic's critique of fashion at the Angevin court. It is offered to illustrate Orderic's appraisal of Fulk as "a man with many reprehensible, even scandalous, habits." The result of all this wickedness, according to Orderic, was that God scourged his people, suffering "mortals to be tormented by disease, harassed by wars and subjected to false rulers."[48]

While monastic authors considered objectionable lay fashions impious and obscene, their critiques of monastic clothing were different. Sometime between 1047 and 1054, the hermit Peter Damian wrote to Mainard of Pomposa about the abbot's "desire for precious clothes." He does not describe the abbot's attire in any detail, but his multiple references to brilliance, splendor, and expense imply silk garments. Damian links the abbot's weakness to his royal service, mentioning the duties of hospitality required of benefice holders and acknowledging that "the great of this world are accustomed to be charmed by the jeweled attire of those who wish to please them."[49] Whereas lay fashions were "brand-marks of Satan," precious monastic clothes only "incite the author of pride" and "open the door to the deceits of evil spirits." Damian was not rejecting the spirituality of sacred vestments, but rather insisting that it be about the cultivation of interior virtues. Indeed, he uses a series of vesting metaphors to admonish Mainard to put on a tunic of chastity, colored in scarlet charity of twice-dyed cochineal, in pursuit of spiritual martyrdom and heavenly joy.[50]

In the twelfth century, this critique is framed in terms of excesses (*superfluitates*). One of the points of controversy between the venerable Cluniac monastic congregation and the new Cistercian order was whether wearing fur was allowed by the rule of Saint Benedict. Bernard of Clairvaux's famous intervention in this debate was his 1125 tract, or *Apologia*, addressed to William, the abbot of Saint-Thierry. Bernard treated a wide range of excesses among fellow Benedictines, from food and drink to the building and decorating of churches. Like Damian, Bernard insisted that inner virtues were the point: "Isn't it better when humility is concealed in furs than when pride is concealed in

48. *EH*, 4:110–11, 186–91, 198–99. On how some of the garment characteristics described may have been achieved, see Jennifer Harris, "'Estroit vestu et manu cosu': Evidence for the Construction of Twelfth-Century Dress," in *Medieval Art: Recent Perspectives; A Memorial Tribute to C.R. Dodwell*, ed. Gale R. Owen-Crocker and Timothy Graham (Manchester, 1998), 89–103.

49. Peter Damian, *Die Briefe*, 1:228 (no. 24); Peter Damian, *Letters*, 1:230.

50. Peter Damian, *Letters*, 1:230–31; Peter Damian, *Die Briefe*, 1:228–29.

robes?" he asked. A monk's clothing should be practical, covering the body and keeping out the cold. Silk or satin were not necessary, nor were concern about the price, color, and style of clothing. Also like Damian, Bernard viewed excessive clothing as spiritually dangerous: "exterior excess is an indication of interior emptiness; soft garments reveal a softness of soul."[51]

When Bernard and other monks considered the clothing of the secular clergy, however, more than spiritual perils were at issue. Although abbots were often also great lords wielding judicial authority and controlling significant estates, their conduct of lordship was not the point of monastic critiques of their clothing. When monks criticized clerical clothing, however, they focused on clerics' exercise of lordship more than the state of their souls. In 1127 the abbot Bernard wrote a long letter to Henry Sanglier, archbishop of Sens, on the conduct and office of bishops (*De moribus et officio episcoporum*). Emphasizing that the office was about ministry, not rule, Bernard advised that Henry honor his ministry "not by *recherché* clothes, grand buildings and a parade of horseflesh, but by moral elegance, spiritual zeal and good works." "Yet how many act otherwise!" he exclaimed, noting that "one may observe in certain prelates a positive cult of clothing, but no, or next to no, cult of the virtues." They should adorn themselves with good deeds rather than the products of weavers and furriers. Note that the critique focuses on the virtues that should be exhibited by an officeholder and, implicitly, on qualifications for office. Bernard invokes 1 Timothy 2:9—which urges women to pray, but not in expensive clothes—recognizing that bishops may take offense at having a judgment applied to women (and laywomen at that) applied to themselves. Still, the abbot compares marten pelts and other episcopal ornaments to "feminine trappings, such as women, who are preoccupied with worldly things and how best to please their husbands, go to great pains and expense to provide themselves with." While this characterization of episcopal clothing as effeminate impugns their fitness to rule, it more directly critiques their subservience to secular lords, the "husbands" that overdressed episcopal "women" seek to please.[52]

And what harm does this do? Repeating his refrain of "not in expensive clothes," Bernard derides expensive horse trappings: "Tell me, priests, what is gold doing, not 'in the sanctuary', but on a bridle?" "Even if the king's court makes no outcry," he alleges, "the penury of the poor still cries out." The naked and the starving cry out,

> Of what use to us, working in wretched conditions of cold and hunger, are all those spare clothes stretched over hangers or folded in travelling chests? What you are squandering belongs to us. From us had been cruelly taken what you idly fritter away. We too come from God's creating hand, we too have been ransomed by the blood of Christ. We are therefore your brothers. Look at what you are doing in feasting

51. Conrad Rudolph, *The "Things of Greater Importance": Bernard of Clairvaux's "Apologia" and the Medieval Attitude toward Art* (Philadelphia, 1990), 254–55, 272–75.

52. *S. Bernardi Opera*, ed. J. Leclercq and H. Rochais, 7 vols. (Rome, 1957–1974), 7:104–5; Bernard of Clairvaux, *On Baptism and the Office of Bishops*, trans. Pauline Matarasso, Cistercian Fathers Series 67 (Kalamazoo, Mich., 2004), 42–44.

your eyes on your brothers' share. It is our substance that goes to make your superabundance. Every addition to your vanities is subtracted from our necessities.[53]

The poor making their lament here are those subject to the bishop's lordship, the dependents and tenants of the lands supporting his see and all the souls committed to his care who pay tithes. The reference to their wealth being "cruelly" extracted may generally denounce the weight of exactions, but perhaps more specifically it impugns the conduct of the episcopal officials who collected tithes, rents, and dues. The reminder that these impoverished subjects of episcopal lordship are "your brothers" pointedly refers to ecclesiastical assertions, like that of Peter the Venerable quoted earlier, that the nature of relations between clerical lords and their dependents was familial, not servile. Bernard of Clairvaux's admonitions "on glorying in one's apparel" constitute a sharp critique of episcopal lordship.

A more global critique of contemporary society, Bernard of Cluny's *De contemptu mundi*, mounts a broader indictment of ecclesiastical lordship. Little is known of this monastic author save that he was active during the abbacy of Peter the Venerable (1122–1156), to whom this long poem in three books is dedicated. The first book follows the conventions of the genre by proclaiming that the Last Judgment is at hand, reminding the reader of the eternal rewards of heaven and the unending torments of hell, and calling all to repentance in light of the vanity of the world. The earnest tone of this first book gives way from the beginning of the second to satire: with biting wit, Bernard offers a comprehensive survey of the depravity of his own times in books 2 and 3. His consistent theme is that none of the orders of society—from bishops and kings to peasants—are fulfilling their duties, so that "wickedness abides and each profession, race, rank and age performs every crime."[54] While he lambasts clerics and priests, Bernard concentrates his critique on bishops and only mentions their clothing. His argument is that bishops are not using their power to correct wrongdoers and bring their people to salvation. "Consider the age and you will see an age destitute of prelates," Bernard laments: "If a prelate exists to promote goodness, to cleanse the rest, the bishop has fled; there is a miter, but the work is lacking, and hence the miter is preeminent." This "preeminent miter" is akin to the "empty suit" in our own parlance: an individual is wearing the costume but incapable or unwilling to perform the functions it represents. The lack of work, the failure to perform pastoral care and do justice, "leaves the people to go to ruin, and they atone for the proud lords on high."[55] As we will see, other critics also focused on the miter and they were certainly responding both to the relative novelty of this episcopal accessory and to the concerted efforts by bishops to raise their visual profile and prominence.

53. Bernard of Clairvaux, *On Baptism*, 45–46; *S. Bernardi Opera* 7:105–6.

54. *Scorn for the World: Bernard of Cluny's "De contemptu mundi,"* ed. and trans. Ronald E. Pepin (East Lansing, Mich., 1991), 96–97 (quote), xi–xx; Rodney M. Thompson, "The Origins of Latin Satire in Twelfth-Century Europe," *Mittellateinisches Jahrbuch* 13 (1978): 73–83. Bernard is also often called "of Morval" (Morlanensis).

55. Bernard of Cluny, *Scorn for the World*, 156–57.

Bernard of Cluny is a conservative social critic in that he has confidence that the ordering of the world is essentially good; the problem is that individuals within the *ordines* are not doing their jobs. But since his ordering of the orders is that for which reformers had fought—that is, bishops by virtue of their care of souls rank above kings—the failings of bishops are most central to contemporary disorder. Bernard believes that bishops have the necessary power to bring their people to salvation, but they are corrupted by wealth and vanity. "If I did not realize that it is burdensome to describe or learn novelties," he confides, "I could describe bishops I know, but I conceal them."

> For them there exist fame, pomp and the arrogance of wealth, and now almost no one strives to be a bridge for souls. The bishop's prelatial garb refuses to loosen bonds or to hold them fast according to the canon, but for money he tears down and for money he builds up.[56]

The bishop's failure to use his judicial powers, to grant mercy or mete out punishment, brings suffering and disorder. Bernard locates the sources of this failure in venality, but also in fear of the rich and powerful. He castigates bishops for not using "the bow of anathema" against the nobility. "They are afraid to proclaim justice," Bernard laments,

> to strike down shameful deeds, to cleanse impurities, to burn what is rotten, to raise up the sick, to search out the feeble, to give Satan those who clearly have been driven onto the sea of death, to endure threats, to endure rapacious acts, to bind together, to stretch out arms exposed to the waves, to stand before the flock.

Their lack of courage is exacerbated by the plague of simony, which allows young boys or incompetent courtiers, with no faith or piety, to ascend to the episcopal office. The bishop "bears his rod of Aaron and crown; a miter adorns his head, and a jewel of India decorates his hand," but he is not busy, as he should be, "with prayer for priest, prelate, duke, magistrate, flock, or himself."[57]

The emptiness of these vestments is no small matter precisely because Bernard accepts the logic of the eleventh-century reforms and investiture conflict: if bishops rank above kings and all others, then theirs is the fundamental responsibility to exercise good lordship. In the midst of his longest section on episcopal failings he identifies bishops as

56. Ibid., 90–93. Pepin here translates *infula* as "chasuble," but this usage becomes common only in the thirteenth century. It retains its more classical sense of ornament or mark of distinction in the eleventh and twelfth centuries and is used to mean episcopal rank or full liturgical attire. That is what is meant here, so I have modified Pepin's rendering to "prelatial garb." Bernard repeats this imagery—"venditur infula pontificalis"—on 169.

57. Ibid., 156–63. The reference to the jewel of India on his hand may refer to the decorative medallions added to episcopal gloves or to a ring. Bishops received rings when "wed" to their sees; surviving late medieval examples do bear gems: Diana Scarisbrick and Martin Henig, *Finger Rings: From Ancient to Modern* (Oxford, 2003), 40–41.

"the impious order of rulers" whose neglect brings famine and disorder. He holds bishops responsible for correcting the king, whom he characterizes as a "plundering fiend" whose "action is tyrannical." This royal tyrant is "bad to citizens, good to reprobates, great to himself." The end result is that "the nation, without a defender and oppressed by a tyrant, is torn to pieces, destroyed by crime, struck by the enemy, burned by fire." The nation suffers under bad monarchical lordship, and "the bishop's stole does not rescue it."[58] Why do contemporary bishops not lasso the dragons tormenting their flocks?

Monastic authors produced most of the critiques of clothing through the mid-twelfth century, and then secular clerics took the lead. But one last monastic author introduces two more important themes. Nigel, in fact, straddled several worlds. He is sometimes identified as "of Longchamp" or "Wirecker" or "of Canterbury," the latter being the surest designation for he was definitely a monk and priest at Christ Church Canterbury in the late twelfth century. He may have been of mixed English-Norman parentage. Although a monk, he moved easily in the world of the secular clergy: he knew Thomas Becket, was a member of his party, and followed him into exile.[59] Nigel is most famous for his *Mirror of Fools* (*Speculum stultorum*, c. 1179–1180), a long satirical poem relating the misadventures of Burnellus the ass, who undertakes a journey in search of means to lengthen his entirely normal tail. The comic odyssey that results allows Nigel to poke fun at a panoply of contemporary abuses. The work was an immediate success and influenced many later writers, including John Gower and Geoffrey Chaucer. Like Bernard of Cluny's *De contemptu mundi*, Nigel's satire left no social group unscathed, and in mocking the secular clergy he, too, concentrated on the episcopate. Although in his ranking of the orders Nigel placed kings at the pinnacle, he devoted nearly twice as many biting lines to bishops and their greed, gluttony, and hypocrisy. While churches throughout their dioceses may be dilapidated and despoiled,

> So many are the bishop's tunics, cloths,
> And copes, that he can't keep account of them.
> The bishop's fingers hold sufficient gold
> And gems for seven men of wealth to own.
> The bishop likes to study marks, not Mark,
> And is more fond of lucre than of Luke.

58. Bernard of Cluny, *Scorn for the World*, 158–59, 92–93.

59. Ronald E. Pepin, *The Literature of Satire in the Twelfth Century: A Neglected Medieval Genre*, Studies in Medieval Literature 2 (Lewiston, N.Y., 1988), 117–18; *Nigellus de Longchamp dit Wireker*, vol. 1, *Introduction: Tractatus contra curiales et officiales clericos*, ed. André Boutemy, Travaux de la Faculté de philosophie et lettres de l'Université de Bruxelles, 16 (Paris, 1959) (hereafter, Nigel, *Tractatus*), 12–34; A.G. Rigg, "Canterbury, Nigel of," in *Oxford Dictionary of National Biography*, 60 vols. (Oxford, 2004); John D. Cotts, "The Critique of the Secular Clergy in Peter of Blois and Nigellus de Longchamps," *Haskins Society Journal* 13 (1999): 138–50.

Underage prelates and simony also drew Nigel's satiric ire.[60] But the miter is most cleverly and obscenely mocked. After studying in Paris, of course, Burnellus the ass fantasized about becoming a bishop. Nigel takes us inside the dim head of the protagonist as he convinces himself that it's the episcopal and not abbatial miter that would suit him. After worrying briefly how it will stay on his head with his large ears, Burnellus muses,

> The miter holds not all the bishop's power,
> Though it's the sacred emblem of his rank.
> The miter then does not concern them most,
> But rather it's the power that with it goes.

Nigel then jests with the differences between mules, which are sterile (here equated with monks), and horses, which are not (here equated with bishops). He was making, of course, a theological as well as ribald joke: bishops could reproduce in the sense that they create priests through ordination, but the unreformed breed also sired children. No sterile miter will do for the ass: "I want to be a bishop with full rights," he brays. Mocking the miter's "horns," Nigel has his protagonist insist that his be reduced in no way: Burnellus must have the episcopal miter, not the abbatial version, since the lappets extending from the latter and its "useless horns" are about as powerful as the mule's genitalia.[61]

While Nigel used his mirror of fools chiefly to lampoon ambitious monks, he turned his focus to the secular clergy in a later work, the *Tractatus contra curiales et officiales clericos* (1193). The work was addressed to a curial cleric—William of Longchamp, bishop of Ely and chancellor of England—but after his fall from grace. Parts of his critique of clerical attire simply reiterate the objections of earlier monastic authors: precious clothing is about unbridled ambition for benefices, rather than piety, and is not the true garb of a good shepherd.[62] But Nigel mounted a new criticism that is key to understanding debates among secular clerics about their own uses of clothing: he mocked the secular clergy's notions of moderation. While excoriating the ambition and greed of clerics serving in the royal court, he accuses them of performing the pretense of piety:

> As a consequence of having cast off all pomp and rejected fine linen, and other ornaments hitherto used, they now dress in moderate attire: namely, linen surplices and lamb fleeces, so that the wolf may conceal his rapacity and the fox his cunning under a sheepskin. They are first at the canonical hours and perform peculiar prayers and angular genuflections.[63]

60. Nigellus of Longchamp, *Speculum stultorum*, ed. Francesca Albini (Genoa, 2003), 160–69 (quote 164); the English translation here is a slightly modified version of *The Book of Daun Burnel the Ass: Nigellus Wireker's "Speculum stultorum,"* trans. Graydon W. Regenos (Austin, 1959), 126.

61. *Book of Daun Burnel the Ass*, 89–91; *Speculum stultorum*, 102–4.

62. Nigel, *Tractatus*, 158, 195.

63. "Abjectis ergo pompis et rejecta sindone, ornamentisque aliis quibus hucusque utebantur, mediocribus vestiuntur, scilicet superpelliceis lineis et pellibus agnanis, ut lupus rapacitatis et vulpis astutiae sub pelle ovina delitescent, horas canonicas praeveniunt et subsequuntur orationes peculiares et genuflexiones angulares." Ibid., 170.

Nigel's reference to linen surplices and lamb fleece must be appreciated in the context of how secular clerics had been responding to criticisms of "superfluity" in their attire. John of Salisbury's account of the Council of Reims in 1148 revealed the lack of agreement among clerics as to what was necessary and what was superfluous: furs, for example, seemed superfluous to those in Mediterranean climes whereas to Germans they seemed necessary. The language of ecclesiastical legislation over the twelfth century pasted over this lack of concord with ambiguous phrases. Note that Lateran II's decree required that clerical clothing "give no offence" without really specifying what was offensive. Lateran III (1179) offered no canons on the subject, but those of regional councils in the late twelfth and early thirteenth centuries began banning particular types of garments, and Lateran IV, in 1215, consolidated these attempts. Significantly, Nigel's reference to linen surplices as "moderate clothing" appears to mock precisely what Lateran IV adopted to address criticism of episcopal attire: "All bishops should wear outer garments of linen in public and in church." The canon didn't touch, of course, what they wore under these plain outergarments. The satirist's specification of lamb fleeces also suggests that prelates who renounced furs substituted very fine shearling in the name of moderation.

While scholars have noted evidence of the influence of John of Salisbury on Nigel's work,[64] in this instance one must recognize a critique of his more famous colleague. Nigel likely knew the author of the *Policraticus* and was certainly fully acquainted with his philosophy of moderation as the "touchstone of an ethically correct (and ultimately, happy) life" and as "the salient characteristic of the good ruler."[65] Immoderate conduct is the mark of tyranny, ecclesiastical as well as secular. Nigel was clearly not alone in his indignation at contemporary ecclesiastical attempts to cultivate moderation. University-educated clerics penned numerous satirical commentaries in the second half of the twelfth and early thirteenth centuries, some of which directly attacked aspects of the ornate style of liturgical attire and the spirituality of sacred vestments. This is what distinguishes the critiques written by the secular clergy: they much more directly challenged aspects of a culture they knew from the inside.

A poem by Gillebert called *On Clerical Superfluity* (*De superfluitate clericorum*), for example, specifically deplored attempts to characterize golden garments as "respectable" (*honestae*). This term was used in the legislation of councils in London in 1175, York in 1195, and Paris in 1208: clerical clothes should exhibit an "honorable example" (*exemplum honestatis*) and every cleric should wear a "respectable habit" (*honestum habitum*).[66] Although these canons appear to refer to clerical clothing worn outside the sanctuary,

64. See Boutemy's introduction to Nigel, *Tractatus*, 123–31. He alleges (124) influence on the passage above, citing John's "Veniunt enim in vestimentis ovium, intrinsecus autem sunt lupi rapaces" from *Policraticus* 7.21, but Boutemy obviously misses the critique of John's position in Nigel's characterization of contemporary ecclesiastical garments as *mediocres* and references to specific practices.

65. Cary Nederman in the introduction to his translation, John of Salisbury, *Policraticus: Of the Frivolities of Courtiers and the Footprints of Philosophers*, ed. and trans. Cary J. Nederman (Cambridge, 1990), xxiv.

66. Mansi, 22:148, 654, 726, 766.

Gillebert targets liturgical garb. While it was the folly of ancient kings to worship golden calves, who among modern men, the poet asks, would not through greed and vices turn their cult of idols into moral behavior?

> For today's cleric, it is respectable
> for the body to be swathed in clothes woven with gold,
> encircled in a pallium and cope with border
> so ample that it could clothe fifteen paupers.[67]

Gillebert's objection is similar to Bernard of Clairvaux's: opulent clothes rob the poor. But while the abbot referred vaguely to "products of weavers and furriers," Gillebert named the prestigious garb of prelates.

This poem survives in a single manuscript, so it can tell us something about clerical critiques of clerical clothing but perhaps little about wider views. Likely more influential was Peter the Chanter's *Verbum adbreviatum*, a popular manual of ethics that survives in at least ninety manuscripts. Peter was from a knightly family with lands on the border between Normandy and the Île-de-France. He studied in Reims and then Paris, becoming chanter of Notre Dame in 1183, an office he held until his death in 1197. In ecclesiastical status, he never exceeded the rank of deacon, but his teaching and administrative experience under Bishop Maurice de Sully of Paris was extensive: he lectured on the Bible, wrote several theological works, and served as a judge and arbiter in cases in northern France.[68] The *Verbum adbreviatum* may have been composed as an aid to preachers since some of its chapters were regarded as sermons. This use is consonant, with Peter's stated purpose to use authorities to rebuke vice and encourage virtue. Two chapters, numbers 81 "Against superfluity in clothing" (*Contra superfluitatem uestium*) and 82 "Against the form of clothes" (*Contra formam uestium*), critique clerical attire.

Each chapter begins with broad principles and objections that could apply to the clothing of either laymen or clerics, but then narrows to more specifically clerical concerns. In 81, for example, Peter argued that simple materials in their natural colors were sufficient for our forebears. Citing Adam and Eve, John the Baptist, Saint Jerome, and Saint Benedict, he reminded the reader of God's decree in Genesis 3:21 that "by the sweat of your brow, you will eat your bread." So, reasoned Peter, by the sweat of our brow we ought to clothe ourselves. Today, he continued, clothes exceed what is necessary in material, dyes, form, composition, diversity, and in their mutations. He mocked fashions in colors, exclaiming that human vanity corrupts even natural beauty, "now in

67. Aureos insania regum antiquorum / adorabat vitulos. Quis est modernorum, / qui per avariciam, cultum ydolorum, / non inclinet viciis honestatem morum? / Honestas est hodie clericalis viri / auro textis vestibus corpus redimiri,/tali limbo pallium vel cappam ambiri, / unde possent quindecim pauperes vestiri. R.B. C. Huygens, ed., *Serta mediaevalia: Textus varii saeculorum X–XIII in unum collecti*, CCCM 171A (Turnhout, 2000), 711.

68. John W. Baldwin, *Masters, Princes and Merchants: The Social Views of Peter the Chanter and His Circle*, 2 vols. (Princeton, 1970), 1:3–16.

red, then reddish, now in green, then in saffron, now in violet, then in whatever other confused mix." In 82, he elaborated that multicolored clothes—whether "bipartite, tripartite, quadripartite, or multipartite"—were excessive, as well as those "in some fashion moving, cleaving, pleating, puckering, splitting, [or] curling."[69]

When Peter turned specifically to clerical attire, he criticized clothing worn outside the sanctuary and within it. Clerics should dress simply, without any vain superfluities such as glittering or perforated garments. Their clothes should be in natural colors, and Peter specifically indicated that the dark/black color of the *cappa clericalis* and white of the surplice were natural. He criticized attempts to subvert the intent of canons on clothing while adhering legalistically to their literal demands. So, for example, Peter condemned clerics who did not dare wear garments trailing behind them—since these were explicitly forbidden—but then pompously added "tails" to copes, including one bishop who decked himself out in ermine tails. Peter also defined as superfluous, however, materials and techniques common in liturgical attire: silk, gold ornamentation, and woven gold cloth. Addressing his fellow clerics directly, Peter wrote, "If you give up multicolored clothing and reddened pelts and the 'violets used in the tabernacle' and temple, and similarly gold, and silver, and whatnot, I assure you that 'when the signs recede, what they signify remains.'"[70] The chanter here not only alludes to Exodus (26:1, *iacinctinas fuisse in tabernaculo*), but also quotes Hildebert of Lavardin's allegorical poetic commentary on the Mass: he counters the scriptural basis for the spirituality of priestly vestments with a refined meaning of the allegorical logic used to link the elaborate garments of Aaron with the attire of the Christian priesthood.

His message was not new, of course. The cleric's virtue, what should be signified by the external signs of vestments, was paramount. But to those who would object that the church already had all sorts "of gold, silver, golden cloths, ornaments and every kind of silk vestment," implying that one might as well continue using them, Peter responded that "it would be better that they be exposed for sale, than the poor to hunger, and better that they be exposed to usury than the poor to frost."[71] He then cites Bernard of Clairvaux's *Apologia*, but note that he goes beyond simply objecting, as Bernard did, that ecclesiastical spending on fine clothing robbed paupers: Peter advocates using the fine garments owned by churches to alleviate the suffering of the poor. He also questioned the relationships that produced clerical garb, although in a somewhat ambiguous fashion. Returning to his initial text from Genesis, he imagines that grammarians might object that we do honor God's decree to produce life's necessities "by the sweat of your brow," only that there's a "transition" between the noun "brow" and pronoun "your";

69. Peter the Chanter, *Verbvm adbreviatvm, textus conflatus*, ed. Monique Boutry, CCCM 196 (Turnhout, 2004), 561–62, 565.

70. "Si obicis uestes uarii coloris et pelles rubricates et *iacinctinas fuisse in tabernaculo* et in templo, similiter aurum et argentum et huiusmodi, respondeo quia: 'Signa recesserunt, significata manent.'" Ibid., 563.

71. "Si etiam obiciatur quod hodie in Ecclesia est superflua uarietas auri, argenti, palliorum aurifrigiorum, ornamentorum et omnimoda uestis holoserica, respondeo quod melius ista exponerentur ad uendendum quam pauperes ad imbrem, melius exponerentur ad usuram quam pauperes ad pruinam." Ibid., 564.

that is, "your" means peasants, proxies, slaves, or helpers. Theirs are the sweating brows that produce clothing. To this, Peter responds, "Such an explanation is distorted and un-Christian."[72] Would the chanter have everyone make his or her own clothes? It doesn't appear so, in that he continues, "And only by their labor and sweat, not in curiosity, sumptuousness, superfluity, and variety!"

Peter the Chanter's critique is not entirely coherent, but it suggests some radical directions that would be developed by the mendicants across the thirteenth century. First, unlike the monastic critics, Peter's censure focused not just on bishops but on all secular clerics. Second, whereas ecclesiastical legislation and monastic critics present the problem of clerical clothing as one of garb worn outside the sanctuary, the chanter and other clerics directly challenged the use of ornate liturgical vestments. Third, while other critics either refrained from saying what should be done about superfluity in clerical clothing or simply urged "moderation," Peter said that precious vestments should be sold or pawned to care for the poor. Finally, he advocated neither moderation nor practicality (Bernard of Clairvaux's position), but simplicity. The models he proffered were extreme: Adam and Eve in the "fur tunics" (*tunicas pelliceas*) that God fashioned for them, Saint Jerome in his "sack" (*sacco*), Saint Benedict in his tunic, and John the Baptist in his goatskin (*pilis caprarum*).[73] He realized, in the end, that the dense web of social relationships—with slaves, servants, workers—that produced cloth and clothing was inescapable. But the fact that he called attention to these relationships and criticized academic arguments that would make light of them is significant.[74] Peter was no marginal figure but a highly placed cleric in Paris whose writings were widely copied and read. And the standard he advocated for acceptable clerical clothing—simplicity—was much more rigorous than the competing establishment models of practicality and moderation.

In fact, the standard that Peter took up had been championed a century earlier, but had been effectively countered by more powerful and conservative clerics. Around 1098 the bishop of Rennes in Brittany penned a carefully worded warning and rebuke to a former archpriest of his diocese. The two men shared much in common: both had been born near Angers in the mid-eleventh century and pursued clerical careers locally. The bishop, Marbode, had entered the clergy and studied at the episcopal school in Angers, later becoming a teacher and then director of the same school. The letter's recipient, Robert, probably began his education locally, then studied in Paris for a period until he was summoned back to Brittany in the late 1080s by Bishop Sylvester of Rennes to help reform the clergy of the diocese. The two certainly met in c. 1093 when Robert was at

72. "Porro quidam nimis gramatici, hunc locum: *In sudore uultus tui uesceris pane tuo*, praue et peruerse exponunt in labore et sudore uultus tui, ut sit transicio inter hoc nomen 'uultus' et hoc pronomen 'tui': tui, scilicet coloni, uicarii, serui, iumenti; que exposicio distorta et non Christiana est." Ibid.

73. Matthew 3:4 and Mark 1:6 describe John's attire as camel skin (*pilis camelorum*, *pilis cameli*).

74. Baldwin demonstrated Peter's influence on a fairly expansive "circle" of theologians, canonists, and preachers and indirectly on several issues debated at the Fourth Lateran Council: *Masters*, 17–46, 315–43.

the Angers school for a period of renewed theological study and teaching. Whereas Marbode had risen steadily through the ranks to the summit—from director of the Angers school to archdeacon of the diocese, then in 1096 bishop of Rennes—Robert jumped ship. He left Angers in 1095 and entered the forest of Craon to become a hermit.

A spiritual crisis was certainly part of what drove Robert into the woods. His first biographer described an "internal conflict, a kind of roar in his mind and a sobbing in the depths of his soul." But disillusionment with a conventional clerical life within the ecclesiastical institutions of his time was surely also a factor. Robert had probably been run out of the diocese of Rennes after the death of Bishop Sylvester in 1093 by the recalcitrant clerics he had been trying to reform. And Marbode in his letter scolded Robert for harshly criticizing the clergy in his preaching, enumerating "the crimes not only of those in orders but even in high offices."[75]

But this letter is most famous for its critique of Robert's clothing. "You ought to be reproached," Marbode wrote,

> for the extreme strangeness of your ragged clothes—and quite rightly, since it seems appropriate neither to the profession of canon in which you started your service nor the priestly order to which you were promoted. . . . They say that you go into the crowd, having discarded your canonical dress, skin covered by a hairshirt and a worn-out cowl full of holes, your legs half-naked, your beard long and your hair trimmed at the brow, barefoot, offering a strange spectacle to all who look on such that you lack only a club to complete the outfit of a lunatic.[76]

Robert had plenty of scriptural and patristic warrant for his dress: John the Baptist, after all, had worn a camel-hair garment, and ascetics for centuries had followed his example. The hair shirt (*cilicium*) Robert wore was more likely goatskin, and he was surely following a long Christian ascetic tradition in adopting this garb. But since ministry to women seems to have had a special place in Robert's wandering apostolate, one wonders whether clothing himself in animal skin was also a rejection of the nexus of clerical relationships with women that produced textiles.[77]

Marbode was fully aware of the biblical and eremitic precedents for Robert's attire, so his condemnation of it is particularly interesting. "For each and every order and profession," Marbode wrote, "there is a fitting and proper dress code, which if violated offends public opinion." Quoting Seneca, the bishop admonished that "reason is to be observed and moderation preserved in the mean and humble guise of common sense and with the authority of custom." To Robert, as a priest and canon, he urged moderation in order to avoid scandal. Marbode seems aware of contemporary criticisms of the ornate

75. Bruce L. Venarde, ed. and trans., *Robert of Arbrissel: A Medieval Religious Life* (Washington, D.C., 2003), 12, 97.

76. Ibid., 95–96.

77. I thank R.I. Moore for raising this possibility, and for his suggestions on the connections with heresy below.

style of clerical attire, but his language very carefully skirts what may be an object of Robert's sartorial critique. Going about decked in finery "seems to pertain to vanity," and "to desire finery" is a sign of dissipation. But going about in "coarse tatters," argues Marbode, is "stupidity" unbefitting religion and modesty.

John of Salisbury went further. Those wearing coarse attire in the name of religion were ambitious hypocrites. In his *Policraticus* (1159) he derided "frauds" who

> fast continually, they pray without interruption and "yet clearly so that a visitor hears," they are clothed in rough and filthy attire and they censure the people. They accuse clerics, they remonstrate about the amendment of the moral characters of princes and powerful men, acquiring evidence of their own justice when they disparage the lives of others.

They have infiltrated the Carthusians, Cistercians, and Cluniacs, according to John. They—not overdressed bishops—are the ones who "come in sheep's clothing, yet inside they are predatory wolves."[78] One can see in this a response to monastic critiques of the secular clergy, but John is doing more than defending his own team, so to speak. He is taking a resoundingly common critique of courtly clerics—that they were ambitious hypocrites—and flinging it at their detractors, who were not only monks but also other secular clerics. John, of course, was the consummate courtly cleric. He had studied in Paris with nearly all the luminaries of the early twelfth century—Peter Abelard, William of Conches, Gilbert of Poitiers—and joined the household of Archbishop Theobald of Canterbury in 1147, where he became close to Thomas Becket. Although he accompanied his friend into exile, he was more inclined to compromise with the king and he remained powerful and well connected after Becket's demise.[79] His *Policraticus*, dedicated to Becket, is in many ways an apologia of the courtly cleric. John's greatest empathy is for the burdens of those exercising power, particularly the Roman pontiff, calling the office "miserable," its burdens horrible even to the most worthy. His friend Adrian IV assured him "that the seat of the Roman pontiff is full of thorns, that his garments are always woven with the most pointed prickles and are of such great bulk that they would weigh down, wear out and crush even the strongest shoulders, and that his crown and mitre deservedly appear to shine since they are on fire."[80] While he argued that immoderate conduct is the mark of tyranny in both secular and ecclesiastical lords, and that members of the polity have a duty to criticize and correct tyrants, he was quite tolerant—in the view of many, overly so—of the foibles of the powerful.

Consider, for example, his discussion of ecclesiastical garb in book 6, chapter 24, entitled "The vices of the powerful are to be tolerated because with them rests the prospect of public safety, and because they are the dispensers of safety just as the stomach in the body of animals dispenses nourishment, and this is by the judgment of Lord Adrian."

78. John of Salisbury, *Policraticus*, 168 (7.21).
79. Cary J. Nederman, *John of Salisbury* (Tempe, 2005), 1–39.
80. John of Salisbury, *Policraticus*, 224 (8.24).

When John was visiting his good friend Pope Adrian IV, the pontiff asked him what men were saying about him and the Roman church. This narrative device gives John the opportunity to summarize many contemporary criticisms of the papacy, among them that Adrian "erects palaces and parades himself about not only in purple vestments but in gilded clothes." Other criticisms of the pope are cataloged, but John demurs: this is what other people say, and he personally has encountered many good and holy men in the Roman church. The pope is charmed, and responds with a lengthy parable about the various parts of the body becoming resentful of the stomach. The eyes, ears, hands, and feet felt that they worked constantly for the good of the whole while the stomach just devoured and consumed. So they decided to stop working and starve the parasite stomach. As the members of the body become weakened and faint, the counsel of the heart convinces them through reason to replenish the stomach. Such is the case also in the body politic. You may not like the prince, but you need him. "Measure not our harshness nor that of secular princes," concluded the pope (and John), "but attend to the utility of all." In sum, since princes of the church are necessary, you shouldn't waste time criticizing them. Do your part for the greater good and give the voracious stomach what it wants.

John, of course, lived through the civil war sparked by Stephen's usurpation of the throne (1135–1154), justly called the "anarchy," and witnessed the results of several papal schisms, and these experiences may have contributed to his caution in the face of the powerful. He also elaborated a political philosophy that emphasized obedience but also refused coercion. As Cary J. Nederman and Catherine Campbell have argued, John's "quietistic" approach to opposing tyranny, counseling prayer and patient correction, was grounded not only in faith in God's inevitable vengeance on the wicked but also in the conviction that individuals had to love justice in order to perform morally good deeds. The Aristotelian notion of moral disposition, or habitus, informed his understanding: "moral qualities were ingrained dispositions not subject to rapid fluctuations," so threats and penalties are not likely to move a morally mature individual to just actions. Thus, John articulated a relatively passive role for individuals and the church in relation to tyranny, and he accorded great leeway to those whom he considered morally good.[81]

John exhibited such an attitude in his direct address to Becket in the final chapter of the *Policraticus* on "What is the most faithful path to be followed towards what the Epicureans desire and promise." Christianity is this most faithful path, of course, to happiness. "Behold that you possess the truest and most faithful path and have achieved the state which is desired by Epicurus," John wrote to Becket. Keep to it and you will be blessed. "And I do not," John continued,

81. Cary J. Nederman and Catherine Campbell, "Priests, Kings and Tyrants: Spiritual and Temporal Power in John of Salisbury's *Policraticus*," *Speculum* 66 (1991): 572–90, but especially 578–83 (quote on 578); see also Cary J. Nederman, "Principles of Liberty in John of Salisbury," in *Beyond the Persecuting Society: Religious Toleration before the Enlightenment*, ed. John Christian Laursen and Cary J. Nederman (Philadelphia, 1998), 53–70.

> prohibit you from wrapping yourself in a variety of glittering garments overlaid with gold, nor from feasting splendidly every day, nor again from occupying the foremost public offices, and—so that I may express much in a few words—from yielding to the times and even perverse morals (even though you are yourself righteous in all moral matters), and from laughing with a world which is amused by its own enticements. For you are so great that you ought not and cannot be captured by these traps (although many have already been taken prisoner by them).[82]

Considered in the context of John's pragmatic philosophy, and the greater good that might be achieved by a moral individual exercising power, his tendency to tolerate indulgence in "superfluities" by curial clerics makes some political sense. Things might well be a lot worse for the poor, for all Christians, and for the church if the secular clergy disengaged from court and abandoned attempts to influence ideas about the exercise of power, especially as monarchical lordship was rapidly extending its reach and sophistication. And John's toleration of human imperfection was accompanied by an insistence on civility, which certainly appealed to many (especially those who felt themselves unfairly targeted by satirists and other critics). But he was also more understanding toward the powerful than those less privileged, and defended propriety in a manner that was surely irksome to poorer clerics: voicing "offences and taunts against men of great power," according to John, was exercising "license more than is permitted."[83]

This rapid survey of loquacious ecclesiastical sources is by no means exhaustive, but it does sufficiently demonstrate both how clothing was used to discuss aspects of lordship and how varied ecclesiastical views were. Critiques of clerical clothing articulated contempt for the hypocrisy and greed of prelates, and fear of the disorder charismatic ascetics might provoke. More important, they also voiced commiseration over the burdens of office, disappointment in the failure of ecclesiastical lords to rule justly, as well as a longing for them to do so. Their very disappointment in the lordship exercised by prelates reveals the influence of the ecclesiastical vision of a more just, less violent mode of rulership accountable to God for good order and peace in Christian society. This is what ecclesiastical lords were being measured against. Could virtue coexist with the exercise of power? John of Salisbury was confident that it could, others like Bernard of Cluny sincerely hoped it would, and the more biting satirists seethed at the very suggestion. No conclusions were reached in this medieval conversation, but the optimistic elitism of John of Salisbury carried the day, providing fodder for satirists down to the present.

These debates over ecclesiastical lordship and clerical clothing, moreover, extended beyond the highly educated sectors of the clergy that have left us records of their opinions. Garments were not just an effete set of concerns, references, and metaphors. Clerical uses of clothing constituted a language about power that was widely enough

82. John of Salisbury, *Policraticus*, 229–30 (8.25).
83. Ibid., 179 (7.25).

understood and compelling enough to contemporaries that it was adopted by competitors. Fleeting traces of their appropriations appear in ecclesiastical denunciations of them. In the life of Saint Norbert of Xanten (d. 1134) written in c. 1155, the author describes the appearance of "a very dangerous heresy" spread by a preacher named Tanchelm. He claims that Tanchelm showed contempt for bishops and priests, and denied the efficacy of the Eucharist as a means to salvation. In the midst of describing how many people flocked to him, and how convinced they were of his holiness, the author relates that Tanchelm "dressed in gilded clothes, and glittered because of the gold twisted into his hair, and the many ornaments which he wore."[84] A sermon of Hildegard of Bingen, in which she castigated the clergy of Cologne for their negligence in the care of souls, describes a different sort of appropriation. She warns the clergy of "disciples and followers" of Satan, who "will come with wan faces and, clothing themselves in sanctity, will ally themselves with great secular princes." They will win over these lay lords by accusing the clergy of polluting iniquities. "The people who say these things about you," she continues, "will walk about in black robes, with proper tonsure, and will appear to men serene and peaceful in all their ways."[85] If these critics, as scholars have thought, were "heretics," then such dissidents were creating their own versions of clerical garments—their own black/dark copes (*cappatus sub nigra veste*)—to express their religious virtue and to claim status and authority for their beliefs and practices.

Other accounts of "heretics" portray them as critical of clerical attire. One from 1165 documents the interrogation by Bishop William of Albi of several individuals calling themselves "good men" (*boni homines*). "They claimed," it recounted,

> that Paul laid down what sort of men ought to be ordained as bishops and priests, and that any who were not ordained according to Paul's instructions are not bishops and priests, but ravening wolves, hypocrites and seducers, men who want to be bowed to in the streets, to have the most prominent seats, to sit at the top of the table at banquets; who want to be called "Rabbi" and "master" contrary to the precept of Christ, who wear albs and white robes, and gold and bejeweled rings on their fingers, which Jesus, their master, did not command.[86]

84. *MGH SS* 12:691; R.I. Moore, *The Birth of Popular Heresy* (London, 1975; repr., Toronto, 1995), 31. The anonymous author of the life was modeling this account on Gregory of Tours's description of the false Christ of Bourges (*Historia francorum* 10.25), but this detail on Tanchelm's apparel is not in the model: *MGH SSRM* 1:518.

85. The dean of the Cologne chapter wrote to Hildegard requesting a written version of the "words of life" she had revealed to them in a recent visit, and she responded with the text quoted here. The date is uncertain, but it seems likely that it preceded and influenced the burning of several "heretics" in 1163. The key passage here reads "Populus autem qui hoc de uobis dicet, cappatus sub nigra ueste incedet et recto modo tonsus, atque omnibus moribus suis placidum et quietum se hominibus ostendet." Hildegard of Bingen, *Epistolarivm*, ed. L. Van Acker, 3 vols., CCCM 91–91b (Turnhout, 1991), 1 (91):40 (40r); *The Letters of Hildegard of Bingen*, trans. Joseph L. Baird and Radd K. Ehrman, 3 vols. (Oxford, 1994–2004), 1:58.

86. Moore, *Birth*, 96; Mansi, 22:159.

Interestingly, in this passage clerical expectations of signs of subservience (bowing, honorific forms of address), as well as special clerical garb, are described as a source of resentment. An even more telling critique of clerical attire is attributed to "heretics" in a treatise dating probably from the 1170s–1180s. Modeled on William the Monk's *Contra Henricum*, this tract is composed of responses to supposed heretical arguments. The ecclesiastical interlocutor declares,

> I do not wish to discuss the appurtenances of priests with you, or the pastoral ring and staff, all of which are sanctioned by authority for the sanctification and regulation of Christian life, or the significance of the array of vestments, the flashing jewels and the glittering gold, or what their origins were. There is no need to justify them and I do not want to argue about these things with you, because there is no doubt that they add to the honour, status and righteousness of the Church.[87]

Honor, status, and righteousness were precisely the issues. Was the wearer of the glittering vestments righteous? Was he truly virtuous? Did he merit, by these garments, a special and higher status? Gregorian claims that even the lowest cleric ranked above all laymen seem not to have been accepted by the "good men." Were clerical orders or offices, such as the episcopate, more ministries or "honors"? The latter term in medieval Latin could mean holy orders and ecclesiastical office, but also public office, a fief, vassal fealty, or lordship. And lordship was precisely what discussions of clothing were about. It is interesting that the orthodox respondent to heretical ideas sees nothing to discuss about ornate vestments and other symbols of ecclesiastical lordship since so many of his clerical and monastic contemporaries had so much to say about them. Everyone, it seems, agreed that clerical clothing mattered, but there was little agreement about how.

87. Moore, *Birth*, 58; Monique Zerner, "Au temps de l'appel aux armes contre les hérétiques: Du *Contra Henricum* du moine Guillaume aux *Contra hereticos*," in *Inventer l'hérésie? Discours polémique et pouvoirs avant l'inquisition*, ed. Monique Zerner, Collection du Centre d'études médiévales de Nice 2 (Nice, 1998), 131, 136.

CONCLUSION

Glittering Tanchelm and the black-robed heretics Hildegard decried were only the first of many who would make their own claims to virtue, holiness, and power using the language of clothing developed by the secular clergy. The dissemination and appropriation of this language over the later Middle Ages and into the modern era is, in large part, why clerical clothing is significant. But before tracing out the long-term importance, let's appreciate these developments in their own time.

In the ninth century, a new and highly ornate style of liturgical attire spread and was affirmed within the Carolingian Empire. Its origins were most likely in Anglo-Saxon England: the earliest documentary and physical evidence of these gold-ornamented vestments made of precious silks comes from either England or the northwestern parts of Francia just across the channel and North Sea. Although Charlemagne and his heir resisted it as inappropriately rich for their clerical servants, their successors from the mid-ninth century embraced the new style, and it bursts into view in the beautiful illuminated manuscripts they commissioned. This new acceptance was fueled by the dissemination from the 820s of a new, more potent understanding of the episcopal office: more than mere servants, bishops were increasingly viewed as collaborators with royal power in the king's special ministry to bring his people to salvation. At the same time, Carolingian exegetes found a warrant for ornate clerical garb in the description of Aaron's vestments, which God had commanded be made from "gold and hyacinth and purple and scarlet twice dyed, and fine twisted linen, embroidered with diverse colors" (Exod. 28:3–5).

This exegesis emerged out of attempts to reform the secular clergy, and it used allegorical interpretations of individual elements of clerical liturgical attire to promote virtues reformers wanted clerics to cultivate: chastity, wisdom, justice, and charity. These symbolic readings of clerical vestments were widely disseminated in the liturgical commentaries used to train the clergy. The response to these educational strategies was highly creative. From the late ninth century, clerics innovated a set of spiritual practices that used vestments, the most notable of which were the recitation of vesting prayers, the bestowal of vestments in ordination rites, and the making and wearing of reliquary vestments. These active, physical practices powerfully connected the cultivation of clerical virtues with the new ornate style of liturgical vestments, their versions of the richly colored, embroidered, golden attire that God had decreed for Aaron and his sons. They also beautified the liturgy and became important unifying elements in clerical culture. They endure to this day among many Catholic clerics.

The new ornate style of liturgical vestments and the intellectual warrant for it developed in northern Europe in the early Middle Ages. This is yet another example of the enormous impact on Western Christianity of its newer converts north of the Alps. Their greater interest in clerical clothing is evident in the ecclesiastical legislation of these early centuries, and their tastes and textile techniques—such as tablet weaving—shaped the new style. Their admiration for the Holy See and its traditions ensured that the new style and its uses developed in conversation with Rome. And, like most masterpieces of early medieval art, these liturgical garments combined classical forms—especially in the types and shapes of the pieces, originally derived from Roman civic attire—with an aesthetic favoring high-prestige objects and extraordinary craft skill.

The artists who created and developed the style were women. Elite women figure most prominently in the documentary recognitions of their talent and generosity, but many common and enslaved women also labored to produce the clerical garments that beautified the liturgy. Women collaborated with clerics in the design of vestments. They facilitated the spiritual practices the clergy had developed around them, not only by producing the garments used but also by repairing them and, in the case of those associated with saintly clerics, incorporating them into wearable reliquary vestments. The inscriptions women wove and embroidered into garments reveal the spiritual character of these collaborative relationships. Hagiographic sources, too, suggest that some women participated in the clergy's spirituality of sacred vestments through their prayerful creation of the garments that were its focus and implements. These relationships surely were spiritually important for some women, but they could be dangerous for them too. Fears of impropriety between clerics and women haunted both parties. The power of defaming rumors fostered practices of secrecy and concealment: women hid their inscribed exhortations to clerics on inner vestments. Male fears are most evident in the emphasis in clerical texts on the virtue of the women makers of vestments and in the anxious insinuations of female influence that surface in the polemical sources of the investiture conflict.

Women very likely did exercise significant influence on ecclesiastical institutions and their reform through their gifts, many of which were liturgical textiles laden with gold. This subject merits further research. The imperial bishops who alleged that Gregory VII was running the church with "a new senate of women" may simply have been seeking to defame him, but then again they may have been reacting to very real and powerful ties. Work on medieval women's cultural patronage has documented their influence on literature and arts such as manuscript illumination and sculpture.[1] Enlarging our view to include the prestigious "crafts" objects favored in gift exchanges among elites can not only enrich our understanding of women's influence but also reveal its political importance. The interest of leading reformers, like Ivo of Chartres, in cultivating spiritual and patronage relationships with aristocratic women arose not only out of his episcopal duty to care for his church but also out of his foundation of new reform institutions. Textiles are clues to such relationships and suggest the network of women supporting reform may well have merited its characterization by opponents as a "senate."

The reform movements of the eleventh century, moreover, affirmed and invigorated the clerical spirituality of sacred vestments. The Carolingian genre of liturgical commentaries was revived and developed to renew efforts to educate and improve the clergy. The continuity this reveals is significant: eleventh-century reformers redeployed a type of educational text developed by Carolingian reformers. But the pattern of development is actually more complex. In fact, the Gregorian era liturgical commentaries were more sophisticated and they drew on the spiritual practices that had been created around sacred vestments. And these practices appear to have emerged in the late ninth and tenth centuries, a period not generally associated with reform. It's the leap from text to practice that is most elusive but also most important. Since I have been able to consult only a fraction of the liturgical manuscripts surviving in European collections, much more work is needed on the diffusion of practices like vesting prayers in order to illuminate the processes that established them within clerical culture. Those processes—the afterlife, in a sense, of Carolingian reforming initiatives—are essential in understanding the relationship between these two major reforming movements.

Reformers embraced the ornate style of vestments even though it was closely associated with the imperial church by the eleventh century. It strengthened ties with female donors and supported cultivation of the clerical virtues that laypeople, as well as other clerics, increasingly demanded. Indeed, while scholars tend to focus on the issues that divided supporters of the papacy and empire in the late eleventh and early twelfth centuries, clerical clothing reveals an interesting common ground of ideas and practices that united the secular clergy. A better appreciation of other forms of shared ideas and practices among clerics may do more to advance our understanding of reform than continued focus on the much-ventilated divisive issues. Indeed, while the ornate style of liturgical garb and spiritual practices associated with it appear to have been widely diffused before the outbreak of the investiture conflict, other aspects of ecclesiastical culture that worked to unify the clergy may well have been products of reforming processes. Culture, I'm suggesting, may be as important as ideology in understanding the reform movements and the investiture crisis. Vestments and their ornamentation, for example, proved a flexible and powerful language to express new ideas and as visual assertions were accessible to a much broader public than texts. Reformers used them to

1. June Hall McCash, ed., *The Cultural Patronage of Medieval Women* (Athens, 1996).

assert the sacredness of all clerics and to claim a status for them higher than any layperson's. They also employed them to distinguish more clearly the different orders of clerics and to heighten visually the status of those who served at the altar and were bound by vows of celibacy. New vestments and insignia, particularly the rationale and miter, were developed to give special prominence to bishops, and papal leadership was also emphasized through distinctive attire. Clerical clothing was key in the articulation of the ecclesiastical hierarchy that was clarified and significantly empowered by reform.

The bases for that power had been established in the mid-ninth century by the Carolingian bishops who successfully devised and disseminated an expansive interpretation of their role as collaborators with secular rulers in the governance of God's people. The ornate style of sacred vestments was associated with this enhanced notion of episcopal authority and became even more meaningful as the temporal powers of bishops grew over the tenth and eleventh centuries. Most bishops were powerful ecclesiastical lords by the advent of the investiture conflict, whether they had been granted temporal powers by their royal collaborators or had seized them in the fashion of local and regional lords all over Europe. The new claims reformers made for clerical status and authority invigorated an important conversation about lordship in which clothing figured prominently. Ecclesiastics used clothing to represent and discuss what they viewed as more just and peaceful modes of exercising power. They denigrated the clothing and lordship of those they viewed as unworthy of the leadership of a Christian society. Clerical attempts to influence lay ideas and practices of lordship were only partially successful, but they contributed to notions of justice, accountability, and official conduct that became central features of Western government.

Clerical assertions of their lordship and power provoked both lay and ecclesiastical criticisms of their clothing practices. The clerical critiques reveal opposition within the ranks to ecclesiastical involvement in royal courts and resentment at the skewed distribution and uses of wealth within the church, particularly the making and use of ornate liturgical vestments when the poor went hungry and raggedly clothed. Lay critiques, mostly evident in the ecclesiastical legislation responding to them, seem to have focused on clerical clothing outside the sanctuary. Although canons from the early Middle Ages vaguely enjoined the wearing of the "priestly tunic" or "clerical clothes" outside of church, only the legislation of the central Middle Ages clarified that this clerical streetwear should be modest and dark in color (the *cappa clausa*, or other suitably humble and "closed" garments). Some laypeople may also have objected to the liturgical finery worn by the clergy, but the enthusiasm for donating it to churches that continues across the later Middle Ages and into the modern era suggests that lay elites supported beautifying the liturgy. The pretenses of the clergy outside of church were another matter. These sensibilities about clerical clothing have been remarkably enduring in Western Christianity. Even the Protestant Reformation did not expunge them: Lutherans, Anglicans, and some other reformed traditions still use vestments in church today that would be recognizable to their medieval forbears and embrace the wearing of dark-colored "clericals" outside of worship services. Catholic and Anglican leaders in the early twenty-first century are still wearing elaborate silk vestments with gold ornament.[2]

For the exercise of authority in the secular realm, the conventions of clerical street-wear and their cultural meanings have had the most enduring significance. Hildegard's observation that religious dissidents in Cologne "clothed themselves in sanctity" (*in omni sanctitate se componet*) when they went about in black robes is just one indicator of the connotations dark, modest attire had. The association of sanctity and virtue with such garb was not only the product of the clerical *cappa*, of course, since monastic habits had been dark, long, and closed for centuries. As a visual shorthand, such attire had long been associated with virtue. Since monks were normally cloistered, however, the more common public presence of such attire was clerical. Although the nobility was eventually influenced, the more immediate impact of the visual culture of clerical clothing was on emerging learned professions and on merchants. To sketch these appropriations, we need to consider points of contact.

Those wearing clerical street-wear were not evenly distributed over the medieval landscape: they were more numerous in centers of power. Kings from the Carolingian era had chaplains in their households, but the number of clerics in royal service skyrocketed from the twelfth century as monarchical bureaucracies expanded.[3] The courts of local and regional lords replicated this pattern on smaller scales. Cities or towns that were the seats of bishops or archbishops had cathedral chapters and considerable numbers of clerics in minor orders studying at the cathedral school. Where clerics would have been most numerous and visually prominent were in the cities where universities developed. In most universities, students entered clerical orders and came under the protection of the local bishop when they enrolled. For their clerical privileges and status to be acknowledged, they had to wear the clerical closed cloak.[4] This use of clerical clothing to protect and foster education had a profound influence on how the literate professions claimed status through attire.

2. While Francis I has cultivated a simpler style, Pope Benedict XVI not only continued Catholic liturgical use of gold-embroidered vestments but even revived wearing of the ermine-trimmed papal cape, or *mozzetta*, and jewel-studded pectoral crosses (both decidedly out of fashion after the Second Vatican Council). In 2003, Rowan Williams wore a gold-embroidered cope for his enthronement as archbishop of Canterbury and one of specially woven velvet cloth of gold for the 2011 royal wedding. A good analysis of the complex development of Reformation attitudes toward special clerical attire is Ulinka Rublack, *Dressing Up: Cultural Identity in Renaissance Europe* (Oxford, 2010), 81–123.

3. Alfred L. Brown presents evidence that the royal writing offices at Westminster employed more than a hundred clerks in the fourteenth century and that the exchequer had a staff of well over a hundred too: *The Governance of Late Medieval England, 1272–1461* (Stanford, 1989), 45, 54.

4. Hastings Rashdall, *The Universities of Europe in the Middle Ages*, rev. ed., ed. F.M. Powicke and A.B. Emden, 3 vols. (Oxford, 1987), 3:385–97. The earliest statutes of the university of Paris required masters to wear the "capam rotundam, nigram et talarem": H. Denifle and A. Chatelain, eds., *Chartularium universitatis Parisiensis*, 4 vols. (Paris, 1889–1897), 1:79 (no. 20). Ecclesiastical leaders did recognize that student clerics were different from the real clergy and modified disciplinary mechanisms in recognition of this fact: Stephen C. Ferruolo, *The Origins of the University: The Schools of Paris and Their Critics, 1100–1215* (Stanford, 1985), 206, 293.

Lawyers and judges are the most obvious example of this influence. While many university graduates continued to be what we recognize as clerics—that is, they took major orders and secured a benefice in a church—others found employment in the nascent bureaucracies of church and state. Systems of justice were among the most precociously developed because they were lucrative, and legal practitioners attained professional status quite early. By the mid-thirteenth century, experienced practitioners were passing on advice in handbooks, and courts established qualifications for advocates admitted to plead before them. Moral character, honesty, and integrity were expected and, indeed, required by the oaths for admission to practice. Not only their educated backgrounds resulted in their continued wearing of the clerical garb that marked them as scholars: the expectation of morality and sobriety did as well. The earliest rules outlining appropriate dress for advocates, which date from the late twelfth and early thirteenth centuries, use the same descriptive language as those for the clergy. Their clothes should be "decent" and reaching to their ankles, with outer garments neither too long nor short. They should be uniform and sober in color (not green or red). Silks and extreme tailoring should be avoided. The medieval successors to Ulpian took the Roman jurist's characterization of advocates as "priests of the law" seriously, and thus they dressed like them.[5] Judges today in many legal systems with roots in the European tradition still wear long, black robes.

Merchants had few of the advantages enjoyed by the new legal professionals but adopted some of the same visual props to cultivate confidence and respect. Although most had a functional literacy and advanced numeracy gained in "abacus schools" and long apprenticeships, their educations did not yield the status that university study did. Still, their profession shared many hazards with the world of scholars and they came to enjoy

5. When coming before a judge, advocates should wear "vestes decentes ad officium pertinentes et talares." Durand counseled that the advocate be dressed *honeste*, and that he "geret vestem sue professioni convenientem, non diversi coloris aut diverse partis . . . nimia brevitate vel longitudine notanda . . . non ex sericis texturis variatam ex variis coloribus ornatam." Reminding the reader that outward appearance reveals qualities of mind, he proffered the example of the unadorned, *honeste* clerical *cappa* as communicating necessary humility. The language of this rule redeployed the wording and concepts of ecclesiastical legislation, which admonished clerics to wear clothing *congruens* to their vocation, not *nimia brevitate vel longitudine . . . notanda* (*Decrees*, 1:243). James A. Brundage, *The Medieval Origins of the Legal Profession: Canonists, Civilians, and Courts* (Chicago, 2008), 285–304 (on professionalization and ethics), 310–11 (on clothing); William Durand, *Principium Speculi domini Guilhelmi Duranti [Speculum iudiciale]*, ed. Franciscus Moneliensis, 4 vols. (Padua, 1479), 1, fol. 131v–132r; see also Michel Pastoureau, *Black: The History of a Color*, trans. Jody Gladding (Princeton, 2009), 95. There are some indicators that royal administrators were also distinguished by a black gown, but further work needs to be done on the liveries these clerks received to determine their appearance. In fifteenth-century England, this group began to include laymen as well as clerics, with the result that the term "gentleman" began to be used to distinguish them. Disputes over the prerogatives of this status indicate that a certain appearance defined it—one involved allegations that individuals had dressed "in the similitude of gentlemen or of thrifty merchants"—and that a black gown furred with beaver was one of its signs. R. L. Storey, "Gentlemen-Bureaucrats," in *Profession, Vocation, and Culture in Later Medieval England: Essays Dedicated to the Memory of A. R. Myers*, ed. Cecil H. Clough (Liverpool, 1982), 90–109, quote on 94.

similar protections. One of the earliest privileges for scholars, Emperor Frederick Barbarossa's *Authentica "habita"* of 1155, granted them safe conduct, since they tended to travel from town to town (as did merchants), and protection, as foreigners in a sometimes hostile environment, from reprisals (also a problem for merchants).[6] Merchants frequented the places where clerics tended to be numerous—courts and towns—and so it is not surprising that they drew on clerical clothing practices for their own needs to communicate trustworthiness. "Wear modest colors, be humble, be dull in appearance," advised Giovanni Frescobaldi, an early fourteenth-century Florentine merchant and poet. As the freewheeling era of the thirteenth-century boom gave way to a riskier commercial climate, good reputation and trust were even more essential to success in trade. Giovanni Morelli in 1393 counseled the wise merchant to have nothing to do with one who gambles, lives ostentatiously, or overdresses.[7] A fifteenth-century observer remarked that the color black "is of high standing and great virtue. That is why the merchants and rich bourgeois, men as well as women, are dressed and adorned in it."[8] Michel Pastoureau dates the adoption of what he sees as "the new black style" by merchants, bankers, and men of finance to the second half of the fourteenth century. Yet he mistakes its primary cause.[9] Sumptuary laws were as much a feature of the merchant republics as they were of northern kingdoms, with nobilities anxious to defend their prerogatives. Merchants did not adopt black merely in response to legislation. The marked growth of commerce in cloth and clothing meant that dress had become "an unreliable signifier of social status" and of the self. Both the proliferation of sumptuary discourses and the merchant's resort to somber attire were rooted in the same unease over the mutability commercialization had wrought.[10] In such a climate, traditional structures of meaning proved attractive.

And merchants understood and redeployed both extremes of the clerical language of dress. Somber, dark, humble attire telegraphed virtue, respectability, and morality in the marketplace. It was good for business. But there were things to be sanctified and

6. Although the earliest manuscript of the privilege protected students from a particular province or region from being held responsible for damage (*delictum*) done by another from their homeland, many later manuscripts change or expand this protection to debt (*debitum*), something students also tended to leave behind. Reprisals against merchants from a certain city or region for the debts of others from the same area was a severe inhibition to trade, and so privileges for merchants, such as those fostering the fairs of Champagne, protected traders against such claims or violence. See H. Koeppler, "Frederick Barbarossa and the Schools of Bologna," *English Historical Review* 54 (1939): 577–607, but especially 593–600; for the earliest text of the decree, Winfried Stelzer, "Zum Scholarenprivileg Friedrich Barbarossas (Authentica 'Habita')," *Deutsches Archiv für Erforschung des Mittelalters* 34 (1978): 123–65.

7. Robert S. Lopez and Irving W. Raymond, trans., *Medieval Trade in the Mediterranean World* (New York, 1955), 423; Iris Origo, *The Merchant of Prato: Francesco di Marco Datini, 1335–1410* (London, 1960), 118–19.

8. Pastoureau, *Black*, 100.

9. Ibid., 96–99.

10. Martha C. Howell, *Commerce before Capitalism in Europe, 1300–1600* (Cambridge, 2010), 208–60 (quote on 214).

celebrated with liturgical pomp. The feast days of saints, of course, were when both clerics and laypeople honored God in splendid attire. Merchants mobilized sumptuous clothing, moreover, to sanctify their own creations too. Their marriages and baptisms became occasions for sartorial display: cloth of gold, precious silks, and elaborate embroidery constructed their public virtue. Did God not smile upon these hardworking families? Their service to their guilds and town governments was also celebrated in brilliantly colored robes trimmed with fur: the civic dignitaries processing in Lorenzetti's *Good Government* wear red, pink, yellow, purple, and blue. To be elected to office was an honor for both individual and family. It signaled the wealth to devote time to the public good and the virtue to exercise power in the collective lordship that urban communes had innovated.[11]

By the sixteenth century, however, governance was a more somber business. Cosimo de' Medici was an early harbinger: the merchant banker wore a black robe in the only contemporary portrait of him and was admired for his shrewd and balanced judgment.[12] Black as the mark of discrete power, wealth, and virtue spread outward from Italy to the courts of northern Europe. The difficulty and expense of producing deep, luxurious blacks allowed for the display of wealth and taste while broadcasting the sober virtue increasingly prized in princes. The dukes of Burgundy cultivated it extensively, and after them the Hapsburgs. The reform movements of the sixteenth century, Protestant and Catholic, solidified the dominance of this moral black.[13] Although the men's three-piece suit emerged in late seventeenth-century France and England as ornate silk court attire, it was tamed by the nineteenth century and claimed by the business and professional classes. "The rising power of the middle classes in the nineteenth century made their Protestant clothing ethic the dominant ideal for high society as well," Diana de Marly observed, with obvious disappointment: "the aristocracy gave up the last vestiges of splendour and started to dress like bank managers."[14]

This is the attire of power in the modern West. We expect our leaders to appear in dark-colored suits at their summits, speeches, and representative functions. Such an appearance of power was hardly a predictable development from the royal finery of the

11. Works on Renaissance dress have focused on this festive attire since artistic representation privileged these high moments and family inventories and records lavished more description on special attire: Carole Collier Frick, *Dressing Renaissance Florence: Families, Fortunes, and Fine Clothing* (Baltimore, 2002); Susan Mosher Stuard, *Gilding the Market: Luxury and Fashion in Fourteenth-Century Italy* (Philadelphia, 2006), 56–83.

12. Dale Kent, *Cosimo de' Medici and the Florentine Renaissance: The Patron's Oeuvre* (New Haven, 2000), 16–20, 315–18.

13. Pastoureau, *Black*, 100–104; Diana de Marly, *Fashion for Men: An Illustrated History* (London, 1985), 37–53.

14. Diana de Marly, "The 19th Century," in Aileen Ribeiro et al. "Dress," in *Grove Art Online, Oxford Art Online*, http://www.oxfordartonline.com/subscriber/article/grove/art/T023637pg8 (accessed May 6, 2011); see also de Marly, *Fashion for Men*, 61–63, 69, 75–87, 89–106; Anne Hollander, *Sex and Suits* (New York, 1995), 63–84, 91–97.

Middle Ages. The desire to foster virtue through clothing and to wed it with governance, however, was remarkably enduring. The medieval clergy originally entwined these endeavors, developing a complex set of practices, ideas, contrasts, and garments that expressed their claims to both virtue and power. Their culture of clothing provided a rich and expressive visual language, deeply meaningful in its own time and with important resonances ever since.

GLOSSARY

alb (*alba*): A white linen or cotton long-sleeved tunic that was the base garment worn during the Mass and other liturgical ceremonies (figure 73). In the early Middle Ages it was also sometimes referred to as a *talaris*, or *tunica talaris*, indicating its full length (*talaris* = of or belonging to the ankles), or as a *camisia* (linen shirt or nightgown). The earliest surviving albs, from the twelfth to fifteenth centuries, were quite full (see figure 45), sometimes with gored inserts of extra fabric on the sides. The alb was worn belted with a cincture, which allowed the length to be adjusted to the height of the cleric by pulling fabric up over the cincture.

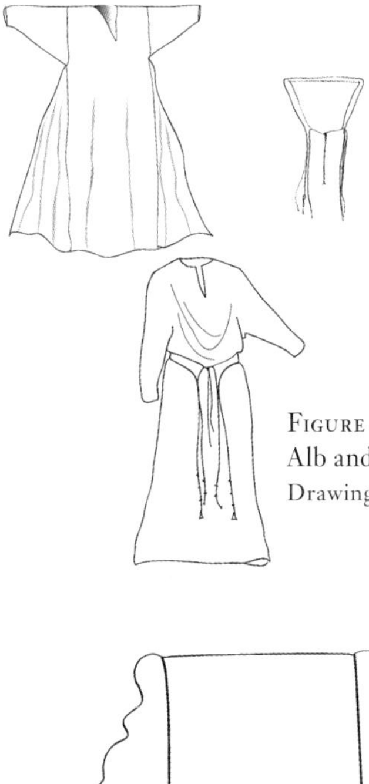

FIGURE 73.
Alb and cincture.
Drawing by Ann Higgins.

amice (*amictus*): A rectangular piece of linen or cotton with ties extending from the long ends of one side (figure 74). It was the first element of liturgical attire to be put on and likely served to protect the neckline of the alb and other garments from grime (the amice being more easily washable than an alb, dalmatic, or chasuble). There were two variations in how it was worn. It could be draped over the shoulders, the ties crossed across the chest, crossed again in back, and then tied in front. Or it could be draped over the head first, pulling the fabric up higher on the shoulders, then secured in the same way. The latter method left a

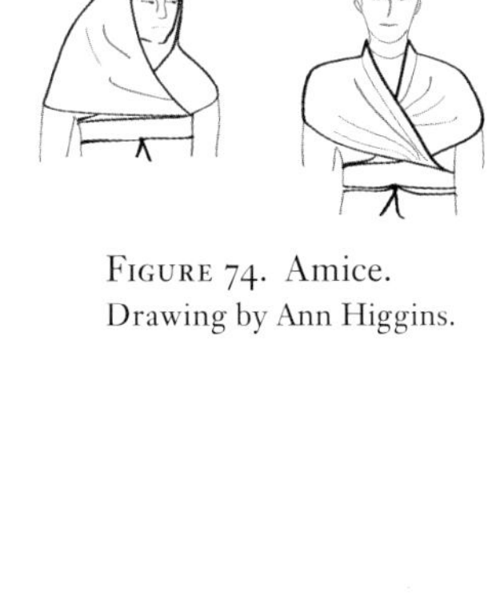

FIGURE 74. Amice.
Drawing by Ann Higgins.

collar of fabric visible above the other liturgical garments put on over it, and from the later Middle Ages ornament was added to this edge of the amice. The amice is sometimes referred to in medieval documents as the *superhumerale* or *ephod*.

amphibalus: An early medieval term for a poncho-like cloak; see *chasuble*.

balteus: See *cincture*.

caligae: Liturgical socks reaching to the knees that were worn by the highest prelates—bishops, abbots, popes—for solemn feasts. Made of linen or silk (see figure 58), they were worn with liturgical sandals.

campagi: Late-antique and early medieval liturgical slippers worn in Rome and in sees accorded papal privilege to wear them. Black and barely covering the foot, they were secured with slender straps across the top (see figures 12–14). They were worn over white stockings called *udones*.

cappa clausa: Long, loose, dark "closed cloak," shut up the front, that came to be defined over the twelfth and thirteenth centuries as the required clerical street attire—that is, what the clergy wore outside of church. Different solutions for accommodating the arms are evident in manuscript illustrations, with the simplest (depicted in figure 75) being two slits through which the arms could be extended.

cappa manicata: A form of clerical street-wear repeatedly banned, the "sleeved cloak" was a dark, ankle-length tunic with narrow sleeves. Its distinguishing feature was an extra piece of fabric—a sort of false sleeve—extending from the shoulder to below the waist (see figure 3).

cassock: An ankle-length long-sleeved tunic, usually black and buttoned up the front. A successor to the closed cloak, it is known from the seventeenth century and is still a common form of clerical street-wear.

chasuble (*casula*, *planeta*): A poncho-like garment that is the outermost vestment worn by the priest to say Mass (figure 76). The earliest depictions and surviving medieval chasubles (see figures 29, 40, 46, and 59) reveal ample fabric in a "bell" shape. From the twelfth century, the form narrowed, leaving the arms less encumbered. The "fiddle-back" form (see figures 53–55), dominant in the early modern and modern eras, was the end development of this process.

chlamys: An oblong mantle fastened at the shoulder with a clasp or brooch (see figure

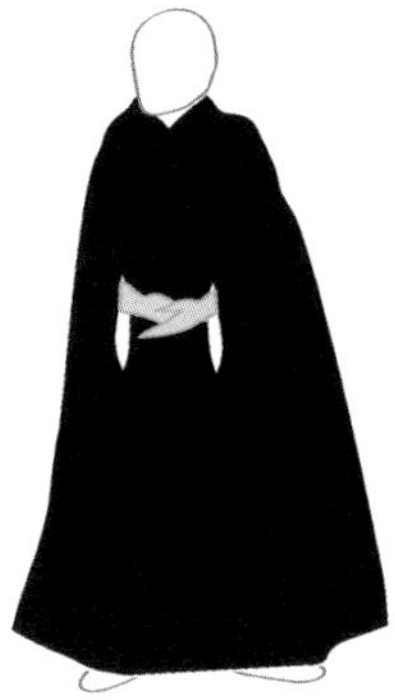

FIGURE 75.
Cappa clausa/closed cloak.
Drawing by Ann Higgins.

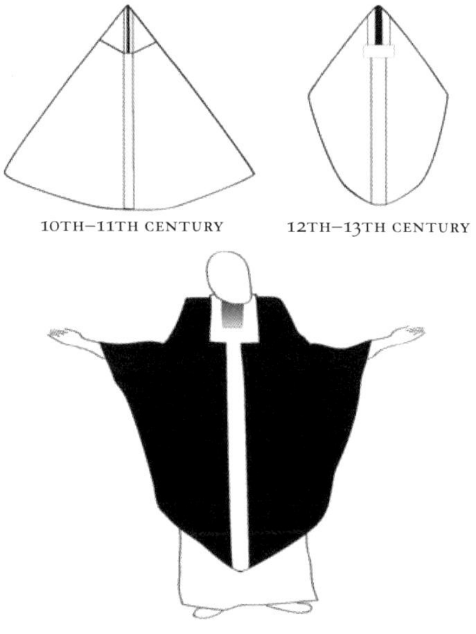

FIGURE 76. Chasuble.
Drawing by Ann Higgins.

12) worn by men throughout antiquity and the Byzantine era.

cincture (*cingulum*, *zona*, *balteus*): A belt worn over the alb (see figure 73). Although there is a leather belt with an ivory buckle in Arles attributed to Saint Caesarius (d. 542), other surviving medieval cinctures are woven and closed with ties.

circulus: A band of decoration around the base of the miter (see figure 69).

clavi: Stripes, usually purple or red, running from each shoulder to the hem on both sides of the dalmatic (see figure 78). Stripes on the sleeves of the dalmatic are also called *clavi.* They derived from the purples stripes on ancient Roman tunics worn by senators and those of equestrian rank to denote their status. The *clavi* are woven into the dalmatic, not sewn on, and in some depictions fringe or tufts of fringe extend from the stripes.

closed cloak: See ***cappa clausa***.

colobia: See **tunic**.

cope (*cappa*, *capa*): Originally meaning generally an ecclesiastical cloak or cape, it developed into the basic street-wear of the clergy as the *cappa clausa*, or closed cloak, and as a liturgical vestment became the normal attire of singers and the prestige garb of prelates (figure 77). Made from a semicircle of fabric, the cope was fastened at the chest with either a band or clasp, the latter becoming highly ornamented in the later Middle Ages. Some originally had hoods, but these quickly became ornamental "shields." The copes worn by bishops were often heavily embroidered. This ornate prelatial cope is also called a pluvial.

corporal: A square white cloth of linen that was placed originally under the chalice and paten during Mass, and later over the mouth of the chalice. It was among the altar linens blessed, along with vestments, for use at the altar.

cowl: A hooded tunic worn by monks.

cuculla, cucullus: See **cowl**.

dalmatic: A type of late Roman tunic, originally from Dalmatia, that became the ecclesiastical vestment associated with deacons (figure 78). Usually calf-length with very wide sleeves, it was distinguished by *clavi*, ornamental stripes (usually purple or red) running from the shoulders to the hem and around the edge of the sleeves. Originally the dalmatic was made of wool or linen, but starting in the tenth century colored silks were used. The sleeves narrowed over the central Middle Ages, making some dalmatics indistinguishable from tunicles.

encheirion: The Byzantine development of the maniple; an ornamental handkerchief worn by Orthodox clergy attached to the cincture.

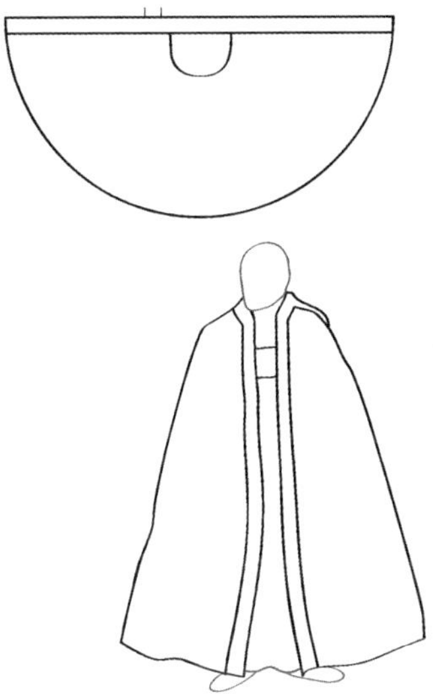

FIGURE 77. Cope.
Drawing by Ann Higgins.

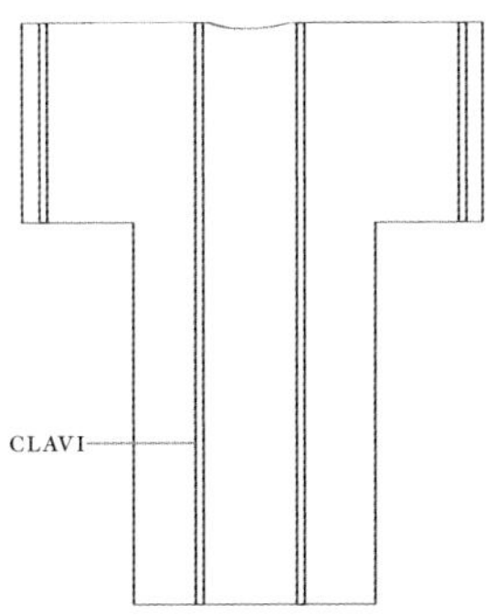

FIGURE 78. Dalmatic.
Drawing by Ann Higgins.

ephod: See **amice**.

epitrachelion: The Orthodox version of the stole.

fanon (*fano*; pl. *fanones*): This term was used to denote several pieces of liturgical garb. The *fano* was a papal amice that developed into a shoulder-cape worn over vestments rather than under them. Used in the plural the term could also denote the two "tails" extending from the back of the miter (usually now called lappets). Finally, *fano* can also mean a maniple.

humeral: See **amice**.

loros: A heavily jeweled wide scarf that was the distinctive garb of Byzantine emperors and empresses.

maniple: This piece of liturgical attire developed from the Roman handkerchief. In form it appears as a band of cloth about a yard long, often with flared ends (a smaller version of the stole) and was worn draped over the left arm (figure 79). It seems actually to have been used like a handkerchief into the Carolingian era, but from the tenth century became ornamental. It was worn by the major orders (bishops, priests, deacons) and became particularly associated with the subdeacon when this order definitively came to be included among the major orders. It is also called in some medieval documents a fanon, *mappula*, sudarium, or *mantile*.

mappula: See **maniple**.

miter, or mitre: A peaked cap worn by bishops. The miter emerged as a piece of distinctively episcopal garb in the eleventh century. Its shape has varied across the centuries, but most commonly in the twelfth through fourteenth centuries it had two triangular peaks, front and back (see figures 69 and 70), and two bands extending from the back (usually called lappets).

omophorion: In Orthodox liturgical attire, a wide outer stole worn by bishops; it is the Eastern development of the pallium.
A length of white cloth (originally wool, but later silk) approximately four yards long and ten inches wide, it was decorated with several crosses.

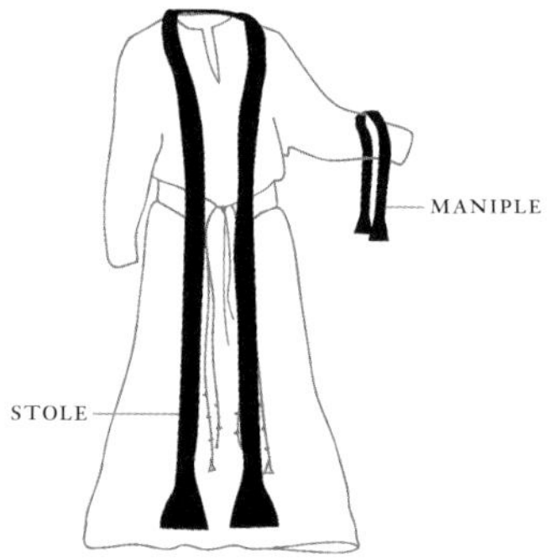

FIGURE 79.
Stole and maniple.
Drawing by Ann Higgins.

opus anglicanum: Although often used to describe all medieval embroideries produced in England, "English work" more specifically refers to a technique called "underside couching" used to attach threads laid on a cloth surface. In the earliest examples of English embroidery from the late eighth to the eleventh centuries, a simpler couching method was used: threads laid on the surface were couched at intervals by other threads stitched over them at right angles that remained visible. In "underside couching," the couching stitches were pulled tightly through to the back or underside of the fabric so that they didn't show on the surface. Pulling the couching stitch through to the reverse created a smooth unbroken line of colored thread on the front surface, a quality that made opus anglicanum highly prized from the twelfth century on.

orarium: See **stole**.

paenula: A term used for the chasuble in the early Middle Ages that also designated a woolen poncho-like mantle covering the whole body, worn for journeys or in inclement weather.

pallium: A term with several meanings. Most generically it means a piece of cloth. It can also designate the gown worn by ancient philosophers (a long piece of cloth wrapped around the body), but in medieval history it usually refers to a white woolen scarf worn by the pope as a symbol of his authority and bestowed by him on other bishops as a particular mark of favor and status. From the sixth to the eighth centuries it is depicted as looped around the neck, across the chest, and then over the left shoulder with one end hanging down the back of the body and the other down the front (see figures 12–14). The ends are usually fringed and decorated with small crosses. From the eighth century, the pallium was affixed with pins to the chasuble at the left shoulder and at the middle of the chest and back to make a Y shape (see figure 25, haloed figure top center, and figure 32, Saint Clement). In the eleventh and twelfth centuries, the original scarf form was lost and the pallium became a circle of white fabric set on the shoulders with tails extending down the center, front and back. In the central Middle Ages it became associated with metropolitan status (that is, with the office of archbishop). The term "pallium" is also used once in the Roman *Liber pontificalis* for cloths (maniples?) worn by deacons over their left arms and by Isidore of Seville for monastic garb.

phelonion: The Orthodox term for the chasuble.

pontificalia: The vestments and insignia of a bishop, cardinal, or other high-ranking cleric.

rationale: An episcopal ornament based on the description of the Jewish high priest's garb in Exodus 28 (see discussion in chapter 2). The term comes from Jerome's Vulgate translation of Exodus, where he used the Latin word *rationale* for the Greek *logion*, or breastplate, of the high priest.

sandals (*sandalia*): Special shoes, more resembling little boots, worn by bishops and abbots for festal liturgies. Surviving pairs are constructed of leather—usually decorated with appliqué work—over cork soles. The most common form has uppers with several tongues of leather converging on the ankle to leave cutouts through which the material of the stockings (caligae) worn with them showed (see figure 67).

soutane: Another term for the cassock.

sticharion: The Orthodox vestment cognate to the Western alb: its sleeves were wider and the sticharion had side openings that could be tied at the hem. Originally made of white linen, in the later Middle Ages silks, sometimes colored, were used.

stockings, pontifical: See **udones** and **caligae**.

stole: A liturgical scarf worn by deacons and priests, but especially associated with priestly status. Usually eight to ten feet long and two to three inches wide (see figure 79), the stole was put on over the alb, resting on the neck, with both ends falling down straight over the front of the body (although in a few areas of Europe, notably Milan, it was worn over the dalmatic). Its ends are usually visible below the chasuble and dalmatic (see figures 24 and 31). Sometimes the ties of the cincture were used to secure it in place. Stoles could be made of linen, cotton, or silk, and were sometimes decorated with embroidery. In Roman usage this vestment was called the orarium, but the term "stole" (*stola*), preferred by the Franks, became more common. From the thirteenth century, deacons wore the stole draped over the left shoulder, across the chest and back, and secured at the right hip.

superhumeral (*superhumerale*): See **amice**.

surplice: A loose white linen tunic with wide sleeves, in the Middle Ages reaching to the shins but in the sixteenth century shortened to just below the hips. Its Latin name, *superpelliceum*, indicates its original purpose as a loose plain garment to be worn over furs. It emerged first in northern Europe in the eleventh century, spreading to Italy in the twelfth. Not properly a liturgical garment, it was worn in choir, for processions and burials, and sometimes for the administration of sacraments.

tablion: In Byzantine secular attire, a decorative rectangle of fabric applied to the oblong mantle called the chlamys. In figure 12, Emperor Justinian has a patterned gold *tablion* on his purple chlamys, and the two officials on his right wear a purple *tablion* on a white chlamys.

tiara: The papal head covering or crown worn in processions and on nonliturgical occasions. This term *thyara* emerged in the twelfth century. Earlier terms used to describe papal head coverings were *camelaucum*, *phrygium* (or *frigium*), and *regnum*. No images survive until the tenth century to help us understand the appearance of papal headgear these terms denoted, but the earliest representations suggest a low rounded cap. From the eleventh century taller triangular shapes (see figure 62) are depicted, until in the late thirteenth century, when the more conical beehive shape with three diadems on it (the *triregnum*, see figure 63) emerged. In the thirteenth century it also appears to have had two lappets extending from the back.

titulus: The vertical decorative band on the miter, extending from the front base to the tip (see figure 69).

tunic: A generic term for a long, loose, straight gown with wide sleeves usually worn over an alb by clerics in minor orders serving liturgical roles (e.g., in processions as crucifers, thurifers, candle bearers).

tunicle (*tunicella*, *subtile*, *tunica subdiaconalis*): Vestment associated with the subdeacon. In form it was very much like the dalmatic only with narrower sleeves and no *clavi*. By the fourteenth century, indeed, it is difficult to distinguish tunicles from dalmatics. Although between the twelfth and fourteenth centuries it came to be bestowed on subdeacons at ordination, in practice it could be worn by acolytes and was sometimes worn by the other major orders. The tunicle could be brightly colored and ornamented (like the dalmatic in figure 66).

udones: White knee-high liturgical socks worn in late antiquity and the early Middle Ages with the liturgical slippers called *campagi*.

zona: See **cincture**.

BIBLIOGRAPHY

Primary Sources

Archival and Manuscript

Archivio della Badia, Montecassino. Cod. 127.

Archivio di Stato, Bologna. Santo Stefano Busta 11. Pergamena 19.

Biblioteca Ambrosiana di Milano H 230.

Biblioteca Apostolica Vaticana. Archivio S. Pietro F 11 A, F 15, H 58; Chigi D V 77; Ottobon. Lat. 6, 576; Reg. Lat. 124, Vat. Lat. 83, 629, 4770, 4775, 7818.

Biblioteca Casanatense, Rome. Codex 614.

Biblioteca Vallicelliana, Rome. Codex Juvenianus B.25/2, Codex B 141, Codex F 4.

Bibliothèque de la Ville, Amiens. MS. 223.

Bibliothèque Municipale de Tours, Diocèse 1.

Bibliothèque nationale de France, Paris. MSS. Lat. 9432, 9436, 12051.

British Library, London. Cotton Tiberius C. I.

Österreichische Nationalsbibliothek, Vienna. Codex 652.

Staatsbibliothek, Munich. Clm. 343.

Stiftsbibliothek, St. Gallen. Cod. Sang. 14, 22, 86, 156, 167.

Published

Ademar of Chabannes. *Chronicon.* Edited by Pascale Bourgain. CCCM 129. Turnhout: Brepols, 1999.

Agnes of Harcourt. *The Writings of Agnes of Harcourt: The Life of Isabelle of France and the Letter on Louis IX and Longchamp.* Edited and translated by Sean L. Field. Notre Dame, Ind.: Notre Dame University Press, 2003.

Amalarius of Metz. *Amalarii Episcopi Opera Liturgica Omnia.* Edited by John Michael Hanssens. 3 vols. Vatican City: Biblioteca Apostolica Vaticana, 1948–1950.

Ambrose. *De officiis.* Edited and translated by Ivor J. Davidson. 2 vols. Oxford: Oxford University Press, 2001.

Amiet, Robert, ed. "Une 'Admonitio Synodalis' de l'époque carolingienne: Étude critique et Édition." *Mediaeval Studies* 26 (1964): 18–82.

Andrieu, Michel, ed. *Ordines Romani du haut moyen age.* 5 vols. Louvain: Spicilegium Sacrum Lovaniense, 1931–1956. Reprint, 1960–1965.

——. *Le pontifical romain au moyen âge.* 4 vols. Vatican City: Biblioteca Apostolica Vaticana, 1938–1941.

Anselm of Canterbury. *The Letters of Saint Anselm of Canterbury.* 3 vols. Edited by Walter Fröhlich. Kalamazoo, Mich.: Cistercian Publications, 1993.

Barsotti, Riccardo, ed. *Gli antichi inventari della cattedrale di Pisa.* Pisa: Instituto di Storia dell'Arte, 1959.

Bede. *Bede's Ecclesiastical History of the English People.* Edited and translated by Bertram

Colgave and R. A. B. Mynors. Oxford: Clarendon Press, 1969.
——. *De tabernaculo.* Edited by David Hurst. CC 119A. Turnhout: Brepols, 1969.
——. *On the Tabernacle.* Translated by Arthur G. Holder. Liverpool: Liverpool University Press, 1994.
Bernard, Cardinal. *Bernhardi Cardinalis et Lateranensis Ecclesiae Prioris Ordo Officiorum Ecclesiae Lateranensis.* Edited by Ludwig Fischer. Munich: Datterer, 1916.
Bernard of Clairvaux. *On Baptism and the Office of Bishops.* Translated by Pauline Matarasso. Cistercian Fathers Series 67. Kalamazoo, Mich.: Cistercian Publications, 2004.
——. *Opera.* 7 vols. Edited by Jean Leclercq and H. M. Rochais. Rome: Editiones Cistercienses, 1957–1974.
Bernard of Cluny. *Scorn for the World: Bernard of Cluny's "De contemptu mundi."* Edited and translated by Ronald E. Pepin. East Lansing, Mich.: Colleagues Press, 1991.
Berno of Reichenau. *Libellus de quibusdam rebus ad missae officium.* In *PL,* 142:1055–80.
Bertran de Born. *The Poems of the Troubadour Bertran de Born.* Edited and translated by William D. Paden Jr., Tilde Sankovitch, and Patricia H. Stäblein. Berkeley: University of California Press, 1986.
Biblia latina cum glossa ordinaria: Facsimile Reprint of the Editio Princeps (Adolph Rusch of Strassburg 1480/81). 4 vols. Turnhout: Brepols, 1992.
Bischoff, Bernhard, ed. *Mittelalterliche Schatzverzeichnisse, Erster Teil: Von der Zeit Karls des Großen bis zur Mitte des 13. Jahrhunderts.* Munich: Prestel Verlag, 1967.
Boniface. *Die Briefe des heiligen Bonifatius und Lullus.* Edited by Michael Tangl. Berlin: Wiedmann, 1955.
——. *The Letters of Saint Boniface.* Edited and translated by Ephraim Emerton. New York: Columbia University Press, 1940. Reprint, 2000.
Boon, Amand, ed. *Pachomiana Latina.* Louvain: Bureaux de la Revue, 1932.
Boretius, Alfred, ed. *Capitularia Regum Francorum.* 2 vols. Hannover: Monumenta Germaniae Historica, 1883–1897.
Botte, Bernard, ed. *La tradition apostolique d'après les anciennes versions.* 2nd ed. Paris: Éditions du Cerf, 1968.
Brommer, Peter, Rudolf Pokorny, and Martina Stratmann, eds. *Capitula Episcoporum.* 4 vols. Hannover: Monumenta Germaniae Historica, 1984–1995.
Bruno of Segni. *Tractatus de sacramentis ecclesiae, mysteriis atque ecclesiasticis ritibus.* In *PL,* 165:1089–1110.
Burchard of Ursberg. *Die Chronik des Propstes Burchard von Ursberg.* Edited by Oswald Holder-Egger and Bernhard von Simson. MGH SSRG 16. Hannover: Monumenta Germaniae Historica, 1916.
Caesarius of Arles. *Caesarius of Arles: Life, Testament, Letters.* Translated by William E. Klingshirn. Liverpool: Liverpool University Press, 1994.
——. *Sancti Caesaru Arelatensis Opera Omnia.* 2 vols. Edited by Germanus Morin. Bruges: Maretioli, 1937–1942.
Columbanus. *Sancti Columbani Opera.* Edited by G. S. M. Walker. Dublin: Dublin Institute for Advanced Studies, 1957.
Coustant, Pierre, ed. *Epistolae romanorum pontificum.* Paris: Ludovicum-Dionysium Delatour & Antonium-Urbanum Coustelier, 1721.
Davis, Raymond, ed. and trans. *The Book of Pontiffs.* Liverpool: Liverpool University Press, 1989.
Décéaux, Joseph, ed. *Le sacramentaire de Marmoutier (Autun 19 bis).* 2 vols. Vatican City: Pontificio Istituto de Archeologia Cristiana, 1985.
Defensor of Ligugé. *Defensoris Locogiacensis Monachi "Liber scintillarum."* Edited by Henricus Rochais. CC 117. Turnhout: Brepols, 1957.
De Vogüé, Adalbert, ed. *La règle du maître.* 3 vols. Paris: Éditions du Cerf, 1964–1965.
Doniol, Henry, ed. *Cartulaire de Sauxillanges.* Clermont-Ferrand: Thibaud, 1864.
Dover, Mary, ed. and trans. *The "Glossa Ordinaria" on the Song of Songs.* Kalamazoo, Mich.: Medieval Institute Publications, 2004.
Drogo van Sint-Winoksbergen. *Vita Godeliph.* Edited by Nikolaas-Norbert Huyghebaert. Tielt: Lanoo, 1982.

Duchesne, Louis, ed. *Le liber pontificalis.* 2nd ed. 3 vols. With additions and corrections by Cyrille Vogel. Paris: E. Thorin, 1955–1957.

Eadmer of Canterbury. *Historia novorum in Anglia.* Edited by Martin Rule. London: Longman, 1884.

——. *Lives and Miracles of Saints Oda, Dunstan, and Oswald.* Edited and translated by Andrew J. Turner and Bernard J. Muir. Oxford: Clarendon, 2006.

Einhard. *Vita Karoli Magni.* Edited by Oswald Holder-Egger. Hannover: Monumenta Germaniae Historica, 1911.

Elizabeth of Schönau. *Liber visionum.* In *Die Visionen der Hl. Elisabeth und die Schriften der Abte Ekbert und Emecho von Schönau.* Edited by F. W. E. Roth. Brün: Druck der Raigerner Benedictiner Buchdruckerei, 1884.

Fainelli, Vittorio, ed. *Codice diplomatico Veronese.* 2 vols. Venice: Deputazione di storia patria per le Venezie, 1940–1963.

Ferrante, Joan, ed. and trans. *Epistolae: Medieval Women's Latin Letters.* http://epistolae.ccnmtl.columbia.edu/.

Francis of Assisi. *Writings and Early Biographies.* Edited by Marion A. Habig. 4th rev. ed. Quincy, Ill.: Franciscan Press, 1991.

Friedberg, Emil and Aemilius Ludwig Richter, eds. *Corpus iuris canonici.* 2 vols. Leipzig: Bernhardi Tauchnitz, 1879–1881. Reprint, Graz: Akademische Druck und Verlagsanstatt, 1959.

Fuhrmann, Horst, ed. *Das Constitutum Constantini.* Hannover: Hahn, 1968.

Fulbert of Chartres. *The Letters and Poems of Fulbert of Chartres.* Edited and translated by Frederick Behrends. Oxford: Clarendon Press, 1976.

Galbert of Bruges. *De multro, traditione, et occisione gloriosi Karoli, comitis Flandiarum.* Edited by Jeff Rider. CCCM 131. Turnhout: Brepols, 1994.

Geoffroi de Charny. *The Book of Chivalry of Geoffroi de Charny: Text, Context, and Translation.* Edited and translated by Richard W. Kaeuper and Elspeth Kennedy. Philadelphia: University of Pennsylvania Press, 1996.

Germanus of Constantinople. *On the Divine Liturgy.* Edited and translated by Paul Meyendorff. Crestwood, N.Y.: St. Vladimir's Seminary Press, 1984.

Gislebert of Mons. *Chronicon Hanoniense.* Hannover: Hahn, 1869.

Goscelin of Saint-Bertin. *Praise of Saint Edith.* Translated by Michael Wright. In *Writing the Wilton Women: Goscelin's Legend of Edith and the "Liber Confortatorius,"* edited by Stephanie Hollis, 23–67. Turnhout: Brepols, 2004.

Götz, George Polycarp, ed. *Liber qvare.* CCCM 60. Turnhout: Brepols, 1983.

Gregory VII. *The Epistolae Vagantes of Pope Gregory VII.* Edited and translated by H. E. J. Cowdrey. Oxford: Clarendon Press, 1972.

——. *The Register of Pope Gregory VII 1073–1085.* Edited and translated by H. E. J. Cowdrey. Oxford: Oxford University Press, 2002.

Gregory of Tours. *Histoire des Francs, livres I–VI.* Edited by Henri Ormont. Paris: Berthaud frères, 1886.

——. *Historia Francorum [Libri historiarum X].* Edited by Bruno Krusch and William Levison. MGH SSRM 1. Hannover: Monumenta Germaniae Historica, 1884.

Gregory the Great. *The Letters of Gregory the Great.* 3 vols. Edited and translated by John R. C. Martyn. Toronto: Pontifical Institute of Mediaeval Studies, 2004.

——. *Pastoral Care.* Translated by Henry Davis. Westminster, Md.: Newman Press, 1950.

——. *Règle Pastorale. 2 vols.* Edited by Floribert Rommel. Sources Chrétiennes 381–82. Paris: Éditions du Cerf, 1992.

——. *Registrum Epistularum.* 2 vols. Edited by Dag Norberg. CC 140–140A. Turnhout: Brepols, 1982.

Grocock, C. W. ed. and trans. *The Ruodlieb.* Chicago: Bolchazy-Carducci; Warminster: Aris and Phillips, 1985.

Guibert of Nogent. *De vita sua.* Edited by Edmond-René Labande. Paris: Belles Lettres, 1981.

Guidi, P., and E. Pellegrinetti, eds. *Inventari del vescovato della cattedrale e di altre chiese di*

Lucca. Rome: Tip. poliglotta vaticana, 1921.

Haddan, Arthur West and William Stubbs, eds. *Councils and Ecclesiastical Documents Relating to Great Britain and Ireland*. Oxford: Clarendon Press, 1869–1878. Reprint, 1964.

Hanslik, Rudolph, ed. *Benedicti Regula*. CSEL 75. Vienna: Hoelder-Pichler-Tempsky, 1960.

Hartmann, Wilifried and Albert Werminghoff, eds. *Concilia Aevi Karolini*. 3 vols. Hannover: Monumenta Germaniae Historica, 1906–1984.

Heiming, Odilo, ed. *Liber sacramentorum augustodunensis*. CC 159B. Turnhout: Brepols, 1984.

Head, Thomas, ed. *Medieval Hagiography: An Anthology*. New York: Garland, 2001.

Hehl, Ernst-Dieter, ed. *Concilia Aevi Saxonici, pars I, 916–960*. Hannover: Monumenta Germaniae Historica, 1987.

Henry IV. *Die Briefe Heinrich* IV. MGH Deutsches Mittelalter 1. Edited by Karl W. Erdmann. Leipzig: Karl W. Hiersemann, 1937.

Hildebert of Lavardin. *De ordinatione clericorum*. In *PL*, 171:926–28.

Hildegard of Bingen. *Epistolarivm*. 3 vols. Edited by L. Van Acker. CCCM 91–91b. Turnhout: Brepols, 1991.

——. *The Letters of Hildegard of Bingen*. 3 vols. Translated by Joseph L. Baird and Radd K. Ehrman. Oxford: Oxford University Press, 1994–2004.

——. *Liber divinorum operum simplicis hominis*. In *PL*, 197:739–1037.

——. *Scivias*. In *PL*, 197:383–738.

Hippolytus of Rome. *The Treatise on the Apostolic Tradition of St Hippolytus of Rome*. Edited and translated by Gregory Dix and Henry Chadwick. London: Church Historical Society / S.P.C.K., 1992.

Honorius Augustodunensis. *Gemma animae*. In *PL*, 172:541–735.

Hrabanus Maurus. *De institutione clericorum libri tres*. Edited by Detlev Zimpel. Freiburger Beiträge zur mittelalterlichen Geschichte; Studien und Texte 7. Frankfurt: Peter Lang, 1996.

——. *Louanges de la Sainte Croix*. Edited by Michel Perrin. Paris: Berg International and Amiens: Trois Cailloux, 1988.

Huygens, R. B. C., ed. *Serta Mediaevalia: Textus Varii Saeculorum X–XIII in Unum Collecti*. CCCM 171A. Turnhout: Brepols, 2000.

Isidore of Seville. *Etimologie o origini*. 2 vols. Edited by Angelo Velastro Canale. Turin: UTET Libreria, 2004.

——. *The Etymologies of Isidore of Seville*. Translated by Stephen A. Barney, W.J. Lewis, J. A. Beach, and Oliver Berghof. Cambridge: Cambridge University Press, 2006.

——. *Reglas monásticas de la España visigoda: Los tres libros de las "Sentencias."* Edited and translated by Julio Campos Ruiz and Ismael Roca Melia. Madrid: Biblioteca de Autores Cristianos, 1971.

——. *Sententiarum libri tres*. In *PL*, 83:537–738.

Ivo of Chartres. *De significationibus indumentorum sacerdotalium*. In *PL*, 162: 520–27.

Jaffé, Philipp, Wilhelm Wattenbach, S. Loewenfeld, F. Kaltenbrummer, and Paul Ewald, eds. *Regesta Pontificum Romanorum Ab Condita Ecclesia ad Annum Post Christum Natum MCXCVIII*, 2 vols. Leipzig: Veit, 1885–1888.

Jerome. *Dialogus adversus Pelagianos*. Edited by Claudio Moreschini. CC 80. Turnhout: Brepols, 1990.

——. *Sancti Eusebii Hieronymi Epistulae*. 3 vols. Edited by Isidore Hilberg. CSEL 54–56. Vienna: F. Tempsky; Leipzig: G. Freytag, 1910–1918.

——. *Select Letters of St. Jerome*. Translated by F.A. Wright. Cambridge, Mass.: Harvard University Press, 1963.

John Cassian. *De institutis coenobiorum et de octo principalium vitiorum remediis libri xii*. Edited by Michael Petschenig. CSEL 17. Vienna: F. Tempsky, 1888.

——. *The Institutes*. Translated by Boniface Ramsey. New York: Newman Press, 2000.

John of Salisbury. *The Letters of John of Salisbury*. 2 vols. Edited and translated by W.J. Millor and C.N.L. Brook. Oxford: Clarendon Press, 1979.

———. *Memoirs of the Papal Court.* Edited and translated by Marjorie Chibnall. London: Nelson, 1956. Reprint, 1962.

———. *Policraticus: Of the Frivolities of Courtiers and the Footprints of Philosophers.* Edited and translated by Cary J. Nederman. Cambridge: Cambridge University Press, 1990.

Julian of Norwich. A *Revelation of Love.* Edited by Nicholas Watson and Jacqueline Jenkins. University Park: Pennsylvania State University Press, 2006.

Kulp-Hill, Kathleen, trans. *Songs of Holy Mary of Alfonso X, the Wise: A Translation of the Cantigas de Santa Maria.* Tempe: Arizona Center for Medieval and Renaissance Studies, 2000.

Liutprand of Cremona. *Die Werke Liudprands von Cremona.* Edited by Joseph Becker. MGH SSRG 41. Hannover: Hahn, 1915.

Lopez, Robert S., and Irving W. Raymond, trans. *Medieval Trade in the Mediterranean World.* New York: Columbia University Press, 1955.

Lothar of Segni. *De sacro altaris mysterio.* In *PL*, 217:773–916.

Mansi, J. D., ed. *Sacrorum Conciliorum Noua et Amplissima Collectio.* 53 vols. Florence: Antonii Zata, 1759–1798. Reprint, Graz: Akademische Druck und Verlagsanstatt, 1960.

Marchegay, Paul and André Salmon, eds. *Chroniques d'Anjou.* 2 vols. Paris: J. Renouard, 1856–1871.

Martène, Edmund. *De Antiquis Ecclesiae Ritibus Libri Tres.* 4 vols. Antwerp: J. B. Novelli, 1763–1764.

Maassen, Frideric, ed. *Concilia Aevi Merovingici.* Hannover: Monumenta Germaniae Historica, 1893.

Mechthild of Magdeburg. *Das fließende Licht der Gottheit.* Edited by Gisela Vollmann-Profe. Frankfurt am Main: Deutscher Klassiker Verlag, 2003.

El "Menologio" de Basilio II Emperador de Bizancio: Vat. gr. 1613. Madrid: Testimonio Compañia Editorial, 2005.

Miller, Maureen C., trans. *Power and the Holy in the Age of the Investiture Conflict.* Boston: Bedford, 2005.

Mohlberg, Leo Cunibert, ed. *Liber Sacramentorum Romanae Aeclesiae Ordinis Anni Circulu (Cod. Vat. Reg. lat. 316/ Paris Bibl. Nat. 7193, 41/56).* Rome: Herder, 1968.

———. *Sacramentarium Veronense.* Rome, 1956.

Mommsen, Theodor E., and Karl F. Morrison, trans. *Imperial Lives and Letters of the Eleventh Century.* New York: Columbia University Press, 2000.

Munier, Charles and Charles de Clercq, eds. *Concilia Galliae, 314–695.* CC 148–148A. Turnhout: Brepols, 1963.

Muratori, Ludovico. *La liturgia romana vetus.* 2 vols. Venice: J. B. Pasquali, 1748.

Nigel of Longchamp. *The Book of Daun Burnel the Ass: Nigellus Wireker's "Speculum stultorum."* Translated by Graydon W. Regenos. Austin: University of Texas Press, 1959.

———. *Nigellus de Longchamp dit Wireker.* Vol. 1, *Introduction: Tractatus contra curiales et officiales clericos.* Edited by André Boutemy. Paris: Presses universitaires de France, 1959.

———. *Speculum stultorum.* Edited by Francesca Albini. Genoa: Università di Genova, 2003.

Odo of Cluny. *Vita sancti Geraldi Auriliacensis: Édition critique, traduction française, introduction et commentaries.* Edited by Anne-Marie Bultot-Verleysen. Brussels: Société des Bollandistes, 2009.

Orchard, Nicholas, ed. *The Sacramentary of Ratoldus (Paris, Bibliothèque nationale de France, lat. 12052).* London: Boydell Press, 2005.

Pertz, George Heinrich, ed. *Chronicon Hildesheimense.* MGH SS 7. Hannover: Monumenta Germaniae Historica, 1848.

Peter Damian. *Die Briefe des Petrus Damiani.* 4 vols. Edited by Kurt Reindel. MGH Briefe Kaiserzeit 4. Munich: Monumenta Germaniae Historica, 1983–1993.

———. *The Letters of Peter Damian.* 7 vols. Edited and translated by Owen J. Blum. Washington, D.C.: Catholic University of America Press, 1989–1995.

Peter the Chanter. *Verbvm adbreviatvm, textus conflatus*. Edited by Monique Boutry. CCCM 196. Turnhout: Brepols, 2004.

Peter the Venerable. *The Letters of Peter the Venerable*, 2 vols. Edited by Giles Constable. Cambridge, Mass.: Harvard University Press, 1976.

Pierucci, Celestino and Alberto Poverari, eds. *Le carte di Fonte Avellana*. 5 vols. Thesaurus Ecclesiarum Italiae IX.1. Rome: Edizioni di Storia e Letteratura, 1972.

Possidius. *Vita Augustini*. In *Vita di Cipriano, Vita di Ambrogio, Vita di Agostino*. 2nd ed. Edited by A. A. R. Bastiaensen. Milan: A. Mondadori, 1981.

Pseudo-Alcuin. *Liber de divinis officiis*. In *PL*, 101:1173–1286.

Pseudo-Germanus. *Expositio antiquae liturgiae gallicana*. Edited by E. A. Ratcliff. London: Henry Bradshaw Society, 1971.

Radice, Betty, trans. and revised by M. T. Clanchy. *Letters of Abelard and Heloise*. London: Penguin, 2003.

Ramon Llull. *The Book of the Ordre of Chivalry*. Edited by Alfred T. P. Byles. London: Early English Text Society, 1926. Reprint, Oxford: Boydell & Brewer, 1971.

——. *Llibre de l'orde de cavalleria*. Edited by Albert Soler i Llopart. Barcelona: Barcino, 1988.

Ratherius of Verona. *Praeloquia*. Edited by Peter L. D. Reid. CCCM 46A. Turnhout: Brepols, 1984.

——. *Praeloquia*. In *The Complete Works of Rather of Verona*. edited and translated by Peter L. D. Reid, 21–208. Binghamton, N.Y.: Medieval and Renaissance Texts and Studies, 1991.

Regino of Prüm. *History and Politics in Late Carolingian and Ottonian Europe: The Chronicle of Regino of Prüm and Adalbert of Magdeburg*. Translated by Simon MacLean. Manchester: Manchester University Press, 2009.

——. *Llibri duo de synodalibus causis et de ecclesiasticis disciplinis*. Edited by F. G. A. Wasserschleben and Wilifried Hartmann. Darmstadt: Wissenschaftliche Buchgesellschaft, 2004.

Robertson, James Craigie, ed. *Materials for the History of Thomas Becket, Archbishop of Canterbury*. 7 vols. London: Longman, 1875–1885.

Robinson, I.S., ed. and trans. *The Papal Reform of the Eleventh Century: Lives of Pope Leo IX and Pope Gregory VII*. Manchester: Manchester University Press, 2004.

Rodulfus Glaber. *The Five Books of the Histories and the Life of St William*. Edited and translated by John France. Oxford: Clarendon Press, 1989.

Roger of Hovedon. *Chronica magistri Rogeri de Houedene*. 4 vols. Edited by William Stubbs, London: Longman, 1868–1871.

Rupert of Deutz. *Liber de divinis officiis*. Edited by Hrabanus Haacke. CCCM 7. Turnhout: Brepols, 1967.

Sabatier, Paul, ed. *Bibliorum Sacrorum Latinae Versiones Antiquae seu Vetus Italica*. 3 vols. Reims: Reginaldum Florentain, 1743–1749. Reprint, Turnhout: Brepols, 1981.

Saint-Roch, Patrick, ed. *Liber Sacramentorvm Engolismensis: Manuscrit B.N. Lat. 816; Le Sacramentaire Gélasien d'Angoulême*. CC 159C. Turnhout: Brepols, 1987.

Schmitz, Gerhard, ed. *Capitularia Regum Francorum n.s.* I: *Collectio Capitularium Ansegisi*. Hannover: Monumenta Germaniae Historica, 1996.

Schneider, Herbert, ed. *Ordines de celebrando concilio: Die Konzilordines des Früh- und Hochmittelalters*. Hannover: Monumenta Germaniae Historica, 1996.

Schütte, Bernd, ed. *Die Lebensbeschreibungen der Königin Mathilde*. Hannover: Hahn, 1994.

Sicard of Cremona. *Mitrale*. In *PL*, 213:11–148.

Sitwell, Gerard, ed. and trans. *St. Odo of Cluny, Being the Life of St. Odo of Cluny by John of Salerno and the Life of St. Gerald of Aurillac by St. Odo*. London: Sheed and Ward, 1958.

Sommer, H. Oskar, ed. *The Vulgate Version of the Arthurian Romances*. 8 vols. Washington, D.C.: Carnegie Institution, 1908–1916.

Sulpicius Severus. *Gallus: Dialogues sur les "vertus" de Saint Martin*. Edited by Jacques Fontaine. Sources Chrétiennes 510. Paris: Éditions du Cerf, 2006.

——. *Vita di Martino.* Edited by Fabio Ruggiero. Bologna: EDB, 2003.

Tanner, Norman P., ed. *Decrees of the Ecumenical Councils.* 2 vols. London: Sheed and Ward; Washington, D.C.: Georgetown University Press, 1990.

Thomas of Cobham. *Summa de arte praedicandi.* Edited by Franco Morenzoni. CCCM 82. Turnhout: Brepols, 1988.

Valverde, José Filgueira, ed. *Cantigas de Santa María: Códice Rico de El Escorial Ms. escurialense* T.I.1. Madrid: Editorial Castalia, 1985.

Venarde, Bruce L., ed. and trans. *Robert of Arbrissel: A Medieval Religious Life.* Washington, D.C.: Catholic University of America Press, 2003.

——, ed. and trans. *The Rule of Saint Benedict.* Dumbarton Oaks Medieval Library 6. Cambridge, Mass.: Harvard University Press, 2011.

Vives, José, ed. *Concilios visigóticos e hispano-romanos.* Barcelona: CSIC, 1963.

Vogel, Cyrille and Reinhard Elze, eds. *Le pontifical romano-germanique du dixième siècle.* 2 vols. Vatican City: Biblioteca Apostolica Vaticana, 1963.

von Glanvell, Victor Wolf, ed. *Die Kanonessammlung des Kardinals Deusdedit.* Paderborn: F. Schoningh, 1905. Reprint, Aalen: Scientia Verlag, 1967.

von Pflugk-Harttung, Julius. *Acta Pontificum Romanorum Inedita.* 3 vols. Tübingen: F. Fues, 1880–1886. Reprint, Graz: Akademische Druck und Verlagsanstalt, 1958.

Wasserschleben, Herrmann, ed. *Die irische Kanonensammlung.* Leipzig: Bernhard Tauchnitz, 1885.

Watterich, Johann Matthias, ed. *Pontificum Romanorum Vitae.* 2 vols. Leipzig: G. Engelmann, 1862. Reprint, Aalan: Scientia Verlag, 1966.

Whitelock, D. M. Brett and C. N. L. Brooke, eds. *Councils and Synods with Other Documents Relating to the English Church, I A.D. 871–1204.* Oxford: Clarendon Press, 1981.

William Durand. *Principium speculi domini Guilhelmi Duranti [Speculum iudiciale].* 4 vols. Edited by Franciscus Moneliensis. Padua: Johann Herbort, 1479.

——. *Rationale Divinorum Officiorum.* 3 vols. Edited by A. Davril and T. M. Thibodeau. CCCM 140A. Turnhout: Brepols, 1995.

William of Malmesbury. *The Historia Novella.* Edited and translated by K. R. Potter. London: T. Nelson, 1955.

Secondary Sources

Adam, Hajo, and Adam D. Galinsky, "Enclothed Cognition." *Journal of Experimental Social Psychology* 48 (2012): 918–25.

Alberzoni, Maria Pia. "'Murum se pro domo Dei opposuit': Lanfranco di Pavia († 1198) tra agiografia e storia." In *Il difficile mestiere di vescovo (secoli X–XIV)*, 47–99. Caselle di Sommacampagna: Cierre, 2000.

Alexander, J. J. G. A *Survey of Manuscripts Illuminated in the British Isles.* 6 vols. London: H. Miller, 1975–1996.

Alexander, Jonathan, and Paul Binski, eds. *Age of Chivalry: Art in Plantagenet England 1200–1400.* London: Royal Academy of Arts, 1987.

Allen, Richard. "'A Pround and Headstrong Man': John of Ivry, Bishop of Avranches and Archbishop of Rouen, 1060–79." *Historical Research* 83, no. 220 (2010): 189–227.

Althoff, Gerd. *Otto III.* Translated by Phyllis G. Jestice. University Park: Pennsylvania State University Press, 2003.

Amiet, Robert. "Catalogue des livres liturgiques manuscrits conservés dans les archives et les bibliothèques de la ville de Rome." *Studi Medievali*, ser. 3, 27 (1986): 925–97.

Andaloro, Maria, ed. *Nobiles officinae: Perle, filigrane e trame di seta dal Palazzo Reale di Palermo.* 2 vols. Catania: Giuseppe Maimone, 2006.

Andreescu-Treadgold, Irina. "The Emperor's New Crown and St. Vitalis' New Clothes." *Corso di cultura sull'arte ravennate e bizantina* 41 (1995): 149–86.

Andreescu-Treadgold, Irina, and Warren Treadgold. "Procopius and the Imperial

Panels of S. Vitale." *Art Bulletin* 79 (1997): 708–23.

Andrieu, Michel. "La carrière ecclésiastique des papes et les documents liturgiques du moyen âge." *Revue des sciences religieuses* 21 (1947): 90–120.

Astell, Ann W. *The Song of Songs in the Middle Ages*. Ithaca, N.Y.: Cornell University Press, 1990.

Ataoguz, Jenny Kirsten. "The Apostolic Commissioning of the Monks of Saint John in Müstair, Switzerland: Painting and Preaching in a Churraetian Monastery." Ph.D. diss., Harvard University, 2007.

Bagliani, Agostino Paravicini. *Le chiavi e la tiara: Immagini e simboli del papato medievale*. Rome: Viella, 1998.

Balbarini, Chiara. "Gli arredi della sacrestia di San Francesco attraverso gli inventari trecenteschi." In *Il Francescanesimo a Pisa (secc. 13–14) e la missione del Beato Agnello in Inghilterra a Canterbury e Cambridge (1224–1226): Atti del Convegno di studi, Pisa, Chiesa di San Francesco, 10–11 marzo 2001*, 117–26. Ospedaletto: Felici, 2003.

Baldwin, John W. *The Language of Sex: Five Voices from Northern France around 1200*. Chicago: University of Chicago Press, 1994.

———. *Masters, Princes and Merchants: The Social Views of Peter the Chanter and His Circle*. 2 vols. Princeton: Princeton University Press, 1970.

Bangert, Michael. "The Metaphor of the Vestment in the Writings of Gertrud of Helfta (1256–1302)." In *Iconography of Liturgical Textiles in the Middle Ages*, edited by Evelin Wetter, 129–39. Riggisberg: Abegg-Stiftung, 2010.

Barnard, Malcolm, ed. *Fashion Theory: A Reader*. London: Routledge, 2007.

Baroffio, Bonifacio, and Ferdinando Dell'Oro, "L' 'Ordo Missae' del vescovo Warmondo d'Ivrea." *Studi Medievali*, ser. 3, 16 (1975): 795–823.

Barone, Giulia. "Chierici, monaci e frati." In *Roma medievale*, edited by André Vauchez, 187–212. Rome: Laterza, 2001.

Barstow, Anne Llewellyn. *Married Priests and the Reforming Papacy: The Eleventh-Century Debates*. New York: Edwin Mellon, 1982.

Barthélemy, Dominique. "The Peace of God and Bishops at War in the Gallic Lands from the Late Tenth to the Early Twelfth Century." *Anglo-Norman Studies* 32 (2009): 1–23.

Barthes, Roland. "Rhetoric and the Image." In *Image, Music, Text*, edited and translated by Stephen Heath, 32–51. New York: Hill & Wang, 1977.

Beaudette, Paul. " 'In the World but Not of It': Clerical Celibacy as a Symbol of the Medieval Church." In *Medieval Purity and Piety: Essays on Medieval Clerical Celibacy and Religious Reform*, edited by Michael Frassetto, 23–46. New York: Garland, 1998.

Bednarz, Ute. *Kostbarkeiten aus dem Domschatz zu Halberstadt*. Halle an der Saale: Stekovics, 2001.

Bedos-Rezak, Brigitte. "The Social Implications of the Art of Chivalry: The Sigillographic Evidence (France, 1050–1250)." In *Form and Order in Medieval France: Studies in Social and Quantitative Sigillography*, 6:1–31. Aldershot: Variorum, 1993.

Bellitto, Christopher M. "Revisiting Ancient Practices: Priestly Training before Trent." In *Medieval Education*, edited by Ronald B. Begley and Joseph W. Koterski, 35–49. New York: Fordham University Press, 2005.

Berman, Constance H. "Women as Donors and Patrons to Southern French Monasteries in the Twelfth and Thirteenth Centuries." In *The Worlds of Medieval Women: Creativity, Influence, and Imagination*, edited by Constance H. Berman, Charles W. Connell, and Judith Rice Rothschild, 53–68. Morgantown: West Virginia University Press, 1985.

Berschin, Walter, and Alfons Zettler. *Egino von Verona*. Stuttgart: J. Thorbecke, 1995.

Bertram, Jerome. *The Chrodegang Rules: The Rules for the Common Life of the Secular Clergy from the Eighth and Ninth Centuries. Critical*

Texts with Translations and Commentary. Aldershot: Ashgate, 2005.

Beumann, Helmut. "Das Rationale der Bischöfe von Halberstadt und seine Folgen." In *Kirche und Reich: Beiträge zur früh- und hochmittelalterlichen Kloster-, Bistums- und Missionsgeschichte*, edited by Irmgard Fees, 39–70. Goldbach: Keip, 2004.

Biddle, Martin. *Object and Economy in Medieval Winchester*. 2 vols. Oxford: Clarendon Press, 1990.

Bisson, Thomas N. *The Crisis of the Twelfth Century: Power, Lordship, and the Origins of European Government*. Princeton: Princeton University Press, 2009.

——. "The Feudal Revolution." *Past and Present* 142 (1994): 14–21.

——. *Tormented Voices: Power, Crisis, and Humanity in Rural Catalonia, 1140–1200*. Cambridge, Mass.: Harvard University Press, 1998.

Blair, John. *The Church in Anglo-Saxon Society*. Oxford: Oxford University Press, 2005.

Bloch, Peter, and Hermann Schnitzler. *Die ottonische Kölner Malerschule*. 2 vols. Düsseldorf: Schwann, 1967–1970.

Blumenthal, Uta-Renate. *The Early Councils of Pope Paschal II, 1100–1110*. Toronto: Pontifical Institute of Mediaeval Studies, 1978.

Bock, Franz Johann Joseph. *Geschichte der liturgischen Gewänder des Mittelalters*. 3 vols. Bonn: Henry & Cohen, 1856–1871.

Boinet, Amédée. *La miniature carolingienne, ses origins, son développement: Planches*. Paris: Picard, 1918.

Borkopp-Restle, Birgitt. *Der Aachener Kanonikus Franz Bock und seine Textilsammlungen: Ein Beitrag zur Geschichte der Kunstgewebe im 19 Jahrhundert*. Riggisberg: Abegg-Stiftung, 2008.

Bornert, René. *Les commentaires byzantins de la divine liturgie du VIIe au XVe siècle*. Paris: Institut français d'études byzantines, 1966.

Bornstein, Daniel. "Spiritual Culture, Material Culture: Church Inventories in Fifteenth-Century Cortona." *Medievalia et Humanistica*, n.s. 28 (2001): 101–15.

Bouchard, Constance Brittain. *Sword, Miter, and Cloister: Nobility and the Church in Burgundy, 980–1198*. Ithaca, N.Y.: Cornell University Press, 1987.

Bowman, Jeffrey A. "The Bishop Builds a Bridge: Sanctity and Power in the Medieval Pyrenees." *Catholic Historical Review* 88 (2002): 1–16.

Bragança, Joaquim O. "O 'Ordo Missae' de Reichenau." *Didaskalia: Revista da Faculdade de Teologia de Lisboa* 1 (1971): 137–61.

Brandt, Michael. *Das kostbare Evangeliar des heiligen Bernward*. Munich: Prestel Verlag, 1993.

Brandt, Michael, and Anne Eggebrecht. *Bernward von Hildesheim und das Zeitalter der Ottonen: Katalog der Ausstellung Hildesheim 1993*. 2 vols. Hildesheim: Bernward Verlag, 1993.

Branting, Agnes, and Andreas Lindblom. *Medieval Embroideries and Textiles in Sweden*. Uppsala: Almquist & Wiksells Boktryckeri, 1932.

Braun, Joseph. *Der christliche Altar in seiner geschichtlichen Entwicklung*. Munich: Alte Meister Guenther Koch, 1924.

——. *Die liturgische Gewandung im Occident und Orient nach Ursprung und Entwiklung, Verwendung und Symbolik*. Frieburg im Breisgau: Herder, 1907.

——. *Die liturgischen Paramente in Gegenwart und Vergangenheit: Ein Handbuch der Paramentik*. Freiburg im Breisgau: Herder, 1924.

——. "Der Paramentenschatz zu Castel S. Elia." *Zeitschrift für christliche Kunst* 12 (1899): 291–302, 343–56.

Brennan, T. Corey. "Tertullian's *De pallio* and Roman Dress in North Africa." In *Roman Dress and the Fabrics of Roman Culture*, edited by Jonathan Edmondson and Alison Keith, 257–70. Toronto: University of Toronto Press, 2008.

Brenninkmeyer, Ingrid. *The Sociology of Fashion*. Paris: P.G. Keller, 1963.

Brown, Alfred L. *The Governance of Late Medieval England, 1272–1461*. Stanford: Stanford University Press, 1989.

Brown, Barton. "'Enigmata Figurarum': A Study of the Third Book of the 'Rationale Divinorum Officiorum' of William Durandus and Its Allegorical Treatment of the Christian Liturgical Vestments." Ph.D. diss., New York University, 1983.

Brown, Warren. *Unjust Seizure: Conflict, Interest, and Authority in an Early Medieval Society*. Ithaca, N.Y.: Cornell University Press, 2001.

——. *Violence in Medieval Europe*. Harlow: Pearson, 2011.

Brundage, James A. *The Medieval Origins of the Legal Profession: Canonists, Civilians, and Courts*. Chicago: University of Chicago Press, 2008.

Budny, Mildred. *Insular, Anglo-Saxon and Early Anglo-Norman Manuscript Art at Corpus Christi College, Cambridge: An Illustrated Catalogue*. 2 vols. Kalamazoo, Mich.: Medieval Institute Publications, 1997.

Budny, Mildred, and Dominic Tweddle. "The Early Medieval Textiles at Maaseik, Belgium." *Antiquaries Journal* 65 (1985): 353–89.

Bull, Marcus. *Knightly Piety and the Lay Response to the First Crusade: The Limousin and Gascony, c. 970–c. 1130*. Oxford: Oxford University Press, 1993.

——. "The Roots of Lay Enthusiasm for the First Crusade." *History: The Journal of the Historical Association* 78 (1993): 353–72.

Bumke, Joachim. *Courtly Culture: Literature and Society in the High Middle Ages*. Translated by Thomas Dunlap. Berkeley: University of California Press, 1991.

Burns, E. Jane. *Courtly Love Undressed: Reading through Clothes in Medieval French Culture*. Philadelphia: University of Pennsylvania Press, 2002.

——. *Medieval Fabrications: Dress, Textiles, Cloth Work, and Other Cultural Imaginings*. New York: Palgrave, 2004.

——. *Sea of Silk: A Textile Geography of Women's Work in Medieval French Literature*. Philadelphia: University of Pennsylvania Press, 2009.

Butturini, Francesco. *La pittura frescale dell'anno mille nella diocesi di Verona*. Verona: Centro per la formazione professionale grafica, 1987.

Bynum, Caroline Walker. *Holy Feast and Holy Fast: The Religious Significance of Food to Medieval Women*. Berkeley: University of California Press, 1987.

Byzantium: An Oecumenical Empire. Byzantine and Christian Museum, October 2001–January 2002. Athens: Hellenic Ministry of Culture, 2001.

Cabaniss, Allen. *Amalarius of Metz*. Amsterdam: North Holland, 1954.

Cabié, Robert. *La lettre du Pape Innocent Ier a Décentius de Gubbio (19 mars 416): Texte critique, traduction et commentaire*. Louvain: Publications universitaires, 1973.

Cabrol, Fernand, and Henri Leclercq, eds. *Dictionnaire d'archéologie chrétienne et de liturgie*. Paris: Letouzey et Ané, 1907–1953.

Camille, Michael. "Word, Text, Image in the Early Church Fathers in the Egino Codex." In *Testo e immagine nell'alto medioevo*, 65–94. Spoleto: Centro italiano di studi sull'alto medioevo, 1994.

Capuani, Massimo. *Christian Egypt: Coptic Art and Monuments through Two Millennia*. Collegeville, Minn.: Liturgical Press, 2002.

Carroll-Clark, Susan M. "Bad Habits: Clothing and Textile References in the Register of Eudes Rigaud, Archbishop of Rouen." *Medieval Clothing and Textiles* 1 (2005): 81–114.

Cavallo, Guglielmo. *Exultet: Rotoli liturgici del medioevo meridionale*. Rome: Libreria dello Stato, 1994.

Cipolla, Carlo. "Il Velo di Classe." *Le gallerie nazionali italiane* 3 (1897): 194–249.

Coakley, John. *Women, Men, and Spiritual Power: Female Saints and Their Male Collaborators*. New York: Columbia University Press, 2006.

Coatsworth, Elizabeth. "Cloth-Making and the Virgin Mary in Anglo-Saxon Literature and Art." In *Medieval Art: Recent Perspectives; A Memorial Tribute to C. R. Dodwell*, edited by Gale R. Owen-Crocker and Timothy

Graham, 8–25. Manchester: Manchester University Press, 1998.
——. "Text and Textile." In *Text, Image, Interpretation: Studies in Anglo-Saxon Literature and Its Insular Context in Honour of Éamonn Ó Carragáin*, edited by Alastair Minnis and Jane Roberts, 187–207. Turnhout: Brepols, 2007.
Cohen, Adam S. *The Uta Codex: Art, Philosophy, and Reform in Eleventh-Century Germany.* University Park: Pennsylvania State University Press, 2000.
Constable, Giles. "The Ceremonies and Symbolism of Entering Religious Life and Taking the Monastic Habit, from the Fourth to the Twelfth Century." In *Segni e riti nella Chiesa altomedievale occidentale*, 771–834. Spoleto: Centro italiano di studi sull'alto medioevo, 1987.
——. "Medieval Charters as a Source for the History of the Crusades." In *Crusaders and Crusading in the Twelfth Century*, 93–116. Farnham: Ashgate, 2008.
——. "The Military Orders." In *Crusaders and Crusading in the Twelfth Century*, 165–82. Farnham: Ashgate, 2008.
——. "The Orders of Society." In *Three Studies in Medieval Religious and Social Thought*, edited by Giles Constable. Cambridge: Cambridge University Press, 1995.
——. *The Reformation of the Twelfth Century.* Cambridge: Cambridge University Press, 1996.
Cotts, John D. "The Critique of the Secular Clergy in Peter of Blois and Nigellus de Longchamps." *Haskins Society Journal* 13 (1999): 138–50.
Couch, David. *William Marshal: Court, Career and Chivalry in the Angevin Empire 1147–1219.* London: Longman, 1990.
Cowdrey, H. E. J. *Pope Gregory VII, 1073–1085.* Oxford: Clarendon Press, 1998.
Craik, Jennifer. *The Face of Fashion: Cultural Studies in Fashion.* London: Routledge, 1994.
Crane, Susan. *The Performance of Self: Ritual, Clothing, and Identity during the Hundred Years War.* Philadelphia: University of Pennsylvania Press, 2002.
Cristiani, Léon. "Essai sur les origines du costume ecclésiastique." *Orientalia Christiana periodica* 13 (1947): 69–79.
Crivello, Fabrizio. *Le "Omelie sui Vangeli" di Gregorio Magno a Vercelli: Le miniature del ms. CXLVIII/8 della Biblioteca Capitolare.* Florence: SISMEL, 2005.
Croom, Alexandra. *Roman Clothing and Fashion.* Stroud, Gloucestershire: Tempus, 2000.
Cubitt, Catherine. *Anglo-Saxon Church Councils c. 650–c. 850.* London: Leicester University Press, 1995.
——. "The Tenth-Century Benedictine Reform in England." *Early Medieval Europe* 6 (1997): 77–94.
Daniell, Christopher. *Death and Burial in Medieval England.* London: Routledge, 1997.
D'Archimbaud, Gabrielle Démians. "Archéologie et vêtement médiéval: Apports et limites des recherches récentes en France méditerranéenne." In *Vêtement et sociétés 2: Actes du colloque national C.N.R.S. "Vers un anthropologie du vêtement," Musée de l'Homme (9–11 mars 1983)*, edited by Yves Delaport, special issue of *L'Ethnographie* 80 (1984): 309–22.
De Blaauw, Sible. *Cultus et decor: Liturgia e architettura nella Roma tardoantica e medievale.* 2 vols. Vatican City: Biblioteca Apostolica Vaticana, 1994.
De Capitani d'Arzago, Alberto. *Antichi tessuti della basilica ambrosiana.* Biblioteca de "l'Arte," n.s., 1. Milan: "l'Arte," 1941.
Deichmann, Friedrich Wilhelm. *Ravenna: Hauptstadt des spätantiken Abendlandes.* 3 vols. Wiesbaden: F. Steiner, 1958–1989.
de Jong, Mayke. "Charlemagne's Church." In *Charlemagne: Empire and Society*, edited by Joanna Story, 103–35. Manchester: Manchester University Press, 2005.
De la Roncière, Charles M. "Condizioni economiche del clero parrocchiale, rurale e urbano, nell'Europa meridionale, XII–XV secoli (osservazioni da lavori recenti)." In *Gli spazi economici della Chiesa nell'Occidente mediterraneo (secoli XII–metà XIV)*, 329–61. Pistoia: Centro italiano di studi di storia dell'arte, 1999.

Deliyannis, Deborah Mauskopf. *Ravenna in Late Antiquity*. Cambridge: Cambridge University Press, 2010.

Dell'Omo, Mariano. "*Litaniae sanctorum, Libellus precum, Ordo Missae* di S. Vincenzo al Volturno (Biblioteca Apostolica Vaticana Chig. D V 77)." *Mediaeval Studies* 70 (2008): 203–74.

Delmaire, Roland. "Le vêtement, symbole de richesse et de pouvoir, d'après les textes patristiques et hagiographiques due Bas-Empire." In *Costume et société dans l'antiquité et le haut Moyen Âge*, edited by François Chausson and Hervé Inglebert, 85–98. Paris: Picard, 2003.

Delogu, Paolo. "L'importazione di tessuti preziosi e il sistema economico romano nel IX secolo." *Roma medievale: Aggiornamenti*, edited by Paolo Delogu, 123–41. Florence: All'insegna del giglio, 1998.

De Marly, Diana. *Fashion for Men: An Illustrated History*. London: Holmes & Meier, 1985.

——. "The 19th Century." In "Dress," edited by Aileen Ribeiro, et al. In Grove Art Online. http://www.oxfordartonline.com/subscriber/article/grove/art/T023637pg8. Accessed May 6, 2011.

Denifle, H., and A. Chatelain, eds. *Chartularium universitatis Parisiensis*. 4 vols. Paris: Delalain, 1889–1897.

Der Nersessian, Sirapie. "The Illustrations of the Homilies of Gregory of Nazianzus Paris Gr. 510: A Study of the Connections between Text and Image." *Dumbarton Oaks Papers* 16 (1962): 195–228.

Deshman, Robert. *The Benedictional of Æthelwold*. Princeton: Princeton University Press, 1995.

Desrosiers, Sophie. *Musée National du moyen âge: Thermes de Cluny, Catalogue; Soieries et autres textiles de l'antiquité au XVIe siècle*. Paris: Réunion des Musées Nationaux, 2004.

Devoti, Donata, and Giulia Meucci. "Il piviale di San Moderanno." In *Il filo della storia: Tessuti antichi in Emilia-Romagna*, edited by Marta Cuoghi Costantini and Iolanda Silvestri, 67–71. Bologna: CLUEB, 2005.

Diez, Ernst, and Otto Demus. *Byzantine Mosaics in Greece: Hosios Lucas and Daphni*. Cambridge, Mass.: Harvard University Press, 1931.

Dodd, Erica Cruikshank. *The Frescoes of Mar Musa al-Habashi: A Study of Medieval Painting in Syria*. Toronto: Pontifical Institute of Mediaeval Studies, 2001.

Dodwell, C. R. *Anglo-Saxon Art: A New Perspective*. Ithaca, N.Y.: Cornell University Press, 1982.

Duchesne, Louis. *Christian Worship: Its Origin and Evolution*. 5th ed. Translated by M. L. McClure. London: Society for Promoting Christian Knowledge, 1956.

Dutton, Paul Edward, and Herbert L. Kessler. *The Poetry and Paintings of the First Bible of Charles the Bald*. Ann Arbor: University of Michigan Press, 1997.

Eco, Umberto. "Social Life as a Sign System." In *Structuralism, an Introduction*, edited by David Robey, 57–72. Oxford: Clarendon Press, 1973.

Elliott, Dyan. "Dressing and Undressing the Clergy: Rites of Ordination and Degradation." In *Medieval Fabrications: Dress, Textiles, Clothwork, and Other Cultural Imaginings*, edited by E. Jane Burns, 55–69. New York: Palgrave, 2004.

——. "The Priest's Wife: Female Erasure and the Gregorian Reform." In *Fallen Bodies: Pollution, Sexuality, and Demonology in the Middle Ages*, 81–106. Philadelphia: University of Pennsylvania Press, 1999.

——. "Sex in Holy Places: An Exploration of a Medieval Anxiety." *Journal of Women's History* 6/3 (Fall 1994): 6–34.

Ericani, Giuliana and Paola Frattaroli, eds. *Tessuti nel Veneto: Venezia e la Terraferma*. Verona: Banca Popolare, 1993.

Evans, Helen C., ed. *Byzantium: Faith and Power (1261–1557)*. New Haven: Yale University Press, 2004.

Falconieri, Tommaso di Carpegna. *Il clero di Roma nel medioevo: Istituzioni e politica cittadina (secoli VIII–XIII)*. Rome: Viella, 2002.

Ferruolo, Stephen C. *The Origins of the University: The Schools of Paris and Their*

Critics, 1100–1215. Stanford: Stanford University Press, 1985.

Field, Sean L. *Isabelle of France: Capetian Sanctity and Franciscan Identity in the Thirteenth Century*. Notre Dame, Ind.: University of Notre Dame Press, 2006.

Filippi, Gabriella Delfini. "Per la storia del restauro musivo nel secolo XIX: L'esempio di Sant'Agnese." *Storia dell'arte* 65 (1989): 87–94.

Fleming, Robin. "Acquiring, Flaunting and Destroying Silk in Late Anglo-Saxon England." *Early Medieval Europe* 15 (2007): 127–53.

Flint, V. I. J. *Honorius Augustodunensis of Regensburg*. Aldershot: Ashgate, 1995.

Flori, Jean. "Chevalerie et liturgie: Remise des armes et vocabulaire 'chevaleresque' dans les sources liturgiques du IXe au XIVe siècle." *Le moyen âge: Revue d'histoire et de philologie* 84 (1978): 247–78, 409–42.

Flury-Lemberg, Mechthild. "Die Adlerkasel in Brixen, ein bedeutendes Zeugnis frühchristlicher Paramentik." In *Am Anfang war das Auge: Kunsthistorische Tagung anläßlich des 100 jährigen Bestehens des Diözesanmuseums Hofburg Brixen*, edited by Leo Andergassen. 298–320. Brixen: Diözesanmuseum Hofburg, 2004.

——. *Textile Conservation and Research: A Documentation of the Textile Department on the Occasion of the Twentieth Anniversary of the Abegg Foundation*. Bern: Abegg-Stiftung, 1988.

——. "Le vêtement funéraire de saint Servais de Maastricht." *Bulletin du CIETA* 70 (1992): 37–44.

Flury-Lemberg, Mechthild, and Gisela Illek. *Spuren kostbarer Gewebe*. Riggisberg: Abegg-Stiftung, 1995.

Flury-Lemberg, Mechthild, and Gabriel Vial. "La chasuble aux aigles de Bressanone, un témoignage important de paramentique du christianism des premiers siècles." *Bulletin du CIETA* 82 (2005): 30–50.

Forey, Alan. "The Military Orders, 1120–1312." In *The Oxford Illustrated History of the Crusades*, edited by Jonathan Riley-Smith, 184–216. Oxford: Oxford University Press, 1997.

Frassetto, Michael. "Heresy, Celibacy, and Reform in the Sermons of Ademar of Chabannes." In *Medieval Purity and Piety: Essays on Medieval Clerical Celibacy and Religious Reform*, edited by Michael Frassetto, 131–48. New York: Garland, 1998.

Freed, John B. *Noble Bondsmen: Ministerial Marriages in the Archdiocese of Salzburg, 1100–1343*. Ithaca, N.Y.: Cornell University Press, 1995.

Freiherr von Reitzenstein, Alexander. "Papst Clemens II. und sein Grabmal im Bamberger Dom." In *Das Grab des Papstes Clemens II. im Dom zu Bamberg*, edited by Sigrid Müller-Christensen, 9–31. Munich: F. Bruckmann, 1960.

Frick, Carole Collier. *Dressing Renaissance Florence: Families, Fortunes, and Fine Clothing*. Baltimore: Johns Hopkins University Press, 2002.

Frings, Jutta, and Jan Gerschow. *Krone und Schleier: Kunst aus mittelalterlichen Frauenklöstern*. Munich: Hirmer; Bonn: Kunst- und Ausstellungshalle der Bundesrepublik Deutschland; Essen: Furhlandmuseum, 2005.

Funk, Philipp. *Jakob von Vitry: Leben und Werke*. Beiträge zur Kulturgeschichte des Mittelalters und der Renaissance, 3. Leipzig: B. G. Teubner, 1909.

Gaastra, Adriaan. "Between Liturgy and Canon Law: A Study of Books of Confession and Penance in Eleventh- and Twelfth-Century Italy." Ph.D. diss., Utrecht University, 2007.

Gabrielli, Noemi. "Le miniature delle omelie di San Gregorio." In *Arte del primo millennio: Atti del II convegno per lo studio dell'arte dell'alto medio evo tenuto presso l'Università di Pavia nel settembre 1950*, edited by Edoardo Arslan, 300–311. Turin: Viglongo, 1951.

Gage, John. *Color and Meaning: Art, Science, and Symbolism*. Berkeley: University of California Press, 1999.

Gamber, Klaus. "Das Superhumerale der Regensburger Bischöfe in seiner liturgiegeschichtlichen Entwicklung." In *Ecclesia reginensis: Studien zur Geschichte und Liturgie der Regensburger Kirche im Mittelalter*, 184–98. Regensburg: Friedrich Pustet, 1979.

Garver, Valerie L. "Weaving Words in Silk: Women and Inscribed Bands in the Carolingian World." *Medieval Clothing and Textiles* 6 (2010): 33–56.

——. *Women and Aristocratic Culture in the Carolingian World*. Ithaca, N.Y.: Cornell University Press, 2009.

Giammaria, Giaocchino, ed. *Un universo di simboli: Gli affreschi della cripta nella cattedrale di Anagni*. Rome: Viella, 2001.

Giandrea, Mary Frances. *Episcopal Culture in Late Anglo-Saxon England*. Woodbridge: Boydell, 2007.

Gibson, Gail McMurray. "The Thread of Life in the Hand of the Virgin." In *Equally in God's Image: Women in the Middle Ages*, edited by Julia Bolton Holloway, Constance S. Wright, and Joan Bechtold, 46–54. New York: Peter Lang, 1990.

Gilchrist, Roberta. "Rethinking Later Medieval Masculinity: The Male Body in Death." In *Mortuary Practices and Social Identities in the Middle Ages: Essays in Burial Archaeology in Honour of Heinrich Härke*, edited by Duncan Sayer and Howard Williams, 236–52. Exeter: University of Exeter Press, 2009.

Gilchrist, Roberta, and Barney Sloane. *Requiem: The Medieval Monastic Cemetery in Britain*. London: Museum of London Archaeology Service, 2003.

Giry, Arthur. *Manuel de diplomatique*. Paris: Hachette, 1894.

Godding, Robert. *Prêtres en Gaule mérovingienne*. Brussels: Société des Bollandistes, 2001.

Goering, Joseph. *William de Montibus (c. 1140–1213): The Schools and the Literature of Pastoral Care*. Toronto: Pontifical Institute of Mediaeval Studies, 1992.

Goldberg, Eric J. "Regina Nitens Sanctissima Hemma: Queen Emma (827–876), Bishop Witgar of Augsburg, and the Witgar Belt." In *Representations of Power in Medieval Germany, 800–1500*, edited by Björn Weiler and Simon MacLean, 57–95. Turnhout: Brepols, 2006.

Goll, Jürg, Matthias Exner, and Susanne Hirsch. *Müstair: Die mittelalterlichen Wandbilder in der Klosterkirche*. Munich: Himmer, 2007.

Gordon, Richard. "The Veil of Power: Emperors, Sacrificers and Benefactors." In *Pagan Priests: Religion and Power in the Ancient World*, edited by Mary Beard and John North, 201–31. London: Duckworth, 1990.

Granger-Taylor, Hero. "The Two Dalmatics of Saint Ambrose." *Bulletin du CIETA* 57–58 (1983): 127–73.

——. "The Weft-Patterned Silks and Their Braid: The Remains of an Anglo-Saxon Dalmatic of c. 800?" In *St. Cuthbert, His Cult and His Community to AD 1200*, edited by Gerald Bonner, David Rollason, and Clare Stancliffe, 303–27. Woodbridge: Boydell, 1989.

Grégoire, Réginald. *Homéliaires liturgiques médiévaux: Analyse de manuscrits*. Spoleto: Centro italiano di studi sull'alto medioevo, 1980.

Gresser, Georg, ed. *Die Synoden und Konzilien in der Zeit des Reformpapsttums in Deutschland und Italien von Leo IX. bis. Calixt II 1049–1123*. Paderborn: F. Schöningh, 2006.

Griffiths, Fiona. "'Like the Sister of Aaron': Medieval Religious Women and Liturgical Textiles." In *Female Vita Religiosa between Late Antiquity and the High Middle Ages: Structures, Norms and Developments*, edited by Gert Melville and Anne Müller, 347–74. Zurich: LIT-Verlag, 2011.

Grossi, Vittorino, and Angelo Di Berardino. *La chiesa antica: Ecclesiologia e istituzioni*. Rome: Borla, 1984.

Guillou, André. "La soie sicilienne au Xe–XIe s." In *Bizantino-Sicula II: Miscellanea di scritti in memoria di Giuseppe Rossi Taibbi*, 285–88. Palermo: Assessorato alla Istruzione della Regione Siciliana, 1975.

Halfond, Gregory I. *Archaeology of Frankish Church Councils, AD 511–768*. Leiden: Brill, 2010.

Hall, Stuart George. "Institutions in the Pre-Constantinian Ecclesia." In *The Cambridge*

History of Christianity, vol. 1, *Origins to Constantine*, edited by Margaret M. Mitchell and Frances M. Young, 414–33. Cambridge: Cambridge University Press, 2006.

Hamburger, Jeffrey F. *Nuns as Artists: The Visual Culture of a Medieval Convent*. Berkeley: University of California Press, 1997.

Hamilton, Sarah. *The Practice of Penance, 900–1050*. Woodbridge: Boydell, 2001.

——. "The Rituale: The Evolution of a New Liturgical Book." In *Studies in Church History* 38 (2004): 75–86.

Hammer, Carl I., Jr. "Country Churches, Clerical Inventories and the Carolingian Renaissance in Bavaria." *Church History* 49 (1980): 5–16.

Harf-Lancner, Laurence. "Les malheurs des intellectuels à la cour: Les clercs curiaux d'Henri II Plantagenêt." In *Courtly Literature and Clerical Culture*, edited by Christoph Huber and Henrike Lähnemann, 3–18. Tübingen: Attempo, 2002.

Harris, Jennifer. "'Estroit Vestu et Manu Cosu': Evidence for the Construction of Twelfth-Century Dress." In *Medieval Art: Recent Perspectives; A Memorial Tribute to C. R. Dodwell*, edited by Gale R. Owen-Crocker and Timothy Graham, 89–103. Manchester: Manchester University Press, 1998.

Harting-Correa, Alice L. *Walafrid Strabo's "Libellus de exordiis et incrementis quarundam in observationibus ecclesiasticis rerum": A Translation and Liturgical Commentary*. Leiden: E.J. Brill, 1996.

Harvey, John. *Men in Black*. Chicago: University of Chicago Press, 1995.

Harvey, P.D.A., and Andrew McGuinness. A *Guide to British Medieval Seals*. Toronto: University of Toronto Press, 1996.

Head, Thomas. "Peace and Power in France around the Year 1000." *Essays in Medieval Studies* 23 (2006): 1–17.

Heid, Stefan. "The Romanness of Roman Christianity." In A *Companion to Roman Religion*, edited by Jörg Rüpke, 406–26. Malden, Mass.: Blackwell, 2007.

Heller, Sarah Grace. *Fashion in Medieval France*. Woodbridge: Boydell, 2007.

Hen, Yitzhak. "Knowledge of Canon Law among Rural Priests: The Evidence of Two Carolingian Manuscripts from around 800." *Journal of Theological Studies* 50 (1999): 117–34.

——. "A Liturgical Handbook for the Use of a Rural Priest (Brussels BR 10127–10144)." In *Organizing the Written Word: Scripts, Manuscripts and Texts; Proceedings of the First Utrecht Symposium on Medieval Literacy, Utrecht, 5–7 June 1997*, edited by Marco Mostert. Turnhout: Brepols, forthcoming.

——. *The Royal Patronage of the Liturgy in Frankish Gaul to the Death of Charles the Bald (877)*. Woodbridge: Boydell, 2001.

Herlihy, David. *Opera Muliebra: Women and Work in Medieval Europe*. New York: McGraw Hill, 1990.

Herrick, Samantha Kahn. *Imagining the Sacred Past: Hagiography and Power in Early Normandy*. Cambridge, Mass.: Harvard University Press, 2007.

Hilkin, Charles. "Necrological Evidence of the Place and Permanence of the Subdiaconate." In *Ritual, Text and Law: Studies in Medieval Canon Law and Liturgy Presented to Roger E. Reynolds*, 51–66. Aldershot: Ashgate, 2004.

Hogarth, Sylvia. "Ecclesiastical Vestments and Vestmentmakers in York, 1300–1600." *York Historian* 7 (1986): 2–11.

Hollander, Anne. *Sex and Suits*. New York: Knopf, 1995.

Honselmann, Klemens. *Das Rationale der Bischöfe*. Paderborn: Verein für Geschichte und Altertumskunde, Westfalens, 1975.

Howell, Martha C. *Commerce before Capitalism in Europe, 1300–1600*. Cambridge: Cambridge University Press, 2010.

Huneycutt, Lois L. "'Proclaiming Her Dignity Abroad': The Literary and Artistic Network of Matilda of Scotland, Queen of England 1100–1118." In *The Cultural Patronage of Medieval Women*, edited by June Hall McCash, 155–74. Athens: University of Georgia Press, 1996.

Izbicki, Thomas M. "Forbidden Colors in the Regulation of Clerical Dress from the Fourth Lateran Council (1215) to the Time of Nicholas of Cusa (d. 1464)." *Medieval Clothing and Textiles* 1 (2005): 105–14.

Jacoby, David. "Silk Economics and Cross-Cultural Artistic Interaction: Byzantium, the Muslim World, and the Christian West." *Dumbarton Oaks Papers* 58 (2004): 197–240.

———. "Silk in Western Byzantium before the Fourth Crusade." *Byzantinische Zeitschrift* 84/85 (1991–1992): 452–500.

Jaeger, C. Stephen. *The Envy of Angels: Cathedral Schools and Social Ideals in Medieval Europe, 950–1200*. Philadelphia: University of Pennsylvania Press, 1994.

———. *The Origins of Courtliness: Civilizing Trends and the Formation of Courtly Ideals, 939–1210*. Philadelphia: University of Pennsylvania Press, 1985.

James, Montague Rhodes. A *Descriptive Catalogue of the Manuscripts in the John Rylands Library at Manchester*. Manchester: University Press; New York: Longmans, 1921.

Jenkins, David, ed. *The Cambridge History of Western Textiles*. 2 vols. Cambridge: Cambridge University Press, 2003.

Johnson, Maxwell E. "The Apostolic Tradition." In *The Oxford History of Christian Worship*, edited by Geoffrey Wainwright and Karen B. Westerfield Tucker, 32–35. Oxford: Oxford University Press, 2006.

Johnstone, Pauline. *The Byzantine Tradition in Church Embroidery*. London: Tiranti, 1967.

———. *High Fashion in the Church: The Place of Church Vestments in the History of Art from the Ninth to the Nineteenth Century*. Leeds: Maney, 2002.

Jolivet-Lévy, Catherine. *Les églises byzantines de Cappadoce: Le programme iconographique de l'abside et de ses abords*. Paris: Editions du Centre national de la recherché scientifique, 1991.

Jones, Ann Rosalind, and Peter Stallybrass. *Renaissance Clothing and the Materials of Memory*. Cambridge: Cambridge University Press, 2000.

Jones, Nancy A. "The Uses of Embroidery in the Romances of Jean Renart: Gender, History, Textuality." In *Jean Renart and the Art of Romance: Essays on Guillaume de Dole*, edited by Nancy Vine Durling, 3–44. Gainesville: University of Florida Press, 1997.

Jordan, Erin L. "Gender Concerns: Monks, Nuns, and Patronage of the Cistercian Order in Thirteenth-Century Flanders and Hainaut." *Speculum* 87 (2012): 62–94.

Jørgensen, Lise Bender. "Textile Industries of the Early Medieval World to AD 1000: The Continental Germans." In Jenkins, *Cambridge History of Western Textiles*, 1:118–20.

Jungmann, Josef Andreas. *Missarum Sollemnia: Eine genetische Erklärung der römischen Messe*. 5th ed. 2 vols. Vienna: Herder, 1962. English edition, *The Mass of the Roman Rite: Its Origins and Development (Missarum Sollemnia)*. Translated by Francis A. Brunner. 2 vols. New York: Benziger, 1951–1955.

Karras, Ruth Mazo. "'This Skill in a Woman Is by No Means to Be Despised': Weaving and the Gender Division of Labor in the Middle Ages." In *Medieval Fabrications: Dress, Textiles, Clothwork, and Other Cultural Imaginings*, edited by E. Jane Burns, 89–104. New York: Palgrave, 2004.

Kay, Richard. "Mansi and Rouen: A Critique of the Conciliar Collections." In *Councils and Clerical Culture in the Medieval West*, 4:155–68. Aldershot: Variorum, 1997.

Keefe, Susan A. *Water and the Word: Baptism and the Education of the Clergy in the Carolingian Empire*. 2 vols. Notre Dame, Ind.: University of Notre Dame Press, 2002.

Keen, Maurice. *Chivalry*. New Haven: Yale University Press, 1984.

Kelly, Thomas Forrest. *The Exultet in Southern Italy*. New York: Oxford University Press, 1996.

Kent, Dale. *Cosimo de' Medici and the Florentine Renaissance: The Patron's Oeuvre*. New Haven: Yale University Press, 2000.

Kessler, Herbert L. "A Lay Abbot as Patron: Count Vivian and the First Bible of Charles the Bald." In *Committenti e produzione artistico-letteraria nell'alto medioevo occidentale*, 647–75. Spoleto: Centro italiano di studi sull'alto medioevo, 1992.

Kirchner, Joachim. *Beschreibende Verzeichnisse der Miniaturen-Handschriften der preussischen Staatsbibliothek zu Berlin. Erster Band: Die Phillipps-Handschriften*. Leipzig: J.J. Weber, 1926.

Klein, Karen Wilk. *The Partisan Voice: A Study of the Political Lyric in France and Germany, 1180–1230*. The Hague: Mouton, 1971.

Klemperer, William D., and Noel Boothroyd. *Excavations at Hulton Abbey, Staffordshire 1987–1994*. Leeds: Society for Medieval Archaeology, 2004.

Knapp, Ulrich. *Buch und Bild im Mittelalter*. Hildesheim: Gerstenberg, 1999.

Koeppler, H. "Frederick Barbarossa and the Schools of Bologna." *English Historical Review* 54 (1939): 577–607.

Köhler, Wilhelm. *Die karolingischen Miniaturen: Im Auftrage des Deutschen Vereins für Kunstwissenschaft*. 7 vols. Berlin: B. Cassirer, 1930–1960.

Köhn, Rolf. "'Militia Curialis': Kritik am geistlichen Hofdienst bei Peter von Blois und in der lateinischen Literatur des 9.-12. Jahrhunderts." In *Soziale Ordnungen im Selbstverständnis des Mittelalters*, 1. Halbband, 227–56. Berlin: W. de Gruyter, 1979.

Körntgen, Ludger. "Ein italienisches Bußbuch und seine fränkischen Quellen: Das anonyme Paenitentiale der Handschrift Vatikan, Arch. S. Pietro H 58." In *Aus Archiven und Bibliotheken: Festschrift für Raymund Kottje zum 65. Geburtstag*, edited by Hubert Mordek, 189–205. Frankfurt: Peter Lang, 1992.

Krautheimer, Richard. *Rome, Profile of a City, 312–1308*. 2nd ed. Princeton: Princeton University Press, 1983.

Kreutz, Barbara M. *Before the Normans: Southern Italy in the Ninth and Tenth Centuries*. Philadelphia: University of Pennsylvania Press, 1991.

Labarre, Sylvie. "Le vêtement dans la *Vie de Saint Martin* (IVe s.): Signe social et valeur symbolique." In *Costume et société dans l'Antiquité et le haut Moyen Age*, edited by François Chausson and Hervé Inglebert, 129–41. Paris: Picard, 2003.

Lachaud, Frédérique. "Dress and Social Status in England before the Sumptuary Laws." In *Heraldry, Pageantry and Social Display in Medieval England before the Sumptuary Laws*, edited by Peter Coss and Maurice Keen, 105–23. Woodbridge: Boydell, 2002.

——. "La critique du vêtement et du soin des apparences dans quelques oeuvres religieuses, morales et politiques, XIIe–XIVe siècles." In *Le corps et sa parure: The Body and Its Adornment*, 61–85. Micrologus 15. Florence: SISMEL, 2007.

Lacy, Norris J. "The Evolution and Legacy of French Prose Romance." In *The Cambridge Companion to Medieval Romance*, edited by Roberta L. Kreuger, 169–73. Cambridge: Cambridge University Press, 2000.

Laffitte, Marie-Pierre, and Charlotte Denoël, eds. *Trèsors carolingiens: Livres manuscrits de Charlemagne à Charles le Chauve*. Paris: Bibliothèque nationale de France, 2007.

Laiou, Angeliki E. "Exchange and Trade, Seventh–Twelfth Centuries." In *The Economic History of Byzantium*, vol. 2, 697–770. Washington, D.C.: Dumbarton Oaks Research Library and Collection, 2001.

Latzke, Therese. "Der Topos Mantelgedicht." *Mittellateinisches Jahrbuch* 6 (1970): 109–31.

Laudage, Johannes. "Rituel und Recht aut päpstlichen Reformkonzilien (1049–1123)." *Annuarium historiae conciliorum* 29 (1997): 287–334.

Laver, James. A *Concise History of Costume*. London: H.N. Abrams, 1969.

——. *Taste and Fashion, from the French Revolution until Today*. New York: Dodd, Mead, 1938.

LaVere, Suzanne. "From Contemplation to Action: The Role of the Active Life in the *Glossa Ordinaria* on the Song of Songs." *Speculum* 82 (2007): 54–69.

Léglu, Catherine. "Moral and Satirical Poetry." In *The Troubadours: An Introduction*, edited by Simon Gaunt and Sarah Kay, 47–65. Cambridge: Cambridge University Press, 1999.

Legner, Anton, ed. *Ornamenta ecclesiae: Kunst und Künstler der Romanik; Katalog zur Ausstellung des Schnütgen-Museums in der Josef-Haubrich-Kunsthalle, Köln, 1985*. 3 vols. Cologne: Schnütgen-Museum, 1985.

Lehmann-Brockhaus, Otto. *Schriftquellen zur Kunstgeschichte des 11. und 12. Jahrhunderts für Deutschland Lothringen und Italien*. New York: Deutscher Verein für Kunstwissenschaft, 1938.

Le Jan, Régine. "Frankish Giving of Arms and Rituals of Power: Continuity and Change in the Carolingian Period." In *Rituals of Power from Late Antiquity to the Early Middle Ages*, edited by Frans Theuws and Janet L. Nelson, 281–309. Leiden: Brill, 2000.

Lemarié, J. "Le Pontifical d'Hugues de Salines, son 'Ordo Missae' et son 'Libellus precum.'" *Studi Medievali* ser. 3, 19 (1978): 363–76.

L'Engle, Susan. "Addressing the Law: Costume as Signifier in Medieval Legal Miniatures." In *Encountering Medieval Textiles and Dress*, edited by Désirée G. Koslin and Janet E. Snyder, 137–53. New York: Palgrave Macmillan, 2002.

L'Engle, Susan, and Robert Gibbs, eds. *Illuminating the Law: Legal Manuscripts in Cambridge Collections*. London: Harvey Miller, 2001.

Leroquais, Victor. "L'Ordo Missae du sacramentaire d'Amiens." *Ephemerides Liturgicae* 41 (1927): 435–45.

Lochrie, Karma. *Covert Operations: The Medieval Uses of Secrecy*. Philadelphia: University of Pennsylvania Press, 1999.

Logvin, Hrihoriy. *Kiev's Hagia Sophia*. Kiev: Mistsetstvo, 1971.

LoPrete, Kimberly A. *Adela of Blois, Countess and Lord (c. 1067–1137)*. Dublin: Four Courts Press, 2007.

Lorquin, Alexandra. "Le costume dans l'antiquité tardive d'après les vestiges textiles coptes." In *Costume et société dans l'Antiquité et le haut Moyen Age*, edited by François Chausson and Hervé Inglebert, 121–28. Paris: Picard, 2003.

Luykx, Boniface. *De oorsprong van het gewone der Mis*. Utrecht: Het Spectrum, 1954.

——. "Der Ursprung der gleichbleibenden Teile der heiligen Mess (Ordinarium Missae)." Translated by Johannes Madey. In *Priestertum und Mönchtum*, edited by Theodor Bogler, special issue of *Liturgie und Mönchtum* 29 (1961): 72–119.

Lynch, John E. "Marriage and Celibacy of the Clergy: The Discipline of the Western Church; An Historico-Canonical Synopsis." *Jurist* 32 (1972): 14–38, 189–212.

MacMullen, Ramsay. *Christianity and Paganism in the Fourth to Eighth Centuries*. New Haven: Yale University Press, 1997.

——. *Voting about God in Early Church Councils*. New Haven: Yale University Press, 2006.

Macy, Gary. *The Hidden History of Women's Ordination: Female Clergy in the Medieval West*. Oxford: Oxford University Press, 2008.

——. *The Theologies of the Eucharist in the Early Scholastic Period*. Oxford: Clarendon, 1984.

Madou, Mireille. *Le costume civil*. Typologie des sources du moyen âge 47. Turnhout: Brepols, 1986.

Malaise-Heger, Christiane. *Le tresor du Prieuré d'Oignies: Chefs d'oeuvre de l'orfevrerie mosane*. Liege: P. Mardaga, 1983.

Mannowsky, Walter. *Der Danziger Paramentenschatz: Kirchliche Gewänder und Stickereien aus der Marienkirche*. Berlin: Brandussche Verlagsbuchhandlung, 1983.

Marnetté-Kühn, Beatrice. *Mittelalterliche Siegel der Urkundenfonds Marienberg und Mariental*. Braunschweig: Sebstverlag des Braunschweigischen Geschichtsvereins, 2006.

Martimort, Aimé-Georges. "Additions et corrections à la documentation liturgique de dom Edmond Martène." *Ecclesia orans* 3 (1986): 81–105.

——. *La documentation liturgique de Dom Edmond Martène*. Étude codicologique.

Vatican City: Biblioteca Apostolica Vaticana, 1978.

——. *Les "ordines," les ordinaires et les cérémoniaux*. Turnhout: Brepols, 1991.

Martin, Ralph P., and Peter H. Davids. "Priest, High Priest." *Dictionary of the Later New Testament and Its Developments*. Downers Grove, Ill.: Intervarsity Press, 1997.

Martindale, Jane. "Conventum inter Willelmum Comitem Aquitanorum et Hugonem Chiliarchum." *English Historical Review* 84 (1969): 528–48.

Martinelli, Patrizia Angiolini, ed. *La Basilica di San Vitale a Ravenna: Atlante*. Modena: Panini, 1997.

Martini, Paola Supino. *Roma e l'area grafica romanesca (secoli X–XII)*. Alessandria: Edizioni dell'Orso, 1987.

Martin I Ros, Rosa. "Les vêtements liturgiques de Saint-Valère: Étude historique." *Bulletin du CIETA* 73 (1995–1996): 63–78.

Matilde di Canossa, il papato, l'impero: Storia, arte, cultura alle origini del romanico. Edited by Renata Salvarani and Liana Castelfranchi. Cinisello Balsamo: Silvana, 2008.

Matter, E. Ann. *The Voice of My Beloved: The Song of Songs in Western Medieval Christianity*. Philadelphia: University of Pennsylvania Press, 1990.

Matthiae, Guglielmo. *Mosaici medioevali delle chiese di Roma*. 2 vols. Rome: Libreria dello Stato, 1967.

——. *Pittura romana del medioevo*. 2 vols. New edition with Aggiornamento scientifico e bibliografia, by Francesco Gandolfo. Rome: Fratelli Palombi, 1988.

Mayo, Janet. A *History of Ecclesiastical Dress*. New York: Holmes & Meier, 1984.

Mayr-Harting, Henry. *Ottonian Book Illumination: An Historical Study*. London: H. Miller, 1991.

McCash, June Hall, ed. *The Cultural Patronage of Medieval Women*. Athens: University of Georgia Press, 1996.

McCormick, Michael. "The Liturgy of War from Antiquity to the Crusades." In *The Sword of the Lord: Military Chaplains from the First to the Twenty-First Century*, edited by Doris L. Bergen, 45–67. Notre Dame, Ind.: University of Notre Dame Press, 2004.

McKitterick, Rosamond. *The Frankish Church and the Carolingian Reforms, 789–895*. London: Royal Historical Society, 1977.

——. "The Palace School of Charles the Bald." In *Charles the Bald: Court and Kingdom*, edited by Margaret T. Gibson and Janet L. Nelson, 326–339. Oxford: B.A.R., 1981. Reprint, Aldershot: Variorum, 1990.

McLaughlin, Megan. "The Bishop as Bridegroom: Marital Imagery and Clerical Celibacy in the Eleventh and Early Twelfth Centuries." In *Medieval Purity and Piety: Essays on Medieval Clerical Celibacy and Religious Reform*, edited by Michael Frassetto, 209–37. New York: Garland, 1998.

——. "The Bishop in the Bedroom: Witnessing Episcopal Sexuality in an Age of Reform." *Journal of the History of Sexuality* 19 (2010): 17–34.

McLaughlin, Terence P. "Abelard's Rule for Religious Women." *Mediaeval Studies* 18 (1956): 241–92.

McNamara, Jo Ann. "The Herrenfrage: The Restructuring of the Gender System, 1050–1150." In *Medieval Masculinities: Regarding Men in the Middle Ages*, edited by Clare A. Lees, 3–29. Minneapolis: University of Minnesota Press, 1994.

Meeks, Wayne A. "Social and Ecclesial Life of the Earliest Christians." In *The Cambridge History of Christianity*, vol. 1, *Origins to Constantine*, edited by Margaret M. Mitchell and Frances M. Young, 145–73. Cambridge: Cambridge University Press, 2006.

Melnikas, Anthony. *The Corpus of the Miniatures in the Manuscripts of "Decretum Gratiani."* 3 vols. Rome: Institutum Gratianum, 1975.

Mercalli, Marica, and Silvia Checchi. I *paramenti liturgici di Castel Sant'Elia: La loro storia e la cronaca del restauro*. Rome: Gangemi, 2012.

Messerer, Wilhelm. *Der Bamberger Domschatz in seinem Bestande bis zum Ende der Hohenstaufen-Zeit*. Munich: Himmer, 1952.

Metropolitan Museum of Art. *The Art of Medieval Spain AD 500–1200*. New York: Metropolitan Museum of Art / H. N. Abrams, 1993.

Miller, Maureen C. *The Bishop's Palace: Architecture and Authority in Medieval Italy*. Ithaca, N.Y.: Cornell University Press, 2000.

——. "The Crisis in the Investiture Crisis Narrative." *History Compass* 7 (November 2009): 1570–80.

——. *The Formation of a Medieval Church: Ecclesiastical Change in Verona, 950–1150*. Ithaca, N.Y.: Cornell University Press, 1993.

——. "The Liturgical Vestments of Castel Sant'Elia: Their Historical Significance and Current Condition." *Medieval Clothing and Textiles*. Forthcoming.

——. "Masculinity, Reform, and Clerical Culture: Narratives of Episcopal Holiness in the Gregorian Era." *Church History* 72 (2003): 25–52.

——. "Reform and New Religious Movements." In A *Companion to the Medieval World*, edited by Carol Lansing and Edward English, 211–30. Oxford: Blackwell, 2009.

——. "The Significance of Saint Cuthbert's Vestments." *Studies in Church History* 47 (2011): 90–102.

Moody, Catherine M., ed. *Gendered Voices: Medieval Saints and Their Interpreters*. Philadelphia: University of Pennsylvania Press, 1999.

Moore, R. I. *The Birth of Popular Heresy*. London: Edward Arnold, 1975. Reprint, Toronto: University of Toronto Press, 1995.

——. "Family, Community and Cult on the Eve of the Gregorian Reform." *Transactions of the Royal Historical Society* 5/30 (1980): 49–69.

——. *The First European Revolution, c. 970–1215*. Oxford: Blackwell, 2000.

Morin, Germain. *Études, textes, découvertes: Contributions a la littérature et a l'histoire des douze premiers siècles*. Belgium: Abbaye de Maredsous, 1913.

Mortari, Luisa. "Il Museo di Arredi Sacri a Castel S. Elia." *Bollettino d'arte* 41 (1956): 275–77.

——. *Il Tesoro della Cattedrale di Anagni*. Rome: De Luca, 1963.

Müller-Christensen, Sigrid. *Das Grab des Papstes Clemens II. im Dom zu Bamberg*. Munich: F. Bruchmann, 1960.

——. "Liturgische Gewänder mit dem Namen des heiligen Ulrich." In *Augusta 955–1955: Forschungen und Studien zur Kultur- und Wirtschaftsgeschichte Augsburgs*, edited by Clemens Bauer, Joseph Bernhart, and Hermann Rinn, 53–60. Munich: Verlag Hermann Rinn, 1955.

Munro, John H. "Medieval Woollens: Textiles, Technology and Industrial Organisation, c. 800–1500." In Jenkins, *Cambridge History of Western Textiles*, 1:181–227.

Muthesius, Anna. *Byzantine Silk Weaving: AD 400 to AD 1200*. Vienna: Fassbaender, 1997.

——. "Silk in the Medieval World." In Jenkins, *Cambridge History of Western Textiles*, 1:325–54.

Nederman, Cary J. *John of Salisbury*. Tempe: Arizona Center for Medieval and Renaissance Studies, 2005.

——. "Principles of Liberty in John of Salisbury." In *Beyond the Persecuting Society: Religious Toleration Before the Enlightenment*, edited by John Christian Laursen and Cary J. Nederman, 53–70. Philadelphia: University of Pennsylvania Press, 1998.

Nederman, Cary J., and Catherine Campbell. "Priests, Kings and Tyrants: Spiritual and Temporal Power in John of Salisbury's *Policraticus*." *Speculum* 66 (1991): 572–90.

Nees, Lawrence. *Early Medieval Art*. Oxford: Oxford University Press, 2002.

Newton, Stella Mary. *Fashion in the Age of the Black Prince: A Study of the Years 1340–1365*. Woodbridge: Boydell, 1980.

Noble, Thomas F. X. *Charlemagne and Louis the Pious*. University Park: Pennsylvania State University Press, 2009.

Nordhagen, Per Jonas. "Working with Wilpert: The Illustrations in *Die römischen Mosaiken und Malereien* and Their Source Value." *Acta ad Archaeologiam et Artivm Historiam Pertinentia*, Series Altera in 80 5 (1985): 247–57.

North, William L. "In the Shadows of Reform. Exegesis and the Formation of a Clerical Elite in the Works of Bruno, Bishop of Segni (1078/9–1123)." Ph.D. diss., University of California, Berkeley, 1998.

Oakeshott, Walter. *The Mosaics of Rome from the Third to the Fourteenth Centuries*. Greenwich, Conn.: New York Graphic Society, 1967.

Origo, Iris. *The Merchant of Prato: Francesco di Marco Datini, 1335–1410*. London: J. Cape, 1960.

Osborne, John. "Textiles and Their Painted Imitations in Early Medieval Rome." *Papers of the British School at Rome* 60 (1992): 312–21.

Otavsky, Karel, and Muhammad A'bbas Muhammad Salim. *Mittelalterliche Textilien I: Ägypten Persen und Mesopotamien Spanien und Nordafrika*. Riggisberg: Abegg-Stiftung, 1995.

Otavsky, Karel, and Anne E. Wardwell. *Die Textilsammlung der Abegg-Stiftung, Band 5: Mittelalterliche Textilien II; Zwischen Europa und China*. Riggisberg: Abegg-Stiftung, 2011.

Owen-Crocker, Gale R. "Anglo-Saxon Women: The Art of Concealment." *Leeds Studies in English* 33 (2002): 31–51.

——. *Dress in Anglo-Saxon England*. Rev. ed. Woodbridge: Boydell, 2004.

Ozoline, Anastasia. *Trésors de la Gaule chrétienne: Histoire et restauration des reliques textiles de saint Césaire d'Arles (470–542)*. Arles: Éditions du Musée départemental de l'Arles antique, 2008.

Palazzo, Eric. "Art and Liturgy in the Middle Ages: Survey of Research (1980–2003) and Some Reflections on Method." *Journal of English and Germanic Philology* 105 (2006): 170–84.

——. *L'évêque et son image: L'illustration du pontifical au moyen âge*. Turnhout: Brepols, 1999.

——. A *History of Liturgical Books from the Beginning to the Thirteenth Century*. Translated by Madeleine Beaumont. Collegeville, Minn.: Liturgical Press, 1998.

Papadopoulos, Karoline. *Die Wandmalereien des XI. Jahrhunderts in der Kirche Panagea ton Chalkeon in Thessaloniki*. Graz: H. Böhlaus Nachf., 1966.

Paredi, Angelo. "Nota storica sui Salteri milanesi del IX secolo." In *Miniature altomedievali lombarde*, by Luigi Santucci and Angelo Paredi, 149–78. Milan: Banco Ambrosiano, 1978.

Parisse, Michel. "Princes laïques et/ou moines, les évêques du Xe siècle." In *Il Secolo di ferro: Mito e realtà del secolo X*, 449–516. Settimane di studio del Centro Italiano di studi sull'alto medioevo, 38. Spoleto: Centro italiano di studi sull'alto medioevo, 1991.

Pastoureau, Michel. *Black: The History of a Color*. Translated by Jody Gladding. Princeton: Princeton University Press, 2009.

——. *Bleu: Histoire d'une couleur*. 2nd ed. Paris: Seuil, 2006.

——. *Jésus chez le teinturier: Couleurs et teintures dans l'Occident medieval*. Paris: Léopard d'or, 1997.

Patzold, Steffen. *Episcopus: Wissen über Bischöfe im Frankenreich des späten 8. bis frühen 10. Jahrhunderts*. Ostfildern: Thorbecke, 2008.

Pavlac, Brian A. "Excommunication and Territorial Politics in High Medieval Trier." *Church History* 60 (1991): 20–36.

Paxton, Frederick S. "Bonus Liber: A Late Carolingian Clerical Manual from Lorsch (Bibliotheca Vaticana MS Pal. Lat. 485)." In *The Two Laws: Studies in Medieval Legal History Dedicated to Stephan Kuttner*, edited by Laurent Mayali and Stephanie A.J. Tibbetts, 1–30. Washington, D.C.: Catholic University of America Press, 1990.

Pelikan, Jaroslav. *The Christian Tradition: A History of the Development of Doctrine*. Vol. 3, *The Growth of Medieval Theology (600–1300)*. Chicago: University of Chicago Press, 1978.

Pepin, Ronald E. *The Literature of Satire in the Twelfth Century: A Neglected Medieval Genre*. Studies in Medieval Literature 2. Lewiston, N.Y.: E. Mellen, 1988.

Petrucci, Armando. "Censimento dei codici dei secoli X–XII." *Studi Medievali*, ser. 3, 9 (1968): 1115–94; ser. 3, 11 (1970): 1013-133.

Pierce, Joanne M. "Early Medieval Vesting Prayers in the *Ordo Missae* of Sigebert of Minden (1022–1036)." In *Rule of Prayer, Rule of Faith: Essays in Honor of Aidan Kavanagh, O.S.B*, 80–105. Collegeville, Minn.: Liturgical Press, 1996.

——. "The Evolution of the *Ordo Missae* in the Early Middle Ages." In *Medieval Liturgy: A Book of Essays*, edited by Lizette Larson-Miller, 3–24. New York: Garland, 1997.

——. "Sacerdotal Spirituality at Mass: Text and Study of the Prayerbook of Sigebert of Minden (1022–1036)." Ph.D. diss., University of Notre Dame, 1988.

Piponnier, Françoise, and Perrine Mane. *Dress in the Middle Ages*. Translated by Caroline Beamish. New Haven: Yale University Press, 1997.

Platelle, Henri. "Le problème du scandale: Les nouvelles modes masculines aux XIe et XIIe siècles." *Revue belge de philologie et d'histoire* 53 (1975): 1071–96.

Pocknee, Cyril E. *Liturgical Vesture: Its Origins and Development*. London: Mowbray, 1960.

Pontal, Odette. *Les conciles de la France capétienne jusqu'en 1215*. Paris: Éditions du Cerf, 1995.

——. "Recherches sur le costume des clercs des origines au XIVe siècle d'après les décrets des conciles et des synods." *L'année canonique* 17 (1973): 769–96.

Prinz, Friedrich. *Klerus und Krieg im früheren Mittelalter: Untersuchungen z. Rolle d. Kirche beim Aufbau d. Konigsherrschaft*. Stuttgart: Hiersemann, 1971.

Puhle, Matthias, ed. *Otto der Grosse: Magdeburg und Europa*. Mainz: Philipp von Zabern, 2001.

Racinet, Auguste. *Le costume historique*. Paris: Firmin-Didot et Cie, 1888.

Radding, Charles M., and Francis Newton. *Theology, Rhetoric, and Politics in the Eucharistic Controversy, 1078–1079: Alberic of Monte Cassino against Berengar of Tours*. New York: Columbia University Press, 2003.

Rashdall, Hastings. *The Universities of Europe in the Middle Ages*. 3 vols. Rev. ed. Edited by F.M. Powicke and A.B. Emden. Oxford: Clarendon Press, 1987.

Rasmussen, Niels Krogh "Célébration épiscopale et célébration presbytérale: Un essai de typologie." In *Segni e riti nella chiesa altomedievale occidentale*, 581–603. Spoleto: Centro italiano di studi sull'alto medioevo, 1987.

——. "An Early 'Ordo Missae' with a 'Litania Abecedaria' Addressed to Christ (Rome, Bibl. Vallicelliana, Cod. B. 141, XI. Cent.)." *Ephemerides Liturgicae* 98 (1984): 198–211.

Reuter, Timothy. *Germany in the Early Middle Ages, c. 800–1056*. London: Longman, 1991.

——. "The 'Imperial Church System' of the Ottonian and Salian Rulers: A Reconsideration." *Journal of Ecclesiastical History* 33 (1982): 347–74.

Reynolds, Roger E. "Clerical Liturgical Vestments and Liturgical Colors in the Middle Ages." In Reynolds, *Clerics in the Early Middle Ages: Hierarchy and Image*, 6:10–15. Aldershot: Variorum, 1999.

——. "Clerics in the Early Middle Ages: Hierarchies and Functions." In Reynolds, *Clerics in the Early Middle Ages: Hierarchy and Image*, 1:1–31. Aldershot: Variorum, 1999.

——. "The *De Officiis VII Graduum*: Its Origins and Early Medieval Development." In Reynolds, *Clerical Orders in the Early Middle Ages: Duties and Ordination*. 2:113–51. Aldershot: Variorum, 1999.

——. "Excerpta from the Collectio Hibernensis in Three Vatican Manuscripts." *Bulletin of Medieval Canon Law* n.s. 5 (1975): 1–9.

——. "Image and Text: The Liturgy of Clerical Ordination in Early Medieval Art." In Reynolds, *Clerics in the Early Middle Ages: Hierarchy and Image*, 7:27–38. Aldershot: Variorum, 1999.

——. "Liturgical Scholarship at the Time of the Investiture Controversy: Past Research and Future Opportunities." In Reynolds, *Law and Liturgy in the Latin Church, 5th–12th Centuries*, 18:109–24. Aldershot: Variorum, 1994.

——. *The Ordinals of Christ from their Origins to the Twelfth Century*. Beiträge zur Geschichte und Quellenkunde des Mittelalters 7. Berlin: W. de Gruyter, 1978.

——. "Penitentials in South and Central Italian Canon Law Manuscripts of the Tenth and Eleventh Centuries." *Early Medieval Europe* 14 (2006): 65–84.
——. "The Portrait of the Ecclesiastical Officers in the *Raganaldus Sacramentary* and Its Liturgico-Canonical Significance." *Speculum* 46 (1971): 432–42.
——. "Rites of Separation and Reconciliation in the Early Middle Ages." In *Segni e riti nella chiesa altomedievale occidentale, Spoleto 11–17 aprile 1985*, 405–33. Settimane di studio del Centro italiano di studi sull'alto medioevo 33. Spoleto: Centro italiano di studi sull'alto medioevo, 1987.
——. "The Ritual of Clerical Ordination of the Sacramentarium Gelasianum Saec. VIII: Early Evidence from Southern Italy." In Reynolds, *Clerical Orders in the Early Middle Ages: Duties and Ordination*, vol. 12 addenda, 19–24. Aldershot: Variorum, 1999.
——. "'At Sixes and Sevens'—and Eights and Nines: The Sacred Mathematics of Sacred Orders in the Early Middle Ages." In Reynolds, *Clerics in the Early Middle Ages: Hierarchy and Image*, 3:669–84. Aldershot: Variorum, 1999.
——. "A South Italian Liturgico-Canonical Mass Commentary." *Mediaeval Studies* 50 (1988): 626–70.
——. "The Subdiaconate as a Sacred and Superior Order." In Reynolds, *Clerics in the Early Middle Ages: Hierarchy and Image*, 4:1–39. Aldershot: Variorum, 1999.
——. "Vestments, Liturgical" and "Liturgy, Treatises on." In *Dictionary of the Middle Ages*, ed. Joseph R. Strayer, 13 vols. New York: Scribner, 1982–1989.
Rhein und Maas: Kunst und Kultur, 800–1400. Cologne: Schnütgenmuseum, 1972–1973.
Riché, Pierre. *Education and Culture in the Barbarian West from the Sixth through the Eighth Century*. Translated by John J. Contreni. Columbia: University of South Carolina Press, 1976.
Rickert, Margaret Josephine. *Painting in Britain: The Middle Ages*. Baltimore: Penguin, 1954.
Rigg, A. G. "Canterbury, Nigel of." In *Oxford Dictionary of National Biography*. 60 vols. Oxford: Oxford University Press, 2004.
Rivard, Derek A. *Blessing the World: Ritual and Lay Piety in Medieval Religion*. Washington, D.C.: Catholic University of America Press, 2009.
Robinson, I. S. *Authority and Resistance in the Investiture Contest: The Polemical Literature of the Late Eleventh Century*. Manchester: Manchester University Press; New York: Holmes and Meier, 1978.
——. *Henry IV of Germany, 1056–1106*. Cambridge: Cambridge University Press, 1999.
——. *The Papacy 1073–1198: Continuity and Innovation*. Cambridge: Cambridge University Press, 1990.
——. "Reform and the Church, 1073–1122." In *The New Cambridge Medieval History*, vol. 4, c. 1024–c.1198, part 1, edited by David Luscombe and Jonathan Riley-Smith, 268–334. Cambridge: Cambridge University Press, 2004.
Rodwell, Warwick. "Lichfield Cathedral: Archaeology of the Sanctuary." *Church Archaeology* 7/9 (2005): 1–6.
Romanelli, Pietro, and Per Jonas Nordhagen. *Santa Maria Antiqua*. Rome: Libreria dello Stato, 1999.
Romano, Serena. *La pittura medievale a Roma. Corpus*, vol. 4, *Riforma e tradizione 1050–1198*. Milan: Jaca, 2006.
Römer, Gerhard. *Die mittelalterlichen Paramente im Kloster St. Marienberg in Helmstedt*. Helmstedt: Marienberger Freudeskreis für Paramentik und christliche Kunst, 1982.
Ronig, Franz J., ed. *Egbert Erzbischof von Trier 977–993: Gedenkschrift der Diözese Trier zum 1000. Todestag*. 2 vols. Trier: Rheinisches Landesmuseum, 1993.
Rosenbaum, Sandra L."The Role of a Dealer in the Development of Collections: Loewi-Robertson, Inc., A Case Study." *Bulletin du CIETA* 67 (1989): 89–101.
Rosewell, Roger. *Medieval Wall Paintings in English and Welsh Churches*. Woodbridge: Boydell, 2008.
Rossetti, Gabriella. "Il matrimonio del clero nella società altomedievale." In *Il matrimonio nella società altomedievale*, 472–554. Spoleto:

Centro italiano di studi sull'alto medioevo, 1977.
Rouse, Richard H., and Mary A. Rouse. "Statim invenire: Schools, Preachers, and New Attitudes toward the Page." In *Renaissance and Renewal in the Twelfth Century*, edited by Robert L. Benson and Giles Constable, 201–25. Cambridge, Mass.: Harvard University Press, 1982.
Rublack, Ulinka. *Dressing Up: Cultural Identity in Renaissance Europe*. Oxford: Oxford University Press, 2010.
Rudolph, Conrad. *The "Things of Greater Importance": Bernard of Clairvaux's "Apologia" and the Medieval Attitude toward Art*. Philadelphia: University of Pennsylvania Press, 1990.
Ryan, John J. "Pseudo-Alcuin's *Liber de divinis officiis* and the *Liber 'Dominus vobiscum'* of St. Peter Damiani." *Mediaeval Studies* 14 (1952): 159–63.
Sabbe, E. "L'importation des tissus orientaux en Europe occidentale au haut moyen âge (IXe et Xe siècles)." *Revue belge de philologie et d'histoire* 14 (1935): 811–48.
Sakrale Gewänder des Mittelalters: Ausstellung im Bayerischen Nationalmuseum München, 8. Juli bis 25. September 1955. Munich: Hirmer, 1955.
Salmon, Pierre. "Un 'Libellus Officialis' du XIe siècle." *Revue bénédictine* 87 (1977): 257–88.
——. *Les manuscrits liturgiques latins de la Bibliothèque Vaticane*. 5 vols. Vatican City: Biblioteca Apostolica Vaticana, 1968–1972.
——. "L'ordo missae dans dix manuscrits du Xe au XVe S." In *Analecta liturgica: Extraits des manuscrits liturgiques de la Bibliothèque Vaticane; Contribution à l'histoire de la prière chrétienne*, 197–221. Vatican City: Biblioteca Apostolica Vaticana, 1974.
——. "Un témoin de la vie chrétienne dans une église de Rome au XIe siècle: Le *Liber Officialis* de la basilique des Saints-Apôtres." *Rivista di Storia della Chiesa in Italia* 33 (1979): 65–73.
Sansterre, Jean-Marie. "Eugenio II." In *Enciclopedia dei papi*, 3 vols., 1:710–12. Rome: Istituto della Enciclopedia italiana, 2000–2006.
Sapin, Christian, ed. *Peindre à Auxerre au Moyen Âge IXe–XIVe siècle: 10 ans de recherché à l'abbaye Saint-Germain d'Auxerre et à la cathédrale Saint-Étienne d'Auxerre*. Auxerre: Centre d'études médiévales and Paris: CTHS, 1999.
Scarisbrick, Diana, and Martin Henig. *Finger Rings: From Ancient to Modern*. Oxford: Ashmolean Museum, 2003.
Schmedding, Brigitta. *Mittelalterliche Textilien in Kirchen und Klöstern der Schweiz*. Bern: Stämpfli, 1978.
Schneider, Herbert. "Rom und die liturgische Vielfalt." In *Roma fra oriente e occidente*, 1101–40. Spoleto: Centro italiano di studi sull'alto medioevo, 2002.
Schoefer-Masson, Marie. "Etude et restauration d'une mitre du milieu du XIIe siècle dont les fanons comportent un décor en tissu dit de Palerme." *Interdisciplinary Approach to the Study and Conservation of Medieval Textiles*, edited by Rosalia Varoli-Piazza, 30–33. Rome: Il Mondo 3 Edizioni, 1998.
Schrenk, Sabine. *Textilien des Mittelmeerraumes aus spätantiker bis frühislamischer Zeit*. Riggisburg: Abegg-Stiftung, 2004.
Schulenburg, Jane. "Holy Women and the Needle Arts: Piety, Devotion, and Stitching the Sacred, ca. 500–1150." In *Negotiating Community and Difference in Medieval Europe: Gender, Power, Patronage and the Authority of Religion in Latin Christendom*, edited by Katherine Allen Smith and Scott Wells, 83–110. Leiden: Brill, 2009.
Schürer, Emil. *The History of the Jewish People in the Age of Jesus Christ (175 B.C.–A.D. 135)*. Revised English ed. 3 vols. Edited by Geza Vermes, Fergus Millar, and Matthew Black. Edinburgh: Clark, 1973.
Schuette, Marie, and Sigrid Müller-Christensen. *The Art of Embroidery*. London: Thames and Hudson, 1963.
Senn, Frank C. *Christian Liturgy: Catholic and Evangelical*. Minneapolis: Fortress Press, 1997.

Somerville, Robert. "The Canons of Reims (1131)." *Bulletin of Medieval Canon Law*, n.s. 5 (1975): 122–30.

——. "The Council of Pisa, 1135." *Speculum* 45 (1970): 98–114.

——. *The Councils of Urban II*. Vol. 1, *Decreta Claromontensia*, *Annuarium Historiae Conciliorum*, supplementum, 1. Amsterdam: Hakkert, 1972.

——. *Pope Urban II's Council of Piacenza March 1–7, 1095*. Oxford: Oxford University Press, 2011.

Somerville, Robert, and Stephan Kuttner. *Pope Urban II, the Collectio Britannica, and the Council of Melfi (1089)*. Oxford: Oxford University Press, 1996.

Southern, R. W. *Saint Anselm: Portrait in a Landscape*. Cambridge: Cambridge University Press, 1990.

——. *Saint Anselm and His Biographer: A Study of Monastic Life and Thoughts 1059–c. 1130*. Cambridge: Cambridge University Press, 1966.

Speciale, Lucinia. *Montecassino e la riforma gregoriana: L'exultet Vat. Barb. lat. 592*. Rome: Viella, 1991.

Spelsberg, Helmut. *Hrabanus Maurus: Bibliographie*. Fulda: Hessische Landesbibliothek, 1983.

Stancliffe, Clare. *St. Martin and His Hagiographer: History and Miracle in Sulpicius Severus*. Oxford: Clarendon Press, 1982.

Staniland, Kay. *Embroiderers*. Toronto: University of Toronto Press, 1991.

Stauffer, Annemarie. *Die mittelalterlichen Textilien von St. Servatius in Maastricht*. Riggisberg: Abegg-Stiftung, 1991.

Stelzer, Winfried. "Zum Scholarenprivileg Friedrich Barbarossas (Authentica 'Habita')." *Deutsches Archiv für Erforschung des Mittelalters* 34 (1978): 123–65.

Storey, R. L. "Gentlemen-Bureaucrats." In *Profession, Vocation, and Culture in Later Medieval England: Essays Dedicated to the Memory of A. R. Myers*, edited by Cecil H. Clough, 90–109. Liverpool: Liverpool University Press, 1982.

Stuard, Susan Mosher. "Ancillary Evidence for the Decline of Medieval Slavery." *Past and Present* 149 (1995): 3–28.

——. *Gilding the Market: Luxury and Fashion in Fourteenth-Century Italy*. Philadelphia: University of Pennsylvania Press, 2006.

Svendsen, Lara. *Fashion: A Philosophy*. Translated by John Irons. London: Reaktion, 2006.

Tavano, Sergio, ed. *La Basilica di Aquileia: Gli affreschi dell'abside maggiore*. Udine: Società per la conservazione della Basilica di Aquileia / Forum, 2008.

Taylor, Lou. *The Study of Dress History*. Manchester: Manchester University Press, 2002.

Temple, Elzbieta. *Anglo-Saxon Manuscripts 900–1066*. London: Harvey Miller, 1976.

Thesaurus cultus et rituum antiquorum. 7 vols. Los Angeles: J. Paul Getty Museum, 2004–2006.

Thierbach, Melanie, ed. *Der Augsburger Dom in der Barockzeit: Katalog zur Sonderausstellung im Diözesanmuseum St. Afra 29. April–26. Juli 2009*. Augsburg: Diözesanmuseum St. Afra, 2009.

Thompson, Rodney M. "The Origins of Latin Satire in Twelfth-Century Europe." *Mittellateinisches Jahrbuch* 13 (1978): 73–83.

Toubert, Pierre. *Les structures du Latium medieval: Le Latium méridional et la Sabine du IXe à la fin du XIIe siècle*. Rome: École française de Rome, 1973.

Trexler, Richard C. *Synodal Law in Florence and Fiesole, 1306–1518*. Vatican City: Biblioteca Apostolica Vaticana, 1971.

Trichet, Louis. *Le costume du clergé: Ses origines et son évolution en France d'après les règlements de l'église*. Paris: Éditions du Cerf, 1986.

——. *La tonsure*. Paris: Éditions du Cerf, 1990.

Tugwell, Simon. "Caligae and Other Items of Medieval Religious Dress: A Lexical Study." *Romance Philology* 61.2 (Spring 2007): 1–23.

Uhlig, Claus. *Hofkritik im England des Mittelalters und der Renaissance*. Berlin: W. de Gruyter, 1973.

Valentini, Roberto, and Giuseppe Zucchetti, eds. *Codice topografico della città di Roma*.

4 vols. Rome: Tipografia del Senato, 1940–1953.

van Buren, Anne H. *Illuminating Fashion: Dress in the Art of Medieval France and the Netherlands, 1325–1515*. With Roger S. Wieck. New York: The Morgan Library & Museum; London: D Giles, 2011.

Van Engen, John H. *Rupert of Deutz*. Berkeley: University of California Press, 1983.

——. "Sacred Sanctions for Lordship." In *Cultures of Power: Lordship, Status, and Process in Twelfth-Century Europe*, edited by Thomas N. Bisson, 203–30. Philadelphia: University of Pennsylvania Press, 1995.

Venturi, Adolfo. "Museo del duomo di Ravenna: La 'casula' di Giovanni Angeloptes." In *Le Gallerie Nazionali Italiane: Notizie e documenti* 3 (1897): 258–60.

Vestiduras ricas: El monasterio de las Huelgas y su época 1170–1340, del 16 de marzo al 19 de junio de 2005 Palacio Real de Madrid. Madrid: Patrimonio Nacional, 2005.

Vodola, Elisabeth. *Excommunication in the Middle Ages*. Berkeley: University of California Press, 1986.

——. "Sovereignty and Tabu: Evolution of the Sanction against Communication with Excommunicates. Part I: Gregory VII." In *The Church and Sovereignty c. 590–1918: Essays in Honor of Michael Wilks*, edited by Diana Wood, 35–55. Oxford: Blackwell, 1991.

Von Giesebrecht, Wilhelm, ed. *Geschichte der deutschen Kaiserzeit*. 6 vols. Leipzig: Duncker & Humbolt, 1877–1895.

Vogel, Cyrille. "Buße und Exkommunikation in der Alten Kirche und im Mittelalter: Ein historischer Überblick." *Concilium* 107 (1975): 446–52.

——. "Les échanges liturgiques entre Rome et les pays francs jusqu'à l'époque de Charlemagne." In *Le chiese nei regni dell'Europa occidentale e i loro rapporti con Roma sino all'800*, 1:185–295. Spoleto: Centro italiano di studi sull'alto medioevo, 1960.

——. *Introduction aux sources de l'histoire du culte chrétien au moyen âge*. Spoleto: Centro italiano di studi sull'alto medioevo, 1973. English edition, *Medieval Liturgy: An Introduction to the Sources*. Translated by William G. Storey and Niels Krogh Rasmussen. Washington, D.C.: Pastoral Press, 1986.

Vogt, Caroline. "Episcopal Self-Fashioning: The Thomas Becket Mitres." In *Iconography of Liturgical Textiles in the Middle Ages*, edited by Evelin Wetter, 117–25. Riggisberg: Abegg-Stiftung, 2010.

Volbach, Wolfgang Fritz, and Max Hirmer. *Early Christian Art*. New York: Abrams, 1962.

von Lerber, Karin. "A Medieval Bell-Shaped Chasuble from St. Peter in Salzburg." *Journal of the Museum of Fine Arts, Boston* 4 (1992): 27–51.

von Schlosser, Julius. *Eine Fulder Miniaturhandschrift der K. K. Hofbibliothek*. Vienna: Jahrbuch der kunsthistorischen Sammlungen in Wien, 1892.

Wackenroder, Ernst, ed. *Die Kunstdenkmäler des Kreises Saarburg im auftrage des Provinzialverbandes der Rheinprovinz*. Düsseldorf: Schwann, 1939.

Walter, Christopher. *Art and Ritual of the Byzantine Church*. London: Variorum, 1982.

Wamser, Ludwig, ed. *Die Welt von Byzanz: Europas östliches Erbe; Glanz, Krisen und Fortleben einer tausendjahrigen Kultur*. Stuttgart: K. Theiss, 2004.

Warr, Cordelia. *Dressing for Heaven: Religious Clothing in Italy, 1215–1545*. Manchester: Manchester University Press, 2010.

Weitzmann, Kurt. *Age of Spirituality: Late Antique and Early Christian Art, Third to Seventh Century*. New York: Metropolitan Museum of Art, 1979.

——. *The Miniatures of the Sacra Parallela Prisinus Graecus 923*. Princeton: Princeton University Press, 1979.

Werblowsky, R.J. Zwi, and Geoffrey Wigoder, eds. "Priestly Vestments." In *The Oxford Dictionary of the Jewish Religion*, 619. Oxford: Oxford University Press, 1997.

Wetter, Evelin. "Defining a Model of Worship: An Embroidered Orphrey with Depictions

Based on the *Cantigas de Santa María*." In *Iconography of Liturgical Textiles in the Middle Ages*, edited by Evelin Wetter, 89–99. Riggisberg: Abegg-Stiftung, 2010.

Wickham, Chris. *Early Medieval Italy: Central Power and Local Society 400–1000*. London: Macmillan; Totowa, N.J.: Barnes and Noble, 1981.

Wild, John Peter. "The Later Roman and Early Byzantine East, AD 300–1000." In Jenkins, *Cambridge History of Western Textiles*, 1:140–53.

Williams, John. *Early Spanish Manuscript Illumination*. New York: G. Braziller, 1977.

Williams, Margaret McEnchroe. "Dressing the Part: Depictions of Noble Costume in Irish High Crosses." In *Encountering Medieval Textiles and Dress*, edited by Désirée G. Koslin and Janet E. Snyder, 45–63. New York: Palgrave Macmillan, 2002.

Wilmart, André. "La légende de Ste Édith en prose et vers par le moine Goscelin." *Analecta Bollandiana* 56 (1938): 5–101 and 265–307.

Wilpert, Josef. *Die römischen Mosaiken und Malereien der kirchlichen Bauten vom IV.–XIII. Jahrhundert*. 4 vols. Freiburg: Herder, 1916–1917.

Winroth, Anders. *The Making of Gratian's Decretum*. Cambridge: Cambridge University Press, 2000.

Witt, Ronald G. *The Two Latin Cultures and the Foundation of Renaissance Humanism in Medieval Italy*. Cambridge: Cambridge University Press, 2012.

Wolter, Heinz. *Die Synoden im Reichsgebiet und in Reichsitalien von 916 bis 1056*. Paderborn: Ferdinand Schöningh, 1988.

Woodfin, Warren. *The Embodied Icon: Liturgical Vestments and Sacramental Power in Byzantium*. Oxford: Oxford University Press, 2012.

——. "Late Byzantine Liturgical Vestments and the Iconography of Sacerdotal Power." Ph.D. diss., University of Illinois at Champagne-Urbana, 2002.

——. "Liturgical Textiles." In *Byzantium: Faith and Power (1261–1557)*, edited by Helen C. Evans, 297–303. New York: Yale University Press, 2004.

Wormald, Patrick. *Legal Culture in the Early Medieval West: Law as Text, Image and Experience*. London: Hambledon, 1999.

Zanker, Paul, *The Mask of Socrates: The Image of the Intellectual in Antiquity*. Translated by Alan Shapiro. Berkeley: University of California Press, 1995.

Zerner, Monique. "Au temps de l'appel aux armes contre les hérétiques: Du *Contra Henricum* du moine Guillaume aux *Contra hereticos*." In *Inventer l'hérésie? Discours polémique et pouvoirs avant l'inquisition*, edited by Monique Zerner, 119–56. Nice: Centre d'études médiévales, 1998.

Zonghetti, Alberto. "Il codice di Gioveniano." *Arte medievale* n.s. 4 (2005): 21–36.

GENERAL INDEX

INDEX OF MANUSCRIPTS CITED